*The Economic History
of Turkey
1800-1914*

PUBLICATIONS OF THE CENTER FOR MIDDLE EASTERN STUDIES
Number 13
Richard L. Chambers, General Editor

The Economic History
of Turkey
1800–1914

CHARLES ISSAWI

THE UNIVERSITY OF CHICAGO PRESS

CHICAGO AND LONDON

Charles Issawi, the Bayard Dodge Professor of Near
Eastern Studies at Princeton University, has taught
at Columbia, Harvard, Johns Hopkins, and the
American University in Beirut. His many books
include An Arab Philosophy of History and The
Economic History of the Middle East, the latter
also published by the University of Chicago Press.

The University of Chicago Press, Chicago 60637

The University of Chicago Press, Ltd., London

Library of Congress Cataloging in Publication Data
Main entry under title:

The Economic history of Turkey, 1800-1914.

    (Publications of the Center for Middle Eastern
Studies; no. 13)
    "Companion volume to [editor's] The Economic history
of the Middle East ... and The Economic history of Iran."
    Bibliography: p.
    Includes index.
    1. Turkey--Economic conditions. I. Issawi, Charles
Philip. II. Series: Chicago. University. Center for
Middle Eastern Studies. Publications; no. 13.
HC491.E26   330.9561'01   80-444
ISBN 0-226-38603-1

To Columbia University and Princeton University
with deep gratitude

Contents

Chapter 3: Trade   74

Chapter 4: Transport

Chapter 6: Industry

Preface

This book is a companion volume to The Economic History of the Middle East (University of Chicago Press, 1966), which dealt mainly with the eastern Arab countries, and The Economic History of Iran (University of Chicago Press, 1971). The present volume covers the area within the boundaries of the Republic of Turkey with the addition of some islands (Samos, Rhodes, Mytilene) and Macedonia, which remained in the Ottoman Empire until the eve of the First World War and played an important part in its economy. The term "Ottoman Empire," rather than "Turkey" has been used to designate the wider area under the rule of the Sultans at the specified date.

As with its predecessors, the primary aim in selecting the material has been to include the best and most interesting texts available, but with emphasis on the less accessible sources. Within this framework, five criteria have been applied. First, no passage from any book or journal in English has been published. This has led to the exclusion of important writings by Eton, Lynch, MacFarlane, Senior, Slade, Thornton, Urquhart, Walsh, White, and others and of works by such contemporary scholars as Berkes, Blaisdell, Chapman, Gordon, Karpat, Earle, Gibb and Bowen, Inalcik, B. Lewis, G. Lewis, Mardin, Mears, Puryear, Rustow, Stirling, and Wolf. Second, preference has been given to unpublished over published material. Third, texts in non-Western languages have been given preference over texts in Western languages, and, within the latter group, non-English texts over English. Fourth, priority has been given to reports and articles over books and to older books over more recently published ones. Last, since the main laws, treaties, and concessionary and other agreements have been reproduced in J. C. Hurewitz, Diplomacy in the Near and Middle East, or are available in G. Young, Corps de droit Ottoman, no attempt has been made to include such documents here.

Of the 126 selections, 100--almost all the English and French ones--are published here for the first time. The texts cover two centuries, the first text having been written in 1790, and the latest in the 1970s. The texts are drawn from English, French, Turkish, German, Russian, Italian, Dutch, Hebrew, and Armenian. The modern Turkish texts were translated by Ahmet Evin and Aygül Sönmez, the Armenian by Hagop Barsoumian, the Hebrew by Marc Brandriss, the Dutch by G. van Wersch, and one of the German texts by Walter Theurer, all of Columbia University. The Ottoman texts were translated by K. Barbir and E. Toledano, of Princeton University. All the other passages were translated by me.

Each chapter of the book is preceded by an essay, and most selections by an introductory note with bibliographical references. The selections and introductions have been

arranged to provide a more or less consecutive narrative and to bring out the salient features of the branch of the economy studied in the chapter. A few explanatory words or sen-
tences, and cross-references inserted in the text or footnotes, are enclosed in brackets.
Otherwise, except for some omissions--which are indicated--no attempt has been made to edit
the texts.

I have used the pound sterling as the basic unit of account, partly because most of
the source material is British but mainly because the pound was by far the most important
currency in international trade and finance. For purposes of conversion, during most of
the period under review the pound was equal to about five dollars, ten gold rubles, twenty
marks, or twenty-five francs. The rates of exchange of the Ottoman kuruş are given in
chapter 7, selection 1, and those of other currencies where they are mentioned in the text.

I have made no attempt to change the fanciful spelling of Turkish words and names, and
of those from other languages, used by the authors of the texts reproduced. In the translated texts and introductions I have followed modern Turkish spelling and usage for names
of places within the present borders, e.g., Izmir rather than Smyrna. For places outside
the Republic I have followed current English usage, e.g., Salonica, Philippopolis. Turkish
terms for weights, measures, and currency have been underlined.

I should like to thank H. M. Stationery Office, Ministère des Affaires Etrangères,
Haus-Hof und Staatsarchiv, the Turkish Embassy in London, and Başvekalet Arivi for permission to reproduce or translate the documents taken from their archives; Professor Enver
Ziya Karal for the extract from his book in chapter 2; the Ben-Zvi Institute for the article by Rofeh, also in chapter 2; and Wolters-Noordhoff Publishing, for the extract from the
book by Brünner in chapter 4. I have received much encouragement from my colleagues J. C.
Hurewitz and Avram Udovitch, and a great deal of help from Bernard Lewis, who read the
manuscript and made many helpful suggestions. Şevket Pamuk helped me with sources and
Timur Kuran with transliteration. Lily Wheeler and Grace Edelman typed a large part of a
messy manuscript. The index of place names was prepared by Yeşim Arat and Sharmin
Batmanghelidj. Above all, I should like to thank my wife, whose help at every stage was
indispensable.

Last, I wish to express my gratitude to the Social Science Research Council which
granted me a fellowship in 1975-76; to Columbia University and Princeton University, whose
financial assistance made it possible for me to carry out much of the work that went into
this book; and to the Rockefeller Foundation, whose hospitality at the Villa Serbelloni I
shall never forget.

Abbreviations and Symbols

FO   United Kingdom, Public Record Office, Foreign Office Series
BT   United Kingdom, Public Record Office, Board of Trade Series
A and P   United Kingdom, Parliament, Accounts and Papers
CC   France, Ministère des Affaires Etrangères, Correspondance Commerciale
BC   France, Ministère des Affaires Etrangères, Bulletin Consulaire
HHS   Austria, Haus-Hof und Staatsarchiv
BVA=BEO   Turkey, Başvekâlet Arşivi, Bab ı Âli Evrak Odası
TE   Turkish Embassy, London, archives, 1836–1914
USDSP   United States, Department of State, Papers Relating to the Foreign
          Relations of the United States
USSC   United States, Department of State, Special Consular Reports
RC   Revue Commerciale du Levant, Bulletin Mensuel de la Chambre de Commerce
          Française de Constantinople
TJ   British Chamber of Commerce of Turkey, Trade Journal
EI(2)   Encyclopaedia of Islam
IA   Islam Ansiklopedisi
IJMES   International Journal of Middle East Studies
JESHO   Journal of the Economic and Social History of the Orient
JEH   Journal of Economic History
JEEH   Journal of European Economic History
EHME   Charles Issawi, Economic History of the Middle East
EHI   Charles Issawi, Economic History of Iran
..   figure not available
--   nil or negligible
()   figure estimated, e.g., (20)
/   between dates indicates fiscal or Muslim years, e.g., 1878/9
–   between dates indicates full period covered by the years, e.g., 1878–80

1

Introduction

The economic history of the Ottoman Empire has still to be written. The scanty published data for the seventeenth and eighteenth centuries make it almost impossible to establish definite patterns or trends, but it seems clear that political decline was accompanied
by at least relative economic decline: compared to both Western and Eastern Europe, the
Empire's economy was much weaker in 1800 than it had been in 1550. It is even possible
that there had been an absolute deterioration, but the evidence for this is much less definite. This change was the result of several powerful forces: increasing cost of armaments
and war; population changes; the great inflation of the sixteenth and seventeenth centuries
and the continuing rise in prices in the eighteenth; technological stagnation in agriculture, transport, and the handicrafts; the shift in world trade routes and the sharp decline
in the relative importance of the Mediterranean; an unfavorable balance of trade with, and
outflow of bullion to, Iran and India; and the effects on the Ottoman economy and society
of increasing contacts with Europe.

The hardening of Austrian, Spanish, Portuguese, Iranian, and Russian resistance to the
Ottoman advance and the great improvement in armaments meant the end of easy conquests,
with their plentiful booty and rising tax revenues, the increasing economic drain of holding the border areas, and the strain on the budget of greater expenditure for arms and
troops.[1] The change in the nature of warfare sapped the basis of the tımar system of land-
holding that had contributed so much to the Empire's strength, and the government's need
for revenue, accentuated by its inelastic tax system, led to increasing use of iltizam, or
tax farming; this adversely affected the cultivators, who had enjoyed much more protection
against extortion in the old system than in the new.[2]

The rapid population growth in the sixteenth century to an estimated 30 million for
the Empire and 8 million for Anatolia around 1600[3] appears to have strained the country's
resources and contributed to the breakdown marked by the Celali revolts of the seventeeth
century.[4] It seems to have been followed by a sharp decline in numbers and depopulation of
the Anatolian countryside--but not the Balkan--probably in the eighteenth century. The
scanty available data suggest that in 1800 the population of Anatolia was distinctly smaller than in 1600 (see chap. 2, sel. 1).[5]

The effects of the price inflation that gathered momentum in the 1580s, and which of
course was part of a worldwide movement, were even more devastating. The silver content of
the akçe was repeatedly reduced, from 0.731 grams in 1566 to 0.384 in 1586 and 0.306 in
1618, and its value in terms of gold dropped correspondingly. Prices of foodstuffs

increased even more, the index (1489=100) rising from 182 in 1585 to a peak of 631 in 1605, after which it fell back to 462 in 1655.[6] However, further debasement of the currency in the seventeenth and eighteenth centuries provoked a new, sharp rise in prices (see 7:1,2). Inflation disrupted Ottoman finances, demoralized the bureaucracy, and disturbed the social equilibrium.[7]

In the seventeenth century, Ottoman agriculture benefited from the introduction of two crops: tobacco and maize; both spread rapidly and by the eighteenth century were important export items.[8] Otherwise, there was no noteworthy change and the Agricultural Revolution had no repercussions in the Empire. Nor did the Industrial Revolution, and the numerous--and until near the end of the eighteenth century flourishing--handicrafts showed no signs of technological progress. Meanwhile European products were becoming not only cheaper but better, and in 1800 Clarke could say that in Istanbul one found only "the worst manufactured wares of the world, . . . unfit for any other market, . . . and yet of the highest price."[9] Shipbuilding techniques also failed to keep up with those of Europe and at least as early as 1789 the Porte was buying, from the United States, Sweden, and elsewhere, both transport and warships.[10] Technological stagnation, together with smaller financial resources and, most important, much greater vulnerability to both Christian and Muslim piracy and the arbi trariness of local officials, explains why Ottoman shippers gradually lost most of the coasting trade to Europeans.[11] But, until the advent of steam, the gap between the merchant navies was not so great as to preclude a revival of Greek, Ragusan, and other shipping between 1740 and 1815, a period during which Europe was mostly at war.[12] Internal transport showed the same stagnation; hard-surface roads, including Roman, were maintained in Rumelia for carts while soft-surface roads were used in Anatolia by camels, but, in contrast with Europe, there was no significant road or canal building and, except for a few carriages in towns and carts in villages, no wheeled transport.[13]

The shift in trade routes also had an adverse effect on the Ottoman economy. The opening of the sea route around Africa diverted only part of the Far Eastern trade, since the Portuguese had limited control over the Indian Ocean. But in the seventeenth century they were succeeded by the Dutch and British, who captured not only the Far Eastern but part of the Iranian silk trade, which was so important to Turkey as a source of both revenue and raw materials for the handicrafts of Bursa and other towns.[14]

Very different, but no less far-reaching in its consequences, was the course of events in the Black Sea trade. In the sixteenth century that sea and its surrounding lands were firmly under Ottoman control, supplying grain, fish, and other produce and carrying some transit trade from Iran and Central Asia; foreign ships from the Mediterranean were not allowed to go beyond Istanbul, which "monopolized the long-distance trade as well as the domestic trade of the Black Sea, acting as a screen between this Mediterranean extremity and the rest of the sea."[15] In the course of the next two centuries the trade of both Russia and Poland through the Black Sea increased considerably; it was carried out by Greek, Wallachian, Armenian, Jewish, Tatar, Turkish, and Persian merchants, mostly Ottoman subjects.[16] The eighteenth century saw a large expansion of trade but also the diversion of Central Asian trade to Russia and the end of the Ottoman monopoly. In 1718, the Treaty of Passarowitz granted freedom of commerce on the Danube to Austrian ships, which however were not allowed to enter the Black Sea. The Küçük Kaynarca Treaty of 1774, clarified by the Russo-Turkish Treaty of 1783, authorized Russia to trade with Ottoman subjects and to send merchant ships through the Straits, a right soon extended to the other Great Powers. The result was that Istanbul was now bypassed and that the Black Sea trade was taken over by Greeks and Europeans.[17]

A further disequilibrating factor was the tightening of economic relations with Europe. In the seventeenth and eighteenth centuries the Ottoman Empire's share in European trade fell drastically: in France from one-half of the trade in the late sixteenth century to one-twentieth in the 1780s, and in Britain from one-tenth in the middle of the seventeenth century to 1 percent at the end of the eighteenth.[18] But this sharp relative decline masks a large absolute increase in the eighteenth century, French trade with the Ottoman Empire rising three-fold and Austrian severalfold while that of Britain and Holland showed a small decrease.[19] European products competed more and more successfully with Ottoman handicrafts; textiles were particularly affected and Ottoman exports shifted from manufactured goods to raw materials--silk, mohair, and cotton; this tendency was accentuated by the increasing preference of wealthy Ottomans for European products, the stagnation of Ottoman crafts, the protective tariffs of Britain and France, and the competition of Indian textiles. In addition, colonial goods, such as sugar and coffee, formerly exported from the Middle East, were imported from overseas in increasing quantities.[20] The path-breaking studies by Genç[21] on the yield of tax farms in the eighteenth century show a sharp and almost uninterrupted rise in duties on foreign trade, accompanied, in the second half of the century, by a marked decline in those levied on such handicraft products as silk, and woolen and cotton cloth. It should be added that the Europeans used their increasing influence to thwart the few attempts being made to promote Ottoman handicrafts.[22] This was facilitated by the indifference of the ruling bureaucrats and military to the interests of the entrepreneurial bourgeoisie.[23] At the same time the opening of new markets for Ottoman and particularly Balkan agricultural produce in Europe encouraged the formation of agricultural estates (çiftliks) and further undermined the timar system. These economic shifts had far-reaching social and political effects. The Turkish Muslims, who had been the backbone of the handicraft groups in the Balkans until the middle of the eighteenth century, were gradually transformed into unskilled laborers.[24] On the other hand a new group of Christian traders, agriculturists, shippers, and craftsmen sprang up and gained in wealth, education, and power.[25] Although some branches of Ottoman trade, e.g., between Anatolia and Egypt, remained mainly in Muslim hands,[26] most of European trade passed into that of foreigners or minority groups (see 2:9).

The weakening of the central authority by the wars with Russia in 1768-74 and 1787-92 encouraged both the struggle for independence of the Balkan nationalities and separatist movements by the provincial paşas and ayans. By the beginning of the nineteenth century effective central government control was confined to a small area adjacent to Istanbul. Arabia, Egypt, Iraq, and most of Syria were virtually autonomous, as were large parts of Anatolia. In the Balkans various notables had achieved autonomy and the Serbian war of independence was under way. And both Austria and Russia had already pushed deep into Ottoman territory.[27] Total disintegration was avoided only because of the preoccupation of the European states with the revolutionary and Napoleonic wars and the determination of Mahmud II (1808-39), who was able to reassert his authority over large parts of his empire with the help of a modernized army and bureaucracy. But this was done only at the cost of provoking resistance among peoples who had become accustomed to local autonomy, notably the Greeks. The struggle for survival was to continue much longer.

The history of the last century and a half of the Ottoman Empire was largely shaped by two forces: the national liberation movement of the non-Turkish peoples and the steady encroachment of the Great Powers. In its attempt to counter these threats, the Ottoman government found itself almost continually at war. Table 1 lists only the major conflicts, and omits such important expeditions as the one against Osman Pasvanoğlu (in Rumelia,

1795-97), Ali paşa of Janina (1820-22), and Hüseyin paşa of Bosnia (1831), the "second conquest of Iraq" in 1831, the campaigns against the Derebeys ("Lords of the Valleys") in
Anatolia, the repeated attempts to subdue the Druzes in Syria, the Kurds in eastern Anatolia, and the Yemenis, and the Cretan insurrections of 1841, 1858, and 1875-78, as well as
the wars waged on behalf of the Porte by Mehmet Ali against the Wahhabis of Arabia (1811-
18). With the possible exception of France, the Empire was more often at war than any
other country in the world.

Table 1

Ottoman Wars: 1768-1923

1768-1774	War with Russia	1853-1856	Crimean War
1787-1792	War with Russia and Austria	1866-1868	Cretan insurrection
1798-1801	French Invasion of Egypt and Syria	1875-1876	Insurrections in Bosnia,
1804-1813	First Serbian War of Independence		Herzegovnia, and Bulgaria,
1806-1809	War with Russia and Britain		war with Serbia and Montenegro
1809-1812	War with Russia	1877-1878	War with Russia and Serbia
1815-1817	Second Serbian War of Independence	1878	Insurrection in Thessaly
1821	Rumanian insurrection	1896-1897	Cretan insurrection, war with
1821-1823	War with Iran		Greece
1821-1830	Greek War of Independence	1912	War with Italy
1827-1829	War with Russia, France, and	1912-1913	War with Bulgaria, Greece, and
	Britain		Serbia
1831-1833	First Turco-Egyptian War	1914-1918	First World War
1839-1841	Second Turco-Egyptian War	1920	War with Armenian Republic
1848	Rumanian insurrection	1920-1923	War of Independence

The sheer cost of these conflicts (see 7:Introduction) goes far to explain the fact
that Turkey made relatively little economic progress during this period. But other factors
were also at work, notably the social and ethnic structure of the Empire, which concentrated political power in groups that had no real understanding of or interest in economic
development, and deprived those that were economically active of support and encouragement.
Another factor was the extent and nature of the political and economic influence exercised
by the Great Powers through the Capitulations and Commercial Treaties (see 3:Introduction).

Almost all the wars ended in defeat. Even when it happened to be on the winning side,
as in the 1841 campaign against Mehmet Ali or in the Crimean War, the Ottoman government
tended to fall into greater dependence on its allies. The result was the steady shrinkage
of the Empire. In 1800 it stretched, nominally, from Croatia, Moldavia, and Wallachia in
the north to Iraq in the east, Yemen in the south, and Egypt in the west; and Ottoman
suzerainty was acknowledged by the North African states of Algiers, Tunis, and Tripoli.
Excluding the Arabian peninsula and North Africa west of Egypt, its territory was some
3,000,000 square kilometres (nearly 1,200,000 square miles) and its population may be
roughly estimated at 25 million. By 1880, the territory had shrunk to under 1,500,000
square kilometres and the population was about 17 million; by 1914 the corresponding figures were about 1,300,000 square kilometres and 22 million.

In this struggle for survival the Ottomans sought salvation in modernization and
centralization--modernization of society to provide the requisite economic and human resources, and centralization to enable the government to appropriate a larger share of these
resources and give it fuller control over the course of events. But here the government
faced mighty obstacles, both internal and external. The archaic and rigid social struc-
tures could not be altered overnight. The ethnic and religious heterogeneity of the Empire,
and its social diversity, which ranged from the cosmopolitan circles of Istanbul through

the Anatolian peasant masses almost untouched by Western civilization to the tribal communities of Kurdistan and Arabia, multiplied severalfold the usual resistance to change. In
every field numerous vested interests stood to lose wealth, power, and prestige from reform.
The reformers themselves had their full share of human weakness; their understanding of the
Western civilization they took as a model was very imperfect and their knowledge of
economics--insofar as they took any interest in that subject--was confined to an acceptance
of Manchesterian free trade.[28] The bureaucracy, which was the main instrument for carrying
out the reforms, was cumbrous, shortsighted, and corrupt. The government's control over
its territory was far from complete and its ability to impose its will and enforce law and
order was very limited not only in such distant provinces as Yemen or Cyrenaica but even in
Syria and the Kurdish areas.[29] Above all, the government was profoundly distrusted by its
subjects, who could not conceive that its reforms could possibly promote their welfare.[30]

The external obstacles were no less formidable. The European powers, which wielded
great influence, were basically opposed to an effective reform of the Empire, whose territory they coveted. As Mordtmann put it so neatly in 1850: "Diplomacy accordingly has the
sad duty to move in a perpetual circle; it must oppose each reform 'because the treaties
are opposed to this or that reform' and revision of the treaties is forbidden so long as
abuses exist in the administration."[31] The Commercial Treaties made it impossible for the
government, until 1911, to raise import duties, a measure desired for both revenue and
protection (chaps. 3, 6, and 7). The Capitulations exempted foreigners and 'protected'
non-Muslims from Ottoman taxation and jurisdiction and gave them a great competitive advantage over Turks (chap. 2); they also made it almost impossible to reform the fiscal system,
since it would have been politically impossible to tax Turks while exempting the foreigners
and protégés who controlled most of the modern sector. When excessive debt led to bankruptcy, the Great Powers set up the Public Debt Administration, consisting of their representatives, which further restricted the Porte's freedom of action; however, the discipline
imposed by that body was on balance salutary and it did help to implement several measures
favorable to agriculture (chap. 5).

In the economic sphere the reforms aimed first of all at assuring the world that all
Ottoman subjects would receive equal treatment and that the government desired economic
progress (decrees of 1839 and 1856).[32] To facilitate economic transactions and further re-
assure foreigners and non-Muslims, a set of codes patterned on Western law was enacted:
commercial in 1850, penal 1858, commercial procedure 1861, maritime 1863. In the 1840s
mixed commercial courts (Ticaret mahkemesi) were established in the main cities; they included Europeans and Muslim and non-Muslim Ottomans.[33] Port Chambers (Liman Odası) were
also set up, to deal with maritime matters. In 1838 committees were established for agriculture, trade, industry, and public works.[34]

Education was slowly reformed and Western-type curricula were introduced. The earliest changes took place, as in many developing countries, e.g., Egypt, at the level of
higher education, with the sending of young men abroad and the opening of medical and engineering schools in 1827. Elementary and secondary schools followed, and by the outbreak
of the First World War there were over 1.3 million pupils (chap. 2).

Attempts were made to promote agricultural development by setting up, in 1838, an
Agricultural and Trade Council (Meclisi Ziraat ve Ticaret)--promoted, after various experiments, to a Ministry of Trade and Agriculture in 1862--by appointing inspectors, and by
seeking the advice of local notables on measures for improvement, but the effect was negligible (5:12). More far-reaching were various measures affecting land tenure, notably the

abolition of tımars in 1831, and the Land Code of 1858 that curbed the extension of vakf (mortmain) and established both the cultivator's right to continued and undisturbed possession and the government's right to ownership.[35] The objective, which was largely achieved, was at once to stimulate agricultural development and increase tax revenues (chap. 5). In 1867, under foreign pressure, foreigners were allowed to purchase land, but the total amount acquired by them remained relatively small (2:11). In the subsequent decades the government, aided by the Public Debt Administration, gave considerable help to cultivators by setting up agricultural schools, model farms and nurseries, and providing extension services and credit.

Efforts to arrest the decline of the handicrafts proved vain and, given the impossibility of providing protection because of the Commercial Treaties, little could be done to promote either government or private industry. It was only in the years immediately preceding the First World War that more active and effective measures were taken. The Mining Laws of 1861, 1886, and 1906 did, on the other hand, encourage foreign investment and led to much development (see below, and chap. 6). A postal service was organized in 1834[36] and telegraph lines laid down during the Crimean War. And although almost all the railways were privately built they relied heavily on the kilometric guarantees and other privileges granted to them by the state (chap. 4).

All these measures helped, but the main engine of growth was undoubtedly the forces of the world market. World demand for Turkish farm produce remained high, and the growth of the population and availability of cultivable land (chap. 2) made it possible greatly to expand agricultural output, especially for certain cash crops, such as cotton, tobacco, and raisins; after about 1890 railways in Anatolia also led to a large extension of grain cultivation (chap. 5). As a result, between the 1840s and 1913 the exports of the area corresponding to that of present-day Turkey rose about sevenfold in real terms while imports, which consisted mainly of manufactured and other consumer goods, increased ninefold (chap. 3). Mineral output multiplied severalfold, its range greatly widening, and in the two decades before the First World War the nucleus of a manufacturing industry was formed (chap. 6). The railway network expanded and began to serve large sections of Turkey; modern ports were built in Izmir, Istanbul, and elsewhere (chap. 4). A rudimentary banking system had come into being (chap. 7). But concurrently with, and only partly related to, this development, Turkey had contracted a huge public and private debt, aggregating some ₤200 million, the servicing of which absorbed nearly a third of its export earnings (chap. 7).

It is unfortunately impossible to measure Turkey's economic growth in terms of national product. Table 2 shows the only available estimates, which cover European Turkey, Anatolia, Syria, Lebanon, Palestine, and Iraq.

The per capita figure of about ₤T10, or $50, per annum is very close to that of Egypt and Greece at that time. Regional breakdowns show the following per capita incomes for 1907: Istanbul and Çatalca ₤T18, Salonica 10, other European 8, Anatolia 8 (ranging from 10 in the Marmara, Aegean, and Mediterranean provinces to 7 in other parts), Syria, Lebanon, and Palestine 9, Iraq 6.[37] Agriculture accounted for over half of gross national product and mining and manufacturing for a tenth. There are no figures on savings and net investment, but it may be surmised that both were positive, though small.

No earlier figures are available, but in view of the large increase in agriculture and in the modern sector--which outstripped the population growth--it is very probable that per capita output and income rose significantly between the 1870s and the First World War.[38]

Table 2

National Income (in millions of Turkish pounds)

	1907	1913	1914
Agriculture, forestry, fishing	113.9	104.2	130.6
Mining	1.7	1.6	1.1
Manufacturing	22.3	25.5	24.4
Construction	6.2	6.1	4.4
Transport	6.9	7.3	6.8
Trade	18.9	21.7	18.3
Finance	2.2	2.7	2.6
Government	13.7	17.7	18.8
House rents	7.4	6.6	6.6
Professions and services	10.2	10.2	11.3
Domestic income	203.4	203.7	225.0
Rest of the world	-1.5	-1.0	-1.0
National income	201.9	202.7	223.9
Indirect taxes	8.1	9.7	7.7
Net national product	210.0	212.4	231.6
Depreciation	9.2	9.1	9.5
Gross national product	219.2	221.4	241.1

Source: Eldem, p. 302.

The level of living continued to be low, particularly in the rural areas, as may be seen from a long and thorough report on northern Anatolia in 1870 (extracts in 2:7). But the available evidence indicates a rise in real wages in the towns (2:6). And even in the rural areas some improvement seems to have occurred during the second half of the period. But there were sharp setbacks, like the 1873-74 famine in the Ankara region, which is reported to have carried off some 90 percent of the livestock and 25 percent of the inhabitants of the area; another 20 percent migrated. The following comments illustrate the change.

In 1838 a memorandum affirmed that the causes of the decay of Turkey were not the loss of Greece, Egypt, and Syria but the internal system. In the Izmir region lands were being left uncultivated and imports were declining: e.g., until 1826 Britain had sent Izmir 800-900 barrels of tin a year, most of which went to the interior for tinning copper pots; but the figure had fallen to 100 because of depopulation and misery that forced the peasants to sell their utensils. Since the destruction of the Janissaries, "who had been born guardians of the interest of the people," the government had become more extortionate, granting legal monopolies that benefited the sultan and illegal ones that benefited the governors, raising taxes and duties and debasing the currency (Considérations sur le tariff, FO 195/152).[39]

In 1845 in Bursa "Numbers of people . . . have been selling their copper utensils and convertible articles of furniture and dress to raise money at any sacrifice in price for the purchase of bread, as the first want to be satisfied" (Administrative Conditions, FO 78/652). But a few years later "There is a change also for the better among the rural population of the District--being no longer harassed and plundered by the ruling authority or by his connivance" (Agricultural Report, 1850, FO 78/868), and selection 2:6 gives a more cheerful picture of the town.

The reduction in warfare seems to have eased conditions. In 1850 in Salonica: "Cotton stockings are more worn by the people of the country than formerly, hence an increased demand for twist" (FO 78/831). In Rhodes in 1859: "The social condition of the agricultural labourer may, on the whole, be considered good. He lives on bread, cheese, salt fish, vegetables and fruit. He seldom tastes animal food."[40] And in a report written in 1858 (FO 78/1637) the following statement is made: "If we compare Turkey as she is with what she was 25 or 30 years ago, the change is marvellous. Men who lived at the former period tell me every day they can hardly credit the state of things now, when they remember what existed in the days of their youth." However, to equal "the first and most civilized states of Europe, the progress she has to make is so immense, that that she has already made appears almost insignificant."

In Kastamonu in 1879 "the country peasants live very poorly, rarely eating meat and consuming only the products of their gardens. They have soup made of rice or flour, sour milk (yogurt), and bread baked in flat cakes. Milk is plentiful everywhere in the vilayet. The townsmen live better, often eating meat. Bread is cheap, and not of very bad quality, 36 paras the oke. The peasants living costs about 2 to 3 piastres per diem, mechanics 5 piastres and the better classes up to 20 piastres. The clothing of the peasanty is generally of home-made canvas, with a small quantity of English cotton manufactures, and rough cloth jacket. The better classes wear different coloured garments of French cloth, lined with furs, and English cotton under-garments."[41]

In the decade or two before the First World War, there are indications of a rise in the level of living. In the poor region of Mamuret ul-Aziz the demand for such articles as bicycles, watches, locks, pumps, saws, and other tools was reported to be rising.[42] In Konya: "There are signs that prosperity is still growing. Konia city grows and new and better buildings are springing up. A corn exchange has been opened. There are new shops and industries. The Bank does better business . . . . Though the bulk of the population are poor agriculturists, the demand for better and more fashionable things steadily increases."[43] There are also signs of capital accumulation and investment: "Excluding the capital sunk in land there is thought to be about ₤200,000 in business in Mersina, ₤300,000 in Tarsus and rather more in Adana."[44]

All this points to both economic growth and development, but in the eyes of the Turks the process had one fatal flaw: the political, legal, and economic changes had given foreigners and non-Muslims an undue advantage and diverted the greater part of the benefits to them (2:17). As a British diplomat and scholar put it in 1900: "But when force does not rule, when progress, commerce, finance and law give the mixed population of the Empire a chance of redistributing themselves according to their wits, the Turk and the Christian are not equal; the Christian is superior. He acquires the money and land of the Turk, and proves in a law court that he is right in so doing. One may criticize the Turkish character, but given their idiosyncrasies, one must admit that they derive little profit from such blessings of civilization as are introduced into their country. Foreign syndicates profit most, and after them native Christians, but not the Osmanli, except insofar as he can make them disgorge their gains."[45]

Turkish awareness was, however, growing and countermeasures were being taken. The banks, public utility, and other enterprises founded by Muslims (2:Introduction) are one indication. Another is the government's attempt to exert more control over foreign companies. But most significant is the far greater attention given by the government to economic matters. A perusal of the archives of the Ministry of Trade and Public Works (BVA-BEO) for 1907-8 shows correspondence relating to the following matters: exemption of machinery from customs duty (6:19); Izmir-Kasaba, Baghdad, and Hijaz railways; various roads; Agricultural Bank; agricultural credit in Adana; electricity supply and electric tramways in Istanbul, Bursa, Trabzon, and Samsun; Şirketi Mahsuse, Bosphorus and Golden

Horn shipping lines; Karasi mines; Istanbul water supply; sending of young men abroad for training; Chambers of Commerce; patent laws; Brussels exhibition; and other matters. And the transport, agricultural, and industrial schemes being implemented (4, 5, 6:Introductions) witness to the quickening tempo of economic activity. Turkey seemed poised for an economic upsurge; instead, it was condemned to eight years of shattering warfare.

1. Lewis, Emergence, pp. 24-27; Barkan, "Price Revolution," which shows the change from budget surplus to deficit; on this, as on other topics, Shaw, History, provides useful information.
2. Inalcık, Ottoman Empire, pp. 107-18.
3. Barkan, "Essai"; Cook, Population; for an excellent study of the data and literature, see Leila Erder, "The Measurement of Preindustrial Population Changes: The Ottoman Empire from the 15th to the 17th Century," Middle Eastern Studies, October 1975; for the whole Mediterranean, Braudel, 1:402-18.
4. Akdağ, Celali.
5. The population decline, and the views of such contemporary observers as Eton and Thornton, are discussed by Issawi in Naff and Owen, pp. 152-57.
6. Barkan, "Price Revolution"; Braudel, 1:137-38, 462-542.
7. The kuruş, which in the mid-seventeenth century was worth 5-6 francs had fallen by 1774 to 2.6 and by 1811 equalled one franc--Novichev, Istoriya, 3:91.
8. EHME, p. 60; Stoianovich, p. 274; Lewis, Istanbul, pp. 133-35, for Peçevi's observations on tobacco.
9. Quoted in Stoianovich, p. 259; see also Issawi in Naff and Owen, pp. 159-61, and, more generally, Gibb and Bowen, pp. 281-99.
10. Despatch from Carmarthen, 15 March 1789, FO 78/10; but good warships were still being built in Istanbul at that time, see Novichev, 2:30.
11. EHME, p. 37.
12. Ibid.; Stoianovich, pp. 273-76; Papadopoulos; and 4:Introduction.
13. Bulliet, passim; EI(2), s.v. "adjala," "Anadolu," "araba"; also information supplied by H. Inalcık.
14. Lewis, p. 28; Inalcık, Ottoman Empire, pp. 44-45.
15. Braudel, 1:110-15.
16. Ibid., pp. 191-202; H. Klimesz, "Poland's Trade Through the Black Sea in the Eighteenth Century," Polish Review, 1970; Grenville, pp. 49-50.
17. Stoianovich, pp. 288-306; Karpat, "Inquiry," pp. 51-54; see also below, 3:2; in 1700 the Porte had rejected Peter's demand for freedom of navigation of Russian ships in the Black Sea and through the Straits--Novichev, Istoriya, 1:191.
18. Davies, in Cook, Studies, p. 203; Masson, XVIIe and XVIIIe.
19. Masson, XVIIIe; Davies, in Cook, p. 203; Stoianovich, p. 260; MacGregor, 2:66-67.
20. Barkan, "Price Revolution"; Issawi, in Richards, pp. 256-58; Gibb and Bowen, 1:296; for the earlier period, Inalcık, Ottoman Empire, pp. 121-39.
21. See the Bibliography.
22. For examples, EHME, pp. 31-32; Stoianovich, p. 258.
23. Issawi, in Richards, p. 251, and sources cited therein.
24. Karpat, "Inquiry"; İnalcik, "Capital Formation," and Jennings, in JESHO, 1973.
25. Stoianovich, passim; the Porte was fully aware of the predominance of non-Muslim Ottomans in foreign trade--see memorandum to British Ambassador, 5 July 1802 (FO 78/36) and CC Smyrna, vol. 86--and Selim III made noteworthy but unsuccessful efforts to reduce the influence of foreigners in trade and transport, to encourage Turkish shippers and merchants, and to curb the issuing of "protection" to non-Muslims--Shaw, Between, pp. 177-79 and 341.
26. Raymond, 1:167-71, 185-89.
27. On this period, see Shaw, Between, especially chapts. XV and XVIII.
28. A few dissenting voices were raised, such as those of Namık Kemal and Ahmed Midhat, who sought to promote industry, or of minor bureaucrats who wished to protect agriculture--Quataert, p. 23 and sources cited, and Mardin, pp. 192-93, 236, 321-23, 369, 388.
29. Many Armenians from Muş emigrated to Georgia because of the oppression of Kurds; in 1841, by abolishing the kişlak, or winter quartering of Kurds on Armenians, the paşa induced many to return (Trade of Erzurum 1841, FO 78/491)--see also 2:13. But the mid-1840s saw numerous Kurdish uprisings (FO 78/832).
30. An example from the Salonica region is illustrative. "The Porte last year directed the Governor of this Province to compel the inhabitants of the rural districts to plant a certain number of mulberry trees. The trees were planted but the peasants suspecting the intentions of the Government and believing that in ordering the plantings its real object was to tax them, resorted to all kinds of devices to prevent the trees taking root, and consequently some of them were never watered and died, some were pulled up during the

night whilst a great number were found to have been mere twigs which could never have taken root" (Trade 1863, FO 195/771).

31. Quoted by Quataert, p. 49; see also Moltke, pp. 414-15, and the views reported by the economist Nassau Senior, pp. 42 and 118.

32. There is an extensive literature on this subject; see in particular, B. Lewis, Emergence; Davison; Ward and Rustow; and Novichev, vol. 3.

33. "Civil suits when relating to trade and various other money transactions are referrable for decision to the Tigiaret or mercantile Tribunals, where existing. But those are confined to some principal ports and internal cities. In the great majority of cases besides, affecting the landed possessions and many other interests of Christians, they remain at the mercy of the law which rejects all but Muslim witnesses against a party of that creed" (Local Administration of Bursa, 1860, 1860, FO 78/1534).

34. Lewis, Emergence, p. 97; Novichev, Istoriya, 2:246.

35. Lewis, Emergence, pp. 89-92, 117; Novichev, Istoriya, 2:225-36; Shaw, History, 2:37, 74, 114 and 230-36.

36. Lewis, Emergence, pp. 93-94.

37. Eldem, p. 305.

38. Eldem, p. 308, estimates that from 1889 to 1914 national income rose at 2 percent a year and population at 1 percent. For a longer period some scattered estimates may be given. In 1846 the gross annual per capita agricultural output of Cyprus was put at about ₺4 (FO 78/661A). In 1862 the gross per capita output of cereals, silk, wool, and tobacco in the sancak of Edirne was ₺2-12-6 (A and P 1865, vol. 53, "Adrianople"), or say ₺3 for all agricultural produce. In 1863 the gross animal and vegetable output of the paşalik of Kurdistan was ₺1-11-0 (ibid., "Turkey"). Around 1880 the gross vegetable output of the vilayet of Trabzon may be calculated at about 130 piastres (say ₺1=?=0) per capita (based on figures in A and P 1882, vol. 70, "Trebizond"). These estimates may be compared with about ₺7 for 1913-14, which implies an increase far bigger than the rise in prices between those dates. These figures are in line with the available estimates for Europe--see P. Bairoch, "Europe's Gross National Product, 1800-1975," JEEH, Fall 1976.

39. Several foreign observers noted that the suppression of the Janissaries removed the major check on the sultan's power to oppress the people, e.g., Slade and Moltke; see Lewis, Emergence, pp. 123-24; Mordtmann, p. 10; Novichev, Istoriya, 2:147-48.

40. A and P 1859, vol. 30, "Rhodes."

41. A and P 1880, vol. 74, "Kastamuni."

42. For details on earnings and demand for foreign articles, see A and P 1902, vol. 110, "Bitlis."

43. Ibid., 1908, vol. 116, "Konia."

44. Ibid., 1909, vol. 93, "Adana."

45. Eliot, p. 153; the growth of wealth and western-style conspicuous consumption in the Turkish upper class also caused much resentment--see 7:9 and Şerif Mardin, "Super Westernization," in Benedict et al., pp. 403-46.

2

Social Structure

The study of social change, as indeed of other aspects of the Ottoman Empire in the nineteenth century, is greatly impeded by the absence or unreliability of statistics. As a well-informed British consul put it in 1847: "It is impossible in this country to obtain correct statistical information, because the government are indifferent to the subject, and because the natives are too ignorant to afford it, or those who can do so, fearing that it might be used to their prejudice, mislead enquirers by erroneous statements" (Henry Calvert, 'Notes on . . . Erzurum," FO 78/703). But matters improved in the following decades, and by the end of the century information becomes much more abundant and reliable.

The population seems to have grown irregularly, at about 0.8 percent a year, over the whole period, but the large territorial losses offset the increase; the total number of inhabitants in the Empire in 1913, some 26 million, was about equal to what it had been around 1800 (2:1). That of Anatolia and Istanbul rose from some 7,500,000 in 1831 to 11,300,000 in 1884 and 15,000,000 in 1913. Available information on regional breakdowns indicates that no great shift took place and that the mass of the population was concentrated in the humid coastal areas.[1] Very little data are available on the numerous nomadic populations, but there is evidence of a considerable amount of settlement in areas that had previously been largely barren and deserted.[2]

The number of people living in towns grew at about the same rate as the total population, and no significant increase in urbanization seems to have taken place; hence, compared to other European countries, Turkey was relatively less urbanized in 1913 than in 1800. There were, however, important shifts in the composition of the urban population: that of the ports rose rapidly, thanks to the expansion of foreign trade, while many inland towns stagnated because of the decline in their handicrafts and trade and some eastern towns actually lost population. During the First World War and its aftermath, a sharp decrease in urban population occurred (2:5). Istanbul continued to tower above the other towns, and supplying its population was, as it had been for long, one of the government's main concerns (2:3, 4).

Little is known about the determinants of population growth. Birth rates were high, as in other preindustrial societies, but there is much evidence that abortion was practiced in parts of Anatolia, particularly by the Turks (2:2). Death rates were also high and the Malthusian checks operated, though not with sufficient force to prevent population growth. Wars were frequent and must have taken a heavy toll among Muslims, though no casualty figures are available. Crops often failed because of droughts, as in 1845 (5:2) and the early

11

1870s (5:Introduction), or because of locusts which, for example, in 1854 destroyed a tenth
to a fifth of the crops of the paşalık of Hüdavendigar (21 June 1854, FO 78/1023), and
famines sometimes ensued. Still more deadly were epidemics. There were many outbreaks of
the plague, especially in the first half of the period;[3] that of 1812 was particularly
devastating, carrying off an estimated 321,000 persons (220,000 Turks, 41,000 Armenians,
32,000 Jews, 28,000 Greeks, and 25 Franks) in Istanbul in six months; the British ambassador saw "no reason to suppose that this calculation is much exaggerated--but it includes
not only Pera and Galata but Scutari and houses on the Bosphorus up to the Black Sea"
(FO 78/81). Other outbreaks of the plague were reported in 1781 and 1783 in Istanbul
(FO 78/2 and 78/4) and in 1828;[4] in 1836 it killed 17,000 of the 90,000 inhabitants of
Edirne and "has been nearly equally fatal in the adjacent towns and villages," affecting
Muslims much more than Christians (12 January 1837, FO 78/314); and in 1841 it carried off
7,455 persons in Erzurum (6,783 Muslims, 404 individuals out of 728 Armenian families, 11
individuals out of 11 Greek families and 51 individuals out of 61 Catholic families--
FO 78/491). Cholera epidemics continued until the close of the century. An outbreak occurred in 1831, in Bursa, Izmir, Istanbul, and elsewhere. In 1847 cholera came from Iran,[5]
through Tabriz and Kars to Erzurum and Trabzon (17 September 1847, CC Smyrna, vol. 91). In
Erzurum there were some 3,600 deaths out of a population of 40,000 (Memorandum, FO 78/753,
and Suter to Palmerston, 3 January 1849, FO 78/796). In Trabzon out of 35,000 inhabitants
12,000 fled to the villages; of the remainder 7,000 "certainly were attacked with cholera,
2,000 of whom received almost regular medical assistance and of whom 1,600 persons were
saved. Of the remaining 5,000 although we had published the mode of proper treatment, and
had visited many once or twice, at least 1,500 of them died" (Memorandum by Dr. Borg,
FO 78/752). The epidemic then reached Zile, where out of 2,000 families "no less than a
thousand persons are reported to have been carried off in a fortnight" (Suter to Palmerston,
18 August 1848, FO 78/753), and Kayseri, where 600 out of a population of about 40,000 died
(Memorandum by Dr. Mordo, ibid.). In Adana cholera caused 700 deaths in a population of
20,000 and in Tarsus 1,355 in a population of 6,000 (FO 78/796). The epidemic then spread
to Izmir, Istanbul, and Salonica; in Istanbul 2,766 deaths were reported, and of the more
than 2,000 persons who entered the eight military hospitals two-fifths died (Report by Dr.
Rigler, FO 781/3). There was another epidemic in 1865. The 1892 epidemic was carried by
Turkish soldiers from Yemen and pilgrims from Mecca and spread to Istanbul, Izmir, and
Trabzon; in the capital 1,200 deaths were recorded in a population of about 800,000--"this
small mortality is surprising."[6]

The reduction in the incidence and deadliness of epidemics in Istanbul and the coastal
towns testifies to the great improvement in medical facilities, part of the military and
civilian reforms. In 1827 a school of medicine was opened and by 1850 Istanbul had ten
government hospitals in addition to four foreign ones and two run by the Armenian and Greek
communities.[7] Hospital accommodations and the number of Ottoman and foreign physicians
practicing in the country continued to increase until 1914. Still more important in preventing epidemics was the installation of a modern quarantine system in 1838, and its extension and improvement thereafter.[8] The force of the other two killers also diminished:
from 1856 to 1911 wars were far less frequent and intense and the improvement of transport
(chap. 4) and growth of food production after the 1870s (5:Introduction) must have greatly
reduced the incidence of famine.

Death rates among Christians and Jews may have been lower than among Muslims, and
this, together with the abortion practiced by Turks, led most observers to believe that the

Turks were rapidly diminishing in number and that the proportion of minorities was increasing (2:2). Official statistics show the contrary, the discrepancy being almost certainly due to migration (2:1). The Russian conquest of the Caucasus in the 1850s and the loss of the Ottoman provinces in Europe caused hundreds of thousands of Muslims to migrate to Turkey; according to Karpat, after the 1877-78 war more than a million moved in.[9] Many were settled in the Arab provinces, especially in Syria and Transjordan, but most remained in Anatolia, where special efforts, e.g., the Konya irrigation scheme (5:14) and in the Çukurova, were made to accommodate them.[10] Concurrently, there was a large and accelerating emigration of Greeks, Armenians, Jews, and Christian Arabs to the New World.[11] As a result, the Empire, which at the beginning of the nineteenth century had had a large Christian minority, became, at its close, overwhelmingly Muslim (2:1).

At the same time that its religious and ethnic composition was changing, the society of Turkey was becoming more complex and differentiated. Two important factors were at work: the growth of foreign trade, transport, industry, and capitalistic agriculture, which generated two new classes, a bourgeoisie (mainly non-Muslim) and an industrial working class; and the spread of modern education, which produced a small professional group and the officials required to run the armed forces, administration, and various government enterprises such as arsenals, steamships, and factories.[12]

Although some non-Muslim communities had opened schools with a modernized curriculum almost two centuries earlier, it was only around 1839 that the government began to establish primary (rüşdiye) schools using European methods; higher professional schools had been set up earlier and included, in addition to various military schools, medical, engineering, agricultural, veterinary, and teachers colleges. By 1900 Istanbul had the nucleus of a university.[13] An important landmark was the founding of the first idadiye (secondary) school in 1855-56 followed in 1868 by Galatasaray, a high school designed to train an élite. By 1876, there were 253 rüşdiye schools, of which twenty one were in Istanbul, and by 1895, fifty five idadiye (of which two were in Istanbul), with 7,200 students.[14] The table below shows the situation in 1896, and brings out both the relatively high school-attendance and the disproportionately large number of students in minority schools and in foreign establishments, most of whose pupils were also non-Muslims.

Schools and Pupils (000) in 1313 (1896)

	Muslim		Non-Muslim		Foreign		Total	
	No.	Pupils	No.	Pupils	No.	Pupils	No.	Pupils
Higher (aliye)	11	..	--	--	--	--	11	--
Secondary (idadiye)	56	5	70	11	63	8	189	24
Primary (rüşdiye)	426	31	687	76	74	7	1,187	114
Elementary (ibtidaiye)	28,615	855	5,982	317	246	17	34,843	1,189
Total	29,108	891	6,739	404	383	32	36,230	1,327

Source: Nezarat umuri ticaret ve nafia, İstatistik umumi idaresi 1316.

The higher educational level of the minorities, their exclusion from military service, the foreign protection they enjoyed, and the opportunities offered by the introduction of Western-type law largely explain their prominence in business and the professions (2:9, 12, 13, and 7:6).[16] The predominance of non-Muslims in finance, and the virtual absence of Turks in that field, may be demonstrated by some figures. In 1912, the number of private bankers in Istanbul was 40; not one of the names listed was Turkish Muslim. Of those that could be identified with a reasonable degree of confidence, 12 were Greeks, 12 Armenians,

8 Jews, and 5 Levantines or Europeans. Similarly, of the 34 stockbrokers in Istanbul, 18 were Greeks, 6 Jews, 5 Armenians, and not one was a Turk.

As for the provinces, in the European parts there were 32 bankers and bank managers: of those identifiable, 22 were Greeks, 3 Armenians, 3 Jews, and 3 Levantines or Europeans. In the Asian parts (excluding the Arab provinces in which many Arab, particularly Christian, names were to be found) there were 90 bankers. Of those that could be identified, 40 were Greeks, 27 Armenians, 6 Levantines or Europeans, and 2 Turks (in Eskişehir and Harput).[17]

A similar situation prevailed in industry, though here one cannot be as precise since many establishments, especially the larger ones, were listed under the names of the firm, not the owner. Turkish Muslim names appear much more frequently than in finance, but still constitute a small minority. In the silk industry, Armenian names prevail and in the cigarette-paper industry, Jewish. In the other branches, the predominance of Greeks is very clear.[18] According to a calculation by Tevfik Çavdar, the capital of 284 industrial firms employing five or more workers was divided as follows: Greeks 50 percent, Armenians 20, Turks 15, Jews 5, and foreigners 10; their labor force was Greek 60 percent, Armenian 15, Turkish 15, and Jewish 10.[19]

In foreign trade the share of the minorities was also overwhelming. At the beginning of the nineteenth century Turkey's trade with Europe was carried out mainly by Greeks and Levantines, and that with Egypt, Iran, and Asia by Muslims. Armenian activity increased in the 1820s, and by the 1860s the Armenian colony in Manchester numbered thirty.[20] A list of the large importers of textiles in Istanbul in 1906 shows 28 Armenian names, 5 Turkish, 3 Greek, and 1 Jewish. In 1910, of 28 large firms in Istanbul importing Russian goods, 5 were Russian, 8 Muslim, 7 Greek, 6 Armenian, and 2 Jewish, and almost all large traders with Russia in the eastern provinces were Armenians.[21] Iraq's trade was mainly in Jewish hands and that of Syria in Christian Lebanese.[22]

A detailed breakdown for 1912, based on various yearbooks, is given by Indzhikyan,[23] whose totals are (in percentages):

	No.	Turks	Greeks	Armenians	Others
Internal trade	18,063	15	43	23	19
Industry and crafts	6,507	12	49	30	10
Professions	5,264	14	44	22	20

The long lead of the Greeks, followed by the Armenians, is evident. A perusal of the more detailed breakdowns clearly brings out the ethnic division of labor, so characteristic of the Middle East, and the predominance of the non-Muslims.[24]

However, the part played by Muslims in the economic life of Turkey should not be underrated. Almost all the livestock and by far the greater part of the land belonged to them, and capitalist landowners, engaged in cash-crop farming, had emerged. Much of the internal trade had remained in their hands, especially in the provinces, as had some branches of foreign trade.[25] There were quite a few Turkish industrialists, owners of handicraft shops, and shipowners. And a perusal of the Ottoman archives from the decade preceding the First World War shows an increasing frequency of Muslim names in applications for concessions, licenses, or tax exemptions in such fields as manufacturing (6:19), mining, electricity, and other public utilities.[26] As the British consul in Izmir put it: "It was only natural that, with the downfall of the old régime, a reaction should set in and a new spirit of commercial and industrial activity in the country manifest itself. . . . Even the Turks themselves have begun to take to commerce and other ventures of an industrial nature."[27]

Even in finance the situation began to change in the few years preceding the First
World War, and still more so during the war itself; from 1909 to 1914, four foreign banks
with a combined authorized capital of ₤T1,860,000 were established, one Armenian bank with
a capital of ₤T100,000, and six Turkish banks with a capital of ₤T382,000; of the latter,
three were in Istanbul and the rest in the provinces. During the war, two foreign banks
(one German and one Hungarian) with a combined authorized capital of ₤T560,000 were established, as were twelve Turkish banks with a capital of ₤T5,215,000; of the latter, five
with capital of ₤T4,345,000 were in Istanbul and the rest in the provinces. Only one bank
was founded by non-Muslims in the period 1914-30, a small Jewish bank in Istanbul in 1923.[28]
And, needless to say, in 1914-22, an enormous amount of property was seized by Turks from
Armenians or Greeks who had been killed, or had fled, or had been deported.

Clearly, the nucleus of a Turkish bourgeoisie had been formed, and its interests were
beginning to be recognized and promoted by the government. But the smallness of this nucleus may be judged from the fact that in Istanbul, in 1922, Muslims owned only 4 percent
of foreign trade enterprises, 3 percent of transport agencies, 15 percent of wholesale and
25 percent of retail firms, and that, in 1919, 73 percent of factories and workshops belonged to Greeks and 85 percent of their employees were non-Muslims.[29]

An industrial working class had also come into being. Data are fragmentary but Eldem
puts the total number of workers in Istanbul and Anatolia in 1913 at 298,000, a figure reduced by Dumont to 200,000-250,000. The latter included some 10,000 in major government
enterprises, like the arsenal and textile factories; about 20,000 miners; some 10,000 railway men; and a smaller number in the Régie des Tabacs. The other factories and larger workshops had some 20,000 workers. Thus a greater number by far were still employed in such
traditional handicrafts as rugs, textiles, leather, shoes, metalwork, and pottery, in spite
of the decline registered in the nineteenth century (chap. 6).[30]

In the second half of the nineteenth century real wages seem to have risen, and although these wages were much lower than those of advanced countries they compared quite
well with those of developing lands (2:6). After 1900 various causes led to a labor shortage which, combined with a sharp rise in prices, the political liberty introduced by the
1908 revolution, and some encouragement from the Unionist government resulted in a wave of
strikes (2:7). The labor movement was, however, undermined by the series of wars between
1911 and 1923, which greatly intensified the antagonisms of the various national working-
class groups.

Lastly, mention must be made of a very important, though numerically small, group--
the foreigners. The number of Europeans residing in Turkey grew quite rapidly during the
period under review but there was no large-scale settlement; if the Hellenes are excluded,
the number cannot have exceeded some 30,000 to 40,000 (2:10). But Europeans played a
predominant part in all fields of economic activity except agriculture, internal trade,
and handicrafts, and their influence was quite incommensurate with their numbers.

1. See map in Akbal for 1831.
2. For examples, see Hütteroth in Benedict et al., pp. 19-47; and the works by
Benedict, Dunstan, Stirling, and Yasa listed in the Bibliography.
3. For the eighteenth century see D. Panzac, "La peste à Smyrne au XVIIIe siècle,"
Annales, July-August 1973.
4. Novichev, 2:162.
5. EHI, p. 21.
6. A and P 1894, vol. 88, "Constantinople" and "Trebizond."
7. For details see Rigler, pp. 381-83; the author, an Austrian professor, had taught
at the medical school in Istanbul. In 1806 a "full-fledged medical school" had been established at the Arsenal--Shaw, Between, pp. 165-66. Foreign physicians were also established
in Pera and elsewhere, but as late as 1835 Bazili (2:188) reported that they treated "almost
exclusively Europeans," Turks being prejudiced against using their services.

8. Rigler, pp. 407-13, and below, 4:11; according to Rosen (1:206) the Ottoman government proposed establishing quarantines in 1834 but were opposed by the Russians who feared it might promote Turkish-European trade, in competition with their own, and succeeded in holding up the project.

The gradual reduction of malaria was also a significant factor, especially in Adana and other southern coastlands; for Muğla province see Benedict, Ula, pp. 56-60.

9. "Inquiry," p. 106; following the Balkan Wars "Some 300,000 refugees are registered as having arrived in Turkey and it is probable that the number is considerably larger" (A and P 1914, vol. 95, "Constantinople") for annual figures in 1876-96, Shaw, History, 2:116-17, 239.

10. Some of the immigrants proved very difficult. In 1845 a British consul reported that migrants were coming to Konya from as far as Ankara and Eskişehir, including Circassians who were "very troublesome to the Greek inhabitants here" (Administrative Condition of Bursa, FO 78/652). In 1878 the consul at Mersin stated: "The country is suffering from another plague, more than 15,000 Circassian fugitives have been sent and distributed throughout the country." They had refused to labor in the fields, and robbed and plundered on the highways (FO 78/3070).

There was also a large amount of internal migration. The lower classes of the Erzurum region, more particularly of Van and Muş, went to Istanbul where they worked as "porters, inferior servants and day labourers. From Van itself, 3,000 migrated in 1848, 2,000 in 1849 and about 900 in 1850" (Report on Erzurum, FO 78/870). In Adana "In harvest time labour is largely supplied by nomadic tribes, who return to the mountains after it is over" (A and P 1909, vol. 98, "Adana").

11. There was also an emigration of Armenians to Russia, put by some sources at 300,000, following the 1828 (5:4) and 1878 wars.

12. For the old social classes see Itzkowitz, and Gibb and Bowen; for the social transformation, B. Lewis, Emergence, Ward and Rustow, Davison, and Karpat, "Inquiry"; and for the evolution of education, Kazamias and sources cited therein.

13. The sending of young men abroad, for training, began much earlier. In 1801 the thirty-year-old son of the hakimbaşi (chief doctor) went to Vienna to study medicine, after overcoming the opposition of his father, and stayed there at least two years (HHS Türkei, 10 July 1801, and 8 September 1803, II/135).

In 1836 two young Turkish officers were admitted to the Dockyard by the British Admiralty, to learn navigation (15 April 1836, FO 78/297); others had come around 1835, to "acquire military instruction" at Woolwich (20 January 1838, ibid.); and in 1838 a young man of the Armenian Duzoğlou family "who always had the direction of the Royal Mint of Constantinople" worked in the London mint as "a common labourer" after studying minting methods in Paris (4 August 1838, ibid.). (For the fate of the Duzoğlou family in 1819, see Bazili, 1:155-57.) For earlier educational developments, see Shaw, Between, p. 190.

14. Kazamias, pp. 67-84; for a detailed account, with many statistics, see Shaw, History, 2:107-13, 249-55.

15. Even Galatasary's students were, at first, mainly non-Muslim, and those of Robert College, founded in 1863 by American missionaries, stayed so until the First World War.

16. They also had an important role in many branches of the civil service; for Armenians and Greeks in the agrarian bureaucracy, and as teachers and students in agricultural schools, see Quataert, pp. 64-128.

17. Marouche and Sarantis, pp. 137-40.

18. Osmanli Sanayii, 1913, passim.

19. Cited by Indzhikyan, p. 166; the latter is a rich source of information on the economic activity of the minorities.

20. Ibid., pp. 186-7; in the eighteenth century, Greeks from Chios (including the Ralli family--see EHI, pp. 101-7) and elsewhere had a far-flung trade, with branches ranging from Amsterdam to Vienna, Odessa, and Moscow, as well as to various European and Ottoman Mediterranean ports. In the 1830s they opened offices in England and by the 1850s had 55 firms in Manchester and 14 in London; by 1870 there were 167 Greek firms in Manchester--S. D. Chapman, "The International Houses," JEEH 6, no. 1 (Spring 1977).

21. Ibid., pp. 206-9.

22. EHME, pp. 184-85; C. Issawi, "British Trade and the Rise of Beirut," IJMES, January 1977.

23. Pp. 211-14.

24. EHME, pp. 114-25.

25. For a breakdown for the eastern and central provinces see Indzhikyan, pp. 146-48, 163-66.

26. Also ibid., pp. 167-70, 269-72.

27. A and P 1912-13, vol. 100, "Smyrna." Two other developments may be noted: a union of Muslim merchants with a capital of over £T100,000 opened 600 shops and the committee of Muslim merchants in Istanbul had 340 members--Indzhikyan, p. 166.

28. Ökçün, "1910-1930 yillari...," in Okyar, ed., Türkiye, pp. 408-84.

29. Tezel, p. 72.

30. See breakdown in Eldem, p. 287; Dumont in La Révolution industrielle, pp. 282-90.

POPULATION

   The 1831 census, described in the following selection, is by far the most reliable
Turkish population estimate for the first three-quarters or so of the nineteenth century.
Karal's tables have been carefully examined and regrouped by Akbal[1] whose totals, multiplied by two (on the basis of Lütfi's statement, given in the selection, that all males,
including boys, were enumerated), are as follows: Rumelia 1,503,000 and Silistria
1,076,000, to which should be added estimates of about 750,000 for Bosnia and 250,000 for
Crete, giving a total for the European provinces of about 3,600,000, with an additional
600,000 for Istanbul (but see 2:5). For the Asian provinces enumerated in the census the
totals were Anatolia 2,378,000, Sivas 641,000, Karaman 527,000, Adana 191,000, Trabzon
273,000, Kars 40,000, and Çıldır 158,000, a total of 4,208,000; to this should be added an
estimate of about 2,500,000 for the districts of Maraş, Diyarbekir, Erzurum, and Van, which
were not included in the census, raising the total for Anatolia to about 6,700,000. The
Eyalet of the Mediterranean Islands, which included Gallipoli but excluded Crete, had
660,000 inhabitants, giving a total for European and Asian Turkey of about 11,600,000. The
following additional estimates may be made: 1,000,000 for Iraq, 1,300,000 for Syria, about
1,000,000 for the parts of Arabia controlled by the Porte, and about 500,000 for Libya;
this gives a total of 15,400,000, excluding the tributary states.[2]

   Another "census" was taken in 1844 but, as pointed out in the selection, the results
are unreliable. The totals were: Rumelia and Silistria (for a comparable area) 8,518,000,
Asia Minor 7,750,000, East Anatolia and Cezire 4,450,000,[3] or say 21 million for the European provinces, Anatolia, and Istanbul. These figures are inconsistent with the much more
reliable ones for 1884 and 1897, discussed below.

   So are the various estimates for the third quarter of the century, based on the 1844
"census," partial enumerations and tax returns, and the resulting figures given in the
Salnamehs. The principal estimates (in millions)[4] excluding the tributary states (Rumania,
Serbia, Montenegro, Egypt, and Tunis) are:

Year	Author	Europe	Asia	Africa	Total
1867	Salaheddin	13.5	16.5	0.8	30.7
1872	Behm	10.5	16.5	0.8	27.8
1876	Ubicini	11	16.5	0.8	28.3
1877	Ravenstein	9.7	16.3	1.1	27.1

   The 1884 and 1897 figures are much more reliable and the 1913 even more so. According
to Eldem,[5] they may be tabulated as follows:

(thousands)

	1884	1897	1910	1913
Rumelia and islands	5,014	5,594	5,949	642
Istanbul	895	1,052	1,056	1,160
Anatolia	10,388	11,430	13,210	13,522
Subtotal	16,297	18,076	20,215	15,324
Syria	2,700	3,001	2,967	3,075
Iraq	1,400	1,550	2,278	2,371
Arabia	..	..	5,570	5,570
Libya	..	1,300	(1,000)	--
			32,030	26,340

   Shaw, History, 2:238-41, gives different but not necessarily incompatible figures. In
1897 the population of the Empire, including such tributaries as Egypt, Tunisia, Bulgaria,

Cyprus, Bosnia-Herzegovina and Lebanon, was 39 million. Excluding the latter and Yemen, Hijaz, Libya, and "parts of the east Anatolian and Arab provinces, the actual population counted for tax purposes came to 19,050,307," of whom 19 percent were under ten years old, 50 percent from ten to forty, and 31 percent over forty. For 1910 he puts the corresponding total at 20.7 million and for 1914 at 18.5 million.

By 1884 the Empire had a large Muslim majority, the enumerated population showing 12.6 million Muslims against 4.5 million Christians and Jews; and by 1900 Muslims formed 74 percent of the total, Orthodox 14, Armenians 6, Bulgarians 4 and Jews 1 percent.[6] An ethnic breakdown for the enumerated population in 1897 shows: Turks 9.8 million, Arabs 3.6, Greeks 2.1, Kurds 1.5, Armenians 1.4, Albanians 1.1, Serbs 0.8, and Jews 0.4; the addition of Arabia and Libya would raise the Arab figure to some 9 million.

Comparison of the estimated 6.7 million figure for Anatolia in 1831 with the "census" figures of 9,826,000 for 1884 shows an increase of 47 percent, or a compound annual rate of growth of 0.75 percent.

Between 1884 and 1897 the population grew at 0.81 percent per annum; the official statistics put the increase of Muslims at 0.88 and that of non-Muslims at 0.64; this contradicts the impressions of most observers (2:2) but may be partly explained by migration.

First there was considerable migration between provinces: thus the Turkish population of Cyprus increased, by immigration, until in 1777 it totalled 47,000, compared to 37,000 Greeks (whose number had been put at 160,000 at the time of the Ottoman conquest), but by 1821 Greeks were again a majority.[7] Similarly, there seems to have been a migration of Greeks from the islands to western Anatolia. Secondly, there was a large-scale movement of Turks from the lost European provinces to other parts of the Empire. Thirdly, there was a large immigration of Muslims from the Caucasus, following the Russian conquests in the 1850s and 60s.[8] Lastly, there was a large, and accelerating, emigration of Greeks, Armenians, Jews, and Arab Christians to the New World in the forty years preceding the First World War.[9] It is impossible to say how these movements--which were largely offsetting-- affected the growth of the population, but they certainly helped to change its religious and ethnic composition.[10]

---

    1. "1831 . . ."; I have also drawn on Engin Akarlı, "Ottoman Population in Europe in the 19th Century," M.A. thesis, University of Wisconsin, 1972.
    2. See EHME, pp. 155 and 209. The estimate for Maraş, etc. was given me by Justin McCarthy, who in a forthcoming article critically examines nineteenth-century Ottoman population statistics. His impression is that the other figures given above are underestimates. He also concludes that the 1884-1913 figures are too low, since women and children are under-enumerated--see his Ph.D. dissertation, "The Muslim Population of Anatolia, 1878 to 1927," UCLA, 1978.
    These figures may be compared with the following estimates quoted by Mikhov (in millions):

Date	Author	Europe	Asia	Africa	Total
1785	"Tabellen"	9	19	4	32
1804	Mentelle	18	9	2.5	29.5
1807	Lichtenstern	11.3	12.3	3.2	26.8
1807	Galletti	11	11.1	3.2	25.3
1822	"Almanachs"	9.5	11.1	3.5	24.1

All these figures include Egypt, Libya, Serbia, Greece, Moldavia, and Wallachia.

In 1819 Dearborn (1:132-35) stated that estimates for European Turkey varied from 5 to 9 million and that Asiatic Turkey, including "Asia Minor, Armenia, Mesopotamia, Chaldea and Syria" had some 10 million. In 1833 Urquhart (Turkey, p. 270) estimated the population for European Turkey and Greece at around 12 million, pointing out that guesses varied from 7 to 22 million. In the 1840s MacGregor (2:7) put European Turkey (excluding Greece, Serbia, Moldavia, and Wallachia) at 7 million and Asiatic Turkey (excluding Syria and "Arabia") at 6 to 7 million.

3. Akyol in Tanzimat, 1:549.

4. Salaheddin, pp. 210–11; his figures are criticized and amended in Ubicini and Pavet de Courteille, pp. 18–20, who give a breakdown by ethnic groups: Turks 14 million, Greco-Albanians 3.5, Slav 4.6, Persian (Kurds, Armenians, Druze, and Metwali!) 3.6, Semite 1.6, Georgian 1; and by religion: Muslims 8.9 million, Christians 9.5, Jews 150,000. E. G. Ravenstein, "The Populations of Russia and Turkey," Journal of the Statistical Society 40 (September 1877), also gives regional breakdowns by race, religion, and crude density. E. Behm, Die Bevölkerung der Erde (Gotha, 1872).

5. Eldem, pp. 50–65, who traces very carefully the changes in boundaries and population during this period.

6. Shaw, History 2:238–41; Kemal Karpat "Ottoman Empire Population Records and Census of 1881/82-1893," IJMES 9, no. 2 (May 1978).

In 1852 the number of Christians in the Ottoman Empire, including the tributary states, as given by the various churches, had been 12,620,000, broken down as follows: Orthodox 10,400,000 (Greeks 2,500,000, Bulgarians 2,000,000, Albanians 1,000,000, Serbians 1,000,000, Bosnians 700,000, and Rumanians 3,200,000); Armenians 1,290,000; Roman Catholics 670,000 (Armenians 230,000, Albanians 140,000, Bosnians 160,000, Croatians 120,000, Frank subjects 4,000, other foreigners 15,000); other Catholics 260,000 (Maronites 135,000, Uniate Rumanians 80,000, Melkites 25,000, Syrians 12,000, Uniate Chaldeans 8,000)   (FO 195/347).

7. H. J. Psomiades, "The Cyprus Dispute," Current History, May 1965.

8. On these two movements, see Karpat, "Inquiry," and ibid. in Abu-Lughod; Salaheddin, p. 213, put immigration of Circassians between 1855 and 1866 at 595,000 into the European provinces and 413,000 into the Asian. Shaw, History 2:116–17, puts Muslim immigration into the Empire in 1876-95 at over 1,000,000.

9. Between 1881, when it began to be significant, through 1914, emigration from the Ottoman Empire was as follows: United States 317,000, Argentina about 100,000, and Brazil 52,000; see annual figures in Imre Ferenczi, International Migrations (New York, 1929), 1:889–91.

10. For additional figures, which are close to but do not quite tally with the ones given above, see Shaw, History, 2:116–17, 239–44.

SELECTION 1. THE 1831 CENSUS

Enver Ziya Karal, Osmanlı imparatorluğunda ilk nüfus sayımı, 1831 (Ankara, 1943), pp. 8–13, 20–22

Censuses in the Nineteenth Century

The first attempt to take a census was made during the reign of Mahmut II, between the years 1826 and 1828, after the abolition of the Janissaries and before the war with Russia. The chronicler of the period says the following about the census:

> After the Auspicious Event, most of the Empire's ancient customs, manners and procedural systems having changed, although the act of census-taking, which is the basic principle of all matters civil, was formerly conducted in the capital, the continual recurrence of obstacles due to war put an end to it.[1]

Michoff [Mikhov], in the above-mentioned book, says that the census took place in 1829.[2] One thing we can be sure of is that this census, which was an experiment for a general census, came to no conclusion because of the war. After the Russo-Turkish war ended in 1831 with the Treaty of Adrianople, the Ottoman government engaged in another census. This time, after large-scale preparations, the census was carried out successfully in the sancaks and townships of Rumelia and Anatolia. According to some foreign sources, this census took place only in Rumelia.[3] In AH 1247, a partial census was taken. Lütfi says the following about it:

> since it was in the proper course of affairs to record once more the names of the entire male population of Istanbul and the Three Cities, officials were appointed and the census taking began. Even after the Auspicious Event, the census continued. Since a great deal of time had elapsed, this meant that there was the necessity to have a new census. The method of recording and other injunctions, which were specified in the decree concerning the census, were proclaimed, and printed sheets containing the information were distributed to the people of the neighborhood and to other residents of the country.[4]

It is curious that those authors who mention population problems do not refer to this census.[5]

After the census attempt of 1831, which will be discussed later in detail, there was another census, in 1844. The 1844 census was taken for military reasons, following the adoption of a lottery system for conscription. Professor İbrahim Hakkı Akyol says the following about it:

The first attempt at having an empire-wide census based on modern standards took place under the direction of the Minister of War Rıza Paşa with the intention of reorganizing the army and the conscription system. Unfortunately, this serious program of the government was met by the skepticism of the people. The census gave rise to rumors that the government would levy [new] taxes according to the population of each province, and in many places the people tried to give figures much below the real ones. The responsible non-Muslim offices, such as the Patriarchate and the Rabbinate, tried to cheat the government, actual population figures were concealed, and because of their incapacity and slothfulness, the census officers did not work as seriously as was required for the job. Most of the time, nobody bothered with physical examination. Thus, one cannot accept as correct the results of modern statistics made under such conditions without control data. When the government realized the mistakes, it did not want to publish the results of the census, but some foreigners who were involved in the census procedure obtained the information from the government semi-officially.[6]

This census, which is referred to as the first census by Professor Akyol, was not really the first. Furthermore, as the results were not published as a whole, we do not have adequate information about it.

There are records of other attempts at taking censuses after 1844. Mikhoff mentions a census in Asia Minor, Syria and parts of Kurdistan.[7]

Cemal Bey mentions that the 1856 census took place in connection with the temettü tax [7:Introduction] and was not carried out successfully. Because the Ottoman government must have felt embarrassed about the earlier unsuccessful attempts, in 1870 an irade for a general census was proclaimed. Yet, because of the internal strife of the empire, the irade was never put into effect. In 1874, a census was taken in the province of Tuna (Danube) only.[8] For the census taken after the Turco Russian war of 1877-78, the counting process in Istanbul lasted six months.

The Ottoman government never published any results of either the small-scale or general censuses. However, the official almanacs of the empire and foreigners who wrote books about Turkey mention general results of these censuses. While doing research in the libraries and archives in Istanbul, this author found some documents concerning the 1831 census. Judging these documents quite valuable, he decided to publish them together, and briefly describe why and how the 1831 census was taken.

The 1831 Census

It now seems that the first census taken in both Rumelia and Anatolia without the pretext of recording land ownership is the 1831 census. If in future we find documents that mention an earlier census, the 1831 census will lose its special significance of being the first. The most important reason why this census was taken was Mahmut II's desire for far-reaching reforms. Since the beginning of the decline of the Ottoman Empire, the Janissary corps obstructed any attempts at reform. After this reactionary corps was abolished in 1826, Mahmut II could exercise the full authority of the throne and gained the possibility of carrying out any reform he wished to make, without fear. The first thing to be done after the abolition of the Janissaries was to form a new army. In order to form a new army, the government had to find out new sources of taxation and the number of draftable males.

At this point the government thought of introducing a yearly personal tax. Lütfi says the following about this new tax:

> It was seen in certain documents that since at that time the imperial government was searching for novel forms of revenue in order to counterbalance expenditures, military and civil, and was considering levying a personal tax on all subjects recorded in the books, among the imperial officials it was said that should an annual tax of 150 kuruş a head--the entirety of which would go to the imperial treasury--be levied in addition to the existing tithes, after dividing up the revenue to meet sundry expenditures, the remaining 196,000 purses [of 500 kuruş each] would be earmarked for such expenditures as would be necessitated by imperial command.[9]

In the explanatory document concerning the census, the taxation problem is discussed in greater detail and the following points are stressed.[10]

1. Because of continuous wars, the public has spent much money and has experienced hardships.

2. As a result of illegal procedures, in some places the basic revenue system governing the taxes to be levied from the rich and the poor and from Muslims and Christians has been adversely affected. Thus while there are people who pay only one-half or a third of the tax they are supposed to pay, there are those who, because of protection and favoritism, do not pay any taxes at all.

3. Under previous orders, certain villagers in Anatolia were exempted from taxes in return for their services of repairing bridges and inns and guarding passes. Although with the passage of time bridges and inns were destroyed and the guarding of passes has become a vocation of no account, the people who were formerly exempt from taxation still do not pay their taxes despite the fact that they are not in the service of the government, and their negligence burdens others.

4. Although the government previously took some precautions to eliminate such injustice, because of wars no satisfactory measure could be effected.

5. But now the wars have ended, and the time has come to find out everybody's true obligations to the state. This would entail the taking of a census.

The explanatory document has the following passage concerning the census.

Since it is a requirement of Our Royal Decree and Imperial Command to secure comfort and repose for all the poor subjects and the destitute of the provinces in our justice-dispensing realm, during deliberations and discussions, all who were present have concurred that a satisfactory accomplishment of the afore-mentioned matter, the introduction of the tax clause and the uniform application of the modification and adjustment clauses, would require information concerning Muslim and non-Muslim individuals in the Ottoman Empire, as was the case previously in the days of our forefathers.[11]

Neither in the explanatory document nor in Lütfi's history is there any mention of military reasons for this census. But, as we shall see later, there was a military aim. In order to determine the procedure of census-taking, a special committee was set up, which prepared regulations.[12]

As a principle, it was decided that the census record the male Muslims and non-Muslims in Anatolia and Rumelia. Since there had not been a general census previously, the officials took into account the possibility of the people becoming apprehensive and appointed religious instead of civil clerks as census-takers.[13]

The clerks came to the Sublime Porte on the day before their departure for the provinces to get their salary and instructions about their duties, which were to be kept secret.[14]

The Ministry of Registry was set up in Istanbul to process and collate the information sent by the clerks from the provinces.[15] After all the reports were received, the contents of each were summarized in one _defter_. This collation, being the last step of the census process, was reported to Mahmut II in the following manner on the first page of the summary _defter_:[16]

Since His Imperial Majesty of rare consideration has always abundantly [provided for] the military corps and matters concerning [Holy] Wars, and since the majestic Sultan of great benevolence frequently expends and disburses on reconstruction of buildings and towns and on the quiet repose and security [of his subjects], it is his exalted desire that the number of Muslim and non-Muslim inhabitants and residents who are present in his domain be recorded and presented to him, and that this matter be expediently effected; according to the wonderful Imperial command and edict which was issued and proclaimed, [the appended is] the final copy of the summary _defter_ compiled by such officials and servants of his as were appointed and sent to Rumelia and Anatolia and to some islands where, under orders, they recorded the information and now submit it to the celestial imperial presence, the details being appended below.

The Extent of the 1831 Census

The Census was taken in Rumelia and Anatolia. The townships and districts where the census was taken according to the summary _defter_ are as follows. . . .

Notes on the Tables

1. The figures in the tables were calculated by adding the details from the text, therefore the totals in the text are corrected with respect to the details.

2. It is understood from the text that the word "non-Muslim" refers to Greeks.

3. Footnotes specify the race of all non-Muslims who are not Greek, Armenian, or Jewish.

4. Gypsies are recorded in a single column, but Muslim and non-Muslim gypsies are differentiated in footnotes.

The Results of the 1831 Census

Because this census recorded only the male population, it is far from being indicative of the exact population of Rumelia and Anatolia. Since, however, it is possible to estimate the number of female inhabitants, given the number of males, one can have a good idea about the population of Rumelia and Anatolia in the first half of the nineteenth century.

The census results indicating the male population were generally broken down according to religion. Thus, the Muslim and Christian populations of both Rumelia and Anatolia were recorded. The figures showing the Muslim population were not broken down into Turkish and nonTurkish Muslims, but the figures for the [nomadic] tribes were recorded separately from the nontribal Muslim population. As for those Christians who were considered _reaya_, the census figures show no distinction of race, religion, or language; as exceptions, the returns for large cities show separate figures for Armenians and Greeks, but in many places non-Muslims were recorded simply as _reaya_. It is impossible to reckon the number of people belonging to separate millets who come under this category. Thus the 1831 census shows us the number of Muslim and non-Muslim inhabitants of two vast areas of the Empire, Rumelia and Anatolia.

We understand from the following passage in Lütfi's chronicle that the census figures added up to almost five millions:

> After the completion of recording of the census and upon the return of the census of-
> ficials, it was shown in the summaries taken from the totals in the census books
> that—apart from the areas which were exempted from census—in those regions where a
> census was taken the victorious soldiers and the male population both Muslim and non-
> Muslim, including children, were nearly five millions.

This result shows a discrepancy with the figures in the record books, in which the population of Anatolia and Rumelia is given as nearly four millions instead of five. It is difficult to explain the discrepancy of one million between the two figures. There is, however, the possibility that the census figures for some sancaks and kazas were not included in the summaries of the record books. As a matter of fact, the census results of a few districts of Kastamonu and Silistre provinces are not shown in the summary book.

In the summary book we see that, of nearly four million males, slightly under a million and a half were living in Rumelia and over two and a half in Anatolia. Disregarding the Jewish and gypsy population, we see that in Rumelia the ratio of the Christian and Muslim populations was two to one: rounding off the figures, there were 800,000 Christians and 500,000 Muslims. Broken down regionally, however, the figures show that, while in some areas there was a vast majority of Christians, in others Muslims were in the majority. In fact, there were 44,959 Bulgarians and 10,920 Muslims in Filibe [Philippopolis]. For Sofia, the figures are 39,692 Bulgarians and 4,161 Muslims. For Western Thrace, however, the following figures indicate a Turkish majority: Sultanyeri, 6,151 Muslims, 51 Christians: Drama, 8,618 Muslims, 3,107 Christians; Gümülcine, 30,517 Muslims and only 5,339 Christians.

As for the census results for Anatolia, we see that Muslims were a vast majority. There were approximately 400,000 Christians, 5,000 Jews and 7,000 gypsies as opposed to 2,100,000 Muslims. . . .

	Census Returns		
	Rumelia	Anatolia	Total
Muslims	513,448	1,988,027	2,501,425
Reaya	811,546	366,625	1,178,171
Gypsies	29,532	7,143	36,675
Jews	11,674	5,338	17,012
Armenians	3,566	16,743	20,309
Totals	1,369,766	2,383,876	3,753,642

---

1. Tarih-i Lütfi, 3:142.
2. Mikhov, Naselenieto; pp. xvii and 274.
3. Rudtorfer, quoted in ibid., pp. xvii and 274.
4. The author has not come across any mention of the 1831 census either in Cemal Bey's İstatistik ve İhsaiyat or in Professor Akyol's article in Tanzimat.
5. Tarih-i Lütfi, 5:109.
6. Prof. Akyol, "Tanzimatta Coğrafya ve Jeoloji," Tanzimat, 1940, p. 548.
7. Mikhoff, op. cit., pp. 156-210.
8. Cemal, İstatistik.
9. Tarih-i Lütfi, 5:146.
10. The following are summarized from the context.
11. Prime Ministry Archives, Box 67, no. 12. The text of the document is to be found in the documents section.
12. Tarih-i Lütfi, 5:142.
13. Tarih-i Lütfi, 5:143.
14. Prime Ministry Archives, Divan Boxes, Box 67, no. 20.
15. Tarih-i Lütfi, 3:145.
16. Istanbul, University Library, İstatistik defteri, B. 29.

ABORTION IN WESTERN ANATOLIA

With the mortality rates prevailing in preindustrial societies, it takes some six to nine births per couple just to reproduce the population. Hence the current religions, mores, and customs encourage high fertility, and most demographers assume that in such societies the birth rate is usually close to the biological maximum. But, even for a region with such high birth rates as the Middle East and North Africa,[41] this assumption cannot be uncritically accepted. A thorough study has convincingly shown that, in the fourteenth and fifteenth centuries, various birth control methods were known to, and used by, the ur-ban middle class of Egypt and Syria, although to what extent remains unclear.[2] It is likely that birth control was also known in other Muslim countries.

As regards Turkey, a large number of foreigners writing at the end of the eighteenth century and in the nineteenth were convinced that the Turkish population was actually de-clining. In addition to epidemics and famines, the causes most frequently given are con-scription, oppression, homosexuality, and polygamy, but there are also hints of abortion. In 1798 Eton stated: "We may add another cause of depopulation, the tyranny of the pashas, who, in some parts of Asia, so much impoverish the people, that they prevent marriages being so frequent as where there is less danger of being unable to maintain a family; and this gives rise to an abominable vice which brings sterility with it, and when men are so degraded as to become habituated to it, they lose the natural instinct in man for the fair sex. Polygamy itself is an institution experience proves to be so little favourable to population, that the Christian families are generally observed to be more prolific than the Mahomedans."[3]

The author of the following selection is equally vague, but his British colleague at Smyrna, writing in 1861 (reply to questionnaire FO 198/14 and 78/1533), was much more definite, attributing the decrease in the Muslim population first to conscription and then to "the horrid system so generally practised amongst the Mussalmans of causing abortion which they do not consider as criminal," and which was carried out by local midwives, mostly Jewish. He adds "the shocking prevalence of unnatural crime amongst the Mussalmans is another cause." In 1850 the consul at Rhodes had stated that Turks were decreasing there as elsewhere, because of increasing abortion (Report, FO 78/833).

The same note was sounded in the capital:

The Mussulman population of the Osmanli race in Constantinople is known to be decreasing. . . . (They are) less able than other races to compete in the struggle for existence. . . . They resort to means for procuring abortion to an alarming ex-tent. On the other hand infanticide is but sparingly practiced, the victims being in such cases of the female sex. Amongst the Mussulman population illegitimacy is never the incentive for these crimes, for it is unknown, together with its corollaries, abandonment of offspring and concealment of birth.

Amongst the Christian population, however, illegitimacy is not infrequent; and factitious abortion, abandonment of offspring, and concealmnt of birth are resorted to. But while the Osmanli Mussulmans are diminishing in number yearly, the Christian and Jewish populations tend to increase in a rapid ratio.[4]

Still more convincing is the government's action in 1888, creating a new post in Bursa to reduce abortion and drawing plans for further efforts to combat it elsewhere.[5]

The impression of a decline in population persisted until the First World War. In 1894, the British Chamber of Commerce in Turkey stated: "it is a well known fact that the tendency of the local population hitherto has been towards diminution rather than in-crease."[6] There seems little doubt that this impression was erroneous, and that in fact the Muslim population was steadily growing, although possibly more slowly than the Greek or Armenian (see 2:Introduction). What the impression does reflect, however, is the rela-tive growth in the number and power of the minorities, and the transfer of much Turkish land in Anatolia into Greek and Armenian hands(2:10, 13).

---

1. Clarke, J., and W. Fisher, Populations of the Middle East and North Africa (New York, 1972), pp. 21-22.

2. Basim Musallam, "Sex and Society in Islam," (Ph.D. diss., Harvard University, in press).

3. Eton, p. 266; similar observations were made by Pouqueville about Muslims in the Morea--see Stoianovich, p. 250.

4. A and P 1878, vol. 74, "Constantinople"; Nassau Senior also reports several remarks on this subject--see pp. 164, 191.

5. Quataert, p. 12.

6. Cited in ibid., p. 12.

SELECTION 2. DEPOPULATION OF COUNTRYSIDE, WESTERN ANATOLIA, 1861

French Consul in Izmir to Minister of Foreign Affairs, 15 November 1861 (CC Smyrne, vol. 49)

What is most striking when crossing the vast plains of Asia Minor is the depopulation of the countryside. Migration from the countryside to the towns can be seen more clearly in Turkey than anywhere else. The causes of this are on the one hand the little encouragement given to agriculture, which is indeed burdened with enormous imposts and often even with extortions, and on the other the abuse of domesticity among the Turks. If one adds to this conscription, which falls exclusively on the Turkish rural population, one can see why the rural Turks are more and more retreating before the Greeks. But the latter, who are much less frugal and hardworking than the Turks, are not such good farmers. They prefer to engage in navigation, work in handicrafts, and control the whole of petty trade. In spite of their increase [développement], the Greeks can therefore never replace the population that is disappearing more and more, nor revive in this part of Turkey the agricultural wealth that existed in the past.

In the neighborhood of Smyrna, many persons have tried to farm with the help of European labor. Swiss, Germans, Alsatians, and even southern Frenchmen specially chosen from among veteran soldiers acclimatized by a long stay in Algeria, have been hired. But in a, so to speak, virgin soil, farming gives forth miasmas which often engender fevers that soon scatter these colonies. And yet new populations are necessary, to give these lands once more the value they had in ancient times. But where can these populations be found? Perhaps among the black peoples of the interior of Africa. For it should be noted that in all these regions there are many blacks, probably descendants of former slaves who have kept their connections with the farms. . . .

GRAIN AND WATER SUPPLY OF ISTANBUL

It has been perceptively pointed out that "the only group outside this ruling segment which exercised any systematic constraint on the economic policies of [Middle Eastern] governments was not the merchants but, curiously enough, the poor in the great cities. Most governments preferred to expend some of their resources on seeing that the populations of their capital cities were fed, rather than face the threat of riot from a hungry mob. Hence an enormous amount of coercion has been applied to the distribution of grain in the Mediterranean in the interests of the great cities of powerful states."[1] Hence, too, some of the apparent anomalies in the Ottoman tariffs (3:Introduction).

The following selection describes the methods used to supply Istanbul with grain in the eighteenth century. The one after that, written by the famous Prussian general who served as adviser to the Ottoman army in 1835-39, describes the no less vital water supply system. In addition, certain other foodstuffs were regarded as essential. Rice and coffee were imported from Egypt, and when communications between the two countries were cut, as in 1798-1801, and again in 1807, there was much distress, followed by corresponding rejoicing when Ottoman authority was restored (Letter of 10 July 1801, HHS, VIII/7/3 and Green to Canning, 4 April 1807, FO 78/59).[2]

Hardly less important was olive oil, the main source of fat in Middle Eastern diets. A dispatch from the British Embassy dated 17 February 1820 (FO 78/94) describes the means used: "With a professed view to prevent the bad effect of private monopoly and of great fluctuations in the price of this necessary, the Turkish Government have assumed the exclusive management of the purchase and sale of oil as well as of corn. Its exportation

is prohibited. Imperial Firmans are issued to the different districts that produce it
ordering the transmission to Constantinople of the quantities necessary for the annual
consumption of the Capital. The quantity is calculated at a Hundred Thousand Quintals a
year, of which Athens is bound to furnish 4,000 cwt, Crete 30,000, Mitylene 32,000 and
different places on the coast of Lesser Asia the remainder. The surplus produce is in no
case allowed to be sold until the proportion required of each district has been previously
forwarded to the capital." The dispatch adds that abuse by the local officials had resulted in a dearth of oil.

As regards grain, the selection confirms the following statement made by an official
of the Levant Company on 4 April 1807 (Green to Canning, FO 78/59). "The supplies of Bread
Corn are derived principally from Moldavia and Wallachia, from the [northern] coasts of
Anatolia and especially from the ports of Salonica, Volo and other places on the coast of
Macedonia."[3] The system described gradually broke down in the first half of the nineteenth
century, with the loss of Ottoman sovereignty over the Danubian provinces and the abandonment of the grain monopoly in them under the Treaty of Adrianople of 1829, the erosion of
monopolies elsewhere--especially after the Treaty of 1838--the great increase in grain exports from southern Russia, and the sharp reduction in freight rates, enabling Istanbul to
draw on supplies from much more distant sources such as Marseilles. Administrative methods
continued, however, to be used in emergencies. Thus in 1821 the government, fearing famine,
ordered that all ships coming from the "Black Sea laden with corn shall not be suffered to
pass, until they have discharged their cargoes at the public granaries, to be purchased by
the Government at the current price, with a fair allowance for profit and freight"--an
action that was promptly protested by the British ambassador (Strangford to Londonderry,
25 May 1821, FO 78/98). And in 1836 the British consul in Salonica reported that "the surplus produce is sent on to Constantinople under the direction of Government Agents appointed for that purpose. I ought however to mention that notwithstanding the precautions
of Government to prevent the exportation, a considerable quantity is smuggled out of the
country, with the connivance frequently of the very persons appointed to prevent it" (Kerr
to Palmerston, 13 January 1836, FO 78/290). But, essentially through private and uncon-
trolled channels, Istanbul continued to draw its supplies--estimated in the 1880s and 90s
at 4 to 7 million kiles a year--from Russia, Rumania, Rumelia, and Bulgaria. However, by
the turn of the century railways had made Anatolian grain highly competitive in the Istanbul market and it soon came to supply the bulk of the city's needs--over 90 percent in
1901, a normal crop year, and as much as 66 percent in the poor crop year of 1903.[4]

Providing a city of over half a million inhabitants with water was a no less formidable undertaking, and in its heyday the water supply system of Istanbul, extended and improved in 1732, was among the very best.[5] Indeed as late as 1831 an American visitor compared it favorably with that of New York.[6] But already Moltke was clearly aware of its
inadequacy, and in the following decades complaints are increasingly heard. In 1878, a
published British report stated: "Stamboul is well supplied with water, but the inhabitants
of Pera and Galata in the summer months occasionally suffer from its scarcity. The prices
charged by the guild of water carriers then become exorbitant, and the poorer classes are
naturally the greatest sufferers. . . . One of these attempts [at improvement] was made
by the municipality; its object was to pump up water from the stream of the Barbyses, at
the head of the Golden Horn, but after the conduits were placed the steam pump was found
to be of insufficient power to force the water up to the required height, and the works
were abandoned." Another project for a company with a capital of £2 million for bringing
water from Lake Derkos, eighteen miles away, was also abandoned.[7]

An unpublished contemporary report is more forthright: "There has been almost a famine during the summer; for fifty days no water came to this Consulate. . . . Pera obtains
its water from two large reservoirs called 'Bends,' situated at the head of the Büyükdere
valley. From personal examination I can affirm that they are not only in a filthy condition from the accumulated mud of years, but also in a dangerous state, the large one bulg-
ing out and leaking."[8]

Two years later it was pointed out that the Bends were "gradually filling with mud,
and the water supply is annually diminishing." In addition, there was great maldistribu-
tion. Of the 33.5 lule (116 million gallons) of rainwater collected annually, 6 were lost
by leakage and evaporation and of the balance 23.5 were appropriated to the imperial palaces and barracks, leaving 14 million gallons for "the 400,000 or 500,000 inhabitants of
the villages and towns. This is at the rate of 28 to 35 gallons per annum per head. I
believe so low a supply of water is not to be found in any other city in the world. Last
autumn 1-1/2d. per gallon was the usual price paid for drinking water."[9]

It was only with the founding of La Compagnie des Eaux de Constantinople in 1882,
with a nominal capital of 20 million francs, that the city began to acquire a modern water
supply system. The company drew water from Lake Derkos and greatly increased the city's
supply.[10] In 1888, the Compagnie des Eaux de Scutari et Cadikeui was founded, with a capital of 1.7 million francs.

---

1. M. A. Cook in The Legacy of Islam, 2d edition, ed. Joseph Schacht and C. E.
Bosworth (Oxford, 1974), p. 224.
2. See also Novichev, Istoriya, 2:108; Shaw, Between, pp. 175-77.
3. See also the description in Thornton, pp. 232-34. The most fertile grain regions,
e.g., Volo, Salonica, Varna, etc., were obliged to furnish to the Porte one-twelfth of
their wheat harvests, at 20 paras a kile of 60 pounds—a contribution known as istira. One
million kiles were thus sent to Istanbul each year and kept in public granaries as a reserve against shortages and high prices.
4. Quataert, pp. 197-202.
5. Shaw, History, 1:243.
6. De Kay, p. 117.
7. A and P 1878, vol. 74, "Constantinople."
8. "Report on Trade with Turkey, Confidential," 1878 FO 78/3070.
9. A and P 1880, vol. 75, "Constantinople."
10. For details see A and P 1883, vol. 74, "Constantinople"; and Thobie, pp. 141-42,
439-41, who gives figures on financial results, showing a rather low rate of profits of
the company; in 1908 the company installed a new pump at Feriköy (BVA BEO 274202).

SELECTION 3: GRAIN SUPPLY OF ISTANBUL IN THE EIGHTEENTH CENTURY

Lütfi Güçer, "İstanbulun iaşesi için lüzumlu hububatın temini meselesi," Istanbul
Üniversitesi İktisat Fakültesi Mecmuası, Vol. 2 (1949/50), pp. 397-411 (footnotes omitted).

Just as it is a problem now, during the fifteen centuries when Istanbul was the capital of the Eastern Roman and Ottoman empires, the supplying of the necessary grain for
bread posed a major problem to the responsible authorities. Although the present study is
concerned with the middle of the eighteenth century, a period long after the Middle Ages
and one when means of transport were inadequate and hindered by banditry on land and corsairs on the seas in all countries alike, it is hoped that it may reflect some of the
characteristics of the older times in spite of the fact that, during the period of our
study, the Ottoman Empire controlled large areas of agricultural production.

In this period Istanbul was a gargantuan metropolis with its palaces, thousands of
slaves and soldiers living in them, students from all over the Empire filling the seminar-
ies, the poor and the needy thronging the welfare kitchens, foreign merchants staying in
the inns, bachelors lodging in special quarters allocated to them, and the ever increasing
number of residents due to the swelling ranks of immigrants from provinces lost to the
Empire during the period of decline, in spite of the fact that a deliberate settlement
policy had been implemented during the period of expansion. Securing the daily bread of
this immense city, being prepared for emergencies, preventing speculation on this most
vital food item and keeping its price at a reasonable level were taken up as serious problems by the administrators. The following statements quoted from opinions found in the

Imperial Records of Grain Supply (Zahire mühimme defterleri), on which this study is based, reflect the importance attached to the administration of victualling by the sultan and government officials: "Since it is necessary and important to secure the daily bread of the servants of God in my felicitous threshold [Istanbul]"; "The grain supply being one of the primary considerations of my Imperial Government"; "Since it is my Imperial wish to increase the bread supply and necessary daily grain supply for the servants of God in Istanbul"; "Since this matter is of the utmost importance in my Almighty Sovereignty."

This study will not discuss the establishment or operation of the institution administrating the grain supply, the liabilities charged upon the areas of production in favor of the Istanbul consumer, and the far-reaching problems resulting from the government's intervention. We shall study only the private and government capital used in the transportation of grain to Istanbul and in the sale of the grain there, where it was purchased by the bakers in the Unkapani exchange.

In order to define this study more precisely, the grain supply must be categorized according to the several consumer groups for which it was earmarked. In fact, the victualling of the palace personnel, Janissary corps, and military guilds was the responsibility of the Imperial Stores (Has Kiler; Kiler-i Amire), a government agency. The victuals for the welfare kitchens feeding the needy and the poor came directly from the farms owned by the pious foundations. Thus, our study will deal only with the grain supplied for the consumption of the public in Istanbul, or in modern terminology, with the financing of the grain supply in the Istanbul exchange.

In the middle of the eighteenth century, capital from two sources, private and governmental, was invested in the grain trade. The extent of private capital was vast, since it was responsible for meeting the daily demand. Government capital played a more limited role, since it was used only in storing the necessary supplies to be drawn upon in emergencies. We shall briefly review the role of the capital from both sources.

The Role of Private Capital

The government determined which areas were to supply grain to Istanbul and established rules governing trade between these areas and the capital city. These rules and regulations, as well as punishments prescribed by them, applied to all merchants involved in the transport of grain to Istanbul. The participation in commerce of private capital owners, however, occurred in two ways.

Some of the capitalists would collectively undertake to purchase grain at the port of export and transport it in their own vessels. They would use their capital for this operation and would stand as each other's surety. A smaller group of merchants would individually purchase and transport the grain under a license issued to them. In our study, we shall separately examine the roles of these two groups.

The Role of Private Capital in Collective Contracts

A collective contract was signed at the beginning of Muharrem, 1169 (7 October 1755) at the Grand Vizirate by the grand vizir, the administrator of the Unkapani exchange, the officials of the Mariners' Guild (the secretary, chief officer, and sergeant), and fifty six owners of 120 ships. A copy of this contract, witnessed by the clerk, Hacı Mustafa, sent by the kadı of Istanbul, was found in the Record of Grain Supply, no. 10 (Zahire mühimme defteri, 10). This original document, recorded by the office of the kadı, contains important decisions which shed light on our study.

According to the contract, 120 vessels, each capable of carrying 700 kiles of grain, were assigned to ferry grain from the Rumelian ports of the Black Sea, extending from Burgas to Odessa (Article 17). These ports exported most of the grain needed for Istanbul. The shipowners promised not to take the grain to any port, especially Anatolian ports, except Istanbul, and stood as surety for each other (Articles 4, 13, 18). The contract did not establish a monopoly for the shippers: should the assigned vessels be inadequate for the task or should other shippers want to work on this route, other sailors could be employed "through the administrator of the exchange and the Mariners' Guild pending the decision of the kadı of Istanbul" (Article 14). This "open door" principle, which prevented a monopoly by making it possible for others to undertake shipping on the same route, shows that the fifty six shipowners could not claim the sole right to grain importation from the Black Sea ports. Article 12 of the contract stated that the ships mentioned in the contract had priority in loading rights over others, but stipulated, at the same time, that the owners of these ships could not prevent other ships from taking on cargo at the Black Sea ports, claiming it to be their right.

Thus, this contract established a concession to supply the necessary grain for Istanbul but barred a monopoly.

We have not found a similar contract concerning Rodosto (Tekirdağ), which was considered the granary of Istanbul, or other smaller ports of Marmara. In some records, however, there are references to contracted vessels carrying grain from the Çekmeces, Silivri, Ereğli, Rodosto, Şarköy, and Gallipoli and to merchants and dealers of those ports having contracts with the Istanbul exchange. Record IX (p. 229, Decision 503) mentions that thirteen rich and reliable merchants, members of the exchange, had agreed to purchase, with down payment at the regular price, such grain as was brought to Ereğli from the vicinity and to transport it to Istanbul, and had stood as each other's sureties. Record X (p. 67, Decision 115) refers to 72 vessels, each carrying a load of approximately 100 kiles, which were commissioned to transport 12,000 kiles of grain daily from Tekirdağ to Istanbul. With this evidence, we can say that the grain trade between the Thracian ports of the Sea of Marmara and Istanbul was made by private investors under the same type of contract that regulated the Black Sea trade.

The role of private investors in fixing grain prices. Article 1 of the above-mentioned contract stipulates that the price of the grain was determined by an official sent from Istanbul, "with the approval of the vendors and shipowners, according to the abundance or the scarcity of the produce, with justice." From this short article, we learn that the shipowners (private investors) took part in fixing the price of grain. Indeed, before the month of Rebiülahir, 1169 (January 1756), the price of grain used to be determined by an official sent from Istanbul, local officials, and the kadı in the presence of the producers and shipowners while the crop was ripening. The decisions made by these commissions, consisting of the above-mentioned officials, who wielded much power, were generally unfavorable to the producer. Thus, a growing number of farmers hid their produce, which led to a black market price for grain above the official price. In January 1756, it was ordered that prices be fixed with the consent of both vendor and buyer. Separate decisions on this matter were sent to Ismail, Akkerman, Kalas, Tekfurdağı, Mihaliç, and other ports on the Sea of Marmara, and Karaharman, and copies of this last decision were sent to Kivarna, Balcik, Mangalye, Constantza, Varna, Ahyolu, and Burgas. The government hoped that as a result of these decisions, which called for mutual consent between buyer and seller, farmers would not hide their produce or shy away from selling it but immediately transport it to the ports for sale at the agreed price.

After this new decision was put into effect, the officials sent from Istanbul would select a port within the area of their jurisdiction, where they would arrange a meeting with the producers, shipowners, captains, stewards, and some "pious people" belonging to none of these parties. Prices were determined after everybody's approval and the consent of the kadı had been secured. Once the power of the officials had thus been reduced, the producers did not settle for reasonable prices but demanded two or three times the price of the previous years for their crop. Thus, bargaining became a lengthy process while empty vessels remained at the ports. This resulted in a grain shortage in Istanbul and the government was forced to intervene. The government, however, did not intervene directly, but "in order to show compassion to the people and pity to the needy, enforce the contracts of and sales by the grain merchants and bakers and end the dispute amongst them," decreed that the merchants and bakers bring their cases to the kadı of Istanbul and abide by his decisions. This decree resulted in small increments in the price of grain wherever there occurred lengthy disputes or producers did not find the offers satisfactory. In fact, 14 aspers per kile was added to the offered price of grain at the Black Sea ports in 1169 when the bargaining could not be concluded; in 1170 the price of grain in Tekirdağ was increased from the offered price of 96 aspers per kile to 106; the same year, an increment of 10 aspers per kile was also granted at the ports on the Black Sea and Danube. In 1171, it was ordered that grain brought from the Danubian ports be sold at 180 aspers per kile, from the Black Sea ports at 150 aspers, and from Tekirdağ at 213 aspers in Istanbul.

To summarize, private capital owners took part in the activities of the regional price-setting commissions (although they were shipowners, they were also represented by their captains and stewards) and voted on such matters as were pertinent to both the price and transportation of grain.

The role of private capital in financing the grain supply of Istanbul. Three different prices were set regionally for three grades of grain: good, medium, and mixed. These prices were publicly announced, recorded in the local courts, and communicated to headquarters in Istanbul. The captains and stewards purchased the grain with a down payment, either at the ports or sometimes in the townships near the ports and transported it to Istanbul. The grain was unloaded at Unkapanı where it was sold to bakers in the presence of the administrator of the exchange. Storage was the responsibility of the bakers. The price at the exchange was decided by the shipowners and bakers by adding the cost of transport according to "ancient custom" and a profit margin "within justice and moderation" to the regional purchase prices (Articles 2,3). The contract stipulated that the price at the exchange was dependent on the consent of the parties and was not to be interfered with. We should note that this stipulation did not mean free trade, for the transportation charges remained nearly constant within the boundaries set by "ancient custom," and the investor's profit was calculated "within justice and moderation." This "just profit margin" was doubtless set by the administrator of the exchange or the kadı of Istanbul, who determined all "just prices" in Istanbul.

The Role of Individually Invested Private Capital Worked by Permission

Private shipowners were allowed to transport grain from the Danubian, Black Sea, and Marmara ports, without contracts but subject to permission, after the collective shipowners met the requirements of their contracts concerning the transport of grain from the above-mentioned areas to Istanbul. Private investors desiring to transport grain to Istanbul were required to state the port from which they intended to bring grain, the tonnage of their vessel, and the type and amount of grain they would transport. They also had to promise not to transport the grain elsewhere but bring it directly to Unkapanı and set up a bond as surety. These formalities completed, they would apply to the administrator of the exchange, who would take the cases to the kadı after registering the bond. The kadı would decide on the case, upon which the Imperial Divan would issue a decree addressing either the administrator or the kadı of the port. When the decree was presented to the local administrator or the kadı, he would record on the reverse side the actual type and amount of the grain loaded on the vessel. Upon the vessel's arrival in Istanbul, the entry on the reverse side of the decree would be compared with the text, and the decree would be taken from the shipowner. Thus, a separate decree was necessary for each run. Apart from those ships permitted by the Unkapanı authorities to transport grains, there were ships which were locally permitted to carry grain and whose bonds were registered locally. All the grain from Mihaliç, the port of Karesi, were transported by such vessels.

The individual shipowners bought the grain at current prices, with a down payment, at the ports.

The Amount of Grain Transported to Istanbul by Private Capital

Unfortunately we have not been able to determine the amount of private capital invested in the grain trade of Istanbul, the transport charges per _kile_, or the profit rate of the investors. We have, however, figures for the type and amount of grain brought from the Danubian and Black Sea ports and the total amount of grain brought from Karesi. In fact, such an important matter as the grain supply of Istanbul prompted the government to keep detailed records on the areas which were required to supply the grain and the ports of these areas. Which port would serve which district was determined and the government worked to establish an efficient operation by sending officials to the ports. Transport had to be organized according to the seasons which permitted shipping. Our findings indicate that until 1161, in order to prevent shortages in Istanbul, ships were sent at random to various ports. Since the availability of grain at the ports was not previously determined, sometimes the ships would wait empty at ports and sometimes they would not appear at ports where grain was ready. A new plan coordinating transport from the farms to the ports and shipping from the ports to Istanbul was put into effect in 1161. Under this plan, called the "comparative system," the average annual shipment from each port was calculated on the basis of previous years' records at Unkapanı, and the ports were accordingly notified. The average annual shipments of districts to the ports were likewise calculated. Thus, once the type and amount of grain to be sent from each port had been determined, the number of ships to be dispatched to each port was an easy matter to ascertain. Furthermore, since the amount of goods arriving in Istanbul was recorded, it was easy to find out whether all expected shipments had come in and, if they had not, to take measures to bring in the grain waiting at the ports.

The "comparative system" was applied permanently to the Danubian and Black Sea ports and from time to time to Mihaliç. This system was not applied to Thracian ports, due to their proximity to Istanbul, which made shipments possible throughout the year, and to the existence in Edirne of the Bostancı[*] corps, which carried out effectively the decrees of the government.

We thus found out the amount of grain shipped to Istanbul by private investors from the regions when the "comparative system" was applied by studying a series of decrees addressed to the officials or the local kadıs. From 1161, the year when the system was inaugurated, to 1171 the amount of grain shipped to Istanbul from the Danubian, Black Sea, and Karesi areas remained constant except for years of shortage. For purposes of comparison with the amount of grain brought to Istanbul by government capital, we shall use the following table which shows the amount of grain shipped to Istanbul by private capital in 1171 (1758). The figures, however, are provisional, and real figures could be found out only from the Unkapanı records, which are not available as yet.

Thus, for wheat and barley combined, a total of 6,510,000 _kiles_ of grain was shipped to Istanbul by private investors in 1758.

---

[*] Gardeners--see EI(2), s. v. "Bostandji."

Danube Ports	Wheat (Istanbul *kiles*)	Barley (Istanbul *kiles*)
Kilya kili	150,000	50,000
İsmail	110,000	40,000
Tolca and Macin	62,500	12,500
İsakça	125,000	25,000
Braila and Kalas	350,000	250,000
Hirişova	62,500	12,500
Akkerman	250,000	100,000
Total	1,110,000	490,000
Black Sea		
Burgas	314,000	59,000
Varna	350,000	100,000
Balçık	300,000	100,000
Kivarna	200,000	50,000
Mangalye	350,000	50,000
Constantza	400,000	50,000
Karaharman	250,000	50,000
Total	2,164,000	459,000
Karesi		
Mihaliç	400,000 (wheat and barley)	
Thrace		
Tekfurdağı	1,800,000 (estimate: wheat and barley)	

Shipment by individual investors, 47,000 (estimate: wheat and barley)

The Role of Government Capital

Every year before harvest time, the government would dispatch agents to the western shores of the Aegean Sea for wholesale purchase of grain and through them buy grain to be "distributed to the bakers of Istanbul in order to prevent any hardship for people" in times of need. Thus, grain for daily consumption was brought to Istanbul solely by private investors, while the government bought and stored grain to be used in emergencies.

Such grain as was purchased by the government did not go to the Unkapani exchange but was shipped directly to the shipyards, where it was stored. This grain, referred to as "state provisions," would sometimes not be used up during the year of purchase, and would be wasted.

The purchasing agents bought the grain either at the price determined by officials in Istanbul or at the current prices in the areas, depending on their instructions. The government determined the prices objectively rather than acting with the benefit of the Treasury in mind, for the Imperial Divan was well aware of the current prices. In fact, the price of grain in the province of Tirhala was 50 aspers per *kile* in 1170, but this price was ordered to be raised to 75 aspers the following year.

The capital allocated for this purchase was either given in cash to the purchasing agents from the Treasury or was transferred, by a bill, from the provincial revenues due for payment at the Treasury. In either case, a down payment in cash was made to the producer.

For the transport of grain, vessels were chartered. If the ships happened to be in Istanbul, the customs administrator would sign the lease of charter and the Imperial Treasury would make the payment. In the provincial ports, such leases were handled by the local kadı. If adequate vessels were not found, Venetian, Ragusan, and French ships would be chartered. In the fall, the galleons of the Imperial Fleet would sometimes stop and take on a load of grain on their way back to their base in Istanbul. The purchasing agents, upon their return to Istanbul, would present their accounts to the petty accounting clerk (Küçük Ruznameci) of the Treasury.

Through studying the entries in the Records, we have determined the amount of grain transported to Istanbul in 1171 by government capital. The following table gives the figures.

Thus, the total amount of grain transported by the government in 1171 (1758) was 560,000 *kiles*. This figure, however, is provisional and will remain as such until, by some happy coincidence, the records of the Granary of the Imperial Shipyards are found.

District	Port	Amount
		(Istanbul _kiles_ of wheat)
Tirhala	Platamona	40,000
Morea	Anapoli	70,000
Serez and Orfani	Orfani	150,000
Salonica, Vardar Yenicesi, and Vodina	Salonica	100,000
Yenişehirfanari	Golos	100,000
Livadya, İstife and Athens	Pireus (?)	120,000
Total		580,000

In the year 1171 a total cargo of 7,070,000 _kiles_ of grain was brought to Istanbul—6,510,000 _kiles_ by private capital and 560,000 _kiles_ by government capital. Thus, while private capital was responsible for 91.4 percent of the grain, government capital brought to the city 8.6 percent of the grain.

We see, then, that the government had not set up a centralized and bureaucratic system governing in the same manner grain shipments from all districts earmarked to supply Istanbul. It regulated this important activity by advantageously making use of existing economic institutions and by appointing capable people to handle appropriate matters. The system neither established direct government control of the trade nor turned the trade over to concessions, but included the participation of the government in the flexible setup that recognized concessions. The government accurately prescribed the extent of its participation as well as the large role given to private capital in this matter.

SELECTION 4. WATER SUPPLY SYSTEM OF ISTANBUL, 1830s

Helmuth von Moltke, _Briefe über Zustände und Begebenheiten in der Türkei_ (Berlin, 1911), pp. 91-98.

. . . Constantinople is built on a rocky height, washed around by the sea, and wells dug there give, in all, only a small amount of brackish flow. Drinking water for more than half a million people who drink nothing but water, the enormous amounts used by the numerous baths, in the mosques, and for the five daily ablutions prescribed by the Muslim religion, must therefore be brought in from outside. For this purpose, the wooded hills of Belgrad, three miles north, are used; in winter and spring clouds pour on them an enormous amount of precipitation, in the form of snow and rain. This water is gathered in artificial reservoirs, made by building a strong wall across a valley and thus creating a dam. Such a reservoir is known as _bend_, a Persian word denoting the wall or dyke and having the same meaning as the German word _Band_.

The conditions that must be met for the building of a _bend_ are that the sides of the valley be high enough to provide a great depth of water and a small surface for evaporation; that they be steep and close to each other, so that the wall does not have to be too long and expensive; that the bottom of the valley behind the wall should not have a steep gradient, so that the dam does not stretch too far back; lastly, that the valley upstream have several branches, thus ensuring a large flow of water, and in general that it lie high enough to provide a powerful fall and make the water flow.

The retaining walls which have to hold back such a large mass of water are 80, or even 120, paces long, 30 to 40 feet high, and 25 to 30 feet thick; they are built of squared stone, filled inside with limestone and uncut stones and covered on the outside with marble, ornamented with inscriptions and kiosks.

When, in spring, the dam has been filled, any further amount of water flowing in goes out through an opening in the upper part of the retaining wall, and is led through masonry channels to the natural river bed. Lower down, in the middle of the wall, there is a gate or vault known as the _taksim_ or division, in which that amount of water which can be constantly maintained flows out of the pool, through a given number of 1½-inch-wide pipes (_luleh_ or _mas_). Naturally, the number of pipes depends on the magnitude of the available reserve of water, which has to last for 8 or 9 months; it should however be noted that in spring, when the _bend_ is full, more water passes through any given pipe than in the autumn, when the pressure is lower because of the lower height of the water. The water flows out of the _taksim_ through vaulted masonry channels, coated with mortar, broken tiles, and limestone, along the sides of the valley.

The duct must slope sufficiently so that the flow is rapid; its slope must be constant, otherwise accumulations and overflows will occur in certain places; and yet the slope must not be so steep that the 10-inch-square stream is not high enough when it reaches the determinate spot from which it is distributed to all the lower parts of the city.

If a duct had to cross a valley that cut its path, the ancient peoples had no other means than to carry it over a bridge across the valley to the other side, and this gave rise to the often gigantic aqueducts which one can still see in Italy, Spain, Greece, and

Asia. The Arabs however knew that water finds its level in communicating pipes and on this
based the simpler and less expensive method of carrying water through lead pipes down one
side of a valley and up the other. This ensured that the water would reach the other side,
but because of friction it flowed slowly and delivered only a very small amount in any
given space of time. But experience showed that friction could be greatly reduced if openings were made in the pipes at given intervals. Where the water is flowing level along the
hillsides, and where the pipe goes underground beneath a swelling in the ground, these air-
holes are like the funnels of a fountain; but where the closed pipes go deep underground
for thousands of paces through a valley such openings can of course not be made, for the
water would flow out at that spot. The means used in such cases is the opposite of a well:
a stone pyramid is built, so high that its apex reaches the general level; such pyramids
are known as _suterazi_ [suterazisi], or water scales. The pipe is brought up through this
pyramid and the water settles into equilibrium, pouring into a small basin at the top of
the pyramid and down again into a pipe on the other side. It is clear that the water does
not, through its descent, gain any force other than that which it lost through its ascent,
and that therefore there is no acceleration. The _suterazi_ is thus nothing but an opening
at the level of the duct, for the diminution of friction. It is also self-evident that
the apexes of the _suterazis_ follow the general declivity of the duct, on hydraulic principles, but in a somewhat greater proportion. The leveling of the first ducts through
such broken ground as that north of Constantinople was certainly no light undertaking, and
was made still more difficult by the fact that the water had to be accumulated in several
bends, which lay at different levels. Their execution does honor to the long past ages in
which they were built.
    The Turks came across the aqueducts among the Romans and the _suterazis_ among the
Arabs,[1] but they employed both in the ducts built by them, the first perhaps only for show.
    The oldest and most important water duct of Constantinople is the one which the Em-
peror Constantine began and which later emperors and sultans extended. It is fed by five
large pools, grouped around the village of Belgrad; the largest, the Büyük-bend, lies immediately below the village inhabited by Bulgarians whose ancestors were transplanted from
Belgrad on the Danube and who gave the name of their hometown to their new abode. This
bend, when full, has a length of over 1,000 paces and by itself holds 8 to 10 million cubic
feet of water and replenishes its stock from a second reservoir, just above Belgrad. The
cut first receives, to the left, the flow from the nearby Eski Sultan Mahmud Bend, which
is distinguished by the height of its walls and the beauty of its wooded banks. It then
gets, through an aqueduct, the flow from the Paşa-Bend, lying half an hour to the west.
The commingled waters then cross the broad valley of the Sweet Waters (ancient Barbyzes)
on a strong aqueduct a quarter of an hour below Burgas (Greek Pyrgos); this is not straight
but forms an angle and, it seems to me, surpasses all the others in architectonic beauty.
Beyond that, the duct receives, from the Baş-havuz (Main Pond) the flow from the Aivat-
Bend, which stands alone in a romantic, wooded ravine. Its water crosses the valley of
the Barbyzes, half an hour above Pyrgos, on the 1,000-pace-long but very irregularly built
Suleyman-Aqueduct.
    In addition to these main sources, a host of smaller source-waters flow into the duct
lower down; these are located in the plateau which comes after the valley of Ali-Bey-köy-
su, the classical Kydaris. This valley is crossed by an aqueduct, which bears the name of
Justinian; it is not the longest but the highest and so durably built that a thousand
years have not shaken the two stories of broad arches which carry the water flow at a
height of 90 to 100 feet above the bottom of the valley. Those who do not suffer from
giddiness can easily walk over the vaulted channel; in this solitude, unbuilt and empty
of men, this monument of the might and love of humanity of a long past age makes a moving
impression. The duct is then carried by a very important aqueduct past Cebeciköy, winds
through the undulations of the plain over several small valleys, goes close behind
Filköprü (Elephant Bridge) and the suburb of Eyub and enters the city at Egri-kapu (The
Corner Door).
    The Greek emperors had seen to it that Constantinople should not remain without a
large water supply within its walls; for this purpose, they built large walled basins,
some open and others underground and covered with vaults resting on hundreds of beautiful
granite and marble columns. These last halls are now used by the silk spinners as a cool
abode in summer while the open reservoirs (Çukur bostan or Lower [sic, read Hollow]
Reservoirs) are filled with gardens and houses, and one can say that as regards such an
indispensable need as water Constantinople is living from hand to mouth. The city could
hardly hold out eight days against an enemy who cut the water stream at any point along
its five-mile course. It never crossed the minds of Mehmet the Conqueror and Suleyman the
Magnificent that their capital could ever be besieged; today it is otherwise, and it is
fortunate that the reservoirs, in spite of their diversion to other uses, are at least
still there.
    The huge population also draws some of its water consumption from the hilly country
west of Constantinople, which is rich in springs, by means of shorter and less imposing
ducts. The most important of these comes from Kalfaköy, passes through the town on a
strong aqueduct, and supplies its higher-lying quarters, the fountains of St. Sophia and
the imperial _serail_. This aqueduct (Bozdoğan kemeri, The Arch of the Gray Falcon) is

attributed to the Emperor Valens; it is built of brick and dressed stone and has two stories of arches but is very dilapidated and damaged. Part of the upper row has been pulled down, on the silly pretext that it hid the Shahzadeh mosque built by Suleyman the Magnificent (from 1543 to 1548). Valens' aqueduct constitutes an excellent walk of over 1,000 paces in the middle of the city, high above houses and mosques, streets and fountains. During my survey of **Constantinople** it rendered me a great service; having exactly determined its two ends I could, undisturbed, fix the position of hundreds of mosques and towers. The city lies like a map before one's sight and the only difficulty arises from the endless multitude of objects.

Lastly I must mention the largest water duct, which supplies Pera and Galata, the Arsenal, Kassim paşa, in short all the suburbs north of the Golden Horn. The reservoirs that feed this duct, the Valideh and Yeni Mahmud Bend, are also located in the above-mentioned wooded hills, not far from Bahçe köy, the Garden Village. The Mahmud Bend was built by the present ruler; the water flow crosses, on a long but not high aqueduct, a ridge between the valleys of Bahçeköy and Büyükdere and winds along the slopes of the latter valley until Kulluk (Guardhouse), where it crosses a narrow valley by means of the Falynis Suterazi. A long row of **suterazis** carries the water through the broad depression to Maslak, a coffee house in the main street, and the three-mile duct ends at the beautiful Taksim of Pera, from where it flows into the numerous city fountains.

However, the suburbs north of the Golden Horn have by now spread so far that the water of this large duct no longer meets their needs. The great drought of this year (1836) made the shortage keenly felt, and the Grand Signior, through the Serasker, ordered me to make suggestions for remedies and to find a spot for a new **bend**. Such a spot was available, but it seemed to me far wiser to increase the capacity of the existing, expensive reservoirs rather than to build a new one. The Binai Emineh (in Arabic, the man entrusted with building) who accompanied me submitted what for the Overseer of all imperial buildings was not a bad suggestion: one could raise the walls of the Valideh Bend by four **arşins**, which would supply a good quantity of water. I took the liberty of showing the Effendi that the walls would, in that case, have to withstand three times as much pressure and made the following suggestions: first, that the reservoirs in Constantinople should be restored to their original use; second, that all ducts should be drastically improved; and third, that the ponds behind the walls should be enlarged and deepened. For every 1,000 cubic fathoms of earth removed, 1,000 cubic fathoms of water would be gained, without having to strengthen the walls in the least. But such unostentatiousness is not to the liking of the Turks; they must have something to show the Sultan (bir göstermek şey lazim); a new kiosk and a dedication ceremony are indispensable. Probably, the building of a new **bend** will be preferred, which could well cost half a million thalers.

---

1. It is also said that the Turks borrowed the **bend** and **suterazi** from the Byzantines.

POPULATION OF TOWNS

The following table shows the population of the main towns of Turkey, within the 1912 borders, at the dates indicated. The reliability of the figures decreases as one goes back; almost all of those for the 1830s-40s are estimates made by the more trustworthy travelers, such as Brant, Moltke, Texier, and Vronchenko, and have been taken either directly from their writings or as quoted in EI, EI (2) or IA. The towns are listed according to their size in 1912.

Although the totals are tentative, they suggest that the urban percentage did not change significantly between the 1830s and the First World War, but that it fell sharply between 1912 and 1927. The table also shows that Anatolia was less urbanized than other parts of the Empire; except for Izmir and Bursa the large cities were either in Rumelia or in the Arab provinces.[1]

Growth was most marked in the ports: Istanbul,[2] Izmir, Salonica, Trabzon, Antalya, Tarsus, Samsun, and Mersin. Eskişehir, and Konya may have benefited from the growth caused by the railway, and Adana was the center of a rapidly developing agricultural region. Other towns, however, stagnated or declined. Edirne had begun to decline early in the eighteenth century, and in 1775 its population was put at 100,000 (HHS, Türkei, V, 26). Many towns in the eastern provinces suffered from the Russo-Turkish wars, the shift in trade routes, and the ruin of handicrafts. Writing in 1836, Brant (FO 78/289) stated that

Erzurum's population had fallen from 130,000 to 15,000, that of Diyarbekir from 40,000 families (sic) to 8,000, and that of Kars from 6-8,000 families to 1,500-2,000.[3] Elsewhere, leading handicraft centers, like Bursa, Ankara, Malatya, Tokat, Amasya, Mardin, Kastamonu, and others (see 6:11) showed little or no increase as imported goods put craftsmen out of business. The sharp fall in the population of several towns between 1912 and 1927 reflects the disruptions caused by the successive wars and the loss of large numbers of Armenians and Greeks.

One more point may be noted--the overwhelming predominance of Istanbul. In the Ottoman Empire, as in preindustrial Europe and the Middle East today, the capital city was several times as large as its closest rival, and the rank-size rule observed in the contemporary Western world did not hold.[4] But the 1975 census seems to show that present-day Turkey's urbanization is beginning to conform to the rank-size rule, the figures being: Istanbul 2,535,000, Ankara 1,699,000, Izmir 636,000, Adana 467,000, Bursa 346,000, Gaziantep 301,000, Eskişehir 258,000, Konya 246,000, and Kayseri 207,000.[5]

Finally, the table shows that, like other parts of the Middle East, Turkey was distinctly more urbanized than most of Europe and North America in the eighteenth and early nineteenth centuries. But unlike them it did not develop large industrial towns, and by the end of the century it had fallen far behind all but the most backward parts of Europe.[6]

Population of Main Towns (000)

	1830s–40s	1890	1912	1927
Istanbul	375[a]	900	1,125	691
Izmir	110[b]	200	300	154
Salonica	70[c]	78[c]	150	245
Edirne	100[a]	87[a]	83	35
Bursa	70[b]	76	80	62
Sivas	40[c]	43	60	29
Urfa	(50)	55	50	29
Kayseri	19[a]-40[b]	72	50	39
Trabzon	33[c]	35	50	25
Konya	25[c]-35[b]	40	45	48
Antep (Gaziantep)	20[d]	43	45	40
Erzurum	15[c]	39	43	31
Eskişehir	4[b]	19	42	32
Adana	12[b]	30	42	73
Bitlis	15[c]	39	40	9
Manisa	18[b]-25[c]	35	38	29
Diyarbekir	54[c]	35	38	31
Afyon	20[b]	17	37	23
Ankara	10[e]-28[c]-45[b]	28	35	75
Aydın	40	36	35	12
Istib	(20)		35	..
Malatya	12[f]	30	34	21
Seres	15[g]	28[c]	32	..
Tokat	30-40[f]-45[b]	30	30	22
Amasya	20-30[f]-22[b]	30	30	13
Antalya	15[b]-16[c]	25	30	17

Population of Main Towns (000)   (continued)

	1830s-40s	1890	1912	1927
Van	(20)	30	30	7
Antakya	17[c]	24	30	(20)
Mardin	15[a]	25	27	23
Zile	3[b]	20	27	15
Muş	7[c]	27	27	4
Isparta	18[b]	20	26	16
Tarsus	4[b]	17	26	22
Erzincan	15[h]	23	25	16
Kasaba	15[b]	23	25	7
Maraş	23[d]	52	25	26
İzmit	20[b]-30[c]	25	25	15
Samsun	4[b]	11	25	30
Adapazarı	(20)	24	25	23
Ayvalık	18[c]	21	25	14
Nevşehir	12[b]		24	13
Burdur	15[b]	27	23	13
Nazilli	6[b]	22	23	9
Kütahya	15[c]-40[b]	22	22	17
Alaşehir	8[c]-10[b]	22	22	7
Tekirdağ (Rodosto)	(15)	20[c]	22	15
Pristina	10[g]		21	..
Bergama	12[b]	15	20	13
Harput	9[c]-20[i]	20	20	(1)
Arapkir	(15)	20	20	8
Merzifon	10[b,c]	20	20	11
Karahisar	(15)	17	20	7
Kastamonu	12[c]-30[b]	16	20	15
Kilis	(15)	20	20	23
Kırkağaç	10[b]	20	20	10
Balıkesir	15[b]	13	20	26
Mersin	j	9	20	21
Total of above	(1,680)	(2,740)	3,304	1,967[k]
Total population[l]	8,000	12,000	15,000	13,648
Percentage	20	23	22	14
Towns of 20,000 or over	(1,390)	(2,590)[m]	3,304	1,700
Percentage	17	22	22	12

Sources: 1927 census; 1912 TJ June 1912; 1890 Cuinet, Istanbul from Eldem, p. 64;
1830s-40s, see Notes.

Notes:

[a] Encyclopaedia of Islam

[b] Vronchenko; Erder, p. 66, gives figures of 60,000 for Bursa in 1831, 36,000 in 1879,
and 77,000 in 1895

[c] İslam Ansiklopedisi

[d] FO 78/1419

[e] Selection 2:5

(Notes continued)

[f]Moltke

[g]MacGregor, vol. 2

[h]Brant

[i]Cuinet

[j]Founded in 1832

[k]Excluding Salonica, İstib, Pristina, Seres, and Antakiya

[l]1912 borders, except 1927

[m]Nearly 3,000,000 lived in settlements of 10,000 or more--Erder, p. 43, based on Cuinet

----

1.   In 1816 official returns put the number of towns with over 20,000 inhabitants in the whole Empire at 47; of those 8 had over 100,000, 7 had 50-100,000, 21 had 30-50,000 and 11 had 20-30,000 inhabitants--Mikhov, 3:139-41.

2.   The figure for 1830s, which like the ones for subsequent years includes the surrounding villages, taken from a highly authoritative source, is much lower than the number usually given. The 1844 "census" put the population at 1,060,000 (Reply from Constantinople to circular, 1870, FO 83/334). Shaw, History, 2:241-42, gives the following figures: 391,000 in 1844; 430,000 in 1856; 547,000 in 1878; 852,000 in 1886; 856,000 in 1910 and 910,000 in 1914.

3.   Writing in 1812, Morier also gives high figures for Erzurum, 150,000 and Diyarbekir, 60,000. Some of his other estimates are Tokat 60,000, Amasya 60-70,000, Kayseri 25,000, Trabzon 25,000, and Urfa 20,000.

4.   Issawi, "Urbanization and Economic Development," in Ira Lapidus, ed., Middle Eastern Cities (Berkeley, 1969).

5.   Devlet Istatiskik Enstitüsü," 26 Ekim 1975 Genel Nüfus Sayim.

6.   Issawi, in Lapidus.

SELECTION 5.   THE POPULATION AND THE TAXES AT ANKARA, 1843.

Memorandum by Henry Suter (FO 78/533)

The population of the whole district of Angora, is at present estimated as not exceeding 48,000 persons:
According to a Census taken in 1839, the Town contained

5,000	Mussulmans
3,395	Catholics
1,066	Greeks
596	Armenians
10,057	Individuals

Since that period a diminution of about 3,000 is calculated, owing to the number of families that have quitted to settle elsewhere.
The following is a comparative statement, of the amount of Taxes exacted annually from the Town, before and since the "Tanzimat-i-Hairiyeh," or Hatti Sheriff of Gulhane, came into operation.

	Prior to the Hatti-Sheriff		Since the Hatti-Sheriff	
	Piastres	Sterling	Piastres	Sterling
Mussulmans	167,360	₤ 1,455	227,850	₤ 1,981
Catholics	82,000	713	231,984	2,017
Greeks	38,102	331	78,312	680
Armenians	9,164	79	16,480	143

The people of Angora are friendly to Europeans, and an anxious desire to imitate European civilization, is strikingly manifest among the Christians. In no part of Turkey have I experienced more civility, or such unbounded hospitality. The trade of the place has much declined, and the misery is extreme among the lower orders, especially among the Rayahs. The Government, instead of affording relief seems to be constantly augmenting the evil by increased taxation, and the present state of things threatens to ruin the place in a few years.

WAGES

It is almost impossible to determine the course of real wages in the hundred, or even the fifty, years preceding the First World War. All available data point to a considerable rise in money wages, particularly in the years 1908–14. But the scarcity of accessible information and the geographical and occupational segmentation of the labor force make it very difficult to establish enough comparable figures to arrive at a quantitative result that could be deflated by a cost of living index--even one as rough as that given in 7:2. It is practically certain that money wages rose sharply in the first half of the century, if only because of the great increase in the cost of living.[1] The figures for 1850–54 suggest a daily wage of 4–5 piastres for common laborers and 9–10 for such skilled workers as masons and carpenters, with other handicraftsmen falling in between.

The figures for 1858, which were provided in response to a questionnaire sent out by the British embassy, reflect the rise in prices caused by the Crimean War. The table shows that wages in Bursa, İskenderun, and Rhodes doubled, or almost. In Mytilene and Antep they went up by 50 percent, in Beirut by 30 percent, and in Antakya by 25 percent. Unfortunately, the figures for 1863, also in response to another embassy questionnaire, do not overlap with those of 1858 so it is not possible to say to what extent the wartime rise in wages survived the postwar decline in prices. The following statement made in Bursa in 1872 does, however, suggest some decline in money--though not necessarily in real--wages: "In the early days of factory labour, between 1846 and 1850, reelers were paid from 3 to 4 prs (5½d. to 7¼d.) per diem. By the year 1857 their wages had advanced to 10 prs. (1s. 6½d.). During the last fourteen years their earnings have fluctuated between 6 and 8 prs. (11d. and 1s 2½d.)."[2]

Wages seem to have held up quite well during the decline in wholesale, and presumably retail, prices that marked the last quarter of the century. Available figures suggest that, at the turn of the century, money wages of unskilled labor were about twice as high as around 1850, which would indicate a distinct rise in real wages.

The 1908 revolution and the ensuing wave of strikes (see 2:8), the rise in prices, the Balkan and Italian wars, and increased mobilization, large-scale emigration, and somewhat greater economic activity, combined to raise money wages sharply in the years immediately preceding the First World War. A few comments from British consuls may be quoted. In Izmir, wages of common laborers were estimated to have risen from 10–12 piastres in 1908 to at least 16 by 1910, matching the general rise in prices.[3] In Ayvalık "the labour question is becoming more serious every day. A few years ago the average daily wage of a farm hand was 1s. Now it is difficult to find men at 2s.6d. This is due to the extension of military service to Christians, who are therefore leaving the country. Out of 300 young men liable to service only 90 responded to the call in this district. This state of things induces farmers to seek a remedy in the introduction of machinery," and examples of this are given.[4] In Salonica, "the strikes, with few exceptions, ended in the successful realization of the employes demands for shorter hours and higher pay; but the general result has been a rise in prices and in the cost of labour, to which is traceable in part a temporary stagnation in trade at the end of 1908, due also in part to the boycott of Austro-Hungarian and Bulgarian commerce."[5] Two years later it was reported: "Owing to the rise in the cost and standard of living, to the increased influence of the Socialist organisations and labour syndicates, and especially to the alarming proportions assumed by emigration, unskilled labour is daily becoming more exacting in its demands. At present a dock labourer frequently obtains from 7s. to 8s. for a day's work, while in harvest time a sufficiency of agricultural labour is not to be obtained at 3s. 6d, rates which 10 or 15 years ago would have been regarded as fantastic."[6]   Indeed the previous year the consul had stated that lightermen and dock laborers "are at present receiving higher wages than similar classes in the United Kingdom, whilst the standard [cost?] of living here is lower."[7]

The following report from Edirne may also be noted: "One of the most noteworthy features of the past year has been the increase in the cost of skilled labour, which has gradually advanced during the past five years until it has reached a rate of three times its cost in the year 1905. Apart from the increased cost of living, which is doubtless in part responsible for it, the main reason for the rise in the past years lies in the number of men who have been employed in the building of barracks for the military authorities, and by a French syndicate which has undertaken the construction and repair of the roads, and in the number of Christian recruits taken annually for the army."[8]

Lastly, there is this report from Izmir: "there was a certain shortage of workers, owing to the large number of peasants called to the colours [in 1912-13], but the women to an almost complete degree supplied the needed labour during the winter."[9]

All of this suggests that, on the eve of the First World War, the bargaining position of labor improved, and it seems probable that the rise of wages exceeded that in prices, at least in the more developed parts of the country.

One final question may be raised: how did these wages compare with those of other countries? In England in the 1860s skilled men earned ₤60-73 per annum, semiskilled ₤46-52, and agricultural and unskilled labor between ₤20 and 41, these figures being slightly higher in money terms and hardly different in real terms from the levels prevailing in the 1840s and 50s.[10]   Taking the average wage for masons and carpenters at 11 piastres a day and assuming 300 working days a year, we can suggest an annual income of about ₤30; for common and agricultural labor the corresponding figure would be 5.5 piastres and ₤15. In other words Turkish wages may have been about half, or a little less, of English wages. But the cost of living in Turkey was surely lower: in London, in the 1840s-60s, the price of bread ranged between 1 3/4 and 2 3/4d. per lb.,[11] whereas in the main towns of Turkey--except during the years of the Crimean War--it seldom exceeded 1d. and in many parts of the hinterland was lower (see 7:2); meat, too, was cheaper in Turkey, and so were several other foodstuffs. It may be indicative of the relatively narrow gap between the two sets of wage levels that in 1858 three skilled English workers, "of good character and experience," were engaged for the Asia Minor Telegraph line at a monthly salary of ₤9 each,[12] or well under three times what would have been paid to a highly skilled Turkish worker.

By the turn of the century, however, both money and real wages in England were some 75 to 80 percent higher than they had been in the 1850s and 60s,[13] and the gap between the two countries had greatly widened. It is doubtful whether the advance in Turkish wages in 1905-14 appreciably changed this relation.

In conclusion, a tentative explanation may be offered for the relatively high level of wages in Turkey. This centers on the factor mix: the abundance of land and the cheapness of the main capital input used in agriculture, draft animals. In the British and French consular reports it is repeatedly stressed that, in the period from 1850 to 1900, land was abundant and could either be bought from private owners at rather low prices or acquired from the government, under Tapu registration, for almost nominal payments (5:Introduction, 6 and 8). The replies to the 1863 questionnaire (5:1), give prices of ₤2 to ₤7 for horses, and ₤3 to ₤10 for oxen and buffaloes. At that time the average wage of a farm laborer was about 5.5 piastres a day or, assuming a working year of 275 days, about 1,500 piastres (say £14) a year. This sum could have bought several acres of land in most parts of the Empire, and two to four draft animals. Since one may also assume that the income of sharecroppers was roughly equal to that of agricultural wage laborers, it may be inferred that there was no very great "push" effect, forcing labor away from the countryside. Available figures on urban population also suggest that there cannot have been a very large influx into the towns (2:5). One may therefore conclude that urban wages were not subjected to any great pressure from the influx of peasants and, hence, in spite of the decline in handicrafts which must have thrown many skilled workers out of jobs (chap. 6), remained relatively high.

---

1. This is suggested by the 1832 figures in the following table. The 1841 and 1842 figures for unskilled labor, however, are suspiciously high and should probably be ignored—they are recorded as having been paid for repairs of the French hospital. In the late 1830s Hagemeister (p. 36) stated that European goods were gaining ground in spite of the lowness of wages in Turkey: $1\frac{1}{2}$-3 piastres a day and seldom as high as 5. Another indicator of trend is the wage paid to the Janissary (guard) at the British embassy in Istanbul: in 1809 it was raised from 10 piastres to 25 piastres a month, by 1816 it stood at 40, by 1825 at 55, and in 1852 at about 222 (FO 78/79, 78/87, 78/147, and 78/902). But, clearly, average wages cannot have risen twenty-two fold between 1800 and 1852 or even ninefold between 1809 and 1852.

In 1850, the British consul at Samsun stated "the condition of the poorer classes has likewise greatly improved, and the price of labor is now more than double what it was two years ago," attributing this to the Tanzimat and greater security (Report, FO 78/835); one may accept his judgment of a rise but hardly of a doubling of wages in two years of, presumably, stable prices.

2. A and P 1873, vol. 68, "Turkey"; see also 6:5.

3. A and P 1911, vol. 97, "Smyrna."

4. A and P 1912-13, vol. 100, "Smyrna."

5. A and P 1909, vol. 98, "Salonica."

6. A and P 1912-13, vol. 100, "Salonica."

7. A and P 1911, vol. 96, "Salonica."

8. A and P 1912-13, vol. 100, "Adrianople."

9. A and P 1914, vol. 95, "Smyrna."

10. S. G. Checkland, The Rise of Industrial Society in England (London, 1964), p. 323; Mitchell, p. 343; A. L. Bowley, Wages in the United Kingdom since 1860 (Cambridge, 1937), p. 10, gives hourly wages of bricklayers in the 1860s as 7-8d. and of laborers as $4\frac{1}{2}$d.; the summer working week was $56\frac{1}{2}$ hours, which suggests a daily wage of 5 to 6 shillings, or say 28-32 piastres, and 3 shillings, or 17 piastres, a day.

11. Mitchell, p. 498.

12. TE, Box 26, 1858.

13. Mitchell, p. 343.

Daily Wages (piastres, decimalized)

Year	Place	Mason	Carpenter	Common Laborer	Agricultural Laborer	Handi-Craftsman	Factory Worker	Source
1831	Salonica	..	..	..	1	..	..	Urquhart
1832	Dardanelles	5	7	3	..	..	..	CC Constantinople, 85
1838	Varna	..	..	..	3	..	..	FO 78/1419
1841	Bursa	..	..	..	3	..	..	FO 78/441
1841	Izmir	12-13	..	5-8	..	..	..	CC Smyrne, 46
1842	Izmir	11-13	..	7-8.5	..	..	..	CC Smyrne, 47
1846	Rhodes	(4-6)	(4-6)	(2.5-3)	(2.5-3)	..	..	FO 78/1419
1846	Jaffa	(7.5)	(6)	(2-2.5)	(2-2.5)	..	..	FO 78/1419
1846-51	Mytilene	..	..	..	..	..	..	FO 78/1419
1851	Rhodes	..	9	4	..	7	..	FO 78/833
1851	Iskenderun	9	9	4	..	..	..	FO 78/1419
1853	Diyarbekir	7	7	2	(3)	..	..	A&P 1865-53
1853	Chios	..	..	..	6	..	..	FO 78/1419
1853	Mytilene	..	..	5	..	7	..	FO 78/1419
1854	Rhodes	9	10	4	..	7	..	A&P 1859-30
1854	Iskenderun	9	9	4	..	..	..	A&P 1859-30
1854	Bursa	..	..	4.5	..	..	..	FO 78/1111
1856	Diyarbekir	6-9	6-9	3	..	..	..	FO 78/1419
1856	Jaffa	15	12	4-5	4-5	..	..	FO 78/1419
1856	Mosul	10	9	3	..	..	..	FO 78/1419
1856	Izmit	..	..	..	1.5-6 plus food	..	..	FO 78/1419
1856	Rhodes	8-12	8-12	5-6	5-6	..	..	FO 78/1419
1856	Samos	10	16	..	8	..	..	FO 78/1419
1856	Chios	8-16	8-16	..	9	..	..	FO 78/1419
1856	Varna	..	..	4-7	8-12	..	..	FO 78/1419
1856	Aleppo	11	11	3	3	..	..	FO 78/1419
1856	Tripoli (Syria)	9-11	9-11	3	..	..	..	FO 78/1419
1856	Maraş	..	..	7	2.5-6	..	..	FO 78/1419
1856	Antakya	9	11	3	2.5	..	..	FO 78/1419
1856	Urfa	(8)	(8)	(5)	3-6	..	..	FO 78/1419
1856	Iskenderun	11-14	11	4.5-5.5	5-5.5	..	..	FO 78/1419
1856	Latakia	9-11	7-9	3	..	..	..	FO 78/1419
1856	Antep	7	7	1.5-3.5	..	..	..	FO 78/1419
1856	Baghdad	7.5	7.5	4.5	..	..	..	FO 78/1419
1856	Basra	12	12	4-6	4-6	..	..	FO 78/1419
1856	Beirut	8-14	8-14	5.5	5.5	..	..	FO 78/1419
1856	Crete	10-12	10-12	3	..	..	..	FO 78/1419
1856	Diyarbekir	6-9	6-9	..	..	..	..	FO 78/1419
1856	Bursa	11	11	9	5.5	..	..	FO 78/1419
1856	Izmir	..	..	..	5.5	..	..	Kurmuş

Daily Wages (piastres, decimalized)--Continued

Year	Place						Source
1856	Mytilene				6		FO 78/1419
1858	Iskenderun	15	15	8	8		A&P 1859-30
1858	Diyarbekir	8	8	3.5-4		12	FO 78/1418
1858	Antakya	11	8.5	3	1.5-5		FO 78/1418
1858	Antep	5.5	5.5	3	3		FO 78/1418
1858	Maraş		6.5	2.5-3.5	(4)		FO 78/1418
1858	Urfa	(6)		(4)	2.5-6		FO 78/1418
1858	Aleppo	11	11	3.5-7	3-6		FO 78/1418
1858	Beirut		8-14	4-6	3		FO 78/1418
1858	Jaffa	15	12	4-5			FO 78/1418
1858	Latakia			2.5-3	4		FO 78/1418
1858	Tripoli	9-11	9-11	3-4.5	3-4		FO 78/1418
1858	Baghdad	7.5	7.5	2.5			FO 78/1418
1858	Basra	12	12				FO 78/1418
1858	Mosul	10	9	4			FO 78/1418
1858	Mytilene	12-14	12-14	3-5			FO 78/1418
1858	Crete	10-12	10-12		6		FO 78/1418
1858	Varna		16.5	8	5.5		FO 78/1418
1858	Rhodes	15	18	8	5.5		A&P 1859-30
1858	Ismit (arsenal)			5.5-11	5-6	12	FO 78/1419
1858	Chio				(6-8)		FO 78/1419
1860	Bursa				6-7	4-5ᵃ	FO 195/700
1861	Bursa				5		FO 195/700
1863	Edirne				(4)		FO 195/771
1863	Istanbul (vicinity)				6-7		FO 195/771
1863	Istanbul (further out)				3		FO 195/771
1863	Enos				4		FO 195/771
1863	Gelibolu				5-6		FO 195/771
1863	Cyprus				5.5		FO 195/771
1863	Cyprus (at harvest)				up to 10		FO 195/771
1863	Dardanelles				4		FO 195/771
1863	Salonica (at harvest)				4-5		FO 195/771
1863	Izmir (vicinity)				9.5-12.5		FO 195/771
1863	Izmir (interior)				7-9		FO 195/771
1863	Izmir (women)				4-5.5		FO 195/771
1863	Trabzon				8.5		FO 195/771
1863	Cavalla				5-6		FO 195/771
1863	Janina (harvest)				4.5		FO 195/771
1863	Janina (harvest, women)				3.5-4		FO 195/771
1863	Jerusalem			4.5	5.5		FO 195/771
1863	Diyarbekir	13					A&P 1865-53
1864	Bursa					(6)ᵇ	A&P 1866-69
1865	Bursa	10-12	5-6		6.5	(5.5)ᵇ	A&P 1866-69

Daily Wages (piastres, decimalized)--Continued

Year	Place	Mason	Carpenter	Common Laborer	Agricultural Laborer	Handi-Craftsman	Factory Worker	Source
1868	Trabzon	10-14	9-12	5-6	..	..	..	A&P 1868/9-59
1870	Izmir	15-18	..	..	9	..	..	Kurmuş
1872	Edirne	..	..	6-8	..	..	3.5-4	A&P 1873-68
1872	Bursa	..	..	..	..	..	6[c]	A&P 1873-68
1878	Istanbul	11	11	8.5	..	..	d	A&P 1873-68
1878	Trabzon	..	..	7.5[e]	..	(11-16)	..	A&P 1878/9-71
1879	Ankara	10-15	10-18	6	..	..	..	FO 195/1161
1883	Philippopolis	..	..	..	5.5	..	..	A&P 1880-74
1886	Erzincan	..	..	..	..	(7)[f]	..	A&P 1880-103
1889	Edirne	..	..	..	(5)[g]	..	..	A&P 1887-82
1893	Salonica	..	..	10	..	..	..	A&P 1890-77
1896	Izmir	15	15	..	..	..	8-11	A&P 1893/4-97
1896	Istanbul	..	..	..	..	7-13	(12)[h]	USSCR 1896/7
1898	Ankara	..	..	4-9[i]	..	..	..	RC 1896
1899	Mytilene	5-8	9	..	(5.5)	..	6.5-16.5	A&P 1899-103
1901	Bitlis	..	..	..	3	[j]	..	A&P 1900-96
1901	Istanbul	..	..	..	..	12[k]	..	A&P 1902-110
1906	Istanbul	..	..	..	..	9-18	..	RC 1901
1908	Adana	..	..	..	7-13[l]	..	5[m]	RC 1906
1908	Adana	..	..	..	5.5-7	..	..	A&P 1909-98
1908	Izmir	..	..	(10-12)	..	..	..	A&P 1908-10
1909	Kastamonu	..	..	..	..	5-8[k]	..	A&P 1911-97
1909	Mytilene	..	..	..	..	9-12[k]	..	RC 1909
1909	Konya	..	..	..	..	4-6[k]	..	RC 1909
1909	Van	..	..	..	..	1.5-5	..	RC 1909
1909	Ayvalik	..	..	..	14	..	..	A&P 1912/3-100
1910	Izmir	16	..	16	..	..	..	A&P 1911-97
1911	Mining, average	..	..	..	..	..	(10)	Eldem
1913	Average	..	..	..	..	..	(12-14)[n]	Eldem
1913	Istanbul	..	..	..	..	..	14.1	Eldem
1913	Izmir	..	..	..	..	..	12.4	Eldem
1913	Coal fields	..	..	..	..	..	10.1	Eldem
1913	Adana	..	..	..	..	..	7.2	Eldem
1913	Beirut	..	..	..	..	..	9.4	Eldem
1913	Damascus	..	..	..	..	..	8.5	Eldem
1914	Carpet industry	..	..	..	..	5.5[o]	..	TJ 1914

[a]Wages paid to girls in silk filatures during depression--"but half their former wages."

[b]In silk filatures, girls earned 4 piastres in winter and 6-8 in summer, superintendents 7 and 13; in 1865, the corresponding figures were 4-4.5 and 6-7, and 6-7 and 10-12.

[c]Silk reelers earned 8 piastres in summer, 6 in spring and 4 in winter, averaging 6, carders and twisters earned as much, sorters and beaters 4; forewomen 8, foremen and engine drivers 12.

[d]In textile factories skilled workers earned 18-27 piastres a week, ordinary workmen 9-14, women 3-5, and children 1-2. "At Constantinople the wages are 20 percent higher than they are in the provinces."

[e]Skilled labor earned 9.5 piastres.

[f]Owners of looms earned about £20 (about 2,200 piastres) a year and apprentices £5 to 10 (550-1,100 piastres).

[g]Labor attached to farms earned £7 7s. (about 8,100 piastres), including (sic-- presumably in addition to) food, casual labor 6-8 d. (3-4 piastres), reapers 1s. 8d. (9 piastres).

[h]Among "factory operatives," firemen earned $15.40 (350 piastres) and millers $13.20 (300 piastres) a month, foremen $44 and engineers $52.80; among railway employees, firemen and clerks earned $19.80, ticket collectors $17.60, and station masters $35.20; among mechanics, tinsmiths and plasterers earned 66 cents (15 piastres) a day, blacksmiths, founders, and plumbers 88 cents, and fitters $1.10. $1.00 was equal to 22.7 piastres.

[i]Unskilled labor earned 9d.-1s. 8d. a day (4-9 piastres), skilled 2s.-5s. (11-28 piastres), men mohair sorters 1s. 3d.-2s. (7-11 piastres), and women mohair sorters 5d. (2.5 piastres).

[j]The yearly income of various groups was estimated, at pounds sterling, blacksmith and shoeingsmith 25-42 (2,750-4,620 piastres), carpenter 23-27, baker and mason 13-23, tanner 17-21, tailor 8-42, shoemaker 8-34, butcher 8-17, porter 10-16, weaver 8-9. In the neighboring villages, blacksmiths and shoeing smiths earned 13-17 and millers 7-8.

[k]In tanneries.

[l]"In harvest time labour is largely supplied by nomadic tribes, who return to the mountains after it is over. The price of labour is fixed each week in the markets of Tarsus and Adana according to the demand. It varies from 30-70 piasters for six days. The employer has to deal only with the headman chosen by each gang. Food is given by the employer and if it is scanty or bad or if there are other difficulties, the men strike at once. Often they are lazy, greedy and inefficient. This rate of wages is the same for harvesters or workers with machines other than the actual mechanics. Each threshing machine tours the country with a gang of 28 or 29 men" (A and P 1909, vol. 98 "Adana").

[m]Cotton spinning; in weaving 280 hands were employed, "the wages bill is about 25,000 (sic) piastres a week"--assuming the correct figure to be 2,500 would give an average of 89 piastres a week or about 12.5 piastres per working day. At Tarsus, in the cotton spinning and weaving factory the average wage was "5 piastres a day for young and old, male and female."

[n]Food processing 11.8, ceramics 13.8, tanneries 13.6, wood 16.9, textiles 6.1, paper 11.7, chemical 13.7, mineral industry 15.0.

[o]Average; skilled weaver "can earn more than" 14 piastres.

SELECTION 6. LEVEL OF LIVING IN BURSA, 1851

Report on the local administration and condition of the District of Brussa in the year
1850-51 (FO 78/868)

The city presents the ordinary signs of an improving and thriving place. A good many
new houses have latterly been built and are in progress, of a much better class than hitherto, and their exterior exhibiting the novelty of some regard to form and appearance.

House rent, especially in the Raya quarters and for European Residents has greatly ad-
vanced--the hire of Shops and Stores in the Bazars and other eligible places of traffic
still more considerably, being in many instances double and even triple what it was a few
years back, and shops have gradually sprung up furnished with many European articles of
general convenience such as were totally deficient on my arrival here, and for some time
afterwards.

The advance and more cheerful aspect of the town have been conspicuous under the administration of the present Governor Sarim Pacha, so that the public voice concurs in as-
cribing to its salutary influence much of the striking change--the more so that he is the
only Governor within memory who has taken a direct active part in promoting the general welfare of the District.

The middling class of Traders and Shopkeepers is in easy circumstances. Wages for
some kinds of work are remarkably high in proportion to the Cost of the necessaries of life,
where Bread is at 2d. the Loaf of 2 3/4 lbs, Meat, of which the lower orders use very little,
2d. to 2¼d. the lb., vegetables and fruits abundant in their Season, and very cheap, so that
a sufficiency of Melons, Grapes and the like may be had for ½d., with which and bread, or
the addition perhaps of some cheese or black olives the workman can make his meal. A Journeyman house Carpenter or Builder receives 12 to 20 Piastres = 2/2 to 3/3 a day. Smiths,
Tailors and Shoemakers if any wise skilful much the same, and a common laborer for any
rough jobwork can scarcely be engaged for less than 13d. to 18d. a day. Some hundreds of
Raya women and children have a further recent resource for employment at the Silk Filatures,
where they earn [6¼d.] to [10½d.] a day,* and Turkish females come to supply the place of
Christian for washing at our houses, from the high wages of 18d. to nearly 2/- a day which
these last must be paid.

Generally speaking, there is no one of any need having the requisite health and
strength to work, who need be at a loss for a competent subsistence by his labor. But unfortunately the intemperate use of ardent spirits, by far too prevalent among the better
classes extends so much to the mass of the population as to be the great bane of their well-
being.

The Mussulmans share with the rest the resources afforded by the exercise of retail
and mechanic trades and the traffic with the surrounding country and the Capital, having
besides the advantage of being exclusively eligible to administrative offices which serves
greatly to enhance their means and sustain their relative station.

The Greeks, altho they cannot be said to have fallen behind in activity and intelligence, do not prosper so well in their affairs as the Armenians. Of their former respectable Merchants and families very few indeed are left, who have preserved the same property
and Credit, owing finally to overspeculation in foreign trade, particularly in Silk when on
the eve of its last extreme depretiation.

The Armenians were more cautious, the business of their chiefs being however mostly
that of Sarafs in advancing money at high usurious rates to the people of the small towns
and villages, and those newly appointed to office there, managing to secure the support of
the ruling authorities, so as to get repaid with accumulated interest.

The Armenian Catholics, forming a separate Community of 80 families differ little except in rite from the larger national Community.

The Jews, few in number, do not count any person of substance amongst them, and from
their usual appearance would be thought in a most abject state; the miserable dwellings or
hovels which distinguish their quarter adding to this semblance of poverty, which there can
be no doubt is to a great extent real. But the aspect of their Community is entirely
changed on their Sabbath and great annual festivals, and no other is so well and decently
clad as theirs, including children, on such occasions.

They as elsewhere practise few mechanic trades, and subsist most by petty traffic,
save a few who rank as Merchants. But they are very illiberally alone excluded from various Retail trades (open to them at the Capital, such as the sale of British manufactures)
by antient local Regulations, which their efforts to supersede, with every aid within my
competence, have failed in doing, notwithstanding the general laws of the Empire and an
express ordinance of the present Sultan place them on an entire equality of rights and immunities common to other Subjects.

There is a small Protestant Community of 17 Armenians, proselytised by American Missionaries here, and in the enjoyment of all the privileges accorded to Protestant Subjects

---

*The figures in square brackets have been inserted in the blank spaces in the original;
they were obtained from the Report for 1851-52 (FO 78/905) and refer to "Young girls Armenian and Greek."

of the Porte by the Edict issued in the time of Lord Cowley's charge of Her Majesty's Embassy.

The public School constructed some years ago by order of the Porte has received its destined organisation, and contains 61 Turkish Boys who are maintained at the Government charge, and wear a distinctive uniform dress, receiving an elementary education in Turkish, to be completed at Galata Serai College at the Capital, for Pupils designed for different branches of the public Service.

The great material improvement anticipated here will be the construction of the Carriage road between this and Ghio, as reported in my Despatch no. 15 of last year, and announced as now about to be commenced.

If really carried out according to the plan agreed upon, and permanently kept in order, Brussa will enjoy advantages not yet possessed by any other city in the Empire. The effect as to agriculture is noticed in my Report under that Title. In the Trade of direct exportation, and of interchange, as well as for personal Communications with the Capital, it will be of the utmost convenience. . . .

SELECTION 7. LEVEL OF LIVING IN NORTHERN ANATOLIA, 1870

"North Eastern Provinces," (FO 83/337)

Classification of Town Industrials and Artizans

The First, and lowest Class, shall comprise day-labourers, porters, job-men having no fixed profession, and dependent on casual employment in the coarser kinds of work, and the like.

The Second Class, somewhat higher up on the social scale, may consist of workmen belonging to a settled, though rough, profession, such as are stone-cutters, common carpenters, boatmen, smiths, bakers, dyers, tanners, and so on.

The third and highest Class, shall include the followers of sedentary professions; tailors, shoe-makers, pipe-makers, weavers, confectioners, ornamental carpenters, silversmiths, and the like. . . .

*
Balances.

We will now strike the Balance for each case [of the First Class] that has been put; proceeding by fair averages within the possible limits on either side of the account.

Married Day-Labourer.

Expenditure.

	Piastres.
House-rent, or Costs,	200
Clothes,	100
Food, self and family,	1,825
at 5 Piastres a day	
Taxes,	60
Sundries,	60

Yearly Total of Expenditures

Piastres
2,245

Earnings.

	Piastres.
Wages, allowing 300	
working days, at 6	
Piastres a day,	1,800
Occasional gains, as	
Night-watch, etc.	450

Yearly Total of Earnings.

Piastres	Ł	s.	d.
2,250	18	15	0.

Balance, in favour of married Day-Labourer.

Piastres	Ł	s.	d.
5	0	0	10.

---

*
Most of the sterling equivalents have been omitted; they were calculated at 100 piastres equals 16s. 8d.

Unmarried Day-Labourer.

	Piastres.
House-rent, or Costs,	Nil
Clothes,	100
Food, exclusive of bread, at 3 Piastres a Day,	1,095
Taxes,	40
Sundries	200

Yearly Total of Expenditure.

Piastres	₤	s.	d.
1,435	11	19	2.

Earnings

	Piastres.	₤	s.	d.
Wages, for 300 working days, at 5 Piastres a day,	1,500	12	10	0.
Occasional earnings,	300	2	10	0.

Yearly Total of Earnings.

Piastres	₤	s.	d.
1,800	15	0	0.

Balance, in favour of unmarried Day-Labourer.

Piastres	₤	s.	d.
365	3	0	10.

Refugee, "Hammal," or Porter.

	Piastres.
House-rent, or Costs,	Nil
Clothes,	100
Food, at 4 Piastres a day,	1,460
Dues, to "Hammal-Bashi," at about 4 Piastres a week	200
Sundries	150

Total of Yearly Expenditure.

Piastres	₤	s.	d.
1,910	15	18	4.

Earnings.

	Piastres.
Wages for 300 working days, at 10 Piastres per day, all included	3,000

Balance, in favour of "Hammal."

Piastres	₤	s.	d.
1,090	9	1	8.

Balances.

Following the same method as in the former instances, I will now strike the Balance of yearly Earnings and Expenditure for each successive sub-variety of this Second Class.

<u>Workman, as Carpenter, Mason, Smith, etc.--Expenditures.</u>

	Piastres.
House-rent, or costs,	350
Clothes,	150
Food, for self and family, at 8 Piastres a day,	2,920
Taxes,	75
Sundries,	100

<u>Total Yearly.</u>

Piastres

3,595

<u>Earnings.</u>

	Piastres.
Wages, allowing 300 working-days in the year at 12 Piastres a day,	3,600
Extra jobs,	200

<u>Total Yearly.</u>

Piastres	Ł	s.	d.
3,800	31	13	4.

<u>Balance, in favour of Workman.</u>

Piastres	Ł	s.	d.
205	1	4	2.

<u>"Kaikjee," or Long-shore Boatman--Expenditure.</u>

	Piastres.
House cost and sundries,	450
Clothes,	150
Food, for self and family, at 6 Piastres a day,	2,190
Dues to "Kaikjee-Bashi,"	500
Sundries,	100

<u>Total Yearly.</u>

Piastres	Ł	s.	d.
3,390	28	5	0.

<u>Earnings.</u>

	Piastres.	Ł	s.	d.
For 260 working days, fair and foul, at an average of 16 Piastres a day,	4,160	34	13	4.

<u>Balance, in favour of Boatman.</u>

Piastres	Ł	s.	d.
770	6	8	4.

<u>Balances.</u>

Taking averages as before, I will now strike the Balance for this [Third] Class; one specimen may here suffice.

<u>Artisan of the Third Class.</u>

Expenditure.

Piastres.

	Piastres.
House-costs, or Rent,	800
Clothes,	180
Food for self and family, at 11 Piastres a day,	4,015
Shop-rent and License,	750
Taxes,	90
Sundries,	150

Total yearly.

Piastres	Ł	s.	d.
5,985	49	17	6.

Earnings.

Piastres.

For 300 working days, at 25 Piastres a day,	7,500

Balance, in favour of Artisan.

Piastres

1,515

This calculation, it will at once be seen, is above the mark of some, and below that of others; but it may, on the whole, be considered a favourable one. . . .

Peasants.

Let us now select an average Peasant, whether Proprietor or Tenant; and let us give him the average allowance of arable land, namely Four Dunems--about Eight English Acres, according to East Anatolian measurement. More than this his rude implements will not permit him to cultivate to advantage. The market value of an acre of land hereabouts is, if for ploughing, 300 Piastres--Ł2 10s. on an ordinary estimate; if for planting, about 130 Piastres--Ł1 1 8.

The materials of the peasant's cottage, wood, stone, or unbaked brick, according to the District, cost him little or nothing; and the construction itself is in part done by his own labour and that of his friends, and is so far gratis. Still much remains towards completion that exceeds mere peasant skill; and the total expense of the dwelling generally reaches 2,000, or even 3,000 Piastres-- Ł16 13 4, to Ł25. Cottages to let are things unheard of in the country villages.

A Barn requires for its construction about 1,000 Piastres,-- Ł8 6 8; and when once built may, like the house, last from twenty to thirty years.

A pair of oxen, here used for drawing the plough as horses are in England, costs from 700 to 1,100 Piastres,-- Ł5 16 8 to Ł9 3 4; the two animals taken together have hardly the strength of one English beast. Buffaloes are preferred where they can be had; the pair costs about 1,400 Piastres,-- Ł11 13 4. A pack-horse too is indispensable, for conveying field-produce to market; the price is from 450 to 800 Piastres,-- Ł3 15, to Ł6 13 4. Agricultural implements and house furniture represent a value of about 2400 Piastres-- Ł20 additional.

It would be almost superfluous to say that every grown-up peasant of these lands is married. His daily food for himself and his family comes to about 3 Piastres,--6d; thus much being spent on purchase; the remaining and the greater part is the produce of his own ground. A complete suit of clothes costs about 200 Piastres,-- Ł1 13 4, and lasts from two to three years. . . .

Peasant Landowner.

Expenditure.

Piastres.

	Piastres.
Food for self and family, at 3 Piastres a day,	1,095
Clothes and Sundries	200
Taxation	320
Expenses for horse, implements, etc.	330

Total Yearly.

Piastres

1,945

Earnings.

	Piastres
Sale of crops,	1,848
Occasional,	200

Total Yearly.

Piastres	Ł	s.	d.
2,048	17	1	4

Balance, in favour of Peasant Landowner.

Piastres	Ł	s.	d.
103	0	17	2

"Muraba'" or Produce-Partner Tenant.

Expenditure.

	Piastres.
Food for self and family, at 2 Piastres the day,	730
Clothes and sundries,	150
Taxation,	150
Expenses for horse, implements, etc.	250

Total Yearly.

Piastres	Ł	s.	d.
1,280	10	13	4.

Earnings.

	Piastres.
Sale of crop, allowing the "Muraba'" two-thirds of the profits,	1,212
Occasional,	200

Total Yearly.

Piastres

1,412

Balance, in favour of "Muraba'"

Piastres	Ł	s.	d.
132	1	2	0.

Tenant on "Tesarref," or Rent.

Expenditure.

	Piastres.
Food for self and family, at about 2-1/2 Piastres a day,	920
Clothes and Sundries,	200
Taxation,	240
Rent, at one-eighth the value of the crop	231
Expenses for horse, implements, etc.,	300

Total Yearly.

Piastres	£	s.	d.
1,891	15	15	2.

Earnings.

	Piastres.
Sale of crops,	1,848
Occasional,	200

Total Yearly.

Piastres

2,048

Balance, in favour of Tenant.

Piastres

157

Note.

No account has here been taken of the mere Day-labourer, because his position, as above explained, is not permanent but transitory only in the agricultural districts.

STRIKES

Various spontaneous and unorganized manifestations of worker discontent seem to have occurred as early as the middle of the nineteenth century, and some form of strike by coal miners in Ereğli took place in 1863.[1] In 1872, there were several strikes in the Istanbul arsenal, the Beyoğlu telegraph, the Ömerli-Yamburgaz and Izmir railways, and the Beyköz shoe factory.[2] In 1872-80, some twenty-one strikes were recorded, but only four in 1881-1906.[3] In 1895, the Union and Progress party founded the short-lived "Osmanlı Amele Cemi-yeti," based on the workers of the arsenal. But it was not until the 1908 Constitution that industrial action on a large scale began; some thirty strikes took place, and in the next two or three years several trade unions were founded, notably in the railways, textile, tobacco, and food and drink industries.[4] Particularly noteworthy was the strike by an es-timated 10,000 tobacco workers for higher wages and a ten-hour day.[5] One may conjecture that among the causes of this wave of strikes was the sharp rise in prices in the immediate prewar days (see 7:2). In November 1908, a law was passed against strikes.

The account of the Salonica strike given in selection 8 may be supplemented by the following analysis, provided by the British consul at Izmir.[6] It is surely not fortuitous that the strike movement began in the country's leading ports, inhabited mainly by members of minority groups whose social awareness must have been greater than that of the Turkish majority. On the other hand, the ethnic and religious heterogeneity of the Ottoman workers must have made it more difficult for them to take united action.

Strikes.--The first awakening to the realities of the altered situation came in the form of labor strikes. The word itself was unknown in Turkey before. Not that the working classes were content with their wages. They knew well enough that they were inadequate, but to concert action and organize demonstrations, to clamor for increased pay--in fact for any object, however innocent--were things not to be dreamt of under the old régime. They would have been considered seditious agitation.

With the advent of liberty, however, proclaimed by the Constitution, the working classes seized the opportunity to assert their right to better their conditions.

Nearly all classes of workers struck, and nearly all succeeded without any difficulty or even question. The whole thing was a very peaceful affair, and the men

obtained, merely for the asking, so to speak, increases ranging from 10 to 25 per cent.

The only instances in which the men's demands met with any opposition were those

of ship stevedores (cargo handlers) and the (British) Aidin Railway Company's employ-

ees. In both cases awkward interruption of shipping and transport operations was the

result, and that too in September, the busiest season.

Realizing the advantages of organized action, all the guilds, corporations,

groups or bodies of kindred workmen and artisans have since formed associations or

unions, so that the future will find them all well prepared for eventualities. The

weak point of these organizations at present is their lack of funds, but this matter

also is receiving attention.

Another interesting appreciation was given, in 1911, by the journal of the British

Chamber of Commerce in Istanbul: "The success of the railway strikes, tramways strikes,

tailors' strike, cabinet makers' strike, lightermen and coal heavers' strike, the strikes

of porters at the custom house and, last but not least, that of the tobacco makers, are all

significant of what is coming on." The congress of the tobacco makers of the Empire had

gathered 21 delegates, representing 37,000 workers. It had included delegates from Macedon-

ia, Drama, Seres, Istanbul, Latakia, and Samsun," and the workmanlike manner in which they

met and passed resolutions showed that there must be some thinking heads guiding them."[7]

1. Guseinov, p. 8.
2. Ibid., and Erişçi, p. 4.
3. Sencer, pp. 147-48.
4. Erişçi, pp. 8-11; see also Dumont in La Révolution Industrielle, pp. 281-307, for
a fuller analysis.
5. Guseinov, p. 10.
6. A and P 1909, vol. 98, "Smyrna."
7. TJ, September 1911.

SELECTION 8. STRIKES IN SALONICA, 1908

Memorandum of 9 September 1908 by Acting Vice Consul Mulock (FO 368/231)

The strike fever which broke out in Constantinople shortly after the declaration of
the Constitution has developed into an epidemic at Salonica, where almost every branch of
commercial and industrial life has been affected by the tendency to discover and air the
grievances of man against master. As in the case of the Capital the Regie employes were
the first to strike, and have not as yet returned to work; but the majority of the recent
strikes have fortunately been of short duration, thanks chiefly to the valuable services
of the Mayor, Osman Adil Bey, as a successful arbitrator.

The strikes, whose duration would have had the most appreciable effect on economic
and commercial interests, are those of the bakeries, which fortunately did not long survive
the threatening stage, and those of the three railways which have their termini here. The
first of these to be affected was the Chemins de Fer Orientaux (Salonica-Uscub-Zibeftche)
whose brakesmen struck on August 23rd, returned to work on August 26th, and went out again
on August 28th. Their example was followed on September 2nd by 200 engine-shop employes;
and, their demands not being satisfied by the Directors' offer of 2 piastres rise on 10
piastres daily wage and 1 piastre on 20 piastres, they persuaded the employes at the intermediate stations to join the movement, with the result that the strike became general on
September 2nd; while the infection spread also to the Monastir and Junction Lines. The
mission of Mr. Steiner, local Managing Director of the Oriental Railways, to Constantinople
to try and arrange matters having failed, the Mayor succeeded for his own part in persuading
the strikers to return to work for 48 hours; and in conjunction with Mr. Mueller, General
Traffic Manager, settled the claims of the brakesmen and workshop employes. As a result of
this the Oriental Railways strike as well as that on the Monastir Line came to an end on
September 4; while a subsequent strike of the former's telegraph and warehouse employes
broke out and was settled on September 6th by the indefatigable Mayor.

The demands of the Oriental Railway employes were as follows:
(1) 30%-40% increase of wages.
(2) Promotion every 2 years, so that 20-25 years' service entitle any man to the highest
grade in his particular branch of employment.

(3) More generous rises of salary.
(4) Shorter hours.
(5) Reorganization of medical service and attendance.
(6) Modification of Pension Fund rules.

Their demands were satisfied by the following settlement made by the Directors on September 4th.

(1) An increase of 3 piastres on wages of 14 piastres a day;
     "   "   " 2   "   "   "   " 15-24 piastres a day;
     "   "   " 1   "   "   "   " over 24 "   " " .
(2) Such employes as have received no increase of wages for several years, or whose turn it was to have their salary raised on January 1st 1908, will receive the regulation increase of 1 piastre a day from September 1st.
(3) Those who have not as yet received any allowance for the increased cost of living will do so on and after September 1st.
(4) Extra working hours, e.g., Sundays and recognized holidays such as Christmas Day, Easter and Whitsuntide will be rewarded by an additional 50% on wages due.
(5) The following scale of wages applies to apprentices:-

                 5 piastres a day during their 1st year,
           8   2nd   "
          13   3rd   "
          15   4th   "

(6) Claims involving alterations of the regulations in force should be subject to a general revision; but it is understood that in case of illness half wages will be paid, while in cases of accidents occurring while on duty wages will be paid in full. In the event of the death of an employe the Directors will, in deserving cases, grant to the surviving relatives an adequate sum in compensation, as has been done hitherto.
(7) The medical staff at Salonica will receive orders to do its utmost to take the greatest and most conscientious care of the sick. Care will therefore be taken to keep two doctors permanently at Salonica and to increase as far as possible the supply of medicines.
      If the doctor in charge of a patient considers an operation in Europe indispensable, then the Company will refund the expenses of his journey.
(8) No employe shall be discharged or molested because of the recent strike.

The strike on the Junction Line, which also began on September 2nd, threatens to continue for some time, as the employes are more intransigeant and difficult to satisfy than those of the Zibeftche and Monastir Lines. A telegraphic offer, from the Company's head office in Constantinople, to raise their salaries by 5% more than that originally demanded by the employes (who had asked for a 15% increase on salaries of 600 piastres a month and 10% on those above that sum) was refused. Arbitration having so far failed utterly, the arrival of Comte Vitalis and M. de Rey, of the Board of Directors, is expected momentarily from Constantinople.

The Bakers' strike referred to above was fortunately a matter of less than 24 hours, thanks once again to the able intervention of the Mayor, who promised that a Commission should at once proceed to investigate and improve the sanitary condition of the night quarters on the bakers' employes. . . .

                    MARX AND ENGELS ON THE OTTOMAN EMPIRE, 1853

Marx and Engels' intense hatred of Russia and their poor opinion of the Slavs (with the single exception of the Poles) predisposed them in favor of those nationalities that constituted an obstacle to Russian expansion, such as the Hungarians and Turks. As regards the latter, a further influence was that of David Urquhart, an eccentric Member of Parliament who had served in the British embassy in Istanbul in the 1830s (EHME p. 42). Urquhart, a passionate Russophobe and Turcophile, even persuaded Marx to start learning Turkish.[1] He repeatedly stated that Marx had a "Turkish intelligence" and "wrote like a Turk," a compliment that was not appreciated.[2]

But if Marx and Engels were representative Victorians in their hostility to Russia and support of Turkey, they were even more typical in their Euro-centrism and deep conviction regarding the antagonism between Western civilization and Eastern barbarism. The following passages, taken from articles signed and sent by Marx to the New York Daily Tribune, illustrate the views of the two men on the structure of the Ottoman Empire and its main ethnic groups. The first, written by Marx and Engels, appeared in the 7 April 1853 issue and the second, written by Engels, in the 19 April 1853 issue. In the Sochineniya (Moscow, 1933) 9:373-75 and 391-92, both articles are attributed to Marx, and the exact date of publication is not given; but they are correctly identified in Marx Engels Werke (Berlin, 1960), 9:pp. 7-9 and 26-27. Both articles, together with many others sent by Marx to the Tribune, were published by his daughter Eleanor Marx Aveling and her husband Edward Aveling, under the title The Eastern Question, by Karl Marx (London, 1897), from which the following selections are taken; in the Avelings' edition, too, all the articles are attributed to Marx.

---

1. Isaiah Berlin, Karl Marx (London, 1939) p. 246.
2. For one example among many, see Marx's letter to Engels of 9 February 1854 (Karl Marx Friedrich Engels Briefwechsel, Berlin, 1949, 2:9): "I had a meeting with Urquhart. The compliment with which he startled me was that the article was such as though a 'Turk' had written it." His account ends with: "Er ist ein kompletter Monoman."

SELECTION 9. THE OTTOMAN EMPIRE AND THE TURKS

Karl Marx, in New York Daily Tribune, 12 and 19 April, 1853

. . . Let us look at the question at once. Turkey consists of three entirely distinct portions: the vassal principalities of Africa, viz., Egypt and Tunis; Asiatic Turkey; and European Turkey. The African possessions, of which Egypt alone may be considered as really subject to the Sultan, may be left for the moment out of the question. Egypt belongs more to the English than to anybody else, and will and must necessarily form their share in any future partition of Turkey. Asiatic Turkey is the real seat of whatever strength there is in the empire; Asia Minor and Armenia, for four hundred years the chief abode of the Turks, form the reserved ground from which the Turkish armies have been drawn, from those that threatened the ramparts of Vienna, to those that dispersed before Diebitsch's not very skilful manoeuvres at Kulewtscha. Turkey in Asia, although thinly populated, yet forms too compact a mass of Mussulman fanaticism and Turkish nationality to invite at present any attempts at conquest; and, in fact, whenever the "Eastern Question" is mooted, the only portions of this territory taken into consideration are Palestine and the Christian valleys of the Lebanon.

The real point at issue always is, Turkey in Europe--the great peninsula to the south of the Save and Danube. This splendid territory has the misfortune to be inhabited by a conglomerate of different races and nationalities, of which it is hard to say which is the least fit for progress and civilization. Slavonians, Greeks, Wallachians, Arnauts, twelve millions of men, are all held in submission by one million of Turks, and up to a recent period it appeared doubtful whether, of all these different races, the Turks were not the most competent to hold the supremacy which, in such a mixed population, could not but accrue to one of these nationalities. But when we see how lamentably have failed all the attempts at civilization by Turkish authority--how the fanaticism of Islam, supported principally by the Turkish mob in a few great cities, has availed itself of the assistance of Austria and Russia invariably to regain power and to overturn any progress that might have been made; when we see the central, i.e. Turkish, authority weakened year after year by insurrections in the Christian provinces, none of which, thanks to the weakness of the Porte and to the intervention of neighbouring States, is ever completely fruitless; when we see Greece acquire her independence, parts of Armenia conquered by Russia,--Moldavia, Wallachia, Servia, successively placed under the protectorate of the latter power,--we shall be obliged to admit that the presence of the Turks in Europe is a real obstacle to the development of the resources of the Thraco-Illyrian Peninsula.

We can hardly describe the Turks as the ruling class of Turkey, because the relations of the different classes of society there are as much mixed up as those of the various races. The Turk is, according to localities and circumstances, workman, farmer, small freeholder, trader, feudal landlord in the lowest and most barbaric stage of feudalism, civil officer, or soldier; but in all these different social positions he alone has the right to carry arms, and the highest Christian has to give up the footpath to the lowest Moslem he meets. In Bosnia and the Herzegovina, the nobility. of Slavonian descent, have passed over to Islam, while the mass of the people remain Rayahs, i.e. Christians. In this province, then, the ruling creed and the ruling class are identified, as of course the Moslem Bosnian is upon a level with his co-religionist of Turkish descent.

The principal power of the Turkish population in Europe, independently of the reserve always ready to be drawn from Asia, lies in the mob of Constantinople and a few other large towns. It is essentially Turkish, and though it finds its principal livelihood by doing jobs for Christian capitalists, it maintains with great jealousy the imaginary superiority and real impunity for excesses which the privileges of Islam confer upon it as compared with Christians. It is well known that this mob in every important <u>coup d'état</u> has to be won over by bribes and flattery. It is this mob alone, with the exception of a few colonized districts, which offers a compact and imposing mass of Turkish population in Europe. And certainly there will be, sooner or later, an absolute necessity for freeing one of the finest parts of this continent from the rule of a mob, compared with which the mob of Imperial Rome was an assemblage of sages and heroes. . . .

. . . The only argument [i.e., by Urquhart] which deserves a moment's notice upon this side of the question is this: "It is said that Turkey is decaying; but where is the decay? Is not civilization rapidly spreading in Turkey and trade extending? Where you see nothing but decay, our statistics prove nothing but progress." Now it would be a great fallacy to put down the increasing Black Sea trade to the credit of Turkey alone; and yet this is done here, exactly as if the industrial and commercial capabilities of Holland, the high road to the greater part of Germany, were to be measured by her gross exports and imports, ninetenths of which represent a mere transit. And yet, what every statistician would immediately, in the case of Holland, treat as a clumsy concoction, the whole of the Liberal press of England, including the learned Economist, tries, in the case of Turkey, to impose upon public credulity. And then, who are the traders in Turkey? Certainly not the Turks. Their way of promoting trade, when they were yet in their original nomadic state, consisted in robbing caravans; and now that they are a little more civilized it consists in all sorts of arbitrary and oppressive exactions. The Greeks, the Armenians, the Slavonians, and the Franks, established in the large seaports, carry on the whole of the trade, and certainly they have no reason to thank Turkish beys and pashas for being able to do so. Remove all the Turks out of Europe, and trade will have no reason to suffer. And as to progress in general civilization, who are they that carry out that progress in all part of European Turkey? Not the Turks, for they are few and far between, and can hardly be said to be settled anywhere except in Constantinople and two or three small country districts. It is the Greek and Slavonic middle-class in all the towns and trading posts who are the real support of whatever civilization is effectually imported into the country. That part of the population is constantly rising in wealth and influence, and the Turks are more and more driven into the background. Were it not for their monopoly of civil and military power they would soon disappear. But that monopoly has become impossible for the future, and their power is turned into impotence except for obstructions in the way of progress. The fact is, they must be got rid of. To say that they cannot be got rid of except by putting Russians and Austrians in their place means as much as to say that the present political constitution of Europe will last for ever. Who will make such an assertion?

EFFECTS OF REFORMS ON STATUS OF MINORITIES, 1840-60

Already by the end of the eighteenth century, the minority groups--Greeks, Armenians and, to a lesser extent, Jews--had obtained a commanding lead in the trade and finance of the Empire. According to a statement made at a meeting of the Turkey Company (17 September 1790, BT 6/73) trade between Istanbul and Egypt--the exchange of timber, naval stores, and arms for rice, flax, drugs, and India goods--was in Muslim hands and had given rise to some fortunes, and Muslims were also active in certain other branches of trade.[1] But although the Turkey Company was not allowed to deal directly with Greek and Armenian merchants in the Levant, it did so indirectly, through Leghorn. Greeks and Armenians "insured to a considerable amount in Holland, which proved that they carried on a beneficial trade with that country," and they dominated the overland trade with Austria (see sel. 11) and that with Russia.[2] The Ottoman government was quite clear in its mind that most of the foreign trade was in Rayah hands, and stated so explicitly (Note to British Minister, 5 June 1802, CC Constantinople 86).

In addition to being helped by their higher level of education, their contacts with Europeans and with their own coreligionists in various European towns, and more generally by the energy and enterprise characteristic of minorities, the Rayahs were also aided by the diplomas of immunity they obtained as interpreters (<u>berat</u>) or servants (<u>firman</u>) in foreign embassies, e.g., in 1795 the British embassy was allowed 39 <u>berats</u> and 78 <u>firmans</u>. "The price of a Russian <u>berat</u>, which secured to the holder the liberty of trading to the Black Sea, was lately as high as 10,000 piastres. That of the English for the last fifty years seems to have varied from 2,500 to 6,000 piastres. The <u>firmans</u> have been sold at

from 500 to 700 piastres" (Liston to Grenville, 25 April 1795, FO 78/16). Diplomas had to
be renewed, on payment of a fee, at the death of the sultan or change of ambassador. Ten
years later a report on berats stated: "The English, Russian, German and French missions
possess the greatest number, each of them having about 40 berats." But since each mission
had begun "to rear up its own interpreters," they no longer needed to employ Ottoman subjects. "Those invested with berats therefore turned the protection they enjoyed to purposes of trade. The most opulent among the Greeks, Armenians, Jews, etc. in Constantinople
and in the provinces made it a point to obtain a protection" (Report, 24 April 1806, FO
78/50). Both for fiscal reasons and because of the use made by the Russians of their
beratlis during their wars and agitations in the Balkans, the Ottoman government tried repeatedly to restrict the number of berats granted and to prevent their abuse, but the government had no success because of the opposition of the ambassadors, for whom it was an important source of income as well as power.

During the Revolutionary and Napoleonic wars, the minorities, especially the Greeks,
improved their position in trade and shipping at the expense of the belligerents. But the
Greek War of Independence naturally weakened the Greek community in the Empire, through
loss of life and property followed by migration (for Izmir, see petition by British merchants, 10 June 1822, FO 78/136, p. 1). Similarly, the Turco-Russian War of 1828 in the
Erzurum region resulted in a large-scale emigration of Armenians and the depopulation of
many towns and villages (see J. Brant, "Report of Journey . . . 1836," FO 78/289).

But a new factor now began to affect the status of a much broader layer of the rayah
population, especially the Greeks--the various Imperial decrees guaranteeing equality to
minorities. Where foreign consular pressure could make itself felt and the government could
exert authority, the removal of the more obvious forms of discrimination, together with
exemption from conscription which was such a heavy burden on the Muslims, gave the rayahs
a great competitive advantage. Numerous examples can be given from British consular reports.

From Erzurum in 1847 (Report on Trade, FO 78/703): "For the moment it [Tanzimat] may
be considered a dead letter. . . . the Rayahs are more favoured by it than the Mussulmans,
and the former, one and all, desire it as ardently as the latter oppose it." But even
there, the following year's report stated (FO 78/796): "The Armenians have more hands, the
Mussulman youth being taken for military service. The Mussulmans do not hire labour and
they are unable to cultivate the extent of land they possess."

In Rhodes (Kerr to Palmerston, 1 November 1850) the Tanzimat "has conferred vast advantages on the Christian population in those parts in which it has been promulgated and
faithfully put in operation. . . . but. . . . while the latter is benefited the Turk, owing
to his indolence, ignorance and apathy, cannot compete. . . . can no longer earn his living,
but sinks into poverty under intelligent rivalry."

The following answers to a questionnaire of 1860 on the status of minorities may be
noted. In Bigha "their [the Christians,] pecuniary means being larger than those of the
Mussulmans, they are constantly purchasing property from the latter. I understand however
that formerly Christians were restricted from so doing; but the prohibition as regards this
province was abolished some years ago, mainly through the instrumentality of Mr. Consul
Calvert. . . . In the Christian villages, the peasantry are decidedly better off in a pecuniary point of view than the Mussulman, being so much more provident and industrious than
the latter. . . . The Muslim population is generally speaking in possession of the largest
and most fertile tracts of land, but their natural indolence prevents them from cultivating
the whole of their property" (FO 78/1525).

In Izmir the general improvement "however is more generally to the advantage of the Christian races who are . . . buying up the Turks." Before Gulhane the large Turkish landlords "lived by a system of oppression and plunder which was put a stop to by the Hatt. The Christians then came forward as cultivators, the numbers increased by newcomers" whereas the Turks, handicapped by conscription, "fall into the hands of some Christian usurious banker [Armenian, Greek, or occasionally European] to whom the whole property or estate is soon sacrificed . . . in the immediate vicinity of Smyrna very few Turkish landed proprietors remain" (FO 78/1533). Christian villagers were better off than Muslim for they paid the same taxes and were exempt from conscription, and "the Turkish villager is, without doubt, more frequently subject to oppression than the Christian" since the latter could more easily bring his case to the attention of "some Consular authority (now more frequently to the Russian than formerly)" (FO 198/14).

In Salonica, on the other hand, Christians, though "better off than five, fifteen or twenty years ago," were more "liable to the irregularities of the Tax and Tithe collectors, and the excesses of the police force, not to speak of the depredation of brigands" and were held by the Muslim landlords, who owned most of the land, practically in serfdom" (ibid). (See also 5:11.)

In Bursa, since 1851, the number of Muslims "has visibly declined whilst that of the Christian subjects has been increasing" (Trade 1860, FO 195/647).

The impression of a decline in the number of Turks was very widespread (2:2) although almost certainly erroneous. One more example will be quoted, from the end of the century. "Every one who has any familiarity with the Aeolic and Ionian coasts knows of many a flourishing Greek village, which not so many years ago was empty or peopled only by Turks. The Turks are losing, or have in places lost, their hold on the coast and on the valleys that open on the coast. . . . As the railway goes inland, the Greek element goes with it and even in front of it."[3]

The influence of the railroad was noted by another observer, twenty years later.[4] A list of the towns with a Greek majority or large minority in Aydın province showed that almost all lay "on the four railroad lines" from Izmir and were "important distributing and collecting centers for the local trade to and from Smyrna." Similarly, in Hüdavendigar province most of the Greek towns were on or very near the Anatolian railroad. Like others, this observer expected Greek influence to spread further, with railways.

This feeling of being overwhelmed and driven out caused much resentment among Turks and helps to account for the intense bitterness and violence in the struggle between Turks, Armenians, and Greeks in the period from 1895 to 1923.

Jews also benefited from the reforms and the protection given by Britain and other Powers (2:6), but their role remained minor. In 1835 Bazili reported: "Among them [Istanbul Jews] are many rich people, many _sarrafs_, but the majority live in misery."[5] Sussnitzki's account, eighty years later (2:15), stresses even more their general poverty and the minor part played by them in business and finance; but in Izmir they were more active (2:17). (See also 2:Introduction, and EHME, pp. 114-25.)

1. See also Raymond.
2. See Stoianovich.
3. W. M. Ramsay, _Impressions of Turkey_ (London, 1897, pp. 130-31.
4. Karl Dietrich, _Hellenism in Asia Minor_ (New York, 1918), pp. 46-49.
5. Bazili, 2:174.

SELECTION 10.   TURKS AND GREEKS IN TRADE WITH AUSTRIA, 1800

HHS Türkei II-127, dispatches from Austrian Internuncio of 11 and 25 January 1802, and
Mémoire sur . . . le Commerce de l'Allemagne à Salonique, 1801"--originals in French

The Turks from the port of Alaye in the Gulf of Satalia, called Alanya by d'Anville,
trading from time immemorial with the Hereditary Lands [Austria] constitute, so to speak,
a body; they meet in a han in Constantinople where they keep their goods and have the center
of their business and the office that sends and pays a considerable quantity of bills of
exchange. As almost all are Janissaries, some of them have used the wealth they acquired
in our country to advance in the military service, and in my time Yeĝen Mehmed who had made
many such voyages as a Janissary-trader from Alaye managed to rise to the supreme dignity
of Grand Vizir.

Now those who are at present in Vienna must have met, in the last couple of years,
difficulties hitherto unknown, both in purchasing ships on the Danube and as regards the
loading and despatching of their goods. Because of this, their partners here have recently
complained to the Reis Effendi, but since that Minister merely advized them to address themselves to me in all frankness and to beg for my help four deputies presented themselves to
me. . . .

[In his next despatch the Internuncio requested the authorities in Vienna to help those
Turks who are "more frugal and in general more thrifty than our nationals and, since they
are willing to accept lower profits, can sell more cheaply and thus multiply the consumption
of our goods. . . ."]

[The Memoir, after pointing out that Macedonia's trade with Germany was growing, that
German steel and Leipzig cloth were replacing British goods but that much of the trade of
the interior with Vienna was conducted overland, and thus did not pass through the port of
Salonica, went on to state:] Macedonia's trade with Germany is entirely in the hands of
the Greeks. Spread throughout both Empires, flexible, nimble and full of intrigues, they
have established themselves as privileged agents in this chain of mutual needs. They sti-
fle, so to speak, the national [Austrian] genius, and get hold of its industry. They always remain foreigners in Vienna, where they come and go, seldom settling down. Dress,
manners, religion are for them rallying points that mark them off and isolate them. In
genius and character, the contrast is still sharper. The peaceful German is good, trust-
ing, easygoing; the turbulent Greek is cunning, suspicious, often deceitful. The courts
are constantly busy with their litigation, as is society with their dissensions. Always
attached to their birthplaces, few indeed are those who after spending some years in Vienna
fail to return to their fatherland, to rejoin their family or form a new one. How often do
they disappear after a fraudulent bankruptcy, carrying with them a considerable fortune
which they bury in obscure villages where justice can no longer reach them. Their avidity
seizes on the least gains and manages to obtain them by every means. Their subtle and fertile genius suggests to them ideas which are astonishing both for the imagination that in-
spired them and the boldness that executed them. Thousands of examples could be given, of
which I shall take one chosen at random. A Greek merchant of Salonica had bought, through
speculation and at a very low price, an antique gold watch studded with diamonds and worth
10,000 to 12,000 piastres. He wished to sell the diamonds in Vienna, but the difficulty
was to get them through the frontier. His agent in Semlin presented himself at the designated government office, declared that he had been ordered to send a watch to Vienna for
repair, and deposited a small sum. After some time, the watch is back in his hands, the
deposit is returned to him, and the diamonds have remained in Vienna.

And yet this is the nation that Germany has deemed fit to welcome and favor by various
means of encouragement and esteem. Once upon a time, Germany's motives may have been well-
founded, but today this is no longer necessary. It can show less predilection for the
Greeks without fearing that they will leave its States. Habits and interest keep them
there, and even if they wished to, they could not transfer elsewhere the links that bind
them to Germany. The trade they carry on in Macedonia pays no duty. If one were levied--
even if only 10 or 5 paras per load, which would be almost nothing for the individual
trader--what advantage would accrue to the State! How many small expenses could be met by
such receipts!

Another privilege which the Greeks enjoy but not our own nationals is to come and go
across the German borders, without passports or any kind of hindrance. This facility is
granted equally to honest people and adventurers; it covers not only travelers coming from
a healthy place but also those fleeing places struck by pestilence. Both are equally admitted to Semlin after formalities [à faire une contumace] that are in neither case rigorous. The passage of goods presents the same dangers. In the precautions taken in the
Lazaret at Semlin, the government follows only general principles and vague notions, the
results of which are merely to prolong or shorten the duration by a few days. At Herman-
stadt and Cromstadt these principles are even more indulgent. Germany is constantly exposed, and does not take heed. And yet in Salonica and Seres, which are the two chief
entrepôts of the German trade and the center of the points from which goods are sent to
spread all over its States, there are vice-consuls who could be charged with delivering
passports to travelers and schedules for their merchandize. . . .

FOREIGN RESIDENTS

It is very difficult to give an estimate of the number of foreigners living in the Ottoman Empire. For 1897, a figure of 172,000 males and 64,000 females, or a total of 237,000, is available; of these 127,000 were in Istanbul, 56,000 in Aydın province, and 33,000 in Baghdad province.[1] But almost certainly the bulk of foreigners in Istanbul and Aydın were Hellenes and those in Baghdad Persians.[2]

Nor are the numbers of those under the jurisdiction of foreign consuls much more meaningful. In Izmir in 1847, they were as follows: Greek 3,376, British 2,258, Austrian about 2,000, French 356, Sardinian 294, Neapolitan 286, Russian 90, Netherlands 89, and Prussian 19--a total of about 8,800; but of the British, 1,944 were Ionians, 211 Maltese, and only 103 British proper (FO 195/288).

More information is available on what were by far the most influential, though by no means the largest, communities, the British and French. In 1853, the number of subjects enrolled at the various British consulates of the Ottoman Empire (including Rumania, Egypt, Libya, and Tunisia) was about 14,000, showing a distinct rise over 1851; but of these only some 1,500 were British, the rest being Ionians, Maltese, Indian, or others. The number within the area of present-day Turkey was about 3,000. Of the British, 390 were in Istanbul and 256 in Izmir (FO 78/976).

The 1861 census returns show that the number of British subjects (excluding Maltese and others) in the Ottoman Empire was 3,608; of these 936 were in Istanbul, 608 in Izmir, 92 in the Dardanelles, 50 in Salonica, 17 in Rhodes, 13 in Bursa, 7 in Trabzon, 2 in Samsun, and 1 in Erzurum. These figures include women and children, and there were almost one and a half times as many males as females (FO 195/700).

In 1886, there were 300 holders of British passports in Istanbul, 164 in Izmir, and 22 in Salonica; these figures exclude the families of the holders and Maltese, Indians, and other subjects (FO 78/4335). Earlier figures for Istanbul are as follows: 1846, 207 British subjects, and 2,001 other; 1849, 331 and 2,737 other, the figures for the years 1847, 1848, and 1852 lying on the trend (see FO 78/699, 748, 793, 830, 866, and 781/4). As for Izmir, when on 15 March 1797 the "Turks premeditatedly set fire to the houses in the Franck street," 35 British subjects suffered losses totalling 1,130,000 piastres, and 16 protégés had losses of 199,000 piastres (see list in FO 78/18). In 1828 it was stated that the number of British residents was eight to ten times what it had been in 1680 (Memorandum, FO 78/171).

As regards the French, 129 persons suffered losses of 680,000 piastres in the Izmir fire of 1797 (CC Smyrne, vol. 1). In 1825 there were 94 adult male Frenchmen registered in the Izmir consulate, plus 20 Genoese who had opted for French nationality, 35 Jews originating from Bayonne, and 23 other persons under French protection (ibid., vol. 42, 31 December 1825). In August 1863, the number of the French in Izmir was 330 men, 388 women, and 330 children (ibid., vol. 50) and in December 1872 the numbers were 304, 368, and 255 respectively, to which the consul suggested adding 50 for underenumeration (ibid., vol. 51). In 1819 there were 15 French males in Salonica (CC Salonique, vol. 18) and in 1863 there were 10 men, 5 women, and 7 children in Adana province (CC Tarsous, vol. 2). Basing himself on the consular records, Thobie[3] puts the number of Frenchmen (excluding Algerians and protégés) in Istanbul at 3,000–3,500 in 1895 and 6,000–7,000 in 1913; for Izmir the corresponding figures were 1,000 and 1,500.[4]

These figures show clearly that, unlike North Africa or Egypt, Turkey attracted few foreigners. The main reasons were that there was practically no settlement in agriculture, industry developed very little, foreign handicraftsmen were few, and trade and finance could be carried out by a small number of enterprises. In agriculture, to quote the British consul in Istanbul in 1872, every attempt by foreigners "either as master or man attempting farming operations in this part of Turkey has been followed by perfect failure; if the old fashioned slovenly systems of working land are pursued by a foreigner he finds that the native is his superior both by being accustomed to his own mode of labour and by the power he has living on a low scale of comfort. If on the other hand the European import improvements, and scientific skill be brought to bear, the inability to maintain them thoroughly and to secure the concert of local assistance for repairs etc. leads necessarily to loss and disappointment" (Industrial Classes, Constantinople, FO 83/378). In the Izmir area British landownership amounted to about 600,000–700,000 acres, but the financial results were not satisfactory, efforts to introduce capitalistic methods had little success, and there was no attempt at settlement.[5] A few vineyards belonging to Germans or Frenchmen are recorded (5:27). The ambitious plans to settle German farmers along the Anatolian railway did not materialize.[6]

Increasing use of machinery had necessitated the employment of foreign mechanics and engineers in the arsenals and steamers. "Every Turkish steamer has one or more English engineers who have come from England on contract" (ibid.). Those employed by the government earned £8 to £25 a month. Other nations were less well represented: "The Austrians and Germans are frequently good engineers but I assume that their number is not sufficiently great to enable them to emigrate from their own country to any great extent. The Belgian, French and Italian skilled workmen if not perfectly content at home with their position do not find in the higher pay they can here obtain a sufficient compensation for the inconvenience attending emigration" while the Americans were "well satisfied at home" (ibid.). Attempts were being made to replace foreign engineers: "it is true that when the native engineer replaces the dismissed Englishman, burnt boilers, broken rods, corroded works and spoiled machinery show the false economy of dispensing with the skilled workman for half instructed mechanics—yet there is a growing and perfectly natural desire to substitute for the foreign the native workman and hence the experiment is frequently repeated though as frequently repented of" (ibid.). But the development of railways, public utilities, mining, and factories must have greatly increased the number of foreign skilled workmen in the following forty years.

Openings for unskilled foreign workers were much smaller. "The ordinary European worker can be beaten in the performance of mere common work by the native and there are many crafts in Turkey where better workmen than the natives are not wanted. . . . there is no place in Turkey itself for competition between native bad work and imported better work, and the latter is only occasionally called for by reason of the unnatural mixture of Oriental and Occidental civilization in Turkey" (ibid.; also 2:15). Yet an earlier report (Industrial Classes, FO 83/334) had given the following number of "artizans" in Istanbul in 1870: Austrians 8,000, Hellenes 5,500, French 2,500, Italians 1,500, North Germans 100, Swiss, Romans, Algerians 1,000, in addition to 40 English "overseers and artizans."

The number of foreigners engaged in trade was small (3:11) and in finance smaller (see 2:Introduction), but both categories must have grown with the development and commercialization of the economy. There were also a few foreigners who supplied professional services, such as physicians, lawyers, and pharmacists. But there seems little doubt that the number of foreigners was not commensurate with their great economic influence.

---

1. Nezaret-i umur-i ticaret ve nafia . . . istatistik umumieh dar 1316, 1897.

2. In 1868 the United States minister put the number of Greek subjects in Turkey at about 200,000, of whom 35,000 were in Istanbul--Morris to Seward, 4 December 1868, USDP.
3. See details, pp. 28-32.
4. In 1848, 168 Italian residents of Istanbul signed a petition against the Austrian consul--P. Herlihy, "Russian Wheat and the Port of Livorno," JEEH, Spring 1976.
5. Kurmuş, pp. 141-50.
6. Wallach, pp. 60-61.

SELECTION 11. THE GREEKS IN ISTANBUL, 1870s

A. Synvet, Les grecs de l'empire ottoman (Istanbul, 1878), pp. 8-12, 32-33, 80-83

Summary

Our research shows that the number of Greeks in the direct possessions of the Ottoman Empire is four million three hundred and twenty four thousand, three hundred and sixty nine:

1) Turkey in Europe

Thrace[a]	728,747
Macedonia	387,860
Epirus	617,892
Thessaly	247,776

Dobruja (former diocese of Preslava and towns on right bank of Danube)	30,000
Moesia, Rascia, Metochia (former dioceses of Rasco--Prisrend, Uskub and Dibra)	40,000

11) Islands of Archipelago and Mediterannean[b]   724,000

111) Turkey in Asia

Asia Minor[c]	1,188,094
Northern Syria, Coele-Syria, Palestine, Phoenicia	125,000
Greek Catholics, distributed almost everywhere	35,000

Total	4,324,369

. . . Constantinople is a cosmopolitan city. The Greeks, its original inhabitants, are--as may be seen from the above table--scattered in the different quarters of the great city. According to the information supplied by the muhtars (mayors)--which agree with the data provided by the Cadastral Administration, the Greek subjects of the Ottoman Empire established in Constantinople number 230,000, including the floating population. This large community is in a flourishing state. It is represented by very able men in high administrative posts and the liberal professions; in banking and trade the Greeks undoubtedly hold first place.

Schools are numerous, widespread, and well equipped, and are supported by generous gifts; it is certain that no community has ever done as much for the propagation of public education. The most important establishments in the capital are: the National School of the Phanar, with 500 pupils and 12 teachers; the Commercial School of Khalki, 260 pupils, 12 teachers; the School of Theology (Khalki) 80 students; the Greek Lycée of Pera, 20 teachers, the Special Lycée and other private schools.

There are 36 Superior Primary Schools, with 1,000 pupils. The Primary Schools, properly speaking, number 50, with 5,000 children. In addition, there is an orphanage where 100 wretched creatures are educated at the expense of the community.

Boarding schools for girls are becoming more numerous each day. Three years ago, two important establishments were founded, Pallas and Zappion, and already they have 400 pupils. In addition to these boarding schools, the Greek community of Constantinople has 15 communal girls schools, with 1,800 pupils.

The Greeks have also founded Syllogues, or scientific associations, which play an important part. There are 20 of them in the city of Constantinople alone.

In brief, the Greeks have, in the capital of the Ottoman Empire, 105 establishments of public education, of which 22 are girls' schools; they are attended by 12,000 children, of whom 3,000 are girls. The number of professors and teachers is 260. The community spends 4,000,000 piastres, or 920,000 francs, on the upkeep of these schools. . . .

The Eparchy or diocese of Derki includes 41 villages in the neighborhood of Constantinople, on the Bosphorus, on the Sea of Marmara, and on the two slopes of Mount Strandja.

As regards education, this Eparchy includes two villages, Therapia and Büyük-dere, each of which has three schools: a high school, a mutual school, and a boarding school for girls. The high school of Therapia was founded in 1780, burnt down in 1840, and was rebuilt in 1843. Today it has 45 pupils. Lessons are given by teachers who follow a program similar to the ones of small gymnasia.

The high school of Büyük-dere was established only in 1845 and has 45 pupils. The mutual schools are very important in the countryside round the Bosphorus. During the sea-bathing season, quite a large number of the better-off Greek families of Constantinople live in Therapia and Büyük-dere, and for three months their children attend the schools in these villages. The girls' schools were founded recently: that of Therapia goes back to 1861 but that of Büyük-dere is only five years old. In the other villages steps are being taken to establish girls schools, for the importance of educating women has been understood.

Two villages, Makri-köy and Kastaniai, have two schools: a high school and a mutual school. Five villages--Yeni-mahalle, Phanaraki, Pyrgos, Kalfa-köy, and San Stephano--have very good mutual schools. The others have only primary school teachers, and in some of the smaller and poorer ones instruction is given by the priest.

In brief, the Eparchy of Derkos includes 40 villages, 39 schools, 3,874 families, and about 25,150 inhabitants, of whom 2,500 speak Bulgarian but have remained faithful to the Greek church. The teaching personnel number 45 and the number of students may reach 1,850. Expenses amount to 155,000 piastres, or 35,650 francs. . . .

a) European part of vilayet of Istanbul and whole of vilayet of Edirne, i.e., including Philippolis, Varna, etc.

b) Including Crete 250,000, Kos 120,000, Cyprus 90,000, Metelin 90,000, Chio 70,000, Rhodes 40,000, Samos 40,000.

c) Including Ionia and Lydia (Izmir, Manisa, Aydin, Alaşehir, etc.) 450,000; Pontus and Paphlagonia (Trabzon, Gumuşhane, Kastambol, Sinop, etc.) 320,000; Bithynia and Mysia (Izmit, Bursa, Balikesir, Dardanelles, etc.) 170,000; Kappadocia (Kayseri, Zinci-dere, Niğde, Yuzgat, Nevşehir, etc.) 130,000; Cilicia and Mesopotamia (Mersin, Tarsus, Adana, Selefke, Diyarbakir, Aleppo) 45,000; Chalcedon (Kadiköy, Usküdar, etc.) 38,000; Pamphylia (Isparta, etc.) 35,000.

N.B. The Greeks inhabiting the Patriarchate of Alexandria (Egypt) and the Danubian Principalities have not been included.

THE ARMENIANS[1]

The three following selections bring out several aspects of the economic activity of the Armenians, which was of very great significance in nineteenth century Turkey. The first describes their important role in various economic, administrative, and cultural fields, the second and third the condition of the peasantry and urban bourgeoisie in the eastern Anatolian provinces which constituted the Armenian homeland.

The number of Armenians in the Ottoman Empire in the second half of the nineteenth century has been variously estimated at between 2.5 and 3 million but, according to Stanford Shaw, the records put their number at 989,000 in 1884 rising to 1,161,000 in 1914. Of these, some four-fifths were rural, concentrated mainly in the paşaliks of Erzurum, Bayazit, Kars, Çildir, Van, and Diyarbekir, but there was also a large population in the Adana and Maraş paşaliks, the remnants of the medieval Kingdom of Cilicia. The main urban center was Istanbul, whose Armenian population had grown, by voluntary or enforced migration, from about 5,000 in 1478 to some 150,000-200,000. Izmir contained around 10,000 Armenians at the beginning of the century and 30,000 at its end and comparable numbers were to be found in such eastern towns as Erzurum, Sivas, Amasya, and others, as well as in Adana and Mersin. Large and active Armenians communities also existed in Syria and Egypt (EHME, pp. 114-25), Russia and Iran.

The growth of the Iranian silk trade in the seventeenth century was crucial for the economic development of the Armenians, who soon came to control it, established contacts with Europe through the transit cities of Aleppo and Izmir, and set up small merchant colonies in places ranging from Amsterdam to India.[2]

Hardly less important was the impact of the Western missionaries. In the seventeenth and eighteenth centuries, Catholic missions were active in the Armenian community, resulting in the conversion of several leading families, the education of many Armenians in medical schools and universities, chiefly in Italy, and the setting up of Armenian printing presses in Istanbul.[3] The marked lead thus obtained by the Armenians was further reinforced by the educational activities of the American Protestant mission that opened in Istanbul in 1831 and penetrated into Anatolia in the 1840s.[4] This foreign competition spurred the Armenian church to open its own schools and educate its clergy.

These two developments largely explain the emergence of the magnates, known as _amiras_, who played a dominant role in the Armenian church and community and an important one in Ottoman administration. One group of _amiras_ consisted of _sarrafs_, or bankers, who furnished tax farmers and other provincial officials with the capital required for bidding (7:6) and guaranteed that the stipulated tax revenues would be paid into the imperial treasury. By the beginning of the nineteenth century, Armenian bankers were prominent in foreign exchange and commercial operations as well. The other group consisted of high government officials, usually in charge of some economic administration or enterprise, such as the customs, mint, powder works, mines, army supplies, and so on. Among the most prominent of these were the Dadian family, who built and managed several factories in the 1830s (6:Introduction).

The bulk of the Armenian urban population consisted of craftsmen organized, like those of other _millets_, in guilds or _esnafs_ (6:12). In the second quarter of the nineteenth century there were some 120 _esnafs_ in Istanbul, over 50 in Erzurum, 30 in Çildir, and several dozen in Van.[5] In 1850, the number of Armenian merchants, artisans, and shopkeepers in Istanbul was put at 36,000. Among the more important trades in which Armenians were prominent were: jewelry, many branches of textiles, gold, silver, and copper work, and shoemaking. (See also the works by Arpee, Dadian, Leart, and Lynch listed in the Bibliography.)

1. In this section I have drawn heavily on Vartan Artinian's dissertation, to which the reader is referred for further details and sources.
2. EHI, pp. 57-62. The collapse of the Iranian economy at the end of the seventeenth century drove many Armenians to Istanbul and Izmir, which became their main commercial centers. "By the middle of the nineteenth century there were over thirty Armenian commercial firms in London and Manchester with their headquarters located either in Smyrna or Istanbul" (Artinian, p. 7).
3. "From 1715-1764 over one hundred-forty books on grammer, geography, logic, philosophy and religious subjects were printed in Istanbul" (ibid., p. 37).
4. One example may be given. In 1871, the number of pupils in government schools in the Erzurum vilayet with an estimated total population of 1,230,000, was 788, in Protestant mission schools 591, in Catholic schools 103, in Armenian schools 400 and in Greek schools 90--"Koordistan," A and P 1872, vol. 58.
5. Artinian, p. 23.
6. Ibid., pp. 5-6.

SELECTION 12. THE ARMENIANS

(Hrachya Adjarian, "Hayots dere Osmanian Kaysrutyean medj," Banber Erevani Hamalsarani, 1967, Erevan)

When Turkey was the Ottoman Empire she had many subject nations, the Arabs, the Kurds, the Armenians, the Greeks, the Bulgarians, the Albanians. . . . The Greeks and Armenians formed a large number even in the capital (Istanbul) and together were 400,000. Constantinople had 1,000,000 inhabitants of which 500,000 were Turks, 400,000 Armenians and Greeks, 100,000 Jews and Europeans. Many Armenians, being well-versed in the Turkish language, reached high administrative positions and played important roles in all fields.

The _amiras_ were the old Armenian government functionaries. Their emergence took place in the following manner. The government would nominate a Turkish Paşa as a governor, the latter would designate an Armenian money-changer as guarantor for the payment of taxes; the money-changer would defray the expenses of the Palace and, after entering these against payable taxes, he would personally collect the taxes from the people. The _amiras_ were mostly from the provinces and, as the most influential people in the country, would participate in all national (i.e., Armenian) affairs. The patriarch and the National Assembly were in their hands. Often _amiras_ were unworthy of their position, but many among them were very helpful. We mention Seghbos amira, the chief merchant (in the 1720s); Shnork amira, a talented man who, in 1790, opened the first Armenian schools in the various districts of Istanbul and a school for young girls; Mkerdich Jezayirlian amira, who founded the Nercisian school at Hasköy and donated 100,000 kuruş; Abraham amira Terzian, who in 1824 established a printing house at Hasanpaşa Han and who distributed in the provinces the books he printed, free of charge.

The general collection of customs duties was entrusted to Hovannes Duzian çelebi, and later to Mkerdich Jezayirlian amira. From 1795 the position of superintendent of powder mills was in the hands of the Dadians, by inheritance. The position of purveyor of bread for the army belonged to the Noradungians. The mint was entrusted to the Duzians, who previously had held the position of Chief Imperial Goldsmith. When they were beheaded on suspicion of larceny, the mint was given to Harutiun amira Bezjian (born 1771), who served for more than ten years with great faithfulness and was rewarded by the sultan with the highest honors. He founded the Armenian National Hospital in Istanbul, rebuilt the cathedral, the patriarchate, the Bezjian school, the church and two schools at Kumkapu, the church at the royal naval yard, the girls school at Pera, the school of the cathedral, and the school, the church, and the fountain of Kartal. Besides these, he willed a guaranteed income for the schools at Kumkapu, paid the 100,000 kuruş debt of the church at Ortaköy, helped the churches at Çanakkale, Gelibolu, Edirne, Malaga, donated 100,000 kuruş for the poor in Istanbul, etc. In 1828 when the Russian army reached Istanbul and demanded 15 million rubles as war indemnity, otherwise threatening to occupy the capital, sultan Mahmud was in disaray, not knowing what to do, for there was no money to pay the indemnity, and no army to continue the fight; Bezjian thought of a new device: he melted the old silver coins found in the mint, mixed copper in great proportion, worked day and night, and cut the coins known as five-six, which he put into circulation, and then gathering the gold kept by the population he paid the indemnity. It is in this manner that the event is related. Bezjian had easy access to Sultan Mahmud, of whom he was considered to be the right hand and the eyesight. When Bezjian fell sick with fever and died, the Sultan came to his funeral in disguise with two chamberlains to see for the last time the face of his dear friend.

Hovannes bey Dadian was appointed general manager of the paper mill at Beyköz, manager of the spinning mill at Eyyub, and superintendent of the powder mill at Azatli. He was sent to Europe three times at government expense, to improve his knowledge of technology, especially in the preparation of gunpowder. After his return he invented a machine to pierce the barrels of a gun. The powder that he prepared was highly esteemed by the French and English commanders during the Crimean War. The leather mill at Beyköz, the [woolen] cloth mill at Nicomedia, the silk mill at Hereke, the linen mill and the iron-smelting mill at Zeytin-Burnu were all built under his supervision.

The imperial architecture was entrusted to Janig amira Serverian and later to the famous Balian family, by inheritance. Nigoghos Balian was sent to Paris and upon his return he built the palace at Dolma Bahçe, which was considered to be the most beautiful adornment of Istanbul. In 1861 Sultan Abdul Aziz replaced Sultan Abdul Mecid on the throne; the former built the palaces, barracks, military schools, etc. at Çraghan, Beylerbey, and on the two shores of the Bosphorus. The 200-feet high tower of the firemen of Istanbul, the Galata-Saray, the palace at Saray-Burnu, etc. are all to be credited to the Balian family. I mentioned Beylerbey in passing, but it is a marvelous piece of work. Imperial painters also were Armenian to some extent. Painter here means mainly decorator, because the painting of figures (faces) was forbidden by the Muslims.

As Turkish pride did not permit entrusting ministries completely to Armenians, the government placed an Armenian by each minister as his counsellor or assistant, but in reality as the true administrator. Thus, Reşat Paşa had Gojigian, Admiral Mehmed Ali Paşa had Hovsep Vartan Paşa, Grand Vezir Ali Paşa had Hamamjian and Seferian, Fuad Paşa had Servichen and Sahag Abro, Mahmud Nedim Paşa had Artin Paşa Dadian, Cevdet Paşa had Vahan Efendi, Midhat Paşa had Odian Efendi, Ingiliz Said Paşa had Nourian, Servet Paşa had Gosdant Paşa, the other Said Paşa had Sarkis Efendi Aghabegian.

The ministry of the Imperial Private Treasury was always in the hands of Armenians (by Private Treasury we mean the Sultan's personal wealth), such as Hagop Paşa Kazazian, Mikael Paşa Portukalian, and Hovannes Sakez Paşa, even during the days of the Armenophobe and perpetrator of massacres Sultan Abdul Hamid. In its most critical condition, the Ministry of Finance was entrusted to Kazaz Hagop Paşa, and many times Dadian and Portukalian served as counsellors. In 1864 Krikor Efendi Aghaton returned from France; the administrations of telegraphs, postal, and public works were in very poor condition. These three ministries were entrusted to him, and this well-known administrator put everything in good order.

The Imperial Medical University was run mostly by Armenians; the principal lecturers were Servichen, Nigoghayos Rousinian, Khentamian, Antranig Bey Gerjigian, Stepan Paşa Aslanian, etc. At the other government schools Portukalian Paşa, Terzian, H. Yusufian, Mihran Karakash, Hagop Boyajian, etc. lectured. At governmental institutions Garabed Karakash, Khederian, and Kuyumjian introduced the double-entry system in accounting; by double-entry system we understand Italian accounting, which is now accepted everywhere. The founders of this system were the Armenian merchants of Chugha (Ispahan). Harutiun Paşa Dadian was the soul of the Foreign Ministry, and although nominally a counsellor he was the true administrator; during the short period of his resignation the official letters sent to the embassies were returned as incomprehensible. The superintendent for mines and forestry was Bedros Kuyumjian. Hovannes Chamich, Odian, Margosian, Aslanian, etc. were well-known in the Ministry of Public Works. In 1864 the military school (Harbieh) at Pangalti was opened, for Muslims only. As an experiment, Sultan Abdul Aziz ordered five

Armenians to be admitted . . .; the government was considering raising them to the rank of general, then it changed its mind and they were kept at the rank of captain. They were the first and last Armenian soldiers to graduate from the military school at Pangalti.

During the Russo-Turkish War the government demanded soldiers from the Christians, too. The Greeks refused. There was a great debate at the Armenian Representative Assembly; Izmirlian and Narbey (both former patriarchs) were completely opposed, arguing that general conscription was based upon equality, that there was no equality in this state, how then could soldiers be given to that government? Patriarch Nerses (the officeholder) agreed to give soldiers in lieu of poll tax (cizye) on condition that the Armenians would not mix with the Turkish soldiers but would have their own units, flag, and commander. Remembering Lazarev and Der-Ghougasov (Armenian generals in the Russian army), the government was afraid and conscription remained unimplemented. Thus, unfortunately, Armenians did not enter the military career.

In 1863 when the Armenians, in twenty steamboats decorated with flags and playing music, were expressing their gratitude to the Grand Vezir Ali Paşa in front of his palace at Bebek, on the occasion of the establishment of the Constitution, the latter told his friends: "I fear the Armenians, they are acting quietly and silently and are in close contact with the Turkish people; I am afraid that one day they will join with the Turks and start a revolution in the country." The Grand Vezir Fuad Paşa also had similar thoughts; he emphasized in his will caution, especially with the Armenians. But Grand Vezir Midhat Paşa, who was a man of ideals and who knew that it was not possible to stop the popular liberal movement, in 1876, during the writing of the Ottoman Constitution, was thinking that when freedom got established in the country the Armenians would benefit most but that they would pull the Turks along with them and that the latter, being numerous and forming the dominant element, would play a primary role

Krikor Odian, counsellor to Midhat Paşa, sought to convince the latter to accept the Constitution. It is reported that the corrected copy of the lawbook in Turkish written by Midhat Paşa at the suggestion of Odian is extant.

When the Constitution was established and the Ottoman Representative Assembly was formed, leaving aside the Armenians of Istanbul who were familiar with parliamentary procedure thanks to the Armenian National Assembly, even the [Armenian] representatives from the provinces (such as Garin-Erzurum, Erzincan, Sivas, Aleppo) amazed the central government by their eloquence.

Armenians played an important role in the trades, agriculture, commerce, and the arts. Shoemaking, carpentry, masonry, and bread-baking were mostly in the hands of Greeks, although there were a few Armenians too. But the other trades were in the hands of Armenians, from goldsmith to mechanic, fine designs on mother-of-pearl, relief engraving. The goldsmiths market at Istanbul was completely in the hands of Armenians, specifically those from Samatia; it is surprising [to note] how the masters had the custom of not keeping foreign (non-Armenian) apprentices. Needlework on velvet with golden thread (dival), widespread in Istanbul, was the monopoly of poor Armenian women for whom it was the main means of earning a livelihood. In agriculture, the Greeks were on the islands of the Archipelago, occupied with viticulture and olive tree plantations, while the Armenian peasants were mostly farmers. Commerce was in the hands of the Greeks and Armenians; while the Greeks were in the import business, that is they were sucking the blood of the country, the Armenians were in the export business, that is they were enriching the country. They took goods from Anatolia and Syria to France, England, and America; the roads were in very bad condition, there were no railways or other means of transport; therefore what the Armenians were doing was equal to martyrdom [i.e., bravery], but they were used to this from very old times and they could not visualize commerce in any other way.

The service that the Armenians rendered in the trades cannot be fully appreciated. The Armenian named Arakel, who established the spinning mill at Eyyub in the 1800s, had learned the construction and operation of spinning machines. The waterpumps of the royal firemen's brigade were manufactured by the Armenian mechanic Nigoghos from Samatia. Kavafian invented a new Greek fire (!) to burn the sea; when the government demanded the secret, Kavafian refused, saying that when a naval engagement took place he would personally execute the orders. Later the government had him poisoned and the invention disappeared with its author. Sericulture is almost an Armenian art, and K. Torkomian was its soul. Kiatibian, Khorasanjian, Peshdimaljian were famous royal and military physicians. Esmerjian became the greatest ophthalmologist in Istanbul. Among the famous lawyers one should mention Vramshabouh Manugian and Krikor Zohrab. In the 1880s there were 300 Armenian physicians and as many lawyers.

Armenians introduced the theater for the first time in Ottoman society; till then the Turks knew only heyal (the plays of Haci Eyvat and Karagöz). Vartovian, Benglian, Rshdouni, Chaprasdian, Fasulyajian, and Mnagian founded the Kedik-Paşa, Vekniçiler and Kadiköy Ottoman theaters in Istanbul; the actors mostly, but the actresses exclusively, were Armenians because Turkish women were forbidden from performing on stage by "amehram." The Turks learned musical notation from the Armenians. The first composer was Baba Hamparzum Limonjian (1768-1839), and in his name the Turks called the notation "Baba Hamparzum notasi." In the school of Beaux Arts there were many gifted Armenian students. The imperial photographers were the well-known Abdullahian brothers.

The first Turkish newspaper (<u>Takvim-i Vekayi</u>, a weekly) was founded by the Frenchman Alexandre Blacque. In the 1860s journalism flourished among the Armenians who, besides the Armenian newspapers, had also Turkish newspapers with Armenian characters for Turkish-speaking Armenians, such as <u>Miunadi</u> or <u>Manzume-i Efkar</u> of Garabed Panosian and <u>Mecmua-i Havadis</u> of Hovsep Vartan. Many Turks learned the Armenian alphabet and read <u>Manzume</u> and <u>Mecmua</u>, where they found European telegraphic dispatches and pictures of the political situation. Through newspapers the Armenian characters were thus propagated among the highest (Turkish) scientific circles who saw their splendid simplicity and advantages in practice. In 1860 Fuad and Ali Paşa had thought of abandoning the Turkish (i.e., Arabic) characters and adopting the Armenian characters officially. The Grand Vezir Reşid Pasa learned the Armenian alphabet to propagate it among the Turks. It is reported that the Ottoman Representative Assembly had accepted the same, but national pride or the quick closure of the Assembly did not allow its implementation. The Armenians published papers for Turks too, such as the famous satirist Hagop Baronian who published the comic paper <u>Teatro</u>; Jevahirjian and Alexan Efendi, <u>Ibret</u>; T. Utujian, the medical journal <u>Sihhat</u>; as well as Boghos Barnasian and Diran Kelegian, who were well-known editors. In the 1890s Mihran Efendi Nakashian, from Kayseri, was the publisher of the official paper <u>Sabah</u>. The publishers, translators, and compositors of Turkish papers were Armenians. Hovannes Muhantisian made and designed the Turkish printing characters. The Arabic printing characters which are in use presently are his work, and the old Turks remember him with blessing. He is the one who created the two kinds of Turkish <u>Taalik</u> characters and 16 point <u>Neskhi</u>, and when he was eighty years old designed the 6 point characters. The Turks, who till then had only one kind of characters, with these [additions] were enriched in the art of printing. Muhantisian was the first to bring from the United States to Istanbul the iron printing press; he also introduced galvanography, stereotype, zincography, etc. In 1844 and 1876 he engraved and printed the paper currencies of the Turkish state, <u>Kaime</u>, <u>Gonsolit</u>, surpassing in a contest the French artist brought especially from Europe.

Armenians played an important role in pedagogy too. Even the first European-style and new-method Turkish-language textbooks were prepared by Armenians. Thus the textbooks by Mihran Apigian, Retig Hoja Saraydarian, and Zeki Garabedian were used in Turkish schools. Mihran Apigian wrote fifty textbooks (<u>Mutavvel Sarf-i Osman</u>).

Armenians were also prominent in folk literature. In this art the best known are the patriarch Hagop Nalian, Manuel Chibukjian, Papa Hagopjan, Mihran Arabajian, Heretig Hoja, who were writer-poets (<u>Kalem şuerasi</u>). The singer poets were Akahi, Chughayi, Lisayi, Serveri, Kurian, Mahjubi, Nami. The last one (the carpenter Hagop from Samastia) one year challenged all the minstrels of Istanbul, even the writer-poets, to come out for competition but no one dared to compete. . . .

SELECTION 13. ARMENIANS AND TURKS IN ERZURUM, 1848

Report on Trade of Erzerum, 1848, FO 78/796

An objection I have heard from Mohamedan peasants, appears to have some force, namely, that the Armenians have more hands, the Mussulman youth being taken for military service. The Mussulmans do not hire labourers, and they are unable to cultivate the extent of land they possess, but the Armenians, keeping their young men at home, are enabled to work all their land, and thus the latter grow rich, while the former do not improve their position. The Mussulmans do not say that they are indolent; that their women and children are above work, while the Armenians work hard, men, women, and children. It may be thought that the call for troops cannot take away all the Mussulman youth; but the number required is greater than it should be; the neglect of the health of the troops, from the want of proper hospitals and medical aid, occasions an enormous mortality, which must be made up by extra levies; and during the term of service, nearly all the men die; such, at least, was the case when the period was longer; perhaps the shorter term now fixed will prevent the same result, and the evil will be to a less extent.

An unequivocal sign of rising prosperity is to be found in the enhanced value of land. Within a short time it has doubled in price. This may be accounted for chiefly by the fairer treatment the cultivators experience under the Tanzimat, and partly by the remunerating prices obtained for grain, arising from the presence of a military force here, and from the increased number of horses and men employed in the transport of merchandise. It is, however, remarkable that the purchasers of land are universally Armenians, and the sellers almost always Mussulmans, a fact of strong significance as to the effect of the Tanzimat on the Christian part of the population, which is evidently rising in prosperity. . . .

SELECTION 14. KURDS AND ARMENIANS IN EASTERN TURKEY, END OF NINETEENTH CENTURY

M.S. Lazarev, <u>Kurdistan i Kurdskaya Problema</u> (Moscow, 1964) pp. 32-37)

. . . The socio-economic structure of the Kurdish tribes in the period under study is characterized by the dominance of so-called nomadic-feudalism. The economy was essentially based on animal husbandry, mainly sheep-breeding.[1] The disintegration of kindred-tribal relationships among the Kurds is indicated by the marked stratification of property within each tribe, as determined by the number of heads of large and small livestock owned by each tribesman.

As regards relationships within the tribe, the vestiges of "warrior democracy" had left a strong imprint. However, the tribal chief (Khan, Bey, Agha) already was not only "first among equals" but had real power over ordinary tribesmen, based on wealth and force although sometimes seeming patriarchal. This was already noted in the 1830s by the author of a fundamental travel book on Turkey, Vronchenko: "The people regard them," said he of the Kurdish Beys, "not only as their judges and tribal lords but as defenders against the oppression of the regional authorities, and even the higher authorities, and as leaders who, concentrating in themselves the power of the tribe, command respect for it."[2]

Socio-economic relationships in Kurdistan had another aspect, pertaining to the inter-relationships between the feudal leaders--who were in overwhelming majority Kurdish--and the settled cultivators, mostly Armenian. During the period under study, the agrarian question in Kurdistan and Western (Turkish) Armenia was inseparable from the national, for social and national oppression went hand in hand, completing and aggravating each other.

The Kurdish feudal Beys ruthlessly exploited and oppressed the Armenian peasants, who were completely devoid of rights. In Kurdistan serfdom, in its harshest medieval forms, flourished. "In the kaza of Sasun," the Russian vice-consul Tumanskii wrote at the turn of the twentieth century, "there is an almost serf-like dependence of Armenians on Kurds, with all its legal consequences: each Armenian is attached to some Kurd or other and obliged to pay him rent; when in need of money the Kurds sell their serfs; should a Kurd kill a serf, the latter's master avenges himself by killing a serf belonging to the murderer." Some Beys even kept, in Armenian villages, the "right of the first night." Armenian serfs, wrote Lynch, were known as "zer-kurri," i.e., "bought with gold." "They are bought and sold by the Kurdish Beys and Aghas exactly like sheep and cattle." The purchase and sale of the serf-peasants took place along with that of the land on which they lived and worked.[3]

This system of relationships--based on serflike dependence of the mainly Armenian peasants on the Kurdish feudalists--was known as "Kafirism," derived from the Arabic word Kafir: unbeliever, godless, used to designate non-Muslims. According to R. Bekgulyants, who made a thorough study of the mode of life of the population of the vilayet of Van on the eve of the First World War, Kafirism signifies "arbitrariness and violence, illegal and unjust requisitions carried out by the Kurdish Beys." He continues: "The agrarian relations between Armenians and Kurdish shaikhs remind one of those between medieval feudal counts and barons and the peasants living on their lands."[4]

Each village, explains Bekgulyants further on, is subjected to its Bey and obliged to pay him taxes in kind. Each family is obliged to work for a specified number of days, without payment, for the benefit of the Bey, who may also impose on the inhabitants money taxes. All this is known as Kafirism and the tax is called the Kafiri tax.[5]

Pointing out, further on, that Kafirism had a harmful effect on the Turkish fiscal system and strengthened the position of the Kurdish leadership, the author noted that neither the Sultan's government nor that of the Young Turks attempted to abolish these rights, and the spontaneous struggle of the Armenian peasants for emancipation made their situation still worse. "In Europe and among us, in Russia," wrote Bekgulyants, "what is happening in Armenia is commonly ascribed to the brigand instincts of the Kurds, but we believe that it has a deeper and more important cause; this cause is the right of Kafirism, to which the Kurdish Beys cling tenaciously and which they do not wish to give up."[6]

Along with the extra-economic methods practiced by the Kurdish Beys to enslave the Armenian peasants, economic mechanisms were also used. The Beys bought land from the Armenian inhabitants; all the livestock was in their hands, and they let the peasants use it for payment in kind. Kurdish Beys who had enriched themselves often farmed the ashar[7] and then, wrote Termen, who occupied the post of Russian vice-consul in Van, "The whole village was in their hands." They advanced to the peasants cash and grain, on advantageous terms, repayable in kind at harvest time. Such loans were known as selem or selef; the selefdars [lenders] soon became rich, by taking over the land of defaulting borrowers. The dispossession of peasants in the eastern vilayets of Turkey was promoted by the mortgage credit advanced by the banks.

The Turkish authorities encouraged the enrichment of the Kurdish feudalists, since they received valuable presents from them. "Thanks to this," remarked Termen, "the whole village passes into the hands of the Kurds; the Armenians starting as miribe--i.e., they receive from the Kurd seed and livestock for working the fields, giving in return half the crop--end up by losing their land and become simple laborers, i.e., serfs of the Kurds." The selef was a source of huge income for the Kurdish Beys. For example, the Armenian village of Haskei, in the valley of Muş, lost through selef 208 fields, 24 houses, and 6 mills, all of which passed into the hands of the Kurdish selefdars. In the formerly prosperous village of Arench, in the kaza of Adilcevaz, out of 115 houses only 70 remained in the hands of the local inhabitants; of these, however, only 55 were held in ownership, the others being miribe.[8] In the village of Marmuss (vilayet of Van) the Kurdish Bey seized all the land belonging to the Armenian community and reduced the Armenian peasants to sharecroppers.[9]

Not infrequently, the authorities settled in Armenian villages Hamidis, i.e., Kurds serving in the Sultan's irregular forces. "These men," wrote the Russian vice-consul in Bitlis, "enjoying the protection of the administration dispensed justice and handed out punishments and, advancing to the ever-needy Armenians funds secured by livestock, horses, and crops, gradually became the owners of the village or Aghas, and the Armenians, performing all their work for them, giving them their girls, supplying them with their best horses and so on, were unable to deliver themselves from the weight of their debts."[10]

Often, the plundered Armenian peasants turned to a "protector" or "defender," in the person of one Bey against another, neighboring Bey. The great Kurdish feudalist, Kazim Bey, extended his "protectorate" over a few Armenian villages on the border between the sancaks of Bitlis and Muş. The Armenian inhabitants were obliged to pay him special taxes, in addition to those levied on them by the Turkish authorities, "in order to protect their lives and fields."[11]

The cruel exploitation by the Kurdish feudalists of the Armenian peasants nurtured dissension between Kurds and Armenians, which suited the Turkish ruling circles--who hoped thereby to strengthen their position in the eastern vilayets of the Empire--and also the Western colonialists, who reckoned on warming their hands at the fire of Kurdo-Armenian emnity.

At the same time--and it is necessary to stress this--the Kurdish peasants or rayah lived at peace and harmony with their Armenian neighbors, and there was no hostility whatsoever between them.[12]

One cannot ignore one further circumstance which facilitated the dirty game played by various reactionaries in the Armenian and Kurdish questions. In eastern Asia Minor, Armenians occupied key positions in trade and business, which facilitated anti-Armenian agitation among the ignorant and backward Muslim masses, and in the first place the Kurds. For example, in the vilayet of Sivas (where Armenians formed 35 percent of the population), out of 166 large importers 125 were Armenians; out of 37 bankers 32 were Armenians, and out of 9,800 small traders 6,800 were Armenians. Armenians owned 130 of the 150 industrial enterprises.[13] In the vilayet of Van, Armenians held 98 percent of the trade, 80 percent of the agriculture, and only 20 percent of the livestock breeding. There were 18 large merchants, all Armenian, 50 moneylenders (30 Armenians and 20 Turks), 20 money-changers, all Armenians, 1,100 craftsmen (1,020 Armenians and 80 Turks), 50 rentiers (20 Armenians and 30 Turks); 80 vegetable merchants (50 Armenians and 30 Turks), 200 fruit merchants, all Armenians. All members of the liberal professions--physicians, pharmacists, lawyers, etc. were Armenians.[14]

These were the objective preconditions for the generation of nationalistic momentum and class contradictions in eastern Asia Minor. However, the existence of such preconditions did not at all mean that class contradictions had necessarily to be subordinated to national ones, that national enmity had to be substituted for class struggle, as Armenian and Kurdish nationalists attempted to prove and actually carried out. The flare-up of Armenian-Kurdish enmity at the end of the nineteenth century had its origins not so much in socio-economic processes as in the circumstances of the internal and external political system, which will be discussed below. For the working masses of Kurds and Armenians the problem stood on a completely different plane. Indeed Armenian peasants and craftsmen were oppressed not by the Kurdish people but by the Kurdish feudal upper class, together with the Turkish officials and the Armenian compradors and middle bourgeoisie.

As for the working-class Kurds, they were plundered not so much by the Armenian bourgeoisie as by "their own" Beys and Khans, not to mention the Turkish and Iranian administrations. The exploitation of the Kurdish tribes was to a certain extent concealed by the strong remnants of "warrior democracy," but it undoubtedly existed and became stronger with the disintegration of the kindred-tribal structure.

In the period under study, a significant number of Kurds settled on the land, or were on the point of settling because of the decline of nomadic animal husbandry, and the consequence was a marked deterioration of the living conditions of the common tribesmen, forcing them to leave the tribe and settle near the towns, as sedentary rayah.

The Kurds became ordinary ploughmen and shepherds, differing very little from Armenian, Turkish, Iranian, or Iraqi peasants. In the words of Linch, "a significant number of (Kurds) were transformed into hardworking farmers and live on the fruits of their labor."[15] "The Armenians," noted the Armyanskii Vestnik, "are oppressed not only because they are Christians--together with them are also ruthlessly exploited the coreligionaries of the oppressors, the Turks, and even their own kinsmen, the Kurdish rayah."[16] The Armenian newspaper Azad-amard stated that "the mass of the Kurdish people lays before its Aghas the same claims as does the Armenian rural population."[17]

1. O. L. Vilchevskii, "Ekonomika kurdskoi kochevoi . . . ," Sovietskaya etnographiya, 1936, 4-5; A. Sh. Shamilov, K voprosu O feodilizme u kurdov, (Erivan, 1936).
2. Vronchenko, 2:225.
3. Kh. F. P. Linch [Lynch] Armenia. . . . (Tiflis, 1910), 2:554.
4. R. Bekgulyants [Severyanin], Po Turetskoi Armenii (Rostov on the Don, 1914), p. 74.

5. Ibid. pp. 74-75. In Bokhtane, wrote the German traveller Müller-Simonis, the local Agha imposed such heavy taxes in kind on the Armenian peasants that the latter were obliged to save themselves by flight--P. Müller-Simonis, Von Kaukasus zum Persischen Meerbusen . . . , p. 228.

6. Bekgulyants, op. cit. pp. 75-76.

7. Ashar or ushr--medieval tithe, levied mostly in kind on the peasants of the Otto-man Empire, officially 12.63% of the crop, but in fact two to three times as much.

8. AVPR [Archives of The Foreign Policy of Russia] Constantinople Embassy, 1908, d. 1595, 1. 4950.

9. De Cholet [Arménie, Kurdistan et Mésopotamie, Paris, 1892], p. 172.

10. AVPR, Constantinople, 1907, d. 4087, ℓℓ. 77-78.

11. AVPR "Politarkhiv," 1907, d. 541, ℓ. 156; also Linch, op. cit., 2:554.

12. De Cholet, op. cit. p. 245. After the Turkish conquest, noted V. A. Gordlevskii, relations between Kurds and Armenians were good. "Gradually, however, the situation of the Armenians deteriorated because the Turks sowed dissension between Armenians and Kurds and, guided by the principle of 'divide and conquer', secretly approved the oppression of the Armenians by the Kurds and the conversion of their flourishing pastures and fields into waste by the Kurdish feudalists; the Kurdish princelets, aware of the powerlessness of the central authorities, ruled in these fields and did what they wished."--Siluety Turtsii, p. 126.

13. A. Dzhivelegov. Budushchee Turetskoi Armenii, "Polozhenie Armyan v Turtsii do vmeshatelstva derzhav v 1895g," Moscow, 1896, p. 174; see also V. A. Gordlevskii, op. cit., p. 127.

14. Tse. G.A.O.R.S.S. Central State Archives, Russian Socialist Republic P. N. Miliyukov , op. 1, kn. 2, d, 1577, ℓℓ. 2-3, Statistical information on the vilayet of Van.

15. Linch, op. cit., 2:540-541.

16. Armyanskii Vestnik, 1917, no. 23, pp. 5-6.

17. Quoted in AVPR, Constantinople, 1910, d. 1599, ℓ.67.

THE JEWS

The two following selections--the first of which was written by an acute observer of Ottoman society[1]--give an unduly somber picture of the Jewish community in Istanbul. By the beginning of the present century, many Jews occupied distinguished positions in finance, commerce, industry, government service, and the professions (2:Introduction).[2] But it is certainly true that they had less wealth and influence than the Greeks or Armenians, and that the vast majority were unskilled laborers, peddlers, or petty retail traders.

Things had not always been so. In the sixteenth century Jewish immigrants, many trained in Spanish, Portuguese, or Italian universities, had introduced printing presses that turned out books in Greek, Latin, Italian, and Spanish as well as Hebrew; cast cannon; established banks; carried out international trade; and served as royal physicians and, oc-casionally, ambassadors.[3] As late as the 1670s, a French monk who visited Turkey stated that there was no "noteworthy Turkish family or foreign merchant who did not have a Jew working for them, either to appraise merchandize and judge its quality, or to serve as in-terpreter or inform them of what was happening--the other Oriental nations, like the Greeks, Armenians, etc. do not have this talent and do not attain their skill."[4] But the reaction caused by the Messianic claims of Shabbatai Zvi (in 1666) caused the Jewish com-munity to turn its back on modern learning and to reduce its participation in outside ac-tivity. The eighteenth century seems to have been a gloomy period for Jews, as for other communities, and saw the abandonment of many crafts they had formerly practiced.[5] A further handicap was the close relations of some Jewish bankers and suppliers with the Janissaries. The years 1815-26 witnessed a fierce struggle between a group of Jewish bankers (Yehazkel Gabbai, Çelebi Carmona, and the three Adjiman brothers) and their Armenian rivals, the three Allah-Verdoglu brothers and Kazaz Aretun; practically all the participants were put to death, but with the destruction of the Janissaries the Armenians emerged as the dominant financiers.[6] Moreover, the Jews were far behind the Greeks and Armenians in taking advan-tage of the opportunities opened by the Tanzimat; they were slower in learning foreign

languages and sent far fewer students, and only relatively late, to such schools as the
Faculty of Medicine and Galata Sarai. It was only in 1854 that the first Jewish primary
school that taught French as well as Hebrew was opened--in the face of strong rabbinical
opposition; two others followed, in 1868 and 1870, but when the Alliance Israélite founded
its first school in Istanbul in 1875 it met much opposition from the community, which
wanted Turkish rather than French as a second language.[7] However, in the last quarter of
the nineteenth century the educational level of the Jewish community rose considerably,
thanks largely to the foundation, by the Alliance, of twenty four schools between 1867 and
1902 within the present borders of Turkey. In 1908 they had over 6,400 boys and nearly
4,800 girls, drawn from an estimated Jewish population of 227,000.[8] As mentioned earlier,
by the turn of the century Jews began to play a significant part in the economic and cultural life of Turkey. This was particularly true of Salonica; half of its population was
Jewish, Jews controlled the bulk of its trade and a considerable part of its industry and
supplied a large proportion of its white-collar and industrial workers and craftsmen.

1. See his essay on "Ethnic Division of Labor," EHME, pp. 115-25.
2. Also Galanté, Turcs et Juifs, pp. 101-35; Franco, pp. 239-60.
3. Galanté, pp. 94-101.
4. Quoted by Franco, p. 115.
5. Ibid., pp. 118, 250.
6. Ibid., pp. 133-40; by 1831 Slade could say (p. 434), "The Armenians are the chief bankers of European Turkey, having supplanted the Jews in that dangerous but lucrative employment in consequence of possessing superior honesty or rather inferior knavery."
7. Galanté, pp. 140-43.
8. Bulletin of the Alliance Israélite Universelle, 1908, cited by Paul Dumont in an unpublished paper; according to Stanford Shaw, the number of Jews in the Ottoman Empire was 184,000 (of whom 22,000 were in Istanbul) in 1884, 256,000 in 1906, and 187,000 in 1914.

SELECTION 15. THE JEWS IN ISTANBUL, 1912

Alphons Sussnitski, "Die wirtschaftliche Lage der Juden in Konstantinopel," Allgemeine
Zeitung des Judentums (Berlin), 8, 12, and 19 January 1912, pp. 16-18

. . . The original residence of Constantinople Jews, at least since Ottoman rule, is
Hasköy on the Golden Horn . . . already in 1483 an Ashkenazi Beni-frank community, bearing
the name of its town of origin, Frankfort, was to be found there. . . . Even in the last
century the richest Jews of Constantinople lived in Hasköy, and the schools and foundations
standing there till this day show that it was always a Jewish cultural center of the capital of the Empire. When, however, business activity in Constantinople surged up, the Jews
also began to settle in other quarters of the city. This was the more necessary for them
because Constantinople, which is not a unitary city but a collective concept for innumerable small places on the Bosphorus, Golden Horn, and Sea of Marmara--enchantingly beautiful in its location but very diverse economically--still suffers from unspeakably poor
means of communication. Of the estimated 80,000 Jews in the metropolis, about 20,000 now
live in Hasköy, 15,000 in Balata, 10,000 in Haydar paşa, Galata, Pera, and Ortaköy, and
5,000 to 6,000 in Kozkancuk. Hasköy and Balata, which lies exactly opposite it on the
other side of the Golden Horn and is the second oldest Jewish quarter, constitute the
Jewish ghetto of Constantinople; but it cannot be denied that Balata, with its somewhat
better-off inhabitants, produces a much less saddening impression than Hasköy. [There
follows Edmondo de Amicis' description of the ghetto.]
  Considerably better, on the other hand, is the impression made by the other quarters,
where the difference between the Greek, Armenian, and Jewish inhabitants is hardly apparent any more; this is particularly true of Galata and Pera, the two outstanding business
quarters of the capital, where the resident Jews are mostly engaged in trade and have developed it most fully.
  Galata and Pera also constitute practically the sole residence of the Ashkenazim, and
it seems to me appropriate to say something here about their settlement in Constantinople.
Of the Frankish and other Ashkenazi communities that lived in Hasköy in the course of time,
nothing has remained. They may well have been absorbed by the Sephardim or, as I believe
more likely, their members may have gone to other places. That no continuous immigration
has taken place shows the sound business sense of those people, who did not mistake possibilities for realities and were thus able to carry out a powerful economic upswing in
their own native lands. Not until the beginning of the last century, when a strong urge

towards Palestine arose among European Jews, did it come about that many of them, particularly from Russia, whose means or strength failed during the journey to the Holy Land--or for other reasons--remained behind in Constantinople and made it their permanent home. But it was only scattered individuals who settled in the Turkish capital in this way.

The Crimean War, however, gave rise to a greater Jewish settlement. Since the port of Kertch, lying at the foot of Mithridate Mountain, had been taken by the Russians, the Jews living there decided to emigrate. They preferred to leave their home city rather than become Russian subjects. And so the few hundreds of families constituting the community, with their rabbi and ritual butchers, went to Constantinople, where the authorities gave them a cordial reception. By an _iradeh_ of the Sultan, the rabbi was granted the title of hahambaşi of the Ashkenazi. Moreover, in Istanbul a very large _han_ was prepared, in which whole families of the community found shelter. In addition, each household was assigned a pension from the government, according to the number of its members. Unfortunately, here too idleness was the root of all evils. Having no need to do anything, the people became lazy, bad, and inclined to intrigue. They concealed the number of deaths and faked the number of births and some denounced the others for such cheating--out of envy. Moreover, an unending conflict began with the rabbi. And when the community sold the cemetery which had been presented to them by the government, the latter lost all interest in and goodwill towards them.

The Crimean War was also connected, in a certain and rather peculiar way, with the expansion of the Ashkenazi colony in Constantinople through the influx of Jewish tailors. The Treaty of Paris of 1856, under which Turkey was received into the European community of states, had stirred powerful ambitions for modernization in the Land of the Crescent. The Turks wanted to become real Europeans. And, following the saying "clothes make the man," their first concern was to dress, as far as possible, in the Viennese and Parisian fashions. Constantinople became the Eldorado for every man jack of a tailor, and many clothesmakers, especially from Austria, rushed there. Their number was so large that they soon gathered together in a new community. Today tailors still constitute the largest contingent of handicraftsmen in Constantinople. It is true that, in the meantime, some of them have gone into purely commercial activity, so that the ready-made clothing business is largely in Jewish hands.

The evolution of Constantinople into a modern city, and more particularly the accompanying increase in foreign visitors, with their dissolute nightlife and their sensual revelry, has also enticed another category of Ashkenazi Jews to the capital: traffickers in women. They too have organized themselves in a separate community; I counted ninety two members in their synagogue, whose president is a veteran of the craft. We shall here, of course, ignore this "industry." It is a melancholy phenomenon and a shame to Jewry. It is an offence to respectable occupations to mention it in this connection.

In the final analysis, the field of activity of the Constantinople Ashkenazim proves to be quite limited: many handicraftsmen, predominantly tailors, of whom some have passed into ready-made clothing; in addition very few merchants, mainly agents, who do business especially with the German-speaking countries. It is perhaps worth mentioning that the numerous tourist guides are mostly recruited from Ashkenazi Jews.

From the economic point of view, the Ashkenazim constitute the élite of Constantinople Jewry. Excluding a small number of Sephardim, who as small bankers or through long-time business relations with the government have reached a certain affluence, the remainder is no better than a miserable proletariat. Match vendors, shoeshines, peddlers, hawkers of frippery, beggars--such were the almost exclusive occupations of the Spaniards some fifty years ago. It was from the immigrant Ashkenazi Jews that they learned to take up handicrafts. Some of them also went into business but, except for a few who had considerable success in textiles, paper, and haberdashery, they did not rise, essentially, above the ranks of shopkeepers. And yet obviously there is scope here for gaining ground from the Greeks and Armenians, whose superiority in the economic struggle is uncontested.

It is truly astounding with what boldness and success these two nationalities have managed to draw to themselves the trade of the Turkish capital, not leaving the possibility for any other labor forces to develop. They have divided everything between them or together dominate the terrain. Practically all that concerns the immediate necessities of life is in Greek hands. All branches related less directly to living but rather to the acquisition of civilization are almost exclusively in the sphere of the Armenians; they have the large textile businesses, the large iron, tin, and zinc businesses, and also all that pertains to the building trade. Only the small fancy-goods, haberdashery, and colonial goods trades are left to the Jews. Even the money business--from large bankers down to paltry money-changers--is, in Constantinople, mainly in Greco-Armenian hands; there are only small Jewish bankers there, and very few money-changers. Even the so-called lustmenschen,[*] otherwise a specifically Jewish phenomenon, are recruited in Constantinople almost solely from Greeks.

There is, however, one more considerable branch which is held by Jews: the antiquity dealers and rug merchants of Constantinople are almost without exception Sephardim. But

---

[*] I presume this is a Freudian slip for Luftmenschen, i.e., a chimerical person.

having evolved from the ranks of peddlers and hawkers of frippery, they still usually pursue their new businesses in the same spirit, however far they may have individually gone ahead and attained remarkable affluence. The buyer's spleen is their only standard for the determination of the price of an object. "Today I had a completely crazy fellow, an Englishman," said one of them to me, laughing, the owner of a large antique shop, "he paid all I asked him for, without bargaining. And I realized that I could ask very much from him because of his idiotic interest in these old things."

A certain change for the better can, however, be already discerned in the situation of the Constantinople Jews. Ever since Jewish youth began to be influenced by an appropriate education, and more particularly by the cultivation of the national tongue, a slow transformation has occurred in this respect. And although the Alliance [Israélite] schools give their pupils only a thin French veneer, many of them have thereby succeeded in obtaining a good position as bank clerks or state employees. But in this respect the activity of the Hilfsverein of German Jews is much more promising. . . .

SELECTION 16. BENEVOLENT SOCIETY OF JEWISH BOAT-OWNERS, ISTANBUL

The Benevolent Society of the Boat-Owners in Constantinople, by Yitzhak Rofeh, Sefunot (Jerusalem, 1966), pp. 621-32

My father, Rabbi Samuel Rofeh, who was the Secretary of the Holy Society [burial society], "The Fount of Life," in the Balat district in Constantinople, brought home twenty years ago a round elongated box made of tin, and within it a rolled manuscript. This box was given to him by one of the survivors of the overseers of the Kaikci Society (boat-owners society). This society was praised in all the districts of the city and it received the favor of the rabbis of the time.

In all cases of weakness in the face of individuals or in the face of the supervisors of the villages, the hands of the heads of the society were strengthened by a Beit Din enactment, "a note of the court." In the manuscript before us [which follows in the original], there are eight notes from the year 5575 [1815] to the year 5654 [1894]. Here I transmit the manuscript with deep thanks to the Ben Zvi Institute for agreeing to its publication, and to its director Dr. Meir Benayahu, who deciphered the ornate signatures of the rabbis of Istanbul and helped in the identification and in the explanation of the concerns of the society.

It is not clear when the Free-Loan [Benevolent] Society of the Kaikci Community (Boat-Owners) in Istanbul was founded. From the first note in the year 5575 [1815], we learn that many years had passed from the time it was founded, and in the hands of the heads of the society were writings "validated by the rabbis" who had already died. It can be assumed that the intention of this phrase pertains to the prescriptions of the society that have been lost. But in note 1 they return to several details, from which we can determine the purposes of the society and its benevolent deeds. Since they recall "notes in their hands generation after generation," it seems clear that the society was established as much as one hundred years before the year 5575 [1815], that is to say, about the year 5475 [1715], over 250 years ago. The society was founded originally by the Kaikcis. Kaik in Turkish means boat. Most of the boat owners who ferried people across the Golden Horn, that wonderful part of the sea that divides greater Constantinople, and is off the Bosphorus, were Jews. It was natural that they would need to set up an organization for themselves, but not for professional purposes, but rather for aid and assistance to its members in time of need. Later, workers in allied occupations joined them--fishermen and fruit vendors, since they often traveled in boats in pursuance of their trades. Also the wine-sellers, who depended on the boats to transport their wares from city to village joined the society.

Each member was required to contribute one Pruta to the society each week; that is to say, one akçe or para, a small coin valued at 1/30th [1/40] of a kuruş. However, the wine-sellers contributed four Mitros of wine per boat-load.

The funds were used mainly to provide aid for festive or mourning occasions for those members who could not afford it; many Jews sailed in the boats and occasionally it would happen that they would drown in the sea. The society would send out members to look for bodies and bring them back for proper Jewish burial.

The activities of the society were recognized by the Constantinople sages as important and, since the income of the workers was small, they exempted them from contributing to other communal charity funds; moreover, in order that individual members would not leave the society, they prohibited the treasurers of these benevolent societies and foundations from collecting funds in the same places, so as not to diminish the income of the boat-owners society. In three districts they permitted collection: (1) "from the village of Hasköy to the village of Yeni Maali" that which is called Tzad Hasköy; (2) "from the border of Aiba Saari (Sarayi) to Balik Bazaar," the side of the Golden Horn that is called Istanbul; (3) "from Galata to Arnaut Köy," the side of the Bosphorus from the district of Galata until opposite Asia. This was an excellent geographic division. It seems that the workers and businessmen who were included in the society lived in these districts. From this we can draw conclusions about the neighborhoods of the various social classes in Istanbul.

The rabbis of Istanbul also imposed on all the burial and funeral-garment societies in the various neighborhoods of Istanbul contributions of 5 percent of their incomes to the needs of the boat-owners, deducting the expenses for funeral garments.

Around the year 5575 [1815] it was agreed with the aforementioned societies to contribute a fixed and regular amount. In the year 5569 [1809], when it became known to the Beit Din that the wine-sellers were not fulfilling their obligations, it obliged them to contribute 60 perutot for every cargo of wine.

In order to insure proper functioning of the society, the Beit Din in Istanbul appointed two learned men as "overseers of all the society's affairs." After the previous overseer died, the Beit Din appointed in 5575 [1815] Rabbi Judah HaCohen and Rabbi Menahem Francis, who was "a man of substance." The appointed were not always recorded in the notes in the manuscript. Besides these two appointees, two other appointments were recorded in the year 5654 [1894]--Rabbi Moses ben Isaac and Rabbi Abraham Mehallel.

Fourteen years after he served his duty, Rabbi Menahem Francis died, in the year 5589 [1829], as he boarded a boat sailing for Israel. The Holy Society of the Galata congregation arranged for his burial. The Benevolent Society of the Boat-Owners complained about this before a Beit Din. Its complaint was that the society's members were attending to the burial of those who had drowned. Several times it happened that they were compelled to attend to people who had died on the boats, and when a rich man died, the society was unable to benefit from his money. The Beit Din recognized the justness of their complaint and ordained that from that time on the Kaikci Society would alone attend to all those who died on boats and large ships, even if they were not connected with the membership of the society, since the deaths occurred at sea. A year later they expanded this regulation and added the stipulation that even if death did not occur at sea but through illness, or if one was rescued from the sea while still alive and died afterwards, no other society but itself alone would attend to it. And if they did this, all the money would be transferred to the Boat-Owners Society.

We learn from the notes that from time to time the treasurers of Holy Societies or one of the communities of Istanbul would encroach upon the jurisdiction of the Kaikci Society, yet the rabbis of Istanbul would always stand by its side in the face of pressures.

It is not known how long the Boat-Owners Society was active. The last document is from the year 5654 [1894]. Elders in Turkey who remember the work of this society inform us that it was in existence until close to the outbreak of the First World War, and afterwards its path is unknown.

There were many societies in Istanbul, yet this society was unique among them in its pursuance of this type of activity by the fact that men have always died at sea. And thus it became necessary to have two burial societies, one for those who died on land and one for those who died at sea. There were undoubtedly many professional associations in Turkey but we do not know about them, as we would not have known about this society had we not found the document at hand. Indeed we do not know about the benevolent societies of well-known professions.

In this period, one of the sages whose signature appears on these notes in the year 5580 [1819], Rabbi Eliezer de Toledo, mentions "the Rufid community of the Siricilik occupations, the work of the cloth weavers." The term "rufid" is also mentioned in the documents before us, "the Rufid community of Kaikci" and its meaning in Turkish is aid or benevolence. There is, consequently, in the publication of these notes a small contribution to progress in research on these societies. . . .

SELECTION 17.   THE IZMIR MARKET IN THE 1900s

Halit Ziya Uşaklıgil, Kırk Yıl, 5 vols. (Istanbul, 1936), 2:14-16

This is not the place to examine the influences and conditions which prevail in the commercial circles of Izmir. But these circles, in which I lived a few of my youthful years, were so miserable that painful awareness pierced through the barriers of my carefree and joyful youth, and what I observed disturbed me.

Almost all the produce from a vast segment of Anatolia connected with Izmir used to come there and fill the large area from the Fruit Market as far as the Customs. And in this area swarmed people of all nations and also those whose origins were unknown but who used to be known as residents of Izmir. These people carried various papers of identification, as if they were Europeans, but their hive consisted of Greeks, Armenians, and especially Jews. This hive had a ceaseless activity, its members buzzing around and endlessly sucking the available honey supply to the extent of flooding their gizzards. There were also a few Turkish shops here and there. There were those gentlemen who used to offer coffee and tea to their customers: they would charge their assistants, who would be members of various ethnic groups, with those aspects of their trade which needed much rushing and fretting.

When the producer in Anatolia was not bound by contract to a foreign export merchant, he would bring the remainder of his crop to the middlemen at the Fruit Market after paying his immense taxes, called tithe (öşür) and quarter (sub'urub); the money for the tax farmer's men, if his property were leased to a tax farmer, which was mostly the case; and God knows how much interest on the money which he might have borrowed. Thus, the Turkish merchants constituted mostly, in fact wholly, this class of people who satisfied themselves by being the middlemen between the producers and the export merchants.

Loads of barley, wheat, chick-peas, millet, sesame seeds, and especially figs, raisins, valonia, sumach, and opium used to come to Izmir to fill the depots of those gentlemen merchants; some of the produce which could not wait would pile up in front of the depots on the streets. Then the export merchants would swarm the area, price the produce, and goods would be weighed and sold.

The price, amount, and so forth was entrusted to the middleman, his honesty and reasonableness, in which the farmer believed.

This short description portrays well the travel of the produce from Anatolia's rich sources to Izmir: the road from the farm to the depot was like an old, punctured, corroded water main which leaked so much that at the end it would yield a mere dribble.

What did the Agricultural Bank do? It was enough to look at the numerous notices advertising farms to let or for sale in the official gazette of the province to grasp the situation.

In this commercial battleground, the producers were the victims; the foreign and semi-foreign elements the profiteers; the Turks the onlookers. Certainly, the strongest, most active, and cleverest were the Jews. . . .

3

Trade

Traditionally the Ottoman government sought to encourage imports and discourage exports. This policy, which puzzled contemporaries--whether mercantilists or free-traders[1]
may be explained by Turkey's social and political structure and the predominance of the
interests of the army and bureaucracy over those of the farmers, craftsmen, and merchants;
by the desire to ensure the provisioning of Istanbul and other cities which had potentially
unruly mobs (2:3,4); by the lower level of prices in the Empire than in Europe and the consequent tendency to have an export surplus in European trade; and by the increasing importance of customs duties on exports. Until about the end of the eighteenth century a uniform duty of 3 percent was levied on both imports and exports (3:7).

This situation was changed by the depreciation of the Turkish currency and the consequent rise in prices (7:1,2), which greatly reduced the real yield of customs duties.[2] The
response was both to request a rise in the duty to 5 percent (HHS Türkei, 125-Ber. 1800-
1801) and multiply the number of prohibitions and monopolies, particularly on exports, thus
creating new sources of revenue. But since the duties were in fact fixed and not ad valorem
(3:3), the continued rise in prices soon meant that the government was collecting much less
than 3 percent, and it repeatedly requested the Powers to consent to an increase (3:4,5).
The latter were naturally reluctant to accept a rise in the duties paid by their subjects,
and were particularly apprehensive that any change might benefit their commercial and political rivals (3:3,4). But, on the other hand, they could not deny the justice of the
Ottoman claim. More to the point, their trade was suffering from the multiplicity of restrictions and the haphazardness with which duties were levied and prohibitions applied.
Their merchants made it clear that they would welcome a small rise in the tariff in return
for less arbitrariness and capriciousness (3:6,9). This fitted the prevalent view in the
industrialized countries that their interests were best served by removal of all restrictions on commerce--the so-called "Imperialism of Free Trade."[3] In 1829 the Russians secured some commercial advantages under the Treaty of Adrianople. But the main thrust was
that of Britain, by far the leading industrial power and the one that was to "open up" such
countries as China in 1842, and Morocco in 1856. Its task was facilitated by the conflict
with Mehmet Ali, whom both the Porte and the British opposed. In return for Britain's help,
which was to prove so effective in 1841, the Sultan consented to grant that country's main
demands, aimed even more at Egypt than at Turkey. The result was the Anglo-Turkish Commercial Convention of 1838.[4] This prohibited all monopolies, allowed British merchants to
purchase goods anywhere in the Empire without payment of any taxes or dues other than import

duty or export duty or its equivalent in interior duty, and imposed duties of 3 percent on imports, 12 percent on exports and 3 percent on transit; in addition to the import duty, British merchants agreed to pay another 2 percent in lieu of other internal duties paid by importers. The Convention was to apply to all parts of the Empire, and specifically to Egypt.

The other European powers soon acceded to the Convention. Thanks to the vigilance of their consuls, its stipulations were swiftly carried out, with only occasional and generally minor infractions, in a nondiscriminatory manner (3:10, and replies to questionnaire, 1845-- CC Smyrne, vol. 91). Its effects on the Ottoman economy were far-reaching. On the one hand it exposed the handicrafts to the full blast of European competition and hastened their decline; at the same time it prevented the government from protecting new establishments and delayed the development of a factory industry (chap. 6). On the other it facilitated the export of raw materials and foodstuffs, benefiting the producers (3:10) and doubtless stimulating the growth of agricultural output (chap. 5). Thus on both sides it contributed to the expansion of foreign trade. It also integrated Turkey more fully into world trade and made her more subject to its fluctuations.

The realization that the Treaty put Ottoman producers at a disadvantage, and the desire for more revenue, led to repeated efforts to modify the rates. In 1861-62 new conventions were concluded with the European countries and the United States, raising import duties from 3 to 8 percent, lowering export duties from 12 to 8 percent, and providing for the reduction of the latter by 1 percent a year until such time as they should fall to 1 percent, which took place in 1869.[5] Thereafter the government repeatedly sought to modify the 1861-62 Conventions, to raise import duties, but the Powers refused their consent even after the Conventions had lapsed in 1890. A few examples are illustrative.

In 1875 the government proposed raising import duties to 20 percent ad valorem; the United States consented to the change but the other powers refused.[6]

In 1881, in view of its great financial difficulties, the government proposed to abolish export and transit duties and to subject imports to duties ranging from zero to 20 percent, but once more failed to secure agreement.[7]

In July 1882 the government declared its intention of denouncing the treaties and made various suggestions including the differentiation of tariff rates on various goods, up to a maximum of 20 percent, calculation of duties on the basis of market values rather than at specified rates, and the collection of duties in gold mecidiehs, at the rate of 100 piastres a Turkish pound. The British Merchants Committee of Constantinople, after examining the proposals, stated: "If we were in Europe and not in Turkey, or if the Administration of the Turkish Customs Houses were given over to competent Europeans invested with full powers, we do not hesitate to say that the best principle to adopt would be the 'ad valorem' coupled with the right of pre-emption"; but given the circumstances, they wished to retain the fixed duties, and they expressed other reservations (22 December 1882, FO 78/3606).

In 1885 the British government consented, in principle, to a tariff of 8-20 percent, and in 1890 the German government agreed to a rise without limit, conditional on the consent of the other Powers. France also agreed to the Ottoman proposals. However, "the negotiations with Russia have been at a standstill owing to her refusal to consent to increased duties on corn and petroleum, or to the creation of a petroleum monopoly" (Memorandum 29 April 1903, FO 78/5381).

In March 1900 the newspapers announced that the government would raise import duties from 8 to 11 percent; on 11 March six ambassadors protested and the proposal was withdrawn

(FO 78/5111). In January 1902 the government declared its intention of applying a new specific tariff but withdrew in the face of protest from the Powers (ibid.).

Finally in 1907, after much reluctance on the part of Britain, Turkey was permitted to raise its import duty by 3 percent, the proceeds of the surtax to be allocated to the Public Debt Administration (7:16).[8] And in 1914, as part of the overall settlement between the Powers (4:17), the duty was raised to 15 percent. In the meantime, to stimulate domestic production, industrial, agricultural, and construction machinery was exempted from duty (6:19).

After 1838 the Ottoman trade régime was one of the most liberal in the world and this, together with population growth and the rise in agricultural output, explains the expansion in the volume of trade.[9] During the Revolutionary and Napoleonic wars and the War of Greek Independence there was a sharp contraction in trade which was not compensated until around 1830 (3:1,11). Judging from the scanty figures for Salonica and the fuller ones for Izmir (3:12,14) there was little increase in the 1830s, perhaps because of the disruptive effects of the wars with Egypt. After that, however, there was a steady rise, and the volume of exports from Anatolia, Istanbul, and Salonica rose over 5 times between the early 1840s and 1873-77 while imports rose 4.7 times (3:1). Since world prices showed little change in this period, the increase in real terms was about equal. Between 1873-77 and 1900 the Great Depression had an adverse effect and the value of exports fell by nearly one-fifth and that of imports by a quarter; this was however more than offset by the drop of one-third in world prices, indicating a continued, though very slow, growth in real terms. From 1900 to 1912 there was rapid expansion, exports rising by 36 percent and imports by 80 percent, while prices rose by only some 10-12 percent, indicating that the real increase was almost as great. Over the whole period, exports rose about 6 times and imports 7.5 times in money terms and about 8 and 10 times, respectively, in real terms. These figures are far below the fiftyfold increase in real world-trade from 1800 to 1914, or the similar figure for Egypt, but are roughly comparable to those for Iran.[10]

It is much more difficult to estimate the value of the trade of the whole Empire, because of territorial changes and different coverage, and for the first half of the period only the returns of the main trading partners have been used. These suggest that the value of exports rose 2.8 times between the 1840s and 1873-77 and 3.3 times over the whole period, and imports 2.8 and 4.6 times, figures that are consistent with the other estimates in view of the great territorial losses. However, there is good reason to believe that the official export figures for both Anatolia and the Empire are greatly undervalued.

The eight to tenfold increase in Turkey's foreign trade was almost certainly larger than the expansion in its gross national product during that period. This shows that its economy was becoming more commercialized and more fully integrated in the world economy. It may also, perhaps, suggest that insufficiency of foreign demand for its products and the limited expansion of its capacity to import were not the major constraints on Turkey's economic growth.

Imports rose more rapidly than exports, and both Turkey and the whole Empire had a consistently adverse balance of trade, estimated at around £T7,000,000 a year in 1907-13. Table 1 presents the main items in the balance of payments as estimated by Biliotti and Eldem, and shows the heavy deficit on current account, only partly covered by new government loans and a small amount of long-term private investment. However, one must repeat that exports were greatly undervalued and that the trade deficit was correspondingly overstated.

Table 1

Items in Balance of Payments (ŁT 000)

	1907	1907/8	1909/10	1913/14
Merchandise trade	(−5,000)	−6,070	−6,640	−8,190
Public debt	−4,600	−3,030	−3,330	−4,090
Railway guarantees	−850	−850	−770	−260
Russian indemnity	−350	−350	..	..
Dividends and profits	−1,000	−2,640	−2,950	−2,600
Tribute	(1,000)	1,010	890	890
Tourism	500	1,000	1,000	1,000
Other receipts[a]	1,000	3,370	4,470	5,030
Balance on current accounts	−930	−656	−733	−822
New government loans[b]	..	526	546	570

Source: Biliotti, pp. 174–75, Eldem, p. 193.

[a]Remittances from Greek, Armenian, and Christian Arab emigrants, income on capital abroad held by Ottoman residents, etc.

[b]Net of redemption.

It will be noticed that the servicing of the public debt, railway guarantees, and private foreign investment amounted to ŁT9,000,000 a year, or about 30 percent of the Empire's export proceeds, a heavy burden.

The nature of Turkey's exports showed little change. Carpets were the only manufactured good of any significance (6:13) and although mineral exports rose considerably they accounted for less than 5 percent of the total in the years immediately preceding the First World War. All the remainder consisted of agricultural raw materials and foodstuffs, as it had done throughout the nineteenth century, but some shifts had taken place. Dyestuffs such as madder, yellow berries, and gallnuts, which had formed a large fraction of exports in the 1830s and 40s, had disappeared (5:Introduction). On the other hand, tobacco, silk, cotton, and hazelnuts had greatly increased their share, and raisins, mohair, opium, and figs continued to be important.

On the import side the most striking change in the first half of the period was the great increase in textiles, especially cotton (3:14,15), and the rise in colonial goods such as sugar (3:1) and coffee. Thereafter their share stabilized—although the amount imported continued to increase—and in 1878–1913 clothing materials accounted for some 25 percent of imports, and sugar, coffee, and tea for about 10 percent.[11] Another major change was the increasing quantity of imports of wheat and flour, which converted the Empire (although not necessarily Anatolia) from a net exporter to a net importer (5:2). More interesting as regards development were the growing imports of coal, kerosene, iron, and copper. Imports of coal rose from 88,000 tons in 1878–79 to 440,000 in 1911–13 and consumption increased greatly (6:10), kerosene imports rose from 27,000 to 178,000 tons, and those of iron and copper from ŁT452,000 to ŁT714,000.[12] Imports of machinery increased, but remained small; an interesting minor development is the rapid rise in imports of sewing machines and typewriters.[13] But, overall, there was little change in the composition of imports between 1905 and 1913, the share of foodstuffs rising slightly to over one-third of the total and that of clothing declining correspondingly to slightly under one-third, while fuels and "investment goods" remained unchanged at 5 and 10 percent, respectively.

Little can be said about Turkey's terms of trade. Import and export prices tended to move together in response to world business conditions, rising in the first quarter of the nineteenth century, declining in 1839–46 (7:2), rising again in the 1850s, falling sharply in the late 1870s and climbing once more in the prewar years. From the 1830s to the 70s, one may assume that, like other primary producers, Turkey benefited from the fall in the price of manufactures, which was greater than that of raw materials. For the period 1878-1913 one can be more definite.[14] Export prices which had declined in the 1870s rose sharply in 1880 and then fell back again, the index for 15 commodities (1913 = 100) rising from 78 in 1878-79 to 110 in 1880 and falling to 84 in 1881-82. Thereafter, there was very little change until 1909, when an upward movement began. The import price index was over 100 in 1878-92 but declined to a low of 85 in 1895 and did not regain the 100 level until 1913. As a result the commodity terms-of-trade index showed substantial fluctuations after 1881, the low points being 81 in 1889-91 and 85 in 1906-7 and the high points 106 in 1897-99 and 109 in 1911, which would suggest that the improvements occurred during periods of world prosperity, when foreign demand for Ottoman products was high, and the deteriorations during depressions. The income terms of trade (commodity terms of trade multiplied by volume index of exports), which show Turkey's capacity to import, rose almost uninterruptedly from 41 in 1878-80 to 115 in 1910-11, or at 3.4 percent per annum, falling back to 100 in 1913.

The growth of Turkey's trade was accompanied by shifts in the channels of trade. Several ports or inland towns that had been quite important in the eighteenth century, such as Rosetta, Acre, Saida, Tripoli, Alexandretta, Aleppo, Antalya, and Edirne, saw their trade diverted (3:11) to Alexandria, Beirut, Izmir, Istanbul, and Salonica, which became by far the leading ports of the eastern Mediterranean (3:12-18). The development of the Adana region led to the rise of the new port of Mersin, which replaced Tarsus. The opening of the Black Sea to European ships at the very end of the eighteenth century (3:2) eventually resulted in the diversion of much of the Iranian transit trade to Trabzon while Samsun became the main outlet for the produce of northern Anatolia (3:19,20). Erzurum retained some of its former importance because of its position on the Iranian route (3:21), but Kayseri's trade declined (3:22).

There were also important shifts in the direction of trade.[15] France, traditionally by far the leading trade partner of the Ottoman Empire, was almost completely eliminated during the Revolutionary and Napoleonic Wars but recovered rapidly from 1840 to 1880. After that it slowly declined in relative importance but on the eve of the First World War was still Turkey's second largest market and fourth supplier (3:25). Britain remained throughout Turkey's main supplier and was almost always its principal market, but its share, too, declined rapidly after 1880 (3:4). The third most important country was Austria, which vied with France for second place (3:1,14). Russia's share of Turkey's trade remained minor, mainly because of the similarity of their foreign trade patterns (3:26). The United States was quite active from 1830 through the 1850s (3:14); its share fell sharply after the Civil War but recovered rapidly at the turn of the century with purchases of tobacco, sultanas, opium, carpets, and other goods, and sales of cotton goods, petroleum, agricultural machinery, shoes, and other items.

But the two countries whose trade increased most rapidly were Italy and Germany. Turkey's annual imports from Italy rose from £T500,000 in 1878-80 to £T1,700,000 in 1899-1901 and £T3,700,000 in 1913, thanks mainly to a rapid expansion in cotton textiles, while exports to Italy were £T100,000, £T700,000, and £T900,000 respectively; as a result, in the years preceding the First World War, Italy occupied fifth place in Turkey's trade. Germany's rise was even more dramatic: according to the German records imports from Turkey rose from 2 million marks (£100,000) in 1880 to 10 million in 1890, 30 million in 1900, 67 million in 1910, and 74 million in 1913; exports rose equally fast, from 6 million to 34 million, again 34 million, 98 million, and 105 million respectively.[16] Both imports and

exports covered a wide range of goods. At the outbreak of the war Germany was Turkey's
third supplier and fourth market.

Table 2

Percentage Shares of Leading Countries in Turkey's Foreign Trade

	Imports			Exports		
	1878–80	1899–1901	1911–13	1878–80	1899–1901	1911–13
Britain	45	35	21	39	35	23
France	16	11	9	31	28	19
Austria	14	20	15	11	10	12
Russia	8	8	8	4	3	4
Italy	3	6	7	1	4	3
Belgium	0.5	3	4	0	1	3
Germany	0.3	3	11	0	4	6
United States	2	0.4	3	1	3	6
Total	89	86	78	87	88	76

Source: Aybar, pp. 18–27.

1. See, for example, MacGregor, 2:13.
2. "In the space of ten years however the current price of the merchandize specified
has so rapidly increased that the Russians do not actually pay two per cent, in many cases
not one, and in some not above one-half per cent for the different articles of their merchandize," instead of the 3 percent stipulated in the 1783 Treaty. The Porte proposed a
"New Tariff more adapted to the state of the times" but the Russians refused to consent to
any change as long as the Treaty lasted (Liston to Grenville, 29 June 1794, FO 78/15).
3. On this subject, see the study by Köymen.
4. Text in EHME, pp. 39–40, and correspondence in A and P 1845, vol. 6 p. 2; see also
an article by Issawi in the forthcoming O. L. Barkan Festschrift, edited by Robert Mantran.
5. Internal duties on produce transported overland were soon abolished, but an 8 percent duty continued to be levied on goods seaborne from one Turkish town to another--A and
P 1878, vol. 74, "Constantinople."
6. Gordon, p. 162.
7. Blaisdell, p. 158.
8. Ibid., pp. 159–73; being "alone among the Powers [to] refuse their assent" was an
embarrassing position for Britain (Memorandum 19 September, 1906, FO 371/144). Its opposition was due partly to its being Turkey's main supplier, partly to the fear that the extra
revenue would be used for "other objects, possibly disadvantageous to British trade, such,
for instance as the Baghdad Railway," and not for their ostensible purpose, reforms in
Macedonia. For Franco-Turkish negotiations, Thobie, pp. 47–53, 501–6.
9. Ottoman trade statistics are very unsatisfactory. The earliest published tables
refer to 1876 (given in Shaw, History, 2:122), and figures for previous years have been
taken from various consular reports. Moreover, even the published figures cover only goods
on which customs duty was paid, which means that a sizeable fraction of both imports and
exports was not recorded (Aybar, p. 13). For 1910 the value of unrecorded exports was estimated at £3,014,000 compared to recorded exports of £20,072,000 (A and P 1913, vol. 73,
"Constantinople"). In addition, there is much evidence that the recorded export figures
are undervalued. The quantitative estimates given in this study are therefore very rough.
10. EHI, p. 70, and EHME, pp. 363–64.
11. Aybar, pp. 47–50. Tea drinking seems to have been picked up from the Russians and
to have spread very fast in the last quarter of the nineteenth century, partly replacing
coffee. In the 1890s the government agricultural school at Halkali began growing tea, an
experiment described as "idiotic" since imports were cheaper and other needs, such as winter fodder, more urgent--see set of articles in RC, no. 285, 1910.
12. Aybar, pp. 45–46. Turkey's consumption of kerosene was put at 2,500,000 crates
(80 million litres) and that of Istanbul at 900,000; "almost the whole population uses
petroleum for lighting," even in Pera where the gas supplied was poor--RC no. 272, 1909.
American and Russian petroleum companies competed vigorously for the Turkish market but
Standard Oil won out--CC Smyrne, vols. 54–57, Trade Reports, and A and P 1914, vol. 95,
"Smyrna." Imports of iron in the mid 1890s averaged about 50,000 tons; Istanbul's consumption was put at 25,000 tons--RC 1898.
13. Izmir's imports of machinery in 1912 were put at £100,000 (A and P 1914, vol. 95,
"Smyrna") and imports of "machinery, carriages and boats" to Istanbul in 1910 was £909,000
(ibid., 1913, vol. 73, "Constantinople"); imports of sewing machines rose from 50 tons in

1905 to 157 in 1912. Imports of typewriters into Istanbul averaged 350–400 a year (RC
no. 279, 1910) and into Izmir 100–150 (A and P 1914, vol. 95, "Smyrna").
    14. Thanks to the analysis in Sönmez.
    15. For further information on the second quarter of the nineteenth century see
Ubicini, Lettres, 1:400–410, and Novichev, Istoriya, 3:96–102.
    16. Wiedenfeld, p. 382, and RC no. 172, 1901.

THE VALUE AND VOLUME OF TRADE

Attempts to estimate the quantum of Turkey's trade in the nineteenth century come up
against almost insuperable obstacles. No overall returns are available before 1876, and
the accuracy of the figures published in 1880–81 and subsequent years, remained very doubtful until the eve of the First World War. Moreover, comparison is made much more difficult
by the drastic changes in the Ottoman Empire's boundaries during that period, which sometimes renders it impossible to know exactly what area is being included. Finally, there
are no satisfactory price deflators.[1]

In the circumstances, perhaps the best way of giving a rough measure of the increase
in the value and volume of trade is a twofold approach. First, the available figures for
Istanbul, Salonica, and the leading ports in Anatolia can be combined and compared for
selected periods. Secondly, a rough check can be made by examining the trade of Turkey
with its three leading partners, Britain, France, and Austria. And, in the absence of Ottoman price indices, the British export and import price indices will be used as deflators
since the United Kingdom was, throughout the period, both the world's leading trader and
Turkey's main partner, and since the values in the tables are expressed in pounds sterling.

The results of the first approach are summarized in table 3. For the four main Anatolian ports, taking the early 1840s as a base, by the mid 1870s imports had risen by about
4.3 times and exports by 3.5 times, or at compound rates of about 5 and 4 percent per annum,
respectively. Between the mid 70s and the turn of the century exports rose slightly while
imports showed a decrease. From the turn of the century to the eve of the First World War,
imports rose by about 80 percent, or at an annual rate of 5 percent, and exports by 30 percent, or at 2.25 per annum. These figures tally closely enough with Quataert's estimate
that between 1876–80 and 1906–8, exports rose by about 45 percent, or at some 1.3 percent
per annum and that "the real gains in export values occurred in the post–1900 period, after
the increase of the 1875–1895 era had been lost in the sharp 1896–1900 downturn. In 1908,
the value of Anatolian agricultural products channeled through these four ports was approximately half again as much as in the late 1870's."[2]

The addition of the tentative estimates for Istanbul does not seriously change the
trend for the 1840–1900 period, suggesting an overall increase of 3.5 times in imports and
4 times in exports. Between 1900 and 1910–12, however, the two series diverge more widely,
because of the apparently greater growth in Istanbul's trade, and the total shows an increase of some 6.5 times in imports and 5.5 in exports over the whole period. Lastly, the
inclusion of Salonica, whose trade grew much more rapidly than did that of Anatolia or Istanbul, raises the overall growth still more, to some 7.5 times in imports and 6 times in
exports. This implies annual rates of growth of nearly 4 and 2.5 percent respectively.

The British export and import price indices given in the table show that there was no
significant change between the early 1840s and early 70s, and that the growth in current
prices represents a roughly equal real growth. In the last quarter of the century, however,
both price indices dropped by one-third, which implies that the stagnation in current values
masks an appreciable rise in real terms. Lastly, in the first dozen years of this century,
the indices rose by about 10 percent, which means that the growth shown in the tables

consisted almost entirely of a real increase in merchandise imported and exported.

Over the 1840-1900 period, the price indices fell by about one-third; this suggests that the real increase in imports may have been about sixfold and in exports 6.5 times. Over the whole period, from the 1840s to 1910-12, the drop in the indices was about a quarter, which suggests that the real growth in imports was about 9.5 times and in exports 7.5 times.

These results may be checked by examining the growth of British, French, and Austrian trade with Turkey. In 1840-43 French imports from the Ottoman Empire averaged 46.5 million francs, or £1,860,000, and exports 18.1 million, or £725,000; the United Kingdom's imports from Turkey were £1,205,000 and its exports £4,358,000;[3] and Austria's imports in 1841-43 were 13,591,000 florins, or £1,359,000, and its exports 8,022,000 florins, or £802,000.[4] Their combined totals therefore indicate that in 1840-43 Ottoman exports to the United Kingdom, France, and Austria amounted to £4,424,000 and imports from those countries to £5,885,000. On the not unreasonable assumption that the United Kingdom, Austria, and France accounted for three-quarters of Ottoman imports and exports,[5] the Empire's total exports were about £5,899,000 and its imports £7,845,000, figures that are not incompatible with those in the table.

In 1896-1900, according to the statistics of those three countries, British exports to the Ottoman Empire averaged £5,701,000 and imports £5,712,000; French exports averaged £1,887,000 and imports £4,080,000; and Austrian £2,431,000 and £1,526,000. Their combined imports were therefore £11,318,000 or 2.56 times the figure for the 1840s and exports £10,019,000 or 1.70 times.[6] Both figures (particularly that of exports) are distinctly lower than the various indices shown in the table, but this is to be expected in view of the fact that the area covered by the later figures was much smaller than that of the 1840-43 totals, which included Greece, Rumania, Bulgaria, Cyprus, and other territories lost between the two dates. Lastly, the estimated totals for Ottoman imports (£7,845,000) and exports (£5,899,000) for 1840 given above may be compared with estimates for 1872-77 and official figures for 1898-9--1900-1 and, 1910-11--1912-13, only the last of which are reliable.[7] The implied rise over the whole period of 4.6 times for imports and 3.3 times for exports is not unreasonable, compared with the other indices, in view of the territorial losses.[8]

In conclusion, a few words may be said about the period before 1840. Quantification, even the roughest, is impossible, but the tables on the trade of Izmir (3:14) indicate the general trends quite clearly. During the Revolutionary and Napoleonic wars, trade was disrupted, particularly that of France, which had been the Ottoman Empire's leading partner. In the first six years of peace, trade recovered rapidly, but the Greek War of Independence once more reduced it drastically, and it is doubtful whether the prerevolutionary level was regained until the 1830s.[9]

---

1. The only attempt at calculating price indices (for the period 1878-1913) is the study by Attila Sönmez; Quataert has also provided data on agricultural exports from 1876-1908.

2. Quataert, pp. 20-21.

3. CC Smyrne, vol. 50, "Notice sur le commerce de la France et de la Turquie" (see 3:25), and Bailey, p. 74.

4. Ausweise über den Handel von Oesterreiche . . . im Jahre 1841 (1842, 1843). The Austrian figures present a major difficulty. They cover only trade across the Austrian border, and it is pointed out that "Trade with Turkey is much more important than is shown here, because in great part it takes place by sea," mainly through Trieste. On the other hand, the figures include Moldavia and Wallachia which in 1871-75, the earliest years when they were shown separately, equalled the figures for all the other frontiers between Austro-Hungary and Turkey, including Serbia and Montenegro (K. K. Statistischen Central

Commission, <u>Ausweise über den auswartigen Handel Oesterreichs im Jahre 1875</u>). I have assumed that these two factors cancel out.

   5. In the first published Ottoman returns, for 1880-81 and 1881-82, combined British,
French, and Austrian imports to Turkey averaged 74.5 percent of the total and exports 77.4
percent--see table in A and P 1885, vol. 76, "Turkey."

   6. A and P 1902, vol. 110, "Constantinople."

   7. "Reports on Trade with Turkey, 1878-79" FO 78/3070 (3:24), and Eldem, p. 186,
converted at Ł=120 piastres, the rate commonly used by the British consuls.

   8. Eldem's index of exports at constant prices rises from 100 in 1885-86 to a peak of
170 in 1911-12, declining to 151 in 1913-14 because of territorial losses--Eldem, p. 183.

   9. In 1783, the French Ministry of Marine estimated the total trade of the Ottoman
Empire at 110 million francs (Ł4.4 million) of which France accounted for 60 million; these
totals were about equally divided between imports and exports (Masson, <u>XVIIIe siècle</u>, p.
416). A breakdown of French trade by ports for 1784, 1787, and 1789 shows that Morea,
Egypt, and North Africa accounted for 20 percent of the total (EHME, p. 36, Charles-Roux,
<u>Echelles</u>, pp. 194-96). Assuming that this proportion also held for the other European
countries, the trade of the area corresponding to the Ottoman Empire after 1830 would have
been about Ł3.5 million. In 1829 British exports and imports to Turkey amounted to
Ł1,826,000 (Bailey, p. 74) and French to 20.5 million francs or Ł800,000 (E. Levasseur,
<u>Histoire du Commerce de la France</u>, 2:151), a total of Ł2.6 million. Prices were about
equal in 1829 to what they had been before the Revolution--see Mitchell, pp. 468-71. See
also 3:11 for British trade.

Table 3

Value and Volume of Trade (Ł000)

	Early 1840's		1873-77		Around 1900		1910-12	
	Import	Export	Import	Export	Import	Export	Import	Export
Izmir	800	1,250	3,700	4,300	2,700	4,000	4,000	4,300
Trabzon	200	100	600	300	500	500	1,500	600
Samsun	150	150	400	300	500	700	1,000	1,700
Adana	40	60	500	600	400	700	700	900
Total	1,190	1,560	5,100	5,500	4,100	5,900	7,200	7,500
Index	100	100	430	350	340	380	610	480
Istanbul	(2,000)	(500)	(10,000)	(5,000)	7,400	2,800	13,500	4,300
Total	3,190	2,060	15,100	10,500	11,500	8,700	20,700	11,800
Index	100	100	470	510	360	420	650	570
Salonica	125	125	1,500	1,600	2,500	1,400	4,500	1,400
Grand Total	3,315	2,185	16,600	11,100	14,000	10,100	25,200	13,200
Index	100	100	500	510	420	460	760	600
Total Trade Ottoman Empire[a]	(7,845)	(5,899)	(22,356)	(16,402)	20,822	12,202	36,436	19,697
Index	100	100	280	280	270	210	460	330
Price Indexes[b]	120	111	126	114	84	73	92	83

Source: See Text and tables, 3:12-19.

[a]After this book had been sent to press, I received from Şevket Pamuk, of Ankara
University, some preliminary results of his research on the trade and balance of payments
of the Ottoman Empire in the nineteenth century. His figures, calculated from the returns
issued by the Empire's main trading partners, are quite close to the ones for the 1840s
and 1870s given in table 3. For later years, however, there are marked differences: while
the Empire's imports agree with those given in the Ottoman returns and shown above, the
figures on exports are much higher, suggesting that the Ottoman returns greatly undervalued
exports and overstated the deficit in the balance of trade.

[b]Averages of Imlah's British export and import price indexes (1880=100) for 1840-43,
1870-73, 1898-1901, 1910-12, from B. R. Mitchell, <u>Abstract of British Historical Statistics</u>
(Cambridge, 1962), pp. 331-32.

SELECTION 1.   RETURN OF SUGARS IMPORTED TO THE OTTOMAN DOMINIONS FROM FRANCE

(FO 78/16)

Consignment	1788	1789	1790	Quintals
Adrianople[a]	3,850	3,850	3,850	11,550
Albania[b]	46	46	46	138
Aleppo	2,245	1,575	1,110	4,930
Athens	70	70	70	210
Cavalla[c]	200	200	200	600
Constantinople	9,027	11,954	9,393	30,374
Egypt[d]	1,000	1,250	1,120	3,370
Morea	225	235	264	724
Salonica	1,842	2,215	1,201	4,255
Smyrna	6,770	6,383	9,340	22,493
Tripoli (Syria)	173	160	216	549
Total	25,448	27,938	26,810	80,196

[a]Via Enos and Rodosto.
[b]Via Carlali and Natolico.
[c]None in the years returned--estimated from previous average.
[d]None received at Alexandria in the year last mentioned which is computed
by average of the two immediately preceding.

Constantinople
31 December 1795   J. Spencer Smith

SELECTION 2.   BLACK SEA NAVIGATION AND TRADE

(Memorandum of 12 March 1803, FO 78/39)

    The number of Russian ships navigating to and from the Black Sea thro' the Channel of
Constantinople are calculated to be yearly on an avarage [sic]   120

Austrian ships   Do. . . .   40

Ragusean since permission has been granted them. . . .   6
in 1802

English. . . .   1

French. . . .   2

    Articles of import to Russia

Wine the growth of the archipelago and places adjacent, upon an
average, Vessels p. annum. . . .   60

Dry fruit of all sorts about. . . .   40
cargos do.

Oranges and Lemons about. . . .   10
Vessels of 50 to 60 tons do.

Drugs, of all sorts, namely Incense of the common and fine sort. . . .   3,000
Kintals do.

Cottons, seven hund. Bales
Kintals do.

Silk, three hund. Bales
_____ do.

Cotton yarn. . . .   500 do.

India Shawls, and India Stuffs about   550 pis.
    p. annum

Stripped Stuffs manufacture of Constple, and plain do. called Ghermessuts
Do. Do. called "alagias" [alaca] Common Barbary Shawls of the Common sort
for the Crimea. . . .   2,000 do.

Red Barbary Skull-Caps   4,000 do.

Articles of European Manufacture sent into
Russia through the Bosphorus
Vizt.

English Shalloons on an Av.	300 pis. p. annum
printed clothes. . . .	500 do.
Tin. . . .	5 cases

French Wines 1 Ship-load sent up this year
by a French Housse upon a Trial

Articles of Export from Russia

Corn. of this article 500 Ship-loads are asserted to have come down and proceeded to different parts of Christendom from the summer 1802 to this date. But this is known to be an extraord.y case. Upon an avarage in the common course of things there may come down every year 50 Cargos of Grain from the Russian Ports.

Butter Skins called "yedecks" [yedek] fifteen hundred being equal to. . . .	12,000	kint^{ls}	pr.an^{m}.
Tallow Do. 80 equal to	650	do.	do.
Tallow candles	200	do.	do.
Wool	2,500	do.	do.
Cavial, 100 Casks equal to	10,000	do.	do.
Dry-fish	2,500	do.	do.
Russian dressed leather called "Tellatyn"[telatin]	20,000	pieces	do.
Do. Do. raw	6,000	do.	do.
Rope and Cables	25,000	Kint.	do.
Tar	500	do.	do.
Sail-cloth called Revendick alias "Musuammaa" [muşamba]	2,500	pieces	do.
Furs	250	Bales, besides what comes overland	
Iron	40,000	Kint. p. annum	
Russian coarse Linnen	200	Bales	do.
Crimea coarse Carpets called Kieces, [keçe] & common cloaks called "yamcies" [yamçık]	6,000	Pieces	do.
Sugar superfine	250	Kint.	do. since the Peace there comes no more from that quarter

Articles exported in Greek or Turkish bottoms from the coast of Europe and Asia in the Black Sea destined for the Consumption of Constple, and which the Turkish Govert. does not allow to be sent elsewhere--
From Varna & Galatz

Honey. . . .	15,000	Kintals p. annum
Cheese. . . .	400,000	do. do.
Butter. . . .	20,000	do. do.
Tallow. . . .	20,000	do. do.
Beeswax. . . .	40	do. do.
Sticks for pipes called "Ghermessik"	10	Boats
Touch Wood. . . .	80	Kintals
Corn. . . .	250,000	Kilos
Barley. . . .	150,000	Kilos
Fowls. . . .	40	Boats p. annum

From Vona [Üngé], Yenissun [Ziresun], Trebizond and Sinop in Asia

Hazel nuts. . . . about 40 vessels load per annum from 500 to 1000 Kintals

Nardenk a sort of preserve composed of apples etc. used by the poor	100 Kintals p. annum
Trays, large and small	80,000 p. annum
Apples. . . .	20 vessels do. of about 1,000 Kintals
Beeswax from Anapa and Abaza	1,000 Kint. p. annum
Box wood. . . .	12,000 do. do.
Lamb skins, white and black	3,000 Pairs do.
Hemp. . . .	80,000 Kint. do.

Timber

The best and cheapest both for ship-building and other purposes comes from the coast of Asia, from <u>Samsoon</u> and <u>Sinope</u> and several other places down to Ackce-Hissar. At the two first places there are regular Dock yards belonging to the Sultan. The best markets therefore for the purchase of Timber are <u>Ineboly</u>, <u>Messet</u>, Facas Bartyn & Ackce Hissar. These places are frequented by Russian Ships, laden with Iron--an article much in demand on all that coast.

Timber also comes from Galatz in Romelia, particularly that quality that is fit for Masts. NB. The Fir of Asia is of a superior quality & cheaper than that which grows in Europe but it is brought down in less quantities, from the difficulty of floating rafts from the Asia coast against the Etesian winds, & current, both of wch. are favourable to the Transport of Timber from the Danube to the Bosphorus.

Altho Sinop be a large Town under the Discipline of a Governor and altho it be the actual Residence of the Russian Consul, its inhabitants are however known to be of so savage a disposition that the best informed persons are of opinion that the four above mentioned places should be preferred as Places of Resort.

The purchase of Timber will at all times be found more practicable and easy with the assistance of a Ferman from the Porte; but it may be effected without that aid by an understanding with the different Turkish Commanders, and by making regular Payments--and as the newly admitted foreign ships are to be exempted from Custom house visits, the Timber Trade (large spars and masts excepted) might be carried on independent of the Turkish Government.

SELECTION 3. EXTRACT OF A LETTER FROM THE LEVANT COMPANY TO ALEXANDER STRATON ESQ., AT CONSTANTINOPLE, DATED 6TH JULY 1802

(FO 78/37)

Sir,

On the 22nd Ultimo we had the honor to receive your Letter dated 17th May accompanied by Copies of the British, Russian and German Tariffs, and of a Letter from the Factory at Smirna to Consul Werry together with your answer to that Gentleman.

The Tariffe being a matter of the highest importance and materially affecting the welfare and prosperity of the Trade of this Country as put in competition with that of other Nations, it behoves us to guard against any innovation by which it can be affected and to take care that in any alteration to be made this Company be put on the same footing with the most favored Nation, and this grand Object we supposed had been obtained by the new formed Tariffe--for as we were not in possession of the Russian and German Tariffes we had had no opportunity of making a Comparison between those Tariffes and that now formed for the British Nation but having carefully compared them by means of the papers you have transmitted we have now to observe that the Russian Tariffe grants many advantages to that Nation over the British--for although on many Articles the Russian Tariffe is higher than the British the difference is on Articles which are all of small value or else such wherein the Russians are little interested as not coming within the extent of their Trade but which form the chief part of our Trade to Turkey--whereas on the principal Objects of our Imports from Turkey and of which a considerable part of the Trade of both Nations consists the Duties are much lower on the Russians than on the British Tariffe--and on these we conceive we have a just claim on the Porte and have a right to insist that the British Export Tariffe <u>from</u> Turkey should be the same as that of the Russians. We subject a list of the articles [omitted here] on which we feel ourselves particularly aggrieved and which we recommend to your serious consideration, and trust you will make them the subject of an application to the Porte claiming to have the Tariffes respecting them reduced to the Standard of the Russian, viz. Cotton, Wool, Silk, Goatswool, Madder Roots, Galls, Opium, Black Fruit, red

Fruit, Figs and Copper and those Articles which are to be charged <u>ad valorem</u> and which in the Russian Tariffe are to be rated at 2 p. Cent. but in the new British Tariffe at 3 p. Cent.

Signed by the Governor & Company of Merchants of England trading into the Levant Seas. . . .

BRITISH TRADE WITH TURKEY

Before the Revolution, France had accounted for a half to three-fifths of the Ottoman Empire's trade (3:25) and Britain for only a fifth to a quarter. The highest point reached was in 1792, with British imports of Ł291,000 and exports of Ł274,000 at <u>official</u> (i.e., 1696) values and perhaps one and a half times as much in real values.[1] In the next fifteen years, trade fell off sharply because of the wars with France and Turkey but began to pick up after 1808, and in 1812 imports amounted to Ł244,000 and exports to Ł311,000, at official values, and in 1818 at Ł369,000 and Ł807,000 respectively.[2] After that, trade rose rapidly and exports at <u>official</u> values (which were nearly 50 percent higher than real values) averaged Ł1,088,000 in 1825-27, and imports Ł875,000, in spite of the disruption caused by the Greek War of Independence. In 1840-43, official exports averaged Ł4,358,000 and imports Ł1,205,000, and in 1854-58 the <u>computed</u> <u>real</u> value of exports averaged Ł4,337,000 and that of imports Ł2,370,000, a high level partly explained by the Crimean War. The coverage of the figures also changed; the earlier figures include much of the trade of Greece, Egypt, Syria, Palestine, and Moldavia and Wallachia while the 1854-58 ones exclude them.[3]

By then Britain was, by far, Turkey's leading trade partner, supplying the bulk of its cotton textiles and taking many raw materials. Its share in Izmir's trade was a little more than a third (3:14) and it accounted for a greater proportion of the trade of Istanbul (3:15-17), Trabzon (3:20), and Salonica (3:13). Overall, Britain may have supplied as much as a half of the Ottoman Empire's imports and taken up to a third of its exports.

These high shares correspond to Britain's place in the world economy. By 1850, Britain accounted for about 40 percent of the world's industrial output and trade, and in such important items as cotton cloth, coal, iron, and steel its share was much higher.[4] Thereafter, its share in industrial output--and more slowly in trade--declined as other nations began to industrialize, although the absolute figures continued to rise, with cyclical interruptions, until 1914. The same process took place in British trade with Turkey, though the increase was checked by the shrinkage of the Ottoman Empire and the fall in world prices. In 1873-77, British exports to Turkey averaged Ł3,291,000 and imports Ł3,926,000.[5] In 1886-90, British exports averaged Ł6,474,000 and imports Ł4,443,000; in 1896-1900, the figures were Ł5,701,000 and Ł5,712,000; and in 1908-10 Ł7,978,000 and Ł5,320,000.[6]

But while British trade was thus rising, its share in Ottoman trade was steadily declining. In 1878, Britain accounted for 49 percent of Turkey's imports and 42 percent of its exports, but thereafter there was a steady decline, Britain's share in imports falling to 43 percent in 1890, 35 in 1900 and 19 in 1913, and in exports to 38,38 and 22 percent respectively.[7] One important reason was that British goods imported to Turkey paid a higher duty than those of their rivals. For duties were, in principle, paid on the prices fixed in the 1861 tariff (3:Introduction), and, in fact, prices fell considerably after that date. The British, whose negotiations for the revision of the 1861 treaty were not completed until 1914, paid 1861 duties on some 75 percent of their exports to Turkey, whereas the French paid such duties on only 60 percent, and the Germans, who renegotiated the treaty in 1891, paid at current, lower prices on all their goods.[8]

But there were also other reasons. Already in 1882, several British consuls tried to explain the greater success of Britain's competitors, especially Germany, Austria, and Italy. The consul at Istanbul stated that continental goods were "gradually edging those of England out of the market. In cotton yarns, grey goods and prints, Manchester still retains the bulk of the trade; but Switzerland and Italy now supply Turkey--red yarns to the exclusion of England, while French and Austrian print goods are gradually working their way into the market. Belgium and Germany push their woolens with success against Yorkshire fabrics; and in the items of hardware, cutlery and small wares, Germany, Austria and Italy have pretty well superseded Birmingham and Sheffield. Two causes have brought this result. One is that in this market cheapness is the first, and quality the second desideratum; the other is that continental manufacturers take much more pains to learn the market than British manufacturers care to bestow. . . . An English commercial traveller is never seen here. . . . In the item of paper Italy has the monopoly which once belonged to England. British glass ware is supplanted by those of Austria and Italy, and the silks of these countries have cut out those of both England and France."[9]

Twenty years later there was this comment from Salonica: "It is an undeniable fact that British trade in Macedonia is rapidly dwindling, nor are the reasons far to seek. Absence of direct relation between Great Britain and this province, high freights, dislike of British merchants to giving credit and increased energy on the part of foreign countries, especially Italy, are among them. Twenty years ago, British merchants being practically the sole importers could dictate their own terms to buyers in Macedonia. But now that Italy, Austria and Germany are so developing their commerce as to easily supply goods once supplied only by England, it is absurd of the former to cling to their ready-money system."[10] The advantages enjoyed by the Germans because of their favorable railway rates and shipping freights were repeatedly stressed.[11] So were those derived by the Germans and Austrians from the presence of their banks in Turkey.[12] No less important was the greater drive and adaptability of the Germans: "The success of the Germans in obtaining a footing in this market must be attributed mainly to the influx of German commission agents and small traders, and to the assiduity with which they set themselves to learn the languages of the country."[13]

The British, on the other hand, showed little flexibility. "It is a poor market. The people want the cheapest things they can buy. It is no use trying to sell them expensive things and telling them that they will last longer. They have not the money to buy expensive things and they do not want them to last forever."[14] Moreover they were handicapped by the fact that, after the dissolution of the Levant Company, "Armenians and Greeks, previously perhaps in the employ of British merchants here, obtained the agency of British firms and entered competition with their former employers"; the result was that the British importers "have almost entirely disappeared" and that the competition had led to a "deterioration of the goods offered."[15]

All of this is very reminiscent of the situation 250 years earlier, when an aggressive England supplanted a mature Venice as the chief supplier of the Levant, providing cheaper, low-quality goods imitating Venetian styles, using techniques adopted from Venice, and helped by cheaper transport and a supportive state.[16]

1. Mac Gregor, 2:66–73; for the ratio of real to official values of goods, see Phyllis Deane and W. A. Cole, _British Economic Growth, 1688–1959_ (London, 1962), p. 317.
2. Wood, pp. 179–95.
3. Bailey, p. 74; A and P 1859, vol. 28; British exports also include goods in transit to Iran (3:119).
4. E. A. G. Robinson, in _Economic Journal_, September 1954; H. Heaton, _The New Cambridge Modern History_, 10:36; E. J. Hobsbawm, _Industry and Empire_ (London, 1968), p. 110.

5. See 3:24.
6. A and P 1892, vol. 96, "Turkey"; 1906, vol. 128, "Constantinople"; and 1912–13,
vol. 100, "Constantinople"; all these figures are taken from British trade returns.
7. Aybar, pp. 18–27.
8. Kurmuş, pp. 264–65.
9. A and P 1883, vol. 74, "Constantinople."
10. A and P 1900, vol. 97, "Salonica"; see also A and P 1909, vol. 98, "Adana."
11. A and P 1906, vol. 128, "Constantinople."
12. A and P 1912–13, vol. 100, "Constantinople."
13. A and P 1901, vol. 85, "Constantinople." On the subject of commercial travelers,
two examples may be quoted from the journal of the British Chamber of Commerce in Istanbul:
"Though I have met no fewer than 43 German commercial travellers, I have not met one single
British-born representative of an English house in any inland city. In the larger seaports,
such as Constantinople, Salonica and Smyrna, as well as Athens, they are occasionally to be
met with. . . . The British manufacturer floods the country with expensively got-up cata-
logues printed in English with prices, dimensions, weights and measures drawn up in our absolutely unintelligible tables" (from the Birmingham Daily Post, 24 November 1908, quoted
in TJ December 1908). And in 1910, the Ottoman government granted 183 licenses for commercial travelors to foreigners: 89 to Austrians, 35 to Germans and 9 to British subjects--
ibid., March 1912. See also Townshend, pp. 174–75.
14. A and P 1908, vol. 116, "Constantinople."
15. Ibid. 1899, vol. 130, "Constantinople"; in 1847 MacFarlane was assured by "a competent city authority" that "no English house can compete with the sharp Greeks and Armenians established among us. . . . One respectable house after another has entirely given up
that branch of commerce within these last two or three years" (MacFarlane, Destiny 1:26).
16. Richard I. Rapp, "The Unmaking of the Mediterranean Trade Hegemony," JEH, September 1975.

SELECTION 4. AN EXPLANATION OF THE NEW TARIFF, 1806

A Statement serving to explain the New Tariff for the British Levant Trade, by which the
Ottoman Duties of Custom are to be henceforth regulated, 1806 (FO 78/49)

The Capitulations or Treaties between the Ottoman Government and the Powers of Christendom,
exact from the Subjects of the latter a Duty of three per Cent, never to be augmented, on
all merchandize entering into their Trade with the Dominions of the former.

In the Year 1794, a Tariff of Rates, never to be altered, was established on this
Principle for the British Trade with the Levant. Before six Years had elapsed, the Diminution in the Value of money and other Circumstances, had so much depreciated those Rates
below the Standard of three per Cent, that the British Government consented in Compliance
with the earnest Intreaties of the Porte, and in Conjunction with the other Christian Powers, to arrange a new Tariff. This was accordingly done; and it was signed the 1st of
July 1800. It was understood, as it had been stipulated, that this Tariff would secure
for the British Trade as favourable Rates as those obtained by any of the others.

The Merchants, however, after they had examined it, pointed out very clearly, that
they were placed by it, in a less favourable Situation than the trading Subjects of the
other Commercial Powers. Its Operation was accordingly suspended, and the British Minister
directed to remedy the Grievances; which were particularly stated in a Letter from the
Levant Company, containing a List of Articles on which they solicited more favourable Rates.

In the meantime, a Treaty was concluded between the French, and the Ottoman Governments, by an article of which the arrangements for their future commercial Intercourse
were indefinitely postponed. From that Period, or nearly from that Period, till the arrival of Mr. Arbuthnot, the Ottoman ministers had in vain attempted to engage the French
to frame a new Tariff; and, until this should be done, the application of the other Tariffs was withheld, and the Correction of the English delayed.

The Consent of the French Mission having at length removed this Obstacle, Mr. Arbuthnot entered on the arrangement of a new Tariff for British Commerce.

In doing so, he felt it to be his Duty to examine all the Tariffs for the Trade of
the different Nations with the Levant; not only that he might secure every fair advantage
to the British; but also with a View to prevent in future such Discussions as had tended
very much to confuse the Subject, and to produce ill humour between the Ottoman Government
and the successive Embassies.

After a very careful Examination of the several Tariffs, Mr. Arbuthnot thought himself authorized to demand those beneficial alterations which are specified in the annexed
List; and which were accordingly granted.

When this Specification is compared with the List sent by the Levant Company in their
Letter to Mr. Straton of July 6th 1802, already alluded to, it will appear that the New
Tariff is much more beneficial than it was then expected in England to be made.

A Detail of various Circumstances will be given in a separate and fuller Statement
for the Use of the Levant Company, which will tend to prove that the new British Tariff is

even more advantageous for our Commerce than it appears at the first View; that it is also much more favourable than would be either the Russian, the French, or the German; and that the latter do not in Fact secure as much for the Trade of those nations, as does ours for the British.

The new Arrangment of the different Exchanges, is one of the Arguments employed to establish the first Position. The Decrease in the intrinsic Worth of Turkish Money has enhanced the nominal Value of all European Coins, when expressed in the Coin of Turkey. The Rate of the English Pound Sterling remains nevertheless unaltered in the new Tariff, while the Monies of France and of Germany are valued much higher than before, in the Tariffs of those Nations. In that of the former, the Increase is 38 per Cent., of the latter, 46 per Cent.

That the _second_ Position is equally well-founded, will be admitted, on recollecting that the principal articles which compose the British Trade with the Levant are different from those in which the other Nations are interested; and on finding, as will appear in the Comparative Statement annexed, that those articles stand generally lower, and in no one Instance higher, than the same Articles in the other Tariffs.

The Truth of the _third_ Position which is of much less Importance than any of the others, can only be proved by a Train of Calculations, too tedious to be introduced here, but of which a general View will be given in the separate Statement already mentioned.

The Preface or Preamble to the New Tariff, it is hoped, will be found better than those of the preceding.

It expresses more clearly the voluntary Consent of the British Government, and of course affords a worse Precedent for another Amendment should the Value of Merchandize again fall, and a more forcible claim to recur to the old Tariff, should it, on the contrary rise.

It stipulates for the universal application of the Tariff throughout the Turkish Empire, whereas the former Tariffs were _literally_ confined to the Factory of Galata or Constantinople and were only extended to the other trading Ports in Consequence of the Energy of the Consuls or Merchants, and of the Forbearance of the Ottoman Customers. They had never been enforced either in Egypt or the Morea, to the great Disadvantage of the British Trade in those Provinces which has hitherto been there taxed according to the Caprice of the Revenue officers. Instead of 3 per Cent. stipulated in the Capitulations, 6 per Cent. has been frequently levied in Morea, and 11 per Cent. generally in Egypt.

But, the Chief Superiority of the Preamble probably consists in the distinct Assertion of our Right, as secured by the Capitulations, to trade throughout the Interior of the Ottoman Empire on the same Principles precisely as those which regulate our Exterior Trade; an Assertion of which the Evasion was attempted in the Preamble proposed by the Ottoman Ministers; a Right which they have for two Years endeavoured to abolish, and of which, at this moment, they affect to deny the Existence.

On the whole, Mr. Arbuthnot is of Opinion that there is not only Reason to be satisfied with the Work now concluded, but that also, from the Precautions which have been taken, there is just reason to be confident that a final End is put to those irritable Discussions which till the present had been so distressing to the Embassy.

SELECTION 5.   LISTON TO CASTLEREAGH, 27 DECEMBER 1818

FO 78/90

My Lord:

The Reis Effendi has repeatedly pressed me to consent to a renewal or at least a revisal and correction of the Tariff which regulates the duties paid upon the exportation and importation of merchandise by British Traders resident in the Turkish Dominions.

The proposal is grounded upon the fact that the present rates were fixed a number of years ago, on the principle that all goods were to pay Three in the Hundred on their value (as is stipulated in the Capitulations;) but that the price of the great majority of the articles has since been so much encreased, that the import now levied does not in general amount to two per cent, in many cases not to one and a half, and in a considerable number not to one per cent upon the actual value.

The Reis Effendi enforced his arguments in favour of what he termed a most reasonable request by stating that the Marquis de Riviere had consented to a renewal of the French Tariff with a considerable augmentation of the duties on almost all the articles it contained;--that his example had been followed by the Internuncio (the Baron de Sturmer) who had with a good grace signed a new Austrian Table of Rates containing all the alterations that had been required;--that the Prussian Minister had given his consent to a similar operation; and that this Government did not expect resistance from Great Britain, whom they considered as their best and surest friend.

I readily agreed to the fairness of the principles laid down by the Minister, and expressed my conviction that the British Government would not, when the case was properly stated to them, refuse their consent to such alterations in the existing Tariff as the change of the times may have rendered necessary, (concessions in which I hope your Lordship will not think I went too far) but that I could not take upon me to do any thing without previous consultation with the parties more immediately concerned, and without receiving express authority from my Superiors.

On taking the opinion of the British Merchants here and at Smyrna, I found among them a pretty general disinclination to making any change in the Tariff, if it could possibly be avoided. And in answer to the argument of the Reis Effendi taken from the example of other Nations, they observed that when we were induced, in the year 1805, to concur in the formation of a new Tariff, our consent to the augmentation of duties was given on the express condition that a similar alteration should immediately be enforced with regard to the French, but that the change had not taken place till within these few months, so that that nation had enjoyed a decided advantage over us for a number of years past, and it was fair we should have our turn.

I explained to them however my opinion that we could not long hold out against the importunity of the Porte, in a case where the demand, in a general point of view, was so well-founded; and I requested information respecting the more important points of the negotiation that must ensue on the subject, a part of which I have already received.

In the mean time, the Ottoman Ministry were hard pressed by the Chief Officers of the Customs, who farm that branch of the Revenue, in different Districts, and who make heavy complaints of the diminution of their income by reason of the inadequate duties paid by our trade; the Reis Effendi appears to have conceived an idea that my situation gave me sufficient power to effect the changes proposed, but that I was kept back by an unwarrantable combination among our Merchants, and a resolution was taken to try whether the progress of the affair could not be accelerated by an act of power on the part of this Government.

Two English Vessels having arrived with cargoes of Iron, upon which we have for some time past paid according to the Russian Tariff, which is extremely low, the Collector of the Customs (with the connivance, no doubt, of the members of the Administration) demanded a higher duty (in conformity to one of the new Tariffs) or otherwise three per cent _in kind_; and on the refusal of payment by the Consignee, prohibited the entry of the Iron at the Customhouse, and sequestered the portion of it that was landed.—I then made a positive demand that the cargoes should be admitted on paying the usual import, and gave the Reis Effendi to understand, that unless matters were allowed,—during the discussion of the question of an alteration in the Tariff,—to proceed upon the ancient footing, I could not venture to transmit any proposals on the subject to my superiors, as I was confident that, in such circumstances, they would not be listened to—The cargoes of Iron were, after some hesitation, allowed to be entered at the Customhouse on the usual terms.

The Reis Effendi then requested I would state in writing the reasons of my conduct on this occasion,—that he might be able to explain, to the satisfaction of the Divan, the real source of an opposition which in their eyes seemed as unfriendly as it was unexpected.

I did so in the enclosed note, and I shall have the honour of addressing your Lordship again on the subject as soon as I have received the information which I wish to collect.
· · ·

SELECTION 6.   MEMORANDUM OF FRENCH MERCHANTS IN IZMIR, 1831

CC Smyrne, vol. 43, 9 July 1831

· · · The Trade would be pleased if a single tariff were applied to all the European merchants established in the Levant. Our relations with France are so greatly reduced that it is indispensable for us to form connections with all the nations that send goods to Turkey or receive goods from this country. If we are to be subjected to a particular tariff, it should at least be on the level of the most favored nations for all merchandise, without distinction, for it is natural that a correspondent abroad should place his orders with those who can effect the greatest savings in the bills of lading; thus, for example, those looking for an agent to ship fruit from Smyrna will seek out a Russian rather than a Frenchman, since the former will charge them for a lower customs duty that the latter, and so on. . . .

It is essential that the Trade know exactly which articles are prohibited, for otherwise speculation is subject to unfortunate miscalculations and to substantial losses. The list of such articles should be appended to that of the Customs duties, or at least it should be formally declared that all non-tariffed goods are prohibited. . . .

The Customs Agents draw up _ilams_ to prove that such and such goods are required for local consumption and request the prohibition of shipping out (_extraction_) for a few months. The Porte, led into error, grants the requested _firmans_. Once the Customs Agents have the _firmans_ they come to some arrangement with the merchants who wish to ship out the articles, exacting a very large gift. The result is that, although the _firmans_ are always valid for only limited periods, the Customs Agents prolong them at will, or maintain them indefinitely, and by this means obtain secure gains, at the expense of the fiscal authorities. Or at any rate if they are sufficiently farsighted, after the expiration of the stated period they give something to the fiscal authorities and keep the greater part. An end could be put to this peculation if the Ambassador demanded from the Porte full knowledge of these _firmans_ and of their stipulated terms, passing on this knowledge to the Trade.

Should the Porte propose to give up its claims to the new duties known as <u>miri</u>, getting compensation from new tariff rates, this concession should extend not only to the European nations but also to its own subjects--in other words, these duties should be entirely abolished, with guarantees that no new duties would be levied under any other name. Failing such a formal promise, the Ottoman Government would soon impose on its subjects new duties, levied on internal trade. In such a case, European merchants would not be able to trade with the interior and would be reduced to that which can be done at secondhand-- as we know from experience. The levying of the <u>miri</u> has given rise to great abuses, for the collector of this duty demands that a permit be obtained from him for any purchases in the interior. He refuses such permits to Europeans, on the pretext that he cannot demand from them the <u>miri</u> duty, but this is untrue since until now he has made those Europeans who have received produce from the interior pay this duty. . . .

SELECTION 7. OTTOMAN DUTIES AND TAXES, 1837

Eyragues to Molé, 25 April 1837, CC Constantinople, vol. 87

. . . For a long time, as your Excellency knows, Turkey has been one of the most liberal countries in the world in commercial matters: no internal customs duties, no indirect taxes, no imposts hindering the circulation of goods, a simple duty of 3 percent on goods coming into the country or leaving it. Turkey was amply rewarded for this system by the abundance and cheapness of goods of all kinds.

But in spite of such a precious advantage the Turkish government, faced with increasing expenditure and obligations while its revenues were diminishing, gave up one day its liberal principles, borrowed from Europe its fiscal system, and entered the complicated path of indirect taxes and taxes on the exchange of goods at the time when that same Europe was beginning to understand the disastrous effects of the imposition of numerous restrictions on trade. But, blocked in these first attempts by his treaties with the European powers, the Sultan--unable to increase the import and export duty of 3 percent--evaded the treaties by imposing duties on the circulation of goods. Thus European goods pay various duties when they leave the hands of our merchants and Turkish products cannot be exported by our merchants until they have paid all the duties on internal trade to which they have been successively subjected.

Indeed soon, harassed by the complaints of the Frankish merchants and the legations, which claimed that the duties imposed on Turkish goods violated the Treaties, the Porte established monopolies on almost all the main products of its soil, in order to avoid discussions in which, according to circumstances, it was sometimes the loser. In setting up these monopolies and prohibitions the Porte based itself on the very letter of the Capitulations which state: exports of goods from Turkey will be permitted on payment of a duty of 3 percent, except for goods whose export is prohibited because they are necessary for the country's consumption.

Thus, in order to get out of the circle in which we thought we had confined it by our Capitulations, the Porte was led to impose duties which it calls duties on internal trade but which are in fact taxes on circulation, and then went further and prohibited the taking out of its main products in order to be free to grant the right to export under the conditions that suit it and according to the whim or needs of the moment. It follows from this state of affairs--and here we reach the heart of the matter--that the Frankish merchants (unable to submit, at least openly, to the payment of duties levied on Turkish goods, since these duties have been in principle contested, although until now with very little result) cannot buy the said goods at the place of production and are forced to acquire them through the intermediary of local merchants who pay these duties, an intervention which is exceedingly costly and full of inconvenience. The impossibility of doing their own business has put our merchants at such a disadvantage compared to the Rayah merchants that, should it continue, the whole export trade and soon the whole of trade would pass into the hands of their rivals. In the opinion of all the merchants, this is the most powerful cause of the decline of most European firms in the Levant, whose business is being taken over more and more by the Rayah merchants. . . .

After having carefully studied the complaints coming from all the ports [Echelles] and the requests of our trade, I realized with pleasure that for our merchants the main question was not so much the amount of the new duties as their equality and stability. For what our merchants are requesting is, as far as possible, the abolition of the monopolies and prohibitions that have diverted almost the whole export trade into the hands of a small number of favored Barataries;[*] being able to buy directly Ottoman products at the place of production; the freedom to sell our goods in all places in the Ottoman Empire; and not having to fear that their wisest and most carefully calculated speculations will be upset by the sudden imposition of a new tax or a new monopoly. In return for this, they would submit without difficulty to the new duties imposed in the last few years, which still leave exporters a large margin of profit. . . .

---

[*][Ottomans holding <u>berats</u>, or letters of protection, from the European consulates.]

[The Chargé d'Affaires therefore suggested continuing the 3 percent duty on exports. Europeans who wished to export goods would in addition pay the internal duties levied on such goods, but these duties would be defined and not changed without long advance notice. Such monopolies as would be retained would have to be genuine and general in their application.]

SELECTION 8. MEMORANDUM ON THE TARIFF, BY JOHN CARTWRIGHT, CONSUL GENERAL, CONSTANTINOPLE, 10 APRIL 1838

FO 78/335

It is not known when it was first agreed with the Porte to reduce to fixed rates the stipulated amount of duty to be paid by Foreign Merchants on Articles of Merchandize imported and exported by them. It is presumeable that long after the commencement of commercial intercourse with Turkey, the duty was levied on Foreign Merchants as it continued to be collected from the Rayah Subjects--by estimating the value of each parcel of goods as it arrived, according to the price of the merchandize at that time. The fluctuation in prices will have been inconsiderable before the Sultans began to adulterate their coin, but the former mode of settling for duties must have been attended with much inconvenience from the attempts of the Turkish Officers to overcharge merchandize. Of this practice frequent complaints were made, as the Capitulations show, in which no mention is made of a Tariff.
The value of the Turkish Piastre appears to have been in the year 1740 between three and four Shillings Sterling. Sultan Mustapha the father of the late Sultan Selim, reduced the Standard of his coin, so much that in the year 1770 the exchange with England was equal to about P8 per £ Sterling, or 2s. and 6d. Sterling per piastre. In 1795 it was P13⅓ and in 1799 at P15 3/4 per £ Sterling. It afterwards declined in consequence of the great amount of Bills drawn for the wants of the British Army engaged in the expedition to Egypt, after the departure of which it again advanced and has continued to rise with the successive depreciations in Turkish Currency--though it has seldom advanced to a comparative par with the intrinsic value of British Currency.
It may be supposed that the introduction of fixed rates of custom duty was previous to the adulteration of the Sultan's Coin, for the Tariff appears to have had formerly more of the character of a Treaty.
The first Tariff was most probably concluded with the intention of preventing further complaints of the exactions of the Custom House Officers and under the impression that the rates would be permanent, for no term was fixed for their duration. The advance in the nominal value of Merchandize, which was produced principally by depreciating the Currency, rendered renewals of the Tariff necessary, but the proposal to advance the rates always met with strong opposition from the merchants, who considered it an infringement of a Treaty. Finally in 1820 Sir Robert Liston advised the Porte to fix a term of years for the duration of the Tariff at the expiration of which the formation of new rates was to be effected. The rates of the Tariff of 1820 were regulated by Commissioners appointed for that purpose by the Porte and the Ambassador.
This change in the manner of reviewing the Tariff was attended with other innovations, in which the Turkish Government did not proceed with the good faith that was observed on former similar occasions. The preceding Tariffs contained merely the changes of rates which those in the value of merchandize had rendered necessary, and the Preambles to them were solely explanatory of the cause of the renewal.
Two clauses were then inserted in the new Tariff, one affecting the nature of the trade in Exports which British Merchants were authorized by the Capitulations to exercise and the other regarding the Interior trade concerning which a stipulation was made in Mr. Adair's Treaty of 1809.
In preceding Tariffs it was stated that the rates of duty were applicable to merchandize imported by British merchants "from their own and other countries," and on those exported by them "to their own and other countries."
In the project of the Preamble which was submitted in 1820 to Sir Robert Liston, then Ambassador, that passage was altered with regard to exports, the insertion of the words "and other Countries" being omitted. The Consul General suggested the apprehension that the omission indicated an intention to interfere with our right to the free exportation of Turkish produce to the Russian Ports of the Black Sea. The subsequent impediments by which that trade was molested and which were not removed entirely until after the publication of the Treaty of Adrianople served to justify the suspicion that had been entertained. Discussion on the subject ended by a compromize. It was understood that the passage should be altered to "which they shall export according to the Treaties."
The existing translation of the Tariff bears the following passage.
"Que d'après ce qui est marqué dans ce Tariff l'on payera exactement les droits de Douane sur les différens genres de marchandises et effets, que les negocians Anglais importeront dans les pays de l'Empire Ottoman de leurs propres pays et des pays d'autres puissances, et qu'ils en exporteront."
When the Firman for carrying into execution the Tariff was delivered to the Embassy it was found to contain the objectionable passage with regard to exports. The Firman was

not accepted, nor were Firmans sent to the Consuls, as it had been customary to do on such occasions.

The clause relative to the Interior trade is as follows:

"Que sur les marchandises, effets et denrées qui seront achetés dans un pays de l'Empire Ottoman et rendus [sic--vendus] dans un autre pays du même Empire on percevra les droits de Douane exactement sur le pied des Negocians sujets Rayas de la Sublime Porte, d'après les règlements du Commerce intérieur."

That article of the Tariff either related to the object of the note of the 5 July 1802 regarding the duties to be paid on Ottoman produce purchased in the Turkish provinces for resale in other parts of the Empire, or it is a distinct separate stipulation.

When the subject was under the consideration of Sir Robert Liston, that clause was regarded as affecting Ottoman produce solely, and the only objection then offered by the Consul General regarded the imposition on British Traders of the Raya rate of duty instead of that levied on Mussulmans.

The Turkish authorities appeared to consider the clause in the same light during several years after the conclusion of the Tariff. In a note from the Reis Effendi to Sir S. Canning dated in June 1827, the application of the duties of Internal Trade to Franks is supported by the plea that every independent Government has a right to tax the produce of its own soil.

During the absence of the Legations from Constantinople in the year 1828, many irregularities were introduced by the Turkish Fiscal Officers and in the year 1830 the pretension to subject Foreign Merchandize (even while it remained in the posession of the Frank Importer) to the duties of Interior trade was published in the "Instructions" addressed by the Porte to the Ihtissap Aga at Smyrna.

The pretension has constantly been resisted, but it is of late strongly persisted in and has occasionally, no doubt, been enforced upon small traders who have submitted to it to avoid the inconvenience of delay in waiting the result of official interference. These attempted innovations affect Frank traders in three points of great importance to them.

1st The application of the duties levied on the trade of the Interior to merchandize purchased in the interior of the Empire for Exportation.
2nd The application of those duties to Foreign merchandize sold to Ottoman subjects or purchased by Foreign Subjects.
3rd The application of them to the Foreign Importer when he removes Foreign Merchandize into the interior of the Empire for sale.

Upon these pretensions it may be observed: First, that there does not appear to be any doubt that the 6th Article of the Treaty of the Dardanelles relates to the Tariff concluded in the year 1805 and to the note of the 5 July 1802 respecting interior trade. The "Tariff of Customs" and the "Article relating to the internal Commerce" are evidently referred to as two distinct documents which it is stipulated "shall continue to be observed as they are at present regulated." The note of the 5 July 1802 announced a pretension of the Porte which the Treaty admitted and confirmed. The regulation announced in that note affects the trade in Ottoman produce purchased in one part of Turkey to be sold again in another part of the Empire. It is not applicable to Ottoman produce purchased in the interior to be carried to the sea ports for exportation to other countries.

In former discussions with the Porte it was asserted by the Reis Effendi that Foreign Merchants were not authorized to purchase merchandize in the Interior unless they payed the duties thereon which were levied on Rayas and moreover that they had not until lately resorted to the interior of the Empire for that purpose.

The practice of two Centuries and various articles of the Capitulations are in opposition to those assertions. The right to trade in the Interior on paying the single duty of 3 aspers in the hundred is clearly stated in the Tariff of 1805, which was signed by the Reis Effendi.

It may be admitted that the Porte possesses the means (as it has also been asserted) of evading the Stipulation by levying the duties on the growers of the produce, but it would be done by an exercise of power rather than of right and the experiment, which would generally be attended with much inconvenience, might also be dangerous if attempted in a district where the population is exclusively Mussulman.

It is difficult to reason on this subject with the officers of a Government that appears to attend so little to the means of extending the Agriculture of the Country. The Ottoman Agriculturists may finally learn how much they are interested in the preservation of Frank commercial privileges.

Secondly. The application of those duties to Foreign Merchants trading in the Interior with Foreign Merchandize does not appear to be authorized by any Stipulation to that effect, with the Foreign Legations, for the note of July 1802 clearly specifies the trade in Ottoman Produce.

No mention is made in the Tariff of 1805 of the "Article" relating to the trade of the Interior or of its object, for the Note of July 1802 had not then been confirmed by Treaty, and the Capitulations only were quoted. In 1820, it was, we may suppose, considered necessary to insert in the Tariff the distinction to be made between the Foreign trade to which the Rates were applicable and the Interior trade which was to be taxed according to the regulations for Interior Commerce. It has been already stated that the passage of the Preamble now alluded to was understood to relate to the trade described in the note of July 1802, but it must be added that the Porte has occasionally declared that a stipulation exists in the Tariff of 1820 by which merchandize of whatever country it is the produce shall, when "purchased and sold" in Turkey by Franks, be subject to the duties payable by Rayas according to the Regulations for Interior Commerce. The paragraph in question certainly does not specify so clearly "Ottoman produce" as it might have done, and its ambiguity would merit censure if the passage of the original Turkish document agreed with the declaration of the Porte respecting it.

The corresponding passage of the Firman which was issued for carrying into execution the Austrian Tariff of 1818 is of the same character: it states, "Che per i prodotti a [sic--e] merci che da qualsiasi parte di quest'Impere [sic--Impero] venissero comprati e si vendessero di nuovo nello stato Ottomano debban pagare la dogana a norma del stabilito relativamente al Commercio interno e come vien pagata dai Sudditi Ottomani."

A Commercial Firman which was procured four years ago for the use of an English Merchant of Aleppo contained two injunctions respecting the duties to be levied on his commercial dealings. One of them is strictly in the sense of the Note of July 1802 respecting Ottoman produce, and the other, with reference to foreign Merchandize, declares that it is inserted in the English Tariff, that English Merchants shall pay on Merchandize of whatever country it is the produce, which has been "bought and sold" by them in Turkey the same duties that are paid by Rayas according to the Regulations for Internal Commerce.

If the Clause in the Tariff is agreeable to that declaration, the Embassy was probably deceived by the translation, but as the Stipulation is not authorized by any Treaty, for the "Article relating to Interior Commerce" which had become a part of the Treaty of the Dardanelles, regards Ottoman produce only, and as the Tariff has a limited term of existence, that Stipulation will of course expire with it. The official Memorandum which was lately delivered to H.M.'s Embassy by the Porte (26 March 1838) represents a new pretension affecting Foreign Merchandize, the tendency of which is more oppressive than former regulations. After stating that Ottoman produce when it arrives at Constantinople and at other places where the Ihtissab duties are levied, if the Merchandize be not accompanied by Teskere's & bear not the Stamp (to show that those duties have already been paid) the Seller (Importer) whether he belong to the several Classes of Ottoman Merchants or be a Frank, shall pay thereon, according to the regulations for Interior Commerce, together with the Customs duty, the other duties of Ihtissab and Damgha (Stamp duty). The Memorandum then proceeds to state that those duties shall be levied on Merchandize the produce of the Foreign Countries of Europe, of Persia and of the Indies in the following manner.

If the Seller be not of the privileged Classes of Ottoman traders nor a Frank, he shall be made to pay the Ihtissap and Stamp duties, but if he belong to the privileged Classes of Ottoman traders or be a Frank, the Buyer shall then pay those duties, and if the Seller and Buyer be both Ottoman privileged Traders or Franks the Buyer shall pay the duties.

The Memorandum does not make any distinction between Ottoman produce arriving at Constantinople & for exportation and that which may be brought for sale. With regard to Foreign Merchandize there is no distinction made between the goods which are sold for the consumption of the Country and those which are purchased for exportation to other Countries.

Thus a Persian trader at Constantinople having purchased British Manufactures from the British Importer of them might be called upon immediately to pay the duties of Ihtissap and Damgha which have hitherto been levied on the Raya retailers and occasionally no doubt on Frank Shopkeepers.

On sending the Manufactures forward to Persia he would be required to pay the Export Duty. The British purchaser of Persian silk or other products of that Country from the Persian Importer would in like manner be called upon to pay the same duties as well as the export duty in Shipping it off for England. Hitherto the export duty only has been claimed, the payment of which, there is reason to suspect, has occasionally been evaded by the purchaser contracting with the Persian Seller, that the latter should ship it for England in his own name. Having succeeded to impose on the Export trade of Ottoman produce the duties of Interior trade, the Porte now attempted to apply them to Foreign Merchandize. Russian Produce imported from the ports of the Black Sea would be liable to the same duties.

The preceding observations refer chiefly to Foreign Merchandize when purchased from the Importers by foreign Traders, and it must be admitted that the latter have of late years (since 1809) paid a second Frank rate of Custom duty when they have removed it from one place to another part of the Empire. No other duty was formerly paid (prior to 1809). Anciently that of Customs was not known to be paid, but whether it was evaded by the seller procuring a Teskere for it in his own name or whether the merchandize itself, being a foreign production, was considered not to be liable to a second duty so long as it remained in the possession of a Frank, cannot now be positively stated. Foreign Merchandize is not mentioned in the note of July 1802.

The Porte will with difficulty abandon the right to levy a second duty when the Foreign Merchandize had become the property of her own Subjects.

According to the Rules of the "Memorandum" the British Seller at Constantinople would have to pay on Ottoman Produce the duties of Interior Commerce as follows:

Custom	5 per cent
Damgha	
1 in 40 or	$2\frac{1}{2}$ per cent
Ihtissab	uncertain

Those duties would not be claimed from him if he produced Teskeres etc. proving the payment of them at the place of purchase, but as he cannot now purchase produce in the Interior in his quality of a Frank unless he pays the interior duties, it follows that they must be paid by him whether he introduces the Merchandize to a Sea Port for sale or for exportation. When he exports it he pays the additional export duty of 3 per cent.

The <u>British Purchaser</u> of <u>Foreign</u> produce at Constantinople would pay thereon

| Damgha Duty | $2\frac{1}{2}$ per cent |
| Ihtissab | uncertain |

and the export duty 3 per cent on exporting it to Foreign Countries, the Import duty having been previously paid by the Importer (or Seller).

In the commercial Firman before alluded to, the duties of Interior trade are declared to be payable on Foreign Merchandize which the English Merchants have bought in Turkey and have sold in Turkey. The "Memorandum" requires that they shall be paid when the merchandize is purchased in Turkey thereby exacting the duties whether the Merchandize be bought for exportation or to be sold again in Turkey.

<u>Thirdly</u>. The pretension to levy a second duty on Foreign Merchandize when the Foreign Importer removes it into the interior of the Empire for sale is so contrary to Stipulation and custom that the proposal creates surprize. It would be destruction of the only means that now remain to guard British manufactures against the imposition of duties that might be so advanced as to amount to a prohibition.

The preceding Statement will serve to show the various pretensions that have been advanced by the Porte respecting the duties to be levied on Foreign Traders since the conclusion of the Tariff of 1820, many of which are generally submitted to and other are enforced on small Traders, who compromise with the Custom House officers to avoid the inconvenience of the arrest of their Merchandize until official assistance can be procured.

The interior duties which it was pretended were applicable to Foreign Merchandize when it was carried by the Purchasers into the Interior of the Country for sale are now levied upon Merchandize purchased by Foreign Shopkeepers for sale in the City and Suburbs. Those duties are strictly enforced on purchases made of <u>Ottoman</u> produce for exportation and will no doubt soon be claimed on <u>Foreign</u> Merchandize purchased for exportation. The Porte ought to feel that if the Capitulations are no longer to have authority, a new Treaty is necessary, whatever stipulations may be made, whether in the form of a convention or of a Tariff, the Conduct of the Porte in the negociation of the Tariff of 1820 and subsequent proceedings points out the necessity of **rigidly enforcing a due observance of them and of not permitting** the slightest infraction.

SELECTION 9.   REPORT BY JOHN CARTWRIGHT, CONSUL GENERAL, CONSTANTINOPLE, 26 SEPTEMBER 1838

FO 78/335

In his report of the 29 April 1835 the Consul General represented the infractions made by the Porte in the privileges granted by the Capitulations to British subjects trading in Turkey by levying extraordinary duties generally on Articles of Turkish produce purchased by them for exportation, and imposing restrictions on the purchase of others.

These innovations commenced partially, soon after the conclusion of the Tariff in the year 1820, but, with the exception of the article of Raw Silk, the Turkish authorities did not oppress the trade in produce of the country by heavy exactions until after the downfall of the Janissaries in 1826.

In 1827, the Porte first attempted to justify the application of the duties of interior trade to the purchase of produce for exportation. In the year 1828 advanced rates of duty were levied generally on articles of produce, the purchase of which in the interior of the country was subjected to new restrictions. It was then that the practice commenced of granting Teskerehs or <u>Permits</u> for the purchase of produce in the interior. They were always issued in the name of Ottoman subjects so that the British merchant who was possessor of a Teskereh could not purchase in his own name.

In 1829 and 1830 the obnoxious system was generally enforced under established regulations. New duties were also then levied on the sale in retail of British imported articles and it was attempted occasionally with more or less success to apply them to Foreign goods sold in Shops belonging to foreign subjects.

The foreign merchants were alarmed by these measures and representations were made to the several Legations at the Porte by the merchants at the outports and the Capital.

A feeling of Consideration for the peculiar situation of the Porte at that momentous period appears hoever to have been entertained by the Legations and the merchants.

The amount of indemnities due from the Porte to Russia appeared to render necessary a resort to extraordinary measures for procuring the means of satisfying her obligations.

The merchants were willing to acknowledge that the long established rate of 3 per cent for duty on foreign Trade, which is a reduction from the ancient rate of 5 per cent, was less than the Trade might support, and considerably below the Rate of duty levied on British imports in other foreign countries.

The British merchants of Smyrna by their memorial in 1831 appeared to acknowledge the necessity of making a compromise with the Porte, by proposing advanced rates of duty, and the project was afterwards under the consideration of those of this city.

As it was stated in the Consul General's former Report, the attention of the merchants was withdrawn from the subject by the conflagration of Pera, and the subsequent revolt of the Pasha of Egypt. The approaching dissolution of the term of the Tariff appeared also likely to afford a good opportunity for claiming the removal of the obnoxious restrictions.

In the meantime the new duties have increased in amount and there is too much reason to apprehend that the subordinate officers have with impunity levied more even than the exorbitant rates fixed by the superior authorities. Such a state of things has become intolerable and a remedy to the Evil is loudly called for. That the necessity of it is also felt by the Porte is apparent in the declaration made by the Turkish commissioners for settling the new Tariff of duties that they cannot proceed in the work with regard to exports without a previous understanding respecting the amount of duty to be levied.

The annexed Table A [not included here] represents the commercial grievances of which the British merchants consider that they now have the right to complain.

The Table B will serve to show the progress which has been made in the advance of duties since the commencement of those unauthorised exactions which have often been increased without any previous notice being given to the merchants, so that the British exporter has had to pay an amount of duty on which he had not Calculated when he made his purchase of produce. This has been occasionally a serious inconvenience and the necessity of permanently fixing the rates of duty is strongly felt.

Table B

Rates of Duty Levied on the Purchase and Exportation of Turkish Produce

Articles	Amount of duties levied at the dates hereunder specified	
Raw Silk of Broussa	In 1824 the internal and export duties paid by the British exporter amounted to 4 7/8 per cent	In 1838 to 20 1/3 per cent
Angora Goats' wool	In 1830 the above duties amounted to 5 1/4 per cent	In 1838 to 21 1/2 per cent
Sheeps wool	In the Tariff of 1820 a conditional restriction on the exportation of wool and the payment of internal duty were admitted which with the export duty amounted to about 6 per cent at that time. No more than the rate of the Tariff was levied until the year 1827	In 1838 the duties amount to 13 per cent
Valonea	In the year 1820 there were no internal duties levied on this article. The British purchaser only paid the Rate of the duty of the Tariff--3 per cent	In 1837 the charge of 55 per cent is admitted by the Customer to have been levied but there is reason for believing that the exactions were still higher
All the remaining articles of produce	Ought to be charged at the rate of the Tariff 3 per cent	The average of the Rates of duties levied in 1838 may be considered to be 15 per cent
Raisins and figs dried	The right of exporting these articles being restricted by the Capitulations to two cargoes, the payment of internal duties has not been objected to.	
Grain, Olive oil and Copper	The exportation of these articles has always been considered as prohibited. Permission to export oil has been procured by the payment of exorbitant duties equal to 33 per cent on the cost. They are not rated in the Tariff of 1820.	

N.B. As some of the internal duties are not rated by <u>centage</u> but by fixed sums on the weight of the merchandize, and as the prices of produce vary, the <u>centage</u> amount of duties is of course affected thereby.

SELECTION 10. THE EFFECT OF THE 1838 COMMERCIAL CONVENTION

A Report drawn up by order of His Excellency Visct. Ponsonby, by Her Majesty's Consul at
Smirna, as to the working of the Commercial Convention of the 16th August 1838, within the
District of this Consulate, and transmitted to His Lordship, for the information of Her
Majesty's Government (1840, FO 195/177)

It is required to be stated, whether the Treaty has been completely carried into execu-
tion. And, if not, in what respects it is not executed at present--
The Information required on these points, will best be given under the four following
Heads, viz.
    1. As to the abolition of Monopolies of Turkish Produce
    2. As to the new internal Duties on Turkish Produce
    3. As to the New internal Duty on Goods imported
    4. As to the application of the Stipulations of the Treaty to Ottoman Subjects

1. As to the abolition of Monopolies of Turkish Produce--
    According to the most accurate Information that it has been possible for the Under-
signed to obtain on this point, all Monopolies of Turkish Produce are entirely abolished,
with the Solitary exception of that of Gum Mastick produced in the Island of Scio. Deputies from the various Mastick Villages have recently proceeded to Constple, for the purpose
of remonstrating against the continuance of this Monopoly, but the effect which these representations to the Porte, on this Subject, have produced is not yet known.
    Teskereas [permits] conferring the privilege of pre-emption are no longer issued by
the Local Governors, but the Cultivators of the Soil, are now at liberty to sell the produce of their labour at the highest price that they can obtain for it.
    No agent of any British Subject has met with the least obstruction in purchasing Pro-
duce directly from the Growers in the Interior of the Country, nor in transporting it from
thence to the places of Shipment.
    As a proof how much the Agricultural population are benefited by this change, while
the Exporters arenot prejudiced thereby, it may be Stated, that the proprietors of Valonea
are now receiving for it, from p. 20 to p.40 p. Kintal (equal to 3s/4d to 1s/8d p. Cwt.)
which previous to the operation of the Treaty, they were forced to Sell to the privileged
Holders of Teskereas from p.7 to p.10 p. Kintal (1s/1d to 1s/8d p. Cwt.) at the same time
the price of the Article in this Market has not since varied. Again, Sheepswool which
during the existence of Monopolies, the Owners of Flocks were compelled to Sell from p.80
to p.90 p. Kintal (13s 4d to 18s/- p. Cwt.) to the Monopolists, brought immediately after
the abolition p.170 to p.180 p. Kintal (28s/3d to 29s/11d p. Cwt.) in consequence of competition among the purchasers, caused by the free Trade in the Article.
    Such facts are most conclusive as to the benefit which the operation of the Treaty has
already conferred on the Agricultural Classes.

2. As to the new internal Duty on Turkish Produce--
    So far as British Subjects are concerned, the Treaty has been completely carried into
execution in this respect. No Duty has been levied in the Interior of the Country on Produce purchased for their Account, tho' [attempts] have been made to obtain the payment of
it, at some places.
    Such pretensions have however been invariably abandoned, on remonstrances being made
against them, by the Undersigned to the Local Authorities.
    On the Arrival at this place of all produce, bought on British Account in the Interior,
no other Duty than that of 9 p.ct. according to the rates established by the Tariffe, has
been levied thereon.
    The Subjects of those Powers which have not concluded Similar Treaties are still li-
able to the payment of the old internal Duties on Produce purchased by them.

3. As to the new internal Duty on Goods imported--
    The only Articles of Import, on which any extra internal Duties are levied, after the
payment of that of 2 p. ct. on their Sale, are Coffee (at some of the places of its consumption in the Interior) and British white Cotton Goods, after they are printed here.
    The only Complaint that has been made to the Undersigned, by a British Subject upon
the former Abuse was brought Some Months ago, against the Pacha of Kutayah, who insisted
on maintaining a Monopoly of this Article in favor of the Tahmis [coffee roasting] (the
privileged and exclusive Seller of ground Coffee) in his District, but the Undersigned
having represented the Case to His Excellency The Ambassador, a Vizerial letter was procured, enjoining the Pacha to desist from so doing, and the Sale of Coffee has since been
free, in that Quarter.
    At Caïssar [Kaisari], the Article is monopolized by the Mouhassil [tax collector] who
compels the Receivers of it to Sell it to him at p.9½ p. oke, and he sells it at p.13.
    This Circumstance having lately been represented to the Undersigned by Several Otto-
man Subjects residing here, who trade with Caïssar, he has submitted the Case to the Consideration of Her Majesty's Ambassador, and it is to be hoped that the Porte will take the
necessary Measures to put a Stop to this abuse of power, which tends greatly to check the
Consumption of Coffee in that District, which is very considerable, and susceptible of increase.

The Duty still levied on British Cotton Goods (imported in the Grey) after they are printed here, amounts to 7½ p.ct. on the value, the consequence is, that the Sales of that description of Goods which were formerly very considerable, have entirely ceased, as Cotton Cloths of the same quality, printed in Switzerland, to imitate the Turkish Work, are imported, and sold freely, without any extra duty being levied thereon.

A Representation has been made on this Subject by the Undersigned to Her Majesty's Ambassador, and it is to be hoped that this Grievance will be redressed. It is in the opinion of the Undersigned an indirect infraction of the Treaty, and the plea Set up by the Turkish Authorities in Support of the exaction of the Duty, Vizt, "that the nature of the Goods is changed by the process of printing," is he conceives totally inadmissable.

An attempt has lately been made by the Appaltador [tax farmer] of Snuff at Magnesia, in virtue of a Firman in his favor of an old date, to prevent the free Sale by an Ionian Subject of Tobacco imported from Europe, but on the representation of the Undersigned to the Pacha of that place, this Obstacle has been removed.

All other Goods imported and Sold by British Subjects as well as by the Subjects of other Powers who have concluded similar Treaties, are freely circulated in the Interior, without being charged with any extra Duties.

On all Goods imported by the Subjects of Powers which have not concluded Similar Treaties, all the old Duties are levied on the transmission thereof into the Interior.

4. As to the Application of the Stipulations of the Treaty, to Ottoman Subjects--

This Stipulation which is contained in the 6th Article of the Commercial Convention, has not yet been carried into execution, Ottoman Subjects of every description, being still chargeable, with all the old Internal Duties, both on Imports and Exports.

The Porte does not derive any advantage whatever from this neglect to comply with its engagements in this respect, for altho' the old rates (a comparative Statement of these duties is annexed) are on most Articles higher than those fixed by the English Tariffe, Turkish Subjects evade the payment of the former, by passing their Goods, which are liable to the higher Duties, in the Names of Subjects of those powers which have concluded treaties similar to ours, and enter in their own Names only, those Goods on which the Duties are lower than the rates of the new Tariffe. Thus the Turkish Revenue is defrauded, and in all Cases the lowest duties are paid by Ottoman Subjects, who are, in a manner, compelled to resort to a demoralizing Subterfuge, in order to maintain an equal footing with their Neighbours and Rivals in Trade.

This Subject merits the Serious attention of the Turkish Government, and has been submitted by the Undersigned to the Consideration of Her Majesty's Ambassador.

The Custom House Authorities put forward the plausible pretext, for not carrying this Provision of the Treaty into effect, of the want of a Firman authorizing them to do so, but there is reason to believe, that their resistance to the Measure, arises from an interested motive.

They now exact from Ottoman Subjects 10 p.ct. on the Amount of all Duties paid by them (which is a perquisite of their own) while all the efforts to obtain the same from Europeans have been fruitless. They apprehend the loss of this perquisite, if the Treaty were made applicable to Turkish Subjects, and are therefore opposed to its execution in this respect.

In concluding this Subject, the Undersigned has to state, that the Treaty has not been carriedinto execution at all at Samos.

The Prince of that Island causes a Duty of 6 p.ct. ad Valorem, to be levied on all Goods imported, and the like Amount on all Goods exported.

As by this Arrangement less is paid, in the aggregate, by British Subjects, than would be levied, if the Treaty were in force, and no complaints have made to the Vice Consul on the subject, he has not moved in the matter, but the Undersigned has represented it to Her Majesty's Ambassador, and awaits His Excellency's Instructions as to the conduct to be adopted by the Vice Consul at Samos on the occasion.

It is only within the last two Months, that the free Exportation of Oil from Aivali, and that Vicinity, has been permitted, by the Authorities at that place.

It is required to be stated, 2nd. whether the operation of the Treaty has been favorable to British Trade--And if not, In what respects it has been unfavorable.

Altho' it is stated in the declaration Signed by the British and Turkish plenipotentiaries, on exchanging the Ratification of the Convention, that it should begin to have effect on the 1st March 1839--Hussein Bey who was the Governor of Smirna at that Period (a most venal public Functionary and the most rapacious Extortioner by whom it was ever ruled), foreseeing that his emoluments would be greatly diminished, so soon as the Treaty should come into operation, and backed by the influence of his Father, Tahyr Pacha, the Grand Customer at Constple, who was equally opposed to it, refused to act upon it, and thereby caused great detriment to British Trade, as the numerous Protests made at the time against his Conduct fully attest.

At length on the 4th July 1839, a Firman ordering the Local Authorities to carry the Treaty into execution, was received at Smirna, which Hussein Bey did not dare openly to disobey, but he still endeavoured underhand to obstruct as much as possible its operation, and resorted to all kinds of pretexts and Subterfuges, to evade its provisions, in order

to continue the System of Spoliation, by which he had enriched himself, and this Conduct
did not cease until he was dismissed from his Office, in November last, to the great Joy
of the population of Smirna, over whom he had been permitted to tyranize for the second
time for Nine Months.

From the receipt of this Firman, Trade which had for a long time previously been extremely depressed, in consequence of the oppressive and arbitrary exactions of Hussein Bey,
immediately began to revive, in a most extraordinary manner, and in the space of Nine
Months, vizt., from the commencement of Sept. 1839, to the end of May in this Year, an increase, varying from 30 to 40 p.ct., and amounting in some instances to 60 p.ct., in the
Sales of Cotton Goods of British Manufacture (by far the most important branch of the Import Trade from Great Britain) compared with the Sales of the Same description of Goods
effected during the corresponding Periods of the two previous Years, took place.

This Assertion is not lightly hazarded, but is founded in Statements that have been
furnished to the Undersigned by several of the principal British Merchants established at
this place, who deal in those Articles, and being extracted from their Books, its correctness may be fully relied on.

The Sales of Iron made by one English House, during the above mentioned Period, exceeded by 40 p.ct., those effected by it during the corresponding Months of 1838--1839.

The Consumption of Coffee has likewise increased very considerably, but it being imported chiefly by Foreigners, the Undersigned has not been able to ascertain with the Same
degree of accuracy, the extent of the improvement, as he has in British Manufactures, but
according to the concurrent Statements of several Merchants, who are well informed on the
Subject, it may safely be estimated at 40 p.ct. A proof is thereby offered that the Condition of lower Class of the population has already been greatly ameliorated, since they
can now afford to indulge in the use of an Article of luxury, while of late years, they
have only been able to supply themselves scantily with the necessaries of Life.

This sudden and beneficial Improvement in the Import Trade, is mainly to be attributed
to the Substitution, by the Treaty, of a fixed internal Duty of 2 p.ct. in lieu of all the
former uncertain, onerous and capricious Imports, as well as the cessation of the number-
less exactions, harassing formalities, and petty vexations, to which Traders with the Interior, and their Goods were previously subjected.

There is not the least doubt but that the demand for British Manufactures, and produce
in general will go on increasing, and their present consumption be at least doubled, when
sufficient time shall have elapsed, to allow the effects of the abolition of monopolies to
be fully felt by the Agricultural population, for the affluence they will acquire by the
operation of this salutary increase will enable them not only to supply their wants more
extensively, but to indulge in Superfluities, and it is then only, that the full benefit
which British Trade will derive from the Treaty will be made apparent.

It having now been shewn in what respects the operation of the Treaty has been favorable to British Trade, it may confidently and emphatically be asserted, that in no respect
has it been unfavorable thereto.

It is required to be stated 3rd--How the Treaty has operated on the Trade of the Subjects of other Powers which have concluded Similar Treaties, and, Its effects on the Trade
of the Subjects of those Powers, which have not made Similar Treaties.

With respect to the Import Trade, the Subjects of those Powers, which have concluded
Similar Treaties, have participated equally with British Subjects in the benefits that have
been derived from the existence of the Convention of 16th Augt. 1838. Their Trade having
increased in the Same Ratio as our own, and the Subjects of those Powers, which have not
made Similar Treaties have been and are forced, to obtain the protection of that Treaty,
by making use of the Subjects of those Powers which have, for unless they had resorted to
this Subterfuge, they could not have continued to carry on their Import Trade.

In the Export Trade, British Subjects enjoy no greater advantages, than the Subjects
of other Powers which have made Similar Treaties, but the Subjects of Russia (which is now
the only Power having Commercial Relations with Turkey, that has not concluded a Similar
Treaty) pay from 1½ to 2 p.ct. less Duty on the Exportation of Produce than British Subjects. But this difference in favor of the former, is not a consequence of the Convention
of 1838.

It arises from this fortuitous circumstance, that the old Russian Tariffe not having
yet expired, is still in force.

An erroneous impression has been entertained, that by the Convention of 1838, British
Subjects have been placed on a less favorable footing, with regard to the Duties payable by
them on Goods exported, than Russian Subjects.

The fallacy of this notion will be obvious, when it is considered, that the Term of
the former British Tariffe, calculated on an old and low valuation, having expired while
the Russian has not, an advantage must be enjoyed by the Russian subjects until their
Tariffe expire and be reformed, but it will then necessarily cease, as it is to be presumed, that the rates of any new Russian Tariffe, will be fixed on the same basis, as those
lately concluded between other Powers and the Porte.

It is required to be stated, 4th, what advantage the working of the Treaty had produced
for British Subjects, compared with the Subjects of any Foreign Power.

All the Information that can be given on this Subject, is comprised under the three preceding Heads. The Undersigned therefore begs leave to refer thereto for the same.

In concluding this Report, the Undersigned deems it expedient to add some information, and to offer some general Remarks, on a few matters connected with the Subject in hand.

With reference to the non-execution of the Treaty, at places not within the District of this Consulate, it may be stated, that Silk is not allowed to be sent freely by <u>land</u> from Brussa to Smirna.

British Merchants residing here, have ordered purchases of this Article, to be made on their Account, but when their Agents attempted to send it by <u>Land</u> to this Port, for Shipment to Europe, the obstacles that were encountered, on the part of the Authorities at Brussa proved unsurmountable, and they consequently were obliged to abandon their purpose.

Ottoman Subjects desirous of doing the same thing, have been openly obstructed, but the greatest facilities are afforded them, when Silk purchased by them is sent to Constple. As the Duty payable by them on this Article is only p.10 p. oke, while that fixed by the new Tariffe is p. 18, all the Silk sent to <u>Constple</u> is passed in the Names of Ottoman Subjects at the Custom House.

Thus by Obstruction on the one hand, and encouragement on the other, the object which Tahyr Bey, the Grand Customer has always had in view, for some Secret purposes of his own, of confining the Trade in Silk to Constple, and which he failed to accomplish by negociation, is attained, and the Freedom of Trade proclaimed by the Treaty, is in this instance destroyed.

Her Majesty's Consul at Brussa will no doubt, in his Report, have thrown Some light on this Subject, and it is to be hoped that the free transmission of Silk by <u>land</u> to Smirna, will not much longer be impeded.

The Undersigned has been credibly informed, that Hassan Pacha, the Governor of Satalia, acting in concert with the Mouhassil of that place, exacts a Duty of p.1 p. oke on Coffee. A Turkish Trader with this place named Hagi Amer. who ventured to remonstrate against this arbitrary Impost, was bastinadoed by order of the Pacha, and compelled to pay it. The Pacha will not allow Indigo to be sold to anybody but himself at his own price, and he levies a Duty of p.1 p. oke on Wax. Hitherto Silk has been monopolized by him, and the Producers have been given to understand, that the same System will be pursued this Year.

As the Military and Civil Governors of Satalia act in Concert, there is no check upon their Conduct, however arbitrary it may be, and consequently they do what they please.

This Hassan Pacha was appointed to the Post which he so unworthily fills, by Tahyr Pacha, late of Aidin, in whose Steps he appears to have been treading, and whose fate he deserves to share.

No other instances of the Contravention of the Treaty, in this part of Asia Minor, have come to the knowledge of the Undersigned.

An opinion is pretty generally entertained by well informed Commercial Men at this place, that the State of uncertainty in which Affairs have so long remained, between the Porte and the Pacha of Egypt, has tended in a great degree to check the progress of Improvement which would otherwise have taken place in the Trade of this Country, and that a Settlement of these differences, would be productive of infinite advantage to the Turkish Empire.

The re-establishment of Peace and tranquillity would doubtless encourage Capitalists to place their Money at Interest, which is now withdrawn from Circulation, as they are afraid of employing it in this manner, owing to the apprehension of hostilities being renewed, and the possibility of the Country being invaded, at any moment.

Paper Money being unknown in Turkey, the want of Capital thus employed is more severely felt than otherwise—it cramps and confines Mercantile undertakings, within the narrowest limits.

Notwithstanding this and many other disadvantages, under which Trade is labouring, and that the Treaty has not been in complete operation quite twelve Months, the effects it has already produced, have been as beneficial to the Commercial Interests of Great Britain, as to those of Turkey, and it will undoubtedly be the means of greatly increasing the Trade of both Countries, when sufficient times shall have elapsed, to allow its influence to extend and to fruitify. . . .

FOREIGN MERCHANT HOUSES

Two circulars were sent out to British consulates in 1849, asking for details about British, French, and American mercantile houses within their areas. The replies (FO 83/111 and 115) may be tabulated as follows. The only American houses were three in Izmir and one in Alexandria. Houses belonging to Ionian or Maltese British subjects or other protégés are indicated in parentheses, and are additional to the other figures.

| | British | | French |
	1842	1849	1849
Istanbul	11	13	31
Izmir and Rhodes	16(2)	13(2)	12
Galatz	4	6	..
Varna	--	--	1
Albania	--	--	..
Salonica	12	8	--
Seres and Larissa	..	5	..
Edirne	1	1	2
Bursa	1	1	1
Erzurum	4	1	2
Kayseri	1	1	--
Tarsus	2	1	2
Samsun	1	1	--
Trabzon	..	..	1
Baghdad	3	5	1
Crete	(1)	(2)	3
Cyprus	--	--	1
Damascus	7	6	1
Aleppo	5	3	4
Beirut	6(2)	5(2)	14
Palestine	(3)	(7)	--
Jaffa	..	1(6)	--
Alexandria	11(9)	11(14)	14
Cairo	4	7(1)	5
Benghazi and Derna	(6)	(6)	..
Tripoli	(7)	(8)	4
Tunisia	..	1	17
Algeria	--	--	..
Morocco	..	7	3
Tabriz	--	--	--
Tehran	--	--	--

It will be seen that the number of British and French houses in the Middle East and North Africa was rather small. For comparison, in 1842 there were 14 British houses in Haiti, 34 in Mexico, 44 in Chile, 40 in Buenos Aires, 25 in Montevideo, 46 in Rio de Janeiro, 33 in Leghorn, and 15 in Trieste.

It is very difficult to find comparable figures for other periods so as to establish a trend. In 1828 MacFarlane wrote: "At present there are about twenty English houses at Smyrna, the number of establishments having increased here, as in many other places, as the business to be done decreased."[1] Kurmuş states that in the early 1840s there were 35 British merchant houses in Izmir.[2] Their number probably rose in the course of the century.

As for the French, in 1825 there were 26 négociants cautionnés in Izmir who were French-born (CC Smyrne, vol. 42, 31 December 1825). In 1837, out of the 44 French "notables" in that town 17 were merchants (ibid., vol. 44). No later figures are available on merchants but the number of notables showed practically no change in the next twenty years.

In a sample of 203 Frenchmen in Istanbul in 1895, Thobie identified 15 percent as "négociants et commerçants"; in a sample of 431 in 1907/8, the figure was 23 percent.[3]

In 1900, the number of Italian trading houses in Izmir was 48 (CC Smyrne, vol. 57, 7 September 1900).

1. MacFarlane, 1:68.
2. Kurmuş, p. 245.
3. Pp. 31-32.

SELECTION 11. SHIFTS IN TRADE CHANNELS OF SOUTHERN TURKEY

Draft Report by Consulate-General, Istanbul, on establishing a Consular Service, 2 December 1831, FO 781/1

. . . In Turkey, foreign trade now confines its principal operations to the Cities of Constantinople, Smyrna, and Alexandria.

The foreign Speculator has preferred resorting to the established general Mart., where he was likely to find the greatest number of Purchasers; and the native traders have increased in numbers in the Same hope of benefiting by a greater competition in the demand for the Produce of their country. Establishments, branches of the great Factories, have been at times formed at places on the Neighbouring Coast, but whether they did not answer the expectations of the concerned in them, or that they could not perhaps compete with the country traders, who had received their stocks from a general Emporium, it is certain that there are now fewer Frank branch Establishments than there were formerly. Nevertheless, there are few Inland towns of the least note, where Articles of Colonial produce, and foreign manufacture, suitable to the wants of the place, will not be seen in the Shops.

Salonica was formerly one of the principal Marts, but its trade has considerably diminished, and it has now little regular, and direct trade, with England.

Aleppo, which was before the Middle of the last Century the most considerable Emporium in Turkey, is now a place of comparatively little commercial importance. The trade began to decline shortly after the above Mentioned period, and in the year 1792 the Levant Company finally dissolved the respectable Establishment which they had previously supported there, the Consul in fact being then the only English Resident in the city, whereas in former times there had been as Many as twenty eight British Merchants attached to that Factory. The towns in Syria have been of late supplied with British Manufactures from the Establishments at Alexandria, but the consumption does not appear to have been sufficiently extensive to encourage any of the trading Houses in that city to form branch establishments on the Syrian Coasts.

The decrease of Trade at Aleppo has been attributed to various causes. The gradual cessation of the demand for the Persian Market, after that Country began to receive Foreign Supplies from the East India Company's Establishments by the Euphrates must be considered the principal cause, and to it may be added the failure of demand in England for Articles which formerly were exported from Syria.

These causes, and particularly the first, are likely to act permanently in regard to Aleppo, for that city would have now in the intercourse with Persia, to compete with this Capital, and with the attempted establishment at Trebizond.

Aleppo is now no longer considered the Supreme Consular seat in Syria, and with the exception of Austria which Government has an honorary Consul General there (a Native of the Country) and the French who still preserve a Consul the other Powers have confided their interests to agents, natives of the Country, that for England being the Brother of the Austrian Agent or honorary Consul General. For the same reasons Beyrout or Acre has been suggested in this report for the residence of the Consul of the Syrian district, but at the same time it is admitted that if unforeseen circumstances should restore the Syrian Market to anything of its past greatness, the city of Aleppo from its Situation and neighbourhood to the Routes of communication with the great Inland Cities, will also resume a part of its former importance and again become the Emporium of that district.

It has been recently attempted to return to this ancient channel for the vent of Merchandize, and two considerable adventures were made during the Summer of last year by direct importation from England, consisting chiefly of Articles of Manufacture, one to Aleppo, and the other to the Port of Tarsus in Caramania.

The Speculators are Greek Merchants, engaged in the British Trade and their object is to supply the Persian Market as well as the intermediate Turkish Provinces with foreign Merchandize making purchases of the produce of Caramania as return Cargoes.

As they are Foreigners, their operations would not, it is presumed be entitled to British protection, and it does not appear that British Subjects are yet inclined to attempt a competition with the Country Merchants in new Establishments.

The final success of these speculations may be considered doubtful, and it is equally so, that considerable establishments will be formed under present circumstances either in Syria or Caramania. A diminished population scattered in distant towns would afford room for a few separate Establishments, for the supply of those places, which might not be in regular communication with Smyrna or this City. The advantages to be expected from the Persian Market are, as it has been already observed, subject to a competition with other channels.

Tarsus is the Port to which Foreign Traders have lately shown an inclination to resort for articles of exportation, many of those of Caramania being in request in the Mediterranean Ports. Some Cargoes of Valonea have also been purchased on that Coast for the English Market, by Agents of the Commercial Houses at Smyrna.

It is the opinion of various persons that Tarsus will become a place of some commercial importance, notwithstanding the want of a commodious harbour.

It may therefore be recommended as a fit station for an experimental Consular appointment, and to provide protection for the Traders who might be inclined to attempt Commercial Establishments in the Interior: another appointment might be made at Cesarea [Kayseri] which from its situation appears to be a favorable central point for communication with Tarsus, and with the large cities and towns of the surrounding districts.

Erzerum, Tarsus and Cesarea are the only stations which it is considered necessary to add to those already adopted and enumerated, Erzerum from its connexion with Trebizond. . . .

TRADE OF SALONICA

The table below indicates that the trade of Salonica, which had been sharply reduced by the Revolutionary and Napoleonic wars, began to recover in the postwar period. However, the Greek War of Independence again disrupted trade, and it did not regain its previous level until the 1840s, when imports and exports averaged about Ł125,000 each. Thereafter trade expanded rapidly, and by the early 70s averaged nearly Ł1,250,000, a tenfold increase implying a compound rate of growth of some 8 percent a year. After that, the two series diverged: imports rose to an average of some Ł4,500,000 on the eve of the First World War, or by more than 3.5 times, implying an annual rate of growth of about 4 percent, but exports showed only a negligible increase. Over the whole period, from the early 1840s until the time Salonica ceased to be part of the Ottoman Empire, its imports increased by a factor of 36 and its exports by one of 10.

Trade of Salonica (Ł 000)

Year	Imports			Exports		
	Total	British	French	Total	British	French
1784		..	78			107
1787		..	58			97
1789		..	180			210
1815		..	34			20
1816	(220)	..	40	140	..	25
1818	(126)	..	..	(114)		
1819	222		53	112	..	45
1820	(149)			(101)		
1830	40			7		
1831	93			13		
1832	(150)			(30)		
1833	..	..	32	..	..	2
1834	..	..	7	..	..	11
1835	..	65	..	..	..	..
1836	..	84	..	..	..	..
1837	91	..	..	137	..	..
1840	86	22	..	114	..	..
1841	136	41	..	140	..	..
1842	166	73	..	163	..	..
1843	112	74	..	106	..	..
1844	..	99	..	..	..	..
1845	..	139	..	..	..	..
1846	..	..	..	312	..	..
1847	243	..	..	522	..	..
1848	338	..	..	244	..	..
1849	351	..	..	218	..	..
1850	324	..	..	261	..	..
1851	490	..	..	181	..	..
1852	599	..	..	490	..	..
1853	572	..	..	695	..	..
1854	745	..	..	1,099	..	..
1864	850	24	333	1,111	35	782
1865	753	58	350	1,193	74	810
1866	597	34	330	1,284	48	920
1867	875	29	440	1,486	82	732
1868	803	39	412	1,769	89	676
1869	1,184	122	672	1,348	206	680
1870	692	226	196	700	..	500
1871	562	301	268	697	27	464
1872	1,259	432	420	943	7	501
1873	1,424	386	372	1,414	21	564
1874	1,651	323	403	1,811	63	632

Trade of Salonica (continued)

Year	Imports			Exports		
	Total	British	French	Total	British	French
1875	1,182	220	403	1,166	3	428
1876	1,311	201	416	1,645	61	188
1877	1,731	..	240	1,782	..	450
1878	1,315	..	184	1,824	..	456
1879	1,224	142	248	1,298	31	308
1880	1,061	130	188	1,371	13	284
1881	1,234	239	247	1,573	..	464
1882	1,413	377	185	1,467	206	300
1883	1,240	387	..	1,191	..	..
1884	1,830	750	260	741	..	116
1887	1,390	..	..	1,084		
1888	1,411			1,225		
1889	1,320			1,440		
1897	1,390			1,084		
1898	1,411			1,225		
1899	2,569			1,651		
1900	2,553			1,221		
1904	2,000			1,300		
1905	2,300			1,250		
1906	2,600			1,450		
1907	2,798			935		
1908	3,254			940		
1909	4,189			1,047		
1910	4,641			1,362		
1911	4,663			1,429		
1912	4,391			..		
1913	3,640			495		

Sources:

1784 EHME, p. 36, includes Kavalla; 1787 and 1789, F. Charles-Roux, Les Echelles de Syrie, pp. 194-96; converted at 25 francs to the pound.
1815-34, C. C. Salonique; 1830-32, 1837- , MacGregor, Commercial Statistics, 2:85; converted at 25 francs to the pound and at the ruling exchange for the piastre.
1835-54, FO, 78 series.
1864-84, BC, 1886, converted at 25 francs to the pound.
1887-1913, A and P, reports from Salonica.

SELECTION 12. TRADE OF SALONICA, 1817

Beaujour to Minister of Foreign Affairs, 16 July, 1817, CC Salonique, vol. 17

. . . The port [echelle] of Salonica has greatly declined from what it was twenty years ago. Of the ten trading firms it then had, only four remain and these four do almost no business. The Greeks have seized the trade of Marseilles, and the French will never get it back unless the Government takes some measures to forbid it to foreigners, or at least to keep them off.

In 1816, Salonica's trade with Marseilles was only 1,300,000 piastres, viz., exports of 500,000 and imports of 800,000 which, at the present exchange rate, is equal to only one million francs in all. Wool, tobacco, and wax are the main export articles and coffee, sugar, indigo, cochineal, caps [fezzes], and silks the main import items. That year, Marseilles sent directly to Salonica only 2 bales of woollen cloth, whereas before the Revolution it sent up to 1,000; but then its total trade with Salonica was 7 million francs, as compared with one million today. The strangest aspect of this trade is that imports [exceeded] exports and that Turkey had a negative balance in its trade with France; but it should be noted that several items were marketed in France through indirect channels and that much wool and wax coming from Salonica and Cavalla was shipped to Marseilles from Smyrna.

Judging from the tables of the first semester of 1817, exports will increase this year because the tobacco of Macedonia, which was formerly sold in Italy, is now being sent to Marseilles, and it would seem that exports will reach at least 800,000 piastres and level with imports. But French trade with Salonica will never exceed 2 million because we no longer control the two main import items, coffee and woollens. It is Trieste that provides Salonica today with Belgian woollens. The trade conducted by the Italians and Germans has held up better, for if it has declined in certain respects it has increased in others. Salonica's trade with Germany today is 5 million francs, viz., 2 million through Trieste and 3 million overland; with Livorno and Genoa 2 million; with Malta one million and with other parts of the world 2 million. Imports fall short of exports and Christian Europe pays to Salonica a balance of nearly 2 million francs, part of which is sent to Alexandria and part to Constantinople, to cover Salonica's [passive] balance with those two Turkish centers.

Livorno and Malta seem to have replaced Marseilles in Salonica's trade, but that is because, owing to the war, those two towns became entrepots for England. Livorno will probably keep part of this trade because it is surrounded by consumers, but Malta, which has none, can flourish only in wartime, as St. Thomas and St. Croix have flourished in the West Indies. This entrepot, which has been so highly praised, should therefore not cast such a shadow on France.

But in general the trade of Salonica, and indeed that of the whole of Turkey in Europe, is diminishing rather than increasing, because the country is becoming poorer instead of growing in wealth.

Exports are almost identical for all countries: cotton, tobacco, wool, wax, silk, hareskins, and sponges, but imports vary between countries. The French bring in mainly caps, silks, and gold lace [gallon]; the Germans woollens, glass, and hardware; the Italians caps, paper, and silks; the English coffee, sugar, cochineal, and cotton cloth and yarn.

In the past Salonica exported cotton yarn and now imports it because English and French yarns are better than its own and less expensive. This is a new branch of trade, which seems destined to make great progress in Salonica as in the other Levant ports.

Raw cotton, which constitutes the main export item, has since the war gone to Germany and Poland and it is likely that it will never find its way back to France and England, because this cotton is too rough for the manufacturers of those two countries. But it looks as if cotton will be replaced by tobacco in trade with Marseilles, because Macedonian tobacco suits us better than Virginian. The French market should therefore be opened to this tobacco, and attempts must be made to prevent it from becoming too expensive there. Now the only means of preventing such a rise in its price is not to buy it in competition with the Greeks. This competition has made everything dearer in the Turkish markets, because it has increased the number [déplacé le nombre] of buyers. Hence the lack of business and the ruin of all the French trading firms.

Such is the trade which Salonica conducts with the various Mediterranean centers, and there is no doubt that France could play a more active part if its trade was better regulated and more protected; but its trade here is badly regulated and not all protected.

SELECTION 13. MR. CONRAD BLUNT'S REPORT UPON THE COMMERCE OF SALONICA, 1835

FO 78/265

Trade with the Port of Salonica has of late years gradually increased, particularly so as regards the import direct of British Cotton Manufactured, and if it may here be permitted, to advance an opinion, will be far more important, when Greece becomes settled.

Amongst the various changes which have taken place, in the internal Government of Turkey, the partial (partial as it is) protection afforded to the agriculturists—the security which the Rayyahs now enjoy—and the abolition of the Despotick powers of the Pachas and minor authorities, may be given as the chief causes of improvement, in the Trade of Macedonia and Thessaly, and that the Port of Salonica, daily becomes of more commercial importance.

The destruction of the Janissaries took place in 1826, but it was long before they were thoroughly subdued in the outposts of Turkey, and before that confidence which their abolition promised produced any beneficial results, at any distance from the Capital.

From the period of the General Peace, 'till 1829, the Trade of Salonica was of little or no importance, as regarded England, and equally trifling with France; with Austria, it was of rather more importance; as regards France but few articles were imported, but they took in return Cotton and Wool for Marseilles. The Austrians brought their manufactures and a few Colonials to the market. Tobaccos and Cotton were the returns to Trieste.

Till 1828/29, what few British Cotton manufactures were imported were upon Commission, from Smyrna and Constantinople, in 1829 the first essay was made of goods direct, and about Fifty Tons of British Goods, principally Cotton Manufactures were imported at Salonica, which left a nett profit to the importers of 20 p. cent, since when the importation has gradually increased.

This simple fact of there being but few Commission Merchants in Salonica and that the Goods imported are by, and for account of Rayyahs, (chiefly Jews) is a proof, that the causes mentioned are producing their good effects, and of the resources of the country and it may here be remarked, that however few minds may be impressed with the idea, of the oppressions of the Local Authorities, and the continual demands of the Porte, it would nevertheless appear that the resources of Turkey are little known, from the numbers of Pilgrims who yearly embark at Salonica for Jaffa. The expenses of these Pilgrims are estimated at from 8 to 10,000 p. each (₤80 to 100₤) which includes all their expences at Jerusalem and their passage back to Salonica.

The Rayyah importers purchase Firmans, which give them the same priviledges as Franks in point of Duties, Customs and Commercial disputes.

Upon the arrival of a Vessel at the Port of Salonica, the Goods are immediately landed and taken to the Custom House and after examination a Permit (or Teskeree) is given, upon sending goods into the interior this Permit is changed at the Custom House. It was formerly the custom to give the import Teskeree with the goods when sold, but this is no longer allowed, the purchaser must pay the inland duty, upon sending the goods into the Interior.

The goods imported at Salonica are chiefly for the Interior, few sales are made on the spot, and soon after arrival, they are sent to Seres, and from thence to the Fairs, where sales are made at from 3 to 8 months' Credit [3:27.]

The Import Trade of the Rayyahs at Salonica, is carried on, by Credits on Vienna (few of the Importers have any Capital). Upon sending orders to England instructions are given to the Agent there to draw upon Vienna. The Agent at Vienna charges at the rate of 6 p. Cent per annum--the current rate of interest at Salonica is 20 p. cent. The goods are generally sold in the interior at an advance upon the Invoice cost, of from 10 to 14 p. Cent, which thereby leaves the importers (provided they make no bad Sales) a profit of from 4 to 8 p. Cent, and their operations being extensive, enables them to live by this speculative and precarious trade. Hence the Jews of Salonica have, by raising money at Vienna, introduced British Manufactures where they were not known before, and where Austrian Manufactures are now unsaleable. Were there any Stocks of British Manufactures sent to the market, as to Constantinople and Smyrna, the consumption of British Cotton manufactures would probably increase, for the Charges of the Commission Merchant are much lower than at Constantinople or Smyrna, viz 4 p. Cent, which includes all Charges of Brokerage, Commission and Remittance. It may here be observed that Seres from its central situation, offers commercial advantages, which might be availed of to a considerable extent, and that no commercial establishment at Salonica can import from England to any extent, without a branch House at Seres.

Salonica being the nearest Port of any consequence to the Confines of Greece would enjoy a trade of considerable more importance, were the transport by land from hence to the Frontiers more secure; were there less to fear from pirates in the Gulf, and were the post in contemplation between Salonica and Greece established; but before any post through the country between Salonica and Greece can be put upon a footing to offer any advantages to Commerce, some changes must take place, as regards Mount Olimpus and its environs, which has ever been commanded by Greeks. The Greeks are allowed this power to keep the country free of Robbers, but are unfortunately the very persons most given to plunder. The post of Chief or Captain is often a sanguinary contest, but the elected is immediately acknowledged by the neighbouring Pachas.

Upon the most minute investigation, it is clearly established that British Cotton Manufactures are now more esteemed than any others in Macedonia and Thessaly, in fact what Goods are consumed are British. The German low muslins are still sent, but are not saleable if there be any British in the market. The only article of British manufacture which has suffered in these districts, as in all parts of Turkey, is the Nankeen, but it would appear that the Saxon manufacturers have lost by their imitation, for there is a decrease of 70 p. Cent upon the quantities formerly sent. Within these few years the Saxons have introduced a new kind of Nankeen, called Demie Caton, the cloth is better with a greater beauty and variety in the stripes, which are brought to resemble the patterns of Silks manufactured at Brussa and Constantinople, and called Stamboul Shalli. These Demie Catons are of very general consumption and are imported both by sea and land carriage. There are three qualities sent to the market, viz.,

1st Fine Bright twilled stripes worth p. 4½ p. yd.	= 10 3/4d
2nd Twilled stripes	do. " 3½ "	= 8 d
3rd Plain stripes	do. " 3 "	= 7 d

These pieces run from 30 to 60 yards in length and 29 to 30 inches in breadth. The yearly consumption in this part of Turkey may be estimated at about 20,000 pieces.

The consumption of these Demie Catons is now so general as to render them worthy the attention of British Manufacturers.

The Consumption of Cotton Twist has greatly increased, and the quantity now imported at Salonica may be about 600 Bales yearly, not including the small parcels which are smuggled in from Leipsic. The quality generally sent to this market is of too high numbers; were the British merchants to confine themselves to the low numbers say Nos. 8 to 14--12 to 20--16 to 24 (Water Twist) there can be no doubt but that the consumption would increase, for the low numbers of the very inferior Egyptian Twist are saleable in this part of Turkey.

The few Swiss Prints sent to Salonica, is scarcely worth mentioning they are too expensive for the market. The Pacha of Egypt has made several attempts to introduce his inferior prints into Macedonia, but as the pieces never render the number of yards marked upon them, that circumstance alone prevents their being saleable.

The Iron mines of Samakoff (near to Philipopolis) formerly satisfied in a great measure all demands for that article in Macedonia and Thessaly, but since the produce of these mines has been monopolised by the Porte, for the Cannon Foundry at Constantinople, the importation of British Iron, has considerably increased.

The Export Trade from Salonica to England is very trifling and what few goods are purchased for the United Kingdom are sent to Smyrna and from thence forwarded.

The French Trade with the Port of Salonica is of no great importance and consists as regards imports in a few Bales of Coarse Cloths called Londrines, Coffee, Sugar, Red Caps, Buonos Ayres Hides, and a few watches; returns are made to Marseilles in Wool, Cotton, Silk, Tobacco and Hareskins. The Returns however bear no proportion to the imports which are but trifling in point of real value.

The Austrian Trade with Salonica is certainly on the decline. It sends from Trieste, Cloths, Nankeens, Demie Catons, Coffee, Sugar, Hides, Red Caps (very inferior), Copperns, Tin, Sulphur, a few Drugs and inferior window glass. The Exports to Trieste are Grain, Hempseed, Linseed, Wool, Cotton, Tobacco, Silk and Hareskins. Salonica exports Wool, Cotton, Silk, Tobacco, Grain, Sesamum, Linseed, Hempseed, Hareskins, Lambskins, Timber, Staves, Beeswax, Hemp, Nuts, Flax.

The Wool is inferior in quality to the Wools of Roumelia, and does not render above 25 p. Cent of first quality, it is likewise less cleanly. The Roumeliott wool only leaves a loss of weight of 3½ to 4 p. Cent, whereas those exported from Salonica have a loss of weight of 7½ to 8 p. Cent. These wools are purchased for the most part for France and Austria, none of late years has been sent to England. When there is a demand for America (that is since the alteration in the American duties) they bring the Salonica wools to cost under 8 cents by mixing them with those of the Negropont, selling the finer qualities and thereby bringing the Seconds to cost under the American rate. This however is at variance with the oath required upon entry into American ports. Upon washing the Salonica wools there is a loss of 45 p. Cent.

The quantity yearly brought to Market is about 1,000,000 lbs.

Cotton. The cottons exported from Salonica are for the most part produced in the vicinity of Seres. The staple is very short and it is seldom purchased for England. The largest shipments are made for Trieste. The quantities produced yearly in the immediate vicinity of Salonica is about 250 to 260,000 lbs.

Seres and its environs sends yearly to market about from 3 to 4,000 lbs.

It was for some time matter of surprise how the merchants at Seres could affort to purchase these Cottons for Trieste at a higher rate than the Trieste market price. This year, this commercial enigma has been solved by the discovery of a band of coiners who have had the Dies at work since 1832, and have distributed immense sums of false Turkish money. The chief of this band was a Russian protégé, but was released from the hands of the Turks by the Russian Consul. The Dies were made in England, and sent by the Greeks to Syra, who sent and landed them on the Coast, near Cavalla, from whence they were conveyed by land to Seres.

Silk. The drawing off, of the Salonica silks, has much improved of late, and the workmen like those of Brussa, can now immitate any silks upon order. Formerly the silks were drawn off in the villages, by the Cultivators of the Worm, but they now find it more to their advantage to dispose of the Cocoons to the Drawers, who from the superiority of their workmanship, obtain a better price for their silks, and can thereby afford to pay the rearers an equivalent for their Cocoons. The Silk Trade is a great source of wealth to certain classes, and there is scarcely a village in the vicinity of Salonica that does not produce more or less of the Cocoons.

The yearly produce of Salonica and its environs may be estimated at from 55 to 60,000 lbs.

Tobacco. The cultivation of this article has much diminished of late years, for which two causes are given 1st. the Constant demands of the Porte for Troops, 2nd the new duty of 6/40 p Oke (1/8 d per lb) which the Cultivator has to pay. The Tobaccos shipped from Salonica are from the vicinity; but those produced at Drama are shipped at Cavalla. The Tobaccos sent to Trieste (where for many years the importation has been a monopoly, purchased by private individuals but now in the hands of the Austrian Government) are the Drama, a Strong mountain Tobacco, and the Qarda Yenneyo, a mild plant, produced in the plains. The mountain plants gain their strength from the goats' manure which is put to the young plants, those of the plains are reared with sheep's manure. Purchases are usually made at the Place of Growth but seldom attempted till the price has been cut at Salonica. The best purchases are made in the month of October. The buyer at that period by making trifling advances is certain that the Tobaccos will not be mixed, which they otherwise do, and with such dexterity that the best judges are sometimes at fault. The racolta of the present year (1835) had been more than usually abundant and is estimated at 2000 Tons, the general racoltas are from 1000 to 1500 Tons.

Linseed is of pretty good quality, though not equal to the Linseed of the North of Russia and has mixed with it a good deal of that spurious white seed, which absorbs the oil in the pressing. It is purchased for Trieste. The yearly produce is about 4,000 qrs.

Hempseed. The quality is good, a good clean full seed; purchases are made for Trieste, but the quantity produced does not exceed 2000 to 2500 qrs. in the Vicinity of Salonica.

Hareskins, exported from Salonica are not equal to those of Anatolia, still they answer for the French Market; and purchases are yearly made for Trieste; about 600,000 Skins are yearly brought to Market; if the winter is severe the quantity is greater and the skins are of better quality.

Lambskins have been purchased latterly for England, not above 25,000 skins could be procured yearly.

Nuts are the produce of Mount Athos and form part of the Revenue of the Convents. Purchases are made of the priests, who are not however, the most honest people to deal with; when there are no orders for England, they are sent to Smyrna. A cargoe was this year (1835) loaded for America. The yearly produce may be estimated at about 400 Tons.

Timber Oak, Elm Beech and Walnut, from the boarders of the Gulf, purchases are made for Egypt, for Gun Stocks and building Timber and for Greece, building Timber.

Staves are purchased chiefly for Constantinople and Smyrna.

Hemp is of very inferior quality, and is for the most part consumed on the spot.

Sesamum is seldom exported, the oil extracted from it is of such general consumption that little is left for Export. The quantity produced yearly averages about 1500 to 2000 quarters.

Wax is collected in small quantities from the Villages, but the best is brought from the Island of Thasos. The principal purchases are made for Trieste. They collect yearly about 100 Tons.

Flax. What is produced in the vicinity of Salonica is consumed. Formerly it was an article of import from Egypt, but since the cultivation of it has increased, it is no longer imported, and may be noted as an article of Export, which it will become, unless unforseen events, should impede the cultivation of it.

Corn Trade, This branch of Trade was formerly of considerable more importance at Salonica than at present; and can never be expected to regain the former value, unless reformation in Turkey should extend so far as to prevent the Pachas making improper uses of the Firmans sent for the supply of the Capital. The prices established by these Firmans generally average from 40 to 50 p. Cent below the market prices. Prior to the arrival of the Boumbiagi or receiving officer from Constantinople, the Pachas avail of the Firmans to force the minor farmers to deliver their grain at the Firman price, the Grain is immediately resold (principally to Greek Captains) at the market price, the buyer also paying 6 p. p killo for permission to Export, which gives the Pachas a clear profit of 100 p. Cent. This system being pretty general at the outports, the prices are so considerably raised at both Constantinople and Smyrna as to encourage the importation of Foreign Grain. The Greek Islands and the Morea are supplied in part by Turkish Grain, the Pachas become wealthy, but all the small farmers are ruined.

The Beys are the most extensive land holders in the vicinity of Salonica, but they refuse to deliver their Grain at the Firman prices. The pachas on the other hand are fearful of reporting them, as they would thereby run the risk of being exposed themselves to the Government.

THE TRADE OF IZMIR

By the end of the eighteenth century Izmir had become the leading trade center of the Ottoman Empire. A breakdown of French trade—which accounted for over half the total trade of the Empire with Europe—showed that in 1784 Izmir's share was nearly a third; for Turkey proper the figure was about one-half.[1] Izmir owed its importance to its rich hinterland, the presence of a sizeable European community and a very large Armenian, Greek, and Jewish population, and the diversion of much of Iran's silk trade from Aleppo to it in the seventeenth century.[2]

In the period under review, Izmir retained its position as the main exporting port, although in the decade preceding the First World War Istanbul caught up with it; in imports, however, it remained well behind Istanbul (3:1). Its trade declined sharply during the Revolutionary and Napoleonic wars but recovered swiftly thereafter and by 1817 had surpassed the prewar level in money, though not in real, terms (table 1). Very soon, however, trade was once more disrupted, by the War of Greek Independence: "The variation in the extent of either imports or exports during the last nine years, that is from the commencement of the Greek Revolution to the termination of the late war with Russia, has been very trifling. Since the Peace, imports, particularly of British cotton goods and twist, have greatly increased" (Trade of Smyrna, 1830, FO 78/194). The wars between Turkey and

Egypt also affected trade but in the 1840s--and doubtless helped by the 1838 Commercial
Convention and the decline in British export prices--a steady growth began. In 1847 the
British consul reported a regular increase in trade: whereas in 1839 only 91 ships aggregating 15,000 tons had loaded for the United Kingdom, in 1845 the figures had risen to 196
ships and 35,000 tons (Brant to Wellesley, 21 January 1847, FO 78/701). In 1848, the
French consul stated: "In spite of a kind of revolution that has been taking place in the
last few years in the trade of the Levant and which has removed from Smyrna a large part of
its operations, taking them to secondary ports, it is still nevertheless through this place
that almost all the goods and produce which the large and rich province of Anatolia buys
from or sells abroad are imported or exported" (Report on Trade, 5 August 1848, CC Smyrne,
vol. 48).

     Table 1 shows that between the 1830s and 1880s imports rose about 7.5 times, or at a
compound rate of over 4 percent per annum, and exports more than 4 times, or at 3 percent.
Since in the meantime British export prices had fallen by almost a half and import prices
by over a quarter, the increase in real terms was much greater, say 10 and 5 times, or at
rates of 4.7 and 3.3 percent. The continued fall in world prices accounts for most of the
decline between the 1880s and the early 1900s but, helped by slowly rising prices and larger volume, the trade figures reached a new peak on the eve of the First World War (table
2). Among the causes of the increase were the railways built in the 1860s, linking Izmir
with the interior (4:15 and 16); conversely, the Anatolian railway probably diverted a
large volume of freight from Izmir to Istanbul (4:17).

     The tables also show the share of Izmir's main suppliers and customers. France never
regained the predominant position it had occupied before the Revolution, falling behind
Britain and, more often than not, Austria. In the first half of the century, the United
States carried on an active trade with Izmir; from the 1820s through the 1850s they occupied fourth place, and occasionally third, but after the Civil War their share declined
drastically and they were overtaken by Italy, Russia, Germany, and other countries. The
United States supplied coffee, sugar, and cotton cloth and took dried fruits, opium, and
wool (CC Smyrne, vols. 44 to 48). Later, they became important purchasers of tobacco (5:
21).

     Selection 14, from an interesting Russian travel book, shows the composition of Iz-
mir's exports in 1834. Raisins held first place, closely followed by cotton; other important items were olive oil, valonea, figs, wool, and madder. In 1776, an Austrian report on
Izmir (HHS V-25) had listed the following items, presumably in order of importance: raw
cotton, cotton yarn, madder, valonea, cotton cloth, Bursa silk, scamony, leaf tobacco,
carpets, alum, Mocha coffee (from Alexandria), printed Indian cloth, etc. The main changes
are the relative decline in cotton yarn and cloth, the disappearance of coffee, and the
diversion of Bursa silk. In 1876, the main products were: valonea, cotton, fruits, opium,
wheat and barley, sponges, and carpets.[3] Here, the main new products are opium, cereals,
and sponges; the rising importance of carpets is noteworthy (5:13) as is the decline of
madder, which had been displaced by alizarin.[4] In 1910 the order was: raisins
(₺1,045,000), carpets (₺735,000), figs, valonea, opium, cotton, barley, and tobacco.[5] It
may thus be said that, except for the greatly increased importance of carpets, in the 150
years preceding the First World War the structure of Izmir's exports showed no fundamental
change.

     As regards imports, in 1784, woollens accounted for half the total; coffee and sugar
were also large items.[6] By the late 1830s cotton cloth had become by far the leading

product, followed by coffee, sugar, woollens, silks, and hardware (CC Smyrne, vols. 45 and 46). In 1876, the order was: cotton cloth, silks, metals and timber, cotton yarn, petroleum, and sugar.[7] In 1910, the main products were still cotton cloth (₤857,000), followed by sugar, cotton yarn, woollens, coffee, hides, and petroleum. However, a few items reflect the development that was taking place in the Izmir region: machinery and tools (₤100,000), ironware (₤136,000), coal (₤53,000), and copper and tin (₤28,000).[8] (See also the works by Georgiades, Rougon and Scherzer, listed in the Bibliography.)

1. EHME, p. 36; in 1787 and 1789 Izmir's share was over a third--Charles-Roux, pp. 194-96.
2. Masson, XVII[e], pp. 371-75, XVIII[e], pp. 604-10.
3. A and P 1877, vol. 83, "Smyrna."
4. "In 1869 Graebe and Liebermann prepared alizarin the colouring matter of the madder root, from anthracene"--W. O. Henderson, The Industrialization of Europe (London, 1969), p. 54.
5. A and P 1910, vol. 95, "Smyrna."
6. EHME, p. 32.
7. A and P 1877, vol. 83, "Smyrna."
8. A and P 1910, vol. 95, "Smyrna."

Table 1

Trade of Izmir (millions of francs)

Year	Imports				Exports			
	Total	British	French	Austrian	Total	British	French	Austrian
1789	21.8	..	9.5	..	30.9	..	12.8	..
1802-3	..	..	6.6	..	..	..	5.0	..
1817	32	9.8	6.4	5.7	29.0	4.7	8.9	7.2
1819	23.6	4.9	5.6	7.9	29.7	6.8	5.7	6.8
1820	(23.7)	(9.6)	(3.6)	(3.6)	(30.7)	(15.3)	(2.2)	(5.8)
1831	(19.3)	..	1.1[a]	..	(20)	..	..	..
1832	17.9	2.5	1.4	2.2	21.7	7.5	2.7	4.0
1833	13.0				19.2			
1834	13.0				28.2			
1835	42.6[a]	..	..	..	..	..	..	..
1836	13.1	2.2	1.0	4.2	27.6	7.5	4.1	7.1
1837	8.1	2.0	0.8	2.3	24.2	7.2	5.8	4.1
1838	14.3	4.0	1.6	3.8	28.4	7.9	6.1	5.4
1839	17.0	4.7	1.1	3.8	35.9	10.5	7.7	7.3
1840	19.3	5.3	2.0	6.0	32.2	12.1	5.7	6.1
1841	18.1	4.7	1.8	6.5	29.9	10.0	5.5	5.6
1842	18.4	4.6	1.7	8.0	33.1	12.1	6.8	5.4
1843	27.6	8.9	2.6	12.5	32.5	13.0	5.8	4.1
1846	12.6	14.1[a]	5.6[a]	5.4[a]	20.0	..	..	..
1850	31.0	..	..	..	36.2	..	..	..
1851	28.5	31.4[a]	8.0[a]	13.9[a]	36.7	..	..	..
1852	30.1	30.6[a]	10.3[a]	13.9[a]	39.3	..	..	..
1854	30.3	..	..	..	35.5	..	..	..
1855	57.1	17.8	7.1	12.4	63.1	18.5	5.9	6.0
1856	71.9	25.9	10.5	12.6	72.2	27.4	8.4	7.9
1857	61.2	18.0	11.3	9.8	62.9	24.5	8.5	7.5
1858	59.2	46.0[a]	15.3[a]	18.3[a]	55.8	..	..	..
1860	59.7	19.3	9.3	7.0	46.2	18.5	6.9	6.6
1862	68.2	81.1[a]	24.6[a]	13.8[a]	113.0	..	..	..
1863	93.5	..	..	..	123.9	..	..	..
1864	63.5	..	..	..	96.1	..	..	..
1871	..	46.0	8.7	10.0	100.6	45.0	14.5	15.0
1872	86.9	..	..	..	121.7	..	..	..
1873	116.7	..	..	..	104.0	..	..	..
1874	112.3	..	..	..	98.5	..	..	..
1875	87.1	..	..	..	97.4	..	..	..

Table 1--Trade of Izmir (continued)

		Imports					Exports		
Year	Total	British	French	Austrian		Total	British	French	Austrian
1876	71.5	..	..	..		115.7	..	..	..
1877	77.1	..	12.6	..		117.1	..	10.6	..
1878	..	..	11.1	..		..	..	9.6	..
1879	117.2	52.2	18.8	16.0		110.2	49.7	18.1	9.9
1880	99.5	38.0	18.2	11.7		96.3	33.5	17.4	7.0
1881	116.4	58.2	23.0	13.7		95.1	37.4	16.0	5.8
1882	116.5	..	..	..		95.5	..	..	..
1883	130.0	..	13.0	..		90.0	..	14.4	..
1889	119.0	43.3	13.2	15.2		135.0	51.0	11.1	10.5
1894	69.4	23.6	12.9	9.2		82.9	38.4	6.9	9.6
1895	65.8	21.0	12.7	9.9		99.9	51.6	7.4	11.0
1896	(73.3)	..	..	..		(98.7)	..	..	..
1897	(81)	..	..	..		(161)	..	..	..
1898	(69)	..	..	..		(76)	..	..	..
1899	73.2	23.3	17.2	..		(103)	..	..	..

Sources: 1789 and 1878--BC 1879; 1883--BC 1884; 1872-77--Georgiades, _Smyrne_; 1833, Bailey, p. 98; 1834 Vronchenko (see selection 14); other figures from CC Smyrne; piastres converted to francs at prevailing rates.

[a]Imports plus Exports.

Table 2

Trade of Izmir (£ 000)

	Imports		Exports	
Year	Total	British	Total	British
1863	3,731	807	4,833	2,858
1864	2,538	1,500	3,842	2,068
1865	2,271	1,054	4,046	2,321
1866	3,763	1,166	3,606	1,520
1867	3,404	1,267	4,408	1,774
1868	3,354	1,366	4,632	1,871
1869	3,587	1,029	4,540	2,015
1870	3,007	845	3,620	1,244
1871	3,760	1,841	4,043	1,824
1872	(3,480)		4,867	
1873	4,518	1,595	4,499	1,881
1874	4,490	1,326	3,940	1,899
1875	3,483	944	3,896	2,062
1876	2,860	1,074	4,630	2,058
1877	3,082	1,244	4,682	1,966
1878	4,140	2,114	3,543	1,514
1879	4,756	2,159	4,407	1,989
1880	3,980	1,520	3,852	1,340
1881	4,656	2,328	3,804	1,498
1888	3,867		2,710	
1889	3,236	1,255	4,536	2,072
1890	3,031	1,006	3,708	1,723
1894	3,158	1,099	4,324	1,992
1897	2,250		3,500	
1898	2,678		3,295	
1899	2,563		3,783	
1900	2,538		4,157	
1901[a]	2,849	997	4,413	2,475
1902[a]	2,805	979	4,275	2,430
1903[a]	2,802	883	4,834	2,734
1904	3,061		4,755	
1905	3,215		5,504	
1906	3,547	1,117	4,973	2,652
1907	3,183	923	4,690	2,401
1908	2,938[b]	884	4,453[b]	2,346

Table 1--Trade of Izmir (continued)

Year	Imports		Exports	
	Total	British	Total	British
1909	3,508[c]		5,036[c]	
1910	4,061		4,500	
1911	4,138		4,400	
1912	3,788		4,000	

Source: A and P, annual reports from Smyrna.

[a]The breakdown between the main countries was (₺ 000):

	Imports			Exports		
	1901	1902	1903	1901	1902	1903
UK	997	979	883	2,475	2,430	2,734
Austria	518	530	482	389	411	467
France	306	307	313	239	214	363
Italy	278	278	268	139	118	137
Germany	119	139	187	220	292	351

[b]₺3,364,000 and ₺4,908,000 if trade of Kuşadasi and Çeşme are included.

[c]Including trade of Kuşadasi and Çeşme.

SELECTION 14. EXPORTS FROM IZMIR, 1834

Mikhail Vronchenko, Obozrenie Maloi Azii. St. Petersburg, 1839–40, 2:311–13

Summary table of the value of the produce of Asia Minor exported from Smyrna and some
other neighboring ports in 1834

	Weight, Measure or Number		Price (piastres)	Value
1) Raisins, red	Kintar	245,600	80	19,648,000
" , black	"	120,900	27	3,264,300
" , Belerce	"	9,450	35	330,750
" , Sultanie	"	12,370	130	1,607,100
2) Figs	"	77,000	75	5,775,000
3) Valonea	"	103,000	70	7,270,000
4) Madder	"	31,000	185	5,735,000
5) Cotton Fibre	"	69,000	340	23,460,000
" Yarn	Oke	30,670	15	460,050
6) Aydin Silk	"	3,900	125	487,500
7) Hareskins	Hundred	3,150	170	535,500
8) Sheepswool	Kintar	28,000	200	5,600,000
toisin	"	2,000	830	1,660,000
9) Goat hair, colored, 1st grade	Çeki	27,000	45	1,215,000
2nd grade	"	17,000	37	629,000
Goat hair, white	"	50,000	39	1,950,000
Fil d'Angora	Oke	41,580	50	2,079,000
10) Salep	"	5,000	11	55,000
11) Yellow grain [maize?]	"	280,000	17	4,760,000
12) Nut-gall	Kintar	2,275	500	1,137,000
13) Gum tragacanth	Oke	50,000	40	2,000,000
14) Aniseed	"	55,000	2	110,000
15) Sesame	Kintar	9,331	74	690,500
16) Sponges	Oke	29,000	55	1,595,000
17) Wax	Kintar	3,220	750	2,415,000
18) Scamony	Oke	3,000	175	525,000
"	"	5,000	100	500,000
19) Alum	Kintar	1,700	55	93,500
"	"	2,000	20	40,000
20) Mastic	Oke	12,600	18	126,800
21) Olive Oil	Kintar	53,000	180	9,540,000
22) Rugs	Square Ells	45,000	21	945,000
23) Skins	Piece	500	25	12,500
"	"	1,000	12	12,000
"	"	1,500	6	9,000

Summary Table (continued)

	Weight, Measure or Number		Price (piastres)	Value
24) Skins	Piece	10,000	50	50,000
"	"	2,000	250	500,000
"	"	8,000	7	56,000
"	"	10,000	22	220,000
"	"	12,000	12	140,000 (sic)
"	"	5,000	13	65,000
Sole leather	Kintar	1,000	400	400,000
	Total			112,694,000

Included are the following goods imported into Asia Minor: Mastic from Chios; 6,000 Kintars of wool from Odessa; 2,000 çeki of goat hair from Adrianople; sponges from Chios.

Total	3,057,800
Exports from interior regions	109,636,200

To which should be added opium and cotton yarn from Aydin sent to Constantinople through Akhissar

	8,136,000
Exports from Asia Minor	117,772,200 piastres

i.e. from those places that market their produce through Smyrna and neighboring ports.

The value of the piastre is continually depreciating. In 1834, 100 piastres were equal to 6 rubles and 49 kopeks, silver (more exactly, 23 rubles 37 kopeks paper); by the autumn of 1835, however, the rate had fallen to only 6 rubles 16 kopeks silver (22 rubles 17 kopeks paper). . . .

TRADE OF ISTANBUL

It is almost impossible to provide even rough figures on the trade of Istanbul. As late as 1893, the British consul stated: "No statistics are published for Constantinople alone, and I have not yet been able to hit upon any means of obtaining even approximate figures for the trade of the capital."[1] Shortly after that, exports and imports from the various customs houses, including Istanbul, began to be published, but the following comment is worth quoting: "But the Turkish returns are of very little use. Besides being out of date, they are manifestly inaccurate. The total imports for 1899 are given as £19,870,000 and the total exports as £12,968,000. The real trade of Turkey is estimated by a careful observer as varying between £40,000,000 and £50,000,000, equally divided between imports and exports. Of this total Constantinople takes from 35 to 40 percent of the imports. The share of the capital in the exports is estimated at from 17 to 20 percent."[2]

This suggests that Istanbul's imports were between £7,900,000 and £9,000,999, compared to the official figure of £7,379,000, and exports about £3,800,000 to £4,500,000, compared to the official figure of £2,842,000.

For earlier years, the situation is even worse. Nevertheless an attempt at a very rough evaluation will be made. Selection 3:17 estimates British imports to Istanbul in 1858 at about £3,300,000 to £3,400,000. Imports from other European countries are stated to be "of small value compared with the importations from Great Britain," so a total of £4,000,000 may be hazarded.[3] It is agreed by all observers that exports were far smaller; a figure of £657,000 for the main exports was given for 1852 and, although the 1858 figure is stated to have been lower, the total may be arbitrarily put at somewhat under £1,000,000.

Selections 3:15 and 16 provide estimates for British imports in 1840-45. The average for these years is £1,565,000, and adding an arbitrary figure of £500,000 for imports from other countries gives a total of, say, £2,000,000. An equally arbitrary figure of

£500,000 may be suggested for exports. In 1847, imports from Britain amounted to
£2,175,000 and in 1848 to £2,839,000 (Report on Trade of Constantinople, FO 195/6 and 7).[4]

If these assumptions are at all correct, the import trade of Istanbul nearly doubled
between the early 1840s and late 1850s, and increased nearly fourfold between the 40s and
the close of the century, or at a compound rate of some 2.5 percent a year. Exports may
have increased rather more, perhaps eightfold between the early 1840s, and fourfold between
the late 50s, and the end of the century, or at about 3.5 percent per annum.

Istanbul's trade rose rapidly in the dozen years preceding the First World War. According to the official publications, in 1899-1900 imports amounted to £7,379,000 and exports to £2,842,000. In 1905-6, imports into Istanbul and its dependencies equalled
£9,476,000 and exports £3,975,000 and in 1910-11 the figures were £13,461,000 and
£4,309,000, respectively. Thus in eleven years, imports rose, in current prices, by 85
percent and exports by 52 percent, or at about 5.8 percent and 4 percent a year, respectively. Adding this growth to that achieved in the nineteenth century suggests a sevenfold increase in imports between the early 1840s and the eve of World War I and a twelve-
fold increase in exports. Since world prices were some 10-12 percent lower in 1910 than
in the early 1840s, the real growth in imports may have been about 8 times and in exports
13 times.

A few quotations from British consular reports illustrate some aspects of the trade
of Istanbul and some of the factors that affected it. First, as regards the large excess
of imports over exports.[5] Imports "are not used only for the consumption of the capital
and its environs, but a large proportion is sent into the interior of Turkey, and to foreign parts, such as Persia, Georgia, Circassia, etc. Some of the Turkish provinces, such
as Brussa, Angora and Adrianople, send their goods to Constantinople for exportation;or else,
although exporting them from a port in the province itself, such as Enos and Rodosto for
Adrianople or Ismid for the province of Brussa, yet have their base of operations in Constantinople. . . . Secondly, Constantinople, being the seat of government, is the place
where foreign goods for the requirements of the army, navy, etc. are bought by the Government, and where, besides, a great number of Government officials reside, also many wealthy
people, who live on the rents of their properties in the provinces."[6]

Another factor noted was "its character as a depot for merchandize. The large fleets
of merchant vessels coming from the Danube and Azoff, with cereals, stop here on their passage for a longer or shorter time, and thus induce some activity in respect of shipping
stores, and the numerous steamers passing and repassing, which lately have enormously increased, induce a large trade in coal."[7]

But steamships also had adverse effects. Until the last ten years "Constantinople
was the emporium for all the produce which found its way from the interior to the Black
Sea and Marmara shores. Small native coasting craft used to collect it and bring it to
Constantinople, and in the Golden Horn therewas a large and active market not only for
Turkish produce, but for the grain, oil seeds, wool, hides and tallow of Southern Russia
and the Danube. Now steamers do the work of the coasting craft. Russian produce is carried straightaway to the western markets . . . and so it is with Danubian and Bulgarian
grain."[8]

The loss of the European provinces after 1878 had an unfavorable effect on Istanbul's
trade, and so did the opening of the Suez Canal. "Large wholesale import houses of this
city, which formerly did business with Persia and Central Asia . . . are gradually disappearing from our centre. . . . Persia, which previously drew a considerable part of her

imports from here, has latterly commenced to make use of Bushire, and the entire trade of Lower Persia is at present centered in that place."[9] Similarly with exports, "the produce of Turkish Kurdistan, estimated to amount to an annual value of ₤320,000, which, two years ago, came through the capital, is now shipped from Baghdad--a route which is considered to be less expensive and safer."[10] In addition, Istanbul "has already lost much of its former importance as a trading centre through the increased facilities of direct communication with other ports such as Salonica, Smyrna and Beyrout."[11] Inadequate harbor facilities were also a handicap, even after the building of a modern port (4:10).[12]

Countering all these adverse factors, however, was a powerful favorable one--the Anatolian railroad. The railway's freight rates were designed to induce growers in the interior to send their produce all the way to Istanbul, rather than to some intermediary point from whence it could be transported to a southern port, like Izmir, or a northern one, like Trabzon. It is not clear whether the railroad succeeded in thus diverting traffic, but it is certain that shipments to Istanbul rose severalfold.[13] One must presume that cheaper transport from and to the interior stimulated Istanbul's foreign trade and at least partly accounted for the large increase in the twenty years preceding the First World War.

1. A and P 1894, vol. 88, "Constantinople."
2. A and P 1904, vol. 101 (p. 1), "Constantinople."
3. Istanbul's imports from France in French ships amounted to 945,000 piastres (about ₤48,000) in 1814 and 1815 combined, and exports from Istanbul to 787,000 piastres (₤40,000). In 1832, imports equalled 1,182,000 francs (₤47,000) and exports 2,835,000 (₤113,000); in 1833 the figures were 1,322,000 francs (₤53,000) and 2,674,000 (₤107,000) respectively-- CC Constantinople, May 1819, vol. 80; 15 February 1833, and 28 February 1834, vol. 85.
4. Selection 3:24 gives an estimate of ₤7,315,000 for Istanbul's imports in 1864 and one of ₤10,000,000 "some years later," both exclusive of the transit trade to Persia and Russia. These figures seem much too high and are inconsistent with the same source's estimate of _total_ imports to Turkey, stated to have averaged ₤10,341,000 in 1873-77.
5. This imbalance had prevailed in the eighteenth century (EHME p. 32) and the first half of the nineteenth (3:15 and 16).
6. A and P 1866, vol. 69, "Turkey."
7. A and P 1868-69, vol. 60, "Constantinople."
8. A and P 1883, vol. 7, "Constantinople."
9. EHI, pp. 83-85.
10. A and P 1889, vol. 77, "Turkey."
11. A and P 1905, vol. 93, "Constantinople."
12. A and P 1913, vol. 73, "Constantinople."
13. On this subject, see the excellent discussion in Quataert, pp. 197-216.

SELECTION 15. BRITISH TRADE WITH ISTANBUL, 1840

FO 78/440

Observations on the accompanying return--
It is not possible to give a return of the invoice value of the cargoes, but the following remarks may serve to give some idea of the nature and extent of British Trade to this port.
The number of vessels in the return are 170, of these:

tons

48 vessels of the burden of	7510	arrd. from Liverpool
31 " " " " "	6573	" " London
39 " " " " "	10348	" " England with coal
22 " " " " "	4255	" " " " iron
3 " " " " "	503	" " Rio Janiero with coffee
11 " " " " "	3113	" " Alexandria with wheat, barley, etc.
3 " " " " "	660	" " Malta with stones and furniture
2 " " " " "	246	" " Trebizond with portion of cargo for England
3 " " " " "	323	" " Galatz with wheat
1 " " " " "	310	" " Toulon with part of cargo
1 " " " " "	162	" " Amsterdam with sugar
1 " " " " "	189	" " Leghorn with marble, oil, etc.
2 " " " " "	366	" " Smyrna with parts of cargoes Turkish produce
1 " " " " "	100	" " Eupatoria with wheat
2 " " " " "	392	" " Cyprus with produce
170 vessels	35050 tons	

The articles imported in the Liverpool vessels are principally British cotton manufactured goods, some woollen goods, colonial produce and a little iron and tin. In the London vessels, East and West India produce and various descriptions of articles of British manufacture.

Of the 48 vessels from Liverpool seven touched at Syra and delivered also portions of their cargoes, the remaining 29 vessels brought full cargoes to this port.

The coals brought to this port by the 39 before enumerated vessels was 14070 tons.

The quantity of iron by the 22 enumerated vessels was 5041 tons.

The cargoes from Liverpool may be estimated at an approximate average of ₤18000, being chiefly composed of British cotton manufactured goods.

Those from London may be estimated at about ₤10000.

According to this calculation the value of the importations by the preceding vessels would be as follows

```
48 cargoes from Liverpool at ₤18,000 each   864,000
   deduct ¼ of 7 cargoes landed at Syra       31,500
                                                      ₤832,500
31 cargoes from London at ₤10,000 each      310,000
   deduct ¼ of 2 cargoes landed at Syra        5,000
                                            305,000
39 vessels with 14070 tons of coals at 10/s.  7,035
22 vessels with 5041 tons of iron at ₤9      45,369
                                          ₤1,189,904
```

30 vessels from foreign ports, the value of their cargoes are not
   noticed not being the produce of Great Britain or the British
   colonies and only affording employment to British shipping

170 vessels

23 vessels were loaded in this port during the present year for Great Britain. The articles of Turkish produce manifested and known to have been exported in them was as follows. It is possible that more may have been exported than what has been declared but it is believed not of any great amount:

```
Part Persian silk bales and cases . . . . . . . .   3382
Angora goats wool bales . . . . . . . . . . . . .   5026
Sheeps wool        "   . . . . . . . . . . . . .    1321
Yellow berries sacks  . . . . . . . . . . . . . .    552
Galls          "      . . . . . . . . . . . . . .    672
Oil of roses cases . . . . . . . . . . . . . . .      11
Salt petre Egyptian okes  . . . . . . . . . . . .228,000
Boxwood  tons      . . . . . . . . . . . . . . .     109
Opium  cases       . . . . . . . . . . . . . . .       2
Bones  tons        . . . . . . . . . . . . . . .     650
Linseed  bags      . . . . . . . . . . . . . . .     741
Valonea  Kints.    . . . . . . . . . . . . . . .   2,968
Hazel nuts  sacks  . . . . . . . . . . . . . . .     252
Lamb skins  bales  . . . . . . . . . . . . . . .      57
Stag horns         . . . . . . . . . . . . . . .   1,200 ⎫
                              & bars.                 11 ⎬ Persian
Old cordage  tons  . . . . . . . . . . . . . . .      20
Oak timber  logs   . . . . . . . . . . . . . . .      90
Liquorice paste  cases . . . . . . . . . . . . .      30
Wheat  quarters    . . . . . . . . . . . . . . .   3,170  Russian
Carpets  bales     . . . . . . . . . . . . . . .       1
```

Constantinople, 31 December 1840

SELECTION 16. APPROXIMATE VALUE OF IMPORTS FROM GREAT BRITAIN TO CONSTANTINOPLE DURING THE FOLLOWING YEARS

| | By Sailing Vessels | | | | | | | | By Steamers | | | |
Years	From Liverpool	From London	From Bristol	From Glasgow	Coals	Coke	Iron	Tin Plates	From London & Southampton	From Liverpool	By Foreign Vessels	Total
1840	₤ 832,500	₤305,000	--	--	₤7,035	--	₤45,369	--	--	--	--	₤1,189,904
1841	1,044,000	227,500	₤10,000	₤18,000	10,000	--	9,674	--	--	--	--	1,319,174
1842	1,109,250	204,167	5,000	--	13,800	--	24,850	--	--	--	--	1,357,067
1843	1,085,020	274,000	--	--	5,922	--	35,057	₤3,321	₤180,000	--	--	1,583,320
1844	1,197,800	277,600	--	--	9,155	--	23,694	810	449,040	--	--	1,958,099
1845	989,930	218,476	--	--	6,170	₤888	43,578	1,440	587,938	₤85,100	₤51,750	1,985,270

Source: FO 78/651.

SELECTION 17. NOTES ON THE TRADE OF CONSTANTINOPLE

Memorandum of 27 December 1858, FO 195/647

It is impossible to furnish exact statistics of the Trade of this Port. The following observations may, however, serve to give some idea of it.

The importation of cotton manufactures and colonial produce from England form the principal trade of this Port. Upwards of 70 large British steamers are entered annually-- bringing goods from Liverpool, and London. Most of these vessels bring from 1400 to up- wards of 2000 bales of Merchandise, and the value of the goods brought in them cannot, I think, be estimated at less than £3,000,000 sterling; a fourth part, however, of the manu- factures comprised in this estimate is destined for the Persian market.

Besides these Steamers about 150 British sailing vessels are also employed in the con- veyance of the more bulky and coarser descriptions of goods, as well as Iron, Tin, Earthen- ware, and Coals, and sundry other articles, the value of which may be estimated at perhaps from 3 to 400,000 pounds sterling. The general opinion among merchants is that the Importa- tion Trade is increasing--and this opinion coincides with my returns of shipping, for I find that whereas 72 British Steam vessels, the tonnage of which amounted to 47,829 Tons, were entered in 1857, 72 vessels entered this port up to the 16 December, the tonnage of which amounted to 52,829 Tons, so that whereas the average tonnage of the Steamers in 1857 was 663 Tons, that of 1858 was 743 Tons. There can, I think, be no doubt therefore that this trade is increasing.

If it is found impossible to give exact statistics of British Trade it is still more difficult to give a satisfactory account of the trade with foreign countries. Goods are imported from France, Belgium, Germany, and Switzerland, but they are of small value com- pared with the importations from Great Britain. They consist principally of cotton, silk, cloth, and other manufactures of a superior quality, watches, hardware and a number of small articles such as glass, china, toys, and other things of which the shops in Pera and many in the Bazaars are now full. These importations are also increasing with the taste for European fashions, and habits.

With regard to the Exports it seems to be the general belief that they have fallen off within the last year or two.

The principal articles of export consist of

Silk	Maize
Goatswool	Rye
Sheepswool and skins	and a variety of Drugs
Opium	Yellow Berries
Wheat	Otto of Roses

The exports of these articles before the War in 1852 were estimated at an approximate value of £657,000 Sterling, but this year the crops of grain have failed, and the demand for Silk in England has been less than usual. The steamers that have brought out goods from England have left this port with only part cargoes or empty, and have proceeded to Smyrna, Salonica or Alexandria to take in, or fill up, their return cargoes. Tiftee or goats wool seems to be the only principal article of export which has afforded a fair re- muneration this year in the British market.

The ballance of trade between Great Britain and this port has therefore been more against Constantinople during this year than usual--no doubt that this difference is made up to Turkey in some measure by the excess of exports over imports in other parts of Turkey --but the prevailing opinion seems to be (although the actual difference cannot be proved by figures) that a ballance remains against Turkey, as well as against Persia which is made up by remitting Specie to Europe.

The principal ports besides those of Great Britain for which produce is exported from Constantinople are Marseilles, Trieste, Leghorn and Genoa. The greatest portion of the silk exported is sent to Marseilles.

This statement may, perhaps, afford some general idea of the trade of this port, but nothing more. . . .

SELECTION 18. TRADE OF EDIRNE, 1835

Kerr to Palmerston, FO 78/265

. . . Adrianople being situated in the centre of Roumelia may be considered as the depot from which the whole of the neighbouring country obtain their supplies, and to which they bring a considerable portion of their produce for sale. Its trade is therefore very considerable, notwithstanding that we now depend entirely for our supplies of goods on either Smyrna or Constantinople, with the exception of the trade in cloth, of which our principal supplies come overland direct from Germany. Formerly vessels came direct from England and France to the port of Enos, but since the year 1817 that port has been blocked up by a sand bank, caused by the River Maritza having broken its course and now the naviga- tion is confined to small boats of the country which trade between that place and Smyrna.

The River Maritza is navigable for boats of from 12 to 40 tons as far as Adrianople during 6 or 8 months in the year and goods from Smyrna all come here by that route--when the river is too dry they are forwarded from Enos by waggons. Goods from Constantinople are forwarded either on horseback, by waggons, or by boats as far as Rodosto, and from thence by waggons.

It is extremely difficult to obtain a correct estimate of the quantity of goods that come here for sale, as the duties having been paid either at Constantinople or Smyrna, the Custom House here keeps no note whatever of them. In, therefore, giving your Lordship the following note of the yearly consumption of our principal articles of import, I cannot be so certain as I could wish of its correctness, tho' I have spared no pains in obtaining my information from persons likely to be best informed on the subject.

Manufactures	annual consumption	average price
		s s
Prints	40,000 pieces	9/- to 20/- p. pce
Handkerchiefs	40,000 dozen	12/- to 16/- p. doz.
Colored Cambrics	20,000 pieces	7/- to 13/- p. pce.
Imitation Shawls	70,000 "	6/6 to 11/- p. pce.
Small square shawls	5,000 dozen	20/- to 30/- p. doz.
Florentines	20,000 pieces	20/- to 22/- p. pce.
Unbleached calicoes	100,000 "	10/- to 40/- " "
East India Long Cloths	10,000 "	22/- to 23/- " "
English " "	30,000 "	17/- to 19/- " "
Muslins	120,000 "	5/- to 9/- " "
Fancy do.	30,000 "	5/- to 15/- " "
Cambrics - 12 yds.	20,000 "	5/- to 7/- " "
do. 24 yds.	20,000 "	17/- to 18/- " "
Cloth	64,000 "	5/- to 15/- p. yd.

Other Articles		
Cotton Twist No. 8/32,	500,000 lbs.	1/4 to 1/6 p. lb.
Coffee	350 tons	60/- to 65/- p. cwt.
Cochineal	2,750 lbs.	9/- to 10/- p. lb.
Cloves	12,000 "	1/3 to 1/4 p. lb.
Cassia Lignea	12,000 "	10d. to 11d. p. lb.
Indigo	100,000	6/6 to 7/- p. lb.
Iron, English	150 tons	£10:10 to 10:15 p. ton
do., Russian	125 "	£13:10 to 14 " "
Nutmegs	12,000 lbs.	6/- p. lb.
Pepper	1,200 cwt.	4 3/4 - 5d. p. lb.
Sugar, crushed	2,500 "	48/- to 50/- p. cwt.
refined	1,200 "	56/- " "
Havannahs	2,500 "	46/- to 48/- " "
East India	3,500 "	44/- p. cwt.
Lead	750 "	28/- " "
Lead shot	500 "	32/- " "
Tin	4,400	100/- p. cwt.
Tin plates	1,000 cases	45/- p. case
Campeachy wood	275 tons	10/- " cwt.
Santha Martha	60 "	32/- " "

The quantities above stated are as near as I can ascertain what are consumed in Adrianople and the adjacent country, which is principally supplied by means of fairs held in all the different towns and villages at stated periods. They commence generally in the beginning of the month of May and finish at the end of October. The most extensive of these is that of Ouzounjovah [3:27], a small village about 50 miles distance from this city, which takes place in the month of September and to which all the dealers of the country around resort, in order to lay in their supplies for the winter.

Of the import articles above mentioned I may state that the cotton manufactures are almost exclusively English. It is true that small quantities both of muslins and florentines arrive from Germany and some of the finer kinds of prints from Switzerland but they are not of much importance compared with the general consumption. The woollen manufactures are almost exclusively German. The other goods come principally from England, tho' America, France, Holland etc. furnish a considerable portion.

In produce this country is very rich and the following may be taken as a list of what is brought to Adrianople for sale.

			s
Hare skins	400,000 skins	price	3/6 p. doz.
Hides, ox and cow, salted	100,000 "		18/- p. hide
Buffalo "	25,000 "		40/- " "
Otto of roses	45,000 ounces		10/6 p. ounce
Silk	115,000 lbs.		10/--p. lb.
Sheep skins	200,000 skins		1/3 " skin
Goats "	60,000 "		3/- " "
Sheeps' wool	125,000 cwt.		4¼d. p. lb.
Goats' "	250		13d. " "
Bees' wax	1,000 "		1/- " "
Yellow berries	2,500 "		16/- " cwt.
Valonea, from Macri	8,000 "		5/- " "
Tobacco	40,000 "		15/- " "
Linseed	20,000 bushels		4/- p. bushel
Cheese	5,000 cwt.		32/- p. cwt.
Brooms	400,000 dozen		3/- p. doz.

The above list is not by any means an estimate of the whole produce of the country, a considerable quantity being sent into Germany direct from the place of growth, and another large portion by way of the Danube to Constantinople. The principal articles sent to England are hareskins, otto of roses, silk, yellow berries, and valonea. Our silk is about 10 per cent inferior to that of Brussa and a large proportion of it is consumed in the silk manufactories at Constantinople. The cultivation is annually increasing here The yellow berries of this country are very inferior and the trade in them is now almost lost to this place, the greatest part of the produce being sent to Constantinople direct from Wallachia. Our sheeps' wool is decidedly the finest in Turkey, but hiterto it has almost exclusively been sent to France. The trade in tobacco and bees' wax is confined to Germany.

This country is also very rich in grain and rice, but the exportation of these articles is strictly prohibited, notwithstanding which a considerable quantity is smuggled out, by means of bribes to some of the inferior government officers. The average produce of this neighbourhood may be estimated as follows, viz.

			s
Wheat	about 200,000 quarters	price	11/- p. qr.
Barley	125,000 "	"	5/6 " "
Rice	40,000 cwt.	"	12/- p. cwt.

and the cultivation might still be very considerably extended were the exportation free.

The import trade is perfectly free in every respect, the only article under any restriction is coffee, of which the sale in retail is monopolized by government, but there is no impediment whatever to the wholesale trade. Goods are not allowed to be warehoused in this country, the duties on them must be paid on their being landed and the navigation of Enos and the other ports of this consulate being almost entirely confined to small boats of the country, there is no tonnage or other port dues levied.

Within the last few years the trade of Adrianople has rather diminished, not that the consumption of the different articles has decreased, but several of the fairs in the interior which were formerly supplied exclusively from Adrianople, now receive a good portion of their wants from Bucharest and Galatz and should the direct trade from England to the Danube continue to increase, this place may be expected to suffer still further.

THE TRADE OF TRABZON AND SAMSUN

The following two selections trace the beginnings of the expansion in the trade of Trabzon and Samsun, including the Iranian transit trade. In the words of a British consular report, written when Trabzon's trade was at its peak, "The importance of Trebizond arises from that, while possessing on the sea-side a fair anchorage and a tolerable shelter, it is placed, for what regards the land side, at the opening of the only gorge affording a tolerable route, practicable in winter as in summer, across the great mountain coast chains to the central lands of Anatolia near Erzeroum, and thence on the Persian frontier."[1] The distance between Trabzon and Erzurum was "66 Turkish hours or about 200 miles" and from Erzurum to Tabriz another 350 miles.

Samsun owed its importance to "its coast position at the exit of the Great Valley, or, at least, of the succession of comparatively low grounds, leading up from the sea to Sivas, a point whence diverge the important routes of Erzinghian, Kaisareeyah, Yuzgat, and Angora, but above [all?] the main route leading to Kharput, to Diar Bekir, Mosool, Bagdad, and Basrah."[2] "Trebizond is thus the point where centre and whence diverge three distinct traffics--one, the Persian; second, the East Anatolian; and, third, the coast trade from Batoum to Cherasund inclusive. Of these three, the first is by far the most important; but the second and third are also of real value."[3]

The Persian trade was carried by:

	Number	Loads	Weights of each load (cwts)	Total (tons)	Average hire Trabzon-Erzurum (£)
Horses	60,000	2	3 1/2	21,000	1-5-0
Camels	2,000	2	7	1,400	1-15-0
Oxen	3,000	2	3 1/2	1,050	10-1
Donkeys	6,000	2	1 3/4	1,050	14-0

I.e. 24,500 tons[4] for a total expenditure of £169,000. The main Persian exports were silk, tobacco, raisins, and carpets and the main imports were cotton goods, tea, sugar, glassware, and hardware. At Trabzon, the trade was chiefly handled by one Swiss, two Hellene, and eight Persian houses but "some Turkish and Armenian houses take also a collateral share." The average total of exports plus imports was put at over £1,300,000 a year.[5]

As for the East Anatolian trade, the main export items were wheat, barley, "potatoes, a new introduction, but already much in use, though the quality is poor," fruit, and skins, for a total of £172,000; since most of this was sent by sailing ship rather than steamer, it did not figure in the export returns supplied by the consuls.

The coastal trade covered the ports between Batum in the east and Fatsah in the west. The main exports were flax and linen, mainly from Rizeh, nuts, fruits, maize, and wheat, for a total value of £423,000. Like the Iranian transit trade, the land and coastal trades "are steadily on the increase," as confirmed also by "the great rise in house-rent and the constant building of new houses at Trebizond." In addition "There existed here, till within the last five years, a fourth and a very important commerce, namely, that from and with the coasts of the Caucasus, not, as has been gratuitously asserted, in slaves, but in the more lawful and profitable articles of grain, hides, wax, oil, wood, furs, and the like. This commerce has now ceased, owing to the well-known depopulation of the Caucasus, and the ruin of its seaports. The cessation gave at first a rough shock to Trebizond, and many bankruptcies were the consequence, but the deficiency has since been filled up from other quarters."[6]

1. "Turkey, Anatolian Provinces," A and P, 1870, vol. 64, p. 341.
2. Ibid., p. 388.
3. Ibid., p. 341.
4. This represents three round trips a year, or about 4,000 tons each way; "reasonable-sized sailing ships of that period" carried 500-600 tons (Braudel, Capitalism, p. 252), so each caravan was equivalent to some 7 or 8 ships.
5. For a detailed discussion of the Tabriz-Trabzon trade, and its course in the period 1820-1914, see EHI, pp. 92-116, and Issawi, "Tabriz-Trabzon Trade," IJMES, 1, no. I (1970).
6. "Turkey, Anatolian Provinces," A and P, 1870, vol. 64, p. 345.

SELECTION 19. RUSSIAN ATTEMPTS TO DIVERT THE IRANIAN TRANSIT TRADE; 1820s

L. S. Semeonov, Rossiya i mezhdunarodnye otnosheniya na Srednem Vostoke v 20e gody XIX v. (Leningrad, 1963), pp. 43-44, 51-52, 75-77, 86-87)

. . . The new "Tariff for Asiatic Trade," approved on May 30, 1817,[1] encouraged the export of all goods and also the import of raw materials and foodstuffs. Under it, a duty of 1 percent was levied on all exports, based on declared values. But the sale abroad of arms, ships, war materials, and rigging continued, as before, to be prohibited. Among imports, silk, wool, and cotton, and also wheat, fish, and livestock, were exempt from duty, and cotton yarn, copper and rice, sugar and tobacco were subject to the low rate of 1 percent. But the tariff restricted somewhat competition in articles produced by Russian industry. Thus the duty on cotton piecegoods was 10 to 15 percent, on silk fabrics 25 percent, and on glassware and a few other goods 20 to 25 percent. Imports of luxury textiles, for instance, gold and silver embroideries, and those European goods which had been prohibited in the all-Imperial tariff of 1816, were prohibited. The tariff was designed to prevent, to a certain extent, the "leakage" of gold and silver abroad: thus foreign coins and ingots did not pay duty on export, but the export of Russian coins was forbidden and the import of Russian and foreign currency was duty free.

The Treaty of Gulistan [between Russia and Iran, in 1813] created possibilities for the development of Russian trade with Iran not only across the Caspian but also over the Black Sea. In a report "Views on Black Sea Trade," prepared, apparently, by N. S. Mordvinov and received for Alexander I in 1817 by Vasili Guriev,[2] it was stated that "the present peace with Iran" would enable Russia, by establishing free ports in Odessa and Kerch, to develop trade with Iran and the Caucasus across the Black Sea--a trade that "hardly exists"--and to "divert the direction of that trade" from Trebizond, Poti, and Batum, so that "Crimean and Odessan commercial houses will rule (upravlyat) its heights."[3] In consequence, stated the report, "caravans from the depths of India and western Persia" gathering in Erzurum would "halve their journey by turning to Tiflis.[4]

By an ukaz of Alexander I in 1817, Odessa was granted the rights of a free port. One should mention that, in its discussion of the question of a free port, the Odessa Chamber of Commerce mentioned among its "proposals" "the draining away of Persian transit trade."[5] In other words, it was proposed to develop trade with Iran through both the Caspian and Black Seas, the second route being intended for transit trade. The Tsarist government reckoned on increasing exports from Russia to Asia, irrespective of the original provenance of the goods. The new customs regulations contained no specific measures for facilitating the export of Russian goods, although they did limit the import of articles produced by Russian industry. Assisting the development of transit from Western Europe to the Middle East could only increase the competition of foreign goods. Hence although the abovementioned opinion of the Department of State Economy mentions the definite importance attached by the government to the sale of Russian manufactured goods, in the circumstances created by the removal of the prohibitive tariff of 1810 on the European borders (tariff of 1816) this should rather be considered as a judgment regarding the possibility of compensating Russian manufacturers in the eastern markets. . . .

In contrast to the previous period, when France tried to oust the English from Iran by giving military aid to the latter while being unable to establish commercial relations, now, in "the period of peace," the struggle between England and France took place mostly in the field of trade.

Taking advantage of the weakening of tariff barriers after the Congress of Vienna and of the ravaged state of the countries of Continental Europe, England, with its more developed capitalist industry, ousted France from European markets. For its part France, which recovered after 1815 part of its previous possessions in India and retained some commercial relations with the Levant--which had been the center of French trade with the East--attempted to restore and extend its position in Turkey and Iran. Taking advantage of its trade relations with Turkey and southern Russia, the government of Richelieu decided to resume transit trade with Iran through the Turkish Mediterranean and Black Sea ports and to "open" trade with Iran through the Russian Black Sea ports.

Trebizond lay on the shortest sea route between Europe and Iran. At the beginning of the nineteenth century, the trade of this port was relatively small because of both the undeveloped state of Black Sea trade and of the unfavorable conditions for European merchants in the depths of Western Asia [Perednei Azii]; for their part, Iranian merchants, trading with Constantinople, preferred the land route. In a report discussed in the State Council in 1816, it was stated that France "desired to divert to Trebizond the trade of Smyrna and Aleppo."[6] However, even though Trebizond had a French consulate--the only European one[7]--the French government chose another route, through Redut-Kale, in the coastal belt of the Caucasus belonging to Russia. This route, in the development of which the Tsarist government was willing to participate, would make it possible, by using the land route to Iran, to avoid a clash with the main competitor, England. The development of this transit route was also connected with French plans for the economic penetration of Russia. Already in 1814 Richelieu had begun negotiations with Russia regarding transit trade across the Black Sea,[8] and it was at his initiative that the route to Iran through the Caucasus had been inspected. In 1817, the "Chief Commissioner of France in the Black Sea," F. Beaujour, visited the Black Sea ports of Russia and Turkey, and the French merchant J.-F. Gamba, prompted by the consul in Trebizond, Dupré, made a "journey in Middle Russia" (1817-1820).[9] At the same time, another French businessman, Joubert, made his appearance in Astrakhan, on the Caspian, in preparation for a journey into the "interior of Persia". . . .[10]

At the same time [1822, following the establishment of a uniform 5 percent tariff on all goods traded between Russia and Iran] a tariff was set for Transcaucasia which granted privileges for imports of Western European goods and their shipment in transit to Iran, and also to persons carrying on wholesale trade in Transcaucasia and with Iran.

Under the _ukaz_ [a translation was annexed to a British report dated December 20, 1823, FO 60/24] of Alexander I of October 8, 1821, granting these privileges,[11] a single 5 percent customs duty was established on "goods from foreign countries," whether imported into Georgia or in transit to Iran (#5). Foreign goods imported "at first" were to be brought to Redut-Kale, on the Caucasian shores of the Black Sea, north of Poti. "Later on, however," went on the _ukaz_ "the local authorities of this region will not fail to use all means to open and equip other safe and convenient harbors" (#6). The quarantine regulations on goods from the Mediterranean which were in force in other Black Sea ports were applied to this port (#7). "Commercial transport" to Tiflis from both Redut-Kale and Baku was to be provided with a "military escort" (#9).

Under the _ukaz_ all those "trading" who, within ten years of its entry into force, "establish in that region commercial houses and engage in wholesale trade" were to receive the rights of merchants of the first guild and were, for the stated period, to be exempt from all but local taxes and duties (#1 and 2). All were authorized to acquire real estate and plots of public land and also, with the assistance of the local authorities, "to build caravan-sarais according to the Asiatic customs" (#3,4,8).

The _ukaz_, which came into force on July 1, 1822, applied to both Russian and foreign subjects, but only within the limits of Transcaucasia ($1,10). Goods transported beyond the crest of the Caucasus paid the duties specified in the Asiatic and European tariffs "according to their origin" (#5).

The elaboration of the tariff for Transcaucasia was the work of the Special Committee on Trade in Georgia, consisting of: K. V. Nesselrode, D. A. Gurev, the Chief Administrator of Georgia, A. P. Ermolov, and M. M. Speranskii, and was presented before the State Council. On the question of transit, consultations were held with the French ambassador in St. Petersburg.[12]

The state of Russian industry and the insufficiency of capital available to Transcaucasian merchants who were Russian subjects made it impossible to increase sharply the export of Russian goods to Iran and the Tsarist government had to fall back on foreign capital. The foreign merchant capital, which was to revive trade between Russia and Iran, entered both directly--thanks to the privileges granted to foreign merchants in transit trade through Transcaucasia (both money-capital and goods-capital being foreign)--and indirectly, when Russian merchants imported foreign goods on privileged terms (goods-capital being foreign and money-capital Russian). By attracting foreign capital into the transit trade through Transcaucasia, the Tsarist government was attempting to meet the competition of English goods in Iran. England was interested in developing transit only through India and Turkey, while France was prepared to use other trade routes to the markets of the Middle East. . . .

Desiring to oust from Iran the goods of other countries and to monopolize its trade, the British ruling circles attempted to direct the flow of that trade exclusively through the Persian Gulf (Bandar Bushire) and Asia Minor (Erzurum, Trebizond, etc.). And if, previously, the market for English goods had been mainly the southern regions of Iran and for Russian the northern, now the principal arena of commercial rivalry of the Powers shifted to northern Iran. Thus, in 1826, British goods worth 4 million rubles a year reached Tehran and Tabriz through the Persian Gulf, i.e. two-thirds of British imports through Bandar Bushire.[13] In the mid-1820s, English goods formerly reaching Transcaucasia mainly through Redut-Kale began to come through Asiatic Turkey and southern Iran.[14]

The increase of exports of goods from England to Iran required the opening of new, shorter sea routes, a development also necessary for the lowering of the price of English goods. The shortest route was through the Black Sea straits. In 1823 England attempted to use the sea route from Constantinople to Trebizond, and from there the old caravan road to Erzurum and Tabriz. But in 1824 and 1825 only about 300 pack loads a year (woollen cloth and glassware) reached Tabriz.[15] A subsequent struggle was to decide which port would become the center of Black Sea transit to Iran, Redut-Kale or Trebizond. The economic factors (costs of transport) were intertwined with the political: under whose authority, Russian or Turkish, would the transit take place? The Tsarist government attempted to expand the export of Russian goods to Iran and Transcaucasia and to redirect European transit through Russia. The English government attempted to oust Russian goods from Iran and to diminish European transit through Russia.

England displaced Iranian goods from their foreign (India and Turkey) and internal markets, which intensified Iran's attempt to subject to its influence Eastern Caucasia, which was increasing its economic links to Russia. The political and economic pressure of England aggravated relations between Iran and Russia. . . .

1. I PSZ, vol. 34, pp. 328-48 (clauses of tariff); vol. 15, sec. 3 (tariff rates); A. Semeonov, _Izuchenie istoricheskikh svedenii o rossiskoi vneshnei torgovle i promyshlennosti_ (St. Petersburg, 1859), pt. 1, pp. 166-67.

2. Mordvinov Archives, 6:227-33; _Sborrik istoricheskikh materialov_ . . . St. Petersburg, 1876, pp. 284-94.

3. Mordvinov Archives, 6:230.

4. Ibid. This idea was adopted in the project of the Russian Transcaucasian company by A. S. Griboedov and P. D. Zaveleiskii: "Caravans coming from the depths of Asia to Aleppo and Damascus, for trade with western countries, will readily cut their journey and their expenses in half, knowing that in the lands between the Caspian and Black Seas they will find what they formerly sought in the various towns of Syria" (A. S. Griboedov, Sochinenie [Moscow, 1953], p. 632.

5. D. Yu. Medzykhovskii, Osvobodnyh gavanyakh (St. Petersburg, 1910), p. 66; see also "Otvety Odesskovo. . . ." (1832), Vorontsov Archives, bk. 39 (1893), p. 35.

6. Mordvinov Archives, 6:227.

7. V. Fontanier, Voyage en Orient, 1830-1833 (Paris, 1834), pp. 191-93.

8. See Richelieu Correspondence, R.I.O, vol. 54 (1884), pp. 410, 419-21, 504.

9. F. Beaujour, Voyages militaires dans l'Empire Ottoman (Paris, 1839); J.-F. Gamba, Voyage dans la Russie Méridionale (Paris, 1826).

10. Severnaya Pochta, 1819, no. 28.

11. I PSZ, vol. 37, no. 28771 (published December 16, 1821). However, the ukaz did not establish a uniform system of customs duties; on the borders of northern Azerbaijan, rahdari [road taxes] remained in force.

12. M. K. Rozhkova, "Iz istorii ekonomicheskoi politiki rossiiskogo tsarizma v Zakavkaze," Istoricheskie zapiski, 18:174; O. P. Markova, "Finansogo-ekonomicheskoe obsledovanie Gruzii," ibid., 30:192-93 [other references, to various archives, omitted].

13. Kommercheskaya gazeta, 1826, no. 62; Tiflisskie vedomosti, 1830, no. 21. Iu. Gagemeister, O evropeiskoi torgovle v Persii i Turtsii (St. Petersburg, 1838) p. 22.

14. See report of Director of Tiflis Customs, June 20, 1824, AKAK, D. E. Zubarev, "O torgovle erivanskoi oblasti, 1828-1829." f. 19, op. 3, d, 101, pp. 347, letter of P. D. Zaveleiski on Caucasia, May 27, 1830, ibid., pp. 188-189.

15. Kommercheskaya gazeta, 1826, no. 62.

VALUE OF TRADE OF TRABZON AND SAMSUN

An estimate of the volume of trade of Trabzon must start by excluding the Persian transit trade, which at one time formed the greater part of the total. In 1834, the British Consul, J. Brant, put Iran's imports through Trabzon at ₺350,000 (Trade of Persia, FO 78/241). In the years 1843-47, Gödel's figures show that imports to Iran through Trabzon were from ₺1,000,000 to ₺1,400,000[1] and French consular figures that in 1848-52 they ranged between ₺1,300,000 and ₺1,900,000. Iranian exports were far smaller, ranging between ₺250,000 and ₺400,000 in 1843-51. The increase in imports between 1834 and the 40's and 50's is roughly consistent with the rise in the number of Persian packages sent through Trabzon from, say, 7,000 a year to 35,000 in 1843-47 and 50,000 in 1848-51.[2]

Deducting these figures from the totals given in the table below suggests that Trabzon's imports, exclusive of transit, may have been around ₺200,000 in the 1830s and the early 40s and in the late 40s about ₺300,000. Trabzon's own exports were probably around ₺100,000 in the 30s and 40s.

By the late 1870s, Trabzon's imports had risen to over ₺500,000 and its exports to over ₺200,000, or slightly more than doubled, implying an annual rate of compound growth of about 2 percent. By the close of the century, imports averaged over ₺800,000 and exports ₺450,000, and the next ten years saw a sharp increase, to about ₺1,500,000 and ₺600,000 respectively. This implies an annual rate of growth of slightly more than 3.5 percent in imports and slightly less in exports. For the period as a whole, between the early 1840s and the eve of World War I, Trabzon's own imports increased by 7 or 8 times, and its exports by 6, in current prices. Deflating by the British import and export price indices, both of which fell by about a quarter over the whole period, suggests that the increase in real terms was nearly nine and sevenfold, respectively.

Samsun's import trade expanded in about the same proportions as that of Trabzon, but exports grew more rapidly. In the 1840s, both imports and exports averaged some ₺150,000.[3] By 1873-77 imports were running at ₺375,000 and exports at ₺308,000 (3:24), compound rates of growth of some 3 and 2.5 percent per annum. Imports averaged ₺625,000 in 1884-85 but declined to ₺514,000 in 1897-1901 and exports about ₺545,000 and ₺707,000, or an annual growth of 1.3 and 3.5 percent over the quarter-century. The upward movement continued, at an accelerated rate, and by 1912 imports had doubled, to ₺1,089,000, and exports more than doubled, to ₺1,700,000, or at rates of 6 and 7 percent.[4] Over the whole period, Samsun's imports rose about sevenfold and its exports over eightfold--in real terms, some nine- and tenfold.

Trade of Trabzon (₺ 000)

Year	Imports			Exports		
	Turkey	Persia	Total	Turkey	Persia	Total
1830			350			..
1831			246			..
1832			492			39
1833			560			45
1834			615			245
1835			1,021			691
1836			1,452			859
1837			1,145			357
1838			1,600			255
1839			1,150			266
1840			1,452			366
1841			1,702			397
1842			1,222			318
1843			1,388			384
1844			1,410			458
1845			1,610			396
1846			1,660			417
1847			1,585			392
1848			1,726			208
1849			2,031			514
1850			2,402			518
1851			2,397			497
1852			2,148			648
1853			1,743			729
1854			2,023			289
1855			2,432			342
1856			2,816			699
1857			3,293			1,483
1858			3,751			1,229
1859			3,256			956
1860			3,417			1,590
1861			2,213			1,266
1862			..			..
1863			..			..
1864			..			..
1865			..			..
1866	256	673	929	521	305	825
1867	421	671	1,092	419	268	687
1868	381	803	1,183	552	404	957
1869	616	844	1,460	371	270	641
1870	716	710	1,426	349	438	786
1871	559	601	1,159	379	390	768
1872	707	676	1,384	448	379	827
1873	769	700	1,469	494	290	783
1874	898	932	1,831	530	286	816
1875	498	895	1,394	478	275	753
1876	566	873	1,439	476	245	721
1877	429	980	1,409	167	408	575
1878	710	1,306	2,016	246	480	726
1879						
1880	644	684	1,328	296	210	506
1881						
1882						
1883	1,264	857	2,121	345	356	701
1884	1,125	944	2,069	318	363	681

Trade of Trabzon (continued)

Year	Imports			Exports		
	Turkey	Persia	Total	Turkey	Persia	Total
1885						
1886	890	783	1,673	271	261	532
1887	720	610	1,330	312	304	616
1888	650	634	1,284	340	233	573
1889	893			354	275	630
1890	788			384	312	695
1891	849	652	1,502	360	265	625
1892	739	535	1,274	287	232	519
1893	818	496	1,315	374	244	618
1894	889	635	1,524	447	214	660
1895						
1896						
1897	792	555	1,347	444	216	659
1898	886	542	1,429	471	208	680
1899	823	502	1,325	418	152	570
1900	919	521	1,441	536	(225)	(761)
1901	1,027	641	1,669	528	163	69?
1902	1,113	656	1,769	484	1//	661
1903	1,029	682	1,710	531	160	692
1904	1,045	499	1,544	542	149	690
1905	1,207	612	1,819	582	234	815
1906	1,565	600	2,165	589	406	995
1907	1,460	363	1,823	581	96	677
1908	867	165	1,032	714	12	727
? 1909	1,352	1,496	2,848	606	2,230	2,836
? 1910			3,084			3,515
? 1911						
? 1912			1,542			644
? 1913			1,355			774

Source: FO 78/3070 and other reports; Annual Reports in Accounts and Papers.

1. Gödel, p. 65.
2. The above figures are taken from CC Trébizonde, vols. 4-6, and FO 78 series, Reports from Consuls in Trabzon--for further details, see Issawi, "Tabriz-Trabzon, IJMES 1, no. 1 (1970)." The figures on parcels shown in the British consular reports do not always tally with those in the French ones, but the trends are similar in both series.
3. The figures were as follows (£000):

	Imports	Exports	Source--FO 78
1841	133	121	492
1842	122	147	533
1843	--	--	--
1844	213	210	615
1845	182	143	655
1846	179	173	704
1847	158	211	753
1848	--	--	--
1849	128	280	835

4. A and P 1886, vol. 66, and 1903, vol. 79.

SELECTION 20. TRADE OF TRABZON, 1836

FO 78/289

. . . It has been placed beyond a doubt by actual results, that it [Trabzon] is the most convenient and economical channel of intercourse between Europe and Armenia and the north of Persia with the circumjacent countries, in proof of which may be adduced the rapid and extraordinary extension of the trade, which has more than quadrupled since 1830.

Previous to that year the trade of Trebizond consisted, First--in the export to Constantinople of the few products of the surrounding districts, as Tobacco, Hazelnuts, Boxwood, Copper, Beeswax, Honey, Butter and Beans; the imports of European manufacture, or Colonial produce from the capital being quite insignificant. Secondly--in a trade with

Abassah [Abaza], carried on in small craft, to which coast were sent Salt, Sulphur, Lead, and considerable quantities of the manufactures of Turkey, receiving in exchange from the uncivilized tribes of the Caucasus, their raw productions as Grain, Hides, Skins, Honey, butter and a vast number of young Males and Females, who were sold as slaves to the Turks--and Thirdly--in a trade with the Crimea and Tanganrog, to the former the manufactures of Turkey were exported to a considerable extent, with a few Nuts and other produce, and from the latter were received Iron and grain. The exports to Constantinople are still for the most part carried by Turkish vessels for although European ships have been allowed by an order of the Government to carry such on freight, yet the nations are forced to forego the accommodation by the insinuations of Turks in power, who are Shipowners, in order not to excite their enmity, thus the permission in favour of Europeans is a dead letter, as far as Turkish subjects are concerned. Deprived of their trade to Abassah the native merchants have turned their attention to the import trade from Constantinople and in consequence that branch has augmented very much. Before 1830 there was scarcely to be found in the Bazars a piece of European manufacture the shops now are filled with them, and upwards of an hundred new dealers in them have opened shops and warehouses.

The strict blockade of the coast of Abassah by the Russians, has nearly put a stop to that trade, but a few boats do still risk a capture, by the blockading squadron, tempted by the large profits to be gained by success, and by the probable chance of escape which, the want of activity and skill in the blockaders favours so much. The export trade to the Crimea in the manufactures of Turkey has fallen off very sensibly and that branch of it with Abassah having been annihilated the sale and stock at Trebizond of these manufactures has so considerably diminished that their use will soon be entirely superseded by the introduction of British goods in their stead. The import of Iron and grain from Russia is nearly as active as ever, the use of the former I had hoped to have seen superseded by the introduction of British, but the immense rise of the article in Great Britain has for the present rendered that hope vain. The trade between Trebizond and Georgia never was active, a want of a Depot of European goods at the former place obliged the Georgians to resort to Constantinople. Soon after the establishment of a British commercial house at Trebizond, a new Tariffe promulgated in Georgia prohibited the introduction into that country of European manufactures. It is expected that a modification of the old Tariffe will be soon substituted for the prohibitory one now in operation in which case, the relations of Trebizond with Georgia will become highly interesting.

The transit trade to Persia is a branch which has grown up since the Treaty of Andrianople previous to which the Persian trade in European goods was not considerable and was carried on wholly by land from Constantinople to Tabreez. The expenses of Transit are materially diminished by the goods being conveyed by Sea from Constantinople to Trebizond but the rapid increase of the trade has not given time for the creation of adequate means of transport, and the consequence has been such a great rise in its price that many articles cannot now be sent into Persia, which were sent when the price of transport was moderate, thus although the trade has so much augmented yet more ample means, and a more moderate rate, of carriage would occasion its immediate further increase. It is presumed that gradually this want of means of transport will be remedied by the supply of additional animals, unless indeed the trade extends itself in the same rapid progression it has hiterto done, when all the increased means of conveyance which can be anticipated will hardly suffice to meet the additional extension of the trade, and the price of carriage will rather augment that decrease. . . .

SELECTION 21. TRADE OF ERZURUM, 1846

Report on Trade of Erzerum, 1846, FO 78/703

. . . Nevertheless the symptoms of an increasing consumption of European Manufactures have been apparent, in the augmentation of the number of dealers in them; and I think there seems less disposition than formerly to push trade beyond its legitimate wants, because fewer failures among the dealers have occurred, and the prices of goods have been better sustained. The facilities of steam, while tending to increase Trade, have had, however, their usual effect of reducing it to one of retail; every petty dealer obtains his supplies direct from the Capital, and the merchant's occupation is gone, for he cannot compete with those who unite the calling of the merchant with that of the retailer. The demand for raw cotton has very much diminished, as well as the production of the coarse cotton cloths manufactured in the country. The reason assigned, and probably the true one, being that the low prices of British Calicoes attract the consumer; and they are now almost universally used, instead of the native, a proof of the extended consumption of this article of our Manufacture.

The Customs were last year collected for account of the Government; this year they have been sold for 2,500 purses, about £12,500 Sterling. For some years these dues were farmed for 1,500 purses, about £7,500. As the Customs are levied on Imports from Georgia and Persia, as well as duties on the produce of the country, it would appear that the Georgian and Persian branches of Trade have increased; for I do not believe there has been any augmentation of production in this or in any of the surrounding districts. . . .

Most of the trades are formed into corporations, which are guided by by-laws of their own. The usual trades exercised in the town of Erzeroom are; tanning; dyeing morocco; preparing sheepskins for pelisses; saddlery; boot and shoe-making; weaving cotton and woollen cloths; dyeing blue and red Calicoes; felting; making cart-wheels; horseshoes and nails, and blacksmith and coppersmith craft. The leather for shoes is dyed red and yellow, by means of logwood, cochineal, fustic, and yellow-berries. Galls are chiefly used in tanning. The dyes employed for calicoes are principally indigo and madder-roots. The red dye is preferred for its cheapness and durability to that used in Europe; the Bitlis red dyed Calico is much esteemed for that reason. The horse-shoe and nail trade is carried on very extensively, not only on account of the great number of horses and mules employed in the traffic between Trebizond and Tabreez, but because of these articles being exported to all the neighbouring provinces, and even sometimes to Persia.

The state of education in this country is at a very low ebb. The learning of the best instructed Mohamedans does not extend beyond a Knowledge of the Koran, and some commentaries on it. Many among the upper classes cannot write, and when anything is required to be committed to paper, they apply to public scribes, few of whom know how to pen a correct letter, grammar being a science not only untaught, but unknown in this country. Everything at school is learnt by rote, and the reasoning faculties of the scholars are not exercised and developed; once they know how to read and write, their education is supposed to be completed. In fact, it is only among those who have been educated at Constantinople that one meets with any degree of literary Knowledge. The Christians of Erzeroom are perhaps comparatively not so ignorant of reading and writing as the Turks, but there are among them also striking examples of ignorance. Some of the members of the Armenian Clergy actually cannot read, nor indeed understand, their religious books, which are written in ancient Armenian, though they daily repeat the contents. The ignorance of arithmetic, too, in educated persons is surprising. Even among the financiers of the State, none know more than addition and subtraction, and to perform simple operations in multiplication, they have recourse to long additions. Very few know what a million is; indeed, there is not a word in Turkish to express the sum, and the European word has been adopted. Ignorance on this point may be thus explained; large sums, instead of being counted by piastres, are reckoned by "purses" (Kesseh), "loads" (yuk), and "treasures" (hazneh); the kesseh being equal to 500 piastres, the yuk, 200 purses, or 100,000 piastres, and the hazneh, 36,000 purses, or 18,000,000 piastres. The terms, yuk and hazneh are not only used in the computation of sums of money, but also to convey to the mind the notion of a large number of anything, thus, 2,000 "purses" represent a million, and a "treasure" eighteen millions. . . .

SELECTION 22. TRADE OF KAYSERI

Report on the Trade of Kaissariah for 1848, and General Remarks on the state of the District by Henry Suter, 26 February 1842, FO 78/492

Kaissariah, or as it is pronounced by the natives "Kaissaryyeh" and more commonly "Kaissary," was formerly the centre of the Commerce of Asia Minor and the emporium to which the Traders of Kurdistan, of Syria, and of Mesopotamia, resorted to dispose of their produce and to obtain supplies of European merchandise. The people are remarkable for great intelligence and activity, and for a spirit of commercial enterprise which leads them to pursue their trading occupations in all parts of the Empire.

The Trade of Kaissariah has been long gradually diminishing, but its decline has been more rapid during the last few years, which by many is attributed to the facilities of communication introduced by Steam Navigation. The more immediate causes appear however to have been the depressing influence of the war with Mehmet Ali, the insecurity of the country owing to the constant disturbed state of the Koords that inhabit the neighbourhood, and the failure for two years of the Grain crops all over Asia Minor. Yet although much reduced from its former importance, Kaissariah is still the seat of a considerable Trade, carried on with the surrounding Districts, with Erzeroom, Tarsous, Constantinople, and Smirna. The intercourse with the two last mentioned places is maintained, partly through Tarsous and Samsoon, but not to a great extent through either, and since the disappointment and loss which attended the Traffic two years ago by the latter route in consequence of the failure of the engagements on the part of the Austrian Steamers, that channel is now but seldom availed of, and the Trade with Smirna, particularly that in Exports, has almost entirely resumed its previous direct course overland. The Merchants have likewise direct transactions with Europe, and there are several who have their own Agents or establishments at Trieste, in the Mediterranean markets, and even in England.

Of Imports, the articles of Colonial and British produce are, Coffee, Refined Sugar, Tin Bars, Selammoniac, Sheet Iron, Copperns, and Indigo, consumed to a great extent; and Cochineal, Dyewoods, Pepper, Pimento, Cloves, Cassia Signea, and other spices, and Tin plates, of which the consumption is more restricted; of British Manufactures, unbleached Calicoes of all descriptions, Muslins, Shawls, Plain and striped Nankins, are very largely consumed; and bleached Calicoes, all Kinds of Printed Cotton Piece Goods, Cotton Velvet, and Cotton Twist, are used, but in smaller quantities.

English Sheet Iron, required to a large extent, is employed in all this part of Anatolia for plates on which the bread is baked. A good deal of Indigo, Cochineal, and Dyewoods, is wanted for the manufacture of Carpets: the remainder, with a portion of the unbleached calicoes imported (which annually exceed 45,000 Pieces) and some of the Muslins,
are worked up in the numerous dyeing and printing establishments, and the produce is distributed throughout the country. Striped and Plain Nankins are worn by all classes, and
very large quantities, especially of the former, are sold. Those from Switzerland, being
provided cheaper, have in some degree superseded the British manufacture. Some Cotton
Twist is consumed for the native manufactures, but the enquiry has fallen off, on account
of many places which drew supplies from this market now obtaining them more easily from
Aleppo and Erzeroom.

Other Imports, consist of Foreign European Articles; as Russian Bar Iron, German
Steel and Glassware, Italian common writing paper, French and Belgian Cloths, Foreign
Silks, and Red Caps or Fezzes, to which may be added, Cotton and Silk Stuffs brought from
Diarbekir, Moossul, Aleppo and Damascus, and Persian Tobacco, Shawls, and Khennah [henna],
brought from Erzeroom.

The consumption of Russian Iron is large for Horse-Shoes, nails, cart furniture, and
implements of husbandry. Common English Iron has been tried, and is not approved, owing
to the difficulty of working it. The quality called "No. 3" would not present that objection, and its cheapness will I hope in time enable its being brought into successful competition with the Russian.

There is a great sale for Paper, as it is substituted for glass in the windows of almost all the houses.

Woollen Cloths are sold in considerable quantities: but few of English make will
answer; those usually sent to the Levant not being of sufficient substance to suit the
general wants in this direction. For this reason the Foreign fabric enjoys a preference,
but I trust, by bringing the proper qualities to the notice of our manufacturers, that
English cloth will become a more important article for this market.

I have confined myself to enumerating the Imports which command the most extensive
and constant demand. There are many others, which are either of uncertain or only limited
demand, and indeed with few exceptions all varieties of European articles used in Turkey,
can be found in small quantities in the spacious and well stocked bazars.

Kaissariah is not fertile in Corn, a plentiful harvest not sufficing for more than
three months consumption of the population. The residue is supplied from Yiosgat and Sivas.
A variety of Exportable commodities are however obtained; vizt. Yellow Berries, Sheep's and
Goat's wool, Raw Cotton, Madderroots, Gum Tragacanth, Anniseed, Linseed, Scammony, Furs,
Skins, Hides, etc. The principal production of the country is the Yellow Berry, to which
the climate and soil of Kaissariah are peculiarly favorable, the quality here being acknowledged far superior to that grown elsewhere. The shrubs which spring spontaneously are the
most hardy and productive, but are few compared with those cultivated. Of the latter there
are large plantations in the neighbourhood of the Town, and of most of the Villages: much
expense and attention are bestowed upon the cultivation, but the return is very precarious.
Shrubs which yield abundantly for several years frequently become suddenly barren, and the
plantations must be renewed. The blossom is often injured by fogs or heavy rain, and the
berry is exposed to many accidents from unseasonable weather before it ripens. A tree in
full bearing will give as much as 6 Okes = 16$\frac{1}{2}$ lbs., but sometimes not more than 1 Oke =
2 3/4 lbs, in fair seasons the average for a fruitful tree is about 3 Okes = 8$\frac{1}{4}$ lbs. After
gathering, the berries are very carefully dried in well ventilated rooms, completely shel-
tered from the sun, any exposure to the influence of which would affect their color: in
the process of drying they lose half their weight. The whole produce of Yellow Berries in
a good season, is estimated at 350,000 Okes = 8,750 cwt., and it has sometimes amounted to
as much as 500,000 Okes = 12,500 cwt. The last year gave a short crop, which did not exceed 200,000 Okes = 5,000 cwt. Of the total quantity of this article annually produced, it
is reckoned, that two-thirds are grown in this District.

Sheep's wool is purchased from the Turkmans and Koords, who in spring bring their
flocks to the pastures in this neighbourhood. About 9,000 Kintals = 500 tons can be easily
collected for Export; and the article is well adapted for England, where it has been sold,
according to the state of the markets, at from 9d. to 11d. per lb. All that does not go
abroad can be easily consumed on the spot, in the manufacture of Carpets, a coarse kind of
cloth and other articles worn by the peasantry.

Large supplies of raw Cotton come from Adana. It is sent thence to Smirna, chiefly
through Tarsous, but a good deal finds its way thither from this place.

Madder-roots are obtained in the adjoining Districts of Caraman, Elegri [Eregli], and
Akserai. The quantity is calculated at about 6,000 Kintals = 6,600 cwt., a part is shipped
at Tarsous for Europe; some go direct, or hence, to Smirna, and some are consumed by the
native dyers. Gum Tragacanth, which abounds in this quarter, is brought to market by the
Koords, and the sorting, performed here, enables the selection of a very fine quality.
Nearly the whole is sent to Smirna and Constantinople for Europe. Very little White Goat's
wool is found here, but it is procurable from the vicinity--of the Gray and Black, or of
mixed qualities, about 40,000 Okes = 110,000 lbs. are annually produced near Kaissariah.

Anniseed and Linseed can be had in considerable quantities. The former, said to grow wild, is gathered by the Koords, and goes to Smirna. Very little Linseed was raised, but the demand for Europe has latterly encouraged its cultivation. Last season upwards of 30,000 Kiloes, about 4,000 Quarters, were exported, and a great increase is anticipated this year. The quantity of Scammony is only small; and of Galls, which come from Diarbekir and Moossul, the supplies are likewise but limited. A good many Fox skins are sent hence to Erzeroom for the dealers from Georgia; and 50,000 to 60,000 Hareskins are annually exported, principally for Trieste. A vast number of Lamb, Sheep, and Goat skins are used here in making yellow and red morocco leather, which forms a great branch of native industry, and many parts of Turkey are supplied with the article from hence. Of Cow and Ox Hides independent of those remaining for local use about 50,000 are available for Export, a great many cattle brought from Erzeroom and Sivas being annually slaughtered for making "Pastoormah." This is Beef which is preserved with Garlic and Pepper and dried in the sun, and is a principal store for winter food. A great deal is sent to all parts of the Country, to Aleppo, and Damascus; and 4,000 or 5,000 Packages, or about 6,000 cwt., proceed yearly to Constantinople.

I subjoin a List of the selling prices of the principal Articles of Import and Export.

The Leech fisheries of Kaissariah, like those of other parts of the Empire, are annually disposed of by Government to the highest bidder at Constantinople. For three successive years they have been purchased by the same parties, Europeans accustomed to the trade who send the Leeches for sale to Marseilles. As the marshes in this direction had not been previously tried the fisheries were sold the first year for the small sum of Ł250. Competition raised the price the following year to Ł800, and last season it was increased to Ł1,200. The purchasers gained a great deal at the commencement, but latterly most of their Leeches perished before getting to market, and besides the risks, the business is attended with so much expense, that on the whole they are not supposed to have made very good profits. The marshes have been much exhausted, nevertheless it is said that 6,000 Okes = 16,500 lbs. of Leeches were obtained last season. The privilege has been this year ordered to be sold on the spot, instead of at Constantinople, but it is not likely to be bought unless on much more moderate terms than those last paid.

Nitre is collected here for account of the Government, by two persons sent from the Superintendent of the Powder Mills at Constantinople. They are not seconded by the Authorities in preventing a trade in the article, and have been unable to procure more than 28,000 Okes per Annum. Natives have offered, if employed, to provide 50,000 Okes = 1,250 cwt. annually, and about as much more is now extracted secretly and sold in this part of the Country.

The Town of Kaissariah numbers 6,451 Houses. . . .

TRADE OF ADANA

The table following shows that in the 1840s imports of Tarsus averaged a little over Ł40,000 and exports a little over Ł60,000, both figures being well above the average for the 1830s. By the 1870s, imports of Mersin were some ten times as large, implying an annual compound rate of growth of about 6 percent and exports thirteen times as large, or at a rate of 6.5 percent. Thereafter there was little growth until the turn of the century, when the Adana region began to develop rapidly, especially in cotton growing and manufacturing (5:16). In 1908-12 Mersin's imports averaged about Ł675,000 and its exports about Ł860,000, or roughly a 50 percent increase over the figures for the 1870s, implying an annual rate of growth of about 1 percent per annum. Exports from the smaller ports also increased, and over the whole period the value of trade, in current prices, must have risen some fifteenfold.[1]

_____

1. Needless to say, other sources give different figures. A letter from Mersin in July 1912 estimated average imports at ŁT700,000; adding goods in transit or not paying duty because they came from other Ottoman provinces gave a total of ŁT1,350,000, i.e., twice as much as ten years earlier. Exports were said to be lower, not reaching the ŁT1,500,000 mark even in good crop years--RC no. 298, 1912.

Trade of Adana (Ŧ 000)

Year	Imports	Exports	Exports Vilayet
1836	64	90	
1830s average	12[b]	40[b]	
1844	31	116	
1845	42	56	
1846	30	29	
1847	60	49	
1847	31[b]	47[b]	
1848	26	80	
1849	84	59	
1851	97	41	
1852	(88)	(82)	
1872	(550)	(700)	
1873	429	675	
1874	405	391	
1875	653	531	
1876	646	977	
1877	421	453	
1878	446	405	
1880	426	562	
1881	464	692	
1882	716	852	
1886	663	789	
1887	393	405	471
1888	365	329	485
1889	355	374	485
1890	404	655	1,007
1891	534	1,082	1,615
1892	591	856	1,062
1893	608	512	562
1894	559	610	
1896	372	780	
1897	296	474	
1898	389	467	
1899	351	657	
1900	269	821	
1901	433	999	
1902	529	..	735
1903	629		1,802
1904	592		1,378
1905	695		927
1908	850	1,000	
1910	612	829	
1911	635	819	
1912	596	795	(1,070)

Source: FO 78/316, 78/615, 78/655, 78/704, 78/753, 78/796, 78/835, 78/908, 78/951, 78/3070, and A and P, reports from Aleppo and Adana.

[a]1836-52, trade of Tarsus; 1872-1912, trade of Mersin--practically all the vilayet's imports came through Mersin but the smaller ports (Ayas, Dörtyöl, Anamur, and Selefke) had some exports which are included in the total for the vilayet.

[b]CC Smyrne, vol. 43, Tarsous, vol. 2; francs converted at 25 to Ŧ.

SELECTION 23.   TRADE AND AGRICULTURE OF CILICIA, 1833

"Etat du Commerce et de la Production de la Syrie," 1 September 1833, CC Smyrne, vol. 43

. . . The caravans of Mesopotamia, Persia and Armenia, which go to Smyrna to sell their goods and take on supplies of European wares, pass through and spend some time in Caesaria [Kayseri] a town of 50 to 60,000 souls, which distributes part of their merchandize to Anatolia. Now the travel time from Caesaria to Smyrna is 190 hours, but to Tarsus only 48 hours.

If, therefore, the caravans went to Tarsus rather than Smyrna, both time and expenses would be cut; similarly if the Europeans took to Tarsus, or even to Caesaria, the goods which the caravans come to Smyrna to buy.

This rearrangement—which is called for by the nature of things—had begun to take place a few years ago; but the trade of Smyrna, fearful of its consequences, succeeded in getting the Porte to impose supplementary duties on goods shipped from Tarsus. It may be that the Egyptian government, which is now master of Tarsus, will find a way of reviving the activity which was stopped by that measure.

The plain of Cilicia, 25 leagues long and 12 to 15 wide, watered by three fine rivers, dominated by mountains covered with good building timber, could easily by itself supply a significant amount of trade, but its population and agriculture have fallen off considerably during the last years of the Turkish regime. In 1824 Adana still produced 8 million francs' worth of cotton and 1 million of tobacco; its present output is however: cotton, 5,000,000 francs, sesame seed 80,000 francs, wool 70,000, yellow wax 50,000. The tobacco, silk and madder crops, which by themselves could make of this a very flourishing region, are today of no value. Olives are abundant, but in the whole region there is not one oil press.

The goods that come from Caesaria, in spite of the obstacles placed by the Turkish government, added to what remains of production, still provide Tarsus with a trade which is not without significance. Tarsus sends to Europe the copper of Tokat and the cotton, wool and wax of its own region: in return it receives only [elle n'est reçoit--sic] its own yearly supply of coffee--600 metric quintals. . . . [In a subsequent table, the average annual exports of Tarsus and Adana are put at 1,000,000 francs, and average annual imports at 300,000 francs.]

TRADE IN THE 1870s

Selection 24 is taken from a set of reports on British trade with Turkey, prepared by the various British consulates at the request of their embassy and issued in a confidential printed report (FO 78/3070). The various returns, averaged and grouped in geographical areas, are shown in the following table. The total figures for imports and exports, excluding Istanbul, differ from those given in the text.

The estimate in the text of Ł10,000,000 for Istanbul's imports may be compared with one of 248 million marks (Ł12,400,000) given by a German source, which put Istanbul's exports at 146 million marks, or Ł7,300,000.[1] In the table on the value and volume of Trade (3:Introduction), Istanbul's imports have been put at Ł10,000,000 and exports at Ł5,000,000.

---

1. Deutsches Handelsarchiv, 1879 (I), p. 389.

Trade in 1873-77 (Yearly averages, in Ł 000)

Geographical Area	Imports	Exports
Major Anatolian ports		
Izmir	3,687	4,329
Trabzon[a]	566	312
Samsun	375	308
Adana	517	562
	5,145	5,511
Minor Anatolian towns		
Gelibolu	102	141
Kastamonu	(850)	(500)
Diyarbekir	(150)	(200)
Minor ports Trabzon vilayet	343	191
	1,445	1,032
The islands		
Scio and Çeşme	92	104
Rhodes and Sporades[b]	668	263
Samos	104	94
Crete	410	377
	1,274	838
The Arab provinces		
Aleppo (Iskenderun)	1,008	716
Beirut	(1,080)	(676)
Jaffa	159	254
Basra	176	329
	2,423	1,975
The European provinces		
Salonica	1,460	1,564
Prevesa	140	53
Scutari	(335)	(144)
Volo	134	285
	2,069	2,046
Grand Total	12,356	11,402

Source: FO 78/3070, except figures for Salonica, taken from table in 3:12.

[a]Excludes transit trade with Persia.
[b]Excludes transit trade of Rhodes.

SELECTION 24. TRADE IN 1878

Reports on Trade with Turkey, 1878-79, FO 78/3070

The want of reliable statistics renders an accurate estimate of the foreign trade of Turkey an impossibility. This want has been alluded to in many published commercial reports, e.g., in that of Sir H. Barron of the 1st of December, 1869, and in that of Mr. Wrench for 1874. At the commencement of the latter it is stated that statistics were to be collected and published by the Porte; the intention, no doubt, existed, but I believe that to this day nothing has been done to carry it out.

From the tables given above it will be seen that the exports from Turkey to Great Britain for the five years, from 1873 to 1877, amounted to 16,456,467 Ł., and the imports from the latter to the former to 19,629,964 Ł. The total exports for the same period amount to 46,292,447 Ł., and the total imports to 51,703,201 Ł. Unfortunately, statistics for the trade of Constantinople are not obtainable [and are not included in the totals--ed.], and consequently we have no information respecting the most important port in the Empire. In 1864, the imports of Constantinople from Europe were estimated at 7,315,113 Ł. exclusive of the transit trade to Persia, Russia, etc., and some years later at 10,000,000 Ł. As regards imports, it is usually said that about 40 per cent come from England, 20 per cent from France, including Switzerland and Belgium, 16 per cent from Germany and Austria, 9 per cent from Russia, and the remainder from Italy, Holland, Greece, and the United States. Under the circumstances, therefore, and in view of the fact that the tabular statements I have given above, cannot convey a really accurate idea of the foreign trade of the Empire, I feel that to offer any comments respecting its fluctuations would not only be useless, but also apt to mislead. As far as the figures go, they show that since 1874 there has

been a falling off in British trade. In 1876 there was a slight recovery, but in 1877, the
year of the war, trade of course was extremely dull. As regards 1878, trade was, at the
commencement of the year, immediately after the cessation of hostilities, extremely active,
and there was a great demand for British produce in those provinces of the Empire which,
during the war, had been cut off from Constantinople. Many persons, however, miscalculat-
ing the amount of the demand, imported so largely that the market became glutted, and merchants find themselves with considerable stocks of unsold goods in their warehouses.

As regards shipping the following is a return of British ships frequenting Turkish
ports since 1873.

In 1873 the figures were as follows:

	British steamers	Sailing vessels	Total
1873	5,085	1,231	6,316
1874	5,032	1,177	6,209
1875	4,515	977	5,492
1876	6,925	733	7,658

In 1877, the year of the war, there was of course a great falling off in the number
of British vessels, especially as regards Constantinople, as may be seen by Mr. Wrench's
published report.

FRENCH TRADE WITH TURKEY

Before the Revolution, France was by far the leading trade partner of the Ottoman Empire. Thanks to its excellent relations with the Porte, the resilience of its economy,
the abundant produce of its colonies, and the supervision and encouragement given to French
merchants by their government, its trade had multiplied severalfold. In the seventeenth
century, French imports from the Levant had exceeded the 10 million livres mark in only
three years. By 1723-29 they had risen to an average of 13.5 million; in 1749-55 imports
averaged 28 million and exports 27 million, and in 1782-85 34 million and 28.4 million
respectively.[1] In the next few years there was a rise to a peak of 38 million and 32 million francs in 1790-91.[2] At that point, France accounted for a half to three-fifths of
Ottoman trade with Europe.[3]

The abolition, by the Revolutionary government, of Colbert's restrictive and regulated
system of trade with the Levant, which opened Marseilles to foreign ships sailing to or
from the area, was resented by the French merchants, who claimed that it was injuring their
interests.[4] The deterioration of relations between Turkey and France also had its repercussions. Still more important, British naval supremacy in the Mediterranean made trade
with Turkey extremely difficult. In 1811 France's total trade with the Levant (exports
plus imports), totalled only 12 million francs.[5] In 1814-15, combined, French exports to
Istanbul on French ships amounted to only 945,000 piastres (about 1,200,000 francs), and
imports to 787,000 (under 1,000,000 francs), and the years 1816-18 showed a further decline. British cotton textiles were pouring into Turkey, Belgian and Saxon woollens were
displacing French ones, and the trade in colonial goods had passed entirely into British
hands.[6] Total French trade with the Ottoman Empire in 1816 amounted to 12 million francs
for imports and 11 million for exports. The Greek War of Independence again disrupted
trade but the figures for 1827 were 23.2 million for imports and 13.9 million for exports.[7]

The following selection, from a report by the consulate-general at Izmir, shows the
rapid progress made between 1840 and 1860. Helped by France's support of Turkey during
the Crimean War and by the massive flow of French funds into Ottoman government bonds,
railways, ports, and other investments, trade continued to surge. By the early 1870s imports ran well over 200 million francs and exports were close to that figure. After that,
however, there was a decline due to the shrinkage of the Ottoman Empire, the general fall
in world prices, and greater competition from Germany, Italy, and other countries.[8] In

the 1880s and 90s French exports stayed around the 100 million franc level and imports were well below 150 million; in 1908–10, exports averaged 116.6 million francs and imports 146.1 million.[9]

According to the first published Ottoman statistics, imports from France amounted to 269.8 million piastres in 1880–81 and 290.5 million in 1881–82, or an average of 15.0 percent of Turkey's total imports, and exports to 290.2 million and 396.3 million, or an average of 34.7 percent. France was thus Turkey's leading market and, together with Austria-Hungary, its second most important supplier. Thereafter France's share in Turkey's exports declined, to around 30 percent at the turn of the century and 19.9 percent in 1913–14, losing first place to Britain in the early 1890s; its share in imports fell to 10 percent at the turn of the century and 8.6 percent in 1913–14, by which time it was behind Britain, Austria-Hungary, and Germany.[10]

---

1. Masson, XVIIIe siècle, pp. 409–16.
2. Letter of 10 June 1830, CC Trébizonde, vol. 3.
3. Masson, p. 416--see also Report in EHME, pp. 31–37.
4. See account of meeting of French merchants in Istanbul of 1 Germinal, year 11 (1804), CC Constantinople, vol. 74.
5. Circular of Ministry of Foreign Affairs, 1812, CC Adrianople.
6. "Diverses Notes," 1819, CC Constantinople, vol. 80.
7. Letter of 10 June 1830, CC Trébizonde, vol. 3.
8. The following explanation was offered by a French observer: the Turks prefer cheap and shoddy goods, which the Germans, Austrians, and Italians willingly supply whereas the French send only fine goods. "Where prices are equal, French goods are always preferred by the natives--so much so that some German and Italian manufacturers put their products under French labels" (Georges Carles, La Turquie économique [Paris, 1906], pp. 32–33).
9. RC, various issues, especially no. 299 (1912).
10. Aybar, pp. 18–27; for fuller details, see Thobie, pp. 53–75, 483–501.

SELECTION 25. FRENCH TRADE WITH TURKEY, 1840-60

Notice sur le commerce de la France avec la Turquie, 1862, CC Smyrne, vol. 50

In 1842, France's general trade with Turkey (imports and exports combined) hardly reached 40,000,000 francs. In 1860 it was almost 200,000,000, increasing fivefold in the space of twenty years. The raw materials which we draw from Turkey amount, at official prices, to 26,000,000 in 1840 and 108,000,000 in 1860, or a ratio of about 1 to 3. Progress has been appreciably greater--and this is a matter for self-congratulation--as regards the products of our industry and also colonial goods and other merchandise drawn from our entrepôts or which only pass through France in transit on their way to Turkey: their value rose from 13,000,000 in 1840 to nearly 36,000,000 in 1860. But, regrettably, of the 13,000,000 in 1840 nearly two-thirds was supplied by our special trade, whereas in 1860 that trade accounted for only one-half.

Trade with Turkey, at official values, in the last twenty years, that is since 1840, in round numbers, appears in the table on the following page.

To make a sound judgment on the progression of our traffic with Turkey it is necessary to take into account the accidental and exceptional circumstances which may have temporarily raised its value; thus in some years a crop shortage made us buy a certain quantity of cereals, and if it is an advantage for us to have been able to obtain them in a country so near to us the need to spend part of resources on feeding ourselves is not a subject for congratulation in good home economics.

On the other hand, during the Crimean War, the needs of a large army caused France's exports to expand considerably, due to quite abnormal circumstances in those years. It is therefore necessary to take into account, in our imports, what was used for public food in certain exceptional periods, and in our exports what was designated to meet the needs of our armies in the field. Having done this, and eliminated all accidental influences, we can soundly judge the real position of our trade with Turkey.

During the twenty years represented in the table, 250 million francs' worth of cereals were imported into France. This gives an average of 12,000,000, ranging from 2,000,000 in 1852 to 55,000,000 in 1847. After 1847 comes 1857 (the year for which we do not have the figures), then 1858, with 24 million, 1856 with 19 million, 1846 with 17 million, 1855 with 16 million, and so on.

Taking into account these different figures, the variations of which followed the food needs of France, we find that normal trade with France amounted to 71,000,000 francs, in

| | (Millions of francs) | | |
	Imports	Exports	Total
1840	26	13	39
1841	40.5	16.5	57
1842	48	17.5	65.5
1843	52.5	20	72.5
1844	45	18.5	63.5
1845	51	25	76
1846	53	25	78
1847	98	28	126
1848	25	29	64
1849	55	34	89
1850	59.5	35.5	95
1851	50	32	82
1852	55.5	29	84.5
1853	68	29	97
1854	52.5	37.5	90
1855	78	90	168
1856	89	88	177
1857	missing	missing	missing
1858	85	70	155
1859	97	74.5	172
1860	109	86	195

official values, in 1847, declining to less than 60,000,000 in 1848. But it quickly rose again in 1849 and maintained itself until the war without great fluctuations, within the limits of 70 and 90 million. For the years 1855 and 1856, when trade was influenced by the needs of our army, one should deduct from the export figures of 90 million and 88 million shown in the table an amount of 100 million in supplies, divided equally between the two years. Thus the figures for total trade (exports and imports combined) are reduced to 102 million in 1855 and 108 million in 1856, while the three last years in the table in which the trade in cereals was not significant show 131 million, 160 million, and 185 million. Thus since the war—which undoubtedly encouraged and stimulated the organization on a large scale of the maritime service of the Messageries Impériales [see 4:5 and 6]—our trade has progressed appreciably and constantly, as may be seen by the results of the last five or six years.

All signs indicate that this progress will continue, and if certain items, for example, silk-worm eggs, show a tendency to diminish or even to disappear—perhaps only temporarily —others will come up, like cotton, the growing of which will be encouraged as long as the American question continues to be unsolved and, hence, prices remain high. Turkey is essentially an agricultural country, and the more is demanded of it the more it can export of its products and the more it will demand, in turn, from the manufacturing countries; for in trade, exports and imports are mutually interdependent. The soil of the different provinces of the Ottoman Empire, its privileged climate which allows the almost spontaneous growth of the most varied crops of the Old World and the New, its geographical position almost between Europe and Asia, should draw to it both the interest of economists and the attention of speculators.

It would seem that, since the war, the taste for French goods and their use have appreciably increased in Turkey, and since then our exports have drawn closer and closer to our imports; it should be noted that the import values given in our statistics include freight and other trade costs required to carry the goods to France, whereas exports are valued at the time they are loaded on board. If, therefore, one adds to the export values freight, insurance, etc. (as one does for imports), the figures of 70 million, 74.5 million, and 86 million shown for our exports to Turkey in 1858, 1859, and 1860 would be very close to those of 85 million, 97 million, and 109 million given for Turkish imports landed in France.

Note, too, that it is our insurance companies that cover almost all risks between the two countries and it is under our flag that, in the main, the most valuable goods sent from France are carried as well as a large part of the goods entering France—and you can form an idea of the advantages derived by our country from its trade with Turkey.

France takes from Turkey cereals, oilseeds, olive oil, silk, wool, goat hair, cotton, raw hides, madder, opium, sponges, gall nuts, and other dyestuffs and drugs.

It sends in return French and Swiss cloth, colonial goods, refined sugar, tanned hides, chemicals, fashionable clothing and other goods from Paris, furniture, and, in general, all the products of our industry.

We shall now examine in detail each of these items. . . .

RUSSIAN ECONOMIC INFLUENCE IN TURKEY

The following extract, from an official report written just before the First World
War, brings out the basic cause of the relatively low level of Russian trade with the Ottoman Empire. Although Russia's industrial output was growing more rapidly than that of any
major industrial country, its products were easily absorbed by the rapidly expanding internal market, leaving little surplus for export and greatly weakening the manufacturers' incentive to push into foreign markets. In Iran, the transport advantage enjoyed by Russia,
its predominant political influence, and the determination of its government to use trade
and investment as a means of penetration, overcame this handicap and enabled it to capture
nearly two-thirds of Iran's foreign trade by 1913.[1] But in the Ottoman Empire such factors
were absent, and although Russia's share of total trade rose slightly--to about 7 to 8 percent of imports and 3 to 4 percent of exports--its rank among importers and exporters remained unchanged, at fourth to fifth, and fifth to sixth, respectively.[2]

No breakdown is available for Turkey proper, but the figures for its largest exporting
and second largest importing port are illustrative. In the late 1830s and early 40s, Russia accounted for just over 5 percent of both Izmir's exports and its imports. Partly because of the disruptions caused by the Crimean War, the percentages fell off slightly in
the 1850s and early 60s. By the 1890s, Russia's share was once more running at 5 percent
and at the turn of the century stood at 7 to 8 percent for imports and 3 to 4 percent for
exports, a level that was maintained in the early 1900s.

Trade was, however, by no means Russia's most powerful lever for exerting influence.
Being a capital-importing country with practically no investments in the Ottoman Empire,
Russia was not a member of the Public Debt Council (7:16); however, following its victory
in the 1877-78 war, it imposed an indemnity of 802.5 million francs (ŁT35,310,000). Since
the Ottoman government was almost always in arrears in its installments on this indemnity,
Russia was in a position to exert considerable pressure.[4] Sometimes this was used for
purely political purposes, as during the Bulgarian crisis of 1908.[5] At others, the objectives were both political and economic, e.g., the securing of a railway concession in the
Black Sea area in order to divert the German line southward and prevent the building in
northern Anatolia of railways that might both pose a strategic threat to Russia and expose
its grain exports to increased Turkish competition.[6]

The Russian steamship line (La Compagnie russe de Navigation à Vapeur et de Commerce)
was founded in 1856; the government owned one-third of its shares and subsidized it heavily,
and its agents in the Black Sea and Levant ports enjoyed consular status. It was strongly
supported by the Russian embassies in Istanbul and Tehran and played a leading part in the
Black Sea coastal trade (4:8).

Like the other Great Powers, Russia took full advantage of the presence of members of
minority groups (mainly Greeks, Armenians, and Orthodox Christian Arabs) who had Russian
citizenship or protection. In the years immediately preceding the First World War, the
Russian government, as part of its new policy of economic penetration of Turkey, backed
the Mavrocordatos, a Phanariot family, in acquiring mining interests and gave initial support to the Armenian oil magnate, Mantashev, who sought to establish a banking network in
the Armenian provinces. In 1910 the government also set up trade committees in Istanbul
and Izmir, opened branches of the Banque russe pour le Commerce étranger and in 1914 made
arrangements for the takeover of a share of the Salonica Bank by the Russian Asiatic Bank.
Negotiations were also started with the Ottoman government by which Russia would have a
representative on the Public Debt Council and be granted various monopolies, including

exclusive rights to railways in the eastern provinces, in return for its consent to the raising of Ottoman customs duties to 15 percent (3:Introduction), to the taxing of Russian subjects on their movable property, and to the imposition of new Ottoman monopolies.[7] The outbreak of war, however, put an end to all these efforts and when relations between the Soviet government and the Turkish republic were resumed it was on a completely new basis.

1. EHI, pp. 142–46.
2. Eldem, pp. 181–82, and Novichev, Ocherki, p. 174.
3. It should, however, be noted that the source from which the earlier figures have been taken points out that the figures for Russian trade are incomplete because the Russian Company, which carried all goods shipped to or from Odessa, refused to divulge the information; CC Smyrne, vol. 50, Report on Trade of 1863.
4. Michael M. Milgrim, "The War Indemnity and Russian Commercial Policy in the Ottoman Empire: 1878–1914" in Osman Okyar, ed., Türkiye, pp. 297–366, on which this account draws heavily.
5. In 1909 Russia agreed to cancel the last forty of the seventy four payments due to it, in return for compensation by Bulgaria, which had just proclaimed its independence-- Shaw, History, 2:277.
6. Novichev, Ocherki, pp. 145–47.
7. See Milgrim, pp. 359–65.

SELECTION 26. RUSSIAN TRADE WITH THE MIDDLE EAST, 1913

V. K. Lisenko. Blizhnii Vostok kak rynok sbyta russkikh tovarov, St. Petersburg, 1913, pp. 14–40

Part I--General

Causes of the relatively slow development of our exports

Being predominantly agricultural countries, with a very low degree of development of factory industry, the states of the Near East hardly need to import any raw materials from abroad and, on the other hand, are completely dependent on the products of foreign industry. Obviously, this more than anything explains the success of West European exports to these countries, and our relative lack of success. At a time when the great development of manufacturing industry in most Western European states makes it necessary to increase by every means the export of manufactured goods to foreign markets, the evolution of our industrial activity has taken place in completely different conditions. The huge extent and consuming capacity of our internal market is still fully sufficient to absorb all the goods produced by our national factories and workshops. The accuracy of this observation is proved by the fact that, until now, we have exported to the Near East mainly the products of those branches of manufacturing which have reached a stage of development that forces them to send the surplus of their production to foreign markets. These are: sugar refining, milling, distilling, petroleum, and others.

Having admitted that the relatively slow development of our exports to the Near East is primarily explained by natural causes, it is nonetheless necessary to state that it is extremely important that we take measures to develop exports further. The progress of all kinds of exports represents one of the main conditions of equilibrium in the balance of payments of our country and of the expansion of its economic power. From this point of view, exports are necessary not only as an outlet for the surplus of our national production but as a powerful motive force making for the modernization of our industrial structure and for the replacement of our exports of raw materials by manufactured goods. Since our exports to the Near East consist predominantly of industrial goods, i.e., of manufactured and semimanufactured goods, they are extremely valuable for us in view of the abovementioned considerations. We must also give this matter serious thought because, owing to their geographic and other conditions, the Near Eastern markets represent our, so to speak, natural markets, the conquest of which would ultimately mark a victory for our economic life.

Our Competitors

At the head of the struggle for economic predominance in the countries of the Near East come Austria-Hungary and Germany. They are followed by Italy, England, France, Belgium, the United States, and others. The first two account for about 50 percent of exports to the Near East, and the others for about 40 percent. . . .

What then are the causes of the success of the above-mentioned countries in selling their goods in the Near East? The main ones are: (1) the high degree of development of their manufacturing industries and the almost total absence of such industry in the Near Eastern countries; (2) the suitability of their goods to the demands of the markets, especially in respect of cheapness, for the Near Eastern markets, with the large amounts they demand, and because of the poverty of the mass of buyers, are not at all concerned with quality; (3) the granting to local importers of large amounts of credit, in most cases for three to six months; (4) strict fulfilment of orders and delivery of goods within the stipulated period; and (5) thorough knowledge of local markets through resident agents, brokers, trading firms, and traveling salesmen.

Main Deficiencies of our Exports

Among the main causes preventing Russian wares from occupying their appropriate place in Near Eastern markets are--along with the insufficient development of our factory industry and the relatively great extent of our internal market--a set of other, smaller, ones which do not constitute serious obstacles to our exports but represent, rather, deficiencies of organization which it is fully in our power to remedy. Among these deficiencies are (1) the sporadic, unsustained nature of our export trade, (2) unsuitability to the needs of Near Eastern markets, (3) faulty implementation of orders and failure to deliver goods on schedule, (4) absence of representatives of Russian firms in the local markets, (5) lack of credit facilities to local merchants.

1. Sporadic nature of our exports. The sporadic, unsustained nature of our export trade is partly explained by the fact that in good crop years--when the purchasing power of the inhabitants increases--we are able to sell our production in our internal markets; when that purchasing power decreases, we give serious consideration to the Near Eastern markets. But such an explanation by no means covers all the cases, and quite often, having established with one or another of the Near Eastern markets ties that offer hope of growing stronger in the future, we suddenly break those ties without any apparent connection with this basic matter.

In the course of our mission to the Near East we learned of many such cases which had undesirable effects on our exports. It is sufficient to mention, in this connection, the highly successful delivery of Russian rails to Serbia in 1907, which unfortunately was not thereafter repeated. The sale by our handicraftsmen of hardware and locks in Constantinople in 1911 was a great success; fifty handicraftsmen went there and, in less than two months, sold a considerable batch of these goods but never reappeared in Turkey. One should also mention here the successful attempt, in 1906, to sell in the Constantinople market a large consignment of Siberian butter (about 600 barrels); although this item still features [in the trade] it does so in very small quantities, and remains insignificant in relation to local consumption. Lastly, one cannot fail to mention the sharp fluctuations in our sugar exports to Turkey and the repeated, but unfortunately sporadic, attempts to export our timber to Palestine, Egypt, and others.

All these phenomena undoubtedly have a very unfavorable effect on our exports and therefore deserve serious consideration on the part of Russian enterprises.

2. Unsuitability to the needs of Near Eastern markets. As already mentioned, one of the causes of the success of West European goods in Near Eastern markets is their suitability to the tastes and demands of these markets. A special virtuosity has been shown in this respect by Austria-Hungary, Germany, and Italy, which have built a whole set of factories and workshops producing specially for export and perfectly copying and preparing articles that can readily sell in the Near Eastern markets, with their capricious tastes. In these three countries, such articles have a special designation: bon pour l'Orient.

In this field we lag far behind our Western competitors, and our goods, with all their advantages over the West European, cannot find general acceptance among Near Eastern customers. First and foremost, most of the articles we export to the Near East are too expensive for the relatively poor mass of Near Eastern consumers. For example, our cotton textiles are 20-30 percent dearer than foreign ones. The same applies to rubber goods, perfumery, timber, and other goods. One must also add that--what is not surprising--Russian wares are too good for the unexacting Near Eastern markets. For instance, our first class flour is used only to flavor the far inferior foreign varieties and is completely beyond the reach of the masses. Our sugar, which ranks high in percentage of saccharine content and degree of refinement, is sold with some difficulty in Near Eastern markets because it dissolves in coffee or tea far more slowly than does Austrian sugar. In the same way, our cotton goods--which are excellent in their quality and artistic designs--are sold in insignificant quantities in the Near East only because the local population prefers the inferior, but cheaper, foreign prints.

In order to remove this obstacle in the path of the development of our exports, it is evidently necessary for us to follow the example of the countries competing with us and to adapt, to a greater extent, the quality and cost of our goods to the demands of the Near Eastern markets. This can be done in two ways: (1) the installation in our country of industries whose products are specially adapted to the above-mentioned markets, which would, of course, entail significant costs for changing many of the technical conditions of present forms of production; and (2) adaptation of Russian goods to the tastes of Near Eastern consumers, independently of change in the techniques of production itself, and hence using simpler methods. . . .

3. Faulty implementation of orders and failure to deliver goods on schedule. Cases of faulty implementation of orders and failure to deliver goods on schedule are, unfortunately, not infrequent among our exporters to the Near East. In order not to seem to be

making unfounded accusations and to back our statement, it is enough to quote the following extract from a written report presented to one of the members of our expedition by the representative of one of our very large commercial-industrial organizations: "In many of the places which the mission visited, I have not only heard but myself ascertained that several Russian firms which received orders fulfilled them carelessly, or with considerable delay or else--which is still worse--not at all." . . .

4. Absence of representatives of Russian firms in local markets. The experience of foreign countries shows that a profound knowledge of the tastes and pecularities of Near Eastern markets can be acquired through skillful and well-organized representation of trading firms in local markets. For this purpose, most of our competitors (1) send out traveling salesmen, (2) appoint permanent representatives of individual firms, and (3) organize joint action by a set of firms or a whole group of industrial and trading firms engaged in the same line of business.

The action of traveling salesmen in any given place has, with few exceptions, a tem-porary character for, having gathered orders on the basis of the patterns they present, they usually move on to another place. Permanent agents of individual firms have, over traveling salesmen, the advantage of staying at the place of import without interruption, and therefore being in a position to study in more detail the tastes and demands of Near Eastern customers, to be in constant contact with them, and to follow closely the doings of their competitors. Such agents usually supply their employers with information on the credit of buyers, on the prices quoted in local markets, and, in general, on the prevalent mood of these markets. Lastly, the collective action of our West European competitors manifests itself either in the form of each industrial group's creating an export union in a given place (for example, Deutsche Export Gesellschaft, the Austrian export association Orosdi-Back in Smyrna, etc.) or else in that of the union of all trading firms in a given place in the Near East, e.g., Constantinople, in the form of a Chamber of Commerce. . . .

So far, we have moved comparatively little in this direction. Nevertheless, very recently, we have taken a few steps forward. Thus some of our firms have sent traveling salesmen to the Near East--the Zaglodin firm of Moscow, which makes brocades, and others. Some Russian firms also have their own permanent agents in the main consuming centers of the Near East, e.g., Nobel Brothers, Treugolnik (rubber goods), Ralli and Co. (perfumery), Naidich of Moscow (spirits), Luther of Revel (plywood articles), Alexeyev, Vishniyakov, and Shamshin of Moscow (articles of gold thread), and many others. Lastly, since 1909, our merchants have shown their initiative by entering the Near East jointly, e.g., The Moscow Export Association, which has permanent branches in Constantinople and Jassy and also agencies in other cities.

Thus it remains only to hope that all our enterprising industrial-commercial class will continue its development further and will follow the example of private initiative, which plays such a decisive role in the field of export.

5. Lack of credit facilities to local importers. The sale of goods on credit--with the exception of foodstuffs, iron, and a few other articles--represents one of the most important causes of the success of Western European trade in the Near East. Our foreign competitors usually grant local buyers credit for three to six months. They have been following this practice for long, and it is particularly widespread in Turkey, where transactions on credit amount to millions of Turkish pounds. Fear that their clients may lack means of payment does not seem to play a significant part because, as already mentioned, most West European firms have their own permanent agents, who supply them with detailed information on the credit and degree of reliability of local importers. Unfortunately, we have followed this example very little. . . .

Significance of Commercial Treaties

West European governments have concluded with most of the Near Eastern countries commercial treaties which fully correspond to the needs of the current requirements of their mutual exchange of goods, and these treaties contain special tariff agreements concerning goods of most interest to both sides. Russia, however, does not have such treaties with the countries of the Near East, since our commercial agreements with Bulgaria and Serbia are based only on the most favored nation clause . . . while the one with Turkey, which has been in force since 1862, is so out of date that it has no real significance for the goods which matter to the two signatory countries. The only exception is our treaty with Egypt, which was concluded in 1909 and presents not insignificant advantages for our exports. . . .

Significance of Banks

The existence in the Near East of numerous foreign banks plays a leading part in the export trade of the corresponding countries. It is therefore even more urgent that we establish there a Russian bank since our exporters have not yet succeeded in familiarizing themselves with all the particularities of the Near Eastern markets and occupying in them a solid position. . . . "The only exception, unfortunately, is a branch of the Russian bank for foreign trade in Constantinople. Such an apathy and inertia on the part of Russian capital is startling. Very many of our banks open branches in the most insignificant

Russian towns, simply because their competitors have conducted successful operations in these places. But to undertake new activities, incur risks, and enlarge their scope--that they cannot get themselves to do. The explanation is, apparently, that our banks like industry to prepare markets for them and guarantee them definite profits. But this mode of operation is hardly the right one. The history of the appearance of foreign banks in the Near East is just the opposite: these banks were pioneers in the export trade of their countries and a main cause of its eventual success. We should adopt a similar point of view, for to continue hoping that some local branch of the Deutsche Orientbank will help our exporters by discounting Russian bills, bills of ladings, etc. is surely not warranted."

We have given below . . . detailed information on the establishment of foreign banks in those parts of the Near East visited by the mission. Here it is necessary to say only that, in the opinion of the majority of its members, the most suitable bases for establishing Russian banks are Sofia and Smyrna. . . .

Trade Museums

In all the large Near Eastern centers, our foreign competitors have trade museums and permanent trade exhibits. This method of acquainting local consumers with the range and quality of their products has been mastered by them for a long time and, apparently, produces excellent results. In this regard, Russia is far behind its competitors in the Near East. All the "Russian trade museums" visited by the mission in Bulgaria, Serbia, and Turkey have nothing in common with those set up by other governments. The persons managing them are there by chance and are little known by the local trading and industrial classes. The objects exhibited in these "museums" make the saddest impression, as regards both quality and quantity. Thus, for example, we saw in a room bearing the sign "Russian Trade Museum" only one samovar, a few penknives (and these, apparently, of German origin), and two or three 5 kopek editions of the works of L. Tolstoi. Agreeable exceptions were provided only by the excellently equipped warehouse of the branch of the Moscow Export Association, in Constantinople, the small exhibits of Russian goods in the offices of the Russian Steamer and Trade Company in Beirut and Smyrna, and the museum of Russian handicrafts organized by our honorary consul in Port Said. . . .

Russian Steamer and Trade Company

The Russian Steamer and Trade Company represents, so far, the main shipping enterprise serving our exports to the Near East. The existence of foreign steam navigation companies like the Austrian Lloyd, Deutsche Levant Linie, Messageries Maritimes, Fraissinet et Co., Paquet, Johnston Line, Khedivial Mail, Westcott and Laurence Line, Société Commerciale Bulgare, Hungarian Levant Line, our own Dobrovolnii Fleet, Severnii Company, and others, does not diminish the immense significance of this company. For it has over the aforementioned enterprises some important advantages, such as direct and regular connections, without transshipments, with most of the Near Eastern ports and, above all, it is able to keep in its own warehouses merchandise given to it for shipping, which foreign shipping companies do only with great difficulty. This fact makes many exporters give preference to the Russian Company, which can with some truth be called a "monopolist" in the carrying of our goods to the Near Eastern ports.

Detailed information on the nature of the activities of the Russian Steamer and Commercial Company is given in an Appendix to this report. . . . Here it is necessary only to mention those measures that would be desirable to coordinate further the activities of the Company with the interests of Russian export trade. The main ones are:

1) The drawing of a regular and permanent schedule for freight rates. . . .

2) Reduction of freight rates. The cost of transporting our goods on the Company's steamers is at present significantly higher than on those of most foreign companies . . . in general not less than 15 to 20 percent. It is interesting to note, for example, that the fairly large quantities of tobacco we have sent to Egypt in recent years were carried exclusively on the ships of the French Messageries Maritimes, solely because the freight rate of the Russian Company from Odessa was 30 kopeks per pud, whereas that of the French company did not exceed 10 to 12 kopeks.[2] The same is true of our spirits, which are often sent to Turkey on foreign ships because of lower freights. Thus, according to information supplied by the Tereshchenko firm, in 1909 20 percent and in 1910 27 percent of the spirits sent by them to the Turkish markets went on Austrian Lloyd ships.

The management of the Russian Company explains this difference by the fact that foreign ships leave Odessa and other Black Sea ports on their return journey, which allows them to charge lower rates and carry large quantities of goods, rather than return in ballast. The Russian Company is in a different position and charges for the various kinds of goods rates based on strict commercial calculations. Whatever be the case, the present Company rates cannot but be regarded as excessive, and some reduction in them would undoubtedly be very helpful to the interests of Russian exports.

3) Establishment of more frequent and regular steamer services between Odessa and the Near Eastern ports. In the opinion of those members of the mission who represented industry, this would be a very helpful measure, since it would enable our exporters to send their goods to local clients regularly, within the stipulated period and in appropriate

batches. This would be particularly important for Bulgaria, on whose ports the Russian Company's steamers call only twice a month, and with much delay.

We should also mention here the desire expressed by some industrialists for the opening of a direct route between Mariupol and Constantinople; this could play an important part in the sale of our iron, coal, cement, and other goods to Turkey. In the opinion of the industrialists, this project should not be too difficult to implement, for the availability of these goods should guarantee that the line will not operate at a loss.

4) Reduction of the fees charged by the Company for loading and unloading goods. According to the industrialists, these fees are very high. Thus, for example, in Salonica, in identical conditions of unloading sugar, the Austrian Lloyd charges 1 franc and 50 centimes per ton and the Russian Company 3 francs 25. . . .

5) More care and attention in handling cargoes. . . . Russian Danube Steamship Line. The Russian-Danube Steamship Line carries our goods mainly to Serbia, Bulgaria and Rumania. . . . [The] figures show that the Russian Line does not yet play a significant part in our sales to these countries. Among the companies with direct sailings on the Danube, the Russian Line comes last in passenger and goods traffic. The largest cargo operations are undertaken by the Austrian and Hungarian companies, and also the Rumanian River Steamers. Only a thorough reorganization of this enterprise will make it possible for our goods to penetrate the Danubian Slav lands, especially Serbia, for whom the Danube represents the only way by which it can deliver itself from the Austrian influence which has captured its markets. . . .

Railway Tariffs for Exports

The question of reducing Russian railway rates on goods exported by us to the Near East was discussed in the commercial-industrial session of 1910, devoted to the development of our trade with the Near East, and also in the conference organized for the same purpose by the Ministry of Trade and Industry at the end of 1911. The participants in these meetings expressed in particular the desire of reducing rates on the following Russian goods: kerosene, from 13 kopeks per pud to 9; flour, increasing the rebate from 20 percent to 50; wood, reduction of exclusive tariff no. 1 by 20 to 25 percent; sugar, extending the southern maritime tariff to all ports on the Black Sea and the Sea of Azov and renewal of the privileges prevailing until September 1, 1911, for Constantinople, Varna, and Burgas; coal, retention of present low rates; metal goods, application of rates charged on coal; matches, at present satisfactory; and a few other goods. . . .

From our discussions with various large foreign exporters, it became evident that foreign railway tariffs are, in general, more suited to the needs and conditions of industry and trade, and hence of exports, than are our own. In this respect we fall behind not only France but even Germany and Austria-Hungary; in the last-mentioned, the attempt to individualize transport rates has led to the granting of widespread rebates (refaktsii) by the railways to exports, for instance sugar and some other goods sent to the Near East. Besides, foreign railway tariffs, unlike ours, have special reduced rates for finished goods and manufactures, i.e., for precisely those goods that are most demanded in the Near East. The difference between the railway rates paid by our exports and by those of other countries is sometimes very great. One example is sufficient; our sugar when sent to the Turkish and Bulgarian ports pays some 40 percent more than does Austrian sugar to those same ports. Our textiles are in the same position in spite of the rebate granted by the railways to textile exports. . . . [There follows a detailed comparison with Germany, showing the rebates granted to exporters by railways in both countries.]

Postal Relations

Our postal relations with the countries of the Near East leave much to be desired. In this respect, we are in a far less favorable position than most of our foreign competitors. . . .

Passport Formalities

Existing passport formalities for persons wishing to go abroad for trade play a not unimportant part in the matter of the development of our exports to the Near East. The prevailing regulations in our country are, in this respect, complicated and inconvenient, and often arouse fully justified complaints from interested parties. . . .

Main Exports to the Near East and Measures to Facilitate Their Sale

Among the main Russian goods that have, or could have, a market in the Near East, the following may be mentioned:

1. Kerosene. In this product we already occupy a very strong position in the Near East: in Serbia we have a monopoly, in Turkey we account for about 65 percent of imports, in Bulgaria 84, and in Egypt 30 percent. However, recently our position has changed drastically and--except for Serbia, where we have a contract with the government monopoly that runs until 1914--imports of our kerosene in the Near Eastern countries have sharply fallen off. . . . The main reason for this is growing competition from Rumania and, especially, North America. which have erected their own storage tanks in most Turkish and Bulgarian

ports, but also the unfavorable conjuncture in our domestic market, i.e., the curtailment of petroleum production and the lack of new oil fields at the disposal of the industry. Among the measures that can increase our sales of petroleum products in the Near East are: (1) the organization of the transport of kerosene, following the example of our competitors, and the building of storage tanks in the main Near Eastern ports, (2) the reduction of the railway rate to Batum from 13 kopeks per _pud_ to 9, (3) the appointment of representatives of Russian firms in the local markets. . . .

2. _Metalwares_ (iron sections and bars, beams, channels, rails, trusses, steel, axles, nails, and other). Total consumption of these goods in Bulgaria, Serbia, Turkey, and Egypt averages about 12 million _puds_ (1910-11). According to V. M. Pulaskii, member of our mission and representative of the Prodamet Company, there are good grounds for assuming that, with the necessary reorganization of our export trade, a significant part of this amount could be replaced by Russian goods; if we assume that Russian iron could account for 50 percent of the total, exports to the Near Eastern markets would amount to 6 million _puds_. In the opinion of Pulaskii, the sale of our metal goods is in any case guaranteed in Bulgaria and Serbia. The same can more or less be said about Turkey, where Russian iron is in great demand and very highly prized for its quality. In Egypt, however, things are somewhat different, for English and Belgian goods are firmly entrenched there and Russian iron would have to engage in a severe struggle with them. . . .

3. _Sugar_. Until now, Russia has sent to the Near East almost exclusively granulated sugar, whose exports, however, do not have a permanent character but fluctuate sharply from year to year. In good years such as 1912, there was practically no granulated sugar in the local markets except Russian, whose quality is preferred to Austrian and which is priced somewhat lower only because of the poor quality of our sacking. But if our exports of granulated sugar are quite satisfactory, one can certainly not say the same about our lump sugar, which until now has been practically unknown in the Near East. In this respect, the Bulgarian and Turkish markets are of great interest. . . .

4. _Spirits_. Russian spirits hold a comparatively strong position in the Near Eastern markets. In Turkey and Egypt—according to the representative of the Russian association of distillers who was a member of our mission—our share of this product is about 80 percent. In Serbia, we shipped 40 railway carloads of spirits to meet the needs of the Serbian monopoly, and our business is only slightly less favorable with Bulgaria, where imports of foreign spirits are steadily diminishing because of greater local production. The further extension of our spirits in all these countries is impeded by the competition of Austria-Hungary, which promotes its exports by granting large export premiums. . . .

1. The percentages refer only to Bulgaria, Serbia, and Turkey.
2. Information supplied by the large importer of Russian tobacco in Alexandria, Mr. Mutasian [Matossian?].

TRADE FAIRS

In the Arab countries and in Iran, fairs—as known in medieval and early modern Europe—played a relatively minor part. "It is within the framework of urban _suqs_, daily or weekly markets in town or country that, under Islam, trade was traditionally carried out in the main."[1] But in Anatolia and the Balkans, perhaps because of Byzantine traditions, annual fairs were frequent and important, becoming more so in the Balkans in the seventeenth and eighteenth centuries with increasing commercial contacts with Central Europe.[2] In 1834, a French consular report listed the following fairs in Rumelia: Seres, Yenica (Yenija, known as St. Lucas) and Petritz in Macedonia, Priştina in Serbia, Perlepe and Sliven in Bulgaria, Philippopoli (known as Marasseon) in Romania, Nevrekop and Uzuncaova (Uzunjuova).[3]

As for Anatolia, a detailed list is given for the 1840s by Lemonidi.[4] First in importance came that of Yapraklı near Çankiri, held for seven to eight days at the end of July.[5] It attracted buyers and sellers from Iran to Bessarabia, who conducted a large volume of business in colonial goods, European textiles, Asian silks, and livestock. The fair of Balıkesir had formerly been the leading one in Anatolia but had lost some of its importance; held for fifteen days in mid-August, and dealing in colonial goods, textiles and household provisions, it attracted business from Istanbul, Izmir, Iran, and other neighboring Asian lands. The third large fair was that of Zile, near Tokat, held for twenty days at the end of September and conducting the same kind of business as the two others. Other, smaller, fairs mentioned are: Ankara, for about fifteen days at the beginning of January; Seres, for twenty days in March; Lüle Burgaz, for seven to eight days in April; Okhri, for seven days in May; Kavarna and Shumla, eight to twelve days at the beginning of June; Yamboli, eight days in mid-June; Varna, twelve to fifteen days starting on July 5; Karasu twelve to fifteen days starting on July eighth to tenth; Karadagh near Salonica, ten days towards the end of July; Tatar bazar, ten days at the beginning of August; Jannina, fifteen days around August 20; Tzirpan (Çirpan?), eight to ten days at the beginning of September, Çatalca, eight to ten days in mid-September; Silivri, eight to ten days starting September 10; Eski Zagra, fifteen days near the end of September; Lukka at Yenice Vardar, twenty days starting on October 8; Kızanlık, fifteen days at the beginning of November. Another fair not listed by Lemonidi is mentioned by Brunschvig, that of Manyas.[6] The same author adds that in these fairs Turks were "hardly represented among the professional merchants; among these there is no doubt that a preponderant place was often held by Jews and Christians--Greeks above all but also Armenians and foreigners."[7]

The volume of transactions at these fairs fluctuated with business conditions. For example in 1857 "the effects of the failures and the monetary crisis spread also through the interior before the autumnal fair of Balukissar [Balikesir], where there was a decrease of one-third in the amount of business done."[8]

The following selection describes the main fair in Rumelia. Further information is supplied by an almost contemporary British report.[9] The town is stated to have consisted of about 200 houses, with a church and mosque, the inhabitants being engaged in agriculture and the fair being the largest and most important in Turkey. The value of the goods brought in 1861 was: foreign ₤721,000 (British 315,000, German 197,000, Swiss 47,000, Belgian 44,000, French 30,000, Persian 33,000, American 28,000, Russian 21,000, Greek 4,000) and Turkish ₤367,000 (260,000 from the European provinces and 107,000 from the Asian). The 1861 figure was some ₤300,000 below that of 1860, because of the "monetary embarrassments and crisis" in Istanbul, in which many Rumelian merchants had been involved.

British goods consisted of manufactures for ₤213,000 and colonials for ₤102,000. German trade had been decreasing, and was estimated to have fallen off by 45 percent since 1846, because of the competition of British cottons; however woolens had held their own. Swiss trade had also declined, but was still important in handkerchiefs and prints while Belgian was increasing and included sugar, window glass, and paper. France supplied silks and fancy articles of dress and Persia shawls, silk stuffs, and tobacco. American goods were mainly furs, brought through Leipzig, and Russian consisted of furs and church books and images, brought through Bucharest. The Turkish provinces supplied furs, tobacco, grain, attar of roses, rice, leather goods, woolen stuffs, iron, and cotton.

Order was maintained by cavalry and police patrols. "Amongst such a multitude of strangers present at the fair only five cases of drunkenness and three of robbery took place. There were about sixty money changers--principally Jews--at this fair. Some of them were to be seen standing or walking about carrying bags full of money in their hands . . . and although they occupied insecure and tempting positions not one of them was molested. This careless display of money was a sign of order and confidence."

The decline in the importance of fairs in Turkey was brought about by the same forces which, earlier in Europe, had shifted the locus of commercial and financial activity from fairs to cities, and which may be summed up as a decrease in transport and transactions costs.[10] Already in 1846 the British consul at Samsun had reported: "The fair of Zile

was a complete failure. No business was transacted but at most ruinous prices, and with
the facilities offered by the steam communication between this and the Capital, ere a lapse
of many years it is probable that the fair will no longer take place, as the greater part
of the trade already prefer going to the Constantinople market, both to purchase their supplies of manufactures and to dispose of whatever articles of country produce they may possess."[11] Of course, the process of decline was much slower than this. The Ottoman authorities did their best to protect and encourage fairs, and as late as 1890 a new one was established, by decree, at Eskişehir, the bifurcation of the Anatolian railway.[12] But the
spread of steam navigation, railways, banking, telegraphs, and information slowly reduced
fairs to purely local functions.

1. Brunschvig, p. 51.
2. Ibid., pp. 65-67.
3. CC Salonique, vol. 21, Report on Salonica, 1 January 1834. See also a list of
the fairs in the Salonica region in the 1830s (FO 78/265).
4. Pp. 200-202.
5. A British consular report gives the date of the fair as 22 September. It states
that "the merchants bring about ₤50,000 worth of merchandise, the Aleppo merchants bring
the most," and that during eleven days at Çankiri "from 7,000 to 8,000 people come daily
to the fair"—A and P 1880, vol. 74, "Kastamuni." In the 1830s Vronchenko (2:278-79) had
put the value of goods sold at Yaprakli at ₤T100,000 and at Balikesir at ₤T150,000.
6. P. 71. Still another fair is mentioned in a British consular report (Stevens to
Brant, 31 December 1840, FO 78/443), that of Tokat. European goods brought to it in 1840
had amounted to not less than ₤150,000, an increase over 1839. They had come to the
"natives of Angora" through Istanbul and Izmit.
7. Brunschvig, p. 68.
8. A and P 1857-8, vol. 55, "Brussa."
9. "Report on Fair of Ouzungiova in 1861" by John Blunt, FO 195/590. For an equally
enthusiastic description, made in 1841, see Blanqui, Voyage en Bulgarie (Paris 1843),
quoted by Brunschvig, p. 70.
10. See Douglass C. North and Robert P. Thomas, The Rise of the Western World (Cambridge, 1973), pp. 134-38.
11. "Trade of Samsun in 1846," FO 78/704.
12. Brunschvig, p. 69.

SELECTION 27. FAIR OF UZUNCAOVA, 1862

Champoiseau to Thouvenel, 8 October 1862, CC Adrinople)

The fair of Uzuncaova, one of the most important in Turkey, which is held in a village
between Adrianople and Philippopolis between 25 October and 5 September [sic, read 25 September to 5 October] has just ended. Here is a table of the commercial transactions carried out:

Foreign furs, mostly from Leipzig; the amount brought in was worth 2,000,000 piastres
and that sold 1,300,000 (a piastre equalled 20.8 centimes at the fair).

Cloth, calico, madapolam of foreign make, mostly from England and Austria; brought in
40,000,000 piastres, sold 25,000,000.

Foreign silk cloth, from Germany and France; brought in 1,000,000, sold 300,000.

Foreign woolen cloth, from Austria and Germany; brought in 1,500,000, sold 750,000.

Foreign hardware, from Austria, France, and a small amount from England; brought in
3,000,000, sold 1,800,000.

Colonial goods, from England and a small amount from France; brought in 1,500,000,
sold 1,200,000.

Foreign cotton yarns, from England; brought in 1,000,000, sold 700,000.

Local products, a total of 6,200,000 piastres was brought in and 5,920,000 was sold.
The main local products that were in demand were:

Aba, or heavy woolen cloth; 1,000,000 piastres' worth was brought in and all was sold.

Lamb and goatskins, raw; 500,000 piastres brought in and all sold.

Iron from Samakoi [Samakov] and Malgara; 200,000 brought in, all sold.

Leaf tobacco; 20,000 brought in, 15,000 sold.

The price of all these goods was between 30 and 50 percent higher than that prevailing last year. This rise is due to the small number of sellers who came to the fair in
1862; almost half the booths in the fair remained vacant.

4

Transport

The absence of navigable rivers in Anatolia has always been a major obstacle to transport, but this is partly offset by the length of the shoreline, the abundance of small natural harbors, and the heavy concentration of population in the coastal rims (4:1). Hence, in the past, the bulk of goods was borne by small sailing ships and the vitally important supply of Istanbul was effected by sea (2:3). Inland, the lack of roads was largely compensated by the efficiency of the camel as a carrier and long caravan routes, with hans built at suitable intervals, that crisscrossed the peninsula (4:12). The chief ones were:

    1. the Trabzon-Erzurum-Bayezıt route leading to Tabriz;

    2. the Samsun-Amasya-Zile-Tokat route to Sıvas, at which point it bifurcated, one branch passing through Kayseri and the Cilician gates to Tarsus and the other to Delikli-taş, Harput and Diyarbekir, and thence to either Mosul, through Mardin, or Aleppo, through Urfa;

    3. the İzmit-Bolu-Tosya route, touching the second route at Amasya;

    4. the Bursa-Akşehir-Konya-Tarsus route leading to Syria.[1]

Carts were not used in the cities or for long-distance travel but were quite important in the economy of many villages.

Thus in the preindustrial period the transport system of Turkey was not appreciably worse than that of Europe, though the high cost of land carriage meant that "a Mediterranean economy was a possibility in a sense in which an Anatolian economy, for instance, was not."[2] But with the development of canals and roads in Europe, from the seventeenth century on, the relative position of Turkey increasingly deteriorated.

Steam navigation came to Turkey in the late 1820s, and in the next two decades numerous steamship lines linked the ports of the Mediterranean, Aegean, and Black seas and connected the country with southern and western Europe, Russia, and the Levant (4:4 to 11). Until the 1850s, steamers were used mainly for passengers, mail, and highly valuable merchandise, but after that they carried bulk goods as well. Practically all Turkey's foreign trade was seaborne, and by the turn of the century only a small fraction went on sailing ships.

The shift from sail to steam greatly helped foreign shipping, since the rising cost of steamers (4:6) made it increasingly difficult for Ottoman shippers to buy and operate them. Local shipping was also handicapped by the government's inability to protect it even in coastal traffic, because of the privileges granted to foreigners by the Capitulations (4:11). Moreover, the fact that most of the ships sailing under the Turkish flag were owned and manned by Greeks made the government hesitant to encourage what was a potentially hostile merchant navy. As a result, the bulk of traffic was carried by foreign ships, although a few Ottoman lines were also active (4:11).

The early steamers did not require any special port facilities other than coal depots, but as their size grew the inadequacy of Turkey's harbors became increasingly apparent. Yet it was not until 1875 that Izmir was provided with a modern port, and Istanbul had to wait until the 1890s (4:10,11). Good ports were also built at Beirut and Salonica, and some docking facilities at Zonguldak and Trabzon. Lighthouses were erected along the coasts (4:11). And shortly before the war surveys were made for the construction of harbors at Tripoli, in Syria, Jaffa, Latakia, Iskenderun, Mersin, Ereğli, Amasra and Rodosto.[3]

The development of sea transport, and the reduction of freight rates (4:11), stimulated foreign trade but did nothing to facilitate the movement of goods from the interior, and, except in a coastal zone that was in most places quite narrow, high transport costs prevented the export of bulky goods such as grain or minerals. A few road projects were considered in the 1840s and 50s (4:13) and a very small amount of work was done on some heavily used roads, e.g., from Bursa to Gemlik and Trabzon to Erzurum, as well as in Lebanon and some European provinces. But the opening of Anatolia had to await the advent of the railway.

Railways are, perhaps, the most important and characteristic single artefact of the nineteenth century. In Lenin's words: "Railways are a summation of the basic capitalist industries, coal, iron, and steel; a summation and the most striking index of the development of world trade and bourgeois-democratic civilization."[4] It is a measure of the low degree of development of the Ottoman Empire that, in 1914, its 1,900,000 square kilometers had only 5,991 kilometers of railways, and that the 740,000 square kilometers of Anatolia had only 2,918--most of the latter having been built in the previous two decades. But this lack of railways also points to something else: the Ottoman Empire was much less subject to imperialist influences than most other parts of the world, a fact due, in turn, partly to the resistance put up by its government and partly to the neutralization of each other's schemes by the various Powers; for example, Russia blocked the building of railways in northern and eastern Anatolia and Britain held up the Baghdad line.

Marxist writers dwell on two aspects of railways. On the one hand, they are "an instrument for oppressing a **thousand million** people (in the colonies and semi-colonies)."[5] This subject is taken up at some length by Rosa Luxemburg, in discussing the Anatolian railways:

> The reverse side of this grand 'peaceful cultural-work' is the 'peaceful' and grand ruin of the peasantry of Asia Minor. The costs of the mighty enterprise were, naturally, advanced by the Deutsche Bank through the ramified system of the public debt, and the Turkish state became, for eternity, a debtor of Messrs Siemens, Gwinner, Helfferich, etc. as it had previously been of English, French, and Austrian capital. This debtor had, now, not only to pump out of the state enormous fixed sums to pay interest on the loans but also to guarantee the gross profits of the railways that had been thus built. The most modern means of transport and installations are here grafted on a completely backward economy, still largely in a subsistence state --on a primitive peasant economy. From the arid soil of this economy, which for centuries has been unscrupulously sucked dry by Oriental despotism and which hardly produces a few stalks for the nourishment of the peasantry over and above the taxes gathered by the state, the necessary traffic and profits for railways can naturally

not be obtained. Commodity trade and passenger traffic are very underdeveloped--
corresponding to the economic and cultural condition of the country--and can increase
only slowly. The provision of the capitalist profits required by the railway companies has therefore to be supplied by the Turkish state in the form of the so-called
'kilometric-guarantees.' This was the system under which the railways in European
Turkey were built by Austrian and French capital, and their system was now, by the
enterprise of the Deutsche Bank, applied to Asiatic Turkey. As a pledge and surety
that this additional payment would be made, the Turkish government handed over to the
representative of European capital, the so-called Public Debt Administration, the
main source of state revenues in Turkey: the tithes of a certain set of provinces.
Between 1893 and 1910 the Turkish government paid some 90 million francs in this way,
for example for the railway to Ankara and for the Eskişehir-Konya line. The 'tithes'
thus pawned, again and again, by the Turkish government to its European creditors are
the ancient peasant taxes in kind: corn, sheep, silk, etc."[6]

On the other hand, railways have a positive function, in accelerating the emergence
of capitalist relations in "feudal" or "Asiatic-type" societies. Marx stated this function
in his often quoted words on India· "But when you have once introduced machinery into the
locomotion of a country which possesses iron and coal, you are unable to withhold it from
its fabrication. You cannot maintain a net of railways over an immense country without introducing all those industrial processes necessary to meet the immediate and current wants
of railway locomotion, and out of which there must grow the application of machinery to
those brances of industry not immediately connected with railways."[7]

In the Ottoman Empire, neither of these effects seems to have been significant. All
the railway equipment was imported and the only stimulating effect on the Turkish economy
was the skills acquired in the railway workshops and the purchase of coal from the Ereğli
mines.[8] On the other hand it is difficult to see how the railways can have impoverished
the Turkish people. The rise in the tithes of the provinces through which the railways
passed (4:17) indicates increased production, not intensified exploitation. And, at any
rate in Anatolia--as distinct from Syria[9] and the Balkans--the railways were built at a
reasonable cost, did not impose undue burdens on the Treasury, and greatly promoted general
economic development.

The first railway in the Ottoman Empire was built by a British group in 1859-60, between Chernavoda and Constanza, and was followed in 1863-68 by the Varna-Rustchuk line,
also British. But the main European line was the Oriental Railway Company, formed by
Baron Hirsch in 1878 with a capital of 50 million francs. It built 1,312 kilometers, and
by 1888 Istanbul had been connected to Vienna. The cost was covered by the 1870 loan of
ŁT34,848,000 issued at 32 1/8--an arrangement that was very costly to the government even
though it was assigned 45 percent of net receipts. Other major lines were the Salonica-
Constantinople Junction Railway (capital 15 million francs) with 510 kilometers completed
in 1896, and the Salonica-Monastir Railway (capital 20 million francs) with 219 kilometers.
Both lines received government guarantees of 15,500 francs and 14,500 francs, respectively,
of gross receipts per kilometer. By 1914 almost all the European lines had been taken
over by the various Balkan states.

In Anatolia, the two first lines, also British, were designed to tap the hinterland
of Izmir: the Izmir-Aydın lines (4:15) and the Izmir-Kasaba line (4:16), both completed
in 1866. The government, however, wanted a line linking Istanbul with the provincial
capitals, and on August 4, 1871, decreed the construction of an Anatolian railway. The

following year a German engineer, Wilhelm von Pressel, drew up a ten-year master plan for
a 2,700 kilometer line "from the east coast of the Bosphorus passing through İzmit, Eskişehir, Ankara, Sivas, Harput, Diyarbekir, Mosul, and Baghdad and reaching the Persian Gulf
downstream of Basra." Two feeder lines were planned: Sivas-Tokat-Amasya-Samsun and Diyar-
bekir-Suwaydia-Aleppo, as well as two first-class branches: Eskişehir-Afyon-karahisar-
Konya and Sivas-Erzincan-Erzurum, totalling another 1,800 kilometres.[10] After some false
starts, the implementation of this plan was entrusted to a German group (4:17), which by
1900 had laid down over 1,000 kilometers of line. The following table shows the constitu-
ent parts of Anatolia's railway network in 1913.[11]

Line	Ownership	Capital[a] (million francs)	Length (kms)	Duration of concession
Izmir-Aydın	British	132	610	1856-1950
Izmir-Kasaba	French	162	701	1894-1992
Mersin-Adana	German	10	67	1885-1935
Mudanya-Bursa	French	4	42	1891-1990
Anatolian	German	223	1,032	1889-2002
Baghdad	German	155	669	1902-2002
		686	3,121	

Source: Hecker.

[a]Shares plus debentures.

It will thus be seen that Germans provided 57 percent of the capital of the railways
in Anatolia and controlled an equal percentage of track. For the whole of Asian Turkey,
the Ottoman government provided 95 million francs for the construction of the Hejaz railway and private companies 840 million; of the latter 46 percent was German, 38 French, and
16 British, the respective shares of mileage being almost identical.[12]

On the whole, the railways in Anatolia were well planned and served the country's
needs. Except for the short Mudanya-Bursa line, they were all of 1.435-meter gauge, and
Turkey was spared the difficulties caused by differences of gauges that have plagued so
many countries. There was little duplication or overlap between the lines: the Izmir-
Aydın and Izmir-Kasaba railways were separated by a mountain range, tapped different areas,
and were fed by caravans; the friction between those two companies and the Anatolian Railway
was being smoothed out in the years immediately preceding the First World War (4:15,16).[13]
Except for the Izmir-Aydın line in its early years, there seems to have been little shady
financial manipulation, and construction costs were reasonable. The rates charged were
far lower than those of traditional transport (4:12) and the railways both raised the price
received by farmers and stimulated extension of cultivation. Thus Kurmuş estimates the
social savings caused by the Izmir-Aydın railway around 1895 at ₺710,000 per annum, one-
half because of lower freight cost on estimated prerailway traffic and one-half because of
the saving on traffic induced by the facilities offered by the railway.[14] And the British
consul at Ankara credited the Anatolian railroad "with raising production 50% and prices
50-100% between 1892 and 1895, an estimate generally substantiated by the scant statistics
available."[15] The rise in the tithe yields of the provinces through which the railways
passed reflects the increase in output induced by the railways, particularly the German
ones (4:17).

The kilometric guarantees paid by the government constituted a heavy burden, but three
points should be noticed. First, the total paid was declining rapidly as traffic and revenues rose: from ₺T900,000 in 1899 to ₺T529,000 in 1911, in spite of the considerable

extension of line between the two dates. Secondly, a large part of the payments was made
to the European and Syrian lines, which were far less efficiently designed and operated
than the Anatolian; thus in 1911 no less than ₤T158,000 was paid to the Salonica-Istanbul
railway and ₤T82,000 to the Damascus-Aleppo line; of the balance, ₤T143,000 went to the
Izmir-Kasaba line, leaving only ₤T145,000 for the German railroads. Lastly, since the
government was obviously unable to finance railway construction, the alternative to kilometric guarantees or a guaranteed return on capital was foreign equity financing, something
that both Abd ul Hamid and the Young Turks wished to avoid.[16] It may be added that both
net profits and dividends were low, those of the German railways standing at about 5 percent (see also 4:15,16).

By 1913 railways were playing the leading role in Ottoman transport. In that year a
foreign expert estimated the total amount of goods carried at 4,700,000 tons, of which
1,900,000 were cereals, 800,000 other agricultural produce, and 700,000 minerals; of this,
2,200,000 tons went by rail, 2,000,000 by road, and 500,000 by sea.[17] The western and
southern portions of Anatolia had been provided with railways, and the implementation of
the concessions granted in 1911-14 (4:18) would have greatly helped the north and east.
The completion of the Baghdad line would have not only developed Iraq but also linked it
more firmly to the capital. But one of the main objectives of its German promoters would
have remained unfulfilled, viz., that of providing a competitive alternative to the Suez
Canal.[18]

The road system, on the other hand, had seen little improvement. At various times
some work had been done on the Samsun-Sivas (Report on Samsun, 1845, FO 78/655), Bursa-
Gemlik (Report on Agriculture, Bursa, 1855, FO 78/1111), Istanbul-Edirne (CC Adrianople,
10 May 1865), Trabzon-Erzurum and other roads, but with little result. Under an 1865 law,
males sixteen to sixty-five years old were required to work for four days a year on local
roads, or pay a substitute tax, but this too had little effect and in 1910 forced labor
was replaced by cash payment.[19] The situation in 1878 may be illustrated by two quotations
(Reports on Trade with Turkey, FO 78/3070): "The arteries of trade leading to Angora are
. . . mere mule tracks," the 250-mile journey to Izmit taking twenty days; and the Beirut-
Damascus road was "the only road in the whole Turkish Empire which is kept in good order;
but it is hardly necessary to say that the repairs and traffic are not managed by the
Turkish authorities, but by foreigners."

In the years immediately preceding the First World War an effort was made to improve
some of the 18,000 kilometers of tracks lying within Turkey's present borders. British
reports from Adana, Izmir, Trabzon, and Erzurum indicate considerable activity.[20] In July
1910 a contract was signed with a French group for the construction of 9,300 kilometers of
road in Asia by 1912, at a cost of some ₤2,000,000 and with a German group for 1,000 kilometers in Salonica and Kossovo provinces. Financial difficulties necessitated the scaling
down of this program to 6,454 kilometers and by 1914 some 600 were near completion and 300
under construction.[21]

Automobiles had just begun to circulate. In 1908 it was reported that "motor cars
are slowly finding their way into Constantinople, and one or two are now daily to be seen
in the Upper Bosphorus villages, but they are not allowed to be driven inside towns. The
Imperial Government is to be congratulated on its decision to no longer prohibit the importation of cars into Turkey."[22] By 1914 there were 110 cars in Istanbul, including a
few taxicabs, 22 in Izmir, and 55 in other provinces.[23] Streetcars, at first horse-drawn
then electric, had been brought to Istanbul (1889),[24] Izmir (1885), and Salonica (1892)

and later to Beirut and Damascus by Belgian and French companies.[25]

The first telegraph line was built during the Crimean War, from Istanbul to Edirne, and was soon linked to the Austrian lines through Rustchuk.[26] In 1856 a British company was formed for laying a line to India along the Persian Gulf and through either Turkey or Syria.[27] But the government decided to build the line itself, and by 1861 it had reached Diyarbekir, Mardin, and Mosul (FO 78/1607) and in 1865, Fao. In the meantime a cable had been laid from Istanbul to Izmir, putting Izmir in touch with Europe (20 August 1859, FO 78/1447 and CC Smyrne, vol. 49, 23 August 1859). The construction of the Iranian telegraph line in the mid-1860s put Turkey in touch with India.[28] By 1882 the Ottoman Empire had 23,000 and by 1900 50,000 kilometers of telegraph line.[29]

Telephones were introduced in 1881 and were in use in a few government and private offices in Istanbul and Izmir; in 1911 a concession was granted to an Anglo-American-French group with a capital of £300,000 for a telephone system in Istanbul and its suburbs,[30] but little progress had been made in this field by the outbreak of the war.

A modern postal service was inaugurated in 1834 and developed in the next decades.[31] In 1914, there were six post offices per 1,000 inhabitants, compared to six in British India and forty in the United States. In addition, since 1721 some foreign powers had had their own post offices. Austria and France had agencies at Aleppo. Jerusalem, and elsewhere. Austria, France, and Russia had offices in the various Mediterranean and Black Sea ports served by their respective steamers and handling mail between the Turkish ports. And Austria, Britain, France, Germany, and Russia had offices in Istanbul that handled mail between Turkey and foreign countries (Memorandum, 1875, FO 195/1059).[32] This arrangement continued until the First World War, and was finally abolished under the Lausanne Treaties.

1. A and P 1870, vol. 64, "Anatolian Provinces," and map in EI (2), s. v. "Anadolu."
2. M. A. Cook, "Economic Development," in Joseph Schacht and C. E. Bosworth, eds., The Legacy of Islam (Oxford 1974), p. 218.
3. A and P 1912-13, vol. 100, "Constantinople."
4. "Imperialism" in V. I. Lenin, Selected Works (Moscow, 1970), 1:674.
5. Ibid.
6. Rosa Luxemburg, Die Krise in der deutschen Sozialdemokratie (Chicago, n.d.), pp. 35-36.
7. "Future Results of British Rule in India," in Karl Marx, Selected Works (London, 1942), 2:661.
8. In 1909 total coal consumption by Turkish railway was 240,000 tons (Eldem, p. 101); "The Aidin Railway still uses British coal exclusively" (A and P 1914, vol. 95, "Smyrna"), but the bulk of consumption came from Ereğli (6:10).
9. EHME, pp. 211-12.
10. Pressel, in EHME, p. 92.
11. For the Syrian, Iraqi, and Hejaz railways, see EHME, pp. 248-57; there were 480 kilometers of line in European Turkey and 789 in Syria, and the Hejaz railway totalled 1,533 kilometers.
12. Hecker.
13. Kurmuş, p. 61; the Anatolian Railway did divert traffic from Izmir and caused a drop in its exports—L. Vannutelli, Bulletino della Societa Geografica Italiana, 1907, p. 205.
14. Ibid., pp. 98-122.
15. Quataert, p. 190.
16. Wolf, pp. 32-33.
17. Eldem, pp. 153-54.
18. See calculations in Mussler, pp. 61-62.
19. Eldem, p. 155; Shaw, History, 2:101, 121-22, 227-28.
20. Lowther to Grey, 3 August 1910, FO 368/472; A and P 1912-13, vol. 100. "Constantinople"; ibid. 1914, vol. 95, "Constantinople," "Smyrna," and "Erzeroum."
21. A and P 1912-13, vol. 100, "Constantinople"; Thobie, pp. 365.
22. TJ June 1908. In 1906 permission was granted for a motor car in Salonica "but the impracticability of the so-called roads in Macedonia will render this kind of locomotion very difficult and even dangerous" (A and P 1907, vol. 93, "Salonica").
23. Eldem, p. 155, and RL, no. 276, 1909.

24. Thobie, pp. 441-46.

25. Eldem, pp. 42 and 170-72. In March 1907 the London United Tramways presented an overall scheme for electric streetcars in Istanbul and vicinity (BVA-BEO 265884). In July 1907 a concession was granted for electric power and streetcars in Bursa; most of the concessionaires were Muslim (BVA-BEO 272522). For a detailed account of the Galata--Pera tunnel streetcar, opened in 1875, see P. Oberling, "The Istanbul Tünel," Archivum Ottomanicum, 4, 1972.

26. Eldem, p. 173; Shaw, History, 2:120.

27. See various proposals in FO 78/1420, Telegraphs 1856-58.

28. See details in EHI, pp. 152-53.

29. Shaw, History, 2:228.

30. A and P 1912-13, vol. 100, "Constantinople." A concession for telephones was also granted in September 1907 to the company founded, mainly by Muslims, for supplying Trabzon and Samsun with electricity--BVA-BEO 273256. The first public telephone service in Turkey was inaugurated in 1913 and, in the same year, wireless telegraphy was introduced for military purposes--Mears, p. 233.

31. Lewis, Emergence, pp. 93-94; Eldem, pp. 172-75.

32. Greece, Egypt, and Italy also had post offices; for details, see Shaw, History, 2:228-29.

SAILING SHIPS AND COASTAL NAVIGATION

With 6,600 kilometers of shoreline (excluding the islands), present-day Turkey has a higher ratio of seacoast to land area than the vast majority of nonpeninsular countries, and this was even more true of the Ottoman Empire in the eighteenth and nineteenth centuries. The value of coastal navigation was further enhanced by the presence of numerous small natural harbors, the absence of navigable rivers in the Ottoman heartlands, the concentration of population on the rims of Anatolia and the Levant, and the fact that Istanbul, to which so much produce flowed, was accessible by sea from almost all the provinces. Sailing ships plying between the various ports and islands were therefore perhaps the most important single element in Ottoman transport.

Already by the eighteenth century European shipping was playing a leading role in Ottoman coastal trade, and in the 1780s some 150 ships sailed to the Middle East and North Africa each year from the Mediterranean French ports.[1] Better vessels, the protection given by the Capitulations, and almost total immunity from the Maltese corsairs--who preyed on Ottoman ships just as the Barbary corsairs preyed on European[2]--put the Europeans in a very strong position. However the long Anglo-French wars greatly reduced European activities and stimulated Ragusan and Greek shipping.[3]

The Greeks soon secured a commanding position in Ottoman waters.[4] Two islands distinguished themselves particularly, Ipsera and Idra, "to which a considerable number of vessels belong and the natives of which constitute a valuable portion of the Marine of Turkey" (Green to Canning, 4 April 1807, FO 78/59). The Greek War of Independence made the Porte acutely aware of the dangers of the situation, and the ferman in the following selection represents an attempt to develop a more dependable merchant navy. The establishment of the Greek state further strengthened the Ottoman Greeks, since they now had a potential refuge and an alternative flag. Restrictions on shipbuilding in Rhodes (4:2) and elsewhere caused hardship, but were evaded. The Rhodians built ships in Greece (Report on Rhodes 1850, FO 78/833) and the shipyards of Mytilene launched each year some twenty vessels of 10-60 tons; the latter were ordered by other ports and had to carry the Ottoman flag (Report on Bursa, 1860, FO 78/1534). The government yards in Istanbul continued to build good warships until at least the 1830s.[5]

Until steam navigation began to account for the bulk of tonnage, the Greeks competed very effectively with the Europeans. This is illustrated by the figures for Salonica (4:3)[6] and by the table below on Izmir. Greek ships were soon over half the total, but as they were much smaller their tonnage accounted for only a quarter to a third. However, thanks to their steamers, the Austrians took the lead, soon to be followed by the French.

French consular reports break down shipping into long-distance and "caravane," i.e., between the Ottoman ports or the immediate neighboring lands such as Greece and the Ionian islands. In 1837-40, the latter averaged 61,000 tons and the former 44,000. Except for the Austrian steamers, practically all the "caravane" was done by Greek and Ottoman ships, the Greeks averaging 23,000 tons (CC Smyrne, vol. 46, Trade Reports for 1837-40). By 1870 sailing ships had almost disappeared except for the coastal trade (4:11).

Shipping at Izmir 1830-40[a]

	Total		British		Austrian		Greek	
	No.	Tons	No.	Tons	No.	Tons	No.	Tons
1830	1,125	94	385	38	147	30	445	4
1831	863	99	279	29	153	31	291	11
1832[b]	630	67	156	19	96	21	276	12
1835	1,255	119	159	20	166	31	770	44
1836	1,045	90	105	14	120	22	711	37
1837	897	88	134	20	145	24	498	24
1838	1,113	115	159	22	191	44	635	28
1840	969	108	113	18	216	41	515	31
1841	951	105	151	23	214	35	410	21

Source: 1835, Bailey, p. 99, 1841 MacGregor, 2:102; Trade Reports on Smyrna, FO 78/194, 78/204, 78/215, 78/229, 78/335, 78/338, 78/369, 78/442.

[a]Tonnage in thousands; Turkish vessels recorded as "none"; British include Ionian and Maltese.

[b]Second half-year only.

Conditions in the other ports were different. In Istanbul in 1863-65, the tonnage of sailing ships, averaging 3,175,000 tons, was still far higher than that of steamers, 701,000; Greek sailing ships, with 760,000 tons, topped the list, followed by Italian, British, Ottoman (421,000 tons), and Austrian.[7] In Trabzon Turkish ships were easily ahead, with 10,000 tons out of 13,000 in 1833, 17,000 out of 26,000 in 1835, and 12,000 out of 22,000 in 1837 (Report on Trade, FO 78/229, 78/287, and 78/338), and even after the advent of steam the Turkish share remained significant (4:7,8). The same was true of Samsun (see ibid.). In Tarsus, which was not served by any steamers until the French inaugurated a service in 1852, "the country vessels predominate" (Commercial Report, FO 78/951). In 1836 out of 166 ships aggregating 13,000 tons 95 were Arab or Turkish (FO 78/316); in 1844 51 ships totalling 3,000 tons, out of 85 totalling 8,000, were Arab or Turkish (FO 78/614); in 1846 the figures were 22 ships and 2,000 tons out of 49 and 6,000, respectively (FO 78/704), and in 1851 they were 273 ships and 25,000 tons out of 298 and 29,000, respectively (FO 78/905). But it may be presumed that, in both the Mediterranean and Black Sea, a large number of the ships described as Turkish were owned and manned by Greeks. As late as 1914 an acute observer, Sussnitzki, could say: "The Greeks . . . dominate large-scale merchant shipping. Equally skilled as seafarers are the Lazes. . . . the Turks, Arabs and Albanians go in for navigation to a much lesser extent and carry only local traffic, although the Turks also produce able sailors."[8]

Much of the coastal trade, however, passed to European steamers. Under the Capitulations, the Ottomans could not reserve the coastal trade for their own flag and this restriction continued until the First World War in spite of repeated protests and attempts.[9] Indeed foreigners exercised not only "grand cabotage" but "petit cabotage": British and

other tugs towed ships and carried passengers in the Bosphorus, and there were loud protests when, starting in 1837, the Porte announced it would stop this practice, a move that
was finally supported by the British ambassador (22 December 1852 and 14 October 1853, FO
195/339). In 1860 the matter had not been settled and the Turkish vice-admiral was complaining that although, eight years previously, it had been agreed to restrict passenger
traffic by steamers in Istanbul waters to Turkish ships, "leaving to foreign steamers only
the right of towing vessels within those limits," now Greek and Sardinian ships were trying
to carry passengers from Istanbul to Kadiköy; he had protested and stopped them (17 June
1860, FO 195/590).

The question was thoroughly examined in a memorandum by a Foreign Office legal expert,
E. Hertslet (15 February 1875, FO 368/228). From the memorandum, it is clear that the Ottoman government had given up objecting to the transport of goods by foreign ships in its
coasting trade; it "admits that its real grievance is against Russia and Austria, for excluding Ottoman vessels from their waters," while their vessels were engaged in the Ottoman
coasting trade. It did object to foreign ships carrying passengers in coasting trade but,
except for the Bosphorus, which "including Constantinople and all the Straits of the Black
Sea was one port," was not seriously attempting to stop such traffic.

Foreign steamers were also active in the Gulfs of Izmir and Salonica, and were supported by their ambassadors against the attempts of the government to reserve this navigation for Ottoman ships.[10]

---

1. EHME, p. 37; in 1788 the French inaugurated a packet service from Marseilles to
Izmir, for letters, passengers, and a limited quantity of goods. Sailings were scheduled
for every fifteen days and the journey took eighteen days (Ainslie to Carmarthen, 26 July
1788, FO 78/9).
2. Peter Earle, passim.
3. EHME, p. 37, and Brune to Talleyrand, Germinal an 11 (1804), CC Constantinople,
vol. 74; Selim III also succeeded in stimulating Ottoman shipping--Shaw, Between, p. 178.
4. For a detailed account see Papadopoulos, pp. 28-44, where Greek ships in 1816 are
put at 615, aggregating 154,000 tons; Russian navigation from the Black Sea was carried
out mainly by Greeks and Ionians (Liston to Castlereagh, 10 September 1814, FO 95/23).
5. Bazili, 1:207-8.
6. See Bailey, p. 106, for full 1835 returns. In 1837, 243 Greek ships, aggregating
12,000 tons, and 38 Turkish aggregating 5,000, entered Salonica out of a total of 329
ships and 25,000 tons; in 1842, the figures were 362 and 23,000 tons, 118 and 7,000, and
561 and 42,000, respectively, but an Austrian steamer made thirty eight voyages, adding
5,000 tons--MacGregor, 2:86.
7. Salaheddin, pp. 233-38.
8. EHME, p. 123.
9. However, it was not until 1911 that the government announced that all taxes on
Turkish ships would be abolished because they were paying more than foreign ships--TJ,
March 1911.
Two of the many incidents caused by unsuccessful Ottoman attempts to reserve the
coastal trade may be given. In 1816 British and French merchants complained about regulations "for the ostensible purpose of checking the contraband trade" but in fact for "favor-
ing their own subjects by excluding foreigners from a traffic to which they are entitled
by Treaty" (Frere to Castlereagh, 9 January 1816, FO 78/86). And in 1889 the British ship
"Euxine," which had been in the habit of trading with the port of Bartin, on the Black
Sea, was not allowed to land its cargo because Bartın, being a few miles up river, was
claimed as an inland port. The ensuing protests and correspondence went on for over ten
years (FO 78/4989, Coasting Trade--also 368/226 and 368/470).
For repeated attempts by the government in the eighteenth century to protect Ottoman
coastal shipping, Raymond 1:170-71.
10. See Young, 3:61-70.

SELECTION 1. FIRMAN GRANTING PRIVILEGES TO TURKISH SHIPS, 1823

FO 78/136, pt. 2

Translated from the French Translation of a Firman granting certain privileges to Turkish
merchant vessels in April 1823. The copy transmitted to the Foreign Legation begins thus.

Whereas it is intended to give encouragement to these merchant vessels for carrying on trade by supplying them with sufficient funds, the merchandize and produce of all kinds shipped by means of the government funds which will be conveyed by these vessels from the Turkish to Christian states, those which they shall bring from foreign countries into the Turkish states as well as those which they may convey from one place to another, shall pay a Custom Duty at the rate of three per cent and the merchandize belonging to Turkish or Rayah merchants shipped upon freight shall pay the regular custom duty according to their ancient tariff with a deduction of one fourth.

The Custom Duty shall only be paid once either at the place of sale or at the place of purchase and the Teskere's or clearances showing that the duty has been once paid shall be valid in all places.

The officers of the Customs at the places where such ships shall touch or call at are not to demand a second or higher duty nor exact any custom house charges "Mastarie" or outward dues, or any other arbitrary duties not even to the value of a farthing and in the event of its being proved that they have received any thing beyond the established duties restitution thereof will be ordered.

Whatever trading posts of the Turkish empire the said vessels may enter, the local authorities shall take care to give them all requisite assistance and protection, so that they may unload before all other vessels, they are to enable them to take in their cargoes, whenever they intend doing so in a Turkish port, before all other vessels, none of which shall commence loading before the former have finished taking in their cargoes and they are also to procure them freight.

As soon as such vessels shall arrive at the port of Constantinople or at those in the White [Mediterranean] and Black Seas and at the time of their passage from the entrances into those two Seas, after their cargoes have once paid the custom duty according to usage, neither the officers of the custom or other officers shall demand any other dues either on the score of gratuity or perquisite or under any other pretence whatsoever.

The Captain upon his delivering a correct and authentic manifest and statement containing an account of the whole cargo with the name of the place of its destination, shall not be subjected to any question, no inquiry shall be made respecting him, he shall not be detained nor made to sustain any prejudice whatever.

With the exception of warlike stores, arms and other prohibited articles such vessels are at full liberty to purchase and convey merchandize and produce of all kinds.

No Customs Duty shall be demanded upon foreign merchandize passing in transit, that is to say: such merchandize and produce which they convey from Russia to other countries in Europe and vice versa--the captains shall not be compelled to land the same nor shall they be detained on that account.

Whenever such ships freighted by Christian merchants shall happen to be loaded with merchandize belonging to Christians, the officers of the Naval department shall freely permit Turkish vessels to tranship the same into Christian vessels and shall not put any hindrance thereto, but in the same manner as Christian vessels are strictly prohibited to tranship any merchandize or produce into any other foreign vessels--all Turkish vessels are equally prohibited to tranship such merchandize into any other Turkish vessel, this permission being entirely confined to take place from a Turkish into a Christian vessel and from a Christian into a Turkish vessel.

Permission is given to such vessels to sell the produce which they may bring to Constantinople from Russian ports, such as Taganrock and Odessa, to Christian vessels and the permission to tranship the same into Christian vessels shall be granted to them by a Firman.

The Sublime Porte grants to Turkish vessels the liberty of freely proceeding to the White Sea with such grain provisions and produce as they may have purchased and shipped in Russia.

Altho' the masters of these ships are persons entitled to confidence they are nevertheless included in the measures which the circumstances of the times have rendered necessary, that of a general search of all ships, and in this respect no distinction shall be made in their favor.

SELECTION 2. SHIPBUILDING IN RHODES, 1850

Kerr to Palmerston, April 16, 1850, FO 78/833

I have the honor respectfully to submit to Your Lordship's consideration a few general remarks on the actual condition of Rhodes, and the adjacent islands, and on the false and ruinous system of policy which, in my humble opinion, the Turkish Government is now rigorously enforcing in them.

Rhodes, which was rapidly falling into that state of decay which is universally the case with all other parts of the Ottoman Empire (except its capital, which is enriched on the plunder of the provinces), and which is the more apparent in places which, like Rhodes, were, in former times, renowned seats of commerce, navigation, civilization, and independence, has sunk into a still more wretched state since the establishment of the Kingdom of Greece.

The political bias of the Greek population of this, and the other Turkish islands of the Archipelago, was very strong in favor of the Hellenes, and revolutionary movements having taken place in some, and strong sympathies evinced in others, the Turkish Government naturally became anxious to suppress any movement that might end in the loss of the richest insular possessions.

Prudent as precautionary measures might be, had they been based on a wise system, I have no hesitation in assuring Your Lordship that the short-sighted policy which is now adopted is producing an effect diametrically opposed to that desired and penetrated as I am with the desire of Great Powers to maintain the integrity of the Turkish Empire, I am as firmly convinced that the Turks are not only plunging these Islands into irretrievable ruin, but that they are at the same time heaping the greatest benefits on the Greek Nation, to the detriment of their own subjects, and rendering to these the desire to be liberated from their yoke more ardent than ever.

Shipbuilding was formerly carried on to a very great extent at Rhodes, Cassos, Castel Rosso, and Symi, of which Your Lordship will be able to form an idea from the astonishing fact that these Islands which (with the exception of Rhodes,) are merely rocks, possess the following vessels, built, owned, and navigated, by their inhabitants, under the Ottoman and Greek Flags, viz.

| | Ottoman Flag | | Greek Flag | |
	Vessels	Tonnage	Vessels	Tonnage
Cassos	63	12,545	51	11,365
Castel Rosso	49	9,675	3	650
Symi	16	3,277		
Rhodes	14	1,129		
	142	26,626	54	12,015

The Turkish Government, considering that the immense resources which these industrious islanders afforded to the Greeks in the construction, and the rapid increase in the number of their merchant vessels, were causes of alarm, and that in the event of a rupture between the Porte and Greece these ships might be employed against the Turkish Government, is now doing all in its power to suppress this branch of industry on which the inhabitants have long depended for their existence: they have prohibited Europeans and Hellenes from cutting the splendid timber with which the coasts of Asia Minor, in the immediate vicinity of these Islands abound, and they have rigorously forbidden the construction of any vessel in the Ottoman islands unless the owner produce a Turkish guarantee that she shall for ever bear the Ottoman flag, which measure has almost entirely put a stop to shipbuilding, and is daily plunging the inhabitants into ruin and despair.

These measures, destructive as they are to the Ottoman Islands, will never succeed in quenching the mercantile enterprise for which the Greeks are so proverbial, nor will they in any degree limit the extent of their mercantile navy. Turks and Rayahs daily purchase and ship Timber on the coast of Asia Minor, and clear out for Egypt or some other Ottoman port, whereas the real destination of the ships is either the Piraeus, Syra--or some of the Greek islands, where shipbuilding goes on in great activity, and the artisans who formerly worked in these islands are yearly deserting their homes, and emigrating to the Greek territory, in which they can find abundance of lucrative employment, leaving their wives and families to satisfy the heavy amount of taxation, and in very many instances totally abandoning them, and remarrying in Greece.

To convey to Your Lordship an idea of the extent to which this ruinous system is carried on, I may state that whereas in the year 1836 the population of Rhodes amounted to 42,000, it does not at this day exceed 28,000: this depopulation has not hitherto continued on the same ratio in the other islands, because, previous to the establishment of the Insular Pachalic, the people of Cassos and Castel Rosso (who are desperate, courageous, seafaring men,) set at defiance the orders of the former Governors of Rhodes, but the present one, having more force at his Command, is enabled to exact the Porte's decrees. . . .

SELECTION 3. SHIPPING IN SALONICA, 1835

Report by R. Blunt, 28 December 1835, FO 78/265

. . . Vessels arriving at the port of Salonica are not subject to any Tonnage or port dues, neither are there any dues upon clearance. Should a vessel be in want of bread, there is a trifling charge of 10 piastres or 2/- for a permit.

It will be observed in the following tonnage lists, that upon the British only there is no increase, the decrease upon other nations (including the Ionians) arises from the increased number of Greek vessels, which carry at a lower rate of freight than any other nation; they are able to do so for they sail cheaper, and altho the Ionians have the same advantages as regards the price of labour and provisions, still the Greeks have less charges. The consular dues for a Greek vessel are only equal to about $P^1/_4$ per ton. The

Greek sailor lives upon olives and bread and is paid according to the freight; the expenses of the voyage are deducted from the gross amount of freight, the captain then takes $2/3$ for the vessel and gives $1/3$ to the seamen for wages, and in the smaller class of Greek vessels, it often happens that the captain and crew are the owners.

It would appear that the Austrians and Sardinians are fearful that the Greek flag will injure their carrying trade, even beyond the archipelago, for the merchants of Trieste and Genoa have advised their agents at Salonica and other Turkish ports that the insurance offices refuse to insure either Greek vessels or goods on board them, but this may also arise from the dishonesty of the Greek captains, for even the insurance offices at Smyrna will not now insure Greek vessels, or goods on board of them, unless the captains be personally known at the insurance office.

The transport of pilgrims to and from Jaffa gives employment to from 50 to 60 sail of Greek vessels yearly from the port of Salonica. The burthen of these vessels average from 50-60 tons and they take from 100-150 pilgrims each. These vessels pay a duty of from 300 to 500 piastres (£3-£5 Stg.) for a permit to embark pilgrims, and the same rate of duty upon their return with pilgrims.

The vessels used in this particular transport trade, are for the most part built at the islands of Scathos and Scopulo and cost to sea from £200-£250 Stg. each.

Tonnage lists of vessels of various nations, arrived at the port of Salonica from the 1st January 1829 to 30 November 1835

		1829	1830	1831	1832	1833	1834	1835[a]
British	No.	1	1	5	5	5	3	7
	Tons	110	124	600	635	612	546	1,168
Ionian	No.	30	23	22	2	8	2	5
	Tons	2,532	1,449	1,566	375	1,174	185	252
French	No.	..	..	2	10	18	14	6
	Tons	...	...	234	1,548	2,612	1,471	761
Russian	No.	..	5	17	6	15	14	6
	Tons	..	1,110	4,400	1,400	3,100	4,100	1,600
Austrian	No.	25	19	28	18	30	34	20
	Tons	4,586	3,563	5,803	3,624	6,588	7,779	4,643
Sardinian	No.	5	7	5	3	6	7	4
	Tons	728	1,235	651	642	1,220	1,130	585
American	No.	..	..	..	..	..	1	..
	Tons	..	..	..	..	..	210	..
Greek	No.	..	..	..	..	..	..	292[b]
	Tons	..	..	..	..	..	..	16,583[b]

[a] To 30 November.

[b] From 4 February, date of establishment of consulate.

SELECTION 4. STATEMENT OF THE NUMBER AND DESCRIPTION OF THE SEVERAL STEAM VESSELS
BELONGING TO THE PORT OF CONSTANTINOPLE

17 February 1838 (FO 78/335)

Name	Where and when built	Tonnage	Length and Breadth	Draught of Water	Built of Wood or Iron	Armament and Extra-ordinary equipment	Carries how many hours fuel, and what consump-tion of fuel per hour	Speed per hour
Crescent, British	Liverpool April 1835	178 28/94	ft. in. 140 · 7 by 20 · 5	Without cargo 8 ft.	Wood	23 men in all	70 hours in her Bunkers 14 cwt. per hour	12 miles in dead water
Essex, British	London in 1830	132	ft. 130 by 18 1/2	about 6 feet	Wood	12 men in all	20 tons in her Bunkers 8 cwt. per hour	10 miles
Levant, British	London 1835	64 30/94	ft. 98 by 15	7 1/2 feet in Ballast	Wood	19 men in all fully equipped	38 hours in her Bunkers 7 cwt. per hour	8 1/2 miles in dead water
Maria Dorothea, Austrian	Trieste 1834	237 builders measure-ments	ft. 135 by 20	6 feet loaded	Wood	21 men in all fully equipped	45 hours coals 8 cwt. per hour	9 miles
Ferdi-nando 1°, Austrian	Trieste 1836	308 builders measure-ments	ft. in. 144 · 6 by 22 · 6	8 feet 6 inches when loaded	Wood	25 men in all fully equipped	28 tons 11 cwt. per hour	9 miles
Prince Metter-nich, Austrian	Trieste 1837	536 tons builders measure-ments	ft. 168 by 26	8 feet un-loaded 9 feet 6 inches loaded	Wood	32 men in all	88 hours coals 16 cwt. per hour	10 miles

Cost	Engines, where built, what horse power, whether high or low pressure	Whether for Sea or River Navigation and Employed for goods or passengers, or both	Voyages, if regular, when – Dates of Starting – Average length of voyage	Charges for Conveyance of passengers	Charges for conveyance of goods
₤20,000	Liverpool 2 sixties low pressure	Sea navigation goods and passengers	Sinope & Trebisond every other Friday 70 hour voyage	P1000 = ₤10 nearly for cabin passengers – for deck pass. P200 = ₤2 nearly – fore cabin P800 = ₤8 nearly	P31 or 6 shillings per package of about lbs. 180 weight
Not known	London 2 forties low pressure	Sea or river navigation goods and passengers	Used as a tug on the Bosphorus	Varies $100 dollars to $200 according to the size of the vessel and the wind	
₤7,500 Iron boilers	London 50 horse power low pressure	Sea or river navigation goods and passengers	Employed chiefly as a tug on the Bosphorus has received sometimes charters	The same as the Essex nearly. Has occasionally charged as high as $250 dollars	
₤11,000	London 70 horse power low pressure	Sea or river goods and passengers	Smyrna and back to Constantinople once a week. 36 hours voyage	Main cabin $15 dollars or ₤3 nearly – Fore cabin $10 Deck P105 or ₤1 nearly	No fixed rate* carries a very small cargo
₤14,000	London 100 horse power low pressure	Sea or river navigation goods or passengers	Galatz twice a month. 60 hours up, 46–50 hours down, with fine weather. Does not go in winter	Main cabin 50 florins – Fore cabin 36 florins – Deck 12 florins	
about ₤23,000	London Bolton & Watts 140 horse power low pressure	Sea or river navigation goods and passengers	Sinope and Trebisond alternate Fridays with the Crescent 70 hours	The same as the Crescent	The same as the Crescent

* Has towed vessels occasionally

SELECTION 5. PREPARATIONS FOR A FRENCH STEAMSHIP TO TURKEY, 1836

Roussin to Broglie, 12 March 1836, in reply to information regarding the intention to establish a steamship service to the Levant, CC Constantinople, vol. 86

I shall assume, first, that our steamers will be perfectly equipped when leaving port and that all that will be necessary will be to keep them in good condition during the voyage and when putting in port here, i.e., to repair slight damage, to replace the coal consumed, and to safeguard their crews from infection when it strikes the country.

I shall also assume that, as far as possible, the management of these steamers will want to be self-sufficient, and to have recourse to the local authorities only in extraordinary cases, ie., very seldom.

Lastly I shall assume that they will have on board an intelligent mechanic, capable of supervising the repair of the machines, should such be necessary, when putting in port here.

Given all this, the steamers will find in Constantinople such help as they may need in the way of unskilled workmen, wood, and iron. As for other naval stores, since the local government has a monopoly, they are not available on the market; among others, copper sheathing (although that metal is abundant here) can be had only at a high price because of the heavy customs duty levied on its export. It would therefore be desirable to stock supplies of copper and also of those parts of machinery which are liable often to break and to require immediate replacement.

Labor is very expensive in Constantinople; there are few naval construction workmen who are paid less than 12 piastres, or 3 francs, a day. Sheathing copper can be found more easily in Smyrna, where the customs are more lenient, but even there it is expensive. The present price is 2 fr. 50 per half kilogram.

Careening is easy in Constantinople, but the large number of ships awaiting their turn often causes delays in this kind of work. It may therefore be necessary, in certain cases, to have this done in Smyrna, where this obstacle does not exist. As for other kinds of repair work, the safety of the port of Constantinople is such that they can be done anywhere. The cove of Stenia, on the Bosphorus, would provide an excellent spot for careening but it is doubtful whether the local authorities would consent to its being used. They refused access to Russia, at a time when the influence of that power was at its height, and it would not be in our interest to press the Porte to yield to such a demand.

Although our merchants are not unanimous on the question of the location of the coal stocks for bunkering our ships, I believe that it would be better to put them in floating vessels rather in warehouses on shore. The first reason is economy, the second is security, because floating storehouses can easily be insured at 3 percent whereas no insurance is available for warehouses on shore, even if they are built of stone and vaulted, which would be difficult to find in case of need, or at least very expensive. The third reason is the need to keep the crews of the ships from having any contacts with the shore in times of pestilence. The vessels would therefore serve as barracks as well as storehouses for the various things which the management would like to have available. . . .

The great decrease in the grain trade having made a large number of ships idle, many vessels of 200, 300, 400, 450 tons are often sold at auction for 5,000, 10,000, or 20,000, or 25,000 francs, and sometimes less. . . .

The management of the two steamers, the Levant (English) and the Maria Dorothea (Austrian) which ply between Smyrna and Constantinople have, after various experiments, recognized the advantage of floating warehouses. . . . Another English steamer, the Crescent, after having used a warehouse on shore, is looking for a vessel; one of 500 tons has been offered for 7,800 francs--it is true it is a little old, but it is still in very good condition. . . .

English coal can frequently be bought here. It is brought from England as ballast, or in special cargoes at £1-10s-6d., i.e., 38 francs 80 the ton of 18 Turkish quintals of 44 okes; this means that the Paris quintal (50 kgs.) costs 1 franc 75. It is said that the cost of that amount of coal in England is 8 shillings and the freight 22 shillings, which means that it yields a profit. But there is no doubt that as consumption increases and arrivals multiply it will soon become less expensive, and anyway it would be easy to get it cheaper by buying in bulk. I should add that the time is perhaps not distant when Constantinople will cease to bring coal from England. Samples of a fine quality of coal have been found near Varna and they are being tested by the Austrian mineralogist in charge. We have been assured that success is certain, but I do not assume it.

A question that deserves consideration is the location of the offices of the steamships. All agree that they should be in the suburb of Galata rather than in Pera. The latter is not suitable because of its distance from almost all European businesses and on the seafront. This distance would impede the transport of bullion, the most lucrative operation for exchange. Should a fluctuation in exchange rates suggest such an operation, it would have to be given up if one were forced to go first to Pera to receive shipping orders and then another time to have the bills of lading signed. Opinion is unanimous on this point. . . .

STEAM NAVIGATION IN THE 1830S AND 40S--THE AUSTRIAN LLOYD

Steam navigation came to Turkish waters in 1828. The Swift, an English ship, after calling at Izmir, entered the Straits on May 20 before immense and astonished crowds "for this was the first steam-boat ever seen in these parts." A few days later it was bought by the Armenian head of the Mint and one or two partners for 350,000 piastres and presented to the Sultan. The English master and engineers were retained with the ship, to train Turkish officers, but apparently with little success. The Sultan also acquired another steamship.[1]

By 1830 the British packets had reached Corfu via Gibraltar and Malta. In 1833 the Russian Odessa Company inaugurated a run to Istanbul and in July 1834 the steamers of the Austrian Danube Company (founded in 1829) reached Galatz (Roussin to Rigny, 12 September 1834, CC Constantinople, vol. 86). Late in 1834 or early in 1835 the Austrian Maria Dorothea arrived, much to the "annoyance of the Porte" which made "attacks and threats" against it; this was joyfully recalled by the Austrian ambassador when, in November 1836, the Sultan travelled on her, the first time that a Sultan had ever been aboard a ship flying a foreign flag (Sturmer to Metternich, 30 November 1836, HHS Türkei, 1836, VI).[2] Two other English steamers, Levant and Crescent, are recorded in 1835 and the Crescent and Maria Dorothea made weekly runs between Istanbul and Izmir.[3] In 1836 the British steamers gave up the Istanbul-Izmir service and a Turkish steamer's attempt ended badly. The Maria Dorothea, however, continued its weekly run, stopping at Gallipoli, Dardanelles, Cape Baba, and Mytilene, and the Ferdinand I sailed between Galatz and Istanbul every fifteen days, stopping at Ilakja, Tulja, and Varna and connecting at Galatz with the weekly Danubian service.[4] By July 1837 the Crescent, now taken over by the Austrians, and the Ferdinand I were making the Trabzon-Istanbul run in 60 hours, the Metternich the Izmir-Istanbul run in 36 hours, and the Maria Dorothea the Galatz-Istanbul run in 80 hours and Sturmer could announce to Metternich that the latter's letter had reached him in only nine days (21 June 1837, HHS Türkei, 1837, 66).

In 1837 the two lines that were to play the leading parts in navigation in the Levant inaugurated their services: the French Messageries (renamed, with the vagaries of French politics, Royales, Nationales, Impériales, and finally, to be on the safe side, Maritimes) and the Austrian Lloyd. In 1835 a French parliamentary commission recommended the establishment of a service every ten days between Marseilles and Istanbul. Ten ships of 750 tons averaging 7 mph would be required at a total capital cost of 6 million francs. Annual costs, including interest, were put at 2 million francs. The round trip to Istanbul would take 21 days, i.e., a reply to a letter from Paris could be received within 29 days, instead of 40 to 50, and diplomatic secrets would be much safer.[5]

The project was implemented and the first ship arrived in Istanbul on 20 May 1837. The ports of call were Livorno, Civita Vechia, Naples, Malta, Syra, and Izmir; another line served Alexandria, connecting with the first at Syra. Although some of the French ships were lost and others damaged (CC Constantinople, vol. 87, and Sturmer to Metternich, 21 June 1837, and 9 September 1837, HHS Türkei, 1837, 66), and although the Austrians proved far abler at meeting local needs and charged lower rates (4:6), the Messageries survived and developed a line (Marseilles-Izmir-Rhodes-Tarsus-Latakia-Tripoli-Beirut-Jaffa-Alexandria being opened in 1852--Niven to Malmesbury, 23 July 1852, FO 78/909) and went on serving the Eastern Mediterranean until the Second World War. It also extended its regular services to the Far East and Australia.

The Austrian Lloyd was founded in 1832 in Trieste by a group of insurance companies

as a news gathering agency.[6] In 1836 it decided to set up a steamship company with a capital of 1,000,000 florins (₺100,000), soon raised to 1,500,000. Three steamers were ordered
in England and the first of these, the 320-ton <u>Ludovico Arciduca d'Austria</u>, left Trieste on
May 16, 1837, and arrived in Istanbul on May 30 with 53 passengers, having called at Ancona,
Corfu, Patras, Piraeus, Syra, and Izmir.[7] First-class passengers were charged 125 florins
(₺12-10s.) and second-class 85 (not including food!). For comparison, in 1835, Greek and
Italian sailing ships took first-class passengers from Italian ports to Istanbul for only
120 francs (₺4-16s.) (see French parliamentary report, cited above). In its first year the
line made twenty one voyages to Greece, Turkey, and Egypt, carrying 8,000 passengers,
35,000 letters, and 4 million florins' worth of money and valuables.[8]

By 1840 the Austrians could announce the following services (CC Smyrne, vol. 46):
Galatz-Istanbul, every 15 days; Kustenje (Constantza)-Istanbul, every 15 days; Istanbul-
Trabzon, weekly; Istanbul-Salonica, weekly; Istanbul-Syria and Egypt, every 4 weeks. Passenger fares were: Istanbul-Trabzon--first-class 30 dollars, third-class 200 piastres;
Istanbul-Salonica--20 and 150, respectively; Istanbul-Izmir--15 and 105; Izmir-Beirut--
33 and 250. In 1844 Lloyd took over the Danube line, raising its capital to 3 million
florins.[9] From 1855 on, the company received a subvention from the Austrian government,
whose mails it carried to the East. With the opening of the Suez Canal it started a run
to Bombay, which was gradually extended to reach Japan in 1893.

The progress of the Company before it opened its Far Eastern services, and by its
fiftieth anniversary, is shown in the following table.[10]

	1840	1850	1860	1868	1885
Capital and loans (₺000)	210	367	2,368	1,999	1,946
Number of steamers	10	30	62	65	84
G. R. tons (000)	3	12	33	51	120
Number of passengers (000)	39	216	354	295	380
Goods transported (000 tons)	3	24	90	215	604

The Company was very well managed.[11] A comparison for 1885 with the three other sub-
ventioned companies sailing the Mediterranean (Messageries Maritimes, Navigazione Generale-
Florio and Rubatino, and Compagnie Russe de Navigation et de Commerce) showed the following
results.

	Lloyd	Florio	Messageries	Russian
Capital & reserves (₺ million)	1.4	2.7	3.3	2.2
Tonnage (000)	120	92	151	87
Income (₺ million)[a]	1.1	1.3	1.7	0.8
Expenditure (₺ million)	0.9	1.3	2.1	0.7
Expenditure per ton (₺)	7-18s	13-19s	13-18s	7-17s
Expenditure per HP (₺)	42-16s	44s	86-15s	77-3s

[a]After deduction of subventions, which were much higher for the other three lines.

The Austrian Lloyd continued to develop until the First World War. After that it was
taken over by the Italians and renamed Lloyd Triestino, serving its old routes until the
Second World War.

Returning to the early days of steam, in 1842 the Peninsular and Oriental line established a Southampton-Istanbul service, via Malta, Athens, Syra, Izmir, Mytilene, and the
Dardanelles (29 October 1842, CC Constantinople, vol. 90)[12] and for a few years also had

an Istanbul-Beirut service, touching at Izmir and Rhodes (31 December 1847, FO 78/715).
Thus by 1844 passengers and mails between Istanbul and London had the choice of five routes
(Report of 7 May 1844, CC Constantinople, vol. 90):

a) Orsova-Vienna-Paris-London: ships leaving every 14 days between April and November;
duration 26 days; cost, including food, 597 francs.

b) Syra-Corfu-Trieste-Paris-London: Austrian Lloyd twice a month; 20 days, 722 francs.

c) Malta-Gibraltar-London: British ships once a month; 20 days, 1,090 francs.

d) Malta-Marseilles-Paris-London: French ships; 30 days, 881 francs.

e) Alexandria-Malta-Southampton-London: 17 days, 1,207 francs.

These services, which took half the time, or less, that sailing ships needed for the
journey, were a great convenience for travelers and mail. For merchandise, however, steamers continued for long to charge much more than sailing ships, and were used only for valuable goods or where speed was essential.[13] A French report of 1850 (CC Constantinople,
vol. 92) gives the following freight and insurance rates from Istanbul:

1) _Marseilles_

a) Sailing ships: wheat, 1.48 francs per hectolitre; silk, 8 francs per metric
quintal; wool, 6 francs per metric quintal; insurance, 1 percent.

b) Steamers (Cie Rostand): silk, 38.5 francs per quintal; insurance, only $\frac{1}{2}$ percent, thus more than offsetting the difference in freight because of the high value of silk.

2) _England_

a) Sailing ships: wheat, 3.30 francs; insurance, $1\frac{1}{2}$ percent.

b) Steamer (P&O): wheat, 35 francs; insurance $\frac{1}{2}$ percent.

3) _Trieste_

a) Sailing: wool, 3.50 francs per metric quintal; 1 percent.

b) Steamer (Lloyd): silk, 30 francs, $\frac{1}{2}$ percent.

One more point may be noted: during the first fifty years of steam navigation in the
Mediterranean, steamers remained small and inexpensive. The French report of 1835 put the
cost of 750-ton steamers at ₤24,000, or ₤32 per ton. The original fleet of the Austrian
Lloyd in 1836 averaged 254 tons at a valuation of ₤47 per ton. The figure for tonnage
rose very slowly, to 397 in 1850, to 526 in 1860, and passed the 1,000-ton mark only in
1874, by which time Lloyd was operating in the Indian Ocean. The valuation per ton fell
to ₤34 by 1850, rose to ₤38 in 1860, and fell back to ₤24 in 1870. Even by 1885 the average tonnage of the Florio Rubatino ships was only 872 and its valuation ₤41 and that of
the Russian line 1,026 tons and ₤10 (many ships being river steamers). Lloyd and Messageries, with their oceangoing ships, averaged 1,426 and 2,606 tons, respectively, at a valuation of only ₤14 and ₤17 per ton.[14]

Lastly, it may be noted that in 1856 the Ottoman government bought the _Silistria_, an
iron-screw steamer of 700 tons and 140 HP built in 1855 and capable of being used in war,
for ₤23,320. This price was in line with these quoted for similar ships.[15] In 1875 the
Aziziye Company (4:11) received an offer from a British firm to build five screw steamers
of 1,250 tons and 1,200 HP, similar to those used by the P&O, for ₤52,500 each.[16] The
size and cost of warships, however, increased rapidly: in 1868 five ironclads (6-inch
armor), with engines of 360-450 HP capable of making 14 knots and displacing 1,200-1,300
tons, were quoted at ₤67,500-98,750 each.[17]

1. MacFarlane, 1:489-91; 2:230-31; see also EHME, p. 47; Bazili, 1:210.
2. In 1837 Mahmud took the Austrian ship to Varna, returning overland by way of
Silistria, Rustchuk, and Edirne--Poujoulat, 1:46.

3. Various issues of <u>Journal de Smyrne</u>, 1835.

4. Advertisement in ibid., 24 September 1836.

5. Report reproduced in <u>Le Moniteur Ottoman,</u> 13 June 1835.

6. Martin Riedlinger, "Das Journal des Oesterreichen Lloyd," unpublished dissertation, Vienna, 1948.

7. Oskar Stark, <u>Eine Versunkene Welt: die Geschichte des Oesterreichischen Lloyd</u> (Vienna-Wiesbaden, 1959), pp. 9-10, and A and P 1887, vol. 82, "Austria-Hungary, Trieste."

8. Stark, <u>Eine Versunkene Welt</u>, p. 10.

9. Riedlinger, "Das Journal," p. 31.

10. A and P 1887, vol. 82, "Austria-Hungary, Trieste."

11. Two appreciations by British observers at Trabzon may be quoted. The initial effect of the Austrian steamer service to Trabzon was to reduce the time needed for Austrian goods to reach Iran to 15 days, compared to up to 2 or 3 months for British goods, and "German merchants turn their capital at least three times pending an English voyage." Hence in 1835-42 German exports had increased by 500 percent and British by only 10 percent (Williams to Canning, 18 April 1842, FO 195/178).

In his Report on Trade for 1859 (FO 78/1335), the consul stated that the Lloyd was doing very well, the French not so well, and the Russians were not paying their way but survived thanks to government subsidies. "The Turkish steamers, on the other hand, enjoy no reputation whatsoever. The owners have allowed them to work without repairs until their state became dangerous. After the loss of the 'Silistria' and 'Kara' in the waters of Alexandria, the Lloyd's of England refused to cover risks by Turkish steamers. The Boats plying on this line, some belonging to Government others to private individuals, were found to be in a sad state." Examples are given. "And thus for several months the Turkish flag under steam ceased to ply between Constantinople and this port,"

12. The estimates of costs and returns submitted for the service were that, with the existing system of 700-ton 140-HP vessels costing £27,000 each, total costs including interest and depreciation would amount to £102,000 a year. Using three 1,000-ton 300-HP ships and six 800-ton 200-HP ships would raise the annual cost to £121,200 (8 May 1840, FO 195/178).

13. However, it should be noted that around 1840 "it was estimated that steam did the work of about five sailing ships for equal tonnage" (Braudel, <u>Capitalism</u>, p. 265).

14. A and P, 1887, vol. 82, "Austria-Hungary, Trieste."

15. TE, Box 16, 1855-56.

16. TE, Box 180, 1876.

17. TE, Box 105, 1868.

SELECTION 6.   COMPETITION BETWEEN AUSTRIAN AND FRENCH STEAMERS, 1837

Challaye to Minister of Foreign Affairs, 19 July 1837, CC Smyrne, vol. 45)

. . . If their rates had been lower, our steamers could have become the channel for correspondence between the whole Levant and Western Europe. But as a result of our high rates, most of the advantage will be retained by the Vienna post. In order to deprive us of the preference which speed gives our steamers, it has managed to accelerate the movement of its couriers, so that for many countries we have no advantage, or hardly any, over it. Since the land route is still considered safer, where prices are equal or nearly so it is assured of preference as regards a good portion of Europe.

Nor is this all. At the very moment when our steamers began their service, a new competitor arose, that of a company called the Austrian Lloyd of Trieste which, like us, sends steam ships to all the principal ports of the Levant. Its rates are lower than ours, for it charges for a letter from Smyrna to Trieste only 36 kreutzers (about 1 franc 65), whereas a letter from Smyrna to Marseilles is charged 2 francs on our steamers. The Austrian Lloyd will therefore take away from us the correspondence of all countries which are as close to Trieste as to Marseilles or closer; indeed, because of its lower rates, its steamers will be preferred to ours for certain other countries.

I have always thought—and I have several times put it down in writing—that, from the financial point of view, the prolongation of our service as far as Constantinople was an unwise operation. Experience has already confirmed this. Here all exchange-operations, with all the European and other commercial markets with which Smyrna has relations, are carried out once a week on a fixed day; this day has been chosen in such a way that statements regarding the results of such operations can reach Constantinople two days before—or at least the day before—the departure of the Vienna post. And it is on this basis that the Austrian steamer of the Danube Company, which makes the run between Constantinople and Smyrna, has set its timetable. Our schedules provide for departures on a fixed day of the month and hence do not coincide with a fixed weekly date; they therefore do not correspond to either the habits or the needs of the two cities. In addition the charge for a letter from Smyrna to Constantinople is only 3 piastres (about 70 centimes) on the Austrian steamers, whereas ours charge 1 franc. The Austrians therefore enjoy an advantage from every point of view and can thus take away from us not only the Constantinople correspondence but all correspondence that has to pass through Constantinople, such as that of the Black Sea, Russia, and others.

Even if all other things had been equal, instead of working against us, the mere formalities demanded by the postal administration would have been enough to give preference to the Austrian steamers. The shore agent of our steamers is required to provide several statements listing every letter and indicating its weight, origin [base] and destination; he is therefore compelled to close his office to the reception of letters long before the departure of the steamer. In the Austrian office, as long as the mail bag is not closed-- and it is closed only a quarter of an hour before the departure of the steamer--there is still time, and even should a letter arrive too late at the office it is received on board the steamer until the moment of departure. . . .

[The consul adds that the enclosed schedule of passenger rates--which is unfortunately missing--shows that they are lower on the Austrian steamers, especially for long distances.]

SELECTION 7. PROGRESS OF STEAM-NAVIGATION AT TREBIZOND, BETWEEN THE YEARS 1836 AND 1841[a]

F. J. Stevens, January 31, 1842, FO 78/533

Name	Nation	Force	Tons	Periods of employment	No. of months running	Tons each Steamer's voyages represent[b]	Total number of tons of all Steamers during year
				1836			
Essex	English	--	132	May to Sept.	5	1,320	
Crescent	do.	140	178	Augt. to Decr.	5	1,780	3,664
Ferdinando	Austrian	100	141	Novr. to Decr.	2	564	
				1837			
Crescent	English	140	178	Jany. to Decr.	12	4,272	
Ferdinando	Austrian	100	141	Jany. to Augt.	8	2,256	8,208
Metternich	do.	140	210	Sept. to Decr.	4	1,680	
				1838			
Crescent	English	140	178	Jany. to May	5	1,780	
Metternich	Austrian	140	210	Jany. to Decr.	12	5,040	9,312
Crescent	do.	140	178	June to Decr.	7	2,494	
				1839			
Crescent	do.	140	178	Jany. to Decr.	12	4,272	
Metternich	do.	140	210	Jany. to May	5	2,100	
Stambol	do.	160	307	June to July	2	1,228	
Metternich	do.	140	210	Augt. to Decr.	5	2,100	12,640
Zibaishy Tijaret	Turkish	120	150	June to Decr.	7	2,100	
Esser Tijaret	do.	140	210	March to Apl.	2	840	
				1840			
Stambol	Austrian	160	307	Jany. to Feby.	2	1,228	
Crescent	do.	140	178	Jany. to Feby.	2	712	
Metternich	do.	140	210	March to Decr.	10	4,200	
Maria	do.	60	100	April to May	2	400	13,922
Crescent	do.	140	178	June to July	2	712	
Stambol	do.	160	307	Augt. to Decr.	5	3,070	
Zibaishy Tijaret	Turkish	120	150	Jany. to Decr.	12	3,600	
				1841			
Metternich	Austrian	140	210	Jany. to Decr.	12	5,040	
Crescent	do.	140	178	Jany. to Feby.	2	712	
Stambol	do.	160	307	March to June	4	2,456	
Crescent	do.	140	178	December	1	356	13,124
Zibaishy Tijaret	Turkish	120	150	Jany. to April	4	1,200	
Iscudar	do.	140	210	May to Decr.	8	3,360	

[a]All running between Constantinople and Trebizond, touching at Sinope and Samsoon.

[b]At the rate of two voyages per month.

SELECTION 8.   REPORT ON THE TRADE OF SAMSOON FOR 1842

R. W. Stevens, December 31, 1842, FO 78/533

By the accompanying Gross Return of Shipping, it will be seen that One hundred and eighty eight Vessels of all nations visited Samsoon during the year. This is a slight decrease on 1841, as in six months alone for which the Return was then made up, the number amounted to Ninety Seven. The difference may be accounted for by the fact, that Steam Communication with Constantinople having been more frequent and regular than formerly, less than the usual employment has offered for Native Vessels.

The Trade under the Austrian Flag appears important for the same reason as assigned last year, vist. the weekly intercourse kept up with the Capital by the Danube Steam Company's Steamers, which call here, both in going to Trebizond, and on their return to Constantinople. Besides two of these, employed throughout the year, the one of 160 horsepower and 625 Tons, and the other of 140 horsepower and 575 Tons, there were two Boats under Turkish Colors, one of 150 horsepower and 570 Tons, and the other, of 400 Tons and 150 horsepower. The two latter began to ply in the Spring, but were frequently interrupted on account of repairs being constantly required in their machinery. An American Steamer of 160 horsepower has likewise just entered the line, but being built for River Service she cannot safely navigate the Black Sea, and may therefore be expected to abandon it very soon.

During the summer a spirited opposition commenced between the Turks, and the Austrians. Reduced fares on one side were followed by reduction on the other, until those for Deck passengers, their principal gains, fell from 24s/- to 2s/-. The parties then entered into an agreement for running at fixed rates, but this was soon violated by the Turks. Finding their rivals enjoyed a preference from the superiority of their boats, and fearing a renewal of the ruinous opposition just mentioned, they applied for assistance against them to the Pasha of Trebizond, who is a shareholder in the Turkish Company. His Excellency commenced by indirectly preventing Turkish subjects from embarking themselves, or their property, by the Austrian steamers. The results of this interference were too evident for it to remain long a secret; the Pasha at length continued it openly, and finally received orders to that effect from Constantinople. This state of things has lasted about two months, causing a loss to the Danube Company of nearly ₤2,000 at Samsoon alone. What decision may be come to, remains to be seen, meanwhile the Turkish Steamers being too small, cannot perform the whole of the work offering. Serious injury to the Trade has been the consequence, and there are now upwards of 4,000 Packages of Produce which have been waiting here a long time for conveyance to Constantinople.

Should the Turkish Government succeed in its pretension of excluding foreign Steamers from the Trade they have hitherto carried on, there will be an end to the hopes entertained of seeing English Boats in the Black Sea; and what is of greater importance, a precedent dangerous to the liberty of European Commerce will be established. The Turks will oppose it whenever they find advantage in doing so without reference to rights which that commerce may have acquired by established usage. I may here mention the opinion general in this quarter, that in the proceedings against the Austrian Steamers, the Porte is acting under the advice of Russia, whose object is to prevent English Boats appearing in the Black Sea. A report also prevails that Russian Steamers are preparing in England, destined to be employed for Commercial purposes in this quarter. They could not however well enjoy privileges denied to the Austrians, unless perhaps, the Russians vary their case, by extending the line beyond Trebizond, as far as Redout Kaleh, thus giving it less the appearance of a Coasting Trade, than that of the Austrians, who run from one Turkish Port to another Turkish Port.

The number of Passengers landed here by the Steamers from Constantinople during the year was 6,500, and of those embarked hence, about 7,000. In 1841 the latter amounted to 18,000, but included 11,000 Troops, of which this year, there were only a few hundred.

Gross Return of the British and Foreign Trade at the Port of Samsoon, during the year ending the 31st December 1842

| Nation | Number of Vessels | Arrived[a] | | |
		Tonnage	Number of Crew	Value of Cargoes
British (Ionian)	2	120	14	₤ 375
Turkish	80	23,972	1,642	" 50,090
Austrian	101	60,896	2,202	" 70,460
Greek	3	750	37	--
Russian	2	320	21	" 1,540
Totals	188	86,058	3,916	₤122,465

Remark. The Turkish entries and clearances comprise 46 steamers. Tonnage 17,080, Crews 1,302. The Austrians were all Steamers. The Greek Vessels arrived in ballast. In the value of Imports I have not included that of Government stores, which I could not ascertain.

[a]The same number of vessels, with the same tonnage and number of crew, departed.

SELECTION 9. THE FEVAIDE OSMANIYE SHIPPING LINE, 1865

Bentivoglio to Minister of Foreign Affairs, 29 March 1865, on the occasion of the Istanbul-
Izmir run by the Fevaide Osmaniye, CC Smyrne, vol. 50

. . . The establishment of the first steam navigation service in Turkey goes back some
twenty five years. The sultan, the Valide Sultana, and a few of the principal paşas were
the only shareholders of this company, which was known as Zecca (Money) because the ships
were owned by the Ministry of Finance. To these ships, which numbered a dozen, were added--
when they were available--those of the Arsenal. But as the latter were withdrawn according
to the needs of the Navy, constant perturbations occurred in the organization of the service. Some lines, including that between Constantinople and Smyrna, were active for a
while but were then given up for several years.

The Fevaide Osmaniye, which was constituted only recently, has only one shareholder,
the Sultan.* It has some twenty ships, of which nearly half consist of the old Zecca
ships, the others belonging to the Admiralty. A former pleasure yacht owned by the Sultan,
the Izzedin--a fast ship--has also been assigned to this line.

When this company was constituted, four months ago, its management was entrusted to
Agha Effendi, who was completely independent and had to submit his statements only to the
Sultan. The ships were put under the command of foreign officers, mostly Dalmatians, and
their internal management was organized on the European pattern. For some time the company's operations were entirely satisfactory to both passengers and trade. In addition to
the Black Sea and Marmara runs, it had a direct and speedy service between Constantinople
and Smyrna. The Izzedin, which was assigned to this service, covers the distance between
the two cities in twenty hours, whereas the Austrian Lloyd and Messageries Impériales
ships take thirty six hours. It should, however, be remembered that these two companies
call on various ports in the Archipelago and that, unlike the Turkish ships, theirs are
not authorized to pass through the Dardanelles Straits by night.

Whatever be the case, the Fevaide Osmaniye was preferred by passengers, who found it
advantageous to spend only one night at sea between Smyrna and Constantinople. In addition, the infatuation which is felt for every new institution made people exalt the merits
of the new service, and it was already being said that all coasting trade would soon be
reserved to the Ottoman flag and the postal service would be in Ottoman hands.

But a sudden change in the organization of the Fevaide Osmaniye has cooled this enthu-
siasm. Agha Effendi was suddenly dismissed--nobody knows exactly why--and replaced by
Salih Bey. The new director has been put under the direct orders of the Minister of the
Navy. This change has led to much more serious consequences, viz., the replacement of the
foreign captains and officers by Turkish officers. This step will be disastrous for the
company, since it deprives trade of all security. The capacity--and still more the vigi-
lance--of Turkish officers is too well known for anyone gladly to entrust them with his
person or even his goods.

Your Excellency will find, enclosed, a Turkish schedule, with translation, of the
Fevaide Osmaniye ships. This document, which is pretty confused, shows only the days of
departure from Constantinople for each destination. It can be summarized as follows:

Two weekly services on the Black Sea, one to Trebizond and the other to Varna and
Kustendje.

A weekly service to Salonica and Volo.

A fortnightly service to Smyrna.

A daily service to Ismit.

Lastly, a few minor services to other ports on the Sea of Marmara. . . .

---

*[Shaw, History, 2:119-20, gives the date of foundation as 1844.]

PORTS OF IZMIR AND ISTANBUL

The following selection describes the building of Turkey's first modern port, the

need for which had been made urgent by the opening of the Aydın railway (4:15). Total cost

of the works described was ₤400,000.[1]

Although British enterprise had initiated the project, the French company which com-

pleted and owned the port gave preferential treatment to French and Austrian ships, which

were charged half the rates paid by others. More generally, although unloading ships on

the quay was four to five times quicker than by lighters, the high dues charged were

strongly resented by merchants, among whom the British were prominent. Hence in 1881 a

British-controlled company was formed to buy the installations and negotiations were pro-

ceeding with Dussaud when, in 1882, the Ottoman government intervened, ordering the reduc-

tion of dues and the ending of discrimination. The company responded to the consequent

diminution of its revenues by refusing to make any further improvements and, to put pressure on shippers, suspended part of its lighterage services. The British merchants reacted
by launching, in 1895, a small fleet of lighters and steam tugs--which in turn were held up
by the company for up to 20 days, while the French and Austrian ships unloaded their goods
onto company lighters in one or two days. Prolonged negotiations led to a settlement in
1911 when, in return for a 20 percent rise in dues, the company agreed to stop discriminat-
ing against British ships. Another company was formed to buy the lighters and tugs belonging to British merchants and, after enlarging its fleet, eventually passed into the control
of the Archipelago American Steamship Company (4:11).

As regards the port company itself, in 1889 negotiations were started for selling it
to the Civil List for 10.5 million francs, but these fell through and in 1891 its concession was prolonged to 1952. Its capital was raised from 10.5 to 11 million francs, enabling it to build storage for alcohol and petroleum (CC Smyrne, vol. 55, 8 January 1890 and
26 May 1891). By the 1890s gross profits had a level of 800,000 francs, of which the government's share was 120,000. Over the period 1894-1913, gross profits averaged 10.3 percent of total capital (shares, bonds, and land) and dividends 7.8 percent.[2]

As regards Istanbul, in November 1890 a concession was granted to Michel paşa who gave
it to a French company, Société anonyme ottomane des Quais, Docks et Entrepôts de Constantinople, with a capital of 23,875,000 francs. The concession ran for eighty five years,
the Ottoman government receiving 10 percent of gross receipts and being entitled to repurchase after 1930, on payment of an annuity equal to 80 percent of average annual gross receipts in the previous five years.[3] Construction began immediately, but estimated costs
soon rose to 29.5 million francs, compared to a paid-up capital of 13 million, and in 1896
the company raised 11 million by issuing bonds. In 1895 some of the Galata docks were
opened to traffic. But the following years showed poor results, and unsuccessful negotiations were undertaken with the government for repurchase.[4] Eventually, the company was
saved by powerful financial backing--in January 1907, the Bank of England on the one hand
and the Ottoman Bank and a group of French shareholders on the other bought 37,500 shares
(Memorandum, March 1908, FO 368/228).

The docks increased the capacity of the port of Istanbul, whose traffic rose sharply:
"Many liners which until lately used to lie out in the fairway and discharge into lighters
are now moored alongside the quays where their operations are much facilitated" (Block to
Hardinge, 22 October 1906, FO 368/58).[5] But constant difficulties arose with the bargemen,
who felt threatened in their livelihood (4:11) and who, as late as 1908 during the wave of
strikes (2:8), prevented the use by British ships of the pontoons built by the company to
facilitate the discharge of goods at Istanbul--as distinct from the quays at Galata which
were mainly used by non-British ships (Lowther to Grey, 6 August 1910, FO 368/470).[6] There
were also recurring difficulties with the government, e.g., over expropriation of land, the
installation of petroleum storage, etc. (Memorandum March 1908, FO 368/228). Complaints
by the shippers were frequent and in 1914 a government commission reported on: insufficiency of quay space; insufficiency of customs depots and warehouses; absence of customs
depots for transit goods; insufficient number and bad condition of lighters; and insufficiency of mooring buoys.[7]

Across from Istanbul, the Germans built ports off the railway at Haydarpaşa and Derince
(4:11,17).[8] In the provinces the only modern ports built by 1914 were those of Beirut and
Salonica, but there were some facilities at the coal port of Zonguldak and, after several
unsuccessful attempts in the nineteenth century,[9] an iron wharf with a crane was installed

at Trabzon.[10] Shortly before the war, a concession was given to a British group to build modern ports at Trabzon, Samsun, and Izmit, to a German group at Alexandretta, and to a French consortium for ports at Jaffa, Haifa, Ereğli, and Inebolu.[11]

1. Kurmuş, pp. 266-72, on whom the section on Izmir draws heavily.
2. Thobie, pp. 132-37, 376-77.
3. Texts in Young, 3:323-42.
4. Thobie, pp. 161-64; 384-91.
5. The traffic of the port of Istanbul itself was some 2.5 million tons in 1901, 3 million in 1902, and 4.5 million in 1903 (ibid.). In addition, some 10 to 12 million tons of shipping called at Istanbul on the way to or from the Black Sea. The efficiency of the port was further increased by the opening, in 1913, of a floating dock at Stenia, in the Bosphorus. An agreement was made in December 1913 for the formation, by the Ottoman government and Armstrong and Vickers, of a large company for building several docks--see 4:11 and A and P 1914, vol. 95, "Constantinople."
6. Conflict with local boatmen began with the introduction of steam navigation. In 1837 two English residents started a steamboat service between Büyükdere and Pera. The kaikcis protested and even plotted to kill the Sultan--Poujoulat, 1:227. In 1851 an Ottoman company, Şirkat Hayriye, was founded, providing service in the Bosphorus--Shaw, History, 2:91.
7. TJ, June 1914.
8. Text in Young, III, pp. 342-51.
9. See, for example, A and P 1878/79, vol. 71, "Trebizond."
10. TJ, March 1914.
11. Thobie, pp. 391-402.

SELECTION 10. PORT OF IZMIR, 1867-88

Report on Port of Smyrna, May 1888, CC Smyrne, vol. 55

. . . Until 1867, because of the absence of a harbor, ships cast anchor in the open roadstead and the loading and unloading of goods ran into all sorts of difficulties. In that year, three English merchants resident in Smyrna obtained, with no financial guarantee from the government, a concession for the construction of a wharf at least 4 kilometers long and 18.75 meters wide along the front of the town. The Ottoman government authorized them, at the same time, to levy a duty on all goods loaded and unloaded, reserving for itself only 12 percent of the proceeds, and in addition granted them full ownership of all land reclaimed from the sea. A five-year period was allowed for construction and the company was to enjoy the right of operating the port for twenty-five years. Installations were to include a tramway, sewers, and, if necessary, a port of anchorage [port d'abri] in a place to be determined. At the end of twenty-five years the wharves, with all their appurtenances, were to revert to the state.

The concessionaires founded a joint-stock company and, for the construction work, called on MM. Dussaud Frères, a contracting firm well known for its work in France and abroad.* Dussaud undertook to carry out the construction work for a fixed sum of 6 million francs, payable in instalments.

Owing to unforeseen difficulties, and notably to the lack of success of the subscription it had opened to sell its shares, the company was unable to carry out its obligations towards the contractors, and the latter began work at their own expense. By the beginning of 1869, the situation not having improved, the company was forced into liquidation and gave up the enterprise. In order to safeguard the considerable sums they had put into this business, MM. Dussaud concluded with the company a convention under which they undertook to refund a large part of the subscribed shares, the company in return making over to them a complete cession of all its rights.

In August 1875 the planned work was completed and ready for operation. A new arrangement was then made with the Porte, under which--in return for certain works of public utility--the original concession was prolonged for 35 years [to 1912] in favor of MM. Dussaud. A tariff was also established for the wharf dues, in agreement with the representatives of the interested Powers.

At present the installations consist of:
1. A wharf 1.50 meters above high-tide level, stretching from the Aydin railway station to the barracks, a distance of 4 kilometers.
2. A dock including about 1,200 meters of wharves, between piers [entre digues]; the total area is 20 hectares and the depth is 6.50 meters at the wharf and 10 to 12 meters at its greatest depth [en pleine eau].
3. A dock under construction, which will have an area of about 12 hectares.

The dock entrance is at the northeastern end; its position is marked by a red light on the right and a green one on the left on the way in. The customs' and other warehouses

*[Its port constructions included Suez (see EHME, p. 414), Port Said, Algiers, and Trieste.]

make it possible to store a large quantity of goods. Merchandise is unloaded by the ships'
winches and machines on to lighters and flat boats and loading is carried out in the same
way. Ships anchor in the places assigned to them, stern to shore, and at distances of
about ten meters from each other. The wharves are lit up the whole night by gaslight.
Rails, used during the day by streetcars, stretch along the whole length of the wharves
and lead to the main station of the Aydin railway. . . .

Each week the port of Smyrna is called at by twelve subsidized steamers of which five
are Austrian (Austro-Hungarian Lloyd), two French (Messageries Maritimes), two Russian
(Russian Steamship Company), one Italian (Florio-Rubattino Company), and two Egyptian
(Khedivial Line). During the same period, seven steamers regularly service the port, viz:
two French (new Compagnie Marseillaise de Navigation à Vapeur, Marc Fraissinet et Compagnie), two Ottoman flag, two English, belonging to Bell's Asia Minor, and one Greek,
owned by the Compagnie Egée. The shipping traffic also includes a large Dutch steamer that
calls at Smyrna each month, a fortnightly Cunard Company steamer, four irregular steamers
a week (mostly English--French ships account for only 6 percent of the total in this category), and, lastly, a large number of coasting vessels and sailing ships providing frequent
communication between Smyrna and the islands.

NAVIGATION AT IZMIR

Izmir was served by the very earliest steamers sailing in Turkish water (4:6), being

connected to Europe through either Syra or Istanbul. By the 1840s Izmir also had steam

connections with the Levant coast and Egypt.[1] In 1860 the following lines called regular-

ly: Messageries three times a week, Austrian Lloyd three times a week; Russian line four

to six times each 15 days; and Cie Hellène. There were also several British and Greek ir-

regular lines as well as a Belgian and a French one (Report on Trade, CC Smyrne, vol. 49).

A French consular report written in 1862 stated that the Messageries led the field in regu-

larity and comfort of passengers but that the trade complained it had less facilities for

transporting goods than the Austrian Lloyd and that its freight rates were too high; that

the Austrian line offered most frequent services; and that the Russian ships were good but

so irregular that they did not attract goods or passengers and could not have survived

without a huge subsidy (ibid., vol. 50).

By 1871, it was reported that sailing ships had almost disappeared except for the

coasting trade, which was carried on by Greek and Turkish ships, and for sailing ships

bringing coal from England. The Austrian Lloyd's steamers had called 170 times during

the year, as against 105 for the French, and the Austrians had a greater volume of activity

and were better appreciated. No German or U. S. ships had called in 1871 (ibid., vol. 51).

The volume of shipping entering the port was over 600,000 tons in the 1860s and passed the

1,000,000 mark in the 1880s.[2]

After an unsuccessful German attempt at establishing a service between Hamburg and

Istanbul in 1880-84,[3] the Deutsche Levante-Linie started a new regular service in 1890,

its first ship reaching Izmir on 22 July (ibid., vol. 55). By 1899, twenty-eight regular

lines served Izmir, and the total tonnage entering the port was 2,180,000. Russian ships

led with 370,000, followed by Ottoman 353,000, British 338,000, French 320,000, Austrian

254,000, Greek 193,000, and German 87,000 (ibid., vol. 57). The prewar peak was reached

in 1909 with 3,018 steamers aggregating 2,804,000 tons. The 1912 figures were lower: a

total of 2,448 steamers aggregating 2,210,000 tons entered; British ships led with 652,000

tons, followed by Russian 432,000, French 327,000, Austrian 192,000, Greek 166,000, German

138,000, and United States 93,000.[4]

The effect of this great increase in shipping was to bring down freight rates sharply.

In 1836, average freight on British vessels was ₤2-10s. per ton; fruits sent to England

paid ₤4 per ton and valonea ₤3, both figures being ₤1 over those of the previous season

(FO 78/287). By 1876, when steam navigation had made its impact, the following freights, per ton, were quoted for England: by sailing ship, dry fruits Ł1–10–0 to Ł2, valonea Ł1–10–0 to Ł2–10–0; by steamer, cotton wool 15s. to Ł1–5–9, dry fruits Ł1–10–0 to Ł2–10–0, valonea Ł1–10–0 to Ł2–2–6, carpets Ł1–10–0, and opium Ł7–15–0.[5] In 1882 the following freights were quoted for Mediterranean ports: 17.50 francs per ton for heavy goods, such as cereals and oilseeds; 45 francs for bulky goods, e.g., cotton and hides; and 150 francs for fine goods such as opium, silk, and rugs. For northern ports, the figures were 30 percent higher (23 June 1882, CC Smyrne, vol. 54). In other words, freights for heavy goods to London had fallen to well below Ł1, and those for bulky goods were not much over Ł2.

The decline continued, with interruptions, until the First World War.[6] In 1897–98, rates of 15 to 45 francs a ton were quoted for the various European ports; chrome and litharge paid 8 to 10 francs for Marseilles and 18 to 25 for the United Kingdom, Antwerp, and Hamburg.[7]

In the early years of this century, a ring was formed among shipping agents providing for a uniform tariff to the Mediterranean and United Kingdom ports, but this frequently broke down. In 1909 the following freights, per ton, were quoted for the United Kingdom:[8]

Wool	Ł1–0–0	to	Ł2–5–0
Figs	17–0	to	1–5–0
Oilseeds		to	15–0
Skins	1–5–0	to	2–5–0
Barley	7–0	to	10–0
Raisins	17–0	to	1–5–0
Valonea	12–6	to	1–0–0

Better connections were also reducing freights to the United States. "Some years ago the freight from New York to Constantinople was Ł2 per ton, with transshipment at Liverpool. The establishment of a direct line brought the freights down to 17s. 6d.".[9]

In addition to these international lines, there were several lines based on Izmir itself and engaged in the coastal trade. A report of 1883 (28 December 1883, CC Smyrne, vol. 54) mentioned the following: Cie Joly, Victoria, a British line founded in 1877, owning eight small ships of 25–40 HP, engaged mainly in transporting passengers in the port of Izmir and its neighborhood.

Cie. Carava, a Greek line established in 1883, owning two ships of 60–80 HP and serving the neighboring islands and the coast of Karaman.

Bell's Asia Minor Co., a well-established British firm with four ships of 100–150 HP, ranging as far as Mersin.

Lastly, the Cie. Ottomane Anonyme Hamidiye, which had just received from the government a thirty-year privilege for cabotage in the Gulf of Izmir and was expected to replace Joly, Victoria.

By 1899 Hamidiye was well established and another Turkish line, Haci Davud, was active (ibid., vol. 57). In 1909, the latter transferred its flag to that of the United States under the name "Archipelago-American Line." "This necessitated a considerable expenditure, as most of the vessels had to be thoroughly overhauled."[10]

---

1. Although steamships greatly helped business by providing speed and regularity, their presence did not, for several years, appreciably raise the total tonnage calling at the port. In 1830–32, annual entries averaged close to 100,000 tons and in 1836–37 89,000. In 1838, by which time both the Austrian and French steamers called regularly, the figure rose to 115,000 and in 1840 it stood at 108,000 (Trade Reports from Izmir, FO 78/195, 201, 215, 229, 314, 338, 369, and 442 and CC Smyrne, vol. 46).
2. A and P 1867–68, vol. 68; 1875, vol. 77; 1887, vol. 86, "Smyrna."
3. Verney and Dambmann, pp. 497–98.

4. A and P 1914, vol. 95, "Smyrna."
5. A and P 1877, vol. 83, "Smyrna."
6. This was in line with general trends. Thus grain freights from the Danube to the UK fell from a base of 100 in 1869 to a low of 26 in 1908 and stood at 38 in 1914--see L. Isserlis, "Tramp Shipping, Cargoes and Freights," Journal of the Royal Statistical Society, 1938, for several series. See also Max Fletcher, "The Suez Canal and World Shipping," JEH, December 1958.
7. RL, no. 149, 1899.
8. A and P 1910, vol. 103, "Smyrna."
9. A and P 1904, vol. 101, p. I, "Constantinople."
10. A and P 1910, vol. 103, "Smyrna" and "Adana."

SELECTION 11. NAVIGATION, 1900s

J. Krauss "Schiffahrt, Güterumschlag und Lagerung," in Josef Hellauer, ed., Das Türkische Reich (Berlin, 1918), pp. 84-98, footnotes omitted.

. . . In 1850 the Turkish Navigation Company (Société de Navigation Turque) was founded and for a long time it distributed high dividends, without making sufficient provision for depreciation and insurance. By 1885 it stood on the verge of collapse and was saved only by the intervention of the state. Its fleet, which had melted away from twenty ships to eleven, was put under the Administration for Sea Trade, in the Ministry of Marine, and has been known by the name of Mahsusseh Company. In the main it carries on long-distance coasting, the larger ships serving for the transport of recruits, reservists, and other troops as well as pilgrims. These Turkish ships do not meet the necessary requirements for general passenger traffic, nor do they play a significant part in goods traffic, for they have been declassified by the leading European ship classification institutes because of their poor condition, i.e., following inspection by experts they were declared unfit and, consequently, the premiums paid on insurance of goods shipped on them are appreciably higher than on those of foreign "classified" ships. Another deterrent to their use for carrying freight is the fact that claims lodged with the Mahsusseh Company for compensation for losses of goods through damage or pilfering have been, as a rule, unsuccessful. Recently, a few better steamers have been acquired and the company's administration has been put in somewhat better order, with the help of a German expert, but this has not succeeded in overcoming the deeply rooted mistrust. However, it seldom attempts to compete with foreign steamship lines. But a certain part in the traffic between Turkish ports is played by the Turco-Greek companies: Hadji Daoud, Courdji & Company, and Cuppa Lambros.

Under the trade and navigation treaties concluded between the Porte and the foreign Powers, navigation in all Turkish waters is authorized for all flags. Cabotage, i.e., coastal trade, is also open to foreign shipping, except where a privileged monopoly has been granted, e.g., in local traffic on the Bosphorus, in the Golden Horn, in the Gulf of Smyrna, and on the Tigris between Basra and Baghdad; in addition, the Mahsusseh Company has the privilege of building piers in the Sea of Marmara for its own exclusive use. Foreign ships do not have to pay any duties other than those imposed on indigenous ships.

The national struggle of the Ottomans, which made its appearance after the promulgation of the Constitution in 1908, has also pushed out into the field of navigation. The boycot of the Austro-Hungarian flag by the Party for Union and Progress in 1908 was, howevery, based more on political grounds, connected with the annexation of Bosnia, than on economic; the exclusion of the Greek flag--which played an important role in the Eastern Mediterranean and Black Seas--was, on the other hand, designed to make room for Turkish shipping. But for this all the necessary prerequisites are lacking: entrepreneurial spirit, indigenous capital, a taste for seamanship among the population, a probability of sustaining a successful competition against foreign flags. The best sailors among the Muslim population in Turkey are the Laz, in the region of Trebizond and Rize, and the Black Sea Turks. The Osmanlis living on the shores of the Aegean Sea, from whom one could have expected great aptitudes for seamanship because of their maritime location, show little inclination for navigation, willingly abandoning it to the Greeks living among them. The Turkish Navy League has carried out much propaganda and the Minister of Marine sent in 1914 a circular to all port authorities, asking them to urge the people to engage more fully in maritime activities. One should not expect much result from this kind of measure.

In order to promote shipbuilding--above all naval construction--the Ministry of Marine has made an agreement with the well-known English shipbuilding firms W. G. Armstrong, Whitworth and Company, and Maxim Vickers Ltd. Already under Abd al-Aziz (1861-76) the Turkish government had set up an arsenal on the Golden Horn, with dockyards, machine-making shops, boiler-making shops, etc., and capable of employing 3,000 men. However, under Abd al-Hamid (1879-1909), the dockyard fell into almost complete dilapidation, and at most can carry out only minor repairs. The Young Turk government attempted to re-equip the state dockyards and make them fit for building warships. For this purpose, they signed a contract with the English firms by which the latter would establish a company Société imperiale ottomane cointéressée des constructions maritimes de docks et arsenaux, with a capital of ₺T 1,485,000 (27 million marks), which would restore the dockyards in the Golden Horn and Izmit and undertake the construction of war and merchant ships. All ships ordered by the Imperial government within the country were to be allotted to this company, but this monopoly did not apply to merchant ships. And if the government wished to build new docks and arsenals, it had to offer a first option to this company. The Golden Horn and Izmit arsenals were to be provided with floating docks with a capacity of 32,000 tons.

The English company also made a pooling agreement with Stenia (Société anonyme ottomane de docks et ateliers du Haut-Bosphore, capital ₺176,000), concerning their installations, of which the floating dock is particularly important; it thus acquired a de facto monopoly over the Constantinople docks.

Through these agreements, the English got hold of the whole Turkish fleet, whose reform had been entrusted to an English commission under Admiral Limpus. Thanks to the German naval officers and men who were taken on by the Turkish Navy, it has become known how the Naval Commission, in cooperation with the Dock Company, used its monopoly. After the outbreak of war, it was shown that it had sought to make, and partly succeeded in making, the Turkish Navy unfit for putting out to sea through planned sabotage. After the outbreak of war, the Turkish government naturally cancelled its agreement with the English Dock Company. The installations of both companies consisted mainly of the three drydocks in the Golden Horn:

```
400/380 feet long, 72 feet wide
285/280   "     "   62  "   "
500/480   "     "   62  "   "
```

The floating dock on the Golden Horn, 245/240 feet long and 48 feet wide; and a floating dock belonging to Stenia, at the exit of the Bosphorus, 449/425 feet long and 70 feet wide, with the necessary auxiliary installations. At the outbreak of war, these facilities were taken over by the Turkish government, and operated with German management and personnel.

. . .

Insofar as the elements required by modern standards for safe navigation have been created, this has been accomplished with European cooperation. They include, in addition to hydrological surveys, the cementing and equipping of the harbor. Mahmud II, whose reign (1808-1839) was filled with attempts--even though carried out by cruel, Asiatic means --to bring the medieval condition of his deeply shaken Ottoman Empire nearer to a European state, in 1838 had the first lighthouses built on the Bosphorus and Black Sea coasts. During the Crimean War (1853-1856) when traffic, particularly of British and French ships, increased in Turkish waters, lighting was found to be inadequate and, by an agreement of 20 August, 1860, a concession was granted to a French lighthouse company, Société des phares de l'Empire Ottoman, part of whose receipts went to the Turkish Ministry of Finance. In the course of time, the company erected some 140 lighthouses, but the rates it charged have often led to disputes between the Porte and the maritime Powers. The Turkish government was too little aware that international ethics [Ehrenpflicht] obligated it not to convert such an aid to navigation into a source of income. The abundance of receipts from lighthouses, under the latest tariff, may be judged from the fact that with the present prolongation of the concession (to November 4, 1924) the Turkish government received an advance of ₺T400,000 (about 7.4 million marks) on its share of gross receipts. The performance of the French concessionary company has also not met reasonable demands: the number of lights is too small, the system of stationary lights only often unsatisfactory, and the power of the lights is in most cases insufficient. The worst thing, however, is the administrative routine: the badly anchored lightships are not infrequently shifted by heavy seas and it often takes months for them to be put back in their right place--a state of affairs that carries great danger for navigation. During the war, the French concession was cancelled. Let us hope that, after the war, this question will be taken up again and the lighthouse administration put in more careful hands.

Not less important for shipping than the provision for the safety of navigation is the sanitary administration of a country; for ships coming from countries infested with epidemics have to go into quarantine when they call on a port, and thereby lose much time. In Turkey, it was the same Mahmud II who also showed himself ready to take the steps in this direction required by European standards. In 1836, when a terrible plague raged in Constantinople, he wished to build a pesthouse. This was threateningly opposed by the ulema (clergy), who said that the plague was God's punishment for the reforms carried out by the monarch, and that it would be godless to try to check it by means of hospitals. And in fact it took two more years before the hospital, headed by two French physicians, was established. An International Sanitary Administration (Administration Sanitaire de l'Empire Ottoman) was set up, and simultaneously quarantine stations were opened for land and sea traffic and a Quarantine Commission, with delegates of the foreign Powers among its members (Conseil supérieur international de santé). These institutions have continued to the present. They are indispensable, for among the pilgrims who come to Turkey many have very little understanding of the requirements of cleanliness and hygiene. Each Easter some 80,000 Russian-Orthodox Catholics (sic), mostly of Russian nationality, make the pilgrimage to Jerusalem, over a quarter of a million Muslims from three continents come to Mecca and Medina, and 150,000 Shii Muslims to Najaf and Karbala in Mesopotamia. All of these are feared carriers of cholera--and in previous decades of the plague--to hold off and fight which is of the greatest importance for navigation, and in general for the welfare of humanity.

Before the war, the Sanitary Council consisted of two Turkish members and delegates from Germany, France, Austria-Hungary, Great Britain, Belgium, Spain, the United States, Greece, Holland, Italy, Persia, Russia, Sweden, and Norway. This body drew its income from the taxes on the health clearance certificates issued to every ship, from taxes on Persian pilgrims and pilgrims to Mecca and Medina, and, in cases of quarantine, from the fees charged by the stations. The European delegates--who usually also fill a subsidiary diplomatic or consular post--receive no remuneration. Receipts ar eused solely to pay the Turkish delegates, the physicians, and other personnel, and to run the stations. Since the promulgation of the Constitution (1908) only Ottoman subjects--carrying diplomas from the School of Medicine in Constantinople which, under German guidance, has significantly improved in the last two decades--have been appointed as quarantine physicians.

On March 14, 1916, the Administration Sanitaire de l'Empire Ottoman was converted into a purely Turkish administration under the name of Administration Générale Sanitaire des Frontières. It is now dependent on the minister of the interior, who also carries the title of minister of hygiene, whereas formerly the minister of foreign affairs was the official president of the International Sanitary Council. Foreign officials are no longer employed in the sanitary service. How the foreign enemy Powers will adjust to this change in the formerly international sanitary service, will have to be determined by special negotiations after the conclusion of peace.

The modest extent to which the interior regions of the Turkish Empire participate in traffic corresponds with the small number of seaports and their lack of modern equipment. In most ports ships have to anchor in open roadsteads, and passengers and goods are carried in boats and lighters, which even in good weather has its dangers. But where the seas are rough or the winds strong, no embarkation or disembarkation is possible. This applies particularly to the ports of the Syrian, Karamanian, and Black Sea coasts, i.e., to most Turkish harbors. In winter, it is a regular occurrence that steamers pass by Jaffa without being able to land or take on passengers, mail, and cargo. Repeatedly, boats carrying passengers have been dashed to pieces on the rocks. Hence it was that our Kaiser, when he visited Jerusalem in 1898 for the dedication of the Church of the Redeemer, did not land at the port of Jerusalem--Jaffa--but in Haifa where however, on the occasion of this high visit, a special landing stage had to be built. It is in large part because of the unsatisfactory shipping conditions in Jaffa that the German and Jewish colonists usually cannot market the produce of their plantations on favorable terms. Loading on to ships, which have often been waiting for ten or more days, takes a couple of days, and the often simultaneously departing steamers carry to the European markets (Trieste, Liverpool, Hamburg) a sometimes excessive supply. Since the fresh fruit is sold by auction, prices are pressed down to a very noticeable extent--sometimes by a hundred or two hundred percent.

Conditions on the coast of Karamania and the Black Sea are similar. In unfavorable seasons, cargo ships often lose a week or more, for loading becomes impossible in open roadsteads. This naturally entails significant losses for shipping, and for the cargo irregularity and disproportionately long delays. Certain goods, e.g., those that are particularly heavy or bulky, can simply not be shipped from some harbors, and from others only at certain times of year. Ships built for traffic with Turkey should include equipment for loading and unloading, because of the lack of facilities in Turkish harbors. Thus several of the steamers of the Deutsche Levante-Linie have derricks with a carrying capacity of 46 tons, in order to be able to unload whole railway cars or machinery on to barges. One cannot make firm calculations regarding sea traffic--natural contingencies are decisive in matters of transport.

In ports of greater international importance, conditions are somewhat better, thanks to European enterprise; there are port installations in Constantinople, Smyrna, Beirut, in the coalfields of Zonguldak and in the stations of the Anatolian Railway: Haydar paşa and Derince. But even in Constantinople itself harbor conditions are thoroughly unsatisfactory. It is true that in 1894 a concession was given to the French Société anonyme Ottomane des Quais, Docks et Entrepôts de Constantinople. But the complaints of shipping companies and merchants have been unending regarding the shortage of space on the wharves and in the customs sheds, the lack of lighters, the disorder prevailing in the port, and the inadequate equipment in cranes for loading and unloading. A contributory cause of this situation has been the opposition of the powerful guild of mahonacis (bargemen), who felt threatened in their livelihood by the building of the quays. When in the mid-1890s a steamer tried, for the first time, to dock alongside the quay, a dramatic, bloody scene ensued: the mahonacis moved their barges between the quay and the French Messageries steamer to prevent the latter from docking. And in fact the steamer had to give up its plans. The mahonacis repeated their action with the following steamer, but the French warship stationed at the disposal of the Embassy was cleared for action and a full-scale fight ensued between the French and the mahonacis. This opposition has, naturally, long since been overcome but complaints regarding payments and conditions in the warehouses have remained. In fact, until the outbreak of war, most ships did not dock alongside the quays but loaded and unloaded in the roadstead.

In the provincial harbors, particularly on the Anatolian coast, the guild of longshoremen terrorized the traffic until recently, and the officials did not take the slightest protective measures against them. In Beirut where, likewise, a French company (Compagnie Ottomane du Port, des Quais et Entrepôts de Beyrouth) was granted a concession in 1888 and by 1892 had completed construction, a lack of space has made itself felt; here the work was transferred to the Société des Chemins de Fer ottomans de Beyrouth-Damas-Hauran. A third French company, Société des Quais de Smyrne, received its concession in 1867, and solved its assigned task in a satisfactory way, but has not developed commensurately with the ever-increasing traffic.

The system of private enterprise in port and warehouse activities has not proved satisfactory in Turkey, a fact which has been keenly felt by the nationalist leaders and has led to the purchase by the Turkish government of the French port installations in Beirut, Smyrna, and Zonguldak. The reason for the failure of the hitherto prevailing system lies not in private organization as such but rather in the fact that the enterprises were French. For, at home, France has clearly shown that it is not fully capable of meeting contemporary demands in matters of shipping, especially in the organizational-commercial field. Slowness and lack of adaptability are as characteristic of French port administration as of French shipping enterprises. It would therefore have been surprising if, in Turkey, the French had measured up to a problem which they had failed to solve in their own country.

What modern enterprise, supported by qualified technical staff, can do may be seen most brilliantly in the port enterprises of Derince and Haydar paşa, built by the Germans for the Anatolian Railway, and which are to be followed by a similar one in Alexandretta. In mid-1895 in Derince, where sufficient opportunity for installation existed, modern grain sheds with grain-cleaning machines and elevators were built. These, the first of their kind in Turkey, did not at first bring much joy to native grain merchants, who were faced with the loss of weight due to the elimination of foreign bodies. In addition, there was harassment of the German enterprise by the French Chamber of Commerce in Constantinople. But soon it could no longer be denied that grain cleaned in Derince fetched incomparably better prices than that containing foreign bodies, which fully compensated for the loss of weight. Much more extensive than the installations in Derince are those of Haydar paşa, the terminal of the Anatolian Railway. For this purpose, the Deutsche Bank founded a special joint stock company, whose debentures have been accepted at the Berlin Stock Exchange. A breakwater 600 meters long ensures quiet water for shipping, and sluices make it possible to regulate the water level at 8 meters; two quays of 300 and 150 meters give extensive scope for loading and unloading, which is facilitated by a crane with a carrying capacity of 35 tons on the bigger quay and three of 1,500 kilograms capacity in the merchandise sheds. For storage, there is a grain warehouse with elevators, with a capacity of 5,000 tons, and two grain sheds, with an area of 3,000 and 500 square meters respectively. A further convenience for trade is the right of the Port Company of Haydar paşa to issue warrants, a process hitherto unknown in Turkey.

In the whole of Turkey there are neither free ports nor customs-free bonded warehouses. All incoming goods are immediately placed under the supervision of the customs authorities; tobacco warehouses—we are speaking here only of exports—are administered by the Tobacco Monopoly [5:20]. Storage fees levied by the customs administration are high, and increase week by week. Should difficulties arise between the authorities and the consignees, the goods generally remain in the customs warehouses and the high storage fees have to be borne by the sender, since the consignee seldom accepts responsibility for them. In the first week after arrival goods are exempt from storage fees; the Oriental customers take advantage of this fact and do not honor bills of lading until eight days after deposition, except for urgently needed goods.[1] An exception is made at the port of Trebizond: goods in transit for Persia have to be placed in special warehouses within thirty-one days of arrival (until then they are exempt from duty) where they are sealed unless they are to be immediately forwarded. Merchandise can be kept in transit warehouses for up to twenty-four months, on payment of increasing fees. After this delay, the owner of the goods is assumed to have refused to take delivery and they are taken over by the customs administration.

Almost all goods traffic with Turkey is seaborne. However, it would be a great error to attempt to judge the value of that flow by the statistics on maritime traffic published by Turkey. Turkish statistics on maritime traffic share a defect with other countries whose main ports are transit ports [Zwischenhäfen], for example, Belgium and Holland with respect to Antwerp and Rotterdam. A steamer sailing abroad from Hamburg or Bremen with a cargo of, say, 5,000 tons which takes on an additional 2,000 tons in Antwerp and on the return journey unloads 2,000 tons in Antwerp will be entered four times in the statistics of Antwerp but only twice in its home port, although its contribution to the goods traffic of Antwerp is only 40 percent of that to its home port.

In the Turkish shipping statistics the situation is still worse. In the statistics published by the Ottoman Sanitary Administration, the traffic of Constantinople includes not only that of the capital itself but also all ships passing through the Bosphorus to the Black Sea--not only to the Turkish Black Sea ports but to those of Bulgaria, Rumania, and sourthern Russia, frequently in ballast on their way to pick up grain--and even those that just sail through the Bosphorus, without casting anchor. On their way back, these ships, and also other ships passing through, are once more entered in the figures for Constantinople. This kind of calculation does not arise from statistical megalomania but from two material causes. First, under the above-mentioned international agreement of 1838, the Sanitary Commission has the right to levy a tax on every ship passing through the Dardanelles, except warships. Secondly, each ship passing through the Dardanelles must get a _ferman_ (authorization) from the Turkish government. This _ferman_ signifies the acknowledgment of the supreme authority of the Porte over passage through the Straits. Moreover, the _ferman_ is not merely a formal right of passage: ships must actually stop at the Turkish ship stationed in the Bosphorus or Dardanelles, according to the direction of their course; only recognized mail steamship lines are granted the privilege of not stopping at the stationed ship but may have the _ferman_ sent to them in advance or later on.

In sea traffic, insofar as it can be put on a regular basis, the modern tendency is to carry it on through shipping lines which serve a given region and make arrangements for a constant, or steadily increasing, value of tonnage. Turkey is one of the countries which, in the main, are served by such lines. Although the country has a national economy that is restricted by a minimal level of consumption, figures on shipping movements occasionally show considerable fluctuations. Large deviations arise not from economic events in Turkey itself but from one of two sets of causes: either the closure of the Dardanelles, for political or quarantine reasons, and the interruption of traffic with the Black Sea and the mouth of the Danube; or a crop failure in Bulgaria, Rumania, or Southern Russia, and a consequent drop in their sales to west European markets--for all ships going to or from the Black Sea are included in the traffic of Constantinople and so in the total volume for Turkish ports.

This can be plainly seen in the two last published sets of statistics on navigation. In [A.H.] 1328, i.e., from 14 March 1912 to 13 March 1913, navigation totalled 44.5 million net registered tons, against 59.9 million for the previous year. This large difference is explained by the fact that the Dardanelles were closed to traffic by the Italian attack on Turkey during the Libyan war.

Just as one cannot judge the total volume of goods traffic by the total value of shipping, one should not draw any conclusions regarding Turkey's trade with different countries on the basis of the entry into Turkish ports of ships carrying their flag.[2] For some states, like Austria-Hungary, France, Italy, Russia, and Rumania, give large subsidies to enable their ships to carry on regular mail services. The flags of these states show up incomparably more often than those of states which do not provide subsidies and which are therefore represented only by cargo ships serving only those ports where a significant goods traffic is to be found. The French Chamber of Commerce of Constantinople--in this case an unimpeachable authority--has pointed out that Germany, which occupies seventh place in shipping traffic, is third in goods traffic.[3]

The statistics of the shipping of various countries in Ottoman ports must be judged with this in mind. The table below shows the share of the different flags.

Nationality	Net Tonnage (000)	Percentage Share		
		1328	1327	1326
England	12,021	26.9	29.3	29.8
Austria-Hungary	7,667	17.2	16.1	15.5
Russia	5,038	11.3	8.5	8
Turkey	5,030	11.3	11.3	8.4
Greece	4,658	10.4	11.3	12
France	3,353	7.5	6.5	6.4
Germany	2,246	5	3.9	3.9
Italy	877	1.9	4.3	8
America	720	1.6	2	1.9
Belgium	690	1.5	1.6	1.6
Rumania	594	1.3	1.5	1.1
Holland	529	1.2	1	1.4
Norway	466	1.0	1.0	1.0
Total[a]	44,536 net registered tons			

[a]Including others.

In the preceding year [A.H.] 1327, total shipping in Turkish waters was 59,967,438 net registered tons; five years earlier, in 1321, it had been 47,826,401, and five years before that, in 1317, 40,786,449 net registered tons. . . .

1. The Oriental importer interprets the conditions of payment agreed upon between him and the European exporter, "payment against bill of lading" to mean thathe has to pay only on delivery of the goods outside the customs house.

2. The figures on sea traffic in Ottoman waters in [A.H.] 1328 show the net displacement of the ships and take no account of the goods they carry. Thus a large steamer of 2,500 tons net registry, calling at four Ottoman ports on its way out and as many on the way back, or eight in all, is entered for a total of 20,000 tons, even if it has loaded and unloaded only 5,000 tons of vargo. On the other hand a small steamer of 500 tons serving a more productive route, may have taken on and discharged more goods and yet will be entered for only 2,000 tons. Hence these tables must be used for what they show, viz., shipping traffic and not movement of merchandize (Bulletin mensuel de la Chambre de Commerce française de Constantinople, XXCII, no. 324, p. 295). [In French in original.]

3. . . . This is because some of the German goods pass through Austrian, Belgian, and Dutch ports. . . . (ibid., p. 291).

TRADITIONAL LAND TRANSPORT

It has been cogently argued that the availability of the camel—which can carry great loads over long distances—inhibited the development of carts and carriages in the Middle East.[1] It is certainly a fact that in Turkey, and even more in Iran and the Arab lands, wheeled traffic was very restricted and that the bulk of goods and passengers traveling by land used pack animals. The selection that follows illustrates the situation on the eve of the First World War in southeastern Turkey and northern Syria and notes the slight improvement in the design of carts and the small increase in their number that had recently taken place.[2] The situation was not essentially different in other parts of Turkey. Thus in reply to a questionnaire of 1863 (FO 195/771), the British consul in Salonica stated that most produce was transported by horses and mules but that ox-drawn carts were also used in the plains; the consul in Izmir that the bulk of transit trade was carried by camels—horses and mules being used only for light weights in the immediate vicinity of the city and for traveling; and the consul in Trabzon that most of the transit trade was carried by horses, mules, and donkeys—camels being seldom used but bullocks being occasionally employed for the transport of grain.

The loads carried by the various animals varied. On the Trabzon-Erzurum road in 1846, the usual camel load was 240 okkas (okes, 680 lbs.), the horse or mule load 120 (340 lbs.), and the donkey load 60 (170 lbs.) (Notes on Erzurum, FO 78/703). On the Diyarbekir-Mosul road in 1858, the maximum loads were: camel 560 lbs., mule 420, horse 364, ox 252, and donkey 168 lbs. (Reply to questionnaire, FO 78/1419). In Edirne in 1864, the usual horse load was 80 to 100 okes and in Bitlis in 1902 it was 120 okes.[3] The usual speed of a mixed caravan was 2.5 to 3 miles an hour—camels being a little slower than horses—and the usual daily stage 15 to 20 miles. To take one example, the Trabzon-Tabriz route of 516 miles consisted of 30 stages, varying from a minimum of 9 miles to a maximum of 27.[4]

Costs per ton-mile for carts are given in the selection as 8d. for the journey from Aleppo to Diyarbekir and 4d. for the return journey, say an average of 6d. Figures for the early 1860s may be calculated from a table giving prices per kantar of 180 okes (506 lbs.) both in 1863 and "in ordinary years."[5] The latter work out as follows (in pence):

Mule from Diyarbekir to Aleppo, 260 miles:	6.7
Camel from Diyarbekir to Aleppo, 260 miles:	3.7
Mule from Diyarbekir to Erzurum, 200 miles:	12.1
Mule from Diyarbekir to Mosul, 215 miles:	8.8
Camel from Diyarbekir to Mosul, 215 miles:	4.4
Mule from Diyarbekir to Samsun, 345 miles:	7.0
Camel from Aleppo to Iskenderun, 87 miles:	8.9
Mule from Aleppo to Iskenderun, 87 miles:	6.7

In Bitlis in 1901 goods from Trabzon cost 7.6d. per ton-mile, and to Trabzon 3.6 per mile; from İskenderun 8d. per ton-mile and to İskenderun 3.1d. per ton-mile.[6]

In 1910 goods sent from Trabzon to Erzurum cost 9.1d. per ton-mile in summer and 11.8 in winter; from Erzurum to Trabzon the cost was 3.6d. in spring and 5.0 in autumn.[7]

The level of these rates may be gauged by comparing them with the cost of other forms of transport. In Edirne, most of the grain was floated down the Maritza River, on rafts, but some was sent by wagons or pack horses. In the early 1860s the cost per oke in summer for the journey to Enos was: by raft 0.05 to 0.06 piastre, by wagon 0.14 to 0.24, and by pack horse 0.5; in other words water transport cost a third to a quarter of wagon transport and one-tenth as much as by pack horse; in winter the differential was still wider, the figures being 0.05 to 0.06, 0.3 to 0.4 and 0.75 to 1.0.[8] It should be added that, owing to the strength of the current, the Maritza could not be used for carrying goods upstream.

The Tigris was also navigable, but only downstream, from Diyarbekir to Mosul and Baghdad by rafts made of skins. Here the cost was one-half that of camel transport and one-seventh that of mule transport.[9]

It is interesting to compare these figures with an eighteenth-century British estimate that canals had a differential advantage over wheeled traffic of 1:12 and over pack animals of 1:16.[10]

Lastly, the costs per ton-mile given above may be compared with those on railways. In England in the 1880s the Midland railway charged for coal and grain rates varying between 1 and 2d. per ton-mile.[11] And in 1907 the Anatolian railway charged for the 750 kilometer journey from Konya to Haydar paşa a rate equivalent to under 2d. per ton-mile for grain carried by the ton; for a carful of grain (15 tons) the rate fell to 0.62d.[12] Needless to add, the average speed of railways was at least ten times that of pack animals.

High transport costs made it unprofitable to carry bulky goods, like grain, over any but the shortest distances by land. The British consular reports are full of complaints about large amounts of grain rotting because they could not be carried to the sea at a cost that would allow them to meet world prices, and conversely in poor crop years prices rose sharply (7:2) and famines sometimes ensued. Five examples of the relation of transport to production costs may be given.

In 1840, the price of wheat in Erzurum in average years was put at 18s. a quarter and in years of abundant crops at 13s. 10d.; for barley, the figures were 7s.8d. and 5s.4d. Carriage to the coast (200 miles), however, was 12s., and freight to England another 12s., to which should be added export duty and shipping charges of 4 to 5s. for wheat and 3s. for barley (FO 78/443). In 1843 wheat cost 6 piastres a kilo or 1s. a bushel in Kutahya, but transport to Bursa (150 miles) cost an equal amount, making export unprofitable (Agricultural Report on Bursa, FO 78/532). In 1858, it was estimated that wheat which cost 35 piastres a _shumbul_ to grow and deliver in Antep cost over 60 piastres by the time it had reached the coast, some 120 miles away.[13] In 1860, Macdonald Stephenson, reporting to the Board of Directors of the Smyrna-Aydın railway, gave the following instances, which may of course not be typical. During the Crimean War contracts "were made for wheat and barley at 85 and 45 piastres, about 14s. and 7s.6d., which were purchased in the interior at the rate of 1s.6d. and 6d. and which from the high cost, and in some cases insufficiency of carriage, were of necessity cancelled." A merchant had told him that he had bought at Konya (350 miles away) grain and paid as transport 2 1/2 piastres or 5d. per kilo, or "upwards of 700% upon the first cost of the grain and exclusive of the loss on the road."[14] And in

1869 wheat and barley which cost 8 piastres per kilo at Alaşehir or Uşak cost 38 piastres at Izmir, some 200 kilometers away, which made export impossible (CC Smyrne, vol. 51, 28 June 1869).

The economic effects of high transport costs were neatly illustrated by the British consul general in Istanbul, Alison, to support his contention that these costs were helping to unbalance Turkey's trade, since most of its imports were light and valuable while its exports were bulky and cheap, and were also severely restricting the zone in which it was profitable to grow export crops. Assuming costs per ton-mile to be 2d. in Turkey and 1/2 d. in the United States, by railway or canal, that the f.o.b. price of wheat was ₤1 and its cost of production 12s. (i.e., it could bear a cost of transport of up to 8s. a ton), then in the United States it would be profitable to grow wheat for export up to 192 miles inland but in Turkey only up to 48 miles.[15]

1. R. W. Bulliet, The Camel and the Wheel (Cambridge, Mass., 1974).
2. Thanks to the improvement of roads, several types of carriage and carts had recently come into regular use in the Aleppo region, including a passenger service to Baghdad. The vehicles were: local landaus and phaetons with imported springs and axletrees; yalieh, a spring carriage with a carrying capacity of 700 lbs., traveling for 10 hours a day at 6 miles per hour; springless wagons, traveling 7 hours at 3 miles an hour; and araba or ox-cart, capable of carrying up to 145 lbs. at 2 miles an hour. (A and P 1908, vol. 116, "Aleppo"). Similar developments took place in other parts of the Ottoman Empire.
3. A and P 1865, vol. 53, "Adrianople," and A and P 1902, vol. 110, "Bitlis." See also EHME, p. 5.
4. A and P 1899, vol. 103, "Trebizond."
5. A and P 1865, vol. 53, "Diarbekr and Kurdistan."
6. A and P 1902, vol. 110, "Bitlis."
7. A and P 1911, vol. 96, "Erzeroum"; in 1889 rates from Ankara to Izmit were 1.44 piastres a ton-kilometer or 4.6d. a ton-mile, and from Konya to Izmit 1.47 piastres--D. Quataert "Limited Revolution," The Business History Review, Summer, 1977; this valuable article appeared as this book was going to press.
8. A and P 1865, vol. 53, "Adrianople."
9. Ibid, "Diarbekr and Kurdistan"; see also Farley, Turkey, p. 180.
10. H. J. Dyos and D. H. Aldcroft, British Transport (London, 1974), p. 111.
11. Ibid., p. 177.
12. A and P 1907, vol. 93, "Konia"; according to Quataert, rates for wheat fell to 0.18 piastres per ton-kilometer, or 0.6d. per ton-mile, on both the Ankara and Konya lines, and discounts of 50 percent were given for filling a railroad car.
13. A and P 1859, vol. 30, "Aintab."
14. TE, Box 41 (1860).
15. "Report on Manufactures," A and P 1857-58, vol. 55.

SELECTION 12. TRANSPORT IN SOUTHEASTERN TURKEY, 1908

Reports by W. B. Heard on Roads and Communications, FO 368/229

. . . Owing to the defective communications of Kurdistan, animal transport is at present almost the only means used for the conveyance of merchandize. Excluding the Erzeroum district, which lies outside the scope of this Report, wheeled transport is only used on the Alexandretta-Aleppo-Diarbekir-Kharput-Samsun route, and that but to a limited extent. Rough ox-carts are employed in most districts for purely local needs, but do not affect the question of foreign commerce. Horses and mules, and, in certain non-mountainous regions, camels carry practically the whole of the import and export trade of Kurdistan.

Wheeled Transport

Vehicles are scarcely used at all for the carrying trade of Diarbekir. Though there is little difference between the prices for wheeled and pack transport merchants prefer the latter, owing to the damage caused to their goods when carried in carts. The reason for the damage is probably to be found partly in the careless packing of the carters, and partly in the jolting caused by the uneven surface of the roads.

The type of cart generally in use is a four-wheeled vehicle known as "yuk arabasi," drawn by two or three horses. The floor space is narrow, and it is furnished with a rigid tilt, supported by irremovable arched ribs, which makes it unsuitable for stowing bulky packages. Its carrying capacity is between 9 cwt. and 13 1/2 cwt.

Similar carts, but better finished and fitted with springs, called "jailis" [Yayli], are used for the conveyance of travellers. A few open waggons carrying a load of from

13 1/2 cwt. to 18 cwt. have been introduced during the last two years.

The journey from Diarbekir to Aleppo is made in eight days, and from Diarbekir to Samsun in about twenty-two days.

Rates. Transport rates (average) per cartload are--

Diarbekir-Aleppo	ŁT. 3 1/2 - 4 (ŁT.1 = 18s.).
Aleppo-Diarbekir	ŁT. 4 - 5.
Diarbekir-Kharput	Medjidiehs 7 - 9 (1 medjidieh = 3s.4d.).
Diarbekir-Samsun	ŁT. 7 - 8.

It is possible that a larger and stronger type of cart, specially constructed for carrying heavy loads and bulky packages, would be found to carry goods more cheaply than do pack-animals at present. Four-horse teams or teams of oxen or buffaloes would probably be able to drag them over the rough bits of road.

Pack Transport

Horses carry loads of from 270 lbs. to 302 lbs.

Mules carry from 369 lbs. to 420 lbs.

The average rate of progress for a caravan is six hours per diem at 3 miles per hour (=18 miles).

Transport prices are governed by a variety of considerations, and vary greatly according to the season, district, and local price of grain.

Thus in spring and summer, when trade is brisk, prices are dearer, but in winter, when trade is slack, muleteers lower their prices, being anxious to save the price of horse-keep. In districts where forage is dear, prices are naturally higher. Thus, in the Bitlis Vilayet they are almost double what they are in Diarbekir. Pack-animals are at times difficult to obtain, as they are liable to be seized by Government for military purposes, or in order to transport grain to famine-stricken districts.

In winter, transport conditions often become very difficult, owing to deep mud or snow. In the higher regions transport ceases for long periods, when the passes are blocked by snow. Hand-sledges are then used by the inhabitants for local needs.

Rates. Average prices of pack transport:

Average Prices of Pack Transport per Kantar (4½ cwt.)

	Ł	s.	d.		Ł	s.	d.
Aleppo-Diarbekir (12 days)							
3 months (winter)	1	5	0	to	1	10	0
9 months	1	8	0	to	1	16	0
Diarbekir-Aleppo							
3 months (winter)	0	10	0	to	0	15	0
9 months	0	13	4	to	1	0	0
(Prices are cheaper this year, as muleteers have gravitated southwards owing to high price of forage in Bitlis, Van, &c.)							
Diarbekir-Kharput (5 days)	0	6	8	to	0	8	4
(this year 16d.8d. to 18s.4d.)							
Kharput-Diarbekir	0	6	8	(this year 10s.)			
Diarbekir-Serè (5 days)	0	10	0	to	0	15	0
Serè-Bitlis (3 days)	0	7	6	to	0	10	0
(this year 17s.6d.)							
Diarbekir-Bitlis via Zokh (7 days)							
6 months (winter and spring)	1	5	0	to	1	10	0
6 months (summer and autumn)	1	0	0	to	1	5	0
Bitlis-Diarbekir via Zokh							
3 months (summer)	0	12	0	to	0	16	8
9 months	0	15	0	to	1	0	0
Diarbekir-Erzeroum via Këghi (9 days)							
Spring and summer	0	16	8	to	1	0	0
Autumn	1	0	0	to	1	6	8
(This route is closed by snow from November to May.)							
Alexandretta-Diarbekir via Killis and Biredjik (15 to 16 days)							
3 months (winter)	1	13	4	to	2	6	8
9 months	1	16	0	to	2	13	4
Diarbekir-Alexandretta via Killis and Biredjik*							
3 months (winter)	0	18	4	to	1	5	0
9 months	1	0	0	to	1	6	8

* This route is not used much for foreign trade, as most of it passes through hands of merchants and commission agents in Aleppo.

Observations

It will be observed that prices for outward journeys are higher than those for return journeys. Muleteers discount costs of delay at their destination, and uncertainty of obtaining loads for their return by adding to their prices.

Certain routes are liable to pillage, but the Aleppo-Diarbekir route has been practically safe for the last three years.

It is evident that foreign trade is much hampered by defective transport. Prices are high and irregular, and fluctuate considerably. The drawbacks of pack-transport, such as small size of packages carried, injury through weather, and ill-usage, &c. sufficiently well known. Delays are often caused when transport is not immediately available. Under present circumstances, it is not to be expected that the natives will of themselves do anything to improve existing methods, which have scarcely changed since pre-historic times.

It is accordingly perhaps worth while discussing whether it would be practicable and profitable for foreigners to undertake the task of improving and organizing the carrying trade of Kurdistan.

The Alexandretta-Aleppo-Diarbekir Route

It is suggested that a beginning be made with the Alexandretta-Aleppo-Diarbekir route. Here we have what is probably the richest trade centre in Kurdistan separated from its seaport by some 310 miles of road, of which some 126 still remain to be made. . . .

SELECTION 13. IZMIR-AYDIN ROAD PROJECT, 1 FEBRUARY 1856

FO 195/460

Table A

Comparative Table of Transit rates from Districts in Asia Minor to Smyrna

Districts	Actual camel rates of transport now paying pr. kilo	Equivalent in Sterling money pr. quarter	Comparative cost of transport over good roads pr. kilo	Equivalent in Sterling money pr. quarter
		Grain		
Magnesia--30 miles	Piastres 5	s. 6/2	Piastres 1	s. 1/3
Aidin--70 miles	" 14	17/3	" 2	2/6
Oushak--140 miles	" 25	30/-	" 4	5/-
Koniah--330 miles	" 45	55/-	" 9	11/-
		General Produce		
	pr. cantar	p. ton p. mile	pr. cantar	p. ton p. mile
Magnesia	Piastres 10	Pence 12 1/3	Piastres 2	Pence 2 1/2
Aidin	" 28	" 15	" 4	" 2
Oushak	" 50	" 12 4/5	" 8	" 2
Koniah	" 90	" 10	" 18	" 1 9/10

Comparative table of Transport constructed on following basis

3 Horses drawing 150 kilos grain or 4 tons goods

Magnesia	60 journeys pr. annum	No back carriage
Aidin	30 " " "	taken into account
Oushak	15 " " "	in the estimate
Koniah	7 " " "	

Keep of 3 Horses at p. 1400 each	Piastres 4,200
One Man's Wages	" 2,000
Interest, wear & tear, etc. ...	" 1,000
Incidentals	" 1,800
	9,000

[Table B]

Comparative Table of Value of Wheat

Districts	Value of wheat at Smyrna pr. kilo		Sundry charges pr. kilo		Actual rate of transport pr. kilo		Balance for the grower pr. kilo	
Magnesia	Piastres	56	Piastres	3	Piastres	5	Piastres	48
Aidin	"	54	"	3	"	14	"	37
Oushak	"	60	"	3	"	25	"	32
Koniah	"	58	"	3	"	45	"	10
			Over good roads					
Magnesia	Piastres	56	Piastres	3	Piastres	1	Piastres	52
Aidin	"	54	"	3	"	2	"	49
Oushak	"	60	"	3	"	4	"	53
Koniah	"	58	"	3	"	9	"	46

Explanations of Tables

Table A gives the actual rates paying, value of Wheat, expenses and Keep of Horses. Table B gives the ordinary rates of transport and average Value of Wheat. Ample Allowance is made for expenses, Keep of horses and Comparative cost of carriage over good roads, as it must be borne in mind that if the Horses are fed on Barley at Smyrna and Magnesia at p. 26 & 18 p. Kilo, they are likewise partly so on the road and in the more distant districts at much lower prices. Moreover no back carriage is taken into account, but left for profits, tolls, etc. The Tables on Government tithes* are merely given to show the effect a general improvement of roads would have on the tithes revenues, which would be increased upwards of 50 p. cent, but as in same proportions growers would be benefitted, it is clear that the Selianes and all fixed taxes—unless augmented—would fall lighter on the people, as they would be assessed on a larger money Value. But the encrease of Government revenue would be far more than the proportion shown by the Tables, as by good roads many articles having a mere local Value at present would become merchantable. For instance, Barley is now worth p.26 pr. Kilo at Smyrna, by reference to carriage and charges in Table A it is evident that beyond Aidin it can have but local Value, whereas with good roads it might be brought with advantage from beyond Koniah. Moreover the encouragement afforded to Agriculture would naturally tend to great increase of all produce. It may also be observed that with the actual high rates of transport, much of the produce will this year remain in the Interior as it cannot afford to pay them, such as Valonia and all the lower Grains, etc.

SELECTION 14.   COMMUNICATIONS BETWEEN INDIA AND BRITAIN, 1857

Backley to Alison, FO 195/460[1]

Constantinople
5th Sep. 1857

I have obtained the necessary information in detail of the route to India via Samsoon and Bussorah and append the same in a tabular form as affording the most ready means of reference.

At present the Telegraphic despatches from Bombay via Cagliari do not reach London under 24 or 25 days--while the written despatches via Marseilles occupy 28 or 30 days in transmission.

As compared with this, the saving obtained by the proposed Samsoon route appears to be from 7 to 10 days.

By this route therefore Telegraphic Messages from Bombay would reach London at the latest in 17 days and would frequently arrive in 14 days and 8 hours--while written despatches from Bombay (by steamer to Kurrachee in 36 hours) would reach the Embassy here in from 16 to 18 days, whence their full contents might be Telegraphed to London without delay.

To carry out this plan on a weekly basis, it would only be necessary to put 2 small steamers on the line between Kurrachee and Bussorah, and at the same time to make proper arrangements at all the ordinary Turkish Post houses on the route between Bussorah and Samsoon, so as to ensure the immediate transmission of the mails from one post to the other. A staff of 4 Inspectors and 8 good Tatars would be required for this duty.

*
These figures have been omitted: they were based on an assumed annual production of 150,000 Kilos for each district and calculated for various hypothetical prices.

The Service between Samsoon and Const^{le} could readily be performed should the Ambassador permit it by the "Coquette" within the time stated.

Should H. E. the Ambassador think this suggestion worthy of trial I should like to have the Service between Samsoon and the Persian Gulf entrusted to my management.

You may place implicit reliance on the information contained in the Tabular statement.

	Utmost time required	Shortest time required	How Transmitted	Nominal distance	Authority for statement
	Hours	Hours			
Bombay to Kurrachee	8	4	Telegraph		Indian Telegraph Department
Kurrachee to Bussorah	96	84	Steamer		Capt. Glynn. "The Times" Correspondent
Bussorah to Bagdad	48	40	Tatar	Hours 48	Mehmet Ali etc. Tatars on route
Bagdad to Samsoon via Mussul etc.	192	168	Tatar	350	Kiamil Tatar and others--Tatars on route
Samsoon to Const^{le}	40	36	Steamer		Mess. Hava, Hanson, Grace, etc.
Constantinople to London	24	12	Telegraph		Lieut. Holdsworth
	408	344			

[1. This report was written during the Indian Mutiny, news of the outbreak of which took from thirty to fifty days to reach London.]

THE IZMIR-AYDIN RAILWAY

The first railway built in Anatolia was the Ottoman Railway from Izmir to Aydın. In 1856 a British company received a concession for a 130-kilometer line, with a gauge of 1.435 meters, between the two cities for a period of fifty years from the completion of construction. The Ottoman government guaranteed a return of 6 percent on the share capital of ₤1,200,000. It was estimated that goods traffic from Aydın to Izmir would amount to 117,000 tons and from Izmir to Aydın to 6,000 (CC Smyrne, vol. 49, 10 January 1857).

Work at first went well (ibid. 5 April 1858) but by 1859 the British consul was reporting difficulties: six bridges had given way, the embankments were of doubtful strength, it was clear that the line would not be completed by the spring of 1860, as planned, and a consulting engineer was sent out at the end of 1859 (Blunt to Russell, 6 September and 14 December 1859, FO 78/1447). In June 1860 work was suspended owing to differences between the contractor and the board of directors; the original estimates had put the cost of the first 45 miles at ₤510,000 (₤300,000 for the line, ₤90,000 for the rolling stock, and ₤120,000 for the docks), but so far over ₤350,000 had been spent and only 30 kilometers of temporary way had been built and "of the docks only some piles have been driven" (ibid., 9 June 1860, FO 78/1533). Nevertheless, by October 45 kilometers, and a year later 59, had been opened to traffic (CC Smyrne, vol. 49, 27 October 1860, 14 October 1861).

In June 1863 a financial reorganization took place; the government's guarantee was increased to ₤112,000 and it was authorized to repurchase the line, in 1910, at original cost.[1] Further difficulties were encountered in digging a tunnel near Ephesus (CC Smyrne, vol. 50, 27 January 1866), but in 1866 the whole line was opened to traffic and soon after the manager was reporting that "traffic by camels has entirely ceased" between Izmir and Aydın (8 October 1868, FO 78/2255).

The position of the company was, however, highly precarious. Construction had been

overelaborate and extravagant, the Izmir station alone costing £64,000 (ibid.).[2] The
government had not paid the promised guarantee (Manager of Railway, 21 February 1867, FO
78/2255). The special commissioner of the Ottoman government complained of shortage of
rolling stock (11 August 1867, ibid.). The report of the committee investigating the railway, presented to the shareholders' meeting of 21 May 1867, concluded:

1) That this line has been essentially a contractor's line.

2) That with the amount of shares subscribed for bona fide the Board were not authorized in bringing out the Company.

3) That the form of debenture (1861) is not in accordance with the terms of the concession. . . .

5) That the manner in which a large proportion of the capital has been issued is most
reckless and reprehensible . . . (ibid.).

Nevertheless the company survived and successive conventions were made with the government in 1870, 1876, and, most important, 1888.[3] These authorized the building of various
branches and prolongations, extended the duration of the concession to 1935, and relieved
the government from paying any guarantee. By 1890 the main line Izmir-Aydın Oaiaykoy-Dinar
was 377 kilometers long, and various branches totalled 139 kilometers. In 1906 the concession was prolonged to 1950 and an extension to Eğridir, of 108 kilometers, was authorized
and completed in November 1912, the government purchase price being fixed at £4,600 per
kilometer (Convention in FO 371/145); by then the main line and branches totalled 610 milo-
meters.[4]

The financial position of the company slowly recovered as the line was extended, although it remained burdened by its high original costs; in 1878, with 135 kilometers of
line, receipts were £50,000, but by 1888, with 237 kilometers, they had risen to £390,000;
by 1883 the government's accumulated debt to the company for guarantees was £600,000 (CC
Smyrne, vol. 55, Report on Railways, 17 December 1888).[5] Receipts fell in the 1890s but
recovered again, the average for 1907-12 being £350,000.[6] Net profits rose steadily, but
not until 1888 did they reach the £112,000 mark at which the government ceased paying a
subsidy; by then the arrears due by the government to the company, exclusive of interest,
were £688,000 (Rothmore to Sandison, 14 November 1905, FO 78/5450). After that only in
one year, 1898, did the railway require a subsidy; its profits rose to a peak of £232,000
in 1910 and the amount it paid to the government increased correspondingly to £45,000.[7]
However, even this represented a low rate of return on the share capital of £1,294,000 and
debentures of £3,064,000 outstanding in 1909,[8] and no dividends were paid to shareholders
after the conversion of debentures in 1898.[9] As regards physical operations, in 1889 the
railway had 28 locomotives, 89 passenger wagons, and 771 freight trucks (CC Smyrne, vol.
55, 13 October 1889). In 1897-99 it carried an average of 328,000 tons (ibid., vol. 57,
Reports for 1897 and 1899) and in 1905-11 an average of 299,000 tons and 2,236,000 passengers.[10]

In June 1914, as part of the overall Anglo-German settlement (4:17), it was agreed
that the Izmir-Aydın railway would be extended to Afyon, and navigation rights were granted
to the company on Lake Eğridir, but the War prevented implementation. In 1935 the railway
was nationalized.

(See also works by Conker, Hecker, Karkar, Kurmuş and Verney, listed in Bibliography.)

1. The share capital was reduced to £892,000 and debentures of £892,000 were issued--
see details in Kurmuş, pp. 48-50; Cuinet, 3:393, and TE, Box 35, 17 April 1863.
2. Hecker's figures (4:Introduction) show that the cost per kilometer was much higher
than that of other Turkish railways. But Kurmuş (p. 58) points out that the cost per mile

for the 81-mile (130 - kilometer) stretch was ₺16,600, which was far below the contemporary average of some ₺50,000 in England. This is explained by lower costs of labor, land, and local materials and by the fact that used rails from the Crimea were employed.

3. Young, 4:202-7; the value of the line was fixed at ₺7,277 per kilometer or ₺3,725,000 in all (Rothmore to Sandison, 14 November 1905, FO 78/5450).

4. Hecker, p. 755; the extension of the Anatolian railway to Konya threatened to cut off the Aydın railway from its hinterland, and in 1899 the Germans proposed the amalgamation and linkage of the two lines, directing Konya produce to Izmir. The British railway refused, reorganized its finances, converted its debentures, and by means of great diplomatic pressure on the Porte (see correspondence in FO 78/5450 and 371/145) obtained the right to build the extension to Eğridir.

5. The French consul estimated construction costs at ₺12,500 per kilometer, i.e., nearly three times as high as those for the Izmir-Kasaba line, partly because of more difficult terrain. Subsequent extensions, however, brought the average down to an estimated ₺10,000 in 1910--TJ, September 1910.

6. A and P 1910, vol. 103, "Smyrna"; 1914, "Smyrna," vol. 95.

7. Table in Kurmuş, p. 321.

8. TE Box 408, Grey to Turkish Ambassador, 12 December 1905, and TJ, September 1909.

9. Young, 4:203.

10. Novichev, <u>Ocherki</u>, p. 279.

SELECTION 15. OPERATIONS ON THE IZMIR-AYDIN RAILWAY, 1868

Letter from General Manager, 14 September 1868, FO 78/2255

Although I have lately reported to the Board on the subject of the large and sudden increase of Locomotive and Rolling Stock demanded by the Turkish Government, I think it may serve to dispel any erroneous impressions as to the adequacy of our present stock which that demand may have produced, if I give you the account of one day's traffic by which will be seen what is the service required of the stock during the busiest season of the year. I will take yesterday Sunday the 13th. The heaviest traffic of the week both goods and passengers always falls on Sunday, extra trips are made for 10 miles out of Smyrna, and it is Market day at Aidin.

An up train with empties to Aidin and Sportsmen to Ayassalook, and Passengers to Aidin Market.

A mixed train both way through with Post, Passengers and goods.

Two down goods trains with Carriages for return sportsmen.

Two trains up to Siedikeuy and one to Devilikeuy and three trains down from same Stations.

The above required four of the large engines to be kept in steam, two others were in shed, and two others were under repair. There are beside two small engines in good repair which were in shed, but could have taken an efficient part in above service if required.

This service amounted to 477 train miles, or, an average of 119 miles per engine. The same drivers, firemen and guards remained by the trains throughout the day and no overtime was made.

The Company's Stock of Goods Waggons is 236 of these 52 came down loaded, the greater part of which had been sent up empty that morning, and they were all discharged the same evening ready for today's work. You will therefore see there was no deficiency in Waggons and not a Ton of goods was left on the platforms.

The day's earning from goods was ₺255 Sterling and ₺48 Sterling from Passengers, or at the rate of ₺2121 per week, the largest week's traffic the line has previously made. The same Service & Locomotive power could efficiently and comfortably have accommodated and earned three times the traffic from passengers and 25% more from Goods, or ₺460, or say at the rate of ₺3,200 per week.

THE IZMIR-KASABA [TURGUTLU] RAILWAY

The early years of the Izmir-Kasaba railway, described in the following selections, were much smoother than those of the Izmir-Aydin line (4:15). The French consul repeatedly stated that it was prudently managed and doing well (CC Smyrne, vol. 50, 27 January 1866, and vol. 51, 28 June 1869). Construction costs were low--about ₺7,500 per mile--operations had been profitable, and the government had had to pay only a small subsidy, for a short period (ibid., vol. 55 Report on Railways, 17 December 1888). Gross receipts rose from ₺79,000 in 1872 (ibid.) to an average of ₺134,000 in 1881-85, and profits to ₺73,000.[1]

In 1885 the arrangements between the government and the company were modified; the latter was to receive 50 percent of gross receipts of the Kasaba-Alaşehir section, built in 1873–75 at government expense, in return for an advance of ₤500,000 it had made to the government.[2]

In 1887 the company was authorized to build, on government account, a 92-kilometer extension from Manisa through Akhisar to Soma, at a cost of ₤5,000 per kilometer. The company was to keep 50 percent of gross receipts, the other 50 percent being earmarked for payment of 6 percent interest and 1 percent amortization of the cost of construction. Debentures totalling ₤500,000 were floated in London, work began in November 1888, and the line was opened in January 1890 (ibid., and 22 January 1890). This raised the total length of the line and branches to 264 kilometers, with 1.435 meter gauge, and the government's debt to the company to ₤T2,208,000.[3] Operations expanded but yielded extremely low revenues on the 40-million-franc investment in the line.[4]

In 1893 the government, anxious not to have both Izmir lines in British hands, repurchased the line for ₤T1,434,000 and granted to G. Nagelmackers a 99-year concession for 50 percent of gross receipts, the other 50 percent to be used for reimbursing the purchase price paid to the company. He was also authorized to construct and work a 251-kilometer extension from Alaşehir to Afyonkarahisar, with a guarantee of ₤T831 per kilometer, to be met from the tithes of the sancak of Aydın.[5] Nagelmackers transferred his concession to the Société Ottomane du Chemin de Fer Smyrne-Cassaba, founded in Paris in 1894 with a capital of 16 million francs. In 1894 and 1895 debentures totalling 126,550,000 francs were issued.[6]

The extension to Afyon was completed on December 1897, bringing the total length to 517 kilometers. In 1899, a working agreement was reached between the line and the Anatolian railway, as part of an arrangement by which French capital participated in the latter; but it was not until 1908 that the stations of the two lines at Afyonkarahisar, a few yards apart, were actually linked.[7]

In 1910, against stiff competition including that of Bellet de Lobel, who claimed to have a concession (4:19), and as part of the general Franco-German settlement, (4:17), the railway was authorized to build a 190-kilometer branch from Soma, through Balikesir, to Bandirma on the Sea of Marmara. The government issued a loan of 38.9 million francs, which raised 34.6 million, providing 175,000 francs per kilometer of line. The line was completed in 1912 and brought the total length of the railway to 707 kilometers.

Traffic showed a steady increase, from 1.5 million passengers and 115,000 tons in 1895 to 3 million and 430,000 in 1913; gross receipts rose from 3.3 to 9.4 million francs and operating costs were low. But although the pre-1895 line showed a profit, the two extensions incurred large deficits, and in 1895–1913 the government paid the company a subsidy of over 60 million francs.[8]

In 1929 the company became Turkish, with a capital of 15 million francs, and in 1931 the government bought the line for ₤T1,260,000.[9]

(See also works by Conker, Hecker, Karkar, and Verney listed in Bibliography.)

1. A and P 1887, vol. 86, "Smyrna."
2. Young, 4:189.
3. Ibid. and Cuinet, 3:396; 19 locomotives were used on the line.
4. Thobie, p. 193.
5. Text in Young, 4:191–201.
6. Thobie, p. 196.
7. A and P 1900, vol. 97, "Smyrna"; Earle pp. 59–60; Thobie pp. 331–34.
8. For details, Thobie pp. 334–41.
9. Conker, Chemins de fer, p. 24.

SELECTION 16. IZMIR-KASABA RAILWAY, 1878

Pelissier to Waddington, 20 February 1879, CC Smyrne, vol. 52

The railway from Smyrna to Kasaba and Alaşehir (ancient Philadelphia) is 169 kilometers long, with a suburban branch to Burnabat of 5 kilometers, or a total of 174 open to traffic. A first section, from Smyrna to Kasaba, of 93 kms. was built between 1863 and 1865 and was opened to traffic in the latter year, as was the branch to Burnabat; it was prolonged in the years 1873-75 to Alaşehir, and thus extended by 76 kilometers.

The "Smyrna and Cassaba Railway Company, Ltd." which operates this line has its head offices in London, 8 Old Jewry. Its representative in our city is, at present, a Frenchman, M. O. Redem a civil-engineer and graduate of l'Ecole Centrale des Arts et Manufactures de Paris. The original concession granted to the company in 1863 covered the line from Smyrna to Kasaba (93 kms.). Its duration was for 99 years and the authorized capital was ₤800,000 or 20 million francs. The Sublime Porte guaranteed an interest of 5 percent on this capital, representing a net annual income of 1,000,000 francs.

Later, in the courseof the years 1873-75, the Ottoman government built at its own expense the section between Kasaba and Alaşehir (76 kms.) and handed over its operation to the Smyrna-Cassaba Company as from 1 March 1875; in return, the company gave up the guarantee of interest, and the duration of the concession was reduced to 16 years, ending on 1 March 1891. Thus at present the company operates the whole line (174 kms.) at its own risk, and its concession has only twelve more years to run. The whole line, with its buildings, material, and equipment will revert to the state on 1 March 1891.

The main stations served by the railway are:

Burnabat, suburban line, 5 kms. from Smyrna, residence of a large number of prosperous Smyrna families, 14,000 inhabitants.

Menemen, 32 kms. from Smyrna--capital of a subprefecture (kaimakamlik), 8,000 inhabitants. Chief products: cereals, cotton, liquorice, valonea; steam factory for cotton ginning.

Manisa (Magnesia ad Sipylum), at the foot of Mount Sipylum, 66 kms. from Smyrna, capital of prefecture (Mutasariflik) of Saruhan, 36,000 inhabitants. Consular agencies, barracks, prison, Turkish and Greek hospitals, lunatic asylum. Main products: cereals, cotton, tobacco, madder. Four steam factories for ginning cotton.

Kasaba, 93 kms. from Smyrna, capital of subprefecture, 6,500 inhabitants. Main products: cereals, beans, cotton, fruits (melons renowned), sesame; 3 steam factories for ginning cotton.

Sardis, 133 kms. from Smyrna, ancient capital of the kings of Lydia, interesting ruins.

Salikli, 131 kms. from Smyrna, capital of subprefecture, one thousand inhabitants. Main products: cereals, valonea from Hermus districts.

Alaşehir (ancient Philadelphia), 169 kms. from Smyrna, capital of subprefecture, 20,000 inhabitants. Main products: cereals, valonea, sesame, liquorice roots; one steam factory for preparation of licorice juice.

The original capital of the Company, ₤800,000, has already been partly amortized;[*] today it stands at ₤716,740, broken down as follows:

Ordinary Shares	₤393,740
Privileged Shares	₤125,000
Debentures	₤198,000
	₤716,740

The distribution of net income is specified as follows in the statutes.

₤198,000 debentures, 7 percent	₤13,860
125,000 privileged shares, 7 percent	₤8,750
393,740 ordinary shares, 2½ percent	₤9,843
Total annual statutory dividends	₤32,453

Any excess receipts, after payment of the statutory interest and dividends, are used for the amortization of capital. They are used first for the extinction of the debentures, then of privileged shares, and lastly of ordinary shares.

The London Stock Exchange quotes:
The ₤100 debentures at ₤105, i.e., 105 percent of the normal value
The ₤20 privileged shares at ₤22, 110 "   "   "   "   "
The ₤20 ordinary shares at ₤12, 60 "   "   "   "   "

The 1878 operations showed:

Gross receipts	₤125,108
Expenses	₤ 60,122
Net income	₤ 64,986

---

[*][The franc equivalents of the sums given in sterling have been omitted in translation.]

This gives a ratio of 48 percent of expenses to gross receipts; gross receipts per kilometer may be put at about 18,000 francs and net income at 9,300 francs.

After payment of the statutory interest and dividends of ₺32,453, a sum of ₺32,533 was available for amortization from the total net income of ₺64,986.

The gross receipts, ₺125,108, were broken down as follows:

Passengers

	Number	Receipts (₺)
Main line	175,393	27,833
Suburban to Burnabat	291,862	5,299
	467,255	33,132
Goods (tons)	95,730	87,538
Luggage, etc. (Messageries)		4,438
		₺125,108

The 95,730 tons of goods carried included: cereals 32,111 tons, seeds 5,415, cotton 2,413, valonea 27,090, others 28,701. . . .

THE ANATOLIAN RAILWAYS

In 1871 the Ottoman government charged a French company with building a 1.435-meter gauge railway from Haydarpaşa to İzmit, 92 kilometers away, and the line was opened in 1873. After managing the railway for seven years, the government, in 1880, transferred the right of exploitation, for twelve years, to a British syndicate, reserving to itself the right of repurchase. In accordance with the masterplan drawn up by von Pressel in 1872 (4:Introduction, and EHME, pp. 91-93), negotiations were started with the syndicate for extending the line to Aleppo and Baghdad, with kilometric guarantees. These fell through, and on 4 October 1888 Alfred von Kaulla, on behalf of the Deutsche Bank, was given the right, for ninety-nine years, to work the line, on payment of 6,000,000 francs, with a kilometric guarantee of 10,300 francs of gross receipts. Kaulla also received the right to build, and work for ninety-nine years, a 486 kilometer line from İzmit to Ankara, with a kilometric guarantee of 15,000 francs (25 percent of any surplus above that sum accruing to the state), and the obligation, if receipts exceeded this sum for three consecutive years, to extend the line to Sivas. The tithes of the sancaks of İzmit, Ertuğrul, Kütahya, and Ankara were earmarked for the guarantee and the government reserved the right of repurchasing the line after thirty years. The company was also granted mineral rights in a zone of 20 kilometers on either side of the railway and the right of eminent domain.[1]

In March 1893 the Société du Chemin de Fer Ottomane d'Anatolie was constituted. It floated the first Anatolian Railway loan, of 80 million francs, through the Bank für orientalischen Eisenbahnen, incorporated in Zurich. The latter soon acquired a controlling interest in the Balkan railways by purchasing Baron Hirsch's share in the Oriental Railways Company (4:Introduction) and became the holding company for all of the Deutsche Bank's railway enterprises in the Near East.[2]

In the meantime the construction of the Anatolian railway was proceeding rapidly, and in January 1893 the first trains reached Ankara. A German-Turkish commission also made a preliminary survey for a railway to Baghdad, which was satisfactory to the Sultan. Hence, on 13 February 1893, the company was granted a concession for a 384-kilometer extension from Ankara to Kayseri (which was given up) and a 445-kilometer branch from Eskişehir to Konya, as well as the construction of quays and warehouses at Derince, on the Gulf of İzmit; the last named were completed in 1893 (4:11). The terms for the Konya branch were less favorable to the company than the original concession: gross receipts of 13,727' francs (₺T 604) were guaranteed per kilometer but the government was not obligated to pay

more than 5,000 francs (subsequently raised to 6,740) whatever the shortfall; 25 percent
of any surplus above ₺T604 was to go to the government. The guarantee was to be covered
by the tithes of the sancaks of Trabzon and Gümüşhane. When receipts had reached a certain
level the company was obligated to extend the line, beyond Sıvas, to Diyarbekir and Baghdad.
The line was opened to traffic in July 1896.[3] Arrangements were also made for linkage with
the Izmir-Kasaba line at Afyon (4:16). However, in deference to Russian opposition to railways in northern Anatolia (3:26), a German commission recommended, in 1899, the abandonment
of the proposed extension through Sivas and its replacement by a line from Konya through
Cilicia and Syria.

In November 1899 the Sultan announced his intention of giving a further concession to
the Germans but it was not until 5 March 1903 that the formal grant was made.[4] The performance of the Anatolian railway had, so far, been very satisfactory. In the areas
crossed by it agricultural output had increased considerably (5:2) and the yield of the
tithes had risen (see below). The kilometric guarantee had not proved onerous: for the
Haydarpaşa-Ankara stretch payment by the government had fallen from a peak of ₺T204,000 in
1895 to ₺T4,000 in 1902 and for the Eskişehir-Konya stretch it stood at ₺T132,000. The
Germans had made every effort to give good service and were politically acceptable.[5]

The concession provided for a line from Konya to Basra of 2,264 kilometers and several
branches, including one to Aleppo and one to the Persian Gulf, totalling about 800 kilometers. A new company, Société imperiale ottomane des chemins de fer de Bagdad, was to
build and operate for ninety-nine years the new lines, and it was formed with a capital of
15 million francs of which the Anatolian railway subscribed 10 percent. The government
was to extend a twofold help (article 35). In addition to a guarantee of 4,500 francs for
every kilometer of line worked it was to grant an annuity of 11,000 francs per kilometer;
the latter was to be capitalized, the Company receiving Ottoman bonds with a nominal value
of 269,000 francs,[6] at 4 percent interest, for each kilometer of line built; for the first
200 kilometers from Konya bonds totalling 54 million francs were to be issued. These sums
were covered by the tithes of the provinces through which the railway passed. Receipts
above 4,500 francs were to be shared, with the government taking 60 to 100 percent. The
equipment and materials used were exempt from customs duty (art. 43). Like the Anatolian
railway, the company was granted mineral rights in a zone of 20 kilometers on either side
of the line, and the right of eminent domain (arts. 6 and 22). The government reserved
the right of repurchase at any time, on payment until the end of the concession of a sum
equal to 50 percent of average gross receipts in the preceding five years (art. 19).

Thanks to the help of the Deutsche Bank, the 54-million-franc loan was successfully
floated, and on 25 October 1904 the 200 kilometer stretch from Konya to Bulgurlu was opened
to traffic. At this point progress was stopped by the ruggedness of the terrain (the
government had insisted that the railway pass through the Taurus Mountains rather than
along the coast, where it would have been vulnerable to naval action), the financial difficulties of the government, and the Revolution of 1908. In the autumn of 1909, a Franco-
German syndicate underwrote the Second and Third Series of a 4 percent Baghdad Railway
Loan, for 108 million and 119 million francs respectively, and construction was resumed:
from Adana westward to the Taurus and eastward to the Amanus Mountains and from Aleppo
westward to the Amanus and eastward to Jarabulus. But it was becoming increasingly clear
that completion of the line to Baghdad would not be possible until much larger sources of
funds had been tapped, and that--since the Ottoman government could not raise its customs
duties without the consent of the Powers (3:Introduction)--this in turn depended on a

settlement of the outstanding political problems: the opposition of Russia, the hesita-
tions of the French government and financial community (on whose savings projectors relied
heavily), and, most important, the increasing hostility of Britain.[7] Eventually, "bargains
were struck." In November 1910 the Potsdam agreement, confirmed by a treaty on 19 August
1911, removed Russia's opposition, in return for recognition of its right to build railways
in northern Iran.[8] On 15 February 1914 a secret convention, signed by French and German
financiers and diplomats, secured French help in return for recognition of France's rights
to railway concessions in northern Anatolia and Syria; the Deutsche Bank also agreed to
purchase from the French-dominated Ottoman Bank the 69.4 million francs of Baghdad Railway
bonds held by it, payment to be made in other Ottoman bonds.[9] Finally, a set of Anglo-
Turkish agreements between July 1913 and June 1914 and the Anglo-German agreement of 23
February 1914 eliminated British opposition.[10] The terminus of the railway was to be
Basra, and an extension to the Persian Gulf would not be built without British consent.
British navigation interests in Iraq were safeguarded.[11] And the Turkish Petroleum Company
was constituted with three-quarters British and one-quarter German capital.[12]

The outbreak of war prevented the implementation of these agreements. At that time
469 kilometers of line had been built in Anatolia beyond Bulgurlu and in Syria, including
a branch to İskenderun, and the 62-kilometer stretch between Baghdad and Samarra had been
opened to traffic on 2 June 1914.[13] Two gaps, however, existed between Anatolia and Aleppo,
in the Taurus and Amanus mountains, and a huge section remained between Tal al-Abyad and
Samarra--825 kilometers in all.[14] During the war the railway was extended eastward to
Nusaybin and the two mountain stretches were completed by the very end of the war, the
first through train reaching Aleppo on 9 October 1918. These operations were expensive:
the German Treasury accounts show payments of 207 million marks (₺10.4 million) for the
Taurus-Amanus stretches and 103 million (₺5.2 million) for the Mesopotamian; one estimate
puts total German wartime expenditure on the Baghdad railway at about 360 million marks
(₺18 million).[15] In the interwar period construction on the line continued in Syria and
Iraq, and in July 1940 the last gap was filled and a through connection between Haydarpaşa
and Baghdad became possible. By then the various sections of the railway had passed into
the hands of the governments of Turkey,[16] and Iraq, and, a little later, Syria nationalized
its stretch.

(See also works by Chapman, Earle, Hecker, Helfferich, Hüber, Karkar, Novichev, Ragay,
Rohrback, Williamson, and Wolf, in Bibliography.)

---

1. Texts in Young, 4:117-63. Already in 1885 the British concessionaires complained
that the government was contemplating seizure of the line, alleging that "we have not paid
the amounts which, according to their sole and arbitrary interpretation of the Convention,
and their mode of making up the accounts between us, they assert to be due to them" (Col.
Alt, 19 January 1885, FO 78/4264). They had protested and asked for diplomatic support.
In 1888 they stated that negotiations with the government had been "progressing satisfactorily when all of a sudden it was reported to them that the Government had contracted
(without, of course, the knowledge of the lessees) a convention with a certain Mr. Kualla
(sic)" (Wilkin to Pauncefoote, 3 August 1888, ibid.). The British ambassador intervened
and a question was raised in the House of Commons. A fusion between the Deutsche Bank and
the British interests was suggested (30 November 1888, ibid.). The Financial News stated
on 9 January 1889: "If the Germans keep on at their present rate they will soon be dis-
puting with the Americans the credit of being the champion rustlers" (FO 78/4265). A mixed
commission awarded the lessees compensation of ₺251,000 (Currie to FO, 8 April 1892, FO
78/4681), but--because the Sultan held out and negotiations dragged on--payment was not
made until January 1895 (Currie to FO, FO 78/4681).
2. Earle, p. 32; in 1913 the Deutsche Bank disposed of its holdings in the Macedonian
Railways and Oriental Railways to an Austro-Hungarian syndicate, reinvesting the proceeds
in the Baghdad Railway, ibid., p. 113.

3. On 10 October 1898 a concession for a 9-kilometer branch between Hamidiye and Adapazar was granted and that line was opened in November 1899; it carried no kilometric guarantee.

4. Text in Young, 4:163-80.

5. Earle, pp. 63-65. In a conversation at the British Foreign Office, von Gwinner, a director of the Deutsche Bank and one of the most active promoters of the Anatolian railway, stated: "It was possible that if they had followed the example of the French Railways in European and Asiatic Turkey of levying high freights, of running as few trains as possible and of claiming the whole of the Turkish guarantee, it might have been so far a greater financial success, but it had proceeded on a sound financial principle. It had developed the country through which it passed. It had obtained the confidence of the Turkish Government who had seen that they had not been cheated, and the Sultan himself was a shareholder in the Company to the extent of 14,000 shares." The importance of the last was underlined by the fact that the Sultan "had not yet allowed any electric lighting or electric tramcars in Constantinople on account of the subtle connexion which in His Majesty's mind must exist between the words 'dynamo' and 'dynamite'" (Memorandum by Lascelles, 24 April 1903, FO 78/5322).

6. Not 275,000, as stated by Earle, p. 77.

7. The diplomatic aspects of the Baghdad Railway have been analyzed by Brünner, Earle, Wolf, and Chapman, among others; for an excellent recent account, see Williamson, pp. 80-110; for the role of French capital, see Thobie, 344-45. There is a great deal of information on railways in "Correspondence Respecting the Affairs of Asiatic Turkey and Arabia," FO 427/178-253.

8. See EHI, pp. 158, 189-91.

9. Text in Earle, p. 248.

10. Ibid., pp. 255-56, 262-64.

11. EHME, pp. 146-53.

12. Ibid., pp. 198-202. At the outbreak of the war the financial situation of the German railways was as follows: Anatolian, capital 59,373,000 francs, debentures 210 million; Baghdad, 15 million and 218 million; Tarsus-Mersin-Adana, 4,700,000 and 3,600,000; Haydarpaşa port, 10,100,000 and 7,800,000--Conker, p. 30.

13. Hecker and EHME, pp. 254-55.

14. Trumpener, pp. 7-8.

15. Ibid., p. 316.

16. In 1920 the nationalist government took over the line; negotiations followed and on 10 August 1928 an agreement was reached by which the government purchased the line for ₺T100.7 million--Conker, pp. 75, 108.

SELECTION 17. THE BAGHDAD RAILWAY

E. R. J. Brünner, De Bagdadspoorweg (Wolters-Noordhoff, Groningen, 1957) pp. 399-406, reproduced by kind permission of the publishers.

. . . 1. Why was this particular route chosen for the Baghdad railroad and did it in fact fulfill the expectations of the Germans and the Turkish government?

2. Did the enterprise come up to the financial expectations of the Germans and the Turkish government and to what extent was it or was it not an exception compared with the other railroad companies in the Turkish Empire?

3. Can one consider the Baghdad railroad as a typical example of German imperialism?

When we look at the physical map of Turkey it appears that, in view of the demand made by the Sultan that the starting point should be in Istanbul, and the impossibility of constructing the railroad from Ankara along the Black Sea to Diyarbekir on account of the Russian-Turkish Black Sea Treaty of 1900, the route from Eskişehir via Konya and Adana chosen by the German Bank undoubtedly was the best one, because there were few natural obstacles in the form of mountains. Consequently technical difficulties were reduced to a minimum and the construction expenses could obviously be held down. Besides the Eskişehir-Afyon Karahisar route was also, for economic-financial reasons, preferable to that from Ankara via Kayseri and Maraş to Aleppo, or that from Ankara, Kayseri, Malatya, and Diyarbekir in the direction of Mosul. Although little is known about the economic situation in the different parts of the Turkish Empire before 1904, the "Vegetations und Kulturkarte" drawn by Banse gives us a reasonable survey.

From this it is clear that the territory of West Anatolia extending from the Mediterranean coast up to the line Bursa-Kutahya-Afyon Karahisar-Konya-Adana indeed belonged to the economically most developed parts of the vast Turkish Empire. A comparison of the routes Ankara-Kayseri-Maraş and Eskişehir-Konya-Adana-Maraş shows that the former route would have led through a vast steppe landscape, with little cultivated land, while the latter route led not only through a more fertile territory but also, in the event of a further extension of the railroad, offered more possibilities for expanding the transport area in a western direction. It is true that Izmir constituted the center of an expanding English and French railroad area, but the coastal strip between Antalya and Adana was nevertheless an almost unexplored transport area along the Mediterranean.

Besides the fact that, by Turkish standards, this West-Anatolian territory produced a sizable amount of agricultural and horticultural products, one should also keep in mind that in this territory the extraction of ore was not unimportant. Anyway one might now have higher expectations of mining ore than in the territory of Cappadocia and West Armenia intersected by the route Ankara-Kayseri-Malatya.[1] To be sure, the mining industry of West Anatolia could not be put on a level with that of Western Europe, but in some cases the ore extracted there constituted a welcome supplement for the ever-increasing needs of the European industrial countries. On the German side, it might legitimately be expected that on the basis of the mining stipulations included in the concession of March 1903, permission would be obtained to open new mines and in doing so both to increase the revenues of the Baghdad railway and to provide German industry with important raw materials. The periods 1888-1903 and 1903-8, however, were too short for the development of the production of ore in the territories crossed by the Anatolian and Baghdad railroad to confirm this by figures.[2] For agricultural production, however, the situation was different.

It has to be postulated that the social structure of the Turkish Empire did not make intensive production worthwhile.[3] Compared with the other parts of the Turkish Empire, however, West Anatolia cut a very fine figure. From the transport figures of the Anatolian and Baghdad railroad companies it appears that the transportation of farm products (in addition to agricultural produce one might mention also cattle-breeding and horticulture) increased greatly after 1893. This fact proves that both the expectation of the German Bank to be able to render the railroads profitable and the expectation of the Turkish government that the economic position of the West-Anatolian population would improve perceptibly was, in great part, being achieved by the beginning of 1908. This was important for the Turkish government not only economically but also financially, because tax revenues increased considerably in the vilayets crossed by both railroads, while those of the territories still lacking railroads remained as good as stationary. Therefore one might answer question 1 in the affirmative for both the German Bank and the Turkish government.

Before answering question 2 one has first to investigate the financial structure of both railroad companies and besides one has to go deeper into the financial situation of the Turkish Empire. With the latter issue the question arises also whether the Turkish government had the right to put the Empire under such heavy financial obligations while the situation of the Turkish Treasury was notoriously bad. In that connection it is necessary to touch for a while on the finances of the Turkish state. . . .

. . . So it was not astonishing that the deficit in the Turkish budget began to show an increasing rather than a decreasing tendency. It was now already difficult enough for the Turkish government to cover current expenditures, but it was still more difficult for it to make new expenditures, as for instance on the construction of railroads, unless the concession applicants were willing to offer special arrangements. This is in fact what happened. Therefore, despite the poor condition of the Turkish Treasury, the Turkish government was able to finance expenditures which otherwise never could have been made. The way the Turkish government and the foreign financiers handled this, however, was very strange.

The construction of railroads by private persons is based on the concession granted by a state, which reserves to itself the right to decide about construction and operation of the railroads. Mostly a preconcession was granted first with a validity of three years, during which time nobody else was allowed to build but which gave the concessionaire only a preferential right. If the final concession was not granted to him, he had no right to compensation. The final concession application had to be examined by different committees. In Turkey it was mostly so, except that the departments of Labor and War, the Council of Public Works, the State Council, and the Council of Ministers had to approve the application. In order to have the Turkish government on their side, foreign concession applicants used Turkish subjects as straw-men. The concession term was mostly from fifty to ninety-nine years. After a certain number of years, the Turkish government had the right to purchase the railroad against a certain amount which, reckoned as an annual payment, was generally equal to half of the average annual income of the railroad.

When one compares the different companies, it appears that they tried to diminish shareholders' risks as much as possible by raising the debenture-stock as high as they could. This meant that the debentures could be issued with a fixed interest at a rather low price. The amount of debenture-loans was mostly used for expenses not directly connected with the construction of the railroad, for instance, the costs of the concession application, technical explorations, compensations to be paid, illicit commissions, etc.

The Baghdad railway company constituted, as it were, a variant on the behavior of the French companies, such as for example the Société Damas-Hamah, or the Anatolian railroad company, because those had first provided the money needed for the construction of the railroad themselves and were repaid afterwards by the Turkish government. The Baghdad railroad company also had a small share-capital and a rather high debenture-stock, but the money needed for construction was obtained by issuing loans calculated according to the costs of construction per kilometer plus interest and redemption. This amounted to 269,111 francs per kilometer, which in connection with the issue price came to 230,000 francs per kilometer.

Because of the uncertain situation in Turkey, the company wanted an income guarantee per kilometer to be paid by the Turkish government, if revenues should not be sufficient to cover expenditures. Those guarantees ranged from 10,000 to 15,000 francs per kilometer, from which was to be deducted operating income. So the company was always assured of a certain remunerativeness of the enterprise itself. In doing so, there were practically no risks, because for guaranteeing the income per kilometer the Turkish government had to assign a number of taxes, preferably grain-tithes, in different districts of the Turkish Empire. These tithes were collected and managed by the Ottoman Debt Administration. From this it is clear that the Turkish state, despite the ever-increasing obligations connected with the progressing construction of the rail net, did not see its payments rise accordingly. This proves that the railroads, despite increased length, did not entail extra taxes for the Turkish Treasury. This appears also from the diagram of the total revenue of the different railroad companies. Despite the fluctuations connected with political unrest or bad harvests, all companies, especially the Anatolian, show a sharp rise in income. This appears also from the transportation figures of the Haydar-Paşa-Ankara line, the Eskişehir-Konya and Arifie-Adapazari line, expressed in tons.[4] And that the two German companies benefited is made clear by the profit-and-loss accounts. That the Turkish government also benefited from it is obvious when one looks at the table[5] on the income of grain-tithes, which shows that the increase of revenue of the vilayets that had railroads was greater than the increase of revenues of those without railroads. Thus the vilayets of Trabzon and Gumuşhane are behind the vilayets of Karahisar, Aydin, and Kayseri. Therefore one can answer in the affirmative the question whether the construction of the German railroads--and the same holds more or less true for the other lines--came up to the expectations of the concessionaires or of the Turkish government. This does not mean that the Turkish government could not have had greater advantages through better handling.

Finally remains the answer to question 3, i.e., whether the construction of the Baghdad railroad up to 1908 may be considered as a typical example of the German imperialism. . . . [The author concludes that it was not such an example.]

1. The Ankara-Kayseri-Malatya route passed through a salt-steppe where only the extraction of salt was undertaken before 1908, while at Eskişehir chromium was found, at Konya mercury, and north of Adana lead and coal.

2. The production of the most important ores in 1907 amounted, for the whole Turkish Empire, to 650,000 tons of coal, 29,000 tons of chromium, and 59,000 tons of manganese. . . .

3. This was mainly caused by taxation, which weighed heavily on the agricultural population. Besides, the Mohammedan religion also plays a role, because people are obligated to help each other, whereby the necessity to take the utmost out of the soil for the sake of livelihood was lacking. Lastly military service was also a serious handicap for the agricultural population, resulting in a lack of needed manpower, which was all the worse because very extensive working methods were used.

4. See appendixes E and F. [Appendix E shows the goods traffic from the year of opening to 1907. On the Haydar-Paşa-Ankara line, the total carried rose from an average of 83,000 tons in 1893-95 to 303,000 in 1905-7; on the Eskişehir-Konya line from 81,000 in 1897-99 to 141,000 in 1905-7; and on the Arifie-Adapazari line from 25,000 in 1900-1902 to 33,000 in 1905-7.

Appendix F shows that by 1905-7, the gross receipts of the Anatolian railway were averaging 10.1 million francs, outlay 5 million, net receipts 5.1 million, and net profits, including the government guarantee, 3 million. For the Baghdad railway, gross receipts averaged 316,000 francs and net profits, including the guarantee, 838,000.]

5. See appendix H. [This gives annual returns of tithe yields for fifteen Anatolian and two Syrian sancaks for the period 1889-90 to 1907-8. Comparing the average of the first three years with that of the last three shows almost a doubling for Izmit and Karahisar and almost a tripling for Eskişehir and Ankara. More generally: "For those portions of Anatolia which were served by the [German] Railway, the amount of tithes had almost doubled in twenty years: in 1889, the year after the award of the Anatolian concession, $639,760 was collected; in 1898 $948,070; in 1908 $1,240,450" (Earle, p. 233).]

SELECTION 18. SUGGESTED MODIFICATION OF BAGHDAD RAILWAY, 1910

Correspondence BVA-BEO 283274

Ministry of Commerce and Public Works
Office of Railroads
No. 85

Subject: the passing of the Baghdad Railroad directly through Aleppo

To the Grand Vezir

This is an address from your most humble servant,

With regards to linking Aleppo to the Baghdad railroad by a branch between Tal Habash and Aleppo, the inhabitants of Aleppo have requested in appeals made to the presidency of the House of Deputies and to the Ministry of War, and in determined telegrams sent to this humble Ministry enclosed herewith, that the main railroad should pass directly through Aleppo. It is shown in a memorandum from the Ministry of War concerning this matter that there is no military objection to the passing of the Baghdad railroad directly through Aleppo, as requested by the local population. The passing of the main line through the city of Aleppo would be beneficial, for it is the center of the vilayet and possesses economic importance. Although in this respect the distance separating Istanbul from Baghdad would increase by approximately 40-45 km., in return, however, the distance between Syria and both Baghdad and Istanbul would decrease. Thus, disadvantages and advantages would balance off one another. Without constructing the original route, i.e., the branch of Tal Habash, the length of the original line reaches 595 km., and having omitted Fatima and Kilis after passing Aqrin, it turns directly to Aleppo and reaches the city. The route is to be extended from Aleppo to the environs of Harran, passing directly through the area of the Kaza of Bab. Thus, passing through Aleppo by constructing the section Islahiyya-Aleppo-Harran, in lieu of the section Islahiyya-Harran plus the branch Tal Habash-Aleppo, would benefit the country and the government. The length of the route, which will be clearly determined in this office, would be shorter than the length of the route according to the agreement and the length of the branch put together. Therefore, construction could be extended forward, past the end point of the agreed section, by adding the difference that will occur in the length of the route to the next section. To this effect, the first clause of the Baghdad Railroad Agreement reads: "The above-mentioned Railroad is to reach Baghdad and Basra passing through, or as close as possible to, the following towns: Karaman, Ereğli, Kardaş, Yili, Adana, Hamidiye, Osmaniye, Bahçe, Quran Ali, Kilis, Tal Habash, Harran, Ras al-Ayn, Mosul, Tiknit, Sadija, Baghdad, Karbala, Najaf, Zubayr, Basra. Upon completion of that route, the Konya line will be extended, and the following branches are to be laid down. (1) from Tal Habash to Aleppo (2) from a point close to the main route, to be determined by the two parties, to Bad and Urfa (3) from Sadija to Haisa (4) from Zubayr to a point in the Gulf of Basra to be determined by agreement between the government and the holder of the concession. The concession to construct the afore-mentioned branches and sections, following the route that will be confirmed by the government, will be granted to the Anatolian Ottoman Railroad Company." Accordingly, following a different route by deviating from the points elaborated in that clause is contingent upon securing the consent of the Company. Thus, an Imperial Decree is requested, in which I will be instructed and informed as to my course of action in undertaking to discuss this matter with the Company following your approval of the observations before you.

21 Cumada II, 1328
[30 June 1910]

Bedros Halacyan Efendi
Minister of Commerce and Public Works

Office of the Grand Vezir
Bureau of Correspondence

25 Cumada II, 1328
[5 July 1910]

To the Ministry of Commerce and Public Works

As for the linking of the Baghdad Railroad to Aleppo by a branch between Tal Habash and Aleppo:

Your memorandum no. 85 of 16 June 1326 included some information and discussed the benefits that would acrue to the country and the government from the passing of the main route directly through Aleppo, as requested by the local population.

The Council of Ministers is of the opinion that your report is essentially reasonable. However, according to the content of the first clause of the Baghdad Railroad Agreement, following a route different from the original one by deviating from the points written into the detailed clause is contingent upon securing the consent of the Company. Thus, while the above-mentioned memorandum is being reviewed by the Grand Vezir, act to inform us in writing and through consultation as to the outcome of the discussion between your Ministry and the Company.

RAILWAY PROJECTS AND CONCESSIONS

For every mile of railway built in Turkey several were projected. Many of these projects were stillborn but several succeeded in obtaining concessions from the government. The motives of the concessionaires were various and mixed: some sought to serve the strategic, political, or economic interests of their own countries, some had no intention whatsoever of implementation but hoped to make a quick financial gain, others reckoned that kilometric guarantees would constitute the source of income for what was obviously not a

paying proposition, and still others had the genuine belief that the projected line would
be both economically justified and profitable. Generally, the government seems to have
got the worst of the bargain, but there were undoubtedly instances in which the concessionaire had a genuine grievance, and the writer of selection 19 may well have belonged to this
category.

Even if the European and Arab provinces are omitted, and the numerous schemes for a
line from the Mediterranean to Iraq and beyond are ignored,[1] a list of the concessions
granted and projects submitted would be very long indeed and, at this stage, impossible to
compile. The following are, however, some of the more significant lines projected.

In 1857, numerous schemes for railways in the European provinces were presented, and
also for a Trabzon-Erzurum line and one from Istanbul to Basra.[2] In the same year, a concession was granted for a Samsun-Sıvas railway, with an authorized capital of £4,625,000,
one-third of which was to be provided by the government.[3]

In 1859 a concession was granted for a line between Üsküdar and Sıvas, with a branch
to Eskişehir and İzmir, and in 1860 the Samsun-Sıvas concession was cancelled.[4]

In 1872 von Pressel drew up his master plan for the Istanbul-Basra line decreed by
the government on 4 August, 1871; this provided for a main line of 2,700 kilometers with
branches totalling 1,800 kilometers.[5] In 1878 the British ambassador, Henry Layard, urged
the Sultan to build a railway from Istanbul to the Persian Gulf, with a branch to the
Syrian coast.

In 1891 a Belgian firm, Cockerill, obtained a concession for a Samsun-Sıvas-Kayseri
line, with the obligation of extending it to Adana and Yumurtalık; it carried a kilometric
guarantee of 13,700 francs. The company sold the concession to the Russian government for
800,000 francs. But the dominant view in Russia was that railways in Turkey--particularly
in the northeastern parts--would be on balance detrimental to Russian interests. Railways
would stimulate Turkish exports of grain and other agricultural produce, in competition
with Russian produce; facilitate the import of European goods into eastern Turkey, Persia,
and Transcaucasia--again at the expense of Russian goods; increase European influence in
these regions; and constitute a strategic threat.[6] In Turkey, therefore, as in Iran,
Russia used its influence to prevent railway building.[7]

In 1892, an application was made for a concession for a railway from Adapazar to Baghdad.[8] This was obviously incompatible with the German projects (4:17) and seems not to
have been pursued further.

In the next few years attention was centered on the Baghdad railway, but in 1909 the
Young Turk government drew up a vast, long-range program, covering 5,695 kilometers in all.
The lines with highest priority were Soma-Bandirma (190 kilometers, opened in 1912--4:16
and 19), Ankara-Sıvas (408 kilometers), Samsun-Sıvas and branches (434), Sıvas-Sarıklı-
Erzurum (542), and Sarıklı-Diyarbekir (390).[9]

Some of these projects formed part of the two last sets of concessions granted before
the First World War--the French concession in northern Anatolia and Syria and the Chester
concession. In June 1911, a provisional agreement was signed with the Régie Générale "for
surveys, construction and operation of the following lines": Samsun-Sıvas, Sıvas-Erzincan,
Erzincan-Erzurum, Erzurum-Trabzon.[10] On 21 September 1911, a preliminary contract was
signed with a Franco-Turkish group for a 120-kilometer line from Giresun to Sebinkarahisar.[11]
Lastly, as part of the general settlement between the Great Powers regarding Turkish railways, culminating in the Franco-German agreement of 15 February 1914, concessions were
granted for French railways in Syria and northern Anatolia. The Société pour la

Construction et l'Exploitation du Réseau de la Mer Noire was to connect ports at Ereğli, Samsun, and Trabzon by railway with Erzurum, Sıvas, Harput, and Van. Connections were to be established at Bolu with an extension from Bulgurlu to Kayseri and Sıvas, and at Ergani with a branch of the Baghdad railway to Nusaybin and Diyarbekir. The government promised to furnish the company up to 140 million francs.[12]

As for Admiral Chester's projects and concession, the first, presented in 1908, for a railway from Aleppo to the Mediterranean, was blocked by German opposition since the line would have crossed an area served by the Baghdad railway. In 1909 Chester eliminated a rival American group, that of J. G. White, which had applied for lines in eastern Turkey, and asked for a concession covering a railway from Sıvas through Harput, Diyarbekir, Mosul, and Kirkuk to Sulaymaniya, near the Persian border. Branch lines were projected to Samsun, Aleppo, and the Mediterranean, and to Bitlis and Van. The total estimated length was over 2,000 kilometers and the cost more than $100 million. The project also included the exploitation of minerals alongside the railway. In spite of some backing from the Department of State, Chester was finally unable to secure a concession and withdrew in February 1914.[13]

On 9 April 1923 the National Assembly did grant the Chester group a concession including an even longer railway network (some 4,500 kilometers), ports, agricultural development, and mineral rights, including oil. However, that concession was cancelled on 18 December 1923.[14]

---

1. EHME, pp. 137-45; EHI, pp. 191-92.
2. TE, Box 22 (1857).
3. TE, Box 26 (1858).
4. TE, Box 41 (1860), 2 April 1859 and 13 May 1860.
5. EHME, pp. 91-93.
6. See report of Russian consul quoted in Novichev, Ocherki, pp. 143-47.
7. EHI, pp. 156, 184-85.
8. TE, Box 281 (1892).
9. For a full list, A and P 1909, vol. 98, "Constantinople," ibid. 1912-13, vol. 100, "Constantinople," and Novichev, Ocherki, pp. 158-59.
10. A and P 1912-13, vol. 100, "Constantinople."
11. Ibid.
12. Earle, pp. 245-46, 272; for more details, Thobie, pp. 355-68.
13. De Novo, pp. 60-87.
14. Ibid., pp. 210-28; see also map in Earle, p. 340.

SELECTION 19. A DISAPPOINTED CONCESSIONAIRE

Camille Vigié to Grand Vizir, 25 June 1909, BVA-BEO 269221

For many years I have studied, in Turkey, a railway scheme, which is described in the enclosed report. . . . Today, there is no longer any reason why my line should not be built. But I have learned that, just now, a person by the name of Bellay (who in Paris calls himself de Lobel) with no scruples, with no regard for what has been granted to me, for what belongs to me, for the lengthy studies and pecuniary sacrifices I have undertaken--I learn that that person has applied to the Ottoman government for a concession for a line which is no other than my own, or part of mine.

I indignantly and energetically protest against this usurpation of my vested rights. I have full confidence in the high justice of the Ottoman Government, which knows what I have done.. . . . .

Statement by M. Camille Vigié regarding his business with the Ottoman government concerning the concession and construction of a railway line from Baba-eski, Gallipoli, and Lapsaki, terminating at Balikesir, with two branches to Panderma and Brusa.

In 1885 I began studying the railway line mentioned above and I had the honor to present to the Ottoman government a technical report with complete information, plans, and studies on the execution, traffic, and importance of this line--a very important piece of work.

In the course of this work, which was studied jointly by the technical commission of the Ottoman government and myself, numerous modifications were introduced because of various remarks made by several ministers, notably the minister of war, who revised part of the scheme; this compelled me to carry out new, long, and important studies.

My work having finally obtained the approval of all the ministerial commissions of the competent departments (in particular the War Ministry), of the Council of Ministers, and of the Council of State, as well as that of the commissions residing in the Imperial palace, the specifications and conventions were decreed by the minister of public works and the irade approved by His Imperial Majesty. At that point, His Highness the Grand Vizier sent for me and informed me of this decision, which was published in all the Constantinople newspapers, notably the Official Journal of the Empire, during the first days of October 1890.

The irade was promulgated on the following bases: the concession granted to M. Vigié will be for a duration of 99 years, a kilometric guarantee of 10,000 francs will be granted to him, and all the other clauses and conditions will be patterned on the concession granted to M. Kaulla for the line from Izmit to Angora (Turkey in Asia).

But shortly after the promulgation of this irade, a change occurred and His Highness the Grand Vizier sent for me in the course of the same month of October 1890, to inform me of the new intentions of His Excellency the minister of public works, who made me a proposal on the following lines: to build the railway on government account—in view of its strategic importance, recognized as indispensable by the Ministry of War—in return for an annual interest of five percent (5%) and an amortization of one percent (1%); as a guarantee, the receipts of the railway and the levying of tithes in the sancaks crossed by the line: in Europe, Adrianople, Rodosto, and Gallipoli, and in Asia, Dardanelles and Balike-sir. As soon as the line had been built, it was to be handed over to the Imperial Ottoman, which would undertake its management. However, until the line had been finally bought back, the concessionary or financial group would be entitled to appoint financial commissions to check receipts.

Later, I was informed that construction of my line wouldnot begin until the Panderma-Konya railway was under way. At a certain time, the latter being on the point of starting, I went to Constantinople thinking that all obstacles had been removed and that I was at last about to obtain satisfaction. The government then gave me to understand that it was no longer necessary to take into account the condition regarding the construction of the Panderma-Konya line, and that it wished to return to the first proposal made to me, by the irade promulgated in October 1890.

I accepted this new proposal and since then have held myself at the disposal of the Ottoman government, being ready to introduce any modifications it might deem useful. I have sacrificed my personal wealth for this enterprise and have gone through all administrative formalities. I have obtained an irade granting me the said concession—in a word, the work is ready for execution, the difficulties have been removed. My only wish is to see this railway scheme carried out; I have worked so long on it that it has become part of myself and I would like to see my forecasts brought to fruition. . . .

The Sublime Porte
The Cabinet

Draft of the minutes of 9 Cumada II, 1327 [28 June 1909]

A memorandum had reached the Ministry of Commerce and Public Works concerning the dispatching of agreement and contract drafts drawn up for the purpose of granting the engineer Mr. Bellay-Lobel a concession, for a period of 75 years, in order to construct a railroad. The basic conditions entail: (a) an obligation to continue with the Manisa-Soma line, starting at Bandırma and passing through Balıkesir; [the line] will be 1.45 m wide, and no guarantee fund or the like are to be given. (b) An option for the construction of branches from suitable points to Bursa, Mihaliç, Sultançayrı, Karamastı, and Balya, for 4 years, starting at the beginning of the construction of the line. The petition of the Public Works and Education Section of the Council of State—containing some corrections and explanations of the agreement in accordance with the memorandum referred to above, [including] granting the concession, within the decided conditions, to the afore-mentioned, [after] having been discussed by the majority and supplemented and confirmed by the General Assembly —was read and studied [by the Cabinet].

It is understood that this line would be built without guarantees, and that drafts of the agreement and contract regarding this subject would follow the basic printed pattern. However, according to announced principles which were determined by the government after the promulgation of the Constitution, in the event that more favorable conditions than these should come up for consideration in the course of recording the basic conditions in the agreement and contract drafts of this line, they would be referred to the Ministry.

In order to announce it [the tender] in the newspapers of Europe and Istanbul and for the applications to be submitted, a suitable period of time will be assigned. If the conditions suggested by one of the applicants are more favorable, the contract will, after careful examination, be granted to him. [The Cabinet] considered writing the Ministry of Commerce and Public Works a memorandum concerning the necessary steps to be followed, enclosing the above-mentioned petition and the texts of the agreement and contract drafts.

Correspondence, BVA-BEO 269221

Ministry of Commerce and Public Works
Office of Railroads
No. 113

To the Grand Vezir

This is an address from your most humble servant,

Thorough examinations have been conducted by the government concerning the applications and petitions submitted for the construction of a railroad from Babaeski to Gallipoli, ending at Dikili and passing through Lapsaki and Balıkesir, and the extension of the branches to Bandırma and Bursa. The enclosed letter was dispatched from Paris bearing the signature of Vigié. It contains some statements alleging the violation of his acquired rights by [our] announcing that a concession had been granted to Mr. Bellay for some of the afore-mentioned lines while the construction of the railroad between the above-mentioned places had been entrusted to him by an Imperial Irade. A report and a map also accompany [this] statement sent [to you].

A memorandum from the Grand Vezir, no. 216 of 25 June 1325, had reached me and was referred to the Office of Railroads, it demanded a report and notification. Upon its referral, we have carefully examined and deliberated the demands of the above-mentioned Vigié relating to dealings that will take place concerning the lines the concession for which is sought by Mr. Bellay. In a letter sent to the Ministry by Vigié, he inquired about [the possibility] of obtaining a contract by another concession requested in order to build a railroad starting at Babaeski and passing through Gallipoli and Lapsaki, ending at Balikesir, with two branches. In a previous memorandum to the Sublime Porte, requesting a ruling and based on an appeal to protect his rights, Vigié asked for a concession to extend the line from Konya to Mudanya and to construct the afore-mentioned railroads.

Construction is according to government plans and is carried out in its name; it is based, to the necessary degree, on local needs. Therefore, the concession was granted to the petitioner on condition that he would raise the means to construct these lines with speed and according to the government plan at the time. This was recorded [extracted] from the requirements laid down by an Imperial Irade. This explanation was communicated in a written form, and registered with the Ottoman Embassy in Paris by a circular note no. 6 of 9--1314. It entailed informing [Vigié] that, in view of the prerogative which the government possesses to grant such concessions at its discretion, and whether another applicant for the above-mentioned lines emerges or not, he will not have the right to object to this matter in any way.

As informing [Vigié] to this effect once again, through the above-mentioned Embassy, is contingent on the view of Your Highness, we request an Imperial Decree on this subject with the return of the enclosed documents.

Minister of Commerce and Public Works

Bedros Halacyan Efendi

6 Şaban 1327 (23 August 1909)
9 August 1325

5

Agriculture

It is difficult to give more than a rough sketch of Turkish agriculture in the nineteenth century or to indicate any but the most general developments that took place in it. Until near the end of the century no overall figures on output are available and information on land tenure and agrarian relations is scanty. It seems clear that, of all branches of the economy, agriculture changed least, but some significant shifts may be noted such as the extension of cultivation, the marked expansion of cash crops, the increase in the proportion of marketed produce, the development of more capitalistic relations, and, towards the end of the period, the improvement of techniques and investment in irrigation schemes and agricultural machinery. Most of this change was the result of market forces, operating through foreign individuals or agencies or through members of minorities, but in the second half of the period the government played a increasingly important part.[1]

Table 1

Percentage Distribution of Cultivated Land by Crop, 1863

	Wheat	Barley	Other Grain	Cotton	Tobacco	Vines	Other
I European Provinces							
Edirne	30	18	35[a]	..	..	5	12[b]
Istanbul	After fallow, land planted to barley in spring and wheat in autumn; succeeded again by wheat if land is sufficiently rich, if not by oats, beans etc.						
Rodosto	65	20	12[c]	0.3	..	2	2[d]
Gelibolu	50	25[e]	..	..	..	..	25[f]
Salonica	38	29	21[g]	0.3	--	--	12[h]
Serres	20	15	33[i]	10	15	..	7[j]
Cavalla	..	..	55[k]	3	8	..	34[l]
Jannina	..	..	100[m]	..	..	..	..
II Anatolia							
Dardanelles (Biga)	45	25	25[n]	--	1	..	4[o]
Diyarbekir	40	30	25[p]	5	..	..	2[q]
Trabzon	6	3	55[r]	--	10	1	25[s]
III Arab Provinces							
Acre	40	9	7[t]	6	2	..	36[u]
Jerusalem	50		..	..	..	..	50[v]

Table 1--Continued

Source: Replies to Foreign Office Questionnaire, 1863 (FO 195/771)

[a]Maize 14, rye and oats 17, rice 4.

[b]Tobacco, cotton, oilseeds, roses and mulberries.

[c]Oats.

[d]Linseed, ecajola.

[e]Barley and rye.

[f]Cotton, maize, oilseeds, tobacco.

[g]Maize 10, rye 6, millet 5.

[h]Sesame 10, haricots and beans 1.7.

[i]Maize 20, rye 10, millet 3.

[j]Sesame 4, aniseed 3.

[k]All grains.

[l]Oilseeds, beans, olives, vines etc. 8; green crops and pastures 25.

[m]Usually maize 50, wheat, barley or oats 50.

[n]Rye and oats 15, maize 10.

[o]Sesame 1, beans, peas, etc. 3--very little cotton.

[p]Rice 20, millet 5. Another estimate for "the percentage of seed sown in the best agricultural districts" was: wheat 47 percent, barley 23, rice 10, cotton 10, maize and millet 7 and oilseeds 3--A and P 1865, vol. 53, "Diarbekr and Kurdistan."

[q]Oilseeds--n.b. rounding error in original.

[r]Maize 52, oats 3.

[s]Beans 10, nuts 5, vegetables 4, potatoes 2, olives 2, mulberry 1, hemp 1.

[t]Millet.

[u]Olives 14, sesame 13, lentils, beans, peas 5, watermelons, vines, figs 4.

[v]Olives, vines, vegetables 25, lentils, sesame, peas, millet, fruit 25.

Table 1 brings out the traditional crop pattern. Even during the 1863 cotton boom, by far the greater part of the land was planted to wheat, barley, and other grains, which were mostly consumed on the farm. It is impossible to determine to what extent output had risen in the previous fifty years, though some growth almost certainly occurred, but in the following half-century there was a marked increase. Between 1879 and 1904 tithe revenues in Anatolia rose by 79 percent and agricultural exports from the four main ports by 45 percent, and in the next ten years tithes rose by over a quarter; in real terms the increase up to 1904 was considerably greater and in 1904-14 somewhat less.[2] This increase in output distinctly exceeded population growth (2:1). Although no precise data are available, it seems to have been achieved almost entirely by an extension of cultivation rather than by a rise in yields.

Helped by the railways and other improvements in transport, cereals cultivation and output greatly increased (5:1 to 3) and in 1913-14 grain still accounted for 5,212,000 hectares, or 80 percent of the cultivated area within the present Turkish borders, while legumes and root crops accounted for 452,000 hectares or 7 percent, industrial crops for 425,000 or 7, and orchards for 411,000 or 6 percent.[3] But the expansion of several other crops had been as large or larger, e.g., cotton (5:15,16), oilseeds (5:17,18), tobacco (5:19 to 21), and, after their recovery from devastating diseases in the 1860s and 1880s, respectively, silk (5:22 to 24) and grapes (5:27). The output and export of opium also increased (5:26).

Some of the minor crops may be briefly mentioned. In the first half of the nineteenth century Turkish madder, yellow berries, and gallnuts were eagerly sought as dyestuffs but were then replaced by chemical dyes.[4] Valonia (oak acorns) was used for tanning and continued in demand; in the 1830s exports from Izmir averaged some 5,000 tons (Report on Trade, 1835, FO 78/287), worth about Ł50,000-100,000 (3:14 and CC Smyrne, vol. 45); in 1880-1908 they averaged about 5,000 tons and brought in some Ł500,000 a year.[5] Hazelnuts were exported from Trabzon and in 1880-1908 averaged some 5,000 tons, worth Ł100,000.[6] Roses were extensively grown in European Turkey for making attar and in Edirne in the 1860s yielded the high net profit of Ł5 per dönüm;[7] from the 1880s on, the government encouraged, with some success, the growing of roses in Anatolia by refugees from the Balkans.[8] Licorice, extracted from a wild-growing root, was much in demand following a series of poor crops in southern Europe. In 1854 the British firm of MacAndrews and Forbes opened a factory in Aydın, followed by three others; it soon came to dominate the market and increased its output severalfold but, towards the end of the period, met increasing German, Russian, and American competition. Anatolia's production before the First World War was estimated at 20,000 tons.[9]

Several minor foodcrops were developed for internal consumption. Potato growing was reported in the Trabzon area in the 1840s. A few years previously "the natives objected to it as food. Of late all classes have commenced to use it" and a cargo had been sent to Istanbul (Report on Trabzon, 1844, FO 78/614). In 1849 potato plantations and consumption were reported on the increase and "a ready sale is never wanting at Constantinople for their surplus however large it may be" (ibid., 1849, FO 78/835). In Bursa, in 1850, "potatoes are very little extending in use" and the carriage to Istanbul was too expensive (Agricultural Report, FO 78/686), but by 1862 the crop was reported as good, with a consequent fall in price (Agricultural Report, FO 195/741). Starting in the 1880s the government made considerable efforts to encourage cultivation, as did the Anatolian railway in the regions it crossed, and by 1913 potatoes were grown on a significant scale and output was about 60,000 tons.[10] With other vegetables less progress was made; in 1911 Turkey's imports were three times as large as its exports and the conservatism of peasants was blamed for the failure to grow off-season produce that would command higher prices.[11] Attempts to develop rice were largely frustrated by shortage of water and labor, and output in 1913 was only 30,000 tons; so were efforts to grow beet and cane sugar, and Turkey continued to be a large importer of rice and sugar.[12]

The evolution of land tenure in the nineteenth century remains obscure.[13] It was determined by the interplay of three sets of factors: natural conditions, market forces, and government policy. The abundance of land in all but a few coastal zones made it easy for farmers to rent, or take possession of and subsequently acquire a title to, a plot; but the erratic rainfall exposed them to great stresses and caused many to fall into debt. The development of market relations with the improvement of transport enhanced the value of land and its output and increasingly attracted urban or rural capitalists. As regards government policy, mention may be made of the heavy burden of taxation (7:11) and the various attempts at improvement referred to in this Introduction. In the field of land tenure three landmarks stand out: the abolition of _tımars_, the Land Code, and the granting, in 1867, of ownership rights to foreigners.

The developments mentioned in Chapter 1--the change in methods of warfare, the rise in prices, the government's need for revenue, and the increase in cash cropping and marketing--undermined the _tımar_ system and replaced it, in many parts, by tax-farming (_iltizam_) or large estates (_çiftliks_). The breakdown of government at the end of the eighteenth

century caused tens of thousands of peasants to flee their masters, further weakening the
tımars, and Selim III converted many of them into iltizams.[14]   In 1818 Mahmud II struck a
blow at the feudal system by prohibiting the corvée in some European provinces, a measure
that was only partly implemented.[15]   In 1831, he revoked all remaining tımars--an estimated
1,000 in Rumelia and 1,500 in Anatolia--the sipahis receiving pensions totalling 60 million
piastres and their lands being leased out to tax farmers.[16]   The effect of this measure on
breaking up large properties is noted in selections 5:6 to 8.[17]   Also important in this
respect was Mahmud's attempt, again only partly successful, to bring all vakfs (pious foundations held in mortmain) under a centralized administration.[18]   While the main beneficiary
of all these reforms was the government, which appropriated the revenues formerly accruing
to the feudal landlords or religious personnel, the lot of the peasants was somewhat eased
and major obstacles to the capitalist development of Turkish agriculture were removed.

   The Land Code of 1858 sought primarily to "tax every piece of land, and therefore to
establish clearly the title to it by registering its legal owner as a miri owner,"[19] i.e.,
one who enjoyed hereditary possession and use of land, confirmed by a deed, the tapu
temesseku, while ownership continued to belong to the state. In pursuit of this aim, the
Code forbade collective ownership or the registration of a whole village as an estate by
an individual. In the Arab provinces these provisions were evaded, and village or tribal
land was registered in the name of a large landlord or shaykh, but this does not seem to
have happened on a large scale in Anatolia. Table 2 shows that in 1863 small ownership
was predominant in the area of the Republic, large ownership being widespread in Macedonia,
Kurdistan, and some of the Arab provinces. The fuller information given in 5:1 indicates
that both ownership and, still more, actual operating units were overwhelmingly small. In
1914, only a handful of peasants were landless and small holdings numbered over 1 million
and took in 75 percent of cleared land; holdings of less than one hectare were 13-45 percent of the total in the various provinces and those of 1-5 hectares 36-67 percent. A
breakdown by provinces shows that the smallest average farm sizes were (in ascending order)
in Istanbul, Erzurum, Trabzon, Canik, Kastamonu, Bolu, and Biga (1-2 hectares) and the
largest in Diyarbekir, Ankara, Aydın, Adana, Karasi, and Bitlis (4-8 hectares).[20]   In
Thrace and Rumelia in 1907, farms of 10 dönüms or under were 34 percent of the total,
those of 10-50 donums 47 percent and those of 50 or over 19 percent.[21]

   Yet a powerful countertrend was under way. The value of land is estimated to have
risen by 75 percent between 1840-44 and 1859[22] and probably went on rising until the Great
Depression of the 1870s, when it fell sharply, but in the two decades before the First
World War it shot up again, particularly in the cotton areas of Adana and Izmir (5:1).
Large landowners, working with hired labor, increased their holdings in these areas (5:16)
and certain others, e.g., Trabzon,[23] but still occupied a relatively small proportion of
cultivated area in 1914.

   These entrepreneurial landlords, most of whom were non-Turks and a few of whom were
British or other foreigners, were largely responsible for the introduction of agricultural
machinery.[24]   Until the First--and even the Second--World War the vast majority of farmers
continued to use the simple tools and follow the traditional methods described in selections 5:3 to 5.[25]   In the 1860s some attempts were made in the Izmir region to use better
implements, but they died out with the cotton boom.[26]   As late as 1878 the situation was
described as follows: "Little or no real progress has been made of late years in the introduction of agricultural machinery and British-made implements. The English firm I alluded to in a former report has energetically strived [sic] to bring them into notice,

Table 2

Percentage Distribution of Farms by Size (Acres), 1863

Consular District	Under 10	10-50	50-100	100-500	Over 500
I European Provinces					
Edirne	26.7	40	30	3	0.3
Istanbul	Within radius of 10 miles mainly market gardens, 2-10 acres Beyond radius of 10 miles mainly 10-500 acres				
Gelibolu	75 percent of <u>farm land</u> in small properties tilled by owners without outside help; 4 percent in farms of 200-250 acres; 1 percent in farms of 400-450 acres; 20 percent over 5,000 acres.				
Salonica	40[a]	10	10		40
Cavalla	50[b]		25[c]	15	10
	2/3 of cultivation done by owner farmers; 1/3 in çiftlik of 100-2,000 acres; let out on métayage.				
Cyprus	In Messaoria "a few peasants" hold 225-375 acres, "a large proportion" 75-225, "a smaller proportion" under 75; "very few as little as 10 acres." In Mountains 50 percent of peasants hold under 75 acres. Overall--farms of 75-225 acres of cultivated land most numerous; about 70 farms of 700-7,000, mostly around 1,200 acres; only 3 or 4 of 4,000 or over.				
II Anatolia					
Dardanelles[d] (Biga)	10,000-12,000	500	20	500	20
	only 1/5 land under cultivation at any given time				
Diyarbekir[e]	--	--	20	30	50
Izmir	"By far the largest proportion of cultivated land is owned by peasants" in farms of 3-20 acres; çiftliks seldom cultivated by owners, let out in small plots to peasants at a rental of 10-20 percent of crop, but sometimes cultivated on joint account with the landlord.				
Trabzon	100	--	--	--	--
III Arab Provinces					
Basra	17	17	..	17	50
Acre	5	74	18	3	--
	Majority of farms, 1 faddan: in hills 36-40 acres, in plains 30-36 acres.				
Jerusalem	In plains mainly farms of 50-100 acres.				

<u>Source</u>: Replies to Foreign Office Questionnaire, 1863 (FO 195/771)

[a]Under 50 acres.

[b]5-15 acres.

[c]15-75 acres.

[d]Number of farms.

[e]Privately owned land in Kurdistan, amounting to 40 percent of arable area; remaining 60 percent government-owned or waste.

going so far as to offer English ploughs, threshing machines, etc. for trial for one or two months without charge, and to impress constantly upon the Government the importance of establishing model farms in the neighbourhood. . . . Perhaps the first thing to be understood is the necessity of admitting all agricultural machinery duty free."[27]

By the 1880s, however, a change was noticeable; in the Adana region, where cotton cultivation was expanding rapidly and labor was scarce, orders were put by the municipality

of Adana for steam ploughs and modern implements at a cost of ₤1,500.[28] Other regions followed suit and the government helped--both directly and through the Agricultural Bank--by
exempting agricultural implements from customs duty, demonstrating new equipment in its
model farms, and encouraging the diffusion of both elaborate machinery and improved tools.[29]
Foreign firms, particularly German, British, and American,[30] pushed the sales of machinery
and improved ploughs and other implements, and set up repair shops. The Anatolian railway
promoted better tools and practices (5:13). But perhaps the most important single factor
was the shortage of labor and steady rise in agricultural wages, particularly in the years
immediately preceding the First World War (2:6). In 1911 it was reported that in Asia
Minor labor was scarce, and "it is said in some places 30 percent of the crops were un-
gathered and rotted in the fields," a further 10-15 percent being damaged by lying in the
open at railway stations because of shortage of trucks.[31] In European Turkey in the same
year, because of the spread of tobacco cultivation and the calling up of reserves, wages
had gone up sharply; a woman harvesting with a sickle was asking 15 piastres a day instead
of 8 and a man 30 to 35 instead of 20; hence machinery had become economical and 80 reapers
and reaper-binders had been bought at Rodosto and 25 at Kırk Kilise; but because of the
weakness of the local oxen two pairs had to be used on each machine.[32] In Adana as early
as 1881 it was reckoned that the cost of an American reaper, ₤T25, was equal to that of
only 164 man-days.[33] By 1913 there were some 300 steam ploughs and threshing sets in the
Adana region, and some 200 to 250 reapers were being imported annually from the United
States as well as many bullock ploughs from Britain and Belgium.[34] By 1910 "A very large
amount of money had been expended in the introduction of Self Binding Harvesters in Asia
Minor" (Massey-Harris Co. to Foreign Office, 20 July 1910, FO 368/471). Imports of agricultural equipment to Izmir and Adana were running at over ₤20,000 a year in the early
1900s.[35] However, in 1923 an authoritative source stated: "The use of the modern plough
is confined to the plains of Adana, Eski Shehr, and in the vilayets of Adrianople, Smyrna
and Brusa. Ploughing with mechanical tractors is very little done in Turkey."[36] (See
Epilogue.)

Government attempts to improve agricultural practices and raise the quality of crops
began quite early (5:12), but achieved almost no success until the Hamidian period, when
an agricultural bureaucracy was set up; schools, model fields, and other forms of extension were established; and the Agricultural Bank was founded (7:6).[37] The Public Debt
Administration helped considerably in silk production (5:22) and the Régie in tobacco (5:19)
while the Anatolian railway did very good work in the regions it crossed (5:13). Starting
in the 1860s, British landowners also introduced some progress in the Izmir region.[38]

The greatest single agricultural improvement made by the government was the Konya irrigation scheme (5:14).[39] The scheme was proposed, studied, and implemented by the Baghdad
Railway Company, which advanced the government 20 million francs to cover costs. Although
the estimated cost per hectare, about 450 francs, was high by international standards,[40]
there seems little doubt that the project was beneficial. It was completed by 1913 and
its implementation encouraged the government to make preliminary contracts for the irrigation of some 400,000 hectares in the Menderes valley, 500,000-600,000 hectares in the Adana
plain, 80,000 hectares in Samsun, 30,000 in the Gediz valley, and 10,000 in Tokat, as well
as in Iraq and Syria.[41] Except for the Iraqi scheme,[42] none of these had been implemented
at the outbreak of war.

Lastly, mention may be made of a branch of agriculture, livestock raising, which has
always played an important part in the economy by providing exports such as mohair and

supplying domestic needs for livestock products (5:28,29). Taxes on livestock were about one-third as large as those on agricultural produce and rose by about a quarter between 1890 and the outbreak of war.[43] Forestry also made a significant contribution; the total area in Anatolia was put at 5 million hectares, the leading vilayets being: Aydın, Bursa, Kastamonu, Bolu, Trabzon, Karasi, Konya, and Adana, in that order. Wood was exported to Egypt and elsewhere, but the Empire was a net importer.[44]

1. See also Novichev in EHME, pp. 65-70.

2. Quataert, pp. 17-23; Eldem, p. 79. The rate of increase was far from uniform. The early 1870s saw "a disastrous series of droughts, grasshopper plagues and crop failures, most notably the famine of 1873-1875." The 1878 war retarded recovery but from the mid-80s to 1895 there was a marked increase in output and exports (Quataert, pp. 209-10). After that the trend in output was upward (Eldem, p. 79).

3. Eldem, p. 73; breakdowns by provinces and major crops in Mears, pp. 284-92.

4. Stich, pp. 78-81. Exports of madder from Izmir, which in 1830 had amounted to 5,000 tons and in 1856 to 7,000 and accounted for 20 percent of total exports, fell by one-half in the early 1860s and in 1901-5 averaged only 94 tons.

The main source of yellow berries was the Kayseri area. In the early 1840s, Kayseri and "the neighboring districts" produced about 450 tons in good years; the figure for 1841 was about 350 tons, 480 in 1842, 500 worth ₤50,000 in 1843, 400 in 1849, and 560 in 1850 (Reports on Trade, 1842 FO 78/533; 1843 FO 78/533; and 1850 FO 78/870). In 1843, 300 tons were sent to Izmir for shipment, mainly to Britain; they were used for dyeing piecegoods for export to China where "yellow being only worn among high classes, the best materials, such as berries of Kaissariah, are probably required."

But demand was declining partly because of "a change in the taste for particular colours" but also from "the discovery of equally efficient and less costly substitutes" (Report for 1842); prices fell from 26 piastres per oke in 1841 to 12-17 in 1842 and 13 in 1850.

5. Table in Quataert, p. 304.

6. Ibid., p. 306.

7. Detailed breakdown in A and P 1867, vol. 67, "Adrianople."

8. Quataert, pp. 314-18.

9. Stich, pp. 75-77; Kurmuş, pp. 195-99.

10. Quataert, pp. 319-26; Mears, p. 291.

11. RC, no. 288; 1911.

12. Quataert, pp. 307-13; see figures on area and output in Mears, p. 291.

13. For a fuller account, see Warriner and Baer in EHME, pp. 71-90, and sources therein; Quataert, pp. 36-48; Barker, pp. 394-412; and legislation in Fisher; Ongley; Padel and Steeg; Tute; and Young, vol. 6.

14. Lewis, Emergence, pp. 89-92.

15. Novichev, Turtsii, 2:225-36, which makes good use of the research carried out in Bulgaria and Yugoslavia in recent years.

16. Lewis, Emergence, pp. 89-92; for comparison, at the end of the seventeenth century there were over 9,000 timars in Rumelia and 12,000 in the three beylerbeys of Anatolia, Rum, and Karaman--Novichev, p. 228.

17. Further information on Bursa is provided in a report of 1852 (FO 78/905). Formerly, forced rayah labor had been used on the "estates of influential Turkish landlords, with stately houses on them, and well fitted with farmyards and stock." But the owners, when they had "to hire and pay all their laborers, could no longer manage these extensive properties," which were therefore abandoned and left waste. "Some compensation on a confined scale is observable in the more extended and thriving cultivation around certain of the villages, almost always those inhabited by Rayas."

18. Lewis, Emergence, pp. 89-92, and Novichev, Turtsii, 2:225-36.

19. Warriner, in EHME, p. 73.

20. Mears, pp. 295-96; also Indzhikyan, p. 265.

21. Eldem, p. 70.

22. Ibid.

23. Quataert, pp. 418-20.

24. In the 1850s, some foreigners acquired land "by purchasing in the name of native subjects," but their attempts "to conduct farming on the English or any other regular system" failed (FO 78/952). In the 1860s, however, Englishmen acquired extensive holdings in the Izmir region and farmed them quite successfully--Kurmuş, passim.

25. One example, among many, may be quoted, from the relatively advanced island of Rhodes: "the implements employed in agriculture are the plough, the spade, the hoe and the sickle, all of which are very imperfect. No machinery has been substituted for human labour" (Reply to Questionnaire, 1856, FO 78/1419). In 1849 the expansion of agriculture in the relatively advanced Salonica region had led to an increase in imports of iron "for those rude agricultural instruments made and used by the natives" (Report on Trade, FO 78/831), but no improvement is implied.

26. In 1861 the Consul at Bursa (Report, FO 195/700) stated that "some of the native cultivators perceiving the manifest advantages of the English plough have given commissions for it" but listed the following difficulties: absence of country blacksmiths for repairs," which can only be done here in town," lack of capital, and "amongst draught animals here only the buffaloes are full sized and vigorous--the breed of oxen and horses is puny and stunted, deficient in strength as well as size."

27. A and P 1878, vol. 74, "Constantinople."

28. TE, Box 208, 19 November 1881.

29. For a fuller discussion, see Quataert, pp. 155-85.

30. The Germans "have already placed large engines on the Mersina-Adana line, established a bank with orders to advance money regardless of risk, bought several houses at Adana and evidently intend to exploit that very rich portion of Asia Minor which has been so absolutely neglected by British enterprise. . . . These plains [Karamania and Cilicia] are the only places where I have seen British agricultural implements employed, as usually America gets the market, their ploughs and reapers being lighter and less expensive. There must be quite a demand for labour-saving machinery all round Mesopotamia, and the Armenians, notably those who have been emigrants to America and have returned, are fully alive to the fact" (Howe to Admiralty, FO 368/470).

31. TJ, March 1911.

32. RC, no. 291, 1911.

33. Quataert, p. 169.

34. TJ, June 1913.

35. Quataert, pp. 164, 167.

36. Mears, p. 292.

37. On all these subjects see the very full account in Quataert; also Shaw, History, 2:230-36; however, it was not until the law of February 1913 that mortgages became easily available--Mears, p. 257.

38. Kurmuş, passim.

39. An irrigation scheme at Kayseri, costing ₤20,000, had been discussed but does not seem to have been implemented (Report for 1842, FO 78/533). In spite of much discussion, nothing was done to prevent flooding around Bursa (Sandison to Palmerston, 18 March, 1841, FO 78/441).

40. A. Theodoli, Bolletino della Societa Geografica Italiana, 1909, pp. 123-28.

41. A and P 1912-13, vol. 100, "Constantinople"; Mears, pp. 270-77.

42. EHME, pp. 191-97.

43. Eldem, pp. 78-79.

44. Mears, pp. 304-9; for exports from Menteşe in 1850, FO 198/11.

SIZE OF FARMS, LAND VALUES, SHARECROPPING

The following eleven selections illustrate various aspects of land tenure, agricultural techniques, and scale and methods of farming in different parts of Turkey. The common features were abundance of land, except on the Black Sea coast and some islands, scarcity of capital and labor, and high transport costs (4:12). Hence, everywhere, inputs of labor and capital were small, implements primitive and inefficient, and yields low; most of the land was left fallow and the bulk of output was consumed on the farm. Irrespective of the prevalent scale of ownership, the units of cultivation in any given region tended to be of similar size, usually equal to the area that could be ploughed by a team of oxen.

The following table summarizes the available information. Naturally, plots were larger in the drier interior regions of Anatolia than in the European provinces or moist coastlands. They were also smaller in the vicinity of towns, where intensive cultivation was practiced, as in Bursa, where the combination of silk-raising, improved roads, and the settlement of immigrants had resulted in small, intensive plots of under four acres, with a required investment of ₤10 per acre for cultivation (CC Brousse, Report for 1893).

But almost everywhere it is stressed that shortage of land was not the limiting factor. In 1840 the French consul in Tarsus reported that the area under cereals was diminishing every year because of the "lack of hands and cash" (CC Tarsous, vol. 2, 30 July 1840). In 1844 a British consul noted "limited cultivation and deficiency of inhabitants" in the Konya area (Notes . . . on Konia, 1844, FO 78/615). In Erzurum in 1846 land sold at about ₤1.5s to ₤4.5s an acre (5:4). In the Diyarbekir region in 1864 government land was being

Year	Region	Area of Cultivation (Acres)	Source
1863	Radius 10 miles from Istanbul	Market gardens, 2–10	FO 195/771
1863	Trabzon	under 10[a]	FO 195/771
1864	Mardin	Çift, i.e., by 4 oxen and 1 man	A&P 1865, 53
1864	Diyarbekir	Çift, i.e., by 6 animals and 2–3 men	A&P 1865, 53
1870	Istanbul	By 1 or 2 pairs oxen, i.e., 20–30	FO 83/346
1870	Dardanelles	By 1 pair oxen, i.e., 20–30	FO 83/346
1870	Eastern Turkey	5–50	FO 83/346
1888	Eastern Rumelia	10[b]	A&P 1888, 103
1890	Edirne	7–12	A&P 1890, 77
1890	Izmir	3–12[c]	Kurmuş, p. 150
1895	Ankara	10–100	A&P 1895, 100
1900	Macedonia	15–25	5:11

[a]All farms.

[b]"Sufficient to maintain a family of five persons, and as much as a pair of oxen can successfully work."

[c]Allotments of land on properties owned by foreigners.

sold, under the Tapu system (5:Introduction), at "perfectly nominal prices"--rates of "40 to 60 piastres for plots large enough to take a quarter of seed" (say 3–4 acres--5:4) being common.[1] In Rhodes in 1859, where "small holdings predominate," land sold at 20 to 120 piastres a dönüm, or about 13s. to ₤4 an acre.[2] In Ankara in 1895, "Apart from irrigated land, which is generally reserved for barley and is always sought after, the peasant does not care much whether he owns land or not. Arable land is more than plentiful and close at hand. Anyone is free to cultivate Crown land and becomes the legal owner thereof after 10 successive years of cultivation. . . . The value of rural property in this province, never very high, has declined 50 percent during the last decade or two on account of the prevalent poverty and scarcity of money. The present prices are: for dry irrigated land, 5s.6d. to 11s. per acre, and for irrigated land, ₤1–8s. to ₤4 per acre; but in the vicinity of towns, where it is adaptable for vegetable gardens, the latter kind of property is worth ₤15 to ₤45 per acre."[3] The same decline had occurred in Edirne: "The value of rural property has been greatly reduced of late years, and the prices vary from ₤2 to ₤4 per acre in the country, and from ₤8 to ₤20 in the vicinity of towns, being as a rule one-fifth as much as the same lands 15 or 20 years ago."[4] In Macedonia, around 1900, land was selling at 50 piastres to ₤T3 per dönüm of 1,200 square meters (5:11). Even in 1908, in the cotton boom areas of Aydın and Adana provinces, land values were low: in Aydın "much of the land is purchasable at from ₤2 to ₤5 per acre" and in Adana "A few years ago large çiftliks changed hands at less than ₤1 per acre. More recently about ₤5 an acre has been asked for large areas on which cotton has been grown."[5] For 1914 a figure of ₤8 per acre for "good cotton land" has been given (5:16).

Few of the large estates were worked directly by the landlord, most being let on some share-cropping system or, less often, on payment of a fixed rent in kind or cash. In Erzurum in 1846, landlords furnished seed and took half the produce (V – 4). In Kurdistan in 1858, the rent equalled 15 to 20 percent of the annual produce (V – 6). In Rhodes in 1859, tenants paid "a fixed yearly rent in kind."[6] In Gelibolu in 1863 the tenant, who provided only his labor and that of his family, received half of net returns (i.e., after

deduction of seed and tithes and taxes) on poor land and one-third or less on good land
(Reply, FO 195/771). In Cavalla the tenant, who "does all the labour required except
ploughing" received half the crop after deduction of tithes (ibid.). In Izmit in 1863,
"the rent was equal to the quantity used for seed" (Reply to Questionnaire, FO 78/1419).
In the Dardanelles in 1870, cash rents were paid on large farms; in share-cropping, the
net produce, after deduction of seed and tithes (12.5 percent), was shared equally between
landlord and tenant, but "further south" the landlord took two-thirds; on small tracts the
amount paid for rent was equal to that used for seed (Reply FO 83/346). In the Mardin
region, under the muraba'a system, the "landowner supplies everything, but neither feeds,
clothes, or pays the Fellahs; but after deducting seed and all expenses, the net produce
is divided into thirds, of which the Fellahs--there are generally in this instance four to
one chift [see above]--would get one third, or Ł10.12s.7d. and the farmer or landlord two
thirds, or Ł20.5s.2d. (sic) after having deducted all expenses and tithe. Another practice
is for Fellahs to provide everything but seed, which is given by a capitalist in the town,
who is also obliged to make them a loan, to be repaid in money or kind at the harvest,
without interest, of 50 piastres for every keyl of wheat or barley they sow; the net produce is then shared equally, giving a sum of Ł18.13s. to the Fellah, and Ł14.4s. to the
capitalist." For cotton cultivation in the Diyarbekir area the owner of the land and water
received 14 percent of the net produce, the rest--after deduction of all expenses--being
shared equally by the capitalist who supplied the seed, the laborer who prepared the ground,
and the gardener who tended the plants.[7] In Edirne "the most common form of contract is
called 'ortaklik' (partnership), and is made for a short term, one year with a peasant,
and three to six years with a farmer. Whilst the proprietor furnishes land, cottage, and
seed, the cultivator provides labour, cattle, and implements. The annual produce, after
payment of tithes, is equally divided."[8] And in Ankara: "the 'outside' partner, who is
generally a wide-awake Greek or Armenian of the nearest town, undertakes to furnish, that
is to say, sell on credit, a pair of oxen valued at about Ł7.10s., and sometimes provisions
for maintaining the peasant and his family till harvest time, viz., 15 to 30 bushels of
wheat. He also advances Ł2 to Ł3 in cash, and supplies the necessary seed at the rate of
20 to 30 bushels per pair of oxen. The peasant, on his part, contributes land, labour,
and implements. In settling accounts at harvest time, the produce, after payment of tithes,
is equally divided. The seed supplied 'dies,' i.e. is not returned to the outside partner,
but the value of the other items is deducted from the cultivator's share. If the oxen lent
for ploughing are not returned, their estimated value has to be given."[9] And in Macedonia
around 1900, the landlord supplied seed and free lodging and took half the crop after deduction of tithe (5:11).

   Few figures are available on the value of gross or net output or for returns on capital in agriculture. In 1836, an Armenian tenant-farmer near Harput had the rather high
gross output of Ł142 on a farm of unspecified size (5:9). In Edirne in 1863, gross output
per dönüm (900 square yards) on a large farm was 38.5 piastres, or 7 shillings; smaller
farms were stated to have been "better cultivated and comparatively more productive" (5:10).
In 1864 near Mardin, the gross output of a çift on which four oxen worked was Ł54.12s. and
the net profits to the landlord, after deduction of all expenses and tithe, Ł28.9s.8d.;
near Diyarbekir gross output was Ł58.1s. and net profits Ł26.5s.[10] In 1865, a 5-acre tobacco farm worked by two families required an outlay of Ł17 by the landlord and Ł15 by the
peasants and, after payment of tithes, brought a profit of Ł80.10s.0d., which was shared
equally by landlord and peasants.[11] In Macedonia, around 1900, share-cropping is said to
have given the landlord a profit of 18-25 percent on his capital (5:11). In the cotton

areas of Aydın province in 1908, "600 piastres per hectare (about £2.5s. per acre) is a usual return for native cotton under primitive cultivation," but great variations existed; in Adana, with similar variations, it was usually "about 300 piastres per hectare (£1.2s. per acre) for native cotton" although with improved methods and American cotton it "should be very much greater."[12] These figures are high compared to the land values given above.

Lastly, some figures may be quoted on the price of what was by far the most important capital item, draught animals. These figures were provided in replies to two questionnaires, one in 1856, at the height of the rise in prices caused by the Crimean War (FO 78/1418 and 1419) and the other in 1863, when prices had fallen a little (FO 195/771). In addition, two earlier sets of prices may be quoted:

Western Anatolia, 1839	Ox up to 120 piastres, milch cow 40 to 100, camel 300 to 500, horse 100 to 1,000, donkey 50 (Vronchenko, 1:169-75).
Erzurum, 1846	Ox 500 piastres, buffalo 500 to 600, pack horse 40 to 500 (see 5:4).

Price of Draught Animals Used in Fieldwork, 1856

Diyarbekir, ordinary value	Ox 150 to 300, horse 600 to 1,000, mule 800 to 1,500, donkey 80 to 180, camel 700 to 1,000.
Diyarbekir, 1856	Horse 1,000 to 1,500, mule 900 to 1,800, camel 900 to 1,300.
Alexandria, 1856	Pack horse 600 to 2,000, good ox 1,200, good buffalo 1,200, good camel 1,500.
Jaffa, 1856	Good ox 900, donkey 300, good horse 1,500, good mule 1,500, good camel 1,000.
Mytilene, 1856	Ox 700, horse 800, mule 1,300, donkey 250.
Rhodes, 1856	Ox 300 to 600, horse 500 to 1,500, mule 500 to 1,500, donkey 50 to 800.
Varna, 1856	Ox £5 to 6, horse £5 to 10.
Aleppo, 1856	Ox £3 to 7, mule £8 to 20, donkey £2 to 10, camel £5 to 10.
Urfa, 1856	Ox 15s to £2-10, horse £8 to 80, mule £2 to 16, donkey 10s to £8, camel £3 to 8.
İskenderun, 1856	Ox £1-10 to 3, buffalo £4 to 6, mule £9 to 16, donkey £1 to 3.
Latakia, 1856	Ox £3 to 6, mule £12 to 15, donkey £3 to 4, camel £8.
Antep, 1856	Ox £3 to 4, mule £9, donkey £1 to 2, camel £7 to 8.
Maraş, 1856	Ox £1 to 2, mule £13 to 18, buffalo £3-10 to £5-10, donkey £1-10 to £3-10, camel £8 to 14.
Baghdad, 1856	Bullock 400 to 1,000, buffalo 600 to 750, mule 700 to 1,000, camel 400 to 600.

Price of Draught Animals Used in Fieldwork, 1863

Edirne	Horse £3-10 to 5-10
Salonica[a]	Horse £4 to 7
Gelibolu[a]	Ox £7 to 12
	Horse £3 to 7, mule £8 to 12
Rodosto	Horse 500 piastres
Istanbul[a]	Bullock and buffalo, £5 to 10
	Horse, mule £5 to 10
Jannina[a]	Ox £5 to 8
Dardanelles	Horse £2 to 4, mule £5 to 8
Izmir[a]	Pack horse £8 to 12, mule £10 to 15

Price of Draught Animals Used in Fieldwork, 1863 (continued)

Trabzon[a]	Pack horse ₤7, mule ₤12, donkey ₤3
Diyarbekir[b]	Horse 600 piastres, mule 1,000, camel 700, Donkey 100
Baghdad	Ox ₤3 to 10, horse ₤7 to 12
Basra[a]	Bullock 300 to 600 piastres; horse, mule 500 to 3,000
Cyprus[c]	Bullock ₤7-10 to 10, horse ₤4 to 6, mule ₤8 to 10

[a]Oxen, bullocks, or buffaloes used for fieldwork; horses, mules, camels, donkeys for transport.

[b]In spring, prices 20 percent above other times, at beginning of winter, cheaper; "when grain is dear, they fall 50 percent and rise in value as it becomes cheaper."

[c]Prices risen sharply because of cotton boom.

[d]Reply to questionnaire, FO 78/1419.

In conclusion, prices for land and draught animals may be compared with wages of farm laborers. The assumption of an average of 5.5 piastres a day (2:6) and a working year of 275 days[13] suggests an annual wage of 1,500 piastres. This sum could have brought several acres of land in most parts of the Empire and two to four draught animals, ratios very different from those prevailing in today's thickly populated underdeveloped countries.[14]

1. A and P 1865, vol. 53, "Diarbekir and Kurdistan."
2. Ibid. 1859, vol. 30, "Rhodes."
3. Ibid. 1895, vol. 100, "Angora."
4. Ibid. 1890, vol. 77, "Adrianople."
5. Dunstan, pp. 9, 12.
6. A and P 1859, vol. 30, "Rhodes."
7. Ibid., 1865, vol. 53, "Diarbekr and Kurdistan."
8. Ibid., 1890, vol. 77, "Adrianople."
9. Ibid., 1895, vol. 100, "Ankara."
10. Ibid., 1865, vol. 53, "Diarbekr and Kurdistan."
11. Farley, Turkey, p. 61.
12. Dunstan, pp. 10, 12; see also 5:22 for silk in Bursa in 1841 and 5:Introduction for roses in Edirne in 1867.
13. In the Izmir area the usual working year was only 260 days, because of religious holidays, but sometimes it reached 304--Kurmuş, p. 148.
14. It is worth noting that in Austria around 1700 the compensation for a dead mercenary was 20 thalers (₤5) and for a dead horse 40 thalers--Nicholas Henderson, Prince Eugen of Savoy (London, 1964), p. 62. In seventeenth century France "a man's daily wage was half a horse's"--Braudel, Capitalism, p. 246.

SELECTION 1. GRAIN PRODUCTION, 1790

Ainslie to Leeds, 22 January 1790

Constantinople 22nd January 1790

My Lord Duke

[Extract for the Committee of Council for Trade]

I was honored on the 12th instant, with your Grace's commands dated 24 November, and I lose no time in transmitting the most accurate answers I have been able to procure for the use of the Lords of the Committee of Privy Council for Trade.

Our last crop of grains say wheat in particular, barley, oats, indian corn, millet, lentils and rice, of which last much is raised in Romelia as well as Egypt, proved not only of good quality, but also abundant over all the Turkish Provinces, excepting only Part of Caramania and those Provinces of the European frontiers, where the cultivation has been more or less neglected by reason of the war, but upon the whole it is presumed was adequate to the consumption of this Empire for two years.

It cannot be doubted, notwithstanding most severe prohibition, that a considerable quantity of wheat, barley and lentils have been clandestinely exported to France and different parts of Italy from the Island of Cyprus and the coasts of Syria, Thessaly, Morea and Albania, and yet the stock of grains remaining in the country is more than sufficient for the consumption of its inhabitants for twelve months to come, nay in some provinces, viz., Mesopotamia, Armenia, and all the interiour parts of Anatolia at a distance from the sea, the best wheat flour sells from a penny to a farthing sterling the English pound.

In case of a real scarcity in the country, which has not happened during my long residence, it is probable that Government would apply for assistance to the coast of Africa, and the merchants to Poland and Hungary, failing of which last (on account of the war) to Great Britain and the Baltick. All sorts of grain are subjected to restriction in their sale by this government, wheat in particular is monopolized by the state who draws a very great income therefrom. The former must all be brought to the publick markets allotted for them and wheat can be disposed of only to the Capan or publick granary, where the contributions of the Maritime Provinces paid in kind are collected at something under two shillings sterling the killo, weighing about sixty pounds English, exclusive of charges in bringing hither. The value of all sorts of grain is fixed by Government, but they bear a higher price in private sale according to its quality, and the demand for different parts distinct from the capital.

The present price given for grain at the public granaries, wheat, the Killo weighing from 55 to 60 lb. English, shillings 5.2 1/2d. Barley. . . . ditto. . . . 48 to 50 lb. . . . 3 . . . and they are sold out again to the bakers, the same measure of wheat at shillings 8 and 2d, ditto. . . . barley. . . . 4 and 1 1/2d, who are permitted to gain about ten p cent from the publick, but commonly mix the wheat flower even with all others of inferiour prices, to increase their profits. The Killo of Carolina rice, weighing in circa lb. English, sells for shillings 4.3 1/4 and that from Egypt about 20 p cent higher. Indian corn and millet, shillings 1.6d. the 60 lb. Lentils, shillings 3 and 6d. the measure of 30lb.

In time of peace no country can I presume furnish grain so cheap as the principalities of Moldavia and Valachia, and the sea coasts of Anatolia (bordering on the Black Sea) from whence this capital is chiefly provided. Wheat in those parts is often sold at one shilling the Killo of sixty pounds English and bartered at half that price. Your Grace will please to observe that all the above evaluations is at the present high rate of exchange which has risen fifteen p. cent by the degradation of the species and all the necessaries of life been increased in the same proportion. . . .

GRAIN PRODUCTION

Very few figures are available on grain production in the first three quarters of the nineteenth century, but some general observations may be made. First, by far the greater part of the cultivated area was sown to cereals, mainly wheat and barley (5:Introduction). Secondly, methods of cultivation remained primitive and unchanged, though there were some minor improvements in the European and Aegean provinces. Thirdly, as the preceding selection shows, the Empire as a whole was usually a net exporter of grain, but it had to import, from various and sometimes distant sources, when crops were poor; this changed later, and in the years preceding the First World War it was a net importer of grain and flour.[1] Fourthly, owing to the very high cost of land transport (4:12), demand and supply conditions and hence prices differed greatly in places which were quite close, and glut and acute shortage often coexisted in contiguous provinces. In seaports and adjacent areas price fluctuations were relatively small, since surpluses or deficiencies could easily be met by shipping grain, but in the interior they were very sharp (5:2 and 7:1).

Illustrations of responsiveness to fluctuations in world demand and prices by grain markets on or near the coast are provided by Edirne and Salonica in the 1830s-40s. The size and price of the main crops in "this neighbourhood" were estimated as follows by the British consul in Edirne (Kerr to Palmerston, 13 January 1836, FO 78/290, and 6 January 1837, FO 78/314), the 1835 harvest being described as "an unusually abundant one."

The surplus was earmarked for Istanbul but in fact there was much smuggling out of the country "with the connivance frequently of the very persons appointed to prevent it." Nevertheless this restriction caused many people "to leave large tracts of country uncultivated" and rear sheep, whose very fine wool ("eagerly bought up for France and England") paid them better than grain. In 1837 the rice harvest was unusually abundant, 45,000 cwt., and the price fell to 14/9 (Agricultural Report, 9 January 1838, FO 78/335).

| | 1835 | | 1836 | |
	Output (000 quarters)	Price (shillings)	Output (000 quarters)	Price (shillings)
Wheat	250	10	180	15
Barley	180	5	120	6
Rice	45[a]	12[b]	36[a]	18[b]
Flour	..	4[b]	..	5[b]

[a] thousands of hundredweight

[b] per hundredweight

Eight years later, in January 1844, the price of wheat was 14/6 a quarter, of barley 6/-, of rye 6/- and of maize 15/- and that of flour 5/6 per cwt. (10 January 1844, FO 78/580). In July 1845, wheat stood at 13/- a quarter, but the news of the potato famine in Ireland and the expectation that the United Kingdom would open its ports to grain imports sent it as high as 22/- to 24/-. The government forbade exports, in order to ensure the supply of Istanbul, but this had little effect on prices, which in January 1846 were: wheat 20/6, rye 13/9, barley 12/4, maize 18/6, and rice and flour 9/6 and 6/11 per cwt., respectively (Willshire to Aberdeen, 20 January 1846, FO 78/651). It may be noted that in Istanbul, too, the price of grain, especially maize, rose in 1846 because of "extensive orders from England" (Memorandum of 31 December 1846, FO 78/699).[2]

In Salonica the consul, in 1846, reported improved methods of cultivation. More attention was being paid to seeds--"in many instances choice seed has been procured from some of the ports in the Black Sea"--and "the winnowing machines introduced have so improved the quality of all kinds of grain exported from Salonica, but particularly wheat, that it is now demanded for the Italian ports, where it was formerly barely saleable" (Report on Trade, FO 78/700). In 1851, the same point is made: "the farmers pay more attention to their seed, and a better kind of grain is produced; this observation is more particularly applicable to maize, which produce from these districts was very recently but little esteemed in the British markets; now, however, it commands a price nearly equal with the maize from the Black Sea" (ibid., FO 78/903).

For the forty years preceding the First World War much more data are available. The grain output of the whole Empire rose by about a third between 1888 and the average year 1913, in spite of the shrinkage of territory; this is confirmed by the fact that the yield of tithes--which included other crops whose output rose faster than grain--increased by 51 percent between those dates.[3]

For Anatolia, the results of Dr. Quataert's painstaking research may be summarized.[4] In the absence of figures on quantity, the volume of cereals exports was calculated by deflating the value of those exports from the four major Anatolian ports[5] by a weighted price index and adding to them the quantities carried by the Anatolian railway. The value of cereals exports rose from an annual average of £523,000 in 1876 to £1,246,000 in 1891-95 and thereafter declined to around £1,000,000 until 1906. The overall increase was achieved in spite of a sharp fall in prices: a composite index of Istanbul cereal prices (1901-5 = 100) dropped from 125 in 1876-80 to 88 in 1891-95, a fall in line with world prices, but then rose much faster than the world price to 129 in 1906-8. The derived quantity of exports of grain from the four ports increased from 87,000 tons in 1876-80 to 287,000 in 1891-95, after which it declined to 203,000 in 1901-5. The quantity carried on the Anatolian railroad rose from 36,000 tons in 1891-95 to 314,000 in 1901-5 and stood at 248,000 in 1906-7. There is every reason to believe that the grain carried on the rail-roads came from increased cultivation in the Ankara, Konya, and other areas along the lines. Adding railway shipments to exports by sea shows a sixfold increase between 1876-80 and 1901-5. This leads Quataert to "suggest that the production of cereals in Anatolia rose at least fivefold during the period 1876-1908." This seems greatly exaggerated: an increase in exports, or in the marketed surplus, implies a far smaller proportionate in-crease in production; and the 500,000 tons shipped by sea or rail in 1901-5 should be com-pared with a rough estimate of nearly 7 million tons of grain output in Anatolia in 1913-14 and 3 million tons of wheat production and consumption.[6]

Finally, for the regional breakdown of grain production the reader is referred to two lists: one for 1890, based on the information on wheat output available in Cuinet's book[7] and the other for 1910,[8] showing tithes collected from the various provinces of the Empire --and it may be taken that in most of them grain supplied the greater part of tithes. The first list, which is incomplete, shows that the major wheat-producing districts in 1890 were the Eastern ones--Diyarbekir, Elazığ, Malatya, Urfa--followed by the Central ones--Sıvas, Ankara, and Konya, which later became far larger producers.

1. Tables in Aybar, pp. 51 and 60.
2. In Samsun in 1841 wheat was purchased in the interior at 13 piastres a kile; transport cost 4 piastres and other expenses, brokerage, and duties raised the f.o.b. price to 17 piastres, or 30/10 a quarter; in "former years" the price in the interior had been 10 piastres. For barley, the purchase prices were 5 and 4 piastres, respectively, and transport and other costs about equal to those of wheat (Trade of Samsun, FO 78/443).
3. Eldem, pp. 75-82; total grain output was put at about 8 million tons in 1913-14 and 10 million in 1914-15.
4. Quataert, pp. 186-216 and 379-90.
5. Izmir "attracted cereals from areas around Konya and as far east as Ankara," in addition to its own hinterland; Samsun "exported cereals from the Yozgat and Sıvas regions while Adana exported the produce of the Çukurova plain and parts of the Kayseri and Konya regions." Trabzon's exports of cereals were very small.
6. Eldem (pp. 72-73) puts grain output within Turkey's present borders at 7,361,000 tons in 1913-14, wheat production at 3,687,000 tons, and wheat consumption at 3,971,000 tons. On the other hand, Quataert (p. 456) is surely right in criticizing Novichev (EHME, pp. 66-70) for stating that in 1899-1912 wheat production declined; the choice of dates is misleading, for by 1899 "a substantial proportion of the increases in cereal cultivation had already occurred. In addition, it is likely that during 1912 . . . large numbers of Anatolian cultivators were serving in the military during the Balkan Wars." Quataert (pp. 209-10) also points out that 1876-80 was a very unfavorable period (5: Introduction).
7. Osmanlı Imparatorluğunda XIX Yüzyılın Sonunda Üretim ve Dış Ticaret (Ankara, 1970), p. 4.
8. Eldem, pp. 86-87.

SELECTION 2. DROUGHT AND SCARCITY OF GRAIN IN ANATOLIA, 1845

Chabert to Stürmer, 26 November 1845, HHS, Türkei, V-1-2, Smyrna--original in Italian

The prohibition on exports of grain from Anatolia published last summer by the Otto-man Porte has been maintained by the Turkish authorities in the various ports of Asia Minor. In spite of the researches made by me, I have had no knowledge of exceptional licenses being granted to speculators. The shipping out of cereals has been stopped not only in Smyrna but also in Scalanuova [Kuş-adası], Satalia, and the other ports of Asia Minor. In the first few days after the publication of the prohibition, a few contrary at-tempts were made by some foreign speculators, but the goods clandestinely exported amounted to only a small amount, since a few weeks after the prohibition new orders were issued from the capital forbidding any shipment of grain. And indeed such rigor was indispensable, since this year's crop failed in Anatolia because of the general drought. Even the city of Konya has requested from Constantinople an aid of 5,000 kantars of flour; the drought has also been felt in Syria, Cyprus, and Crete. Water was also almost everywhere insuffi-cient for the mills, hence Smyrna took about 800 bags of flour from Trieste, an unpreced-ented event till now.
The price of grain has risen this year from 18-22 piasters to 23-27 piasters per kilo, measure of Constantinople, and it is feared that it may go up to 30 piasters, since the

new crop is still far off. The vegetable, haricot bean, and broad bean crops have also been poor and their price has appreciably increased. Anatolia, and particularly the city of Smyrna, would have experienced great shortage if exports abroad had been allowed and if it had not been able to draw on the resources of European Turkey and Russia. This year Rumelia produced a large quantity of wheat, maize, and barley, and a considerable amount has come here by sea, especially from Gallipoli, the Gulf of Orfano, and Salonica. The last named has also been able to continue exporting to the European countries, especially Trieste and Genoa, but the demand has raised prices in Salonica by about 25 percent in the last month. From Russia, several cargoes have arrived, part being consumed locally and part re-exported; in the present season shipments from the Sea of Azov have stopped and the cereals of Odessa are demanded in Europe, to which they are directly sent. At present there is in Smyrna a stock of about 15,000 kilos of grain from Russia (Odessa and Taganrog) and Galatz. There are also about 20,000 kilos of Anatolian grain, designed for local consumption, and new consignments are arriving from the interior.

In Crete, Rhodes, Beirut, etc. Rumelian grain is also in demand, for exports from there arenot prohibited, and even those from Asia Minor are prohibited only if destined for foreign countries, and not for other Ottoman provinces.

A few days ago, the English house of Routh tried to export a cargo of 12,000 kilos of grain from the port of Melemen [Menemen], but the heads of corporations in Smyrna objected and that house was prevented from shipping the cargo and had to transport it to Smyrna and sell it there for local consumption.

From this it is clear that speculators have not been able to get around the prohibition, in spite of the great demand that has made itself felt this year in Hamburg and also in London for the needs of Ireland, partly because of the potato failure. In Italy, the crop is one-third below average. . . .

GRAIN YIELDS

Official returns of the main crops show that, in an area closely corresponding to that of the Republic, wheat yields averaged 1.28 metric tons per hectare, barley 1.42, and rye 1.65 in 1913 and 1.66, 1.38, and 1.29, respectively, in 1914.[1] The figures are of doubtful accuracy and may be compared with the more reliable ones for 1934-38: wheat 0.99 tons, barley 1.09, and rye 0.96.[2]

For the period under review, the scanty data on yields are almost always in the form of the return on seed, as in selection 3. Further information gathered from various British consular reports is shown in the table below. The 1836 figures are from the report of James Brant on his tour through Armenia and Asia Minor and seem to be too high.

If we disregard the 1836 figures, wheat seems in average seasons to have given a five- to six-fold return on seed, a reasonable figure; yield per acre seems to have been a little over 30 bushels (or about 2 tons per hectare) in the European provinces--a surprisingly high figure, unless very thick sowing be assumed--and less than half that amount in Ankara.[3] The data are too scanty and unreliable to show a trend, but it seems highly probable that no significant change occurred.

These yields may be compared with figures for other countries and periods. In Roman Italy a fourfold yield, equivalent to 9 bushels per acre, was regarded as normal.[4] In Europe, yields rose from 3- to 4-fold in the Middle Ages to around 6 in the eighteenth century, or about 700 kilograms per hectare, but were higher in The Netherlands and England. It was not until the nineteenth century that British wheat yields exceeded 30 bushels an acre.[5] In Austria in the eighteenth century, a 3- to 5-fold yield prevailed[6] and in Russia, in 1800-1870, the average was 3.5 or about 500 kilograms per hectare.[7] In China in the 1920s, unmodernized agriculture yielded 14 bushels per acre.[8] In the fertile and irrigated soil of Egypt, wheat yielded about 15-fold, or 2,300 hectolitres per hectare, around 1800, 16 bushels an acre around 1880, and 30 around 1900.[9]

In the light of these figures, the yields per acre shown in the table, if correct, show a surprisingly high level of output.

Year	Place	Return on Seed			Yield Per Acre (bushels)			Source
		Wheat	Barley	Rye	Wheat	Barley	Rye	
1836	Erzurum, mountains	6-8	..	..	..	..	..	FO 78/289
1836	Erzurum, plains	12-15	..	..	..	..	..	FO 78/289
1836	Harput, poor land	6-8	..	..	..	..	..	FO 78/289
1836	Harput, good land	12-16	..	..	..	..	..	FO 78/289
1836	Tokat, bad land	7-8	..	..	..	..	..	FO 78/289
1836	Tokat, good land	10-12	..	..	..	..	..	FO 78/289
1836	Arapkir	12	..	..	..	..	..	FO 78/289
1836	Ulaş	10-12	..	..	..	..	..	FO 78/289
1836	Arganeh	16	..	..	..	..	..	FO 78/289
1846	Erzurum	5	6-7	4	..	..	..	FO 78/703
1862	Edirne, large farm	6	10	10	32	..	..	Selection 5:10
1863	Diyarbekir	5	5	..	..	..	..	A&P 1863-53
1887	Philippopolis	6	..	..	32	..	..	A&P 1888-103
1889	Edirne	6-10	12-18	8-10	24-40	..	..	A&P 1890-77
1894	Ankara, average	5	..	..	10-15	..	..	A&P 1895-100
1894	Ankara, favorable soils, good seasons	15	35	..	30-45	..	..	A&P 1895-100

1. Eldem, p. 75.
2. FAO, Yearbook, 1950; in the two villages studied by Stirling (p. 44) wheat yields were about 5 to 1 (1 ton per hectare) in one and slightly higher in the other; in Diyarbekir in the 1960s "a yield of five to tenfold is considered to be normal," or 1 to 1.3 tons of wheat per hectare--Yalman, p. 192.
3. These figures may be compared with the following for European Turkey: "Eight times is considered an average crop, ten times good, and twelve times very good, but I have had fourteen times the seed from rye. About three bushels of wheat are sown to the acre, two and a half bushels of rye, four bushels of barley and four bushels of oats" (Barker, p. 407).
4. Cambridge Economic History of Europe, 2d ed. (Cambridge, 1971), 1:104, 125; M. I. Finley, The Ancient Economy (London, 1973), p. 83.
5. Braudel, Capitalism, pp. 78-82; Eric Kerridge, The Agricultural Revolution (London, 1967), pp. 329-31.
6. Ernst Wangermann, The Austrian Achievement, 1700-1800 (London, 1973), p. 24.
7. P. Lyashchenko, History of the National Economy of Russia (New York, 1949), p. 324.
8. Mark Elvin, The Pattern of the Chinese Past (London, 1973), pp. 307-8.
9. EHME, p. 377; P. O'Brien in P. M. Holt, ed., Political and Social Change in Modern Egypt (London, 1968), p. 169.

SELECTION 3. GRAIN CULTIVATION IN ANATOLIA, 1860s

P. de Tchihatchef, Klein Asien (Leipzig, 1887), pp. 66-68

. . . The growing of cereals, and hence cultivation in general, is unfortunately--with a few local exceptions for maize--rather neglected in the peninsula. Leaving aside the rude agricultural instruments, which often recall primitive times, hardly a quarter of the productive land is put under cultivation; yet where a relatively high degree of development has been reached, namely, in the western and central parts of the peninsula, the unmanured soil yields ten to twenty times the amount of seed-corn. This is, for example, the situation in Ankara, where the land is planted to summer wheat in May and winter wheat in December, is never manured but only left fallow after two years, and produces fourteen grains for one. In Sivas, whose climate is unfavorable not only for vine but also for tobacco growing, in good years fifteen to twenty grains are yielded for one, particularly when the soil is properly fertilized with sheep manure; rye costs there 20 paras an oke (about 25 centimes per kilogram) and barley 10 paras an oke. In the neighborhood of Tokat, where the soil is manured, grain yields 10- to 15-fold. In the Meander valley winter wheat, which is usually sown in December, yields 15- to 20-fold; the same applies to the Kaikus valley (Bakur-çay) and although only part of it is under cultivation it exports, through the two ports of Aivali and Çanderlik, some 800,000 kilograms a year to Trieste, Genoa, and Marseilles. In Samsun the soil, which is not manured but left fallow for two years after each crop, yields 15 to 20 grains for one. The beautiful, large plain of Çukurova in Cilicia, which stretches from Tarsus to Adana, yields without manure 30 and even 60 grains. In the province of Canik, where the soil is likewise not manured but left fallow for two years, wheat, rye, and barley yield 20- to 30-fold and Turkish wheat has reached such a degree of development there that I have often seen stalks with two ears of corn, each of which bore 300-350 grains. Lastly, the districts (sancak) of Amasiya, Merzifan, Zille, Çorum, Tahova, and Bozok send some 5 million kilograms of wheat and 2 million kilograms of barley to Istanbul.

These examples, to which I could easily have added, show sufficiently what brilliant results could be achieved by agriculture in Asia Minor, particularly if it be noted that the localities mentioned by me should not be regarded as exceptional. For among the considerable wastelands there are some that fulfil all the conditions required to crown the farmer's efforts with extraordinary success. To give only one example, which I will take from the neighborhood of Istanbul itself, there is the beautiful plain between Adapazar and Sukumeni (Bithynia) which stretches about 10 kilometers from east to west and about as many from north to south. It consists of black, rich humus and could easily be converted into large, luxuriant fields of grain and yet--at least when I last saw it, in 1869--it is a waste. Similar examples meet us at every step in the interior of the peninsula, where among the deserted, untilled areas one finds others whose soil consists of pulverised volcanic rocks like trachyte, dolerite, basalt, etc. which contain all the minerals required for the growth of cereals.

We have numerous and telling historical evidence that all these deserted lands were once fully cultivated and that, consequently, not only in Greek and Roman times but also under the Byzantine Empire Asia Minor, like Sicily, was considered to be an inexhaustible granary. . . .

SELECTION 4. FARMING IN ERZURUM, 1846

Henry Calvert, "Notes on the . . . Pashalik of Erzeroom," 1846, FO 78/703

The agricultural products of this Province consist principally of wheat, barley, rye, lucerne of two qualities, linseed and vetches; besides small quantitites of lentils, peas, beans, millet, and hemp.

Wheat and barley are sown as early in the spring after the disappearance of the snow, as the dryness of the ground will admit of; this occurs sometimes about the middle of April, but frequently not until the end of May. Wheat is likewise partially sown in autumn, but as this practice is attended with the risk of the crops rotting from a protracted damp spring, it is not general. Rye is always sown in autumn; and barley, in spring. The grains are all sown broadcast; the sower precedes the plough, scattering over the field the seed, which is then ploughed in; after that, a heavy beam, on which the driver stands, is drawn transversely over the field, to break the clods and level the ground.

The plough is of simple construction and is managed by a single labourer, who dexterously guides his oxen with a long slender stick. To increase the depth of the furrow, the yoke is shifted towards the extremity of the beam, which causes the point of the share to depress more vertically into the soil.

The fields are not enclosed with hedges or palings, but occasionally they are surrounded by a ditch. They are usually left fallow every other year, the system of a rotation of crops being unknown.

Barley fields are often manured with the ashes of dung that has served as fuel, as well as with those of reeds and rushes, after they have been used in heating the public baths. The manure is either strewn over the field and then ploughed in, or else thrown gradually into the rills of water with which the land is irrigated. The soil is never manured for wheat. The usual produce of these grains is as follows:

Wheat (average crop) 5 fold: (good crops) 9 to 10;
Barley (do.) 6 to 7 do.   (do.)   12
Rye (do.) 4 do.   (do.)   6 to 7

The relative proportion between the quantity of wheat and barley sown on the same extent of land, is 8 parts of the latter, to 5 of the former.

Grain sown here in the spring, by reason of the heat, vegetates so rapidly, that when accompanied by drought, the ears are formed while the straw is yet short. In many instances it does not exceed the height of 18 inches.

There are four qualities of wheat cultivated in this province; namely,
Topbash boogdai ("Round-headed wheat")
Bearded hard red wheat. This quality is the most extensively sown of all.
Kiltchiksiz boogdai ("Beardless wheat")
Beardless hard white wheat. Not much sown. Ripens early in the season. The flour made from it is very white.

Kizzil boogdai ("Red wheat")
      Bearded soft red wheat.   Often mixed with the ak boogdai.
Ak boogdai ("White wheat")
      Bearded soft red wheat; called white, from its being a shade lighter than the Kizzil boogdai.
      The harvest commences about the middle of August, but as the ripening of the grain depends materially on the position of the fields, some crops are often not gathered in before the beginning of October. After the sheaves have remained a short time stacked in the fields, they are conveyed in carts to the harman, a circular threshing floor, where they are spread out, and the grain is separated from the straw by being trodden on by cattle, which are made to drag thick boards studded underneath with sharp flints. The drivers stand upright on these planks, and by repeatedly guiding the cattle in every direction over the floor, the straw is cut up into short lengths, and is then in a state to be used as forage. The threshing floor is in the open air, the corner of a field, or a level piece of turf, being prepared for that purpose. Thus exposed, it is of course liable to injury from rain and damp; but on the plain of Passin, the villagers are most provident, and perform this labour under shelter. This mode of treading out grain is, I believe, practised all over the East, and the mosaical law of not muzzling the oxen is still adhered to. The winnowing is effected by tossing the grain in the air; and as this is done in the immediate vicinity of the threshing floor, the cattle employed are often blinded by the minute particles of chaff and dust.
      Bread is made in this country by rolling out the dough into thin sheets, and either baking it in an oven, or else applying it to the internal sides of a large circular earthen vessel, called a tandoor, buried in the floor and previously heated by fuel placed within it.
      Lucerne is mown in the middle or end of June, and again in September; but, unless the first crop be early and the summer showery, the second is not at all abundant. When first sown, the seed is mixed with wheat, which the natives suppose causes the lucerne to take firmer root. The next year the soil is lightly harrowed, and more lucerne seed sown, until the plants become sufficiently thick. A field of this forage lasts about fifteen years, after which time it requires to be renewed.
      Linseed and Hemp are exclusively grown for their oil, and are chiefly produced on the Passin plain. Compression is used to extract the oil.
      The vetches are ground, and given to cattle in the shape of meal.
      According to the quality of the soil and its position, the value of land varies from 500 to 2,500 piastres (£5 to 25) for an extent about 200 paces long by 100 broad, which, it is calculated, will exactly require a somar [9 7/8 bushels] of barley to sow it. Where water exists for irrigation, a certain right of using it, is attached to each field, and is sold with it. These privileges were formerly granted to landed proprietors in proportion to the influence enjoyed by the then owners, and have not been altered since. The most favored fields are watered once every ten days, others less so, once a fortnight or three weeks.
      These water-rights are all legalised at the Mehkemeh, or Court of Justice, and in case of dispute, the register is consulted.
      The most usual way with landed proprietors who do not cultivate their grounds is to furnish seed to the poorer peasants, who undertake all the agricultural labour, on condition of receiving half the produce of the harvest.
      Before the Armenian emigration of 1829, the plains of Erzeroom and Passin were more extensively cultivated than they now are; but as the present produce of the land is more than sufficient for local consumption, and as there are no carriageable roads to cheapen the means of transport to neighbouring provinces, or to the sea coast, it is easy to believe that the peasantry have little inducement to bring more land into cultivation. It has occasionally happened that adjoining Pashaliks have suffered from scarcity, and though the harvest of this province was unusually abundant, no supplies of grain could be sent to the distressed districts, for the reasons above given: exportations can only be made when famine prices exist.
      On an inspection of the map herewith, it will be observed that extensive marshes occupy the Eastern extremity of the plain of Erzeroom. This tract can, however, hardly be considered as waste land, for it produces vast quantities of various kinds of reeds, rushes and coarse grass, which require no care and are a source of profit to the husbandman. Some species of these products afford a good fodder for cattle and sheep during the winter; others, that are not relished by these animals, are either made into mats, twisted into haybands, or used for roofing houses, and for heating baths. If the marshes be overfilled in spring, and the time for mowing the reeds and rushes approaches, without the water having sufficiently subsided, it is customary for the villagers to collect large herds of buffaloes, and drive them through certain parts of the marsh, and by this means, the water, which had been impeded from flowing, by the accumulation of weeds and decayed vegetable matter, is afforded an outlet, and in a few days the ground is drained, but in many places this mode is impracticable, the mud and water being so deep that the mowing can only be done when the water is frozen.

Part of the town of Erzeroom, is surrounded by kitchen gardens, cultivated with considerable neatness by gardeners who come every spring from the vallies beyond Tortoom, and return to their homes on the approach of winter. These vegetable gardens usually produce lettuces, cabbages, parsley, tarragon, Jerusalem artichokes, spinach, mustard, and potatoes. Besides these vegetables, the following are sown in fields in larger quantities: turnips, beetroot, common and French beans, peas, chickpeas, coarse carrots, onions, pumpkins, and cucumbers. When the autumnal frosts set in, the edible roots are buried deep in the ground, from whence they are dug out as they are required. Turnips are sown in considerable quantities in the autumn, after the corn has been reaped. A few are also sown in the spring. Erzeroom receives its supplies of fruit from Erzinghian and Tortoom; this climate being too cold to produce any.

After the fields are sown, the peasants occupy themselves and their oxen in bringing native soda, rock salt, and wood, to town; birch and dwarf oak are obtained from the mountains in the neighbourhood of Ashkala, and pine from the Soghanlee Dagh near Kars. The pine is brought in the shape of beams, which are sometimes so large as to require two pair of oxen or buffaloes to drag them. The forward extremity of the beam is connected to the yoke by means of strong thongs of raw hide or iron chains, and the hinder end is supported on a stout axle and wheels, constructed by the woodcutters, and being only intended to last as far as Erzeroom, they are very rudely made, and without any iron fastenings. They are sold with the timber, and are broken up for fuel. Deal boards and shovels are also brought from the Soghanlee Dagh on carts of somewhat similar construction.

Charcoal is made in this neighbourhood; it is not much consumed for culinary purposes, except by a few rich Turkish families, its principal use being for smiths' forges, and as fuel for braziers to warm apartments.

The carts used for agricultural purposes are of substantial build. The wheels are made of stout solid deal planks, bound together by iron tires. A full-sized pair is worth about 500 piastres (£5). The axle, which is likewise strong, passes under the body of the cart, and turns with the wheels, grease being used to diminish friction; and when the axle wears out, it is replaced by a new one; thus, a pair of wheels is made to last a long time. These carts are drawn by a pair of buffaloes or oxen, and being low, and the wheels far apart, they can go over very uneven ground without upsetting.

Sledges of most primitive construction and drawn by a single ox between shafts, have lately been in use during the winter, generally bringing grain from Kars. They are however as yet only partially adopted, the peasants being peculiarly averse to deviating from the customs of their forefathers. . . .

The prices of domestic animals are as follows:
Buffaloes, fit for labour (at 3 years old) each p.500 to 600 (£5 to 6)
Oxen   do.   do.   p.500   (£5)
Milch Cows   p.100 to 150 (£1 to £1.10)
Horses for burden p.400 to 500 (£4 to 5)
Mules p.500 to 600 (£5 to 6)
Asses p.20 to p.500 (4s/- to £5)
Sheep p.45 to 50 (9s/- to 10s/-)
Goats p.30 to 35 (6s/- to 7s/-)

The poorer classes of peasantry live chiefly on milk diet, and occasionally on preserved meats called pastoorma and kavoorma. Pastoorma is prepared by curing beef with a mixture of salt, pepper, garlic and other ingredients, and then drying it in the sun. Kavoorma is mutton or beef, cut into small pieces, fried. . . .

Although there has been material decline, rates are still far above an average in times of but ordinary plenty:

	Wheat			Barley		
	Per Constantinople		Per Imperial	Per Constantinople		Per Imperial
	Kilo	=	Quarter	Kilo	=	Quarter
In 1844	p. 7 1/3	=	10s/7d.	p. 4 1/6	=	6s/1d.
1845	p. 20	=	29s/6d.	p. 12	=	17s/7d.
1846	p. 11	=	16s/-	p. 6	=	8s/9d.

Hitherto appearances have been most promising for agricultural prospects next season, and should these be realised, trade will improve and the country revive from the deplorable distress that has prevailed for nearly two years past. . . .

SELECTION 5. AGRICULTURE IN KURDISTAN, 1908

Memorandum by W. B. Heard on Agriculture in Kurdistan, 1908, FO 368/229

. . . Very fine soil is to be found south of the Karaja Dagh and Jebel Tor ranges, which mark the boundary between Kurdistan and Mesopotamia.

In general it may be said that the country is much under-cultivated and should produce vastly more than it does at present. The reasons for this deficiency, briefly stated, are, the general insecurity, the want of export facilities, and the sparseness of the agricultural population. Many of the most fertile regions which fringe the northern extremity of the great Mesopotamian plain are left entirely untilled owing to the lawlessness of the roaming tribes of Kurds and Arabs, whilst many other districts, owing to Government maladministration, are being gradually deserted by their inhabitants. Agriculture, then, cannot be regarded as very flourishing in Kurdistan, though much of the country is potentially productive. Innumerable streams, which, starting in the central highlands, flow down to meet the Tigris and Euphrates, cross the plains in every direction, and supply abundance of water.

The soil too, is generally rich and productive whilst the climate leaves little to be desired from the farmer's point of view. Little, however, is done to profit by these natural advantages. Agricultural methods are extremely primitive, the people are ignorant, unenterprising, and for the most part lazy, and such soil as is tilled does not yield anything like the return which it might be made to give if properly cultivated.

On the enclosed map an attempt is made to indicate the most fertile districts and to distinguish between the cultivated and uncultivated areas.

The Diarbekir Vilayet may at present be called the granary of Kurdistan. When the harvest in Mosul or Baghdad is short, those provinces draw on Diarbekir to make good the deficiency, and it is believed that ŁT100,000 is not too high an estimate for the value of the grain surplus which Diarbekir, in average years, is able to spare for export. When corn is not required elsewhere it is stored in underground granaries. In 1907 some ŁT30,000 worth of corn was exported to Bitlis and Van, where great dearth exists, in spite of the heavy transport charges which double the price of corn when brought to these markets, and it is probable that a still greater amount will be exported thither during the present year.

The following are the chief agricultural products of Diarbekir.

Wheat. Sown from September to December (a small quantity in spring) reaped during June and July. Stored by end of September.

Barley. Sown from November to end of February. Reaped before the wheat.

Millet. (white and red) Sown in March. Reaped in July. (This cereal is much in favour with the Kurds, as it requires little labour and gives quick returns. It is also taking the place of corn in some of the richest agricultural districts in the Bitlis Vilayet, where the population has grown too poor to afford seed corn.)

Rice. Sown in March. Reaped in September and October. Grown chiefly in Silivan and Bisheri and on the Ambar Chai.

Tobacco. Grown in Sewerek and Silivan.

Cotton. Sown from March till May. Gathered in September and October. Chermuk produces most cotton. Some is also grown in the Silivan, Bisheri and Redvan districts, which have black soil and abundant water. A good deal is also grown in Kharput. Probably large areas are suitable for cotton-growing, but the population is too indolent for this culture, which requires much care, and in general it grows only enough for its own needs.

Sesame is grown and reaped with the cotton.

In the uplands of Bitlis and Mush the harvest is about a month later than in Diarbekir.

Prices (1907) per "eulchek" [ölçek] (about 38 lbs.).

Wheat sl/6-sl/10 (average years 10d-sl/4) in Diarbekir. In Bitlis and Mush from 20 piastres (s3/4) upwards. In Van slightly higher. In Kharput s2/4-s2/8 (in average years about the same as in Diarbekir).

Barley 11d-sl/1 (average years 5d-6d) in Diarbekir. In Bitlis s2/8.

Cotton per batman (17 lbs.) s6/8 in Diarbekir.

Rice (per batman) 2/-2/4.

Prices for grain were high during the past year in Diarbekir, owing to large export to famine stricken districts.

Agricultural methods

Ploughs require 2 yoke of oxen or buffaloes, each yoke working for one spell of 4 hours per day. The oxen are weak and undersized and draw a lighter plough than the more powerful buffaloes. The plough-share is of the primitive arrow-headed shape and cuts a furrow of from 8 in. to 1 foot. In some Provinces a big heavy plough, drawn by several yoke is used for turning hard soil that has lain fallow for long.

The soil is cross-ploughed from 3 to 7 times. Seed is sown broadcast and then ploughed into the soil.

Harrowing is unknown (except for cotton).

Manure is not used in Diarbekir (except for water-melon growing). In Kharput, stable manure and human excreta are extensively employed. Crops are reaped with sickles. It is said that one man can reap 1 Kile (5-6 cwt.) in 10-12 days.

The corn is trodden out by oxen. Flails and threshing machines are unknown. 10 kile are trodden out by 8-10 oxen working 16 hours per day in 4 to 5 days.

In most districts rough ox-carts are used to carry the corn to the threshing floors. In Diarbekir, however, there are no ox-carts, and the corn is carried by animals.

Winnowers of local manufacture are used in many districts, though not in Diarbekir. The corn is ground in water-mills, and the flour is of indifferent quality. It is husked

by a mill-stone revolving on its edge in a circular groove, and worked by horse-power.
Corn-crushers, of local manufacture, introduced some 5 or 6 years ago, are now made in
Kharput and Diarbekir.

In Diarbekir the land lies fallow for two years and is ploughed in the third. In
Kharput it is tilled every year and crops are grown in the following rotation: corn, barley, cotton. Under existing conditions the best land gives a return of 6-10.

The only attempt made at irrigation consists in leading shallow channels from the
nearest stream over the fields, where the lie of the land permits it. Any system of dams,
whereby water may be stored up for the dry months, is unknown. Water-wheels are nonexistent.

In short, agricultural methods in Kurdistan are such as one might expect from a people
on a very low plane of civilization. It is probable, however, that though utterly incapable
of introducing any improvement into existing methods on their own initiative, they would
not disdain the use of agricultural machinery and labour-saving appliances, once they had
been shown, by practical demonstration, the profit to be derived from the employment of
such new-fashioned devices.

SELECTION 6. LAND TENURE IN KURDISTAN, 1858

Reply by Holmes to Questionnaire, FO 78/1419

Tenure of land, Public or Private, Crown or Common?
I. What are the different kinds of tenure of land and in what proportions are they,
respectively, in use in your district?

About 20 years ago this part of Koordistan, which had previously been more nominally
than really in the hands of the Turkish government, was wrested from the Koordish Beys,
and the whole of the land, with the exception of some few parts the ownership of which was
confirmed to its ancient proprietors, was confiscated to the Crown. Since then a portion
has been sold and become private freehold property, a considerable portion is let as short
leases of a year or two, a great deal has become Church property or "Vakouf," but the
greater part remains the property of the state and is waste and uncultivated. The owner
of land either lets it to a farmer, or cultivates it himself by means of hired laborers,
or cultivates it in partnership with a farmer or several small farmers to whom the proprietor advances a certain sum of money and the necessary seed. The farmer finds the animals
and labor; and after the harvest, the net produce, all taxes having been paid, and the advance in money refunded, is equally divided. In this manner land is held and cultivated
throughout this pashalic.

II. Which of them is most favourable, and for what reasons, to the developement of Agriculture or Commerce?

The tenure under which land is held makes no difference in the developement of agriculture and commerce. All are subject to the same taxes and one system of agriculture is
common throughout the Pashalic.

III. What is the condition of vakouf and other public lands as compared with that of
freehold property?

Every individual takes care of his own private property to the best of his ability
but the vakouf and crown lands are entirely neglected. They are merely let to the best
bidder at short leases and are never improved or in any way cared for. Consequently freehold property is usually in a much better condition than any public lands.

IV. What special privileges and exemptions are attached to any particular tenure?
If lands purchased from the State are poor and unreclaimed it is often granted that
no taxes shall be paid on the produce for one, two, or three years, according to circumstances. I am aware of no other privileges attaching to any particular tenure.

V. In what manner and under what restrictions are the sale and transfer of land effected
at present?

In case of an individual wishing to purchase any portion of the land belonging to the
state, he applies to the defterdar who arranges the conditions, and then applies to the
Porte for the document describing the sale and making over the property to the purchasers.
This constitutes the proprietors' title deed to the possession. The transfer of land from
one individual to another is effected by making over the original title deeds, which constitute the seller's right to the property, to the purchaser, and also giving a paper par-
ticularising the land sold and the terms of the sale, which paper is sealed by the witnesses to the transaction. I am aware of no legal restrictions with reference to the sale
or transfer of land in this Pashalic. The Moslems, however, when it suits their purpose
often protest against the sale of <u>Mussulman</u> property to Christians as unlawful on the
strength of certain ancient firmans, the virtual repeal of which they affect to ignore.

VI. How far might such transactions be facilitated by abolishing restrictions and sim-
plifying forms of procedure?

The fact of there now being no restriction should be made distinctly apparent. The
forms of procedure appear to be as simple as possible.

VII.   What races or classes in the Community are disqualified from being landowners?
None.

VIII.   What constitutes a legal title deed to land under each kind of tenure?
Papers obtained from the Porte for the sale of crown lands. Papers from the local
government for the lease of the above. In case of the sale of Vakouf lands, papers from
an officer called the "Evcaf Nazir" or Government superintendent of Vakouf property, in
conjunction with the special guardian of the property appointed by the Mosque to which it
belongs. In case of the lease of such lands papers from the "Mutevelli," or guardian above
mentioned, suffice. In case of the Church lands of the Christian communities, papers from
their respective Bishop constitute legal title deeds.

In case of the sale of private freehold property the original title deeds and a witnessed written statement of the sale is sufficient.

IX.   What are the laws or usages in force as to the inheritance of land, and how far is
land subject to testamentary dispositions?
Land can be inherited by direct descent. It can be also transferred by gift during
life, but it cannot I believe by testamentary disposition be made over to any one out of
the family of the proprietor. In case of the absence of an heir the property reverts to
the crown.

X.   By what courts of justice are lawsuits concerning the ownership of land decided in
your district?
Sometimes the Mekemeh and sometimes the Municipal Council or Medjlis.

XI.   Are large estates or small holdings predominant, and what are the causes which most
affect the distribution of land?
Small holdings predominate. The cause chiefly affecting the distribution of land is
the presence of water. The only property in this pashalic for which a purchaser can be
found is that which contains a stream of water, or the right to a certain portion of one,
available for irrigation. The country at present out of reach of irrigation may be cultivated by anyone who will take the trouble, the government only claiming ten per cent on
the produce. This arises from there being vast tracts of land which no one will either
rent or purchase, it being out of reach of irrigation. All this land could be made most
valuable property by the cutting of canals for irrigation from the various rivers which
intersect the Pashalic, by making cart roads and introducing carts, and by the introduction
of a more just and efficient government capable and willing to afford security and protection to its subjects.

XII.   What is the nature of the rent on leasehold property?
Sometimes it is paid in kind by special agreement, and sometimes in money.

XIII.   What relation does the rate of rent on such property bear to the annual produce of
the land, and in what degree has it varied during the last ten years?
The relation that the rent on leasehold property bears to the annual produce of the
land may be calculated at between 15 and 20 per cent, and I do not learn that there has
been any material variation during the last ten years. Altogether this question cannot be
satisfactorily answered as the rent to be paid for a property is often based on a variety
of considerations besides the value of its annual produce. No farmer in this country could
tell the annual value of the average produce of his farm. He keeps no accounts, he cultivates most unscientifically and he only is aware of success by the amount of grain he is
enabled to put by for the winter's provisions and the sum of money at his disposal to begin
operations the following spring.

Remarks

The above answers have reference to the customs prevailing in this Pashalic rather
than the Turkish law on the subject. The latter is exceedingly difficult to ascertain as
it is generally administered in the most arbitrary manner, and it seems to be purposely
made as vague and uncertain as possible.

SELECTION 7. AGRICULTURE IN BURSA, 1841

Report on Agriculture of Bursa, 1841, FO 78/490

I have the honor to report to your Lordship on the State of Agriculture in this District for the past year 1841.

The previous Season for the labor and seeding of the Soil had been so adverse from
long continued droughts that a deficient crop of Grain necessarily ensued, in proportion
to the extent of land usually under tillage.

But other circumstances have continued in operation which for several years have been
diminishing Corn Agriculture. Experience is so far from enabling the large Proprietors to
manage their Farms with success that additional Estates of this nature are constantly offering for Sale from the losses attending them. They appear only to be kept up by the
owners from the impossibility of disposing of them so as to reimburse the Capital expended

on them, or for a price at all approaching their former value a few years back.

Mr. Hanson an English Merchant at Constantinople who bought an Estate of some thousand Acres near Ghio for about £2,000 with Expences of Title Deeds, brought but little land into culture last year, as there was little time after he entered on possession.

The ensuing Season if not unfavorable from natural causes connected with the weather etc. will bring the fact to the test whether Europeans can cultivate the Soil here to more profit. It is the general opinion however that without the aid of a good practical British Farmer which Mr. Hanson has not, it will be impossible for him to direct such an extensive Property on a good system. And if this opinion should be verified it will tend still more to discourage native Proprietors, as well as have the same effect in regard to other Europeans who might have in view similar Investments.

In case of a favorable result on Mr. Hanson's Farm even in two or three years if the best practicable means are pursued in the experiment a very considerable changè may be anticipated for the improvement of agriculture and of the value of land in this part of the Country.

It is to be observed that the present largest owners of Farms are either the Successors of those to whom they belonged when productive, or persons of rank or influence who became purchasers when the Peasantry could be compelled to labor for them without wages. None of these Proprietors are themselves versed in agriculture, nor have their Deputies or Managers a sufficient interest in its prosperity or the Knowledge and disposition requisite for the direction of landed Estates.

In these parts of the District where Grain is raised in the greatest quantity, and which may be called corn growing Departments as Yenisheir to the Eastward of this more particularly, it is the peasantry who are the Producers on small tracts, as the only means of turning the soil to account from the nature of culture for which it is best adapted, or the large Farmers are chiefly men trained to the occupation from infancy, and themselves the working Superintendents.

In the Department of the District under the immediate jurisdiction of this City the decay of Corn agriculture affects rather the individual owners of land and their families than the community. The profits which the lands yielded were wrung mostly from vexations exercised towards the peasantry, who left to themselves naturally find means of turning their labor to better account, and living more at ease. Exertion is wanting, more particularly among the Turkish part of the population, otherwise the condition of the peasantry, in scarcely any instance bordering on extreme distress, often exhibiting substance and generally a sufficiency for subsistence, might be much superior to what it is.

Wherever the Mulberry thrives they need not, if their Plantations and dwellings are sufficiently extensive for raising Silk, be at a loss for a livelihood. In the mountainous tracts where the Mulberry grows but scantily at the highest elevation the nurture of their flocks and the product of some patches of Corn lands furnish additional resources. The supply of wood and Charcoal for this City is the main dependence of some Villages I have visited on Mount Olympus and found in easy or thriving circumstances.

The wealth which was accumulated in the antient great families and shared by their Dependants and Servants has almost disappeared. But as the sources from which it was derived are left more free to flow in their natural channels the general wealth of the Community must rather have increased than suffered. Fewer individuals and families than formerly rise above mediocrity. But the same causes which explain the decay here of the Land Owners apply generally to the great who lived by vexations and abuses under a more arbitrary regime, up to the latter years of Sultan Mahmoud. Hence that comparative poverty, or diminution of luxury, which is generally observed here as in other parts of Turkey within these six years past--How much the rest of the population may have gained or how much of their burthens has been lightened is less remarked, and capable of direct proof.

This part of the District is always able to pay for the Surplus Corn it requires, and as a Market may be as useful to other parts of the Country as these are to the rest in contributing to its Supply.

A great part of the Soil in the plain of Brussa is from being too sandy and marshy little adapted for the Growing of Wheat. As it can easily be irrigated in most places it answers well for the culture of Rice.

The prohibition against this within ten or twelve Miles of the City having been relaxed so as to become obsolete, and Rice plantations being found profitable, greater preparations for them are making this Season than at any former period within these twenty years. The public health as experience seems to prove is liable to suffer in proportion to their extension, but the immediate effect may be a considerable Income to the Land owners and accession of Revenue to the Government (or whoever may be Receivers in its stead) from the Tithe.

Tobacco as observed in the Commercial Report is also becoming more cultivated since the removal of the Land Tax upon it of about 5 Shillings per Turkish measure called the Denume [dönüm] of 300 [sic; read 30] yards square or 900 yards superficies. This was taken off for last years Product, and everywhere throughout the District except in the hilly or mountainous Soils I find there are preparations for raising Tobacco in greater quantity. I have already transmitted details on the subject to Her Majesty's Consul Gl as desired by the Embassy.

With respect to the State of agriculture in the adjoining Department of Mohalitz [Mihaliç] I have had occasion to report on the special causes of its diminution from inundation of the Soil. The same evil continues to operate with undiminished or rather increased effect as no remedial measures have been employed. But the pressure of Taxes on that part of the District which is disproportionately burthened is most injurious to production of every sort.

I have the honor of enclosing Copy of my Report to Her Majesty's Ambassador on this Subject, and embracing various other particulars relative to the administration of the District.

I also transmit enclosed for Your Lordship's information a list of the prices of Grain and provisions in this District.

These have been moderate and the supplies ample of grain brought from Constantinople and the Districts to the Eastward which are the usual contributors.

SELECTION 8.   LAND TENURE IN EASTERN TURKEY, 1870

Report, FO 83/346

Modification of Tenancy

. . . But while direct Proprietorship, or Landlord Rights and Profits, have been thus affected, sub-Proprietorship or Tenancy has not escaped.

We have already stated that the greater number of the Fiefs, while yet entire, were cultivated on a semi-Feudal System; the peasants holding the position of personal, though not of territorial, serfs; giving labour in return for maintenance and protection; retaining a not very accurately defined share of the Produce in requital of Services and Dues not more accurately defined; and enjoying a permissive occupancy right seldom interfered with. All this ceased, of course, on the suppression of the Fiefs themselves.

Where the Estates left in Life-Tenure to their original Proprietors were small; and where confiscation followed by piece-meal Sale came into action, that is, in about four-fifths of the Fief-lands, the Muraba', or Produce-Partnership System immediately replaced every other. Where however submission or weakness allowed Estates of considerable bulk, no longer privileged indeed against future Division, yet entire for the moment, to remain in the hands of the original Proprietors; or where some wealthy purchaser took up the Estate on confiscation whole and undiminished, it became necessary to fill up the void left by Serfage in other ways.

In some cases, but not numerous ones, hired labour at fixed wages per diem was introduced. The Peasants retained, as a rule, the prescriptive occupation of their houses, and even of the little gardens often attached to them; but lost all right, legal or moral, in the ploughed lands and in the partnership of the Crops, which they henceforth cultivated on hire for the Land-Owners. This arrangement still subsists here and there; but as the Estates are, from inheritance and other causes, being themselves constantly frittered down to smaller and smaller dimensions, the Class of Hired Labourers diminishes every year; and Muraba's or Produce-Partners take their place.

In a somewhat larger number of instances the peasants have retained their quasi-right in the Land they till, and have become Tenants on the Tesarref system; either at Life-Leases, or, more ordinarily, on renewable Leases, as explained already.

The Wakf, or Endowment Lands, having, though with some difficulty, escaped the sweeping confiscations of Sultan Mahmood and his Successor, continue so far to be cultivated in the manner before described. But the actual tendency of the Executive, which in this country partly includes and wholly controls the Legislative, being to diminish, and even, when possible, wholly to break up these Endowments, the Wakf Estates have also undergone a considerable, though gradual, alienation and subdivision; in consequence of which the Muraba' System, one readily adopted by indolent Trustees or Proprietors with small plots of ground, has come in latterly here also.

Lastly; a similar group has been at work on the Meeré, or State-Lands; originally cultivated on Tesarref by Tenantry; now daily sold off in small lots, to meet the exigencies of an ill-administered and always exhausted Treasury; and thus more and more passing away into little fractional Estates, cultivated by Muraba's.

Metrookeh, or Pasture and Forest Common Lands remain much as they were; Mubah, or Unreclaimed, is on the increase.

Further Effects of the Subdivision and Equalization of Land

By far the greater number of Landlords being, from the combined influence of the causes above enumerated, too poor to employ hired labour on a profitable scale, have now adopted the Muraba' System; so that at the present day three-fourths of the cultivated Surface is split up into an almost infinite number of small Farms, worked either by the pauperized Proprietors themselves, or by associated Peasants, who stand to the Landlords in a numerical proportion of about three to one.

Thus Landed Property is still, as before, one vast Limited-Liability Association, with this difference however that, in a general way, the Partners are now all small, and almost all bankrupt.

The Backbone of the old System, I mean the Large Entail Estate Proprietors, men able to meet a demand, to support a failure, to lift their lesser co-Landlords over a difficulty, being gone, the entire mass is fast collapsing into a chaos of feeble land-owning or produce-sharing beggars too slender the most to bear the yearly burden of expenditure and taxation, and utterly crushed by a single bad harvest. No one has strength to carry out, or even to undertake any real improvements on his wretched little plot of ground; no one feels that firm enough under his feet to attempt any superstructure of Capital on it; no one cares to better what if bettered is only so for the increase of Government Dues, and the ultimate ruin of legal and hereditary partition.

Such is the condition into which the greater part of the Landowners in Eastern Turkey are already sunk; and into which the small and decaying remnant of the better sort are rapidly sinking. Meanwhile Agriculture wanes on every hand, its quality and its quantity alike deteriorate and diminish; pasture-land encroaches on plough-land, waste land on both; cottage-roofs drop in; and the country population emigrates, or dies away. A sad landscape, but a true one; I have seen the original in 'Irak from Bagdad to Mosool, in Syria from Damascus to Aleppo and in Anatolia from Erzeroom to Angorah, and can neither forget nor overdraw it.

If any one wishes to know the effects of Estate-titles annulled, Property subdivided, and Landlords and Tenants placed on a level, let him travel a few years in Eastern Turkey, the lesson is unmistakable.

It may be asked, is there any hope in the end? I answer, None under the existing Land Legislation. . . .

SELECTION 9. FARMING IN HARPUT, 1836

James Brant, "Report of a Journey Through a Part of Armenia and Asia Minor," 1836, FO 78/289

Regarding the situation of the agricultural population, I will state what I learnt from an Armenian farmer in the plain of Harpoot. He had 10 pair of Draught Oxen, a few Cows and Sheep.

His produce was

Wheat	375 Bushels valued at 4/-		£75
Millet	50 " " 1s./2³/4d.		3
Cotton	1155 lbs.	6d.	28
Grapes	3300 lbs.	4/10d.	6

Sundries as Lentiles, Beans, Seed for Oil butter) etc. all used in the family or consumed by Guests)   30
                                                                                     £142

His expenditure

125 Bushels Wheat furnished the mines	£25
200 Bushels furnished to Guests	40
495 lbs. Cotton paid to the Lord of the Soil	12
Tax to the Pasha 10 per Cent	14
	£ 91

Remains for the maintenance of the Farmer) and his Family)   51
                                                                   £142

The Millet 50 Bushels and 50 Bushels wheat, the grapes and the sundry produce were consumed by the Farmer and his family. The Cotton sold, after the Lord of the Soil had taken his rent, was about sufficient to pay the tax to the Pasha. The man received occasionally something from his guests which as it would be paid in money was probably saved. This was the statement made by the man himself, and, as is universally the case, he no doubt represented his position rather worse than it really was. Nearly two thirds of the whole produce was thus consumed in Rent, taxes and entertainment of strangers. I was not informed how much land he had in cultivation, there is no measure of land, it is estimated by the quantity of seed used in sowing or the number of Oxen necessary to plough it. They do not manure much but allow the land to lie fallow every alternate year this is the general system of agriculture throughout Armenia.

SELECTION 10.   A FARM NEAR EDIRNE, 1863

Reply to Questionnaire from Consul at Adrianople, FO 195/771

. . . In the following statement I give an account of the value, cost of management, and revenue of a farm of 2000 donums in extent (a donum is 900 square yards), soil middling and situated about 15 miles from the town of Adrianople.

The 2000 donums with farm and store houses, were sold in 1862 for Ł.stg.1200
cost of livestock:

60 bullocks at Ł5	each	300
40 horses " 3.10 "		140
10 cows " 3 "		30
Agricultural implements		25
10 wagons at Ł1 each		10
Repairs, etc.		50
		Ł 1755

cost of management:

1 "Nazir"--bailiff	per annum	Ł 30
1 "Anahtarji"--storeman	" "	14
1 "Odaji"--cook		13
1 "Tchiftchi"--head ploughman	" "	15
1 "Kuruji" [Korucu]--herdsman	" "	10
1 "Hergeliji" [Hergeleci]--stableman	" "	10
20 "ergats" [Irgat]--ploughmen at Ł10 each	" "	200
"Oraktchies" [Ortakci]--temporary labourers during harvest time		75
Contingent expenses including land tax (Ł8.10), repairs etc.		25
		Ł 392

In the above statement of wages, board and perquisites are included.

Revenue

Of the 2000 donums only 1000 were under cultivation in 1862, the produce of which was sold for about Ł700--as follows:

500 donums in wheat gave

	killoes	3000	the 2200 killoes	Piasters
deduct	300 " tithe		fetched at	
"	500 " seed	800	20 piasters	
	800	2200	per killo	44,000

300 donums in barley and Indian

corn gave	killoes	2300	the 1770 killoes at 10 piasters	
deduct	230 " tithe		per killo gave	17,700
"	300 seed	530		
		1770		

200 donums in rye, oats beans
and sundries gave

	killoes	1700	the 1330 killoes at 7 piasters	
deduct tithe	170 "		the killo gave	9,310
" seed	200 "	370		
	370	1330		

Straw and hay   6,000

                                    Total piasters   77,010

Piasters 77,010 equal to Ł.stg. 700.1.9 3/4

8 killoes per Imperial quarter

110 piasters per Ł.stg.

It has been remarked that small farms, varying from 20 to 50 acres in extent, kept by peasant proprietors, are generally better cultivated and comparatively more productive than the farms in which hired labourers are employed. . . .

SELECTION 11. FARMING IN MACEDONIA, 1900s

Draganof, La Macédoine et les Réformes (Paris, 1906), pp. 48-53.

. . . From the legal point of view, farmers consist of:
1) Landowners
2) Çiftçis (sharecroppers)
3) Laborers and domestic servants.

The first group, who are masters of the çiftçis, are the Muslim beys; the second are the Christian villagers.

There are also Christian landowners, but they have only small holdings, not exceeding 200 dönüms (of about 1,200 square meters each); beyond that limit, landownership is mainly in the hands of the beys. Small holdings are predominant in mountainous regions, large holdings in the plains. Large Christian landowners are a rare exception, represented by Greeks who own vast estates in the cazas of Serres, Drama, and Salonica.

The price of land varies greatly; an idea may be given by the following method:
a) Land used for rice-growing (in the regions of Kotchani, Kratovo, etc.), from ŁT15 to 20 per dönüm.
b) Land used for other crops, from ŁT½ to 3.
c) Meadows ŁT3-6.
In regions where population density is greater--as in Kalkandelen (Tetovo) where Christians, subjected to successive attacks by Albanian bands, have come down to the plain--the price of land has greatly increased.

The cost of cultivation to the owner is:
a) For rice paddies, per dönüm:

1) Ploughing (twice)	10 piastres	
2) Sowing	5 "	[9?]
3) Harvesting	10 "	
4) Transport of grain	15 "	
5) Threshing	24 "	
6) Tithe	30 "	
Total	98 [sic] piastres	

A dönüm of rice paddies yields 240 okes of rice, which at 30 paras an oke gives 180 piastres. The difference between the sale price and cost of cultivation (98 piastres) represents the net profit on a capital of 1,500 to 2,000 piastres (price of the paddy field and the 98 piastres laid out on the cost of cultivation).
b) For other crops: wheat, rye, etc.

1) Ploughing (twice)	10 piastres
2) Sowing	9 "
3) Harvesting	10 "
4) Transport	7½ "
5) Threshing	12 "
6) Tithe	15 "
Total	63½ "

A dönüm of wheat yields on average 120 okes which, at 30 paras an oke, gives an income of 90 piastres. The difference of 27 piastres is therefore the net profit on a capital of 63½ piastres (cost of cultivation) and the price of the land.

This method cannot satisfy landowners since the profit it yields is insufficient. Only small Christian landowners use it, when they cannot till a field themselves. Large landowners, the beys who hold çiftliks, have recourse to sharecropping, çiftçilik--equal sharing of produce, which covers three quarters of the arable land.

Sharecropping is one of the main causes of the awful misery of the Christian rural population, for it gives rise to permanent arbitrariness and abuses by the bey, against whom there is no recourse. In theory, sharecropping works thus: the bey, who owns the land, hands it out in plots according to the number of families in the çiftlik--a family tills 60-100 dönüms, depending on the number of its members. The bey also advances the seed and provides free lodging. The produce, after deduction of the tithe, is divided in equal parts between the owner and the cropper. Such a sharing can provide the landowner with a profit varying between 18 and 25 percent of his capital. But, more often than not, the landlord is not satisfied with such a share and--as absolute master of the fate of his Christian sharecropper, whose labor he exploits according to his pleasure-- he manages to seize from him, by threats and violence, the better part of what is due to the latter.

Arbitrariness and iniquity on the part of the beys are frequent. In several regions they have made the sharecropper carry the whole burden of the tithe. The latter is forced:
a) To transport the bey's share wherever the latter wishes. Very often, the bey sells his crop 80 or 100 kilometers away from the village and the sharecropper is forced to deliver it there. One should note that the livestock and all agricultural implements belong to the sharecroppers, who have to cover their cost.
b) Each sharecropper must deliver to his bey four cartloads of firewood a year.
c) The sharecropper is obliged to work, with no remuneration, for ten days a year on the bey's own fields, if the latter has kept some land for himself apart from the plots let out to sharecroppers, or if he owns some in another village.
d) If the bey owns a mill, which often happens, its upkeep as well as all the work on the waterducts falls on the sharecroppers, who in return may grind, free of charge, the grain they consume.
e) The village watchman, with whose help the bey terrorizes the villagers when he wants to impose unforeseen obligations, is paid almost always exclusively by the sharecroppers.

These obligations as well as many others of the same kind, which vary according to circumstances and the bey's whims, have put the whole output of the villagers at the bey's mercy. Thanks to this, in many çiftliks the villagers, in spite of their very modest needs, have contracted debts with their beys, which have reduced them almost to slavery.

The situation of domestic servants receiving annual wages is even more miserable than that of sharecroppers. These domestics, or "farm-boys" as they are called, are almost always married and have numerous children. . . . They cannot become sharecroppers since they do not own livestock, and hence have no share in the fruits of their painful labor. They receive annual wages amounting to: 80-100 kiles of grain (a mixture of wheat, rye, and maize), 100-120 piastres in cash, 3-5 liters of kerosene, some ten okes of haricot beans. This wage is the pay for the work of the head of the family, helped by his wife and young children, whose work is never remunerated. It represents the whole family income when the bey strictly keeps his word. But the farm boy is sometimes dismissed before the end of the year, without receiving the corresponding wage. He must then wander off, with all his family, and live on charity until he finds another place, as inhospitable and insecure as the first.

Farm boys working for Christian landowners are better off. They receive 500-600 piastres as well as food and shoes. But the number of Christian owners who need outside labor is very limited; hence very few of those who offer their work have a chance of finding a good job.

Christian landowners are, in the main, Bulgarians. As we said earlier, their holdings seldom exceed 200 dönüms. They till the land themselves and could have enjoyed a certain well-being if taxes were more equitably assessed and more honestly levied and also if insecurity were not a constant threat to the lives and property of Christians. . . .

SELECTION 12. ORDINANCE FOR THE ADVANCEMENT OF AGRICULTURE, 1844

Report by D. Sandison, 4 December 1845, FO 78/612

During last Summer, Inspectors of Agriculture under the Title of Ziraat Naziris had been appointed from among the residents in the different Divisions of the District. But up to the end of the year they had performed no duties, and I was assured they had neither received Instructions for their guidance, nor had funds at their disposal, for making advances to the peasantry.

However this might be, a Circular address in the name of the Sultan was received by the Authorities here in March, complaining that the Imperial Mandate in aid of the Agriculturists had not been obeyed, and accompanied by a requisition for Delegates to proceed to the Capital, to answer Queries on the Subject.

One of the Turkish notables of this City [Bursa] called on me at the time, saying they were all embarrassed what answers to return--admitting that they had been authorized to make outlay for various public purposes, as the repair of roads etc., besides affording aid to Cultivators, with the necessary funds at their Command.

These the receipts from the Local taxes and Duties might amply supply, but it is not clear whether the particulars of any proposed outlay were not first to be submitted to the Sublime Porte, and the amount, such as it might sanction then to be remitted at convenience, or ordered to be paid over here to the Agricultural Inspector.

The Government plan embraced the drainage of flooded lands, embankment of rivers, and the repair or formation of roads, causeways, and bridges, according to the exigencies--towards which nothing had been done, either from indifference or neglect.

On my enquiring why the Loans had not been granted to the peasantry, as designed and ordered by the Government, the Turkish official already mentioned replied, "That does not suit us. We get 20 per Cent. from the people of the villages for the use of our money, during five or six months (as is perfectly true) and as the interest on these State Loans is fixed very low, 10 per Cent per annum (more correctly, I believe, 12 per Cent.) this would destroy our own Incomes."

He also alledged that the Members of the Municipal Court were called on to give a Guarantee under their Seals for the reimbursement of the Monies, so to be advanced, which would be paid over to the heads of each Village or Commune leaving to them the distribution among the inhabitants, for which they would take the necessary Security.

I remarked that as these rural Primates, whether Mussulman or Raya, were wont to commit every Sort of abuse, it was not advisable to make them Trustees or apportioners, nor was it necessary.

And I am assured that at Mihalitz the Inspector notified that the Firman directed pecuniary aid to be granted to each individual separately, on his presenting a suitable recommendation, and security from some of his neighbours.

The rate of Interest was declared, as further stated, to be 12 per Cent. for the year, at which the Cultivators might be furnished with money for the purchase of Seed, Cattle, Implements of husbandry, etc. But the Inspector had also to inform applicants, that he was waiting for funds and orders from his Superior, the Inspector in this City, who it has been seen, is much in the same position.

The Delegates from hence, two of whom are Rayas, concerted with the other members of the Municipal Council before their departure at the end of last month, the Report to be made to the Government, and I learn from a party present, worthy of entire Credit, that when one of the intended Raya Delegates asked his Turkish Colleagues, what would be the nature of the Queries at the Capital, to prepare for them, he was told "Are you so foolish as not to know, that all you have to do is to bow in assent to what we say."

They carried with them a Drawing in illustration of a plan to be proposed for the drainage of some marshy lands lying near the small river which runs through the plain of Brussa, and of the embankments connected with this, suggesting that the Soil thus to be reclaimed, and taken into culture, would, by the Tithe on its product, bring in a considerable Revenue to the Government.

The project would have the merit of some ingenuity and novelty, as well as of apparent solicitude for the interests of the Imperial Exchequer, whilst it may exhibit how so much surface of the plain has from progressive overflooding become unfit for yielding crops.

The chief advantage of the enterprise would however be the conversion of so much marshy or sandy waste into useful meadow fields, if properly managed. And there is a vast portion of the lands around already free, and adapted for corn crops lying fallow, for want of hands and spirit to cultivate them. Hence it may be inferred how little the extension of arable surface is likely to increase the Government Revenue, or annual production of Corn.

But the Surveyor and Projector has a Farm of his own lying contiguous to the river, which would be improved I understand by the Embankments. He would also have the direction of the work, affording a sure scope for overcharged outlay, of which a portion is usually shared among the other municipal authorities, having to pass the Accounts.

A far safer medium of preliminary expenditure, and more urgent for the public convenience, would be the improvement of the internal Communications where often personal safety is endangerd, animals imbedded, and the rude wheeled vehicles of the Country broken down, for want of a few planks or stones at particular places. At others Bridges and Causeways are wanting or defective, and many of these suited for service left out of order and neglected.

To remedy this in great part, a mere trifling expence is necessary, which would scarcely be felt in the shape of an extra tax even, on each part of the District directly benefited allowing for the overcharge inseparable from such labors, and the damage and loss of time, to which the inhabitants are exposed by these negligencies, amount really to more.

For costly roads and bridges the traffic and amount of population scarcely warrant an outlay. It is different to make the best of existing communications, instead of disregarding exigencies, and permitting the progress of decay.

The Deputies gone to the Capital were further provided with lists of different villages in the District, the number of families in each, and a note affixed of their condition. The Turkish are mostly, if not all I understand, marked "Harab," or decayed, a description but too just, with scarcely an exception, and which is not applied to the Raya villages. If the distinction is also to denote, as surmised by my Informant that these are so prosperous as to stand in no need of pecuniary aid from the Government, it would be a fallacy.

In general the Raya Communities of villages, as well as many of the residents individually for their own account are encumbered with Debt, of which the enormous ordinary Interest increases the pressure.

They may surpass their Turkish neighbours for the most part, in activity and ingenuity, when they do labor, but partake much of the same recklessness and indolence, spending their time, and no little of their money at holiday feasts, and in the Taverns. And such, though not universal, is but too commonly their mode of life.

So the production of Silk, requiring but a few months toil and tendance throughout the year, and almost alone affording to many thousands resources for a livelihood, is often the parent of idleness. The rest of the year will be wasted, and the gifts of providence in bestowing a Soil and Climate so happily adapted for obtaining this valuable product, are perverted by Numbers, instead of being made available by all within their range, for increased ease and comfort.

The habitual indifference so widely diffused among the people here to bettering their condition, or extricating themselves from difficulties, by any extraordinary effort, stands not a little in the way of realizing the designs of the Sublime Porte in this Quarter, and whilst all the peasantry might be eager to obtain Loans of money at less than half the common rate of Interest, there is need for every caution against its being misapplied or dissipated.

The proposed advances if well regulated, might be bestowed with due regard to this prevalent character of the rural population, and are not the less needed, and calculated to be of extensive benefit to the District and Government.

That better qualified and more disinterested parties than the Local Inspectors of Agriculture, could best, or at all, carry out these measures efficiently, may be deduced from various circumstances now detailed, to which others might be added. But the Expence of employing special Superintendants with Salaries such as might be selected the most competent or suitable, may be a material consideration in regard to such appointments. The disadvantages of any other, unless subjected to a vigilant and permanent control, may be at least sufficiently obvious.

In case of the announced intentions of the Sublime Porte being put in execution it occurs to me that the good results contemplated might be greatly enhanced, by the Government providing a supply on previous specific applications of various agricultural implements and vehicles of carriage, of European model or Structure, such as could be most easily and usefully worked, without being over costly. From information furnished to me I believe that a limited number of some of these would now be bought at comparatively high prices. And instead of the whole being in money, the Government might stake part of the advances to Cultivators in such materials, at fixed and moderate, but remunerating prices.

Even if it were too much to hope for immediate or general success, in opposition to routine practice from ages immemorial, the experiment might be well worth trying. There would be a chance of the visible advantages leading some new parties to attempt imitation and rivalry. And one step might be gained to prove progressive, in departure from the established most defective and wasteful methods of husbandry.

SELECTION 13. AGRICULTURAL PROGRESS, 1899

Report on Smyrna for 1899, CC Smyrne, vol. 57

. . .Agriculture. Although far from being very enlightened in matters of farming, the peasant of the interior regions is, nevertheless, less ignorant regarding our methods of cultivation; little by little, he is giving up his ancient working habits and is often willing to adopt newer and more profitable ones. Of course we are far from seeing all the land being farmed, or all the old errors given up. To quote only one, not very important, example, the methods of picking olives at present being used in the south of France are still unknown in these regions, and the olives are still struck down with long sticks. The result is that, since the following year's shoots are already sprouting at the moment when the fruit of the current year is ready for picking, both fruit and shoots are struck down simultaneously, with the same blow of the stick, and one year's crop out of two is thus gratuitously lost.

However, certain facts are clear: agricultural machines, introduced from America a few years ago, are becoming more numerous every year; peasants do their best to fight the diseases that hit their crops; each day they strive harder to obtain better seeds and to sow new ones, hitherto unknown or not widespread in the region.

The initiative behind this progress is not solely due to the Anatolians, whose hopes of ultimate gain would not be strong enough to stimulate this zeal. Europeans established in the region encourage them strongly in the path of progress, and in this connection the part played by the Ottoman railway of Anatolia deserves to be mentioned.

As is known this German company, realizing that the development of the agricultural wealth of the country would have beneficial effects on the growth of its traffic, decided to establish an agricultural service as a supplement to its main business. Headed by an agronomist, this service attempts to help the inhabitants of the region through which the railway passes to make the fullest use of their soil. In his latest report, dated last April, Mr. Scheiblich, the company's agronomist, describes the efforts he made and the results obtained in 1899. . . .

Mr. Scheiblich is under no illusions regarding the difficulties he will have to overcome before obtaining "rational ploughing, turning the soil to a depth of 30 or 40 centimetres"; but he observes that the inhabitants are interested in these experiments and willingly take up the ordinary steel ploughs which at present are being supplied by the company to farmers. This is the important point that deserves attention. The company does not merely provide the "riparian" farmers with an adviser to help them improve their lands-- in a way it acts as their banker and supplies them with instruments of work, the cost of which they gradually pay back. Not only does it supply them with ploughs but also, under similar arrangements, with wheat and potato seeds--one can say that to all intents and purposes, it is the company that introduced potatoes in the vilayet of Koniya. Everywhere it has obtained the greatest trust of the people, who have shown the highest degree of good will in repaying the advances made to them. "Of the total amount due on the sale on credit of ploughs, and which was payable after the last crop, about 88 percent has already been received, without its being necessary to have recourse to the law." Encouraged by these results, the company is planning to supply kerses, machines for reaping and threshing wheat. . . .

SELECTION 14. KONYA IRRIGATION SCHEME, 1908

Wylie to Eyres, 23 February 1908, FO 368/229

Beyshehr Canals:

Length: The principal canal is to be 200 kilometres long. Of this 102 kilometres are to be newly excavated.

The subsidiary canals are estimated at 2,000 kilometres. The principal canal will follow the existing river from where it leaves Beyshehr lake to Karaviren. The bed of this river is to be deepended to 1½ or 2 metres. From Karaviren a canal will be dug round the Sogla or Karaviren lake, to join the Beyshehr river with the Charshumba. This canal is to be 30 kilometres long, 25 metres wide, and 1½ metres deep. After the junction the course of the Charshumba will be followed to Yalid Chitflik. From Yalid Chiftlik to Choumra the water will be carried on an aqueduct, or embankment above the present river bed.

Barrages: There will be a barrage built at the Beyshehr entrance 60 metres long, and 4 metres above lake level, with 15 sluices. From Karaviren to Yalid Chiftlik, where the present Charshumba has a fall of 50 metres in 25 kilometres there will be 5 or 6 barrages.

Amount of water: The canal can contain 10,000,000 cubic metres of water. 200,000,000 cubic metres are required to irrigate the land proposed. The lake gives at present in the driest years: 230,000,000 cubic metres
Last year   600,000,000   do (heavy snow)
Two years ago   420,000,000   do

Area to be irrigated:
        In Konia plain   46,000 hectares
        Bed of the Sogla lake   7,000   do (seems small figure)
        53,000 hectares

It does not seem impossible that this figure will be exceeded in years when a very high lake gives water for lands on the fringe of irrigation, particularly at the waste water end near Choumra.

Expenses: Expenses are calculated at 400 francs a hectare. This comes out at 21,000,000 francs as against the 20,000,000 of the loan.
        The canal will take five years to construct.

Population: 5,000 agricultural immigrants are to be settled on the lands and there are some existing villages.* It was stipulated that at least half the lands were to be sold before work began. From local accounts, there is none now for sale. Foreigners are only allowed to hold 500 deunums or 5 (sic--read 50) hectares each.
        If the 5,000 immigrants are found, and well and liberally settled, if the canal is well looked after, and if the water supply is cheaply and effectively regulated, the benefits should begin in about one year after completion, i.e. in 1914. It is probable that the Anatolian railway has effective guarantees for the preservation of the canals, and the regulation of the water supply, and no doubt the benefit to them has been calculated by skilful engineers. But these calculations are not available.
        The following would be some of their considerations:

Area: The farmer of to-day, who makes very little manure and can not buy artificial fertilizers, only tills half his land. Fallow is necessary every other year. Thus the 53,000 hectares must be halved in considering the harvest. Some land must be deducted for houses, gardens, roads, subsidiary canals &c. as well as for small crops other than those exported, such as vetch for plough bullocks, maize, tobacco, or mulberries for sericulture.
        Not more than 23,000 hectares would yield harvest for export in any one year.

Crops: As for crops, cotton and sesame have not so far been found to be a success at this altitude. Rice which grows in the Angora province, might be tried, if enough water was afforded. It would pay better than wheat. But the wheat and barley which are grown to-day, are the only crops on which a rough calculation can be based. Their present proportion to each other is 70 wheat to 30 barley.
        Barley does not at present, on unirrigated land, do well in the Konia plain, but irrigation may alter this, and there will be the bed of the Sogla lake, and mountain land near Yalid Chiftlik, which will probably yield heavy barley crops.

Yield by hectare: An irrigated hectare gives in a good year 25 Konia killehs of wheat or 40 of Barley, in a bad year only 10 of wheat or 20 of barley. (Konia killeh is six times that of Constantinople.) With irrigation good harvests should be more common, and some allowance may be made for the superior industry and intelligence of the promised Roumeliote. However the average cannot be put at more than 20 killehs of wheat and 30 of barley. From this is deducted roughly 33%, 16% for seed + 17% for the family's food.
        No allowance is made for tithes, which paid in kind are themselves ultimately exported: nor for the local market which is already supplied.

---

*Figures were taken from a Turkish source, but they are not official.
[*"In the last five years there have been settled in Akshehr (a barley district) 300 families of Russian and Roumeliote peasants. In Karaman and Konia, which are probable centres of future barley cultivation about 800 families, and in the whole of the province perhaps 2,000 families have been settled. This settlement is daily and rapidly increasing, fostered by the Government and the Anatolian railway alike. These men, in so far as they are agriculturalists, are far superior in education and industry to the Turkish peasant. They improve methods as well as find labour." Annexed letter.]

Gain to the railway:

	Killehs
17,500 hectares wheat give, deducting 33%	234,500
7,500 hectares barley give, deducting 33%	150,750
	385,250

83 killehs of wheat and 90 of barley go to the truck.

Thus the number of trucks is roughly 4,500 one quarter of which go to Smyrna by Karahissar, and the rest to Haïdar Pasha. Karahissar ŁT15,750, Haïdar-Pasha ŁT67,500, total ŁT83,250.

The average proportion of cereals to other goods carried is 70% and in the irrigated lands this might be 80%. The freight for wheat is only ŁT20, but for other goods much higher. Sugar, manufactures, hardware and iron are ŁT43 by truck, wool is ŁT60, mohair is ŁT72 and petroleum oil is ŁT32. An average of ŁT45 will be a safe figure to take. Of the 1,125 trucks, one quarter would be to and from Smyrna, Karahissar ŁT9,835 and Haïdar-Pasha ŁT37,980 give ŁT47,815.

The grand total of gross profit to the railway would thus be ŁT131,065.

In these figures I have reduced the freight of barley to that of wheat, which is a probable event. But it is unnecessary to look forward to a reduction in the differential rate against the Cassaba railway to Smyrna. In fact the present working arrangement of through fares for the Baghdad Railway is, I hear, shortly to cease.

Beyond possible additional rolling stock, the canal traffics bring no extra expenses to the Baghdad Railway.

Railway connection with Mersina, by altering freights would of necessity alter all these calculations.

Gain to the Government: By taking the average prices of wheat and barley for the last three years, and deducting 20% for the tax buyers profits and expenses, the Government appears to make from the new lands, a tithe of ŁT47,600, taking the tithe at 10.5 per cent and not counting the extra tax for the military and the Public Instruction funds. There will be also land tax, 4 per mille, on 53,000 hectares worth say 800 piastres the hectare ŁT1,696. Also house tax on 5,000 houses, worth ŁT30 each at 5 per mille ŁT750 bringing the annual income up to ŁT49,046. Tithe on garden produce cannot be calculated, nor the tithe on supplementary crops (a large tax if there be much opium). The road tax ŁT1,300 has been omitted, but the sheep tax should be added. The ordinary stock on 5,000 small farms would be 150,000 sheep or goats. The tax on these would be ŁT6,750.

Grand total of taxes is ŁT55,796 payable 6 years after the installation of the immigrants.

Water tax: Whether the canals be managed by a company under the Railway Company or by the provincial officials, there is likely to be a charge for water. The sum of 10 piastres a deunum, which pays 2.8% on the capital sunk, is a possible one. Out of this ŁT25,000 would come the salaries of the officials and the upkeep of the canals and barrages. Reductions and exemptions are possible, and not more than ŁT10,000 a year net profit may be taken. This brings, the Government gain to ŁT65,800 a year, without counting the reduction in the railway guarantees.

Government expenses: Immigrants pay no taxes for their first six years, possibly not even a water tax. It will probably take a long time to find the immigrants and they will be slowly settled during the five years of the construction work. Labour on the canal should feed them till their holdings are ready, which is a gain to the Government. On the average it does not seem likely that taxes will be paid in their entirety before 1918. During these 10 years the Government has to pay ŁT53,742 a year for the interest and sinking fund on the canal loan, a large lump sum to instal the immigrants and a further sum representing interest on this money, until it is repaid.

Installation of immigrants: Each family receives a house, a pair of bullocks, the first year's seed corn, free transport and food nominally till the house is completed. In this case food would be only given till work was found on the canals. The houses are put at ŁT30. The Government failed to get a contract accepted a few years ago for ŁT25 at Serai-Öni. For transport, the immigrant fare from Haïdar-Pasha is 61.2 piastres a head. 25,000 souls comes to ŁT15,312. This has been doubled for the transport from Roumelia, which I am unable to calculate. Bullocks and seed would not be given till the last minute, so that interest on their cost is counted for 8 years only, as against 10 for the houses &c.

5,000 houses at ₤T30	150,000
Transport from Roumelia	30,000
Food for 2 months	15,000
	195,000
deduct Agricultural Bank lottery and aid from immigrant Commission	85,000
	110,000
add ten years compound interest	69,987
	179,987
5,000 pairs of bullocks at ₤T8 pair	40,000
Seed corn for 25,000 hectares	50,000
	90,000
add compound interest for 8 years	42,970
	132,970
Add from above	179,987
Interest & sinking fund canal loan 10 years	537,420
Expended by Government Grand Total:	850,377

There are three obvious factors to lessen this sum, which I cannot put in figures:
    1) The whole of the 20,000,000 francs loan will not be at once expended, so that there would be interest on some of it for some periods.
    2) The settlement of the immigrants will be pushed on as fast as possible, so that some will pay taxes before 1918.
    3) The funds at the disposal of the Immigrant Commission.

    To set against this initial loss, the government has the ₤T65,800 option already set out, and a further sum of ₤T77,000 a year, the difference between the gross profits on the railway and the interest and sinking fund on the canal loan. This ₤T77,000 is the amount by which their guarantee is lessened.
    The initial loss with interest is met in 1925 by the payment of the 143,000 a year. After this the Government will have a benefit of ₤T143,000 annually, which in 1943 when the canal loan is extinguished rises to ₤T196,000.

Gain to commerce: The construction of the canal will employ an army of workmen for 5 years. There is to be a telegraph line as well as a road, fit for motor traffic, along the canal bank. Presuming that the Anatolian Railway Company has already arranged for all appliances required for the construction, tools, explosives, materials for bridges and barrages, shops for workmen and thousands of picks and shovels, there still remains the fact that this large army of men will powerfully stimulate every branch of local trade. The workmen will want clothing and shoes, food and necessaries of all kinds. They will be well paid and have money to spend.
    The permanent gain to commerce is very large though it will not be evident for some years.

Wheat & Barley: The wheat and barley crops alone, if the average of the last three years be maintained, will be worth every year after 1914 ₤T557,000. The export of wheat will be worth ₤T260,550 and that of barley which goes largely to England, ₤T118,575. The smaller crops will have their importance. Probably there will be opium and silk, rye and linseed, maize and peas.

Wool and Mohair: Allowing for a proportion of black goats the clip on 100,000 sheep is worth ₤T7,000 and on 20,000 mohair goats ₤T3,000.

Wood: The canal will to some extent tap the forest country. If it be possible to float timber down the canal, a most valuable trade will be done, or at any rate for small timber and firewood there will be the road along the canal bank.

Immigrants: When the canal is finished there will be a permanent increase in the population of 5,000 families: 25,000 souls. These people must be clothed and fed. 5,000 farms will require ploughs, carts and spades. A large number of reapers will ply for hire, and possibly thrashing machines also. These latter will be able to move along the new road along the canal bank. One of the difficulties in their introduction at present has been the difficulty of moving them away from the railway.

Purchasing power of the immigrants: From a calculation too long to set out here, the conclusion may be taken: After the immigrant has paid all his taxes including Piastres 10 per deunum for water, after he has paid not only the upkeep of his stock and tools but a sinking fund also to replace them, after he has provided for his own and family's food, and for the seed corn, the average man, if a fair year, in fair soil, and at fair prices, would spend ₤T15 on clothing and boots, sugar and lighting and coffee for himself and children, and still have ₤T20 over. It is very little, but in the aggregate it comes to a very considerable purchasing power, ₤T15 for clothing &c is ₤75,000 on all the immigrants. ₤T20 saved is ₤T100,000. Of this latter sum much would be saved as insurance against the inevitable bad seasons. Perhaps one quarter may be spent on the collective hire of a threshing machine, or still better on manure.

General profits: In Konia trade will circulate the large profits on cereals, wool, mohair, meat, hides, manufactures, sugar, coffee, leather, and oil.

Railway guarantees: It appears that the money earned on the railway by the carriage of the irrigation crops is to be put on one side, and after payment of the ₤T53,742 interest and sinking fund on the canal loan, the surplus is to be deducted pro tanto from the guarantee on the Baghdad Railway. This surplus, if these calculations can be accepted, is ₤T77,000 subject to such percentage as it may be considered fair to deduct for any unforseen contingencies. . . .

A failure to find good and sufficient immigrants, the presence of any large proportion of alkali tainted land in the irrigation area, a dishonest or incapable administration of the water, these taken singly or together would render nugatory the benefit of the Beyshehr canal.

In the background stands the spectre of bad farming. Canal water will leave no rich deposit behind it, as of Nilotic mud. The Porte, the Railway and the farmer, to reap their harvests, must turn their minds to fertilizers.

COTTON

The two following selections indicate the trends in cotton production and export in Turkey and their relation to changes in world markets. Until the end of the eighteenth century the Levant--i.e., Macedonia, the Izmir region, Syria and Cyprus--was Europe's main supplier of cotton.[1] The output of the Salonica region in 1780 was put at 9,000 tons and its annual exports in the 1780s--chiefly to Austria, Saxony, and France--at 6,000 tons.[2] Around 1800 production was about 7,500 tons, of which 2,500 went to Germany, partly overland and partly through Trieste, 650 to Italy and a variable quantity, never exceeding 1,250 tons, to France; exports to Britain were negligible.[3] As for Izmir, cotton was its principal export (Ainslie, Memorandum to the Porte, December 1792, FO 78/13, and "Nota delli diversi prodotti di Smirna," 1776, HHS Türkei, V-25). In the 1780s the output of the region was put at 42,000--44,000 bales," of which 12,000-13,000 are sent to France, 5,000 to Italy, 8,000 to Holland, 3,000 to England, and the rest stays in the country."[4] Output and exports must have subsequently risen, since a French consul states that exports had at one time been as high as 60,000-70,000 bales or 15,000-17,500 tons (CC Smyrne, vol. 48, Report on Cotton, 1851).[5]

American competition was, however, squeezing Turkish cotton. Izmir's exports fell to 4,600 tons in 1838, less than 3,000 in 1840, and 600 in 1846; in 1851 exports rose to 2,000 tons but declined again to 700 in 1857 and 1,200 in 1858 (CC Smyrne, vol. 49, Report of 8 December 1861).[6]

Another factor affecting production was the decline in the local textile handicrafts and their reduced demand for cotton. Thus the British consul in Edirne stated that before 1828, "when our cotton manufactures were scarcely known in this country, the cultivation of cotton was very considerable in some districts" and was all used for local consumption. Then imports of textiles "rapidly increased and cotton culture diminished in proportion" (Reply to Circular, 28 May 1863, FO 195/771). In Gelibolu, output had fallen from some 2,350 bales in 1845--all used for local consumption or sent to textile workshops in Izmir or Rumelia--to 250 bales in 1860 (ibid.). In Acre, exports had fallen from 600 tons in 1852 to nil by the end of the decade and land had been shifted to sesame and wheat (ibid.). And by the 1850s Salonica's production had fallen to a little over 1,000 tons.[7] Taking Anatolia as a whole, in 1851 output was put at about 30,000 bales, of which 12,000-15,000 were exported, 8,000 remained in the interior, and 10,000 were consumed by the workshops of Manisa, Menemen, Kasaba and Aydın (CC Smyrne, vol. 48, Report on Cotton, 1851). Ten years later Turkish production, including that of Cyprus, was estimated at 12,000-15,000 bales (ibid., vol. 49) 8 December 1861.

An attempt to improve the situation had been made in 1846, when Dadian, on behalf of the Sultan, had requested the United States legation to send American experts who would carry out experiments with American cottonseed in Turkey. The legation agreed, but it is not clear whether the project was in fact implemented (Brown to Buchanan, 5 January 1846, FO 195/290). More important was the founding in 1857, of the Cotton Supply Association,[8] which sought to reduce Britain's overwhelming dependence on American cotton by developing other sources, including Turkey.[9] But the real stimulus was provided by the "cotton famine" caused by the Civil War in the United States and the enormous rise in prices. As in so many countries in the Middle East and elsewhere,[10] cotton cultivation in Turkey greatly expanded. This comes out clearly in the British consulates' replies to a circular in 1863.

In Izmir, whereas the 1860 crop had been "trifling," the 1861 crop was 15,000 bales and the 1862 crop 42,000 bales, or nearly 7,500 metric tons, and the area sown to cotton in 1863 was more than five times as large as in 1862. Exports amounted to 13,860 tons in 1865.[11] In Cyprus, exports in 1857-61 averaged 1,000,000 lbs., but output rose to 1,500,000 in 1862. In Gelibolu, production rose from 250 bales in 1860 to 600 in 1861 and 1,300 in 1862. In Edirne and Bulgaria, the cotton acreage in 1863 was more than twice as large as in 1862. In the Dardanelles there was a 10- 15-fold increase in the area sown to cotton. In Diyarbekir the landowners were apathetic. "They do not feel certain of a regular market so as to encourage them in devoting increased tracts of land to that culture. The fellahs have been so long accustomed to the routine of crops that without some pressure or special agreement they would hardly desert it for an article, which at present can be imported from other places cheaper than they can produce it themselves." Nevertheless, here too output in 1862, at 750 tons of "clean cotton," was twice as high as in 1857.[12] In Trabzon attempts were being made to grow cotton, using Egyptian and American seed. In Damascus much more than usual was being sown, and even in Basra some farmers were introducing cotton. In Salonica, output rose from 25,000 cwt. to "ten times that quantity."[13] Production also increased in Adana.

In all, cotton production in Anatolia rose to 80,000 or "even 100,000" bales during the Civil War, but with the sharp fall in prices that followed the end of hostilities production dropped, to about 50,000-60,000 in the 1870s.[14] Prices continued to drop in the Izmir region from 8.11 piastres per oke in 1876-80 to 4.88 in 1896-1900, and in Adana from 7.48 to 4.65, but after that they rose sharply, to 6.90 and 6.34, respectively, in 1906-8.[15] Production responded to prices in Izmir, falling from about 40,000 bales (of 150 kilograms or 330 lbs. each) around 1890 to a low of 25,000 in 1903 and rising again to over 40,000 on the eve of the First World War. But in the Adana region output rose steadily and rapidly, from under 20,000 bales (of 170 okes, i.e., 217 kilograms or 481 lbs.) around 1890 to 118,000 in 1912-14.[16] On the other hand, production in Salonica continued to decline, falling from 3,800 tons in 1889 to 2,200 in 1907 and 1,000 in 1910.[17] Turkey's exports showed a steady and considerable increase, from an average of 6,276 tons, worth ₤T314,000, in 1878-82 (3.3 percent of total exports) to 11,042 tons, worth ₤T543,000 (3.8 percent) in 1890-94 and about 17,200 tons, worth ₤T900,000 (4.3 percent) in 1908-13; in 1913 exports were the highest on record, at 23,500 tons and ₤T1,206,000.[18] In addition, local production met the needs of the growing textile industry (6:14).

Among the factors encouraging cotton-growing in Adana were a more active government policy after 1900, when seeds, credit, and technical information were supplied. The Deutsche Levantinische Baumwolle Gesellschaft, founded in 1904 by the Baghdad Railway Company, also played a significant role.[19] So did improved transport (4:17), which rendered the region independent of Izmir for marketing purposes. The opportunity presented by the soil and climate of the region was seized by a group of medium and large landowners, mainly from minority groups, who overcame the labor shortage both by hiring workmen from other regions and by using machinery on a large scale; little advantage was, however, taken of the possibilities for irrigation offered by the rivers.[20]

One more, rather minor, development may be noted. The rapidly growing demand for cotton in Russia resulted in the diversion of the output of eastern Anatolia to that market, by caravan through Erzurum, instead of the much more distant one of Izmir.[21]

In the interwar period, cotton expanded slowly and after the Second World War became Turkey's largest single export (tables in Epilogue).

(See also works by Bruck, Dunstan, Fesca, Kurmuş, Hellauer, Herrmann, Quataert, and Todd, listed in the Bibliography).

1. See Ralph Davies, <u>Aleppo and Devonshire Square</u> (London, 1967); Britain's imports from Turkey rose from 667,000 lbs. in 1725 to 4,407,000 in 1789--Kurmuş, p. 76.
2. Theodossi Robeff, <u>Die Verkehrs -und Handelsbedeutung von Saloniki</u> (Lucka, 1926).
3. A and P 1873, vol. 67, "Salonika."
4. "Etat du commerce du Levant en 1784," translated in EHME, pp. 31-37.
5. The consul stated that the bale varied between 200 and 300 kilograms, and that a camel load consisted of two bales.
6. Another source puts exports in 1851 at 12,000-15,000 bales (CC Smyrne, vol. 48, Report on Cotton, 1851. Izmir's exports in 1852 were only 800 tons; nearly half went to Central Europe, nearly a third to France, one-sixth to Russia, and under 2 percent to Britain--Stich, pp. 83-88.
In Adana, Muhammad Ali's attempts to develop cotton production in the 1830s were unsuccessful--EI (2), s.v. "Filaha."
7. A and P 1873, vol. 67, "Salonica"; for a similar trend in Syria see EHME, p. 229.
8. In 1858 it was announced that the company had sent 75 barrels of cottonseed for distribution among cultivators in Bursa and 25 to those in the Dardanelles, and that the Porte had instructed the customs authorities to exempt the barrels from duty (April 1858, FO 195/590). It also sent American seed to Izmir, with encouraging results (Kurmuş, p. 76), although labor shortage was a severe handicap (CC Smyrne, vol. 49, 8 December 1861).
9. For a spirited expression of resentment of Britain's dependence on "this turbulent democracy," see EHME, pp. 144-45.
10. See EHME, passim, and EHI, pp. 144-45.
11. Stich, p. 84.
12. A and P 1865, vol. 53, "Diarbekr and Kurdistan."
13. A and P 1873, vol. 67, "Salonica."
14. BC 1879, pp. 644-45 and CC Smyrne, vol. 52, 2 April 1879.
15. Quataert, p. 280.
16. Eldem, p. 85; according to Stich, p. 84, the output of the Izmir region fell from 15,000 tons at the beginning of the 1870s to 9,000 at the beginning of the 1890s. Eldem's figure of 135,000 bales in 1914 differs sharply from the one of 85,000 in 5:16.
17. Robeff, <u>Die Verkehrs</u>.
18. Aybar, p. 62.
19. Quataert, pp. 279-88; also 5:13, 16. In 1910 the Ottoman Chamber of Commerce of Manchester stated that the German company had "done remarkably well"--TE, Box 463 (1910), Memorandum of 5 October 1910. For the French concession in the Çukurova in 1912, see Thobie, pp. 424-25.
20. For a detailed description of varieties of cotton, machinery, and labor problems, A and P 1909, vol. 98, "Adana"; and Dunstan.
21. Stich, pp. 84-85; also EHI, pp. 244-47.

SELECTION 15. ATTEMPTS TO ENCOURAGE COTTON PRODUCTION, 1860s

Birinci Köy ve Ziraat Kongresi, Türk Ziraat Tarihine Bir Bakış (Istanbul, 1938, pp. 120-37)

Agricultural Measures taken after the Crimean War and the American Civil War and Cotton Production in Turkey

English textile manufacturers were thrown into a panic when in 1861 the dispute between the northern and southern states of America grew and the danger of war became apparent. For, if cotton imports from the States were to stop, the English factories would have to close down. Thus, the English thought of importing cotton from Turkey. Although Turkey's climate is fit for growing cotton, at that time neither was production large enough nor was quality good. The English applied to the Ottoman government and asked that it take serious measures regarding the volume and quality of cotton production in Turkey. They also sent agents to Turkey to help bring about better cotton production, and had articles published in Turkish papers.

Before the American Civil War began, an article appeared in Ceride-i Havadis (13 January 1861) with regard to Turkish Cotton:

"Whereas such importance is attached to the disorders in the United States of America, whereas these disorders have occasioned higher rates in the London exchange and the question has been raised whether they would affect all of Europe, we shall now explain this matter. England has a great many factories. The raw materials for the goods produced in those factories are bought and imported from abroad and afterwards the goods are exported. If wool, cotton, and other such materials cannot be imported, the factories would close, people would not find means of subsistence, and the government would be incapacitated and embarrassed. The English annually purchase 40 million lira worth of cotton from the fifteen states of America which employ slave labor and, after manufacturing textiles from it, export the same commodity for 55 to 60 million lira. While twenty years ago the annual cotton import of England from the United States was 2,177,000 bales, in 1860 the estimated cotton import reached 4,500,000 bales; also while twenty years ago there were 20 million spindles in Europe, now there are 70 million. The quantity of cotton now available is not adequate for such a number of spindles, which can process an extra million bales of cotton. Should there be a revolution in the United States due to the slavery problem, such a revolution would hurt the cotton trade, force textile factories in England to close down, and cause unemployment for several millions of workers whose livelihood depends upon the textile industry. The English cotton trade has such a great volume that should the price of one kiyye [okka=2.83 lb.] of cotton be raised by 40-50 para, the textile industrialists will incur a loss of 5 to 10 million lira. A great number of vessels are commissioned to transport cotton from the United States to England; since shipping depends on various forms of labor, it is evident that very many workers will be affected, should the cotton trade be stopped. As the English government and nation realize that if the cotton trade were to be solely dependent on American export any interruption thereof would cause difficulties, for the past three years they have been exploring possibilities and taking precautions to avert any danger of interruption. A company was set up in London consisting of civil servants, merchants, and industrialists and a considerable sum of money was raised. This company has sent special agents to parts of Europe, Asia, and Africa in order to encourage cotton-growing in those regions. One such agent has come to Istanbul and is still here. To the farmers who will grow cotton, these agents supply seeds free of charge and machinery at low prices, and they even train farmers in cultivating cotton. In various parts of Anatolia and on the island of Cyprus, cotton was grown from American seeds. Upon examination in England, the produce of these regions was found to be third-grade. But, it was hoped that the produce could be improved and therefore the afore-mentioned company has sent agricultural machinery to Cyprus. Yenişehir, Kavalla, and Latakia. Since special efforts were made in Egypt in cotton cultivation, last year that region raised a crop of 100,000 bales and now it is hoped that Egypt will be able to produce up to one million bales of cotton annually. Both the planting and growing of cotton need attention and hard work throughout the year. Yet, the profits of cotton growing are proportionate to the efforts needed."

Since Ruzname-i Ceride-i Havadis was published by an Englishman, it contained several noteworthy articles about cotton cultivation. The day after the previous article appeared in the paper, another on the same topic, written by Mr. Sanford the agent of the English company, was published in Ceride-i Havadis. After dwelling on the importance of cotton in trade, Mr. Sanford said:

"Until recently over 50,000 bales of cotton were shipped annually from Izmir to Europe, but now only 2,000 bales are shipped. This is low-quality produce and cannot be used for textiles; it is used only for manufacturing wicks. Thus, although in the beginning it was primarily carried on in Asia, in the past few years cotton cultivation developed in America and became a source of wealth and prosperity for that country. Since cotton products are cheaper than silk or woollen products, a great majority of people use them. Cotton goods are so much in demand that the output of so many factories [in Europe] does not meet this demand. Textile industry is the main reason for the prosperity and wealth of England, France, Germany, and Switzerland. In addition to its domestic sales, England, last year, exported 48-million-lira-worth of cotton products. Last year England imported 2,475,000 bales of cotton worth 24,750,000 lira at 10 lira per bale. After products necessary for domestic consumption were manufactured, the remainder was exported at twice the price paid for the import. The United States, last year, exported 4,500,000 bales of cotton worth 45,000,000 lira. Until recently annual American exports amounted to only four to five hundred thousand bales, but the development of shipping and the textile industry facilitated the rapid growth of American exports. Previously, the cotton produce of Asia was much in demand, but now the volume of cotton produced in Asia has decreased and it is evident that the development of shipbuilding in Europe helped to make textiles cheaper. The cotton produce of Asia has declined because there have been uprisings and revolutions there and the people therefore could not attend to farming; nor have the governments there facilitated the cultivation of cotton. In America, there has been order and security; the government has shown every consideration possible to facilitate cotton cultivation and has not levied customs and other duties. Thus, American cotton production has come to its present level." After mentioning how much care and attention cotton cultivation needs, the article continues, "Last year, cotton was grown in the late Ilhami Paşa's land in Egypt with the greatest care. The produce, which amounted to some 1000 kantars,[*] was of such high quality that it was exported at a higher price than American cotton, and thus other farms in the area started paying attention to cotton cultivation with the utmost care. According to the results of research, in addition to the afore-mentioned quantity of cotton, Egypt last year produced 140,000 bales of cotton, 7,000 of which were grown in Ilhami Paşa's farm. Egypt has imported about three hundred machines from London to gin and clean the cotton crop. A hundred of these machines were located at one place, each can clean one kantar of cotton a day. Manually, it takes six days to clean one kantar of cotton. It is evident that such methods of cultivation will be of great profit and increased trade if applied in Anatolia, Rumelia, and the Damascus area, the latter being especially suitable. Should cotton cultivation be started in those regions, it is possible to obtain seeds free of charge and machinery at factory prices; there is in Istanbul an agent of the English company to advise and instruct cotton growers."

Another article concerning cotton produce was serialized in Ceride-i Havadis on 10 March, 12 March, and 14 March 1861:

"It is a matter of importance that the present situation in the United States of America which, at present, is of deep concern to England and France, should immediately be taken into consideration by the Ottoman Empire. It is evident that should some attempts be made to take advantage of the present revolutionary situation in the United States, such profits and wealth could now be realized as would be difficult or impossible to obtain at other times." The article then summarizes the development of cotton cultivation in America: "For the first time in 1784 cotton was shipped from North America to England. But since at that time this commodity was banned, the shipment was confiscated at the Liverpool customs. Under English rule in America, the cultivation of cotton was barred; yet in 1785 on three vessels five bales, in 1786 on two vessels six bales, in 1787 on five vessels 109 bales, and in 1788 on six vessels 282 bales of cotton were shipped from the States to England. After that, the export increased:

Year	Bales
1825	568,248
1830	976,845
1845	217,835
1850	2,728,596
1860	4,675,577

In 1860, England alone imported 5,554,000 bales of cotton, 84% of which came from America. At present, 810,000 bales of cotton are annually used in England. In addition, nearly all of the cotton imported by Europe comes from there. Although Europe imports cotton from other countries as well, compared to imports from America, which make up about 75 percent of the total, other imports are negligible. As was pointed out earlier, as cotton cultivation developed, cotton consumption increased proportionately, and cotton became the chief agricultural and industrial commodity in England as well as in America. It is clear that without cotton America would lose a major portion of its foreign trade, and in England many factories would close, one-fourth of the population would lose their jobs and become poor and needy. Although it cannot yet be conjectured to what serious degree the present situation in the United States will affect the produce, the current cotton stock in America can meet European demand for only three months. We understand from the present trend that next year there will be a scarcity of cotton crop." The article goes on to point out that the Civil War would affect cotton growing and further states that "If slavery is abolished, the price of cotton will increase. Thus, although up to now America has been able to produce cotton cheaply, thanks to black slave labor, after [abolition] it will not be able to do so. Since the English textile factories would close down in case cotton is not available, the resulting unemployment among workers might lead to civil disorders. Thus, England will have to purchase cotton elsewhere. . . . No country in the world is better suited for cotton cultivation than the Ottoman Empire. Although cotton at

---

[*] An Egyptian kantar was, at that time, equal to 99 lbs.]

first appeared in Eastern lands and grew without much attention paid to the crop, at present its cultivation has almost been abandoned in the Ottoman Empire. It is clear that should cotton be grown properly in Tirhala, Salonica, and Serez in Rumelia, in many places in Anatolia and Arabia, and in Crete and other islands of the Mediterranean, the produce would be adequate to meet the demand in Europe and would take the place of American cotton. Yet, these areas produce only 13,700,000 kiyye of cotton annually. Of this amount, 5,990,000 kiyye is consumed domestically and 7,710,000 kiyye, equivalent to 48,187 American bales, exported." The article then explains why Turkish cotton could not compete with American cotton: "Heavy taxation has caused the scarcity of Turkish cotton: apart from land tax, tithes, and customs duties levied on the produce, transportation of this commodity is also difficult in Turkey. Land taxes in America are low, no customs duties are levied, and matters of transportation have been greatly facilitated. Thus, naturally, Turkish cotton has not been able to compete with American." The article further states the changing of this situation: "The present situation in the United States conveniently paves the way for the Ottoman Empire to get out of its deplorable inferior situation. Because of its proximity to Europe, the Ottoman Empire will doubtlessly become one of the major cotton-producing areas. Time must not be wasted; measures must be carried out immediately to take advantage of the present situation in America. By the time slavery has been abolished in America, peace made between the people of the north and the south, and things have returned to normal, the Ottoman Empire must start producing large quantities of cotton, find foreign purchasers, and make textile industrialists use Turkish cotton. Since cotton-growing does not take a long time to begin, even if the present unrest in America does not continue for long, before the situation is normalized in America, cotton cultivation in the Ottoman Empire can be properly established."

The article elaborates further on the agricultural measures which needed to be taken quickly: "First, the cotton produce of Rumelia and Anatolia must be exempt from customs levy when exported or transported from one province to the other. Secondly, tithes must be abolished for cotton produce. Thirdly, land planted to cotton must be declared exempt from all taxation for a ten-year period. Fourthly, Tatars and other immigrants who are given land must be required to cultivate cotton on one-fourth of the land if it is suitable. Fifthly, in order to lessen the cost of transport, both in Anatolia and on the islands, government-owned lands near ports, wherever possible, should be made available for cotton cultivation. Sixthly, farmers who are given land to cultivate must be made to keep up the roads from the farms to the ports. Seventhly, all possible encouragement must be given to landowners to cultivate cotton.

"It is clear that the customs duty levied on the increased imports as a result of cotton export will offset the loss from the tax exemptions.

"It is evident that if the above-mentioned precautions are taken, cotton cultivation in the Ottoman Empire will improve and most of the cotton for the European market will be produced here. Also, a great deal of silk, corn, dye, and tobacco which are in demand can be produced in the Ottoman Empire.

"These comments, based on experience in trade and scientific research conducted in all countries, are not of questionable veracity; in case such advice is taken into consideration, it will doubtless lead to an increase in the domestic wealth and international power of the Empire." The end of the article once more calls attention to the importance of this matter and the necessity of taking action quickly: "while such an opportunity has presented itself due to some unexpected circumstances, it must be taken advantage of; yet since taking advantage of this situation is dependent upon speedily taking measures, not even a minute must be wasted. If the above-mentioned measures are delayed, the United States will come out of the present state of sedition and disorder and return to normal. At such time the Ottoman Empire will not be able to compete with the United States in cheap cotton cultivation. If the Empire neglects this matter now, success later will be improbable. India, Brazil, the Gulf of Mexico, and some other areas will take the place of the United States in export and will therefore be able to reap great profits."

New Commercial Treaties

It is interesting to note that one and a half months after the appearance of this article, which was undoubtedly written by an Englishman, the Ottoman Empire signed a series of commercial treaties with England, France, and other nations. These treaties, dated 29 April 1861, superseded the 1838 Commercial Treaty. They called for an 8% customs duty on imports to Turkey, and on exports from Turkey an 8% customs duty which would be reduced by 1% each year successively. The customs levy on exports was reduced compared to the 1838 Treaty, probably because the English and French factories were in a state of crisis due to the Civil War and wanted to obtain the necessary raw materials cheaply from Turkey.

Publications on Cotton Cultivation

At about this time a great many articles on cotton cultivation appeared. An article published in Ceride-i Havadis on 9 December 1861 dealt with the areas and methods of cotton cultivation, the precautions that have to be taken in cultivating cotton, and the means of exterminating worms found in cotton fields.

On 10 July 1861, <u>Ceride-i Havadis</u> reported that as a result of the efforts of the committee in Manchester to encourage cotton production everywhere in the world, new shipments of cotton had arrived in England. These shipments included 700 bales sent from Izmir and 800 bales from Iskenderun.

On 21 February 1862, <u>Ceride-i Havadis</u> reported that in order to promote cotton cultivation in the Izmir area, large amounts of American cottonseed had been sent there and distributed to the farmers free of charge.

There was an article in <u>Ceride-i Havadis</u> published on 30 September 1862 concerning the amount of cotton that could be produced in Turkey. This article was based on reports received by the Foreign Office from English consulates in Turkey: "While there have not been any previous shipments of cotton from Gelibolu to England, last year 750 liras' worth of cotton was exported from there. The produce was well-liked and preferred to those of other areas. Around Gelibolu there are areas favorable for cotton cultivation. If sustained efforts are made to grow cotton and improve the produce, a large crop of better quality than American cotton could be produced there. Cyprus used to be a great source of cotton production; when the island was under Venetian rule, over 30,000 bales of cotton used to be exported from there. Last year only about 6,000 bales were grown. While Cypriot cotton was found to be of low quality and in need of improvement, if efforts are not spared both its quantity and quality would improve. With imported American seeds, a good cotton crop was grown in the Bursa area. Since the people of that region have not spared any effort in cotton cultivation, it is evident that in the future more produce will be grown there. With the constant encouragement of the imperial administration, persevering efforts are being made to cultivate and grow increasing quantities of cotton in Diyarbakir, Birecik, and other parts of the Empire. The people of these areas will produce more cotton and their present efforts indicate that one-third of the English demand can be met by them."

Measures Taken by the Government to Promote Cotton Cultivation

The English efforts to promote cotton cultivation in Turkey had some influence on the government. The imperial decree of 27 January 1862 summarized some of the measures taken.

1. To those who attempt to cultivate barren areas, such lands will be distributed without charge and no tithes will be collected from the first year's crop. If the land cultivated had been rock beds, tithe exemption will be given for two years. These measures, already existing in the Code of Title Deeds, will be amended so that those who cultivate cotton in such locations will be exempt from tithes for five consecutive years.

2. It is decided that the customs levy on cotton produce will remain the same for ten years and the same rate of duty will be applied to all qualities of cotton.

3. In the districts where cotton is grown, those highways from the farms to the ports that need repair will be repaired in order to facilitate transport.

4. No customs duty will be levied on machinery imported for sorting and cleaning cotton seeds.

5. The state will import sample machinery and cotton seeds from America and elsewhere, and these will be distributed free of charge.

6. Pamphlets and manuals on cotton cultivation will be published and disseminated in such areas as grow cotton.

7. Annual fairs will be held in cotton-growing areas and the producers of the best crop will be given prizes.

8. It is decided that henceforth the government will help cotton cultivation in all ways possible.

The Application of the Measures Concerning Cotton Cultivation

As a result of this promotion, in the Serez province a successful crop was grown from the sowing of American cotton seed. <u>Ceride-i Havadis</u> reported on 24 December 1862 that, according to the governor of Salonica, each seed yielded 200 pods. It was decided that "in order to show appreciation to these farmers and encourage their colleagues, a medal be struck, and one medal given to each farmer who produced such a crop, and the governor be [sent a letter] of appreciation."

The 2 January 1863 issue of <u>Ceride-i Havadis</u> reported that a commission consisting of Manchester textile manufacturers had published a pamphlet to promote cotton cultivation in Turkey. The proceeds from the sale of this pamphlet were to be distributed among the needy workers in the textile factories of Manchester. . . .

Cottonseed Distributed Among Merchants

In April 1863, <u>Ceride-i Havadis</u> reported that 226,843 <u>okka</u> of cottonseed had been imported from Egypt to be distributed free of charge in various parts of Turkey.

The same paper quoted the following statistics from <u>Takvim-i Vekayi</u> on 18 April 1863. The figures, showing the amount of Egyptian cottonseed distributed, were supplied by the Ministry of Commerce:

Distributed in	Okka
Izmir	89,000
Bought for merchants and sent to Izmir	20,639
Edirne	75,000
Salonica	28,500
Amasya	6,000
Kastamonu	3,000
Sinop (experimental)	350
Trabzon "	300
Karahisar "	150
Tolci "	150
Sofia "	150
Vidin "	150
Silivri "	7,000
Biga "	10,000
Bursa	3,000
Balikesir	1,000
Mediterranean islands	2,000
Crete	10,000
Damascus	2,500
American seed to Izmir	2,400
Salonica (second shipment)	2,400
	264,829

Cottonseed and Agricultural Machinery Exempted from Duty

On 29 May 1863, Ceride-i Havadis published an official notice, taken from Takvim-i Vekayi, which proclaimed that, in order to promote cotton cultivation in Turkey, cottonseed and agricultural machinery imported to Turkey would be exempt from customs duty for a period of ten years.

Cotton Produce Arriving in Europe

Ceride-i Havadis of 30 December 1863 published the following statistics on the amount and value of cotton imported by Europe that year:

From	Bales	Lira
India	1,650,000	51,975,000
Egypt	300,000	17,531,000
From those parts of the US not blockaded	140,000	6,673,000
Ottoman Empire and its possessions	140,000	4,025,000
Brazil	190,000	3,911,000
China	200,000	334,000
Italy	15,000	632,000
Other areas	30,000	975,000
	2,765,000[sic]	88,656,000[sic]

"Egyptian bales weigh 180 okkas, and Ottoman bales, 100; American bales, 150; and other bales weigh 70-80 okkas. The best produce is American and Egyptian; secondly, Turkish, thirdly Brazilian and Italian. Indian and Chinese cotton are of the worst quality."

Machinery Imported

A memorandum sent from the Porte to the Office of the Chamberlain on 8 July 1863, included the following passage: "For the time being the purchase of fity small and ten large machines to be used in cotton cultivation is considered adequate. For the immediate purchase of these machines, in order to insure their arrival at the time of reaping, 100,000 kuruş will be forwarded from the exalted treasury to the Ministry of Treasury." A decree was issued confirming the decision not to levy duties on imported machinery and cottonseed and ordering that the matter be proclaimed through public notices in the newspapers.

A Factory for Ginning Cotton in the Adana Area

In a memorandum sent from the Porte to the Office of the Chamberlain on 21 September 1864, the grand vizirate ordered that a license be issued to a James Kot, merchant, to build a cotton sorting factory in the Adana, Tarsus, and Mersin area. According to the license, the machinery imported for the factory would be exempt from duty, the project would come under the Factories Regulations, for each steam engine a boiler tax of 10 lira would be levied, the owner of the factory would not have the right to create a monopoly, and would come under Turkish laws, whatever his nationality.

On 14 November 1864, the Porte instructed the Office of the Chamberlain to issue a similar license to a Mr. Edwards, who had asked permission to build a cotton ginning factory near Kirkağaç in the Balikesir province [see 6:14].

Article on Cotton Cultivation

Takvim-i Ticaret, no. 2, on 10 February 1866 began serializing "An Article on Cotton Cultivation," parts of which appeared in nos. 3, 5, 7, 8, 10, 11. This article mentioned how suitable Turkey was for cotton cultivation, which did not hurt grain cultivation, and how much better American cotton was compared to other types. The article continued to explain that if American type cotton should be grown in Turkey, because of Turkey's proximity to Europe it would be exported to Europe even though the war in America had ended. Several matters relating to the cultivation of cotton were also discussed.

Medals for Cotton Growers

The main points of the regulation "Concerning the rewarding of those who help promote cotton cultivation in the Ottoman Empire, of those who sow the seed, and of those who initiate the use of machinery to sort cotton," dated 27 January 1866, are given below as quoted in 10 February 1866 issue of Takvim-i Ticaret: [the awarding of gold and silver medals]. . . .

Distribution of American Cottonseed

Takvim-i Ticaret reported on 31 March 1866 that a shipment of 60 tons of American seed, out of a total of 300 tons ordered by the Ministry of Commerce through the Turkish Embassy in London, had arrived and been distributed as follows:

To	okka
Salonica	50,000
Amasya	10,000
Izmir	20,000
Bursa	10,000
Istanköy	2,000
Imperial farms	1,000
Rusçuk	2,000
East Karahisar	200
	95,200

On 23 June 1866, Takvim-i Ticaret reported that 45,000 okka of American cottonseed had been distributed free of charge among farmers in Anatolia.

Inflammable Materials in Cotton Bales

Takvim-i Ticaret reported on 1 December 1866 that the cotton bales exported from Turkey contained sulphurous material that caught fire due to friction, and some other chemicals that started burning due to heat. Whereas these bales occasionally caused fires, insurance companies were losing money, and the merchants of Liverpool and Manchester were complaining. The Porte ordered provincial governors to prevent such incidents and punish those who caused them.

Decline of Cotton Cultivation in Turkey

The effect of the measures taken to promote cotton cultivation with the encouragement of the English declined after a while. The government did not seriously continue its efforts, and cotton production in Turkey declined. The Levant Times of Istanbul published an article about the decline of cotton production in Turkey.

"It is very regrettable that a decline in cotton production in Turkey is being observed. While because of the nature of the land the production of cotton should have increased, the export records for 1871 show that the produce has declined. The local governments have neglected to distribute fresh seed among the farmers, to train the farmers in such methods as best apply to growing cotton in those areas, to build dykes to divert rainwater and prevent swamps, and to take other similar measures.

"The farmers make two major mistakes in understanding and promoting cotton cultivation as the most profitable form of cultivation: first, instead of planting in April, the most suitable time, they delay sowing until June; secondly, they sow cottonseed in the same manner as they sow wheat and barley, yet for barley they plough the land twice, for cotton three times. Their ploughs are made of wood, six feet wide and nine inches deep. After ploughing the field, they take care to sow the seeds deep, thinking that that gives better results. This way poor crops result but they think that it is a matter of bad luck. Had the government appointed people to teach methods of cultivation, instead of 50,000 bales, 400,000 bales of cotton could have been exported from Izmir. . . .

"In 1871, 20,128 bales of cotton were exported to Spain; 18,385 bales to Austria,

4,605 bales to England; 1,804 bales to France; 110 bales to Russia, and 28 bales to Holland from Izmir. The total export from that port amounted to 51,345 bales. . . ."

SELECTION 16. COTTON PRODUCTION IN THE ADANA AND IZMIR REGIONS, 1910

W. F. Brück, "Türkische Baumwollwirtschaft," <u>Probleme der Weltwirtschaft</u>, no. 29, Jena, 1919, pp. 58-79

Adana

. . . In the last few years before the outbreak of war, production in the Adana region rose considerably, thanks to more suitable cultivation of the soil and also to easier credit supplies to peasants. The crops show the following increase (in bales of 200 kilograms):

1903	40,000	1910	64,000
1904	42,000	1911	80,000
1905	45,000	1912	100,000
1906	50,000	1913	105,000
1907	60,000	1914	85,000
1908	75,000		

Before the war and in the early war years, the crops would probably have been better had they not suffered from natural calamities. Once it was hail and another time a cloudburst that damaged the crop and again locusts left hardly a stalk standing in many districts. After that, the war began to affect the crops adversely: in 1915, the crop was 50,000 bales, in 1916 35,000, and in 1917 still lower; this year's crop is estimated at 20,000 bales at most.

Of total Turkish production, 95 percent comes from a cotton plant locally known as Yerli--a variety of <u>Gossypium herbaceum</u> which has been acclimatized in Asia Minor--and 5 percent from an American variety imported within the last few years and known in Adana as i hane ("foreign"). The Yerli has adapted itself well to the climatic conditions of the country in the course of the long period during which it has been cultivated; its main advantage is its timely ripening, before the rainy season. We shall discuss its other characteristics later. It is said that the Yerli is native to Syria and North Arabia. This short-staple variety dominated the European market until the 17th century, and was known as Levant Cotton. It is still occasionally grown in Europe--in Macedonia, southern Italy, and southern Spain. Immigrants took it to North America, but after that date it was progressively driven out by the long-staple Upland variety from Mexico. In addition, a set of experiments was carried out in the Adana plain with foreign plants (i hane), principally from American (partly from America and partly from the region of Smyrna) and Egyptian seeds. A definitive judgment cannot be made on the experiments, but those in charge believe that the proceeds of these products do not justify the higher costs of production. On the other hand, some individual successes have led to great hopes, which however have not been fulfilled for reasons that have no essential connection with the natural conditions of cultivation. Promising beginnings have been spoiled by mixture with other varieties, arising partly out of defective organization and partly from the fact that the peasants are not accustomed to handle pure seeds.

The war put an end to attempts at improving seeds and introducing new plants. The Deutsch-Levantinische Baumwoll-gesellschaft had carried out a set of attempts at improving native cotton and planting varieties of different origins--according to the statements of the company, with varieties imported directly from America and Russian Asia and with all the better Egyptian varieties. It had also carried out, for many years, experiments with Caravonica--and all of this under the direction of a cotton expert who had been brought over from Egypt for this specific purpose. The results announced by the company were that Egyptian varieties developed very well, especially where they could be irrigated, but that with few exceptions they did not ripen at the right time, and hence worms got into the bolls and seriously damaged the cotton. According to the company, it is out of the question to aim at the high-class Egyptian product. Experiments with American seed and with American varieties grown in Russian Asia were completely successful. But after some years, during which the farmers were induced with considerable difficulty and expenditure to use American seeds and the population seemed gradually prepared to buy such seeds, the experiments had to be given up. The lack of labor and inexpert handling prevent orderly picking. The lint often fell out of the boll, was dirtied by wind and dew and lost much of its market value. The company's model farms also carried out experiments for improving native varieties, but the costs incurred were not in proportion to the increase in value of the improved cotton. Only a planned organization, which provides expert selection of the seed and supervision of the crop from harvesting until sowing, can produce results. We shall make some recommendations on this subject in our final chapter. But it is clear that the adverse circumstances prevailing until now stand in the way of rational work and outstanding success. . . .

Comparisons of fiber yields show that, until now, Asia Minor cotton has fared badly.

In a table published by the Deutsch-Levantinische Baumwollgesellschaft, the following figures are given on lint yields:[1]

Adana plain	75 lbs. per acre	(84 kilograms per hectare)
Russian Asia	170 " " "	(190.5 " " ")
America	183 " " "	(205.8 " " ")
Egypt	340 " " "	(381.1 " " ")

Thanks to improvements carried out by the company, yields in 1912 were raised to 95 lbs per acre, according to the same report. For anyone who knows the heights of the various kinds of cotton plants and the stem on which the boll rests (Kapselansatz), and also the methods of cultivation in the above mentioned countries, it is no cause for surprise that the cotton of Asia Minor compares so badly with the others. One should add that it is of much shorter staple than the other varieties.

Compared to the methods of tillage used in the interior of Asia Minor, cultivation in the Cilician plain can already be termed advanced. In that plain, as in the whole of Asia Minor, cotton is a summer crop. A kind of three-field system prevails, under which in the first year cereals are planted and in the second cotton only, or sesame and cotton, or sesame only. The third year, the land is left fallow, or fallow and pasture. Frequently, the fallow period is prolonged considerably. This is due to the fact that there is much land available, from which individual plots can be taken for cultivation, and in addition farmers are highly dependent on available labor. The longer the fallow lasts, the more the field is filled with weeds, and the higher the costs of ploughing, hoeing, etc. when planting it once more to cotton or other crops. This will take place after the war, for the fields have been covered with weeds owing to the lack of cultivation due to the shortage of labor. It also happens frequently that fallow is not practiced and that a plot of land is planted to the same crop for 8 to 10 years without a break.

Among the cereals grown in the Adana region wheat, barley, and, occasionally, oats are prominent. Millet, maize, and durrah [sorghum] are of less significance. For example, in October-November wheat is sown, and reaped the following June or July. In March or April cotton, the next crop in the rotation, is sown (by itself or with sesame) and picked in October. In a mixed rotation, sesame comes a month earlier than cotton. This double culture is inherently very unsuitable; it is used because, should one crop fail, the peasant at any rate receives some income from the other crop. Sesame, which is a highly productive crop, draws away too much nutrient from the soil. And during the harvesting of the earlier crops the ground is trampled, which injures the cotton crop and diminishes the lint yield. It should, however, be noted that sesame is being planted less and less in combination with cotton. Watermelons are also planted together with cotton. Fruits, which contain up to 80 percent water, also deprive cotton of this important building material [i.e., water] when planted with it.

In general, the soil is neither manured nor deeply ploughed. But one should admit that, in the last years before the outbreak of war, the importance of modern methods for securing higher yields has been increasingly recognized by individual large landowners; among these, few are pure Turks, but rather Greeks, Armenians, Syrians, and so on. In the decade preceding the war, the number of machines imported into and used in the Adana vilayet was not less than about 1,000 reapers, 100 steam threshers, 25 double-steam ploughs, 85 single-steam ploughs. Unfortunately, the German share in these machines was small. . . .

In general, the productivity of the soil has sharply decreased, because of continuous planting without manuring. Deep ploughing is also restricted to a few individuals. Tillage generally consists of 6 to 8 ploughings with the Turkish pointed plough, whose blade does not turn but only loosens the soil. The agricultural implements, which are very primitive, are described on pages 22-23 of this work. Soskin[2] says, rightly, that on some estates European ploughs are to be found, but most are thrown away as scrap. For the workers and the peasants prefer to work with their traditional ploughs, and the indolence of the managers is such that they cannot accustom the people to using European ploughs, of whose utility they themselves are not convinced. Near Adana, the Turkish government set up a model farm, which I visited. . . .

Until now, extensive areas have remained uncultivated in the plain, because of a shortage of capital. There is a great number of large landlords, but most of them are not in a position to exploit their estates with paid labor and take on a partner (ortak) whom they provide with land, seeds, and occasionally also draft animals. Sometimes, the landlord also advances loans to the cultivator. The latter undertakes the whole work of ploughing, sowing, and harvesting. After deduction of the tithe [see 7:11] due to the government, the crop is divided in kind between landowner and ortak. If conditions are favorable each side gets its due. . . .

As we showed earlier, Turkey lacks the good, efficient, easy credit system required to complement agricultural capital. In particular, the absence of a highly capitalized mortgage bank has had very adverse effects on farmers. A branch of the Agricultural Bank exists in Adana, but most of its capital is loaned to the government, leaving little for the support of agriculture. The inevitable consequence is that farmers turn to usurers-- Armenians, Greeks, Syrians, and, unfortuantely, also Europeans. In most cases the farmer cannot pay the high rates of interest charged on the mortgage, which unavoidably leads to the sale of his land--unless the usurer himself takes it over. This explains, to a large extent, the fact that land is left uncultivated. The farmer who has invested all his fortune in a plot of land has to borrow--at 15 or sometimes 30 percent or more--to acquire the necessary implements, draft animals, or seeds; this means that hardly one year gives him clear profit, for he is all the time servicing his old debt. Thus he works mostly for his creditor, for he is not able to cover an interest rate of 10-20 percent in addition to his living expenses.

The deterioration of cottonseed and fiber is closely connected with this obvious defect in the credit system. For only too often the farmer gets the seeds from the usurer, who wherever possible owns the ginnery. He therefore receives from various points bolls, cotton, or seeds, and, with no consideration for selection, purity or quality, gives seeds to farmers for planting. Protection against this usurious exploitation, and simultaneous upgrading of the fiber, can be carried out only by a large-scale organization, and a specific program for this purpose is given on pages 107 ff. The capital of the Agricultural Bank should also be increased, so that it can supply large landowners, too, with credit. The largest amount the bank was allowed to advance before the war was ₤T150, the interest rate was 6 percent, and the loan was repayable in 1-10 years.

The distribution of landownership may be briefly discussed. Before the war, there were a few large landlords who owned estates of one thousand to, exceptionally, five thousand hectares. Of these, however, only part was cultivated. There were medium landowners with 200 or 500 or 600 hectares and a much higher number of small owners with only 10 hectares. Overall, one-third of the land was held by large owners. Those farmers who used modern methods--those with 100 hectares of land or over--had their own machinery, while those with 50 hectares or less rented machines from each other. The Anatolische Industrie und Handelgesellschaft also successfully rented out German machines to the farmers.

One should also point out that, so far, Europeans have seldom been landowners, participating only in the role of merchants. The Deutsch-Levantinische Baumwollgesellschaft rented land for short periods and farmed it with modern methods, doing pioneer work in this field. But Europeans in general have been rather suppliers of loans and buyers of crops while farming operations were carried on by the native farmers. The Deutsch-Levantinische Baumwollgesellschaft, together with a few big Greek and Armenian firms, was among the principal buyers of the crops, while the Deutsche Orientbank was a particularly large supplier of loans.

The above-mentioned improvements in cultivation, as well as those in further preparation--and to a certain extent the replacement of hand gins by rotary gins--and others, including longer-term loans to farmers, have greatly raised the level of cultivation in the last few years, which can be clearly seen in the figures given above on the increase in crops. The Yerli cotton, which as stated constitutes 95 percent of the crop, is regarded in world markets as a low value product; it has a very short, coarse fiber, of uneven length and is thus inferior to middling Indian varieties. The low value of this cotton is shown by the fact that a large part is used as stuffing and packing material, and when spun gives only the lower numbers of 4 or 6 or 8. Somewhat higher numbers, allegedly up to 20, can only seldom be spun, from special varieties. But these native varieties have one great advantage--they are well suited to the climate of Asia Minor and northern Syria. It is not necessary to pick the lint, as with American, Egyptian, and Indian cotton, for it can be plucked along with its boll and the picking can be done in winter, by the townsmen in their homes. So far, all the better varieties that have been tried out in the Adana vilayet have not offered this advantage, which is closely connected with the labor question. The American cotton variety that has been introduced--the above-mentioned hane--requires three pickings, in other words a large number of workmen precisely during the harvesting season. This fact changes the basis of all calculations, when drawing up future plans for the introduction of higher-quality cotton. But one should also bear in mind that the quality of the already low-value Yerli is deteriorating year by year and, therefore, some other variety will have to be introduced in the future.

Before the war, land prices ranged between 50 and 500 marks per hectare, varying according to the location (proximity to a town, railway, etc.) and goodness of the soil. A hectare of good cotton land cost about 400 marks before the outbreak of the war.

Before the war, labor was provided by members of every imaginable nationality of Turkey, the most important and ablest being the Armenians.[3] Of the others, mention should be made of, among Muslims, Çerkes, Kurds, Turkomans, Arabs, and Nogai, in addition to the Muhacir (immigrants) and other Turks; and among followers of other religions Nusairis, Syrians, and fellahin.

The gathering of the crop begins in autumn, as soon as the desired number of bolls is available. For American varieties, which have to be picked, harvesting begins earlier. For this, all available labor is gathered from town and country, and relatively high wages are paid. Most of the picking is done by women and children. From the end of September, the poorer townsfolk, with their families, spread over the countryside. Payment is frequently made in kind.

The crop is then bought by native merchants (Kosaci), who give the cotton a first cleaning. For this a drum operated by hand is used, which separates the bolls from all impurities such as leaves, pebbles, dust, etc. In Adana, there are over 200 such cleaning drums. At this point cottage industry takes over: the bolls that have been cleaned in drums, the kosa, are worked over further in homes, i.e., the lint is picked out of the bolls by hand. Before the war, 7 piastres per çeki (32.05 kilogrammes) was paid at the beginning of the season and 4 piastres at its end, in other words a relatively high price. Nearly all the thousands of poor people live on this home work.

After this separation, the cotton, which is still attached to the seed, is sent to the ginnery for ginning and cleaning. Before the war, there were some 800 gins in the vilayet. The ginned cotton is then packed in large bags. The owner receives from the ginnery in which his cotton is stored a bond showing the amount belonging to him. With this, the merchant negotiates with the exporter, who buys the goods by samples, and receives the bond, which authorizes him to withdraw the goods from the ginnery. The cotton is then pressed: almost every large exporter has his own hand-operated hydraulic press. The sister company of the Deutsch-Levantinische Baumwollgesellschaft, the Anatolische Industrie-und Handelsgesellschaft, has built a steam press near its ginning factory, which presses bales of 250 to 270 kilograms; the bales of the hand-operated presses, on the other hand, usually weigh not more than 200 kilograms. This company owns, in addition to gins, separating machines, the so-called décorticateurs, like the ones used for cotton in Transcaspia and Transcaucasia. Should Yerli cotton continue to be planted, a more general use of such machines would save much labor. For American varieties, where the cotton is picked in the fields, such machines are, of course unnecessary. But, as has already been mentioned, such cotton requires much more labor for harvesting than does Yerli. . . .

My investigations have led me to the following conclusions: using modern farming methods--selected seeds, deep ploughing (about 30 centimetres) with a steam plough, etc., low-cost loans to farmers--one can harvest a 200 kilogram bale per hectare. The data given by Soskin (p. 338), showing that at present the average yield per hectare is only 125 kilograms, and those of the Deutsch-Levantinische Geselleschaft, show how far from this ideal we still are. Until now, only about 30,000 hectares have been worked in a relatively modern way. In other words, for a crop of 100,000 bales of 200 kilograms, around 100,000 hectares would have to be planted to cotton each year in the Adana region. This represents about 15 percent of the total cultivable area of the vilayet, which is put at 1.5 million hectares; the rest consists of mountains, swamps, etc.[4]

Until now Adana varieties have been rain-grown, and have not received artificial irrigation. The largest crops recorded--insignificant as they are in the world market-- could not have been harvested with the labor force available in the vilayet of Adana: 60,000 to 70,000 additional seasonal workers had to be brought in from Van, Erzurum, Diyarbakir, Mosul, etc. for this purpose. . . .

At present there is much talk of irrigation projects: the idea is to regulate the flow of three rivers, the Tarsus-çay, the Seihun, and the Cihan, and to water an area of 250,000 to 300,000 hectares in their basins. A few years ago, the firm of Philipp Holzmann and Co. presented a project to the Turkish government but was not asked to implement it. Until now, other studies have also not made any advance towards the fulfilment of the scheme. . . .

As regards the cotton textile industry, one may note that there are two spinning mills in Adana and two in Tarsus. The Adana mills had, before the war, 10,000 spindles and 200 looms and 6,500 spindles and 50 looms, respectively; in Tarsus there is a spinning mill with 5,700 spindles and another with 15,000 spindles and 600 looms in the attached weaving shed.

Oil-pressing from cottonseed has been carried on in a few presses in the vilayet; before the war, there were also two enterprises producing on a factory scale.

Smyrna

As mentioned earlier, before American cotton became naturalized in the European consuming countries, the crops of Smyrna, Macdeonia, and also some southern parts of Sicily and Spain covered European consumption. But Smyrna cotton stood far ahead of the others. Here, too, the cotton was Yerli, a variety of Indian Gossypium herbaceum. As in the Adana region, plants of various origins were introduced, mostly American but more recently some Egyptian varieties. But hardly 10 percent of the cultivated area is accounted for by American varieties, while Egyptian cotton is only occasionally planted. It is reported that in the 1870s some 75,000 bales were exported from Smyrna, but in recent years the production of this region has not exceeded 52,000 bales of 200 kilograms each--in 1911-12. Among other factors, the unfavorable relations resulting from the war and political events have caused cultivation to decline more and more, so that in 1916 the crop was estimated at a bare 7,000 bales. This corresponds to the quantity consumed by German spinning mills in a single day. The development of production has been as follows (in bales of 200 kilograms):

1905-6	42,000	1911-12	52,000
1906-7	33,000	1912-13	40,000
1907-8	45,000	1913-14	30,000
1908-9	38,000	1914-15	ca. 10,000
1909-10	35,000	1915-16	ca. 10,000
1910-11	34,000	1916-17	ca. 7,000

In the last few years the cotton crop has become hardly worth mentioning, for much of the area has been shifted to cereals, tobacco, and other crops.

In peacetime, 10,000 bales were used for internal consumption, i.e., for the spinning mills of Smyrna, the neighboring Greek islands, and Salonica. The rest went to Spain and France; Austria was an occasional buyer but Germany did not come into the picture at all. Previously, Smyrna had also been the market for Adana cotton, but in the last few years Adana has completely emancipated its trade from Smyrna. In 1911 the Smyrna exporters got together, to rescue their threatened business, and formed the Asia Minor Cotton Association Ltd., with a capital of 20,000 pounds. At present, this company is in liquidation. . . .

The cotton zone of the vilayet of Aydin consists of three regions [the Gediz basin, the Burgas Ovasi, and the plain of the Menderes] which have several common characteristics: all three are floodlands of large rivers and, being not more than 100 kilometers distant from the sea, are exposed to the sea breezes so that cotton can be grown without artificial irrigation. Annual precipitation averages 50 to 60 centimeters. The summers are rainless but humidity is provided by the sea breezes and heavy dew. . . .

As regards the distribution of landownership, the following may be said: the predominant form is small ownership, of about 20 to 30 hectares, belonging mostly to Greeks but also to Turks. The workers are mainly Anatolian and fellah migrants, who have mixed with the local farmers. In the last few years before the war, there was also a large inflow of seasonal workers from the eastern parts of Turkey. In addition, some large enterprises exist--we refer to farms of 1,200 to 1,500 hectares. More recently, a few experimental farms have been established near Akhisar, among others by the Khedive [of Egypt] and a Jewish company, Or Yehuda. Small-scale operation is best suited, for given the primitive methods of cultivation, the labor of the owner and his family is adequate. Because of the large number of children in Greek families--and in those of the fellahin, who have several wives who provide them with labor--wages are low. Methods of cultivation differ in the region. We find the three-field system, alternation with grain, and repeated planting to cotton. Cultivation is unbelievably primitive, mainly with a wooden plough which only scratches the soil, seldom with an iron ploughshare. Heavier ploughs cannot be used, for the draft animals are not strong enough. The cultivation of the soil is not as developed as in the vilayet of Adana. . . .

The yield per hectare is much higher than in the Adana region. . . .

As in the Adana region, ginning is carried on partly by farmers and partly by medium and large enterprises run by intermediaries and buyers. Before the war, there were 12 factories in the Menderes plain, with 270 gins (Platt Brothers system). In Magnesia there were the largest factories, with about 20 gins, and in the Kaystros plain 6 factories with 90 gins. All these establishments did not deal exclusively in cotton processing but usually had olive presses and grain mills. As regards the pressing of the bales, what was said about Adana applies here, except for the fact that there are no steam presses yet. Two large spinning and weaving factories in Smyrna process cotton. The first has 20,000 spindles and 100 Cabot looms, and can process 6,000 bales a year working on one shift (Tagesarbeit); in normal times, its work-force is 600 to 700. The other factory has 8,000 spindles and 300 looms and processes about 4,000 bales. Smyrna cotton (about 1,500 bales) is also spun in two mills in Mitylene, with 3,000 and 1,000 spindles respectively. . . .

1. The calculations are those of the author. The figures for Adana are too low and much higher figures for average yields in America (around 250 kilograms) have been given. In any case, the difference between yields of Adana cotton and that of other varieties is very great.

2. In Tropenflanzer, 1917.

3. In his calculation of costs of production, Soskin provides information on the workmen, their activity and their mode of payment; we refer to his description. . . .

4. The main crops are:

a) Wheat: area in 1912, 115,000 hectares; of the gross production of about 250,000 tons one-third is exported, leaving about 500 kilograms per capita; most of the export is to Turkish ports.

b) Barley: the area of 85,000 hectares gives a crop of 140,000 tons, of which one-third is exported.

c) Oats: the 45,000 hectares planted to oats give a crop of around 70,000 tons, of which more than half is exported.

OLIVE OIL AND OILSEEDS

Olives and olive oil have supplied the bulk of the fat consumed in Mediterranean countries for thousands of years, and the western and southern rims of Anatolia, together with the adjacent islands, have always been large producers and exporters. In the nineteenth century two other sources of oil were developed, cottonseed and sesame. But during that period Mediterranean oils had to meet increasing competition from the tropical regions of Asia and, subsequently, Africa.

On the eve of the First World War, Anatolia's olive crop was estimated at about 175,000 tons. The main centers of cultivation were Aydın and Bursa provinces, with 90,000 and 70,000 tons. About one-seventh of the crop was exported, by Greek firms, mostly to Rumania, Russia, Bulgaria and Egypt.[1]

An important technological innovation was the introduction, in the 1880s, of hydraulic presses for oil. These were far more efficient than the traditional presses, but they required much larger investment and led to concentration of oil-pressing in a few places and the development of capitalistic relations in the industry. By the First World War, there were some 260 such presses in Anatolia, 60 percent of the capacity being in the sancak of Izmir; they produced some 95 percent of the average output of 30,000 tons of olive oil a year. In the export trade a leading role was played by foreign firms—British, Italian, and German.[2] Exports declined from an average of 14,900 tons in 1878-82 to about 11,200 in 1908-13, but, thanks to higher prices, their value rose from ₤T456,000 to ₤T480,000.[3]

As the two following selections show, the cultivation of sesame developed rapidly in the early 1840s, in the Izmir region, and still more so in Cilicia, owing to a rise in price. The subsequent upward trend may be judged from the quantity of oilseeds sent from Izmir to France, which was almost the sole importer. Starting on a large scale in 1840, when 2,000 metric tons were exported, the yearly averages rose as follows: 1840-44, 5,600 tons; 1845-49, 10,700 tons; 1850-54, 13,100 tons; 1855-59, 14,000 tons. One reason given for this rapid expansion, in contrast to the failure to extend cotton-growing until the American Civil War, was that oilseeds demanded less labor than cotton (CC Smyrne, vol. 49, 8 December 1861).

Output must have somewhat declined in the next two decades, since Turkey's total exports of sesame in 1878-82 averaged only 11,200 tons, worth ₤T153,000. But exports rose sharply thereafter, reaching a peak of 23,000 tons, worth ₤T301,000, in 1892-96. In the years preceding the First World War exports were lower, perhaps because of increasing domestic processing of oilseeds in Cilicia and Izmir (6:Introduction), and in 1908-13 exports of sesame averaged 14,000 tons, worth ₤T256,000.[4]

The production of cottonseed oil also increased, together with that of cotton (5:16); when ginned, cotton yields roughly two pounds of seed for one of lint.

---

1. Stich, pp. 44-46, citing Fickendey.
2. Ibid., pp. 47-49.
3. Aybar, p. 61; "But the methods of extracting the oil are so crude that the product is usually acrid and easily becomes rancid. The low quality of the oil is the obstacle to serving a foreign market" (Mears, p. 287).
4. Aybar, p. 61.

SELECTION 17. OILSEED PRODUCTION IN IZMIR REGION, 1844

Reply to Questionnaire, 7 August 1844, CC Smyrne, vol. 47

1. What is the state of the production of oilseeds today?

The cultivation of oilseeds in Asia Minor includes sesame, poppy seed, and linseed; except for the first, it is at present very limited.

Smyrna supplies about 1,500 metric quintals of linseed, but Kayseri and the neighborhood of Tarsus could provide another 10,000 metric quintals.

Poppy seeds are produced only in the neighborhood of Uşak and Karahisar. In an average year, output may be about 15,000 metric quintals, but it can be exported only if a very high price is offered, to withdraw it from local consumption, which absorbs it entirely.

As for sesame, one can estimate its output in Asia Minor (Smyrna, Scala Nuova, Caramania, and Tarsus) in a good year at 50,000 metric quintals, or 225 to 240 thousand kilos of Constantinople, of which local consumption absorbs 60 to 80 thousand kilos.

2. What is the cost of the different seeds and their selling price at the place of production?

In 1842-43, prices of up to 40 piastres a kilo of Constantinople were paid at the place of loading on board ship, customs duty included. In 1843-44 29 to 33 piastres (add 5 percent for the brokerage fees, commissions etc. of the exporting firm).

Linseed sold at 56 paras per oke in 1842-43 and 44 in 1843-44.

Poppy seed 2 piastres an oke and 55 paras, respectively. Prices at the place of production vary, according to distance.

3. Is the planting of sesame being extended? What is the present situation?

Purchases of sesame seed for Marseilles and the high prices paid at the producing places have led to a great development of the cultivation of this seed. However, since not all soils are favorable to this crop, it can hardly be extended further.

In addition, the considerable transport costs (from 3 to 5 piastres per Constantinople kilo, according to distance), the enormous duties paid on cultivation, viz., 10 percent for tithe and 10 percent tax on income, which because of the estimates used for prices come to 15 percent and 18 percent, plus 12 percent customs, prevent the planting of sesame from going beyond certain limits. It is even probable that it will stop as soon as prices fall to 25 piastres a Constantinople kilo and 30 paras per oke of linseed.

4. What are the relations between this crop and cotton? Is it true, as has been claimed, that the gains arising from it have led to the giving up of cotton, or at least have stopped the development of the latter?

Soils which are suitable for cotton are equally suited for sesame, or roughly so. The sowing of both plants is carried out at the same time and the methods of cultivation of both are similar and require the same care. However sesame is more subject to atmospheric influences. It is not correct to say that the planting of sesame has resulted in the giving up of cotton. The same field often holds both crops intermixed, the farmer thus having two chances instead of one. But the low esteem with which, for a long time now, Anatolian cotton has been regarded in the French and Swiss markets, has gradually led to a decrease in production. The resulting improvement for the country has, however, been very precarious, for the profits made on sesame can only be very small--for the reasons given under 3, above--and because that plant, being extremely frail, seldom gives a large crop.

5. What are the freight rates for oilseeds shipped on Greek, Sardinian, Austrian, or Tuscan vessels to Nice, Genoa, Leghorn, and other ports?

Generally, there is a difference of 50 centimes per metric quintal between French and foreign ships in favor of the first.

N.B. 1 Turkish piastre equals 40 paras; 170 paras equal one franc.

1 metric quintal, or 100 kilograms, equals 4 3/4 kilos of Constantinople.

1 oke equals 1 1/4 kilograms.

SELECTION 18.   OILSEED PRODUCTION IN CILICIA, 1844

Reply to Questionnaire, 29 September 1844, CC Tarsous, vol. 2

1. The cultivation of oilseeds, and especially sesame, has considerably expanded, being stimulated by the ease and favorable terms with which they find buyers. It is only since 1841 that the planting of this seed has revolutionized the system of cultivation of this region. Until that time, planting was confined to local consumption, which limited output to about 150,000 kilograms. Since then, it has expanded so prodigiously that if the hopes pinned on the present crop are not shattered by some accident, the output of this district should be nearly 1,875,000 kilograms.

2. The low cost of producing this crop and the high export price almost always obtained for it have effectively contributed to determine the farmer to exclude all other products from his fields and to allocate the latter exclusively to sesame. When this seed was grown only for local consumption, its selling price ranged between 10 and 12 francs per 100 kilograms. In 1841, when for the first time trial shipments were sent to France, the price rose to 30 francs. The first shipments were so successful that they probably exceeded the hopes of the exporters.

In 1842 the price reached 40 francs. The crisis that hit sesame in Marseilles, because of too great shipments and a considerable decrease in processing, struck a heavy blow at operations in this product; severe losses were incurred and speculators were discouraged.

In 1843, sales for export, while not excessively great, rose to not less than one million kilograms. The whole crop was not cleared, and quite a large part of last year's harvest is still in the warehouse.

Everything leads one to believe that this year sales will be large. We have here several trade agents from Beirut, Smyrna, and Constantinople who have already laid out large sums in advances. It is believed that the price offered to growers will range between 28 and 32 francs per 100 kilograms.

3. The answer to the first question contains also the answer to this question.

4. The cultivation of sesame is very similar to that of cotton; both crops are planted at much the same time, i.e., in March. Not infrequently, cotton and sesame are to be found in the same fields, planted in the same season and by the same methods. Two powerful causes have hindered the growing of cotton. The first is its decline in the European markets, where its poor quality puts it well below American cotton. Since production of cotton was only called upon to meet the consumption of the interior of Anatolia and Caramania--which is, incidentally very considerable--it had necessarily to decrease, and farmers immediately preferred sesame as being more advantageous than any other crop and as requiring very little expense for cleaning and depositing in warehouses.

5. Ships belonging to the nations mentioned in Question 5 have loaded some oilseeds here, but only for Marseilles, and no shipments have been made to any Italian port.

On French ships, the freight is 4 to 5 francs; on ships flying the Greek, Sardinian, Austrian, or Tuscan flags, freights to Marseilles are 2.50 to 3.50 francs and to the Italian ports 2 to 3 francs.

If I had to state to Your Excellency the general opinion prevailing in the trade on transactions in sesame seeds, I would have to say that most merchants here consider it a very risky business and that, most often, excessive competition in this market has made such transactions very unsatisfactory, especially in the last few years; fears have even been expressed that this branch will be lost to French trade if numerous duties are put on sesame imports to France.

TOBACCO

Both the smoking and the planting of tobacco came to the Middle East at the beginning of the seventeenth century.[1] As in other countries, smoking was prohibited, more particularly by Murat IV (1623-70), under whom, in the words of Katib Çelebi, "many thousands of men were sent to the abode of nothingness." But capital punishment did not have the desired effect, and taxation was tried instead, under Süleyman II (1687-91). By then, cultivation was well established in Syria and the Balkans and by the eighteenth century tobacco was being exported from Salonica,[2] Trabzon, and Latakia[3] (see also selection 19). Soon the Black Sea region, from Sinop to Trabzon, became the main center of production; in 1840 Bafra's output was estimated at over 800 tons (Stevens to Brant, 15 February 1840, FO 78/401) and in 1841 Canik's was put at over 2,200 (Trade Samsun FO 78/492). In 1847 it was reported that the French government had made a trial purchase of Samsun tobacco: "The quality was greatly approved of, and another quantity of one hundred bales has been ordered to be shipped to Marseilles" (ibid., 1847, FO 78/704). In that year the output of the Samsun region was estimated at 2,250 tons;[4] much of its crop was sent to Istanbul.

As an exporter, however, Turkey did not attain world significance until the 1850s. As late as 1848, British exports of tobacco and products to Turkey, at 471,000 lbs., greatly exceeded its imports of 5,000 lbs. therefrom. But by 1850 Britain's exports had practically disappeared while its imports shot up, to 3,388,000 lbs., worth £71,000, by 1854 and rather smaller amounts through the rest of the decade.[5] The American Civil War greatly increased the demand for Turkish tobacco[6] and in 1862 Samsun and Sinop exported 3,250 tons. The mechanization of cigarette-making further stimulated demand, and Greek and Jewish emigrants from the Ottoman Empire helped to familiarize American and European consumers with Turkish tobacco, which came to be increasingly used for blending. In response, cultivation began to spread, in the 1870s, in the Izmir region. By 1902 western Anatolia was producing some 3,200 tons and by 1911 about 10,000.[7]

In the meantime the tithe and other taxes on tobacco were making a significant contribution to the Ottoman budget.[8] In 1860 tobacco became a state monopoly. Following the 1876 financial crisis, tobacco revenues were ceded first to the Administration of the Six Revenues and then to the Debt Administration (7:16). In 1883 the latter signed an agreement with the Régie Cointéressée des Tabacs de l'Empire Ottoman, a consortium with a capital of 100 million francs set up by the Ottoman Bank, the Kreditanstalt of Vienna, and

Bleichröder Bank of Berlin. The Régie was to pay the Debt Administration a fixed annual fee--from 1885 on this amounted to ₤T750,000.[9] After distribution of a certain proportion of profits, net profit was to be divided, according to a sliding scale, between the Régie, the government, and the Debt Administration. "The Régie received the right to control the cultivation, processing, purchase and sale of tobacco products; to it accrued the fees from licenses necessary to sell tobacco in retail shops; as well as the duty on tobacco imported into Turkey or exported to other areas of the Ottoman Empire, including Egypt, Crete, and Tunisia."[10] It was obligated to buy all tobacco produced for local consumption in Turkey (that for export could be sold freely, but its cultivation was also under Régie control); to provide interest-free loans to farmers who offered tobacco as collateral; and to set up warehouses for storage. In return, its permission was required for growing tobacco-- although it had no legal power to limit cultivation; together with the planters it fixed the price paid to the latter; and it alone set the retail price.

As selection 20 indicates, the immediate response to the Régie was an immense amount of smuggling, which continued until the First World War.[11] The government, whose revenues from the Régie were disappointingly low, does not seem to have made any serious attempt to stop contraband, and relations between the two remained strained.[12] Another initial response seems to have been a fall in output, but this was soon reversed and production rose steadily, to 31,000 tons in 1900 and a record of 63,500 in 1911.[13] Moreover, some observers claimed that the low prices set by the Régie had led farmers to plant inferior qualities and neglect their land, resulting in a deterioration of the tobacco.[14]

Exports also rose appreciably, from an average of 10,971 tons in 1879-83 to 13,073 in 1890-94 and about 25,700 in 1908-13,[15] and tobacco had become Turkey's leading export item, going to Britain, the United States, Germany, and various Mediterranean countries. The export of cigarettes suffered from the competition of the Egyptian industry, founded in the 1870s by Greek emigrants from Izmir and other parts of Turkey, and when Turkish prices rose too high various consumers, including Britain and Egypt, shifted to tobacco from "Greece, Bulgaria, China, Japan and elsewhere."[16] Another important factor after 1900 was the entry of the American Tobacco Company, which soon came to play a dominant role in the Izmir market (5:21); by 1912 it was spending $10 million a year in buying and preparing tobacco in the Ottoman Empire and exports of tobacco to the United States from Izmir were $2,388,000 in 1913.[17] Nevertheless, thanks to increasing world consumption, export prices and values continued to rise.

During the First World War and the War of Independence tobacco cultivation in the Black Sea region was disrupted by the emigration of Greek growers,[18] but after that it spread in the Bursa and Izmit regions, to replace the destroyed mulberry trees. In 1925 the Régie was abolished and replaced by a government monopoly. Since then both output and exports have continued to increase, the latter rising to 43,500 tons in 1938, when they represented 27 percent of total exports. By the late 1960s output averaged some 160,000 tons, exports about 80,000 tons, and tobacco ranked second only to cotton as an earner of foreign exchange.

(See also EHME and works by Quataert, Philips, Günyüz, Kahyaoğlu, and Brooks, listed in Bibliography.)

---

1. For Iran, EHI, pp. 247-51.
2. Salonica's exports at the beginning of the nineteenth century were put at 1,000,000 l. (lbs.?)--A and P 1873, vol. 67, "Salonica."
3. Bailey, p. 111; Gibb and Bowen, 1:304; in 1725 tobacco guilds were formally recognized; Gibb and Bowen, 1:291.
4. Stich, p. 71.

5. A and P 1854-55, vol. 52, and 1859, vol. 28, Statistical Tables on Foreign Trade; the figures exclude Greece, Moldavia and Wallachia, Egypt, Syria and Palestine, Tripoli and Tunisia.

6. EHME, pp. 60-64.

7. Stich, pp. 71-73; Benedict, Ula, pp. 173-204.

8. The situation in 1847 was as follows (Memorandum, FO 195/289). Snuff was bought from the manufacturers by the Ministry of Finance, which resold it by auction at a price agreed with them. The exclusive right to sell the snuff cost 1,000,000-1,200,000 piastres (Rumelia 500,000 and Anatolia 600,000 in 1846) and could be resold on a provincial basis; Istanbul had to be supplied at cost, the guild (gedik) of tobacconists (6:12) buying it from the customs house at 30 piastres an oke and reselling it at the price they chose. Export was authorized for those who had bought the required license from the government.

Tobacco growers paid a tax of 250 piastres, a tithe in cash, a transport tax, and, until recently, a tax of 7 1/2 piastres per dönüm. They could sell their produce freely, but the buyer had to pay excise duties ranging from 52 to 100 paras per oke, depending on quality; after which he could sell freely. The number of tobacconists in the gedik had, in the past, been strictly limited but in recent years had fluctuated, since entry was allowed on payment of 1,000-2,000 piastres.

In 1852 the government decided to abolish the tithe and special taxes on tobacco, replacing them by a 20 percent tax payable by growers. Traders were to be exempt from all taxes other than customs duty. The British government consented to this change which, however, does not seem to have been implemented--TE, Box 7, 1852.

9. Text in Young, vol. 5; the following account is based on Quataert, pp. 261-77.

10. Quataert, p. 264; Heidborn, 2:202-3.

11. A and P 1899, vol. 103, "Constantinople."

12. Quataert, pp. 266-72; after an initial loss in 1884-86, the Régie's profits showed a steady rise, except in the years 1896-98, to £T469,000 in 1906; ibid., p. 397.

13. Eldem, p. 83; according to one source, before 1884 tobacco output had been 10,000-13,000 tons--RC 1907, no. 243.

14. For example, the Russian vice-consul in Samsun in 1901, quoted by Novichev, Ocherki, pp. 73-74.

15. Aybar, p. 70.

16. Brooks, p. 240.

17. De Novo, p. 39.

18. For 1914 and 1920 figures, Mears, p. 287.

SELECTION 19. TOBACCO, 1789

Ainslie to Leeds, 22 December 1789, FO 78/10.

Weather has rendered this Residence remarkably sickly. The Dutch Ambassador has been seriously indisposed, though now out of all danger, as also my Secretary and Mr. Daniels, but we have had the misfortune to lose our worthy Chaplain, Dr. Charles Nicolson, a most respectable character, who died the 13th instant of an inflamation in the lungs, exceedingly regretted by all who knew him.

. . . In obedience to your Grace's command, I have now the honor to subjoin the most accurate and precise information that I have been able to procure on the different points contained in Your Grace's Dispatch dated the 16th October.

1mo The duties imposed and actually levied on unmanufactured tobacco imported into Constantinople is divided into three distinct rates according to its quality. The best sort pays 8 Paras per oke of 400 Drams

Second sort   6 Ditto

third sort   4 Ditto

40 Paras make a Dollar or Piastre, and 142 Drams make the English Pound of sixteen ounces. Snuff or manufactured tobacco pays no duty at the importation, but must be sold to the Farmer general, who alone has the privilege of vending snuff, which of course is equivalent to a prohibition. There is no excise or internal duty on tobacco, manufactured or unmanufactured, nor is any part of the duties paid back when the said articles are reexported.

2do No port duties are levied on manufactured or unmanufactured tobacco when imported or exported.

I presume that tobacco will never constitute an object of importation into this country, where so much is grown and where the price is so cheap, but here follows the charges established on imports and exports.

Imports

Freight on tobacco must run high, being an object bulky and light. Custom, if the capitulations are inforced, is only 3 p.ct. on the value.

Porterage, boathire, steeving, weighing and warehouseroom, about one piastre p hundred weight.

Commission, brokerage and loss on money 54 p thousand.

The above charges first deducted, the net produce is charged 1 1/2 p cent for provision on remitting the cash, but when the factor himself invests the net produce the 1 1/2 p cent is not charged.

Exports

Custom: the Levant Company's rates amount to about 2 p cent on the value.
Shipping charges are trifling, and would not exceed piastres 1 per hundred weight.
Brokerage, 1 per cent.
These charges added to the first cost of the goods, the factor charges 3 p cent for commission and warehouse room on the amount of the invoice.

3$\underline{°}$ No measures whatever are taken in Turkey to prevent tobacco cleared out for reexportation from being relanded in the country from where they are exported, and consequently no proofs are required of such articles having been landed in the country for which they were cleared out. I take the liberty to add, that tobacco is grown in I believe every part of this Empire, but the importation here from various parts of Turkey is very great, by reason the small quantity of cultivated lands in the neighbourhood of this capital is more advantagiously [sic] employed, and the consumption is very considerable. The greatest importation here is from Latachia, and all the coast of Syria, Salonica, and the environs of Durazzo in the Adriatic. The current price of tobacco in Turkey varies according to its quality, and the different qualities are produced from the different parts of the same Plant and the care taking in drying. At Constantinople the price in retail varies from twenty Paras the Oke to one hundred and twenty, whilst at Salonica it sells from five to twelve Paras the Oke. The manufactured tobacco or snuff is farmed out by Government, and is consequently subject to strict regulations. The price fixed by the farmer is 4 1/2 Piastres per Oke--and is retailed at 5 Piastres. Mr. Peter Tooke, from whom I received the greatest part of the above information is of opinion that a contract might possibly be made with the Farmer general for a certain quantity of tobacco manufactured into Snuff.
. . .

SELECTION 20. TOBACCO MONOPOLY, BURSA REGION, 1886

Report of March 25, 1886, CC Brousse

. . . It is true that every day we see the <u>zaptieh</u> (<u>gendarmes</u>) walking through the town, escorting the <u>kolcu</u> [customs guards] who are charged with fighting contraband; personally, however, I am convinced that the intervention of the public authorities has not succeeded in appreciably reducing fraud, which at present is carried out on a very large scale. In spite of all these efforts, such large quantities of tobacco are marketed in this way that one is almost inclined to believe that, alongside the Régie, there is another body set up to compete with it by offering consumers good quality tobacco at very reasonable prices!

In this field, the outcome of the struggle cannot be in doubt. For, given all the different kinds of expenses it has to incur. the Régie cannot possibly sell its goods at 10 or 20 piastres an oke, i.e., 28 a kilogram; it is forced to quote prices of 190-120-80-50-30-16 or 10 per kilogram, depending on whether the tobacco is of the first, second, third, fourth, fifth, sixth, or seventh grade. The managing board of the Régie seems to have understood that the best way to ensure success was to divert the custom of the producers from the smugglers to itself. Hence, all the branch managers have been authorized to supply each year, free of charge, a certain quantity of Yenice and Samsun seed, in order to raise the quality of the tobacco grown in the province. This service, which costs little, renders it possible for an intelligent farmer to make fairly large profits, since on an area of one dönüm he can harvest about 150 okes which, at an average price of 5 piastres, fetches 750 piastres or £T7½. The average used to reckon this amount seems to be based on the prices fixed by the Régie for the five different grades of tobacco grown in the <u>vilayet</u> of Bursa, and which--according to the information I have been able to obtain--are as follows in French currency:

3rd grade about 2.65 francs a kilogram
4th   "   "   1.50   "   "   "
5th   "   "   0.90   "   "   "
6th   "   "   0.45   "   "   "
7th   "   "   0.15   "   "   "

These figures, although not necessarily accurate, were given to me by a person who is generally well informed in these matters. He added that it was also usual to make two advances to the peasant-farmers, one of 20 percent at registration and the other of 30 percent when the leaves were picked. These advances, totalling 50 percent, are deducted when the Régie finally settles accounts with the farmer, who is obliged to hand over to it his crop before the end of July. This deadline, which may not be extended, is almost never reached by the grower. For, since he picks the leaves in October and November, his enlightened self-interest makes him deliver to the Régie as soon as possible, in order to avoid storage costs, and take what is owed to him after deducting the 50 percent advances already received by him. . . .

[The Report adds that the Régie obtained from the 1884–85 crop 860,000 kilograms of tobacco in the vilayet, of which 500,000 were in the Bursa district.]

SELECTION 21.   TOBACCO IN IZMIR, 1910

FO 368/471

Smyrna tobaccos known commercially as Aromatic Ayasolouk are cultivated throughout the region stretching to the East and South of Smyrna, that is to say in the districts of Sevdikeuy, Eudemish, Sokia [Söke], Ayasolouk (anc. Ephesus), Scala Nuova [Kuş-adasi], and Melissus [Akhisar].

During the last few years the plant has also been grown fairly extensively in the districts to the North of Smyrna, but the products of those parts are not so highly prized. Smyrna tobaccos are exported to nearly every country in the world and their consumption has notably increased recently.

The warehouses of the Smyrna merchants are at present empty. There are no stocks left over from the 1909 crop, while the same may be said for the consuming countries. At Dresden, Hamburg, Bremen and in London, in Russia, in America and in Egypt an identical state of things exists. Manufacturers abroad who held large reserves have had to break in on them; so the nature and quantity of the Smyrna 1910 crop is pregnant with interest for the Tobacco world.

The crops of the last three years were largely below the average, while the demand for Smyrna tobacco has been getting keener every year. The total amount of the new crop will only be known exactly when the Ottoman Tobacco Régie has finished their second estimation of the crop, but it is given as approximately 6 million kilograms or roughly 5 million okes—the largest since 1903. Despite this large crop, buying operations started unusually early, in fact quite two-thirds of the tobacco was still standing in the fields at the time. This early buying is a habit which has grown up in the last 3 or 4 years, because buyers live in fear of not being able to secure the quantities they desire owing to the huge purchases effected by the American Tobacco Co., before the crop is cut—as took place for instance last year. From the opening sales the market was very animated owing to the competition of this American Tobacco Co., which sent a large number of new agents in different directions to make purchases simultaneously. Lively competition followed and prices went up rapidly. The first offers were directed to villages where the cutting of the crop was more advanced and the tobacco considered better: later the movement becoming general, all the growing districts were tapped, so that even inferior tobaccos which had been neglected during the first purchases were not only bought but fetched good prices.

Prices paid in the Eudemish district (Pastal) average 20% dearer than those of 1909 but the Sevdikeuy crop (strung) fetched as much as 25% more. An instance may be made of the purchases made at Ak-keuy and Jerondo in the Sokia district. The crop had been very successful and a spirited contest ensued between buyers. The two villages between them produced some 500,000 kilograms which were secured in a few days at prices 30% above those paid last year. And it should be borne in mind that the 1909 prices paid to farmers themselves constituted a record. The purchase price was particularly high in second and inferior qualities, being double and sometimes even three times those of last year. The competition in purchases all round must of course be attributed to the American Tobacco Company operation.

On the 6 million kilograms available from the crop it is estimated that this company alone took from 3¼ to 3½ millions. As these tobaccos are destined for the exclusive usage of the Company's own factories in Europe and America, this huge quantity may be considered as abstracted from the world's market. The same applies to the half to three quarters of a million kilos bought by the Ottoman Tobacco Monopoly (Régie). There are thus left barely 2 million kilos on the market for the purposes of the general dealers in Smyrna Tobacco throughout the world, till the 1912 crop is gathered. It is extremely unlikely that this quantity will be sufficient, and the lack of tobacco will be still more keenly felt in some few months.

Selling prices are very firm with a decided tendency to rise; and as this movement is fully justified by events it may be expected that prices will stiffen progressively as the season advances. In sales too some qualities are fetching double and treble what they did last year.

As regards quality, the whole crop is free from disease except round Scala Nuova and Ak-Hissar where traces of "bassara" have been found.

The crop is by now completely gathered and the drying of leaves terminated. As the weather was favourable, gathering took place under the best conditions.

The quality is good. . . .

SILK

Sericulture was introduced into the Western world around A.D. 550, when two Nestorian monks smuggled silkworm eggs out of China, and the Byzantine Empire had a flourishing silk industry.[1] But by the eleventh century, the main source of raw silk both for Anatolia's own industry and for re-export to Europe had become northern Iran, from where caravans came through Erzurum first to Constantinople and later to the great silk emporium of Bursa. The prolonged Turco-Iranian wars of the sixteenth and seventeenth centuries, however, led to frequent and costly interruptions of trade, and early in the sixteenth century the Ottoman government began encouraging the production of silk within the Empire--in Albania and Rumelia--and by 1587 silk was being grown in Bursa.[2] A further impetus was probably given by the collapse of Iranian silk production at the beginning of the eighteenth century.[3] By the middle of that century appreciable amounts of silk were being grown in Madedonia, Morea, and Lebanon, as well as in the Bursa region, and exported to Europe. In the mean-time, the Persian silk caravans had been diverted to Izmir, to avoid the duties levied at Bursa, and Armenian merchants tended to replace the Muslim merchants of Bursa who had pre-viously handled the trade.[4]

An Austrian consular report of 1775 (Türkei 5:26) gives some interesting information on Bursa's silk production. Crops ranged from not less than 1,500 bales to up to 4,000 bales, i.e., roughly 165,000 to 440,000 kilograms.[5] Part of the raw silk was woven in Bursa, part was sent to Istanbul, Izmir, Aleppo, Damascus, Egypt, and other provinces, and part exported to Europe. England took 700-800 bales, "France less," and Italy bought silk when its silk crop failed. In 1775 silk sent to Europe fetched 28 to 29 piastres a teffe and the finer qualities, used in Bursa or sent to other Ottoman towns, 34 to 35 piastres. In a good year the silk crop brought in 4 million piastres (nearly ₤500,000).

Increasing European demand led to the regulation of 1806 by which a portion of Bursa silk was set aside at a fixed price for the tradesmen of Istanbul; the rest could then be sold to Europe.[6]

After 1815 rising world demand led to an expansion of production in many parts of the Empire.[7] In Edirne increased British purchases raised prices sharply and exports to Europe were established on a firm base.[8] There was also some technical improvement and in 1838 the British consul reported: "The improved manner of winding the silk, which since my ar-rival here I have been endeavouring by all the means in my power to induce the cultivators to adopt, is gradually becoming more general and I expect that of the next raccolta full one half will be wound in that way" (Report on Trade, FO 78/368). The increase in output and exports was accelerated in 1851 by the ravages caused by the pebrine disease in Europe. Mulberries were planted on a large scale in the neighborhood of Edirne, Demotika, and Mustafa paşa and output grew by 15-20 percent a year. The value of the silk crop rose from some 3-4 million piastres to 10-15 million in 1854 and 1855 and to 22 million in 1856 and 1857.[9] At that point the disease hit the Edirne region and the output of fresh cocoons fell from over 900,000 kilograms in 1857 to 640,000 in 1858 and went on declining to 230,000, worth 7 million piastres, in 1866.[10] In the 1880s, however, production began to revive (see below) and in 1890 output of fresh cocoons was put at 450,000 kilograms. Of this, 40 percent was reeled by three steam factories in Edirne and the rest sent to Italy and France.[11]

In Salonica, as the two following selections show, there was also rapid growth begin-ning in the late 1830s (also Trade Report, FO 78/441). The Trade Report for 1846 (FO 78/700) put the value of silk exports at ₤91,000 (compared to ₤22,000 in 1840) and mentioned great improvements in methods: "attention paid to the cultivation of worms. . . . and introduction of improved system of drawing. . . . in many instances machinery has been brought from Europe."[12]

In Amasya, as selection 5:24 shows, there was a certain amount of silk-raising and in the mid-1850s a filature was installed by a German firm. Disease, however, almost wiped out silk-growing, the filature was transformed into a flour mill,[13] and production began to revive only at the very end of the century. Output in 1900 was worth ₤15,000, for a quantity of perhaps 150,000 kilograms.[14] In Harput exports of cocoons rose from 5,000 kilograms in the 1880s to 19,000 in 1902 and 136,000 in 1907, and Diyarbekir's production from 4,000-7,000 to 160,000.[15] Izmir's output increased from 25,000 kilograms in the 1890s to about 250,000 in 1909. Lastly, mention may be made of developments in Adana. Output in the province rose a hundredfold in twenty years--from 64,000 kilograms in 1896 to perhaps around 1,300,000 in 1907--thanks to the efforts of a Lebanese physician who introduced silkworms in the villages.[16]

But the main center of production remained the Bursa and İzmit regions. In Bursa, improved reeling machines were installed in peasant houses--an estimated 8,000 by 1856.[17]-- steam was introduced in 1838, and in 1845 a filature "on the French model" was established (Report on Trade, FO 78/652) and was soon followed by many more (6:15). This greatly improved the quality of the silk produced, and "in the English market silk reeled in the common manner is only from 12/- to 15/- per pound, while that which is reeled in the manufactories is sold at 23/- to 25/- per pound" (Cumberbatch to Ross, 11 August 1852, FO 195/382). Indeed the British consul stated that the "silks of the Bursa filatures have attained a rank in the markets of sale equal to those of any other country," that the cocoons were judged "as in some localities finer than any in Europe," and that the native reelers were producing "from year to year a greater proportion of the finer sorts as more advantageous though requiring extra expense and labour." By then France, which until recently had taken only a third to half as much Bursa silk as England, had become the main customer, buying three-fifths of the output, with England taking the rest (Report on Trade 1852, FO 78/952). By 1854 France was taking four-fifths of production (ibid., FO 78/1111).

Figures on output of raw silk in the 1840s and 50s do not show any clear trend.[18] In 1840 the output of the district of Bursa was put at 196,000 kilograms; the addition of İzmit, Bilecik, and Kütahya, plus an estimate for contraband, raised the total to 460,000 (Report on Trade, FO 78/441). In 1843 the figures were 123,000 and 304,000 kilograms, respectively (ibid., FO 78/570). In 1844 the crop was put at 305,000 kilograms or 3,844 bales of 170 lbs. each, in 1845 at 250,000 kilograms, in 1846 at 275,000, and in 1847 at 290,000 kilograms (ibid., FO 78/652, 78/701, and 78/750). The 1851 crop, at 410,000 kilograms, was the largest since 1839 "if not within memory" and was worth ₤624,000, to which should be added ₤17,000 for the raw cocoons sold (ibid, FO 78/952).[19] The 1855 crop was 218,000 kilograms, of which 25,000 were kept for local consumption and the rest exported to France and England (ibid., 78/1209), and the 1857 crop was 369,000 kilograms.[20]

A description of sericulture in Bursa at that time may be quoted (Agricultural Report, 1860, FO 78/1534). "The method of hatching and treating them till the completion of their process is now considered by some enquirers from their researches as more conducive probably to preserving the brood in a healthy state than the practice in France and in Italy. Here the leaves are not gathered from the trees and distributed for the food of the worms ranged in layers, requiring also to be constantly cleansed of the impurities voided by the worm. But twigs or branches are cut off with the leaves upon them and placed on the beds where the worms lie, which naturally ascend to reach the fresh food and are protected by the twigs from being intertwined with the deposit underneath. As they increase in size they are separated into other beds to afford the necessary space, and the same mode of feeding precisely persists until the time when they refuse nourishment and are ready to spin the cocoons. For this purpose branches of dwarf oak are provided on which they climb and finish their process. Everything is superintended by the simple peasant who neither uses nor possesses any thermometer for ascertaining the temperature--rears the worm in his ordinary dwelling or any adjunct he can contrive for the purpose, ventilates or introduces heat as the weather and condition of the worms indicate to be most suitable. But there are no regular establishments such as those called in France and Italy 'magnaneries' for rearing silkworms."

Two differences from Europe were noted: "Bringing home the leaves attached, instead of picking them in the field, saves here a great deal of time and labour--and the trees thus annually lopped remain usually low to be conveniently accessible without the aid of a ladder." But the trees did not grow to full size or yield such a large amount of leaves. Also, trees were planted too close, though one could have planted other crops in between them.

At that point, when mulberry trees were increasing at 5-10 percent a year, the disease reached Bursa and output dropped to 192,000 kilograms by 1864 and fell to around 100,000 in the early 1880s. Simultaneously, the opening of the Suez Canal and the entry of Japan in world markets increased competition. Many Bursa filatures closed and mulberry orchards were cut down and planted to cereals and other crops.[21]

Some relief was afforded by the use of Japanese and other eggs,[22] but revival was due mainly to the efforts of the government and the Public Debt Administration, to whom all the silk tithes had been successively granted in 1881 and 1888. These efforts were more comprehensive and successful than for any other crop.[23] Strict inspection procedures, based on Pasteur's discoveries, were applied first to imported and then to homegrown eggs. The Institut Séricole was founded at Bursa in 1888; largely staffed and attended by Armenians and Greeks, it played an important part in diffusing improved methods. Exemption from tithes and other taxes was granted to mulberry growers and silkworm raisers. Mulberry bushes were distributed and over 60 million trees were planted on 130,000 acres of land-- in Bursa alone, in the seven years following the foundation of the Institute, 15 to 20 million trees were planted (CC Brousse, 29 May 1896).

These measures, and a sustained world demand for silk resulted in a sharp increase in output until 1913 although Japanese competition tended to keep prices low. Bursa's production rose from an average of 283,000 kilograms of raw silk in 1892-93 to one of 347,000 in 1896-99 (CC Brousse, annual reports). The output of fresh cocoons in Bursa and İzmit rose from 1,168,000 kilograms in 1888-89 to 3,173,000 in 1903-5.[24] Output of fresh cocoons in the whole Empire, including Lebanon, went up from 7 million kilograms in 1888 to a peak of 20 million in 1910-12.[25] And exports of raw silk increased from an average of 302,000 kilograms worth ŁT396,000 in 1878-79 to 1,390,000 worth ŁT1,701,000 in 1909-11, while exports of cocoons rose from 472,000 kilograms worth ŁT207,000 to 1,916,000 worth ŁT860,000.[26] The silk tithes increased correspondingly.

During the First World War and the War of Independence silk production was badly disrupted by the deportation or exile of Armenians and Greeks (6:15) and by military operations.[27] In 1923 Bursa's output of raw silk was only 60,000 kilograms and in 1924 90,000.[28] After that, Turkish silks, like others, suffered from the competition of rayon and played a minor part in the economy.

---

1. Haussig, passim.
2. See the excellent account in EI(2), s.v. "Harir"; and Dalsar, passim.
3. EHI, pp. 12-13.

4. "Harir" and EHME, pp. 32-33.

5. Bales sent inland, on horseback, are stated to have weighed 40 teffes of 610 drachms or dirhams each, i.e., 98 kilograms; those shipped to Europe weighed 60 teffes, i.e., 146 kilograms. An average of 110 kilograms has been assumed. İnalcık states that around 1806 European demand for Bursa silk was 28,000 kilograms--"Harir." All figures given in okes or pounds have been converted into kilograms, at 1.283 and 0.454, respectively.

6. Ibid.

7. For Lebanon, EHME, p. 230; for Iran, EHI, pp. 231-38.

8. A and P 1868-69, vol. 60, "Adrianople."

9. Ibid.

10. Ibid.; figures on output and consumption for those years in CC Andrianople differ only slightly from those in the British report.

11. A and P 1890, vol. 77, "Adrianople."

12. For details, see Urquhart, pp. 179-81.

13. Stich, pp. 36 and 96.

14. A and P 1901, vol. 85, "Sivas."

15. Quataert, p. 257.

16. Stich, p. 100, and Almanach d'Orient, 1907 (Constantinople 1907), p. 134.

17. EI(2), "Harir."

18. In spite of the sharp rise in the price of mulberries ("they are now at 90 piastres or 16/3 per thousand, being the triple of their general cost last season"), returns on silk-raising were high: "The lowest estimate is 20 to 25 percent profit in purchasing plantations arrived at maturity and erecting buildings for rearing the worms, all the rest of the labor besides being paid for on hire." Wheat land was therefore being shifted to mulberries (Sandison to Palmerston, 18 March 1841, FO 78/441).

19. For the earlier years those figures do not tally with those on silk production in Bursa in A and P 1873, vol. 68, "Turkey"; it may be that the latter include cocoons from other provinces brought to Bursa for reeling. After 1851 the series are very close.

20. A and P 1859, vol. 30, "Bursa."

21. CC Brousse, 1 July 1881, and Quataert, pp. 246-47.

22. Stich, p. 98; by 1870 a wide variety of eggs was being used: native, Japanese, Persian, Rumelian, Armenian, Caucasian, etc. (CC Brousse, 16 July 1870).

23. See the excellent account in Quataert, pp. 245-61.

24. Ibid., p. 394.

25. Eldem, p. 84.

26. Aybar, p. 64.

27. The growing of mulberries and reeling of silk was largely carried out by Greeks--Dietrich, p. 50, and EHME, pp. 116-17.

28. Stich, p. 101.

SELECTION 22. GROWTH OF SILK PRODUCTION IN SALONICA, 1838-1840

Blunt to Palmerston, 5 August 1840, FO 78/411

As regards the productions of the Country, the Convention may be said to have had a very beneficial effect upon the article of Silk--the Cultivation or rather the rearing of the Silk-worm having very considerably increased, and not being aware of any increase of Commercial demand for the article, it may be allowed to infer, that the advantages derived from a fixed rate of duties, and the total abolition of abuses, on the part of the Minor Authorities, have induced people to give more of their attention to the article. Before the Convention, and the Hatti Sheriffee, it was impossible to calculate what was, or was not, the rate of duty generally fixed by Firman was [sic] 10 per cent, but when did the Collectors ever content themselves with that rate? for it is a well known fact, that many of the rearers of the Silkworm had to pay 25 to 30 per cent upon their Cocoons--It is not yet two months since the Silk drawing has commenced at Salonica, for this year, and the number of Factories for drawing of Silk is above that of last and former years. There were in Salonica in 1838:

10 Factories --	280 Reels --	625 persons employed	
		1839	
12 do.	346 do.	739	do.
		1840	
17 do.	397 do.	987	do.

and should there be any demand for the article more Factories will be opened.

The Silk drawing Factories in Salonica were formerly entirely in the hands of the Jews, and the Silk produced was very inferior, latterly the Franks of Salonica have given their attention to Silk drawing, and the qualities now produced, fetch a good average price in European markets, compared with other silks the produce of Turkey. . . .

SELECTION 23. SILK IN SALONICA, 1845

Mr. Consul Blunt's report upon the Trade within the Jurisdiction of the Consulate of Salonica during the year ended the 31st December 1845, FO 78/651

. . . The increase in the production of Silk pods in the interior is now so considerable, that there is enough for Export and in 1845 agents were sent to Salonica from some of the Italian ports to purchase Silk pods. The gradual increase, and improvement in the production of Raw Silk, is clearly shown in the following table. The persons employed in drawing Raw Silk are for the most part poor Children, averaging from 14 to 15 years of age, who work for about 14 hours a day, so that the value of this Trade has been most advantageous to the lower orders of Christians and Jews, which is the more evident when it is considered, that 2 children of a poor family, can earn in the space of 6 months' p. 1890 or Ł17.3.6, when perhaps the expense of the Keep of the whole family during the year does not amount to that sum. In 1840 the whole amount paid for wages was Ł2373.19, whereas in 1845 the amount was Ł23,280.3.7.

Years	Number of Reels	Persons employed	Total amount of wages to the silk drawers		Quantity produced for export	Gross value of silk exported		Market price at Salonica	Market price in London
			Currency	Sterling	lbs. English	Currency	Sterling	Currency p. oke	Sterling p. lb.
1840	429	1058	301,080	2737	38,000	2,550,000	23,182	170-180	16/-
1841	459	1103	322,530	2932	41,000	2,725,000	24,773	"	17/-
1842	500	1237	352,430	3204	46,750	3,145,000	26,773	180-200	18/-
1843	590	1447	412,100	3746	55,000	3,700,000	33,636	"	19/-
1844	600	1470	520,800	4735	66,000	5,400,000	49,091	215-230	20/-
1845	795	1977	2,561,260	23,280	107,250	10,140,000	92,181	260	21/6 & 22/-

SELECTION 24. AGRICULTURE AND MINING IN AMASYA REGION, 1841

Report by R. W. Stevens, 30 November 1841, FO 78/491

. . . The crop of silk at Amassia, was this year abundant, and the quality very good,
compared to that of last season. It is calculated the total produce, amounted to 36,000
okes (or lbs. 99,000) being 6,000 okes (=lbs. 16,300) more than what is considered a tolerable crop. The price fixed for repaying in silk those who had previously advanced cash,
was p.40 per litra of 125 drams (=9s/3d per lb.), but this was looked upon as too high, and
very few took the article in payment, preferring to receive back their money with the customary interest, an option allowed those who advance money. The silk was then sold for
exportation at p.25 per litra (=6s/- per lb.) gradually advanced to 36 per litra (=7s/9d.
per lb.) but soon again declined to p.32 (=7s/3d. per lb.), which was its value when I
visited the place. The improvement in the quality of this silk seems to have recently attracted the attention of Europeans, and a Swiss commercial house, with a view to that object, has been established at Amassia. The conductor of it told me that although the quality might be made much finer, and rendered fit for the consumption of some of the markets
of Europe, still he did not think it could ever be brought to equal the silk of Broussa and
Adrianople, owing to the description of the mulberry leaves on which the worms are fed. He
intended to give the article a trial next season, which will prove how far the object of
improvement can be attained. An English Merchant at Constantinople, sent men from Broussa,
who purchased cocoons, and wound them off in the mode practised at that place. The produce
was better than that prepared by the natives, but it bore no comparison with the quality of
Broussa. The cocoons were bought at p.80 per Batman (6 okes) = 1s/- per lb. They gave 250
drams of Silk, which, without calculating the attendant expenses, made it cost p.40 per
litra, or p.15 per litra more than purchases could at the same time have been made in the
market. The people of Amassia complain very justly of the high Export duty to which their
silk is subjected, there being no difference made between their quality, and the more valuable ones of other places. The duty fixed by the new Tariff of p.24 per oke (or 12 p. Cent.
on p.200) amounting to 24 per Cent, the value of an oke of Amassia silk, not being now more
than p.100. On a short crop, and on a great demand, it is seldom above p.140 per oke, so
that the duty as it now stands would under any circumstances come to nearly 18 per Cent.
Besides this, the local authorities levy duty from the growers of 10 per Cent, in lieu of
all former duties, which amounted to 17 per Cent. I am told that the Silk which is sent
hence to Aleppo, is shipped to France, as the produce of Syria, and pays according to the
Tariff p. 14½ per oke; thus, the exporters through Aleppo have an advantage over those who
export direct from Amassia of 10 per Cent on the duty. A petition praying for a reduction
in this charge has been forwarded to Constantinople, and it is to be hoped that the Government will examine into the matter and render justice to the people, so as to encourage them
to cultivate Silk more extensively and improve its quality, an object of importance to
Amassia, as it produces no other article for exportation to any extent.

There was hardly any business doing at Tokat, partly owing to its being Ramazan, and
partly because by this time of the year, the traders have usually disposed of their stocks,
and prepare to go to Zilleh to purchase new ones. I could therefore not learn much of the
Trade, which however from the size of the bazars, and the accounts I heard, must at other
seasons be considerable and active.

The cultivation of the yellow berry is extending very much, and the attention of all
natives is directed to its production. One person told me that three years ago he purchased a piece of ground, and planted it with these trees; the plantation had altogether
cost him Ł400, and he had recently refused an offer for it of Ł2,000. There are several
qualities produced: of the best, which is even superior to the berry of Kaissar, it was
this year expected that 2,500 batmans (=375 Cwt.) would have been produced, but unusually
cold weather in the spring caused great injury to the trees, and only 500 batmans (or 75
Cwt.) were collected. It was sold at p.25 per oke (=Ł10 per Cwt.) for exportation to Constantinople, where it realised the high price of p.38 per oke (=Ł15.4 per Cwt.). The
second quality comes from Deumoorteh, a village on the plain, five hours from the town,
and is worth p.14 per oke (=Ł5.12 per Cwt.) at which it was this year all sold to merchants
of Kaissar, to mix up with their own yellow-berries, previous to sending them to Constantinople. There is a wild sort collected in the neighbouring mountains, and worth only p.5
per oke (=Ł2 per Cwt.); this is too inferior for European consumption, is used by the dyers
of Tokat, and is forwarded to Moossul and Baghdad, where it is employed in the manufactures
of those places.

The Turkish Government are building at the skirts of the town a large establishment
for refining copper, under the superintendence of Mr. Gustave Paulini, a Hungarian Engineer,
with sixteen assistants of the same nation. It will cost about p.1,000,000 (or Ł10,000)
when terminated, but this expense will be compensated by the great saving it will secure
to the Government, in the refining process, which employs at present 1,000 men, while in
the new Establishment the operations will be completed by machinery, worked by water power,
and it is said that 20 men will be sufficient to conduct them. The copper refined here is
brought from Arganah Madem [Ergani-maden]. In 1839 the quantity was 170,000 batmans
(1,275 Tons), and this year, it will amount to 120,000 batmans (900 Tons). The deficiency

after smelting is from 17 to 20 per cent; the copper in its rough state costs at Arganah p.6 per Batman (= 8 s/- per Cwt.) to which must be added the transport to Tokat, where, after it is refined, it is worth p.72 per Batman (= 86s/- per Cwt.). A good deal is worked here, which is the only portion allowed to be sold on the spot, unless a Firman is procured, authorising the sale of a further quantity; with this exception the whole is forwarded to Samsoon, for shipment to Constantinople on Government account.

Mr. Paulini has discovered a silver mine two hours from Tokat, near a Turkish village called Ilbisteh. His men have been working it for the last two months, and the ore appears to be very rich, giving 25 per Cent of Silver. Mr. Paulini's absence at Constantinople prevented my obtaining any particulars on this subject. . . .

Annex A

Table showing the average produce of the crops of wheat and barley in the following districts; the proportions consumed, and those available for Exportation.

In Imperial Quarters

Districts	Quantity of an average crop		Quantity consumed		Quantity available for exportation	
	Wheat	Barley	Wheat	Barley	Wheat	Barley
Amassia	4,500	2,000	2,500	1,200	2,000	800
Marsovan [Merzifon]	6,500	1,500	3,250	750	3,250	750
Zilleh	8,000	1,300	4,000	750	4,000	750
Tchoroom	7,500	2,500	2,500	1,250	5,000	1,250
Tashovah	1,200	1,200	600	600	600	600
Bozook	15,000	7,500	5,000	2,500	10,000	5,000
Total Impl Quarters	42,700	16,200	17,850	7,050	24,850	9,150

FIGS

Turkey's figs are grown mainly in the Menderes valley and have been shipped from Izmir at least as early as the eighteenth century (HHS V Türkei, 25 "Nota delli diversi prodotti di Smirne," 1776). In the nineteenth century demand and prices rose and production and exports increased correspondingly. The Istanbul price for figs rose from 2.36 piastres per oke in 1876-80 to 4.03 in 1901-5 and 4.01 in 1906-8.[1] Output increased very fast, from about 6,000 metric tons at the beginning of the 1860s (selection 5:25) to an average of 9,000 in 1871-75 and 30,000 tons in 1906-10.[2] Exports grew correspondingly, from an average of 8,500 tons, worth ₤247,000 in 1876-80, to nearly 14,000, worth ₤346,000, in 1896-1900 and nearly 30,000 tons, worth ₤676,000, in 1906-8,[3] but fell off slightly after that.[4] By far the greater part of the crop went to Britain, but the United States was also an important customer and Europe took significant amounts, especially of the inferior varieties.[5]

In 1912, the packing and export firms formed a combine, the Smyrna Fig and Packers Ltd., with a capital of ₤200,000, and sought to dominate the market for both figs and crates. The combine suffered, however, from mismanagement and corruption and was dissolved by the government in 1914.[6]

---

1. Quataert, p. 301.
2. Stich, p. 63; Eldem, p. 83, whose series, however, exclude Hurda, or low quality, figs. The latter formed about a fifth of the total crop--A and P 1910, vol. 103, "Smyrna," which gives figures for 1897-1909.
3. Quataert, p. 301; in 1834 exports had been 4,300 tons, worth about ₤580,000--3:14.
4. Aybar, p. 67.
5. Stich, p. 64.
6. Ibid.

SELECTION 25. FIG-GROWING AND TRADE, IZMIR REGION, 1862

Report on Trade, 1862, CC Smyrne, vol. 50

. . . Various fruits, and especially figs and raisins, constitute without doubt the principal export of Smyrna. They are of superior quality and widely sought for in the whole world. Each year, numerous clippers and steamers come from America to load dried fruit in Smyrna. They come here in ballast, or bring at almost zero freight rates products of American industry, such as armchairs and chairs made of fluted straw (paille cannelée) which are sold very cheaply in Smyrna. But the greatest amount of export of figs and fruit goes to England. The best qualities are sent there, and it alone takes nearly half the crop. Austria also plays a significant part in this trade; each year, at harvest time, the ships of the Lloyd Company, which makes the run between Smyrna and Trieste, stop at Çeşme, on the coast of Anatolia opposite Chios, and load the fruit that comes there from different parts of the interior. Fairly large quantities of dried fruit are also exported to Constantinople and other Turkish ports. France holds only fifth place in this item.

The province of Aydin, of which Smyrna forms part, provides the whole fig crop of Asia Minor. It is difficult to give precise figures on the average size of the fig crop for, on the one hand, there are often enormous differences in crops and, on the other, the quantity exported varies with price. The higher are prices on the Smyrna market, the greater is the amount supplied by the interior; should prices however fall, growers prefer to send their produce to the interior, where they do not have to pay customs, commissions, etc. The 1861 crop was 23,000 loads, i.e. 92,000 quintals or 4,968,000 kilograms (the Smyrna quintal weighs 54 kilograms). That of 1862 was 35,000 loads, i.e. 140,000 quintals or 7,560,000 kilograms. In the last fifteen years, the largest crop was 42 to 43,000 loads and the smallest 11 to 12,000.

The wide difference between the various qualities of figs makes prices vary enormously. In 1861 selling prices ranged from 15 to 44 francs a quintal of Smyrna, and in 1862 between 12 and 38 francs. There are moreover small quantities of choice figs called eleme which are more expensive and sometimes fetch up to 70 francs a quintal. The most appreciated quality is that of the sancak of Erbeily, twelve days journey beyond Aydin.

Figs arrive to Smyrna on camel, the transport cost varying between 4 and 7 francs a quintal, depending on the size of the crop. Last year, part of the crop was carried by the Smyrna-Aydin railway; but as operations are confined to half the total distance, the company had the goods carried on camel back as far as the station of Ayasoluk (Ephesus), where they were loaded on the railway wagons. Caravans make the journey between Aydin and Smyrna in five days, but when the railway is completed it will take one day. It has however been said that railway transport is not suitable for this kind of goods, for the bags are piled on top of each other in the trucks and the figs, thus squeezed, soften, break and lose their value. . . .

OPIUM

Opium has been grown and used in Anatolia since ancient times but its cultivation expanded greatly in the nineteenth century with the opening of overseas markets. Turkish opium was, and still is, prized because of its high morphine content (10-15 percent), and in the early nineteenth century its consumption spread eastwards and westwards. In 1835 the Dutch took 40 percent of the crop (Report on Trade of Smyrna, FO 78/287) and in 1839 over 40 percent of Izmir's exports, mainly for the use of the Netherlands East Indies, while one-third went to America, one-tenth through England to China, and the rest to Trieste, Livorno, and France.[1] In 1848 the French consul in Izmir reported that, for the last three years, half the crop had been shipped directly to China by the P and O line (CC Smyrne, vol. 48, Report on Trade, 1848) and in 1852 Britain sent about three-fifths of Izmir's crop to China. But in the latter half of the century the bulk of the crop went to Europe and America, Chinese demand being met from India and other sources.

The main centers of production were Bursa and Konya provinces, which supplied a little over, and a little under, a third, respectively, of the total crop, but opium was also grown elsewhere.[2] Two main qualities were distinguished. The finest, incemal, was used for smoking or the extraction of morphine; it was grown principally in Sivas, Ankara, and Mamuret-ül Aziz provinces, but some 1,800 hectares were also planted to opium in Salonica and other parts of European Turkey. The second quality, used mostly by druggists, included yerli, adet and other varieties; the main growing centers were Konya (especially the Afyon Karahisar district), Bursa, Aydın, Geyve, Kastamonu and Ankara provinces. Istanbul, which received opium directly by caravan and later by railway but also by sea from Samsun, was the main source of export of the finer quality and Izmir, followed by Istanbul, of the second, but Macedonia—where output rose from about 150 cases in 1880 to 1,500-1,700 on the eve of the First World War—increasingly exported directly and some quantities from Malatya and Harput were sent through İskenderun. During the nineteenth century London was the main warehouse for Turkish—as for Persian—opium but Germany increasingly replaced it as the main supplier of Europe. However, half of Turkey's output went to the Americas, being used for morphia in the North and for smoking in the South. The trade was mainly in the hands of Armenians and Jews and was avoided, as too speculative, by Turks who had a saying: "Afyonun ağacı alçaktır, düşen parçalanır"--"the opium tree is low, but those who fall from it are broken in pieces."[3]

Some figures are available on exports from Izmir. In 1831 the French consul reported that, in ordinary years, the value of the opium crop had been at least 15 million piastres, or say ₤150,000 (CC Smyrne, vol. 34, Memorandum). Whether because of a monopoly imposed in that year or for other reasons, exports from Izmir in the late 1830s were low, averaging the equivalent of ₤47,000 in 1836-39, but, perhaps aided by the application of the 1838 Commercial Convention, they picked up to an average of ₤121,000 in 1840-43 and in the 1850s higher figures were recorded, including ₤269,000 in 1857 (CC Smyrne, vols. 45-49, Reports on Trade of Izmir). A figure equivalent to ₤640,000 was given for 1871 (CC Smyrne, vol. 51) and one of ₤631,000 in 1877 but these seem to have been exceptional and in most years exports ranged between ₤150,000 and ₤300,000.[4] In 1900 they were ₤283,000, in 1901 ₤300,000, and in 1910 ₤415,000 (A and P 1902, vol. 110, and 1914, vol. 95, "Smyrna").

There are also a few figures on the quantity of exports. The opium crop of the Izmir region was estimated at 2,000 baskets of 140 lbs. each in 1835 and 1,000 baskets in 1836, or 127 and 64 metric tons respectively (Trade of Smyrna, FO 78/287). In 1857 exports were put at 214 tons (CC Smyrne, vol. 49, Report on Trade). In 1882-86, exports averaged 3,210 cases or about 212 tons, 205 tons in 1897-1901 and 2,427 cases or about 160 tons in 1905-8.[5] In 1910-12 exports averaged 183 tons.[6] It would therefore seem that the quantity exported rose appreciably until about the 1870s and then stabilized.

As for total exports from Turkey, they averaged 387 tons that were worth ₤T643,000 in 1878-82, 412 tons worth ₤T686,000 in 1890-94, and about 450 tons worth ₤T700,000 in 1908-13. As a proportion of total exports, opium fell from 6.7 percent to about 3.9 percent.[7]

There is some evidence that production of opium increased considerably in response to a rise in price and then stabilized when prices fell. The table below summarizes the available information.

The following selection describes the situation in 1881, which must have been very close to a peak. Between 1876-80 and 1901-5 internal opium prices fell by more than a half, from 259 piastres per oke to 124 in Malatya, and from 235 to 109 in Geyve. This seems to have offset the rather feeble attempts by the government to encourage cultivation by exempting opium growers from the tithe after 1881, and production showed little change between the 1880s and the early 1900s. After 1906 prices started rising again and output increased.[8]

---

1. Stich, p. 68; a large part of American purchases was resold to China and the East Indies--MacFarlane, 1:65.
2. In 1852 the British consul at Bursa had reported that "opium is raised chiefly within the limits of this Province, and a portion in various parts of the Pachalik," i.e.,

Hüdavendigar. "The finest or purest of all at Levke and Gheve. The rest is obtained throughout a large range of country towards Kutahia and Smyrna, and extending over the Sangiak of Karrahissar where the most is produced, to Konia in that direction" (Report on Trade, FO 78/905).

3. The above is based mainly on an article in TJ, March 1913; also EHI, pp. 238-41; according to the French Chamber of Commerce of Istanbul, Salonica shipped its own opium and of the rest 60 percent went through Izmir and 40 percent through Istanbul (RC, no. 62, 1900).

4. Table in Quataert, p. 402, and Reports in CC Smyrne, vols. 56 and 57.

5. Quataert, p. 402; the case weighed 145 lbs.--A and P 1894, vol. 88, "Turkey"; the figures given by the French consul are higher, ranging between 400 and 500 tons in the 1890s (CC Smyrne, vols. 56 and 57).

6. A and P 1914, vol. 95, "Smyrna."

7. Aybar, pp. 62 and 73. Britain's share in 1893-97 averaged 154 metric tons, or 40 percent of the total--A and P 1899, vol. 103, "Constantinople."

8. For prices, Quataert, pp. 297-300; for output, Eldem, p. 82.

Year	District	Baskets	Tons	Source
1832	Turkey	300,000 çeki	229	Hagemeister, p. 11[a]
1834	Turkey	160,000 çeki	122	Hagemeister, p. 11
1835	Turkey	120,000 çeki	92	Hagemeister, p. 11
1836	Turkey	80,000 çeki	61	Hagemeister, p. 11
1847	Afyon	270	21	FO 78/750[b]
Mid 1850s	Sancak - Bursa	270	182-273	A & P 1859, 30[c]
1863	Karahisar	1,800	120	A & P 1864, 31[d]
1877	Afyon	..	96	CC Brousse, 1877[e]
1877	Balıkesir	..	38	CC Brousse, 1877
1877	Kütahya	..	38	CC Brousse, 1877
1877	Bursa	..	13	CC Brousse, 1877
1877	Hüdavendigar	..	192	CC Brousse, 1877
Until 1869	Asia Minor	Not over 4,000	310	CC Brousse, 1877
1877	Asia Minor	8,000	620	CC Brousse, 1877

[a]Decline attributed to imposition of monopoly.

[b]"Adverse season."

[c]"The bulk of the product comes from Afyon"; prices 160-240 piastres per oke.

[d]Prices 210-220 per oke.

[e]Increase attributed to rise in prices.

SELECTION 26. OPIUM CROP, 1881

Report on Agriculture in Smyrna Region, 30 September 1881, CC Smyrne, vol. 54

. . . From the point of view of trade, no crop in Anatolia is as important as opium. This year's crop has been quite exceptional. Being short of seeds because of the extreme dryness and the ravage wrought by locusts in the maize, wheat, and barley fields, farmers turned to poppy-growing, and have sown it in almost all parts of the region. It is therefore not only the main producing centers--Uşak, Kutahya, and Afyon Karahisar, whose opium enjoys the greatest reputation--that have supplied this crop in abundance but all the localities where it was grown.

According to the most conservative estimates, this year's crop should amount to 10,000 baskets of 80 kilograms each, worth 2,400 francs apiece; this represents a total value of 24 million francs. Adding the poppy-seed, of which it is reckoned that some 15 million kilograms, worth 5 million francs, should be exported this year, one reaches a total of 29 million francs for this crop alone. . . .

GRAPES

Asia Minor's grapes and wines were famous in antiquity, and cultivation continued after the mass of the population became Muslim. This was in sharp contrast to, for instance, Egypt and North Africa where vinegrowing practically disappeared, and was no doubt partly due to the presence of a large Christian population; however, as the following selection shows, Muslim villages also had large vineyards. Grapes were grown all over Anatolia, but the main centers of cultivation were the Izmir, and to a lesser extent the Bursa, regions. Grapes are consumed fresh, as raisins, as wine, as distilled liquors (e.g., raki), and boiled juice (pekmez).[1]

No overall figures on grape production are available until 1888, but some trends may be discerned. In 1862, the oidium disease struck the vineyards of the Bursa region (Report on Bursa, first half of 1862, FO 195/741) and those of other parts of Asia Minor (see selection 27) and caused great damage. But since French and other European vineyards were soon after attacked by phylloxera, the demand for grape products rose and Anatolian growers responded by planting much larger areas to vines, especially in the Gediz valley where they replaced cotton, whose price had dropped sharply after the end of the American Civil War[2] (5:16). "In consequence of increasing French demand, the number of vineyards in Aydın province rose tenfold."[3] This process was helped by the introduction of an improved variety of vine by a German firm in 1884.[4]

In 1885, however, phylloxera reached Asia Minor and caused great damage in the Izmir and Bursa regions, although other parts of the country seem to have escaped quite lightly. The government sought to aid growers by spreading technical information, exempting new vineyards from taxation and, helped by the Debt Administration, most effectively by establishing nurseries and distributing millions of American shoots which, as in France, had proved themselves immune to the disease.[5] However, production had hardly begaun to recover when it was hit by a new blow: the French tariff of 1892, which raised duties on grapes and grape products. In the Izmir region, much land was shifted from vines to legumes. In 1900 the British consul reported: "The vineyards have suffered terribly of recent years from phylloxera and mildew. Moreover, the taxation on grapes and wines is very heavy--12 per cent on grapes as fruit, 15 per cent in addition on wine, and a further 8 per cent on all wine sent to other parts of Turkey, or 4 per cent on that sent abroad." Nevertheless he estimated the vineyards of Aydın province at 200,000 acres and noted that "American vines have been introduced in most districts to combat phylloxera with good results."[6] Output of raisins in the Aegean region fell from over 40,000 tons around 1890 to 36,000 in 1897 and then recovered to a peak of 69,000 in 1913.[7]

For much of the period under review, grapes and grape products were Turkey's leading export item. Fresh grapes were shipped from Bursa to Istanbul, and from Izmir to Istanbul and Egypt,[8] but very little went outside the Empire. Wine was exported from Izmir in the 1850s to Russia and the United States, in the 1860s to Italy, and then to other European countries.[9] In the late 1870s, some German firms began to develop the wine industry, by introducing modern methods, in the Marmara, Izmir, Erenköy, and other regions, and French capital also played an important part. This resulted in larger exports, but after 1900 protective measures in France, Italy, and Austria, and the competition of Greek wines, had an adverse effect. In 1909 Izmir exported 1,800 tons of wine, mainly to Germany and the Nordic countries.[10]

But by far the most important grape product exported was raisins, of which the finest were known as sultanas. These penetrated various European markets as early as the

fifteenth century[11] and in 1784-90 Izmir's exports to Britain alone averaged 7,400 tons a
year (BT 6-73). In 1834 Izmir's exports amounted to 22,000 tons worth about ₤250,000 (3:14)
and in 1855-56 they averaged about 10,700 tons worth some ₤176,000 (CC Smyrne, vol. 49, 28
November 1856).[12] Thereafter there must have been a considerable increase since Turkey's
total exports of raisins averaged 54,200 tons worth ₤T1,154,000 in 1878-80 and continued
rising to a peak of 74,000 tons worth ₤T1,886,000 in 1891-95. After that, a rise in price
offset the decline in quantity, and in 1908-13 exports averaged about 57,200 tons worth
some ₤T1,787,000.[13]

The rise in raisin exports was accompanied by a shift in markets; France's share, which
had risen sharply after the phylloxera had ravaged its vineyards,[14] declined sharply and
that of Britain increased.[15] Here Turkish raisin exports met keen competition from Spanish
raisins and Greek currants, and when on 1 May 1890 the duty on all currants was lowered
from 7s. per cwt. to 2s., while that on raisins remained at 7s., the Ottoman government
made repeated attempts to secure a similar reduction on their raisins. The British government refused, pointing out, first, that Turkey was increasing its share of the British
market,[16] secondly that the total value of imports of raisins from Turkey had shown a constant increase (FO 368/471), and thirdly that the unit price of Turkish raisins had always
been above that of currants (ibid.).

---

1. Greeks accounted for the bulk of grape production and for wine and liquors; the
Turks consumed their grapes fresh or made raisins--Dietrich, p. 50; EHME, pp. 116-17.
2. Stich, p. 58.
3. Quataert, p. 217.
4. Kurmuş, p. 286.
5. Quataert, pp. 217-36.
6. A and P 1901, vol. 85, "Smyrna."
7. Eldem, p. 82; after 1908 many Izmir growers shifted from olives to vines--Quataert,
p. 240.
8. Stich, p. 58.
9. Ibid., p. 60. In 1859 the British consul-general in Istanbul reported: "The export trade of native wines from this district has very much fallen off of late years, but
still about 5 or 6,000 hogsheads are every year sent to Russia--and some of our Ionian
merchants are engaged in it" (10 February 1859, FO 195/590).
10. Stich, pp. 61-62.
11. EI(2), s.v. "Filaha."
12. Some indication of the trend is given by the fact that total exports of dried
fruits (of which raisins accounted for by far the greater part (3:14 and Report on Agriculture, 30 September 1881, CC Smyrne, vol. 54) averaged ₤136,000 in 1836-37, ₤115,000 in
1841-43, and ₤309,000 in 1851-52. The main markets were Britain, Austria, and the United
States and, in the mid-1850s, France (CC Smyrne, vols. 45-47, Annual Reports on Trade).
13. Aybar, p. 66; for figures on grape and raisin exports from Izmir, see Quataert,
p. 391.
14. From August 1878 to January 1879 Izmir exported 10,000 tons of raisins to France,
worth 3 million francs--CC Smyrne, vol. 52, 10 February 1879).
15. Quataert, p. 242.
16. Between 1888-94 and 1901-4, British imports of raisins from Turkey rose from
13,900 to 14,800 tons, while imports of raisins from Spain remained unchanged and those of
currants from Greece declined--FO to Turkish Ambassador, 9 December 1905, TE Box 439 (1908).
By 1905-7 Turkey's share had risen to 18,100 tons while those of Spain and Greece further
declined to 13,300 and 60,700 tons, respectively (Statement, 13 November 1908, FO 368/231).

SELECTION 27. VINE-GROWING AND WINE-MAKING IN BURSA REGION, 1880

"Etat de la viticulture . . . dans le vilayet de Hudavendighiar, Turquie d'Europe," BC,
1881

The sancak of Bursa has always been famous in the Orient for the abundance and quality
of its wines.
The disease that hit the vines of Asia Minor, about twenty years ago, has however
greatly damaged the vineyards of Bursa. This disease, called külleme in Turkish, had all
the characteristics of oidium (vine mildew): from the moment they were formed, the grapes
began to shrink; they continued nevertheless to grow but, instead of acquiring juice, they

dried up; at picking time, the bunches were well-formed but black and dry as though they had been put in an oven. Many attempts, at first unsuccessful, were made to stop the progress of this disease. It was only after quite a long time that the use of sulfur was recognized as perfectly efficacious. But by then a large number of vine-growers, justifiably scared, had pulled out their vines and sown instead wheat, maize, etc. while others had completely abandoned their fields. Thus, by the time the remedy had been found, the number of vines had diminished by half.

Other factors also caused the vineyards of the _sancak_ of Bursa to decrease in importance. We can mention, among others, the earthquake of 1855 that shattered the greater part of the town, and the great fire that destroyed the best wine cellars.

Today, the külleme has disappeared; thanks to the widespread use of sulfur, vines are no longer hit by disease; no trace of phylloxera has yet been seen; earthquakes seem to be less frequent; as for fires, although they are still numerous, as in all Turkish towns, they can no longer reach in Bursa the scale of that of 1863, since the greater part of the town has been rebuilt along wide and straight streets.

The grape harvest of the _sancak_ of Bursa should therefore--while falling short of its former size--be sufficient to reconstitute the wines that have disappeared. For if these wines no longer exist, that is not because of the lack of grapes (the harvests are still very large) but because of the lack of development of the wine trade in this country, which does not receive the indispensable help it needs. This industry does not exist, and has to be entirely created. But we are certain that the day private enterprise takes up this matter it will, so to speak, lay its hand on a mine of still unexploited riches.

The following table, whose figures were gathered with great care and checked whenever possible--in spite, and because, of the difficulties met in Turkey in any attempt to obtain the slightest information--shows clearly that there is no shortage of grapes in Bursa for producing wines of the desired quantity and quality.

Production of the Vineyards of the Sancak of Bursa, Within a Maximum Radius of 40 Kilometers from the Shipping Ports of the Gulf of Gemlik

Location	Turkish or Christian area	Black Grapes okes	kilograms	Approximate Production White Grapes okes	kilograms
Kızıklar (5 villages) . . .	Turkish	..	..	500,000	625,000
Ak-Su	Idem.	..	..	200,000	250,000
Gözede and Çataltepe . . .	Idem.	..	..	10,000	12,500
Dimboz	Idem.	..	..	15,000	18,750
Kestel	Idem.	..	..	15,000	18,750
Dödakli and Bazarköy . . .	Idem.	..	..	150,000	187,500
Karakidir and Narlidere . .	Idem.	..	..	200,000	250,000
Cidir, Kazikli and Aga-Köy	Idem.	100,000	125,000	200,000	250,000
Kelessen	Christian				
Dimirdeş.	Idem.	400,000	500,000	400,000	500,000
Alaşar	Turkish				
Kara-Balçik	Idem.	..	..	50,000	62,500
Seteş-köy	Idem.	..	..	50,000	62,500
Çurdane	Idem.	..	..	150,000	187,500
Filadar	Christian	100,000	125,000	1,100,000	1,375,000
Aksungur	Turkish	..	..	15,000	18,750
Ahmed-Bey	Turkish	..	..	120,000	150,000
Plain of Bursa	Turkish & Christian	..	..	100,000	125,000
Bursa, Missi, and Çekirge	Idem.	..	..	1,800,000	2,750,000
Demirci-köy	Turkish	..	..	300,000	375,000
Çali-köy	Idem.	..	..	300,000	375,000
Fodra and Yalacik	Idem.	..	..	400,000	500,000
Tahtali	Turkish & Christian	..	..	500,000	625,000
Kayapa	Turkish	..	..	500,000	625,000
Hasan-Aga	Idem.	..	..	500,000	625,000
Akçaklar	Idem.	..	..	200,000	250,000
Dansari-Gurukle	Christian	25,000	31,250	575,000	718,750
Quitte	Turkish	..	..	200,000	250,000
Yenice-köy	Idem.	..	..	15,000	18,750
Dere-Tehkuşu	Idem.	..	..	15,000	18,750
Total		625,000	781,250	8,480,000	10,600,000

In other words, the town and neighborhood of Bursa produce, on average, nearly 1,000,000 kilograms of black grapes and nearly 11,000,000 of white grapes, a total of 12,000,000 kilograms. It should be noted that the table includes only those vineyards that are connected by passable roads to Bursa or the shipping ports of Mudanya and Gemlik. The closest are 5 kilometers from the shore, the furthest about 40 kilometers.

There are five main kinds of white grapes, locally known as: <u>gerence</u>, <u>eksenes</u>, <u>doğru-cibik</u>, <u>amasya</u>, and <u>çauş</u>. The last two are excellent dessert grapes, especially <u>çauş</u> which is a large, fragrant grape, very similar to the <u>chasselas</u> of Fontainebleau. Bursa has been producing this variety for only a few years; it was imported from the Bosphorus (Asian shore), where the <u>çauş</u> is grown for consumption in Constantinople. Black grapes consist of two varieties: <u>cabata</u> and <u>dimrit</u>; their taste is not very pleasant. One-third of the amount of white grapes given above is sold in the town and eaten as fruit. The other two-thirds are used for making (1) wine, (2) a kind of thick juice known as <u>pekmez</u>, which is used for making household jams. These jams play an important part in the towns and villages of Asia Minor. They are of two kinds: <u>beçel</u>, a jam made of fruits mixed with certain vegetables; and <u>bulama</u>, a yellowish, very thick paste, which in certain areas takes the place of sugar or, rather, molasses. Some regions of the interior trade extensively in <u>beçel</u> and <u>bulama</u>.

The grape marc obtained by all these processes is used for making <u>raki</u>, a kind of marc brandy flavored with aniseed and resin, which is consumed on a large scale. The inhabitants drink this liquor as an apéritif, and also as an aid to digestion. For them, <u>raki</u> takes the place of the various liquors used in France, which will never be able to provide serious competition in this country.

Black grapes are used exclusively for making wine.

The price of these various kinds of grapes sold in the towns (price of delivery at the buyer's house) varies, from year to year, between 50 and 80 piastres the 100 okes, or 11 to 18 francs per 125 kilograms (the oke equals 1,225 grams and the piastre 22 centimes).

Each year, the government sells, at set prices, the vineyard tithe. It would obviously have been desirable to give here the sale price for each locality; however, the grape tithe is generally sold together with the wheat tithe, so that it is almost impossible to determine the amount of tax levied by the government on grapes. Each year the government fixes a price for the oke of grapes, which serves as a basis for levying taxes.

The Turkish vinegrowers usually sell their grapes, or use them for making <u>pekmez</u>. It is Christian growers who make wine.

In Bursa, there are wine-makers and wine merchants, grouped in a corporation consisting mainly of Greeks. Most of them have made vats out of the old baths, which provide well-fitted premises for this industry.

In Bursa and its suburbs wine-making is, so to speak, still in its infancy. The methods used are of the simplest. Only crude [<u>brut</u>] wine is made, without further processing. After the bunches of grapes have been pressed, the juice is poured into barrels where it is left to ferment for about two months, then it is decanted in other barrels and the wine is ready.

White wines are usually colored, almost golden. Originally, they are sweet and very heady. Some vineyards produce wines that have the same qualities as those of Spain and of Madeira. A Hungarian, recently established in Bursa, has had the idea of using certain kinds of grapes to make wines which, after being bottled for several months, have all the properties of Rhenish wine.

The four Frenchmen resident in Bursa also make, for their own use, dry white wines which, being better processed [<u>fabriqué</u>] are very similar to our French wines and leave nothing to be desired in the way of taste and flavor. Such wines can be preserved and easily transported. The same is true of black wines, which are very rich in alcohol, sweet, and very heady.

Another local method is the making of cooked [cuit] wines. As soon as the grapes are pressed, the juice is cooked until it almost thickens into a syrup; it is then put into barrels, where it can keep indefinitely. In this way the wines of certain districts can be aged. But this process causes the liquid to lose all its qualities and gives it defects that make it unfit for continuous use.

As we said earlier, grape marc is used to make <u>raki</u>. The marc is put in open barrels where it is left to ferment for twenty to twenty-five days. It is then put in a still without a spiral pipe; when it starts boiling a certain amount of aniseed is added, and different degrees of marc brandy are thus obtained.

The average price of processed wines is as follows: white wine costs 40 to 80 para (1 to 2 piastres) an oke, or 22 to 44 centimes; black wine costs 60 to 100 para (1½ to 2½ piastres) an oke, or 33 to 55 centimes; <u>raki</u> costs 4 to 10 piastres an oke, or 80 centimes to 2 francs 20 centimes; old wines sell for up to 10 piastres an oke, or 1 franc 75 centimes per litre.

All the above figures refer only to vineyards with good transport to the coast and not more than 40 kilometers away. The following is a list of the main grape-producing areas in the whole <u>vilayet</u> of Hudavendighiar. It should however be remembered that the lines of communication between these localities and both Bursa and the ports on the Gulf of Gemlik are either nonexistent or so rough that the costs of transport would exceed the profits one could hope to make by exporting. The _vilayet_ of Hudavendighiar is divided into four _sancak_:

1. _Sancak_ of Bursa--this includes the _kaza_ of Mohalitz, Gemlik (coast), Bilecik, Mudanya (coast), Ainegöl, and Yenişehir. The first and last of these _kaza_ (Mohalitz and Yenişehir) do not grow vines; the four others produce large quantities, notably Bilecik, twenty hours away from Bursa, whose black grapes are highly prized for wine-making.

2. _Sancak_ of Karesi--this includes the _kaza_ of Ayvalik, Erdek, Bandirma, Edremid, Bihadiz, Kemer-Edremid, and Sorma. Except for the last but one, all these _kaza_ grow vines.

3. _Sancak_ of Karahisar--this includes the _kaza_ of Sandıklı, Çal, Bulvadin, and Azizie; except for the last two, all these _kaza_ grow grapes.

4. Sancak of Kutahya--this includes the _kaza_ of Uşak, Gediz, Simari, and Eskişehir. Uşak is the only _kaza_ producing wine.

As may be seen, 13 out of the 21 _kaza_ constituting the _vilayet_ of Hudavendighiar are vine-growing areas. Since transport is lacking, each region consumes its grapes locally, and prices are naturally far lower than in Bursa and its suburbs.

General statements on vineyard production in the whole _vilayet_ would, of course, be very interesting but could be compiled only on the spot, and even then only with great difficulty since local administration in the interior has few documents from which statistical data could be drawn.

MOHAIR

Mohair, the fleece of the Angora goat, has been used for a wide variety of articles of clothing, carpets, and household furnishings. In Turkey it was "produced in a district covering from 60,000 to 80,000 square miles, and comprising, roughly speaking, the vilayets or provinces of Angora and Kastamuni, though portions of the provinces of Broussa, Yozgat, Koniah, and Sivas must also be included in the mohair-producing area." The finest quality came from the district of Beypazar, in Ankara province, and an inferior quality was also produced in Van.[2]

Until the beginning of the nineteenth century, the mohair clip was absorbed domestically, supplying several thousands of looms in the Ankara and Kastamonu regions; significant amounts of yarn were sent to Europe, but the export of both raw hair and Angora goats was prohibited.[3] In 1820, however, the first shipment of raw hair was sent to England and by 1839 exports amounted to 1,240,000 lbs, greatly exceeding those of yarn, as is noted in the following selection. The result was a great decline in the number of looms in Ankara, to only a few hundred by 1867.[4]

The rapidly rising demand led to a sharp increase in exports of mohair, chiefly to Bradford in England, and a corresponding expansion in production. In selection 28, average shipments from Istanbul--which accounted for the bulk of exports--in the early 1850s were put at 12,000 bales, or some 2,500,000 lbs. In 1866 the total Angora mohair clip was put at 25,000 bales, or 4,200,000 lbs., to which should be added another 4,000 bales from Van. Between 1866 and 1873, "with a succession of fine seasons, the clip rose steadily from a total of about 30,000 bags to nearly 50,000." In 1873 a drought followed by a severe winter killed nearly one-third of the goats and reduced the total clip to 33,000 bags. The consequent sharp increase in prices seems, however, to have helped to stimulate a speedy recovery: in 1876 output rose to 38,000 bags and in 1877 to 48,000.[5] This level seems to have been more or less maintained: in 1873-82 annual exports averaged 35,000 bags, or about 6 million lbs., and in the 1890s over 8 million lbs. for a value of about ₤500,000.[6] On the eve of the First World War, output was estimated at 5,000-5,500 tons (11 to 12 million lbs.) and exports in 1913-14--mainly to England--amounted to 4,600 tons of which 3,900 went through Istanbul.[7]

This increase in production and exports was accompanied by two changes in the structure of the market. The purchase and export of mohair in Turkey passed increasingly from Armenian to British hands: "within the last few years two of the most important manufacturing houses in Yorkshire have established agencies here for the purpose of pur-chasing mohair, and the experiment seems to have been a success."[8] Far more important, Turkey, which hitherto had enjoyed a monopoly in mohair, began to meet increasing competi-tion.[9]

During the Crimean War, the British secured permission to ship some goats (see the selection) and shortly after that the production of mohair was developed in the Cape and Natal, receiving a stimulus from the rise in prices caused by the American Civil War. In the following decades herds were also raised in the United States (Texas, New Mexico, Cali-fornia) and in Queensland in Australia. Of these, the Cape and Natal provided the most serious competition, although the quality of the hair was inferior to that of Turkish. In 1875 British imports from South Africa were about one-fifth of their imports from Turkey—1,100,000 lbs. compared to 5,300,000—but by 1885 they were almost equal—5,300,000 lbs. against 6,800,000.[10] Cape prices were about one-third below Turkish[11] and—together with the slackening of demand for bright lustre materials—forced the price of the latter down. In 1870-73, before the drought, the price of British imports of Turkish mohair averaged 3s.6d. a pound; by 1883-85 the average had fallen to 1s.10d.[12] The opinion of the British consul in Istanbul was that: "Even at so low a price as 1s.6d. per lb., some mohair would, no doubt, be still produced by the smaller growers, who can keep goats at less expense; but should the price decline still further, and remain for any length of time at, say, 1s.3d. per lb., even the small grower could not cover the cost of production, and mohair trade of Turkey would infallibly disappear. This, it is believed, is only a question of time, as the Turkish producer cannot compete with those of the Cape and Natal."[13] British import prices for Turkish mohair did indeed fall as low as 1s.2d. in the early 1890s,[14] but they recovered thereafter[15] and production and exports continued.

1. A and P 1899, vol. 103, "Constantinople"; "the Mohair is purchased by local mer-chants from the owners of the goats in its unwashed state, frequently several months before the shearing season (April). It is sorted in the warehouses into four classes called whites, yellows, colours and inferiors. . . . Though the whites are supposed to be packed separately, a scrupulous attention to this matter is not the rule, and gives rise to seri-ous complaints from Bradford and other purchasing centres" (ibid., 1895, vol. 100, "Angora").
2. Ibid., 1878, vol. 74, "Constantinople."
3. Stich, p. 116, Texier, pp. 458-62.
4. Stich, p. 116, and A and P 1899, vol. 103, "Constantinople."
5. Stich, p. 116, and A and P 1899, vol. 103, "Constantinople."
6. A and P 1883, vol. 74, "Constantinople," and 1899, vol. 3, "Constantinople."
7. Stich, p. 118; Mears, p. 290.
8. Stich and A and P 1899, vol. 103, "Constantinople."
9. Attempts had been made in the eighteenth century to raise Angora goats in Sweeden, France, Austria, and Italy but all had failed because of the climate—Stich, p. 117.
10. Because of the tax on goats and—until the building of the Anatolian railway—high transport costs, it was impossible "for the Anatolian flockmaster to lay down his mo-hair in Constantinople as cheaply as the South African flockmaster can lay it down at Capetown or Natal"—A and P 1883, vol. 74, "Constantinople."
11. Information supplied by British Board of Trade to Turkish Ambassador, TE, Box 237 (1886).
12. Ibid.
13. A and P 1883, vol. 74, "Constantinople."
14. Computed from table in A and P 1899, vol. 103, "Constantinople."
15. See numerous quotations in TJ, 1908-14.

SELECTION 28. THE MOHAIR CLIP, 1854

Hardy to Clarendon, May 6, 1854, FO 781/4

. . . The additional inquiries I have recently made show that the annual clip from these animals, in proportion as they attain full age is, from the Ewes, from 1 to 2 okes. The Rams produce more than the Ewes, and at two years old, at which age they have attained their full growth, they give 2 to 2½ okes, and fine specimens, that have passed that age, have been known to yield 3½ to 4 okes. They are in their prime, as regards both quantity and quality of the wool at from 3 to 5 years old. The wool from the Ewes is finer than that from the Rams which is longer as well as coarser. The shearing takes place generally towards the end of April, but varies a little according to the season.

This is the proper time to buy the animals, as they are, naturally, cheaper after they have been shorn of this valuable produce. Ewes of 2 years old may then be bought at from 80 to 100 piastres, or 12 to 15 shillings. Rams of the same age would cost 120 to 150 piastres or about 18-23 shillings. Those of four years are worth from 200 to 300 piastres, or 30 to 45 shillings, and fine specimens sometimes obtain a higher price. The Spring and the Autumn are equally proper times for the animals to make the journey, whilst both summer and winter should be avoided. The direct route from Angora to Constantinople should be preferred to any other. The expenses of the journey would be but trifling, and were rather overrated in my first report. In that Report I stated that the Rams should form a proportion of 10 p. cent: but this would be a larger provision than would be necessary, except to provide against accidents--5 to 6 p. cent being amply sufficient for use.

The passage home should be made by steamers, of which there are now almost weekly departures for England and at very reasonable freights. I confirm, however, my former recommendation that this had better be arranged by anticipation with the managers in England.

The quantity of Goats wool exported from Constantinople during the last five years has averaged no less than 12,000 Bales. Each Bale used formerly to contain about 60 okes, but I find that they have, for sometime past, contained from 70 to 80. The oke is equal to lbs. 2 3/4 English.

The first cost of the article here (Constantinople and Angora) during the last three years has been as follows, viz.

in 1857 from p. 24 to p. 25 per oke
   1852   "   23 to   26
   1853   "   28 to   30

This year's clip is only now beginning, and is not yet at market. The price is expected to be unusually low, say under 20 piastres.

The Exchange on London may be calculated at 130 piastres the £ Sterling.

The selling prices in England during the above period have been as follows, viz.

          s d   s d
in 1851 from 1/5 to 1/11
   1852   " 1/6 to 2/-
   1853   " 2/- to 3/-

but the value of it there at present, is only about 1s.6d.

I should not omit to add that the article of "Mohair Yarn" manufactured in this country from Angora wool, and which, in former years, formed no inconsiderable an item in our Exports, has now been entirely superseded by the raw material, thereby transferring the manufacture of it into yarn entirely to our own country. . . .

SELECTION 29. LIVESTOCK RAISING IN ERZURUM AND DIYARBEKIR, 1860s

Charles Issawi

Livestock breeding played an important part in the economic life of Turkey. As in other parts of the Middle East, there was practically no "mixed farming" in the sense of raising animals on the farm and feeding them with forage crops grown specially for that purpose. Herds were tended either by nomads or by peasants who took them to graze on land lying outside the area cultivated by their fellow villagers. The average net value of animal products in the whole Empire in 1913-14 was put by Eldem at £T26.8 million, compared to 84.8 million for vegetable produce.[1] The breakdown of the returns for the tithe (aşar) and animal (ağnam) taxes shows that the gross value of vegetable products in the area corresponding to present-day Turkey was about £T48.3 million in 1913-14 and that of animal products 14.0 million. It also shows that animal husbandry was a relatively minor occupation in the moist coastal areas, such as Trabzon, Kastamonu, Hüdavendigar, İzmit, and Adana, and a much more important one in the interior provinces, such as Ankara, and the eastern ones: Diyarbekir, Van, Erzurum, etc.[2] But the European provinces had also been large raisers of livestock and it was from them that Istanbul had drawn its supplies of meat.[3]

Livestock raising was carried on in a traditional way and practically no attempts were made to improve pastures or breeds or to combat the diseases that took such a heavy toll.[4] Nevertheless in many parts of the country it was sufficiently profitable to attract capital from townsmen. A detailed account shows how this was done in Erzurum around 1870, under a sharing system known as Kome.[5] The capitalists "are supposed to have purchased a pasture, affording ample grazing for 800 sheep in spring and summer, and yielding them a sufficiency of cut dried fodder for winter, together with the rude mud buildings for housing animals in rigorous weather, and a cabin for the shepherd . . . assisted by two boys paid by him, and four dogs." The capitalist also paid the tax (2 piastres on full-grown sheep) and provided salt and medicines, while all the labor was supplied by the shepherd. The initial outlay consisted of ₤600, for 800 sheep (45 piastres, or 8s., each), a pasture-ground (28,000 piastres or ₤255), and 16 rams. The calculation was based on the following assumptions: average animal mortality 10 percent; yield per sheep 1½ okes of butter at 7 piastres and 1½ okes of cheese at 2 piastres; yield of wool half an oke rising to 1½ okes.

Expenses in the first year consisted of 12 percent interest on capital, ₤70, value of shepherd's perquisites 1,500 piastres (₤13-12-8), taxes, forage, medicine, and salt for a total of ₤117. Income from butter, cheese and wool amounted to ₤127, leaving a profit of ₤10. The second year's expenditure was ₤143 and income ₤128, showing an apparent loss of ₤15 which, however, was offset by the increase in the flock. The third year's expenses were ₤145 and income ₤186, but the sale of 338 two-year-old males at 50 piastres each brought in another ₤154, giving a profit of ₤194. Furthermore the sale of 952 surplus ewes and rams fetched another ₤406, which brought the total profit for the three years to ₤611 "or more than 25 per cent per annum on the original ₤600 capital."

Townspeople owning only a few sheep and no pasture-ground would hand the sheep for the period May-November to a villager who charged them 2½ piastres for each sheep and gave them all the lambs and wool and 1½ okes of butter and 1½ of cheese for every sheep. An account for 100 sheep showed income at 2,290 piastres and expenses at 1,780, leaving a profit of 510 piastres on a capital of 4,400, or under 12 percent, plus the female lambs born during the year. The main items of expenditure were 1,200 piastres to the pasture owner, 250 to the shepherd, and 200 in taxes.

Sheep farming in the Diyarbekir region "is not so expensive as in this neighborhood, but the profits are less, owing to higher taxes, comparative distance from large markets, inferior quality of pasture, and greater heat of the climate, which lessens and deteriorates the produce." In summer and autumn sheep were pastured in the mountains, subject to payment to the Kurdish tribes, and in summer in the Mesopotamian plains, where the Arab chiefs exacted a small fee. "A thousand sheep require three shepherds, who receive annually 100 piastres each, their food costing 1½ piastres, about 1½d. (sic), and a suit of clothes, the whole not exceeding 500 piastres (₤4-10-10) for each." An account for 1,000 sheep costing 40,000 piastres showed expenses of 11,120 (including interest of 4,800 and taxes of 3,000) and income of 14,300, leaving a profit of 3,180 piastres or 8 percent above the interest on capital.

A few years earlier, in 1858, the consul in Diyarbekir had stated that sheep cost nothing to the grazier and gave an average profit of 5 piastres a head. The average annual yield of an Arab sheep was 1½ to 1¾ okes of wool, which was sold by the fleece at about 5 piastres an oke. Kurdish wool, which was coarser, was sold at 15 to 25 piastres per batman of 6 okes, or about 2 to 3d. per lb. (Reply to Questionnaire, FO 78/1418).

1. Eldem, p. 282.
2. Ibid., pp. 86-87; the number of sheep in 1910-11, within the present borders, was put at 16 million and that of goats at 12.7 million--ibid., p. 274; for 1913 and 1919 figures, Mears p. 289.
3. A and P 1878, vol. 74, "Constantinople."
4. In 1842 the sultan bought 2,400 merino sheep from Odessa (12 November 1842, FO 195/178) but no significant results are recorded.
5. A and P 1871, vol. 71, "Koordistan."

6

Industry

The industrial evolution of Turkey in the nineteenth century was very similar to that of other underdeveloped countries. Because of the competition of foreign machine-made goods the decline of the traditional handicrafts accelerated, and it was only in the two or three decades preceding the First World War that a significant factory industry rose to take their place; the development of mineral resources also started at about the same time. This delay is somewhat surprising, since Turkey had more of the prerequisites of industrialization than most countries.[1] It had a sufficiently large and not very poor population, providing an internal market; abundance of coal, iron, copper, lead, and other minerals; and a wide range of agricultural raw materials, notably cotton, silk, wool, wood, leather, tobacco, fruits, and oilseeds. The inadequacy of its transportation system was largely offset by the concentration of the population along the coastal rims and the fact that almost all the big cities were on or close to the sea. And the presence of a large number of handicraftsmen provided a source of skills that could have been tapped for factory work. The main obstacles were social and political. There was first the lack of a native Turkish middle class with capital, enterprise, and managerial skills;[2] this gap might have been filled by the non-Muslims or foreigners, who in fact were responsible for most of the industrialization that took place, but who were inhibited by a feeling of insecurity in dealing with the government and were diverted from investment in industry by the attraction of rival fields that promised quicker returns, such as government loans, money lending, trade, or the purchase of real estate in the rapidly growing towns. And organized industrial credit was practically nonexistent. The low educational level of the masses and their aversion to industrial work made the recruitment of labor more difficult, while at the same time wages were relatively high.[3] The opposition of the guilds was strenuous, and often effective. The government's inability to protect national industry, because of the Commercial Treaties, until near the end of the period was a still more serious obstacle, which was aggravated by the internal duties on sale and consumption of manufactured goods (see, e.g., 5:27). But perhaps most important was the government's lack of interest in economic development in general and industrialization in particular. This in turn was partly due to the social structure of the country and the fact that the government reflected the views of the military and bureaucracy, rather than the very small and largely non-Turkish entrepreneurial middle class. In part it was due to the prevailing belief that Turkey could not be industrialized: even a well-wisher, the distinguished Orientalist Vambery, stated in 1873 that "European factories can only exist on the basis of the climatic and social relationships of Europe" and that the spirit of application and hard work which had made possible Europe's factories "never have been nor ever will be conceivable amongst Moslems of Asia."[4] But in large part it was due to the unwieldiness and corruption of the bureaucracy, its ignorance of economic matters and its preoccupation with fiscal considerations to the exclusion of development policies (see, for one of many examples, 6:14).[5] International rivalries also played their part, by preventing or delaying the granting of concessions for railways and public utilities.

Mining developed more rapidly than manufacturing. Both the Balkans and Anatolia have numerous, though generally not large, deposits of a wide variety of minerals, and the Ottoman Empire was one of Europe's main producers. "According to fermans written in the years 1551-1784, the most important silver, copper, and iron mines were located at Gümüşhane, Espiye, Keban, İnegöl, Ergani, Kiği, and Bilecik; and salt-peter mines at Akdağ, Karaman, İçel, Maraş, and Kayseri. In the European part, the most important mines were at Novoberde, Serberniche, Kiratova, Sidre Kapsi, Rudnik, Kamengrad, Kochanya, and Taşoz."[6] The state was mainly interested in securing silver and gold for minting, copper for guns and anchors, and saltpeter for ammunition (6:1). In the sixteenth century the mines were exploited by private enterprise, the state receiving a share of the refined metal. As the central government became weaker and unable to supervise operations, it forced neighboring villagers to take over the mines and share their profits with it. This proved onerous to the peasants, who began to desert their villages, so the government compelled them to assign quotas of forced labor, fuel, and transport to their members (6:2 to 8). Usually, the government took five-eighths of gross output, but arrangements varied. Newly discovered deposits were sometimes leased out on ten- to twenty-year concessions, the government receiving one-fifth of output. Refining was a government monopoly, its share being also one-fifth of the refined ore.[7]

This system was not calculated to promote development, and all reports agree that the villagers worked with great reluctance, corruption was rampant, techniques were primitive and wasteful of natural resources, and productivity was very low. According to Ubicini, as late as 1853 the gross output of mines was only 4 million francs (6:5).

After the Crimean War there was a flurry of foreign interest in mining,[8] and various concessions were granted, including many to speculators who had no serious intention of developing the mines but merely hoped to resell the concession or force the government to pay them an indemnity.[9] To curb some of these abuses the first mining law was promulgated in 1861; it provided for the granting of concessions for not longer than ten years and the payment to the government of one-quarter of gross receipts. This was replaced in 1869 by a law based on the French mining law of 1810; among its features were that taxes on exports were twice as high as those on output and that the government retained the right to annul concessions for not very clearly specified reasons.[10] A new law, in 1886, was still regarded as too restrictive by capital, but under it much development took place. Following foreign protest and prolonged negotiations between the government and the embassies, the mining law of 1906, which was regarded as much more satisfactory, was promulgated. Conditions for prospecting and exploiting mines were clearly specified, the duration of concessions was not to exceed 99 years (art. 5), and the government was to receive a small ground-rent and a royalty of 1 to 5 percent of output of minerals extracted from shafts and galleries, like coal, copper, and lead, and of 10 to 20 percent of those which were found not in seams but in lodes (amas), like chrome, boracite, and petroleum (arts. 47-51).[11]

The table below, compiled by Eldem, shows the extensive investment of foreign, particularly French, capital within the 1910 borders of Turkey in the thirty years preceding the First World War (also 6:9,10).

Foreign Capital in Mining Sector, 1914

Establishment	Year	Mineral	Share and Bond Capital	Investment
			million piastres	
French				
Balya-Karaaydın	1892	silver-lead	29.0	49.2
Kassandra (Salonica?)	1893	manganese, etc.	19.8	25.0
Ereğli	1896	coal	138.6	186.0
Seniçer (Jannina)	1891	tar	3.5	5.0
Karasu	1900	lead, zinc	22.0	25.0
			212.9	290.2
British				
Borax	1887	boracite	27.5	39.5
Paterson & Partners	1885	chrome	..	10.0
				49.5
German				
Sarıca Mines	1900–1913	coal	10.0	13.5
Krupp, Rochling	1911	chrome	..	7.5
				21.0
Italian and Greek				
Kozlu Kömür	1913	coal	3.0	6.0
Russian				
Ottoman Minerals	1910	coal	6.0	4.0
			259.4	370.7

Source: Eldem, p. 96.

The result of this investment was the exploitation of a wide range of minerals and a large growth in output. Between 1885 and the peak year of 1909, output of coal, in constant prices, rose from 59 million piastres to 180 million, and of other minerals from 29 million to 132 million; between 1885 and 1913, coal output within the 1913 borders increased by 8.7 percent a year and other minerals by 15 percent. Turkey had become an important producer of chrome, boracite, copper, coal, and other minerals (6:10), and there were some 25,000 permanent workers in the mines and another 30,000 in quarries and salt extraction. The main producing regions were Bolu, Karası, Aydın, and Hüdavendigar.[12] The government continued to exploit directly the following mines: copper in Ergani, silver-bearing lead at Bulgar Dağ and Gümüş Hacıköy, meerschaum at Eskişehir, and clay at Mihalıçık, near Ankara.[13]

Mining in Turkey was developed by Europeans, primarily for their own benefit. Their share in mineral output rose from 51 percent in 1902-3 to 76 in 1910-11, while that of minority groups fell from 5 to 4 percent and that of ethnic Turks from 43 to 20 percent[14] and their profits must have been substantial. But they also made a significant contribution to economic development. Turkey was almost self-sufficient in fuel (6:10) and minerals constituted some 5 percent of its exports. Skills were generated, although since a large proportion of workers were non-Muslims (6:9) many were subsequently lost. Above all, when under the Republic foreign interests were taken over (Epilogue) Turkey had a wide and solid basis of mining on which to build its industrial development.

As regards manufacturing, the main development for many decades was the decline of the handicrafts. Already in the eighteenth century Ottoman crafts had been hurt by the growing imports of European woollens and other goods, by protective duties on woollens, silks, and cotton cloth and yarn in Britain and France--which led to a shift to exports of raw cotton (5:15)--and by the competition of finer Indian cloth. But, writing in 1807, Thornton could still pass this enthusiastic judgment: "I know not whether Europe can equal, but certainly it cannot surpass them in several of their manufactures. The satins, and silk stuffs, and the velvets of Brusa and Aleppo, the serges and camelots of Angora, the crapes and gauzes of Salonica, the printed muslins of Constantinople, the carpets of Smyrna, and the silk, the linen and the cotton stuffs of Cairo, Scio, Magnesia, Tokat and Castambol [Kastamonu], establish a favourable but not an unfair criterion of their general skill and industry. The workmen of Constantinople, in the opinion of Spon, excel those of France in many of the inferior trades. They still practise all they found practised; but from an indolence with respect to innovation, have not introduced or encouraged several useful or elegant arts of later invention. They call in no foreign assistance to work their mines. . . ."[15]

After 1815, however, mortal blows struck the handicrafts. Machine-made textiles and other goods poured in from Europe and became increasingly competitive after the conclusion of the 1838 Commercial Convention (3:Introduction) and the introduction of steam navigation and lowering of freight rates (4:6,11). The devastating effect of the Treaty on Ottoman industry was thus described by the Austrian consul: "Now a Belgian manufacturer pays 5% on goods sold in Turkey; a Turkish merchant pays 12% for exports or even for transport from one of the Ottoman states to another."[16] The results are described in selections 6:11 and 12.[17] Only one craft managed to thrive in the new circumstances, carpet-making, which responded to rising overseas demand by greatly increasing output and exports and attracted foreign capital that soon came to dominate it (6:13).

Attempts to establish state factories, mainly to supply military needs, began in the 1830s and met with only limited success (6:14).[18] In 1845 the British consul reported that imports of British machinery were "entirely for account either of the Ottoman government or of Pashas at the head of Public Departments, no importation having taken place for account of private companies or individuals"; in 1843-44 600 tons, plus an amount valued at £7,000, had been imported from Britain (Cartwright to Aberdeen, 22 February 1845, FO 78/611). The first successful private factories were in the simple processing of raw materials: silk reeling (6:15), cotton ginning and pressing (6:14), wheat milling and cotton textiles (6:14). The description of Istanbul's industry in 1863 (6:16) shows how tiny it was, and a contemporary account of Izmir lists: a silk filature; a chiffonerie; steam presses for cotton, madder, wool, and cocoons; and twelve mills driven by water, wind, or steam; almost all these establishments were in European hands (CC Smyrne, vol. 50, 1862).

Not very much progress was made in the following decades. In 1871 the French consul in Izmir reported that in the last two years three foundries and forges for iron and copper had been established, one by an English engineer and two much larger ones by Greeks; they could make all kinds of ordinary repairs on steamers and one had even made a small steamer of 20 HP "whose hull and machine will be entirely built here" (ibid., vol. 51, 1871). An account of industry in Istanbul in 1891 lists, in addition to gun powder and tobacco, four government factories for tanning, woollens, cotton cloth, and fezzes; all of those had high costs--fezzes cost twice as much as those imported from Austria--and quality was low. As regards private industry, there were many tanneries, including two well-equipped ones at Yedikule; several good steam mills; two good brick factories at the Sweet Waters and

Büyükdere which had replaced bricks imported from Marseilles; two poor gasworks at Dolmabahçe and Yedikule; two glassworks at Beyköz and Yedikule, reported to import sand from
Norway and producing low-quality glass; and a woollen and silk factory at Yedikule which
was very well equipped but had not yet started production.[19] At about the same time the
situation in Izmir was summed up as follows: "the only significant industry here is that
of carpets. Cotton manufactures and olive oil factories are of little importance; exports
of licorice juice dwindles day by day; as for the tanneries, flour mills and factories
making furniture, shoes, soap and dough products, their output is mainly sold in the region
where it is produced. If we add gasworks, some foundries--rather well equipped--a factory
for processing paper and an ice factory we have mentioned all the industrial establishments
of the region" (CC Smyrne, vol. 57, 1899).[20]

The fact is that industry could make little headway as long as it was unprotected
against foreign competition and subjected to administrative harassment. The following
passage from Izmir (CC Smyrne, vol. 51, 2 May 1879) is eloquent: "In this same spot,
where water is abundant and can provide motive power, several attempts have been made to
establish first a paper mill, then a glass factory, a spinning mill, and a tannery. But
all these attempts remained fruitless for one reason or other but especially because of
the difficulties which the entrepreneurs met at the hands of the Government. It may seem
incredible, but it has been observed more than once: by its inept and vexatious measures,
the Government has always paralyzed the attempts that have been made to introduce industries
in Turkey."

By the 1900s, however--and more particularly after the 1908 revolution--a change is
noticeable. The government began to encourage industry and to exempt its imports of machinery from custom duties (6:19); moreover in 1911 import duties were raised to 11 percent
and in 1914 to 15. In response there was a considerable amount of investment, mainly by
foreigners or minority groups, and several well-equipped factories were set up. In Istanbul
the following were noted around 1912:[21]

Founded	Capital	Branch
1886	£46,000	Cotton and woollen textiles
1909	£T15,000	Carbonic acid
1910	£T77,000	Grain mill
1910	650,000 francs	Bricks
1910	£T75,000	Cement
1911	£T90,000	Cement
1911	4,000,000 francs	Beer
1911	£T20,000	Shoes
1911	2,000,000 francs	Shipyard

There was also a stearin factory, a paper factory (6:17) and canning, dough products
and glassmaking factories. In Izmir there was the Oriental Carpet Manufacturers with a
capital of £500,000 and a cloth factory with £81,000. And in Cilicia there was a rapidly
growing complex of industries based on cotton: ginning, spinning, weaving, and cottonseed
oil.

The overall situation, and the accelerating rate of investment, is brought out in the
table below.[22]

One industry that, surprisingly, did not develop was sugar refining. In 1900 the
"Sultan authorized a ten year tithe exemption for either beet or cane sugar cultivation
and duty-free import of machinery for a projected sugar processing plant in the Adana area"
but this did not materialize, and "in either the immediate pre-World War I or early war
years, the Germans were assisting in the construction of the 'first' sugar processing plant,

at Sıvas," which also does not seem to have been completed.[23]

It is impossible to say whether this impetus of industrialization, which was provided almost exclusively by foreigners and non-Muslims, would have survived in Turkey's increasingly nationalistic atmosphere. In any case, the war and its aftermath completely changed the situation, and when industrialization was resumed, in the 1930s, it was on a different basis (Epilogue).

Private Industries, Year of Foundation

	Until 1880	1881-90	1891-1900	1901-15	Total
Food	15	6	7	38	66
Ceramics	1	2	3	5	11
Tanneries	3	1	3	4	11
Wood	3	--	6	15	24
Textiles	17	4	6	18	45
Paper, printing	17	6	6	21	50
Chemical	--	--	1	6	7
	56	19	32	107	214

---

1. For Egypt, EHME, pp. 452-60; for Iran, EHI, chap. 6.
2. In the 1913 industrial census only one-third of the establishments had any sort of bookkeeping. "In one factory, where more than 100 workers were employed, it was found that all accounting and production records had been written on one of the walls of the administration office"--Kurmuş, p. 175, quoting census.
3. Consequently, foreign engineers and skilled workers had to be imported (2:10). In the 1860s the British entrepreneur J. Gout had eight Europeans in his various factories--Kurmuş, p. 174. But many of the foreign technicians proved unsatisfactory and either could not or would not train Turks--EHME, p. 47.
    Some of the larger enterprises tried to train their workers, e.g., the Aydın railway recruited each year 400 young people for training; only a small number remained with the company but many set up on their own, a phenomenon comparable, on a very small scale, to Aramco's activities in Arabia in the 1940s and 50s.
4. Quoted by Kurt Grunwald, "Industrializing the Middle East," New Outlook, January 1961. One of the very few dissenting voices was that of J. L. Farley, Turkey.
5. Two good examples are given by Kurmuş, p. 172. In 1874 it was reckoned that a British subject planning to open a textile factory worth ₺6,000-7,000 should be prepared to pay an annual minimum of ₺1,700 in taxes and dues, irrespective of the volume of output and profits. In 1881 MacAndrews and Forbes were informed that the local authorities were raising the tax on their licorice paste by 167 percent, retroactive to 1879, and were demanding ₺40,000; they appealed, but the authorities ordered them to suspend production, which was disrupted for two months and was restored only by the intervention of the British ambassador.
6. Refik, p. V; Anhegger, passim.
7. Brandt, pp. 64-68.
8. "Till now all native Mines have been inaccessible to Europeans as direct lessees, and the privilege confined to Ottoman subjects. But I am aware that some British subjects are concerned in Lead Mines which are being worked in Thessaly" (Report on Reforms, Bursa, 1855, FO 78/1209).
9. Morawitz, p. 213.
10. Brandt, pp. 69-74.
11. Brief note and text of 1906 law in Young, 6:15-44.
12. Eldem, pp. 93-107; Mears, table, p. 325; A and P 1902, vol. 110, "Constantinople," and 1903, vol. 76, "Smyrna"; for the French mines, Thobie, pp. 143-45, 404-16.
13. RC, no. 284, 1910.
14. A. Gündüz Okçün in Prof. Yavuz Abadana Armağan, Ankara Üniversitesi Siyasal Bilgiler Fakültesi Yayınları, no. 280, (Ankara, 1969).
15. Thornton, pp. 23-24; under Abdül Hamid I and Selim III attempts were made both to encourage the consumption of local, rather than imported, goods and to revive the handicrafts--Shaw, History, 1:257; EHME, p. 52.
16. Puryear, p. 127.
17. For further details, see EHME, pp. 41-55; for the parallel process in Iran, EHI, pp. 258-78.
18. See EHME, pp. 55-57, and Clark, who gives a thorough and detailed account. The

factories, all equipped with European machinery, included a spinning mill near Eyüp, a leather tannery and boot works at Beyköz, a cloth factory at Hünkar İskelesi, a fez factory, a wool-spinning and weaving mill at İslimiye, a sawmill and copper-sheet rolling mill near Tophane, steam power at the Tophane cannon foundry and Dolmabahçe musket works, a large foundry and machine works and a cotton-cloth factory at Zeytinburnu, a cotton-spinning and weaving factory at Bakırköy together with forges, a machine shop, and a boatyard to the construction of small steamships, gunpowder works at Küçük Çekmece, a woollen-cloth factory at İzmit, a cotton and silk factory at Hereke, and a silk filature at Bursa (6:15). These were followed by other plants. In all, they employed some 5,000 hands in addition to European engineers, foremen, and skilled workers. The factories were managed by the Armenian family of Dadian until 1849, by which time most had ceased operating or were being abandoned.

19. BC 1891, pp. 484-85.

20. In 1886-7 the total number of workshops (fabrika) in the Empire was 1,103, of which 141 were in the Istanbul area; the breakdown in the vilayets was: Aydın 111, Hüdavendigar 106, Kastamonu 96, Salonica 82, Edirne 54, Islands 43, Adana 35, Konya 16, Sıvas 12, Trabzon 9, Erzurum 9, Van 5, Ankara 4, Mamuret ul Aziz 4, Diyarbekir 2, and Bitlis 1, and there were 25 in the mutasarrıflık of Izmir, 5 in Biga, and 3 in Çatalca--MS no. 80872, Abdul Hamid collection, Istanbul University Library.

21. Marouche and Sarantis, pp. 80-94; RC, nos. 278, 282, 283, 289, 290, and 298.

22. Eldem, p. 121; see pp. 111-47 for detailed information, and Stich, passim.

23. Quataert, pp. 311 and 475.

MINING

The eight selections that follow describe various mining operations carried out in the traditional way and include a comprehensive study (6:5) made by a foreign expert for the Ottoman government; the next two concern foreign enterprises that entered mining at the end of the century. Until the revision of the mining law (6:Introduction) and the influx of foreign capital, mining methods remained essentially unchanged. The state owned and generally managed the mines, either allowing or compelling the neighboring villages to extract the minerals. Techniques were inefficient and productivity was very low. The information in the selections may be supplemented by the following.

Ergani copper mine (6:3,4). The output of this ancient mine declined, from 6,400 tons in 1780 to 3,200 in 1819 and 1,050 in 1836, largely because of lack of fuel (Report on Diyarbekir, FO 78/3070).[1] A large amount of unsold ore must then have accumulated because in 1883 some 2,200 tons of previous years' production was offered on auction (TE, Box 218, 1883). In 1902, the following description was given:

"The Arghani Maden mine is the richest copper mine in Turkey. The average ore contains 30 per cent copper, 40 per cent. iron, and 30 per cent. sulphur, also a very small quantity of gold. It is worked in a very primitive manner. After smelting, the residue, containing about 90 per cent. of copper, is sold on the spot to a Government representative at the rate of 2d. per lb. (2 pias. the kilo.) it is transported to Alexandretta at the rate of $\frac{3}{5}$ d. per lb. (25 paras per kilo.), and sold there for $7\frac{9}{10}$ d. per lb. (8 pias. the kil.). The mines produce annually about 13,000,000 lbs. of crude copper. Water-power is close at hand, but fuel which is growing more and more scarce each year has to be brought from a distance of 30 miles, and its price has doubled in the last three years."[2]

From 1889 until the war, almost every year varying amounts of copper, with a content of some 75-80 percent, were offered and sold at Liverpool, at prices ranging from £30 to £60 per ton (TE, various boxes). Costs of production were estimated at: purchases by entrepreneurs £T21.90, labor 2.18, transport to İskenderun 7.50, transport to Europe 5.00, or a total of £T36.08 (sic),[3] leaving a handsome profit in all but exceptional years. Output fell from an average of over 800 tons a year between 1850 and 1880 to a low of 474 in 1896; after that output was almost always above the 1,000 mark, with a peak of 1,566 in 1903.[4]

Copper refining. "The copper refinery managed by Hungarian engineers, under M. de

Pauliny, recently commenced working, but has not succeeded so well as had been anticipated, the metal being but indifferently refined" (Brant to FO, 1843, FO 78/533).

Copper mines of Trabzon. "The rich mines of this province, especially those of Elévé in the immediate vicinity, have been farmed out by the Government to various individuals, Europeans and natives, but they have no knowledge of mining. The product of this year was sent to Marseilles where previous to smelting it was expected to realize 70 per cent of copper, in lieu of which 30 to 33 per cent would be obtained. There is no doubt that if the miners were intelligent and provided with machinery the produce would increase considerably. The alum cisterns of Karahissar, a district of this province which formerly supplied all Turkey, have been neglected of late years. The silver mines of Goomooshhane are quite abandoned" (Trade of Trebizond, 1859, FO 78/1535).

The previous year's output of copper had been 200 tons and of lead 50 tons.[5] In 1851 the figures had been 340 and 34 tons (ibid., 1851, FO 78/909) and in 1850 it had been stated that the ore "which had been accumulating for some time past" had been sold off by the government and shipped to Europe: 1,100 tons had fetched £50,000 and 500 tons more were offered (ibid., 1850, FO 78/870).

Lead Mine of Keban Maden (6:2). There were some 400–500 families "all more or less employed in the working and superintending of the mine or in supplying the wants of the miners and their families. The greater number are Greeks, natives of the mountains between Gumushhaneh and Trebizond, but likewise some Armenians and Turks. The latter are generally the directors of the various departments, the Armenians are artisans and the Greeks are the miners" (J. Brant, "Report . . . 1836, FO 78/289).

Divrigi iron mines. In 1836 these were not regularly worked; anyone who wished to could extract ore but this was "not done on any important scale" (Brant, Report, FO 78/289). Saltpeter (see 6:6). In 1836 the annual output of Boğazlıyan, some thirty miles from Kayseri, was estimated at 30,000 lbs. (13 tons), which the government bought at 1 piastre an oke (Brant, Report, FO 78/289). In 1869, the Kayseri refinery sent to Istanbul 125 tons, at £20 a ton; the saltpeter came chiefly from Boğazlıyan.[6]

Silver. In 1836 the Akdağ mine, near Yozgat, employed 300 families and sent to Istanbul 300 okes of silver (825 lbs.), worth £3,000 (Brant, Report, FO 78/289).

The Bulgar Maden "have an average annual yield of 7,050 lbs. of silver, 7,000 drams of gold and 400 tons of lead. They have been worked for 75 years. They belong to the peasants who work in them, but cannot be alienated. The buying of the produce is a Government monopoly. The peasants extract the ore as they please, carry it to the furnaces (1 to 3 1/2 hours) find fuel and smelt it themselves. The Government pays 12 3/4 piastres for one dram of gold, 38 paras for 1 dram of silver and 16 paras for one dram of lead."[7]

Silvan iron mines. This "was worked under Hefiz pasha by a French Engineer, he died and the work has been since abandoned; it was skilfully and scientifically conducted during the Engineer's life. The iron is very good. . . . There is no doubt whatever that veins and deposits of ore in this Country are everywhere to be found and it is not improbable that if the Turkish Government permitted Europeans to work mines on paying a moderate seignorage, adventurers would not be wanting to enter on such undertakings" (Brant to Aberdeen, 24 January 1842, FO 78/491).

Chrome (6:9). Deposits were discovered at Harmancık, near Bursa, by Professor Lawrence Smith in 1848, and exploitation soon began (6:8).[8] In 1854 some shipments from Gemlek to Istanbul were reported, "but to no great extent" (Report on Trade of Bursa, 1854, FO 78/1111). Modern methods of production were introduced by the British firm of Paterson, founded in 1885 (6:9), and by the end of the century Turkey was meeting over half the world's demand. Output peaked at 41,000 tons in 1901. The discovery of chrome in Rhodesia in 1910, however, affected Turkey adversely and its share fell to 10 percent. Just before the First World War Krupp began to take an interest in Turkish chrome and during the war exploited some deposits.[9]

Emery was shipped from Izmir, and in 1837 total exports were 12,000 kantars; but the ore came from the Greek island of Naxos, not from Asia Minor (CC Smyrne, vol. 44, 14 September 1837). In 1844, however, deposits were discovered, first near Gemlik and then near Izmir, by George Hiller, and, starting with Abbot in 1865, three British firms entered the industry and produced the bulk of the output. The large-scale emigration of Greeks and Armenians, who provided most of the miners, after 1908 (when non-Muslims became subject to conscription) strengthened the position of the British firms against the small Ottoman concessionaires (6:10), and raised their share of output to over 90 percent. In 1911 the leading British firms merged.[10]

Boracite (6:9,10). The deposits at Yıldız, near Bandırma, were discovered in 1815. "In 1868 a Frenchman obtained the concession of a quarry of gypsum, only eight acres in extent, and from it he extracted annually from 3,000 to 4,000 tons of boracite, which he exported to France for many years as 'plaster of Paris.' The value of the boracite was ₤60 per ton, while the cost did not amount to more than one-tenth of the value. Subsequently the discovery of large deposits of borax in California caused a temporary fall in its value to ₤28, but afterwards it rose to ₤40, at which figure it stands at present. Meanwhile it transpired that the so-called plaster of Paris from the quarry at Yıldız was boracite, and several persons commenced to 'prospect' in the neighbourhood for boracite, with invariable success."[11]

In 1887 the concession was taken over by the powerful British company, Borax Consolidated, which in 1899 formed a syndicate with the main American producers.[12]

(See also works by Anhegger, Brandt, Eldem, Mears, Rafik, Stich, and Vronchenko, listed in Bibliography.)

---

1. Part of the ore was sent to Tokat, where it was refined and used in government ordnance works--Mears, p. 322.
2. A and P 1902, vol. 110, "Diarbekir."
3. Brandt, p. 103.
4. Eldem, pp. 102-3.
5. A and P 1859, vol. 30, "Trebizond."
6. A and P 1870, vol. 64, "Anatolian Provinces."
7. A and P 1908, vol. 116, "Konia."
8. Eldem, p. 91; Brandt, p. 88.
9. Eldem, pp. 105-6; Brandt, pp. 88-90; Stich, pp. 131-32.
10. Kurmuş, pp. 225-33; Stich, pp. 134-35.
11. A and P 1880, vol. 75, "Constantinople."
12. Eldem, pp. 106-7; Stich, p. 134.

SELECTION 1.   PRODUCTION OF SALTPETER, 1790

Ainslie to Leeds, FO 78/11

. . . Salt-Petre is produced in various Parts of Turkey in Europe and Turkey in Asia, in sufficient quantities to supply the wants of this Government and of Individuals, consequently little or none imported into this Empire from other Countrys. It's price governs according to the quality, from twelve to fourteen pence Sterling the Oke, equal to forty four Ounces English, and the Duty, if imported by Subjects of Christian Powers, would be three per Cent on an estimate, always under the Market price, but for Turks and Rayas, Christian Subjects of this Empire, it is from four to five per Cent. The Princes of Valachia and Moldavia collect all the Salt-Petre produced in their respective Provinces for the exclusive use of Government, and towards the breaking out of the present War, a large quantity was imported from Morocco to supply deficiencies at all Events.

Gun-Powder is manufactured in Turkey and in sufficient quantity for the use of Government, and of Individuals, during times of Peace. Its price governs from four Pound ten to five Pound Sterling the Kintal, of one hundred twenty four Pound English, in the Market, but obtained by means of forced Contract at two Pound ten for account of Government. The Duty when imported by Subjects of Christian Powers, is three per Cent or an estimate of fifty Piastres the Kintal, or four Pound ten Sterling.

In the years 1780 to 1784, this Government imported from the Coasts of Italy and France, about twelve thousand Kintals of Gun-Powder (in addition to an extraordinary quantity Manufactured at home for the use of their Frontier Places) which was delivered by Contract at fifty Piastres per Kintal. Since the above Epoch, it is supposed that France, Spain and Venice, have furnished to the Porte about ten thousand Kintals, mostly landed in Albania and Morea at the same price. Some thousand Kintals have also been received as a Present from the late Emperor of Morocco. One to two thousand Kintals imported from Holland (which proved inferiour) and in circa sixteen thousand Kintals from Great Britain, which sold upon an average at fifty seven Piastres.

I take the liberty to add that most Parts of Romelia produce plenty of Salt-Petre, which is chiefly consumed in the Manufacturies of Gun-Powder about Salonica, and that great quantities are sent hither from Asia Minor, and some from Egypt for the use of the Capital Manufacturies established Here and at Gallipoli; and I beg leave to observe, that throughout this Empire, little use is made of Salt-Petre for preserving Viands, and still less Gun-Powder expended by Sportsmen or in Salutes upon publick Occasions.

SELECTION 2. KEBAN MADEN MINE, 1836

Memorandum by James Brant, FO 78/289

The whole population of Kebban Madem is occupied in the working or superintending the mine or in supplying the wants of the miners. There may altogether be about 300 or 400 persons employed, and the miners are paid 50 paras (equal to 3d) per diem, a sum they could not exist upon, but to compensate this low rate of wages they are supplied with bread at 4 paras (¼d) per Oke (2 3/4th lbs) a price about a quarter its real value. The neighbouring districts are obliged to furnish a certain quantity of wheat without payment and likewise wood and charcoal, and these contributions were estimated by the saraff, who was likely to know the truth, at about ₤10,000 sterling.

The mine is argentiferous lead, the Government takes all the Silver at 50 paras or 3d per dram, exactly one half its real value, the lead remains to the managers of the mine, out of which they pay the wages of the miners. At present the mine yields annually to the Government 200 Okes of Silver worth ₤2000 Sterling, but as it pays half the value it only really derives a nett revenue of ₤1000 Sterling from the mine. Thus while the country is taxed directly about ₤10,000, the government receives only ₤1000, a most improvident waste of revenue it must be admitted, besides the mode of obtaining the supplies of wheat, wood, and charcoal is a great source of oppression to the people, as is likewise the procuring miners who are not volunteers but must be furnished by the districts they inhabit. It has been suggested to the Porte to give up working the mine and to tax the districts which now supply the materials and miners, but the higher employes who are Turks and rich Armenian Saraffs, probably, misrepresent matters to the government, for those persons have been in some way or other always enriched. Their arguments are plausible as they are founded on facts. At one time the mine was very productive indeed, it then fell off and gave less than at present, it afterwards recovered and for a series of years the annual produce averaged 1000 Okes of Silver (2750 lbs). The government is induced to continue the work in the hope the produce may again increase. There is so much concealment and interested misrepresentation in all matters an European enquires into in Turkey more particularly regarding mines, that I cannot be at all certain I was correctly informed, and it may be very possible that this mine under a proper management might be profitable though it would appear from what I heard that it is now a ruinous concern. I feel a conviction that if the workings of mines in Turkey were given up to private persons and a Seignorage paid to Government out of produce, and if European Capital and Science were allowed to be applied to the work, the mines would be a fruitful source of revenue to the state and of wealth to the population, but so long as the management is in the hands of Government Agents, so long as the system of forced labour and of contributions of materials from the neighbouring districts be continued, mines must inevitably be the source of intolerable oppression and ultimate ruin to the people, they cannot be highly beneficial as revenue to the State and the advantage now derived will be progressively diminishing. The government as well as the people would be gainers by abandoning this mine and imposing a tax on the districts which now supply the materials. If after that any individuals were bold enough to work it at their own risk, a Seignorage might be demanded.

SELECTION 3. ERGANI MINE, 1836

Memorandum by James Brant, FO 78/289

The Arganah Madem is the richest and most productive mine in the Turkish Empire, it has
been worked nearly two hundred years. At the commencement it was argentiferous lead, but
the Ore became so poor in Silver that it was not thought worth working and Copper having
been discovered that metal was thenceforward alone sought after. The present beds of Copper Ore were after a time found and the older ones abandoned. The former lie about sixty
fathoms below the surface, and would appear to be inexhaustible. The actual produce of
this mine is estimated at one hundred and forty thousand batmans of not very impure Copper
equal to 1050 Tons, 20 years ago it equalled 1500 tons. The directors told me there would
be no limit to the production could fuel be obtained. Wood and charcoal are at present
brought on animals from places twelve to eighteen hours distant, formerly the whole country
was covered with forests which by want of attention and improvident use have been exhausted,
and the cost of production has been proportionately advanced. The managers of the mine are
Greeks originally from Gumushanah they have directed it from Father to Son since its first
discovery, but most of the present persons were born on the spot. At one period a fifth of
the produce was allowed them for their trouble and remuneration, the whole expense being
defrayed by them, they were permitted to dispose of their share as they pleased. Afterwards the conditions were altered, the government took all the copper and allowed to the
managers a fixed price to face the expenses and remunerate the directors. This price has
varied very little since it was first fixed, but on account of the depreciation in the
Turkish currency, it is now not at all adequate to the expense of production. The managers
have therefore for some years been losing money. They are allowed seven and a half Turkish
piastres (1s/6d sterling) for a Batman of Copper (16½ lbs). They say it costs them 2s/-
admitting that they make their position something worse than it really is, yet the copper
can scarce cost so little as they receive, they are now getting into debt with the government after having expended the accumulations of better times. They are not allowed to retire from the management, but they all asserted they would rejoice to do so. What can be
so unjust or so impolitic as to follow a system which must render the mine unproductive,
for as the managers lose the more, the more they produce they are interested in raising as
little as they possibly can. One of them confessed that by proper conduct on the part of
the government the produce could without difficulty be increased to upwards of 2000 Tons.
There is an Adit to drain off the water from the mine, and this water is so strongly im-
pregnated with copper as to be of a deep green colour. Yet it is allowed to run to waste,
one of the directors observed that they could not be expected to buy Iron at p. 36 per
Batman to convert it into copper for which they would receive 7½ Turkish piastres. The
ore is roasted and smelted on the spot, but for want of fuel it is conveyed to Tokat to be
purified, and hence acquires the name of Tokat copper. The Turkoman tribes who winter near
Angora perform the transport, they are obliged to furnish five thousand beasts to convey
the copper from Arganah Madem to Tokat, and I believe the Service is not paid but exacted
as a tax.

The town at the mine contains 743 houses, 270 Greek, 173 Armenian and 300 Turk. The
Greeks and Turks work in the mine, the Armenians are all artisans. About 700 men and boys
are employed, they work under ground in raising the Ore in winter and are employed in
cleaning, roasting and smelting it in Summer. The miners receive from two (5d.) to five
(1s/-) Turkish piastres per diem according to their skill. I believe that the neighbouring
districts are not obliged to furnish Wheat and wood gratuitously, but that the managers pay
for the requisite supplies at the market prices. The Ores appeared to me very rich, the
poorer are picked out and thrown aside, but they would I apprehend be considered good Ores
in England. Many improvements might be suggested in the mode of managing and working the
mine, but nothing would be of any avail while it is under such an intolerably oppressive
system. It is true that no system could be devised which would give such a present large
share of the produce to the government, but the natural consequence of it must eventually
be to put an end to all production. Until the Porte adopt a system of liberality in the
management of their mines, new ones which abound everywhere, will not be worked, at the
same time that the old ones will be gradually becoming less productive, but by a change to
a more equitable management although the revenue raised directly from the mines might at
first be less than at present, yet it would probably increase afterwards, and would certainly be more permanent than it can be expected to be under the existing system.

SELECTION 4. MINING IN EASTERN ANATOLIA, 1841

To Brant, 20 December, 1841, FO 78/491

Mr. Gustave de Pauliny, Director-General of Mines in Turkey, recently passed through
Samsoon on his way to Constantinople, and I obtained some information from him which perhaps may not prove uninteresting to Her Majesty's Government.

M. de Pauliny has just returned from Arganah, where he went to establish some Hungarian
Engineers in the Turkish Service, now employed in working the Mines of that District. He

visits the Capital, to represent to Government the absolute necessity of a change in the system now pursued, of supplying the mines with fuel by forced labour. The people are obliged to furnish it at p.3 = 6½d. per horse-load, and such as do not themselves possess horses hire them from others at p 10 = 1s. 9½d. per load, or 1s.3d. more than they receive. The consequence is, misery and discontent among the natives, which, added to the exhaustion of the forests in the neighbourhood, has made the work a matter of great difficulty, and unless the proposals of Mr. Pauliny be attended to, the mines will gradually become lost to the Empire. He made a tour in search of wood, and the only forest which he found, and which could be made available, is at 12 hours distance. Mr. de Pauliny proposes to make charcoal on the spot, and send it to the mines instead of wood. A load of wood of 120 okes = 3 Cwt., is equivalent in power to 10 okes = 27½ lbs. charcoal, which, at the rate now paid for wood, would cost p36 = 6s.5d. per load; but he says that the people would readily furnish charcoal at piastres 15 = 2s/8½d. per load, and thus by substituting charcoal for wood, the cost of the fuel would be reduced by 21 piastres = 3s.8½d. per load. An important saving would therefore be secured, the people would be amply remunerated for their labour, and the working of the mines would be rendered comparatively easy.

The forest alluded to, Mr. de Pauliny supposed, would furnish sufficient fuel for the next 20 to 25 years, after which the mines must be abandoned, unless the Government adopt the only possible method, the replanting of the woods near Arganah, which formerly supplied the fuel, a plan that has been repeatedly suggested by Mr. de Pauliny, and by Hafiz Pasha, when the mines were within the jurisdiction of his Pashalik.

Mr. Pauliny intends to make one more effort to shew the indispensable necessity of adopting in time the only means which can prevent so serious a loss to the revenues of the Country.

The average quantity of Copper which the Arganah mine yields is 140,000 Batmans = Tons 1,050 per annum.

Since the establishment at Constantinople of the "Conseil des Mines" the Arganah mines have been withdrawn from the dependence of the Pasha of Diarbekir, and placed under the charge of a Turk appointed by that Council. This arrangement produced great jealousy between the two officers; the one by his influence and intrigues thwarted the other in his duties, and the Director having no authority in the Country, had no means of obliging people to obey his orders. Delay in getting fuel resulted from this discord, and, as a natural consequence, less work was performed than ought to have been accomplished.

Zaccharia Mehmed Pasha, the Pasha alluded to, has been recently removed from Diarbekir, and as his successor has entered on his administration without any authority over the Mines, he and the Director may agree better, and render the Mines more profitable to their Government.

Mr. de Pauliny is anxious to get the Porte to authorise him to construct a rail-road between the forest and the mines, and as the trees are felled, he would replant them, to make the rail-road a permanent advantage. The undertaking will require a heavy outlay, but it would soon be covered by economy in the expense of transport.

Mr. de Pauliny tells me that there are copper-mines yet unexplored in many parts of Asia Minor; some of them in the immediate vicinity of Tokat. He intends recommending the Porte to allow European Companies to work them, the Porte receiving a seignorage.

He visited the Sivan mountains near Harpoot, to report on the iron which is found there in great quantity. The ore is exceedingly rich, rendering, according to a trial he made, 75 per Cent pure metal. He has discovered similar Iron, equally abundant on some mountains near Kemmak. a place on the Euphrates, equidistant between Erzinghian and Eghin.

I put a few questions to Mr. de Pauliny about the silver mine he discovered two years ago at Tokat. He seemed rather reserved on this subject, merely saying that the ore was rich, and that the work had been so far very satisfactory.

On every other topic he was obligingly communicative. . . .

SELECTION 5. MINING IN ANATOLIA, 1836

Report by G. Pauliny, HHS Türkei VI-66, January 1837[*]

On behalf of the Imperial Turkish Government, I visited all the lead, copper, and silver mines as well as the smelting works of the Turkish Empire in Asia Minor. The trips took a thousand hours over seven months. My instructions did not require me to visit iron smelting works. The iron smelting works are not under the administration of the Defterdar, but rather under the Kapudan Paşa. The "Porte" currently owns 9 silver, 3 lead, and 4 copper smelting works. Attached to the copper smelting works, there are also 3 copper schleiss[1] smelteries.

Table 1 gives the location and current yearly metal production.

[*][Footnotes added.]

Table 1

Silver Mines

Mines	Location	Production
Hacı-Köy	8 hours from Merzifon, produces yearly	1,350 Marks[2]
Itrmudely	12 hours south of Ordu on the Black Sea	100 Marks
Korum	4 hours north of Gümüşhane	100 Marks
Gümüşhane	24 hours south of Trabzon	560 Marks
Keban on the Euphrates	48 hours north-west of Diyarbekir	4,250 Marks
Ada-Maden	12 hours from Tokat and from Sivas	1,600 Marks
Gümüşgen	18 hours south of Tuzgat (Yozgat)	100 Marks
Bulgar-Maden	8 hours from Niğde	100 Marks
Bailly (Ballya) -Maden	Between Bursa and Izmir	200 Marks
	Total:	8,360 Marks

I was not commissioned to visit the last one of these mines. Anyway, it is said to be of no importance; I know of its production only by hearsay.

Table 2

Lead Mines

Mines	Location	Production
Fatsa (Foça)	On the Black Sea, produces yearly	40 Zentners[3]
Bereketle-Maden	6 hours from Nigde	5,000 Zentners
Puskir (Bozkır)	Near the Taurus, 12 hours south of Konya	100 Zentners
	Total:	5,140 Zentners

Note. Asia Minor has no real silver mines; this precious metal always occurs in a compound of a lead ore, of hexahedral galena [du plomb sulfuré]. At all of these silver smelteries, first the lead containing the silver is extracted and then the two are separated by refining. It is thus obvious that lead is also produced at the silver smelteries here. This lead is also sent to the treasury and, with the above-mentioned 5,140 Zentners, makes 15,000 Zentners.

Table 3

Copper Smelting Works

Mines	Location	Production
Küre	12 hours north of Castambul (Kastamonu), has no ores of its own but only smelts the old wastes which still contain lead and produces yearly	800 Zentners
Ezeli-Maden	10 hours south of Tirebolu	3,700 Zentners
Helnaly	12 hours west of Erzurum	2,000 Zentners
Ergani-Maden	18 hours from Diyarbekir	13,000 Zentners
	Total:	19,500 Zentners

Note. The regulus of copper (impure copper) from Küre is purified at Kazakli-Dağ, that from Ezeli-Maden at Trabzon, but that from Ergani at Tokat. At these towns, therefore, there are copper refineries.

These mines are all in a deplorable state. They are run with great ignorance and therefore at considerable expense. Nature has provided Asia Minor, especially the Taurus range, with appreciable ore deposits. The ignorance is such that, to give only one example, silver of 9 "loth"[4] and 12-pound copper ore is dumped, whereas in the Austrian Empire silver of 2 "loth" and 3-pound copper ore is profitably smelted. The mines of Asia Minor are run with no consideration for practical extraction of the ore or for drainage. The machines which we in Europe for centuries have found indispensable to help in these matters are completely lacking here. There are neither shafts nor tunnels, just a labyrinth of clay-bed burrows, in which it is impossible for a man with a fully-loaded wheelbarrow [brouette] to work and in which a machine for extracting the ore could be built only with great difficulty. The dug ore is carried topside with great effort by children in small sacks. The water in the mines in general restricts the scope of possible mining methods, since they have not even dreamed of a solution to this problem yet.

However poor the mining methods may be, the smelting methods are even worse, if that is possible. The ores, dug with such great effort, are smelted, with great losses, in tiny smelteries. Whereas there are smelting furnaces in Europe 20-30 feet high, here they are often only 2 shoes high. Bellows are used to fan the furnaces,[5] even though water, which would be necessary to operate a proper blast furnace, is often used in the immediate vicinity to run a grain mill. Properly run furnaces and the use of water power to facilitate smelting are unknown here. An expert would be astounded to see the poor smelting conditions and then to hear that nevertheless appreciable amounts of metal are produced. Of course this is achieved only at great cost and with great losses in production. A third of all the metal in the ore is lost through these unsuitable processes. It is obvious that an immediate reform is necessary. Were one to run things as they are in Austria, for instance, funds running into millions would hardly be enough. If I were commissioned to regenerate the Turkish mines, I would restrict myself, in the existing mines, to facilitating the methods of extraction and to introducing the best possible methods of mass production. In the new mines, where there are many possibilities for improvement, one would introduce the most modern methods.

In the smelteries the problem is not so easy. Here it is imperative to construct many new installations, the benefits of which would soon be obvious, in which one would greatly increase production with less energy and smaller losses. Towards that goal, it would be necessary to construct 12 silver, 9 copper, and 3 lead blast furnaces. Since building materials cost almost nothing in Asia Minor and a thousand poor people must work as unpaid laborers, these new constructions would cost much less than they would in Europe. Preliminary calculations indicate that 500 piasters [sic] would cover these costs. A sum of almost the same magnitude would of course be necessary to purchase the cast-iron parts needed for various mining and smeltery machines, which must be imported since there are no iron-casting works in all Turkey.

Accepting all these reforms, silver production could be increased by 40% and lead and copper production doubled.

The most likely spot for the first new installation would be Gümüşgen, near Tuzgat [Yozgat], where the effects of European production methods would be most obvious. These works have, up to now, not produced more than 50 Marks of silver, whereas it would not be unreasonable to expect some 1,000 in the same time-span.

One real problem for the Turkish mining industry is that Nature, so generous in its distribution of minerals, was not similarly generous in distributing fuel. At most spots there is either a complete lack of wood or overcut woods, the replacement of which no one considers. The barrenness is extreme. Both conditions demand quick relief and improvement.

The administrative conditions of the country are a major restriction to the flourishing of the mining industry in Asia. The Paşas of the provinces put the income of the mining districts to other uses than the expenditure of the state, as determined by the Grand Signior. Therefore, they deliver less and less metal every year to the Imperial Treasury, resulting in its decline. These governors of the Eyalets, holding in their hands all the reins of administration, without any controls and therefore fearless, without any sense of duty for the welfare of the state, keep the greater part of the revenues and of the metal production for themselves. This national trait of the Turks, tending towards greed and stinginess, makes the implementation of strict controls in the mining districts highly desirable. The opportunity is too enticing; without any negative influences, the state treasury would certainly always be favored. One must realize, however, that it is this reform which will cause the most opposition. The first reforms which have been made in this direction can be promising only for the future. I recently felt it my duty to inform the minister of the treasury, in a report which I sent from Trabzon, of these abuses. The result was that the Osman Paşa of Trabzon was relieved of the direction of four of the more important mines. In his place, officials named by the minister of the treasury are soon to be sent to these mines.

One other condition must be mentioned which has a very negative effect on the expansion of the Asian mining industry. I refer to the system by which ores are traded. The mines here are mostly the property of private persons, who must meet all the expenses of the mines, and who then deliver the ore to the smelteries where it is smelted on the account of the Aerar. For the mined silver the mine owners receive, after a 20% allowance for the unpaid laborers [Frohne] 5f30x OMu per Mark of silver, whereas in Austria the unpaid labor charge is only 10% and the owners receive 23f36x OMu for a Mark of silver.[6] The mining industry can hardly flourish under these oppressive circumstances, and I intend to introduce a system of selling ore which is more advantageous to the owners of the mines of Asia Minor.

It is known that every reform implies expenses and other sacrifices. Therefore, funds must be made available if one is to implement my suggestions. Now, it is not my duty to name the sources for these funds, but I was requested to suggest a way to the Porte by which the state treasury would not have to provide the slightest amount of money. One should use the income of the mining districts themselves, which are not sent to the treasury anyhow under present conditions. In this manner all current expenses could be met and the improvements could be financed without the Grand Signior anticipating any great expenses to the treasury.

Aside from these mines, the Grand Signior has none, with the exception of the iron mines.

There is very little gold in the ores of Asia Minor, and each year only the unimportant amount of 12 Marks is obtained from the silver of Gümüşhane, extracted by wet process. The copper of Ergani, which is traded mostly through Marseilles, and the meerschaum mines of Karaman cover a portion of the gold requirement, which is imported and coined at Istanbul.

If one figures the Mark of silver at 24f, the Mark of gold at 370f, a Zentner of lead at 15f, and a Zentner of copper at 50flMu (prices at Istanbul) the income of the mines of the Turkish state are as follows:

8,360 Mark silver at 24flM	200,640f
12 Mark gold at 370flM	4,400f
15,000 Zentner lead at 15flM	225,000f
19,500 Zentner copper at 50 flM	975,000f

Total: 1,405,080f 1Mu

I am to first of all send a complete report on these matters to the minister of the treasury, who will then bring it to the attention of His Majesty, the Grand Signior. If one can believe what is said, the <u>Defterdar</u> as well as the minister of the treasury are greatly interested in these matters; they constantly assure me that there are no obstacles to the realization of these plans. One must now await the decision of His Majesty and his ministers.

1. The technical term <u>Kupferschleisshüttenwerk</u> is unclear. What is implied is an abrasive or wearing-down process of smelting copper, perhaps by means of water.

2. A "Mark" is a measure of precious metal, being 1/2 pound, in silver, specifically, 8-ounces troy or 160 grams.

3. A "Zentner" is a hundredweight, here 50 kilograms.

4. A "loth" of silver is 1/2 ounce troy, or 10 grams.

5. It is implied that these bellows are operated by some primitive means. Precisely by what means is unclear--one word is illegible.

6. The currency referred to is presumably the Austrian florin, or gulden, exchanging at about 10 to the pound sterling.

SELECTION 6. NITER REFINERY IN KAYSERI, 1844

Memorandum by H. Suter, 18 May 1844, FO 78/573

The soil throughout the District of Kaissariah, and especially the plain in the immediate vicinity of the town, furnishes a great deal of Nitre. The article is collected exclusively for account of the Government, and an establishment for refining it has been formed here within the last two years. The refining is carried on in an old building neatly repaired for the purpose, which is situated at the North-West extremity of the town, in a convenient position for receiving the Rough Nitre as it is brought in. The building consists of a long arched apartment, about 30 feet wide, fitted up on each side with copper and stone tanks, and having at its extremity opposite the entrance, a large stone reservoir. Attached to this apartment are two stores for depositing the Nitre in its rough state, and that which is refined, and there is also a small room containing 3 large copper boilers encased in stone, and heated by fires from beneath, in which the refining is completed.

The process, which I witnessed, is simple. The Rough Nitre is placed in the copper and stone tanks alluded to on the sides of the arched apartment, and repeatedly washed with water, which, after the contents settle, being run off, frees them from some impurities. The produce is then placed in the reservoir mentioned, and after being therin further washed and turned about for some days, is finally transferred to the refining room. While the boiling proceeds there, the boilers are very carefully skimmed, and when no more scum rises, the operation is terminated. The contents of the boilers are then ladled out into moulds made of sheet iron about 18 inches by 12, and 3 deep, in which the Nitre soon hardens into beautiful transparent cakes, very much resembling alabaster. These cakes, to the weight of about 140 lbs, are packed with dried reeds to prevent their breaking, in strong cases, which are covered either with a dry hide, or with a felt wrapper, and afterwards another of common hair sacking, to protect the contents from wet on the journey to Constantinople. The expeditions are always made thither by camels or mules, overland. The route by Samsoon, which would be much shorter and less expensive, is not resorted to, because the Nitre, it is said, would be injured by the sea air.

A Nazir, or Superintendent of the Refinery (a Mussulman) is named by the Authorities of Kaissariah, but it is merely to secure him the benefit of a small salary. He has no particular charge, and takes no part in the management, which is in the hands of an Armenian

Director, and two others under him, sent from the Baroot haneh or Powder Manufactory, at Constantinople. I have not been able to learn what pay any of these persons receive. The others employed are 12 labourers, who get from p. 80 to 110, or from 15s/- to 20s/- per month. With the view of obviating misunderstandings which might arise from Mussulmans serving in situations subordinate to Christians, the orders from Constantinople were, to employ only Rayah labourers, but they have not been adhered to. The Director complains that this occasionally mars his efforts when work has to be expedited, but admits that the Turk labourers work as well as others, and though sometimes impatient at being ordered by Christians are not very troublesome.

The Refinery was completed about 18 months ago. The repairs and fitting up of the copper boilers, which were procured from England, and the other utensils, are estimated to have cost p250,000 or about ₺2,270.

The establishment is only at work during the Autumn, and part of the Winter and Spring. The rough Nitre is furnished by persons who make it their business to collect it, but they do not supply for Government as much as they might. It was said that in 1842, only 28,000 Okes, or about 700 cwt., could be obtained as the management was not well seconded by the Authorities, and a great deal was extracted and sold secretly. The following year it appears more attention was paid, and that about 140,000 Okes or 3,500 cwt., were procured. When I visited the establishment recently, it contained about 40,000 Okes, or 1,000 cwt. of prepared Nitre, in the cakes described, ready for transmission to Constantinople, being the result of the work of the past winter, and present spring.

The Rough Nitre is supplied at the price fixed by the Authorities of Kaissariah, of 112 paras per Oke, or about 20s/- per cwt. The loss in refining, which is sometimes as much as 30 per cent, and never less than 22, is calculated to average 25 per cent. If the quantity of Rough Nitre does not yield full 3/4ths Refined, the Government is discontented.

The Directors estimate that the refined Nitre costs the Government p.6 per Oke, or about 44s/- per cwt., delivered at Constantinople including all charges and wages, cost of fuel, and every expense attending its preparation, but without comprising any allowance for interest on the outlay for the repairs of the building and value of the utensils.

The arrangements in the Refinery are orderly. It appears creditably conducted, and the managers, especially the principal Armenian director, very zealous, and more anxious to acquit themselves well, than is usually the case with natives employed in such undertakings in Turkey. . . .

SELECTION 7. LEAD MINES OF KULAK BOĞAZ (TAURUS), 1845

Memorandum by John Clapperton, 19 November 1845, FO 78/615

These mines are situated on the summit of the second range of mountains known by the name of Bulghar Dagh, about 5 hours ride to the North of the pass of Koulek, from which, at one hour's distance, the road leads through the village of Koulek Boghaz, where are situated the smelting furnaces. These mines have now been regularly worked during the last eighteen months, for account of the Ottoman Government. The produce last year was but limited, owing to the many obstacles incident on new undertakings, and the want of proper furnaces and smelting implements. The Director of the Mines however expects that at least one hundred thousand Okes (=2,500 Cwt.) of metal will result from this year's operations.

The Director, Reshid Effendi, calculated the cost of the Lead, laid down in Constantinople (for the Government will not permit the sale of any part on the spot) at 65 paras per Oke = about 12s. 6d. per Cwt., which appears to be reasonable enough, as the quality is very good. A sample of the Ore, as well as one of the refined metal, is sent herewith; 260 Okes of the former produce 100 Okes of pure lead. Reshid Effendi thinks that some silver may be found in the lead, but is not provided with the means of separating it. Until now none of the lead has gone forward to the Capital, but a considerable quantity is already down at Mersine (the Port of Tarsous) waiting a vessel; and more is daily being sent thither.

The mine, which is horizontal, has five galleries, of which the longest may measure about seventy paces.

The ore is brought down to the smelting furnaces, a distance of 4 hours from the mine, by mules, at an expense of about p6 per 100 Okes = about 2½d. per Cwt. There are as yet only two furnaces at work, but it is probable that next year more may be erected; the quantity of wood on the mountains in the immediate vicinity providing fuel in abundance.

The miners, of whom there are generally about 50 employed, are for the most part Greeks from the environs of Trebizond. They have constructed temporary houses at the entrance to the mine. As the snow on the mountain is too deep in winter time to permit the mines being worked, they at that season repair to their homes with the fruits of their labours, and remaining until the spring, when the snow has so far melted as to permit them to recommence operations, return to Koulek Boghaz about the month of May.

The wages of the miners are as follows:

```
The chief miner, has . . . piastres 10 = 1s. 9 3/4d per day
The principal under miners    "     8 = 1s. 5 ¼d. per day
Others of less capacity       "     6 = 1s. 1d.     "   "
Labourers                     "     4 = 8½d.        "   "
```

The Director of the whole establishment, Reshid Effendi, who resides at the furnaces in Koulek Boghaz, enjoys a salary of p.3,000 (about £28 Stg.) per month.

SELECTION 8.   CHROME MINING IN BURSA, 1851

Supplement to Report on Trade for 1850-1, FO 78/868

About two years ago a Mine of chromatic substance had been discovered in the Sangiak of Kutahia. But it is only latterly on commencing its extraction that it has come to the knowledge of the public.

The quantity is represented to me by the Pasha to be unlimited, at a place called Korum Dagh, the Korum mountain, 22 hours, about 75 miles distant from hence, the surface of the mountain containing entire masses of it.

The mineral is a dark blackish solid substance, very ponderous, with shining particles and reduced to Dye by being baked in an oven with the adjunct of saltpetre. It then crumbles to powder, with small pieces or flakes intermixed, exhibiting six or seven distinct varieties of colouring matter in shades of yellow from pale to deep, and some with a reddish and greenish tinge, of which I have seen small samples sent from Constantinople, but not of the pure Green also produced from the same substance, and far the most valuable.

The worth of the others was stated to be about 70 Piastres = 4/6 to the 1b. and that of the fine green to be as high as 400 Piastres the oke = 26/5 the 1b. The relative proportions of the Dye of each tint from any given quantity of mineral I have not ascertained. But the primitive substance is said to be of one uniform appearance, as described from a specimen before me, similar to which there was one amongst the Products sent from hence for the Exhibition, but presenting nothing remarkable to the eye.

Samples of the Dye obtained were to be forwarded from the Capital, where only two ovens constructed for the purpose were being worked under the direction of a Greek Priest, alone found competently acquainted with the process, each oven yielding about 50 okes, together 100 okes, or 2½ cwt. per day.

The Dye is said to be adapted for coloring all materials of Silk and Cotton, but not imbibed by Wool, nor consequently Cloth, and alike unsuited for House painting, from rubbing off when dry. But my information on this head is not so satisfactory as to be relied on, and no experiments have been made here to afford a test.

The Pasha added that the mineral substance had been found to contain nearly all pure Dye—losing only 60 Drams in the Oke of 400 Drams, or 15 per cent in the baking process; that he had suggested to the Porte the expediency of establishing ovens here, or rather at the site of the Mine, where wood was at hand cheap, and a great Saving in the Cost of fuel thus to be effected; that the labor of removing the Mineral from its bed and expence of carriage to Ghio came to 15 Paras the oke, about 2/9 the cwt. and that the Porte had contracted for the delivery of a large quantity at that Port at 45 Paras the oke = 8/2 the cwt. to some Party unknown. This agreement I have further learnt is for 100,000 Turkish Quintals (5,500 Tons) and the Contractors would seem to be favored so as to secure to them an enormous profit, according to the quotations given of the value of the Dye. It is observed that the Porte gains 200 per Cent, amounting to £30,000 on the Contract made, and having at command an inexhaustible supply it derives a considerable Revenue from selling at such a very moderate rate, yet having free power to regulate the supply, it is not obvious why it should not limit this according to the demand so as to sustain the cost of the Mineral for Purchasers at the most advantageous level.

As yet about 1000 Camel Loads at 5 cwt. each, making 250 Tons, have been conveyed to the coast at Ghio. But the transport continues, and its extent may most depend on the number of Camels to be obtained on hire, of which there had been some difficulty in obtaining a sufficiency.

These are all the particulars I can now furnish relating to a matter which excites some interest and of which further time only can shew the real importance.

Memdm By subsequent information from the Pasha, the whole 5,500 Tons are intended for Shipment to England where the value of the Mineral is stated to be only about 24/- the Cwt.

SELECTION 9.   MINING IN BURSA REGION, 1901

CC Brousse

Chromium Mines

An English firm is working two mines in this vilayet, located on the spurs of Mount Olympus. The first, known as the Atranos (Adrianus) mine, produces about 15,000 tons of ore a year, with a content of 52° to 54°. The ore is shipped from the port of Gemlik; from Atranos to Gemlik transport is by camel or mule.

The cost of production, free on board, can be roughly broken down as follows:

Extraction (exploitation, proprement dite)	5 francs
Administration and overhead	2 "
Government dues	11.45"
Transport	47
Customs 1% and sundries	1.15"
Loading	2.30"
	68.90 francs

Sales are made on the basis of a minimum of 90 to 95 francs a ton, with a premium of 3 fr.10 for each degree above 50°. This mine is reputed to be one of the richest in Asia Minor. It could produce more than 15,000 tons per annum if better transport were available.

The second mine, which is worked by the same English firm, is known as the mine of Karli Yer and is near Aynagöl; it produces about 2,000 tons a year. Its ore is not as rich as that of the first mine, but its content is nevertheless above 50°.

Another chromium deposit, near Kutahiya, is worked on behalf of an Ottoman notable of Constantinople. It produces about 10,000 tons a year, with a content of 52° to 54°. The ore is carried to Kutahiya station (about 70 kilometers) on camelback. The f.o.b. cost is about 85 francs. This is one of the best deposits in the country, and the financial results of the operation are very good.

Lastly, there are other chromium mines in the same region, worked by private individuals and producing 300 to 500 tons a year, with a content of 48° to 50°. . . .

Antimony Mines

An antimony mine, located near Kutahiya and producing about 300 tons a year, is at present being worked by a native. The ore is sold at 160 to 230 francs f.o.b.

Another antimony deposit, discovered about 72 kilometers from Bandirma [Marmara], belongs to a concession holder who is waiting for capital willing to buy his concession.

Lastly, there is a third antimony mine, at Orancik near Kütahya, from which some 50 tons have already been extracted, as a sample, and which produces good results.

Here is the analysis of a sample of antimony ore, from a mine near Bursa, made by a French chemist who owns the mine: metal antimony 68 per cent; sulphur 26.733; insoluble substances and losses 5.267, total 100.

Silver-bearing Lead Mines

An important silver-bearing lead mine at Balya-Karaydin is being fully worked by a company whose shares were issued in France. In 1899, this mine produced 62,497 tons of crude ore. The average lead content was 14.5 percent, of zinc 10.6 percent and of silver 1,735 grams in 1899. The gold content of the lead metal [plomb d'oeuvre] was 8 grams, crude, per ton. In the mechanical preparation workshop, 60, 133 tons of crude ore were processed, producing:

6,446 tons of galena
2,359 tons of blende
2,112 tons of secondary blende

The lead workshop processed 30,141 tons of slag [lit de fusion], from which 2,596 tons of lead metal [plomb d'oeuvre] were extracted.

Here, in addition, is a breakdown of expenses during the financial year 1899, which I think I should give in detail in order to provide a picture of the rational operation of mining operations in this part of the country:

Fixed and proportional dues	₤T6,931
Operating costs	2,105
Overhead and administration	5,602
Major repairs to installations	771
Interest and discounts	1,894
Interest on debentures	4,622
Amortization of building costs	284
Amortization of buildings and equipment	2,700

The profit balance was ₤T50,830.

Another deposit of silver-bearing lead, zinc, and copper has been discovered near Yenişehir, about 60 kilometers from the port of Gemlik and at a height of 360 meters: The concession has been granted to some local people, who are looking for capital willing to buy it from them.

Boracite Mines

The powerful English company, Borax Consolidated, is at present successfully working the rich boracite deposit in the valley of Sultan Çayir, about 75 kilometers from the port of Panderma. This company has amalgamated with the various companies that had obtained concessions for these mines, more particularly with the Société lyonnaise des mines et usines de borax de Lyon, whose shares it bought up at very high prices. At present, the

English therefore hold a monopoly of borax and have raised its price from ₤13 to ₤18 a ton.

Mines of Magnesium Silicate or Meerschaum

For a long time, hydrated magnesium silicate, commonly known as meerschaum, has been extracted at Eskişehir, on the German railway. Annual output is about 10,000 crates.

Tin Mines

Production will soon begin at a tin mine discovered near Eskişehir and the concession for which has been granted to a native capitalist. . . .

COAL MINING AND CONSUMPTION

Coal was discovered at Ereğli, on the Black Sea, in 1829, and soon after that the deposits began to be worked by Montenegran and Croatian miners,[1] with a view to supplying Black Sea steamers (4:7). The first results were not encouraging. In 1844 the British consul at Trabzon reported: "No native coal was brought from the Heraclea mines. What the Steamers' agents had in store from previous years' importations has been thrown out as unfit for use" (Report on Trade 1843, FO 78/572). The following year, "Two cargoes of native coals were brought from the Heraclea mines. These consisted of 300 tons and are intended to be mixed with English as a trial and with a view to economy" (ibid. 1844, FO 78/614). But by 1849 it was stated that the mines were being worked for the Turkish steamers (ibid., FO 78/832) and two years later that miners had been brought over from England "and much advantage has already been obtained therefrom. The coal is better than before. The cargoes were this year imported for the use of the Turkish steamers, amounting together to 900 tons" (ibid. 1851, FO 78/909). A further impetus was given by Allied needs during the Crimean War, when the mines were put under a British engineer and annual output rose to over 30,000 tons.[2] During this period the mines were under the supervision first of the Evkaf and then, from 1865, of the Ministry of Marine, the income accruing to the Civil List. The Ministry worked some seams directly and let others out on small concessions, charging 10 piastres a ton and taking 30 percent of output.[3] It also had a first claim on output, and this was of great help to the Ottoman fleet, which took 50,000 tons during the war of 1877–78. But the primitive methods used and the lack of incentive had resulted in the flooding or breakdown of pits and machinery and the ravaging of the surrounding woods that supplied timber. "The working of the mines is at a complete standstill and the Turkish and Croat colliers, together with the contractors for the working of the mines, are plunged into utter misery, as the Government owes them long arrears of wages, amounting it is said to ₤200,000."[4] In 1882 the share to which the Ministry was entitled was reduced to 60 percent.

In 1878 the Duke of Sutherland proposed founding a large company for the exploitation of Ereğli coal but, after being discussed by the Council of State, the project fell through (TE, Box 193--Minister of Foreign Affairs to Turkish Ambassador, 19 September 1878). In 1896, however, a French company, Société des Mines d'Héraclée, with a capital of 10 million francs subsequently raised to 15 million with debentures of 10.9 million, received a concession to work some of the fields. The company made heavy investments in the mines and built a small railway and a breakwater,[5] and the output of the fields shot up, from 101,000 tons in 1886 to a peak of 904,000 in 1911, after which the Balkan wars reduced it to 827,000 in 1913 and 651,000 in 1914; employment also rose to some 10,000 by 1911.[6]

Further foreign capital was also being attracted to the coalfields just before the First World War, including Italian and Greek. In 1913 a Belgian company absorbed a British one, Ionian Private Company. The Belgians' capital (6 million francs) being insufficient, they made arrangements with the Stinnes group to take it over and raise their capital to 10.5 million francs.[7]

For some time Ereğli coal was only just competitive with imported British, its cost of production of 10s. a ton comparing with an average British export price of 10s.2d.[8] But by 1909 the British consul in Izmir stated that "unless some vigorous steps are taken British coal will soon be completely ousted by the native Heraclea coal. . . . Cheapness principally accounts for the preference shown to the native fuel but . . . the quality of the coal has steadily and greatly improved of late years, partly owing to natural ameliora- tion at the greater depths, but more so we should think owing to improved methods of manipu- lation and washing." The c.i.f. price for good Ereğli coal was 17s.-18s. a ton, compared to about £1-2-0 for British, partly because freights from Ereğli were about 3s. below those from Britain.[9] "The Aidin Railway still uses British coal exclusively, but in normal times Turkish coal forms the bulk of the Smyrna import."[10]

On the eve of the First World War, Turkey's consumption was over 1 million tons a year, of which some 240,000 was used by the railways, 300,000 by ships and 150,000 by factories.[11] Istanbul's consumption was about 500,000 tons[12] and imports to Izmir rose from an average of 36,000 tons in 1885-87 to 102,000 in 1903-8.[13] By far the greater part of consumption was covered by domestic production, imports averaging 290,000 tons a year in 1908-11, com- pared to 231,000 tons for exports.[14]

Coal was also discovered in other parts of Turkey, especially Bursa, but although con- cessions were granted no production took place (see selection 10).

Lignite deposits--thought to be coal until tested by a British engineer in 1855--were discovered near Gemlik. Attempts to work them in the late 1840s failed because of poor quality and high costs of transport (Sandison to Clarendon, 7 March and 21 July 1855, FO 78/1111). In 1901 the Société de Balia set up modern installations and produced 25-30,000 tons (see selection 10). During the First World War lignite was used by the Anatolian railway.[15]

1. Stich, p. 135, Brandt, p. 80.
2. Eldem, p. 98.
3. Brandt, p. 80.
4. A and P 1878, vol. 74, and 1880, vol. 75, "Constantinople."
5. A and P, 1902, vol. 110, "Constantinople"; for details, Thobie, pp. 411-15.
6. Eldem, pp. 101-2, whose figures are lower than those given in other sources, e.g., 6:10 and Brandt. In 1897 there was a decline in output because of flooding and "labour troubles among the miners" (A and P 1899, vol. 103, "Constantinople").
7. TJ, March 1914.
8. A and P 1901, vol. 85, "Constantinople."
9. A and P 1910, vol. 103, "Smyrna."
10. A and P 1914, vol. 95, "Smyrna."
11. Eldem, p. 101.
12. Details in A and P 1901, vol. 85, "Constantinople."
13. A and P 1910, vol. 103, "Smyrna."
14. Eldem, p. 101.
15. Stich, p. 136.

SELECTION 10. MINING, 1900-1914

"Charbonnages de Zongouldak et autres annexes: Annexe au Rapport Economique du trimestre décembre, 1919-février, 1920," typescript, with handwritten additions, Stanford-Hoover Library, Turkey M483a*

I. Coalfields of Zonguldak

Coal mining in the coal basin of Zonguldak is actively being pursued, in spite of the disturbances that have continued to prevail in this region, and shows the following figures:

*Document kindly supplied by Professor Enver Ziya Karal of Ankara University.

	Financial Year 1919-1920 [Metric tons]		Financial Year 1919-1920 [sic, read 1918-1919]	

<table>
<tr><td>December 1919</td><td>57,287</td><td>December 1918</td><td>4,291</td></tr>
<tr><td>January 1920</td><td>56,520</td><td>January 1919</td><td>19,785</td></tr>
<tr><td>February 1920</td><td><u>55,872</u></td><td>February 1919</td><td><u>24,209</u></td></tr>
<tr><td></td><td>169,779</td><td></td><td>48,285</td></tr>
<tr><td>Mining, 1 March-</td><td></td><td></td><td></td></tr>
<tr><td>30 November</td><td><u>339,312</u></td><td></td><td></td></tr>
<tr><td></td><td>509,091</td><td></td><td></td></tr>
</table>

For the preceding years (1 January to 31 December) the figures were:

	Tons
1919	444,184
1918	194,519
1917	140,104
1916	267,591
1915	454,579
1914	713,929
1913	750,477

The main regions in the Zonguldak basin are: valley of Zonguldak, Kozlu region, Çamlı region, Acılık region, Çatalağzı region, Kilimli valley, Amasiya [sic, read Amasra] region. The regions whose mines are served by a railway and which are being worked most actively are: Kozlu, with a railway of 3,000 meters; Zonguldak, with a railway of 7,300 meters; Kilimli, 2,400 meters; and Çatalağzı, 7,200 meters.

The Zonguldak basin, which is regarded as one of the leading ones of Eastern Europe, should easily regain its prewar level. The following figures show the number of concessions and their output until 1912.

Kozlu region--32 concessionaires, of whom 24 are Turks, 7 Greeks, and one Bulgarian.

		Output
	Tons	Turkish pounds
1909-10	107,877	50,566
1910-11	104,106	49,114
1911-12	134,276	61,997

Zonguldak region--12 concessionaires, in addition to Société d'Heraclée, of whom 6 are Turks, 5 Greeks, and one Armenian. The four main concessions are:

			Tons	₤T
1.	Société d'Heraclée	1908-9	356,787	210,419
		1909-10	466,145	354,051
		1910-11	389,112	206,229
		1911-12	418,929	324,670
2.	Greek Concess.	1908-9	48,158	28,402
		1909-10	72,214	54,849
		1910-11	64,330	34,095
		1911-12	91,377	70,817
3.	Greek Concess.	1908-9	14,733	8,689
		1909-10	21,728	16,503
		1910-11	18,066	9,575
		1911-12	23,786	18,434
4.	Armenian Concess.	1908-9	16,439	9,695
		1909-10	20,652	15,685
		1910-11	33,161	16,436
		1911-12	21,664	11,697

Çatalağzı region--the concessionaire is the Société d'Heraclée.

	Tons	₤T
1909-10	5,750	2,433
1910-11	20,580	12,153
1911-12	2,728	1,682

Amasiya region--concessionaires: Two Greeks and one Turk, whose mines produced 3-4,000 tons and 4-5,000 tons per annum, respectively.

Çatalağzı--14 concessionaires, of whom one is Greek; the output of the two most productive mines was:

	Tons	₤T	Tons	₤T
1908-9	41,405	24,840	19,652	11,731
1909-10	33,020	19,322	26,529	15,523
1910-11	46,360	21,280	13,709	6,855
1911-12	55,565	30,506	25,070	13,789

The output of the other mines ranges between 2,000 and 4,000 tons a year.

Kilimli region--11 concessionaires, 4 Turks and 7 Greeks. The largest of these mines
(Turkish) produced:

	Tons	£T
1908-9	16,500	9,900
1909-10	6,698	3,349
1910-11	17,370	7,295
1911-12	24,970	11,486

The output of the others ranges between 2,000 and 7,000 tons.

Coal is also to be found in the vilayets of Konya, Kastamonu, Mançilli and Erzurum
(mines of Kirtipan, Kukurlu, Şitke, Bartek, Koldağı, Şivşi) and especially in Bursa, where
the number of concessions granted totals several hundreds. But capital is lacking. The
main deposits are at Gemlik and Kormasti (Bursa), Söğüt (Ertuğrul), Kütahya and Karasi.
Annual output and exports of Turkey were:

| | Coal | | | | Coal dust | | | |
| | Production | | Export | | Production | | Export | |
	Tons	£T	Tons	£T	Tons	£T	Tons	£T
1902-3	374,193	187,096			13,930	2,368		
1903-4	424,974	208,237			28,814	5,187		
1904-5	465,858	228,269			52,326	12,797		
1905-6	522,725	256,135			67,354	12,797		
1906-7	544,108	272,054			66,848	12,201		
1907-8	703,098	421,859			32,662	9,799		
1908-9	659,692	395,815	317,710	190,626	37,997	11,399	12,220	3,667
1909-10	794,808	652,998	119,481	84,634	38,403	12,984	24,116	8,154
1910-11	726,590	381,190	188,539	98,541	38,428	8,997	15,956	3,851
1911-1912	857,850	605,580	241,040	175,900	45,934	11,462	16,102	4,026

II. Other Mineral Riches of Turkey

Meerschaum

Almost all the meerschaum consumed in the whole world comes from the region of Eskişehir; this mineral is embedded in friable rock, of dark gray-red color. The deposits are
inexhaustible, but in quality they are inferior to those of Greece and Hungary. Extraction
is carried out, in a primitive way, by the inhabitants of the neighboring villages. Before
the war, nine-tenths of output was sent to Vienna, in crates of 30 to 35 kilograms. Here
are figures on production:

	Tons	£T
1907-8	130	106,172
1908-9	125	40,003
1909-10	152	78,514
1910-11	115	67,435
1911-12	128	78,868
1914-15	20	10,871

Pandermite (Boractic)

This gets its name from the town of Panderma. The richest deposits are mined by an
Anglo-American company, Borax Consolidated Company, with a capital of £2,239,740; they are
located near Sultan Çayır (Tyrt village) and produced:

		Tons	£T
in	1909-10	15,281	113,991
	1910-11	11,352	83,200
	1911-12	13,400	97,338
	1914-15	10,465	82,146

Emery

The largest deposits are to be found in the vilayet of Smyrna and, during the last
few years, were worked--under firmans obtained from the government--by 48 concession holders, some of whom managed to extract 200 to 500 tons; these concessionaires were: British
26, Ottomans 12, Greeks 5, French one, Italian one, Egyptian 2, Armenian one.

The main mines are at Gümüş-dağ, Serdi-köy, Alacalı, Palamut-dere, Tirçol, Kabak Köy-
dere, Nebi-köy, Kacica, Kekre, Kaya-dere, Kosağaç, Karaca-su, Elmacık, Kara-köy, etc. All
these mines are in the vilayet of Smyrna. The concession with the highest output is that
of Gümüş-dağ (British) in the kaza of (Söke); it produced:

	Tons	£T
1908-9	8,595	30,942
1909-10	7,724	27,806
1910-11	6,845	24,642
1911-12	7,473	26,902

Emery is usually mixed with chalky soils, and the two are separated by hand. Total annual
output was:

	Tons	₺T
1908-9	24,476	88,112
1909-10	25,200	91,080
1910-11	27,665	99,565
1911-12	29,430	106,940
1914-15	19,088	65,074

of which the following was exported:

	Tons	₺T
1908-9	24,466	88,076
1909-10	25,299	91,076
1910-11	27,657	99,550
1911-12	29,430	106,940

Lignite

This mineral is abundant in Anatolia, especially near Gemlik, Soma, Söke, Scala-Nuova
(seam: 10 kilometers, 2 meters thick), Karağaç, Afyon Karahisar (in the mountains, at a
height of 1,840 meters), Lampaque, Eskişehir, Mosul.

In the Constantinople vilayet, lignite is found at Ağaçlı at Ergine-çiftlik, at
Kissirmon-dere, at Adrinople, near Salacık; at Sıvas, near Çoltok.

In the kaza of Balia, near Mancilik, the Société de Balia Karaaydın mines a rich seam
of 5 kilometers, with a thickness of 10 to 20 meters, whose output was:

	Tons	₺T
1908-9	26,665	10,666
1909-10	29,940	11,976
1910-11	34,151	13,661
1911-12	25,662	10,265

Total annual output of lignite was:

	Tons	₺T
1908-9	26,965	10,816
1909-10	35,844	14,890
1910-11	42,283	16,197
1911-12	38,375	14,146
1914-15	8,834	2,832

Petroleum

Abundant sources have been spotted at Bayburt, at Alexandretta, and especially in
Mesopotamia, but their rational exploitation has not yet begun. Crude output was:

	Tons	₺T
1910-11	73	280
1911-12	68	410
1914-15	741	6,070

This industry seems assured of a brilliant future, especially in Mesopotamia.

Naphtha

Abundant sources south of Mosul, near the Tigris; methods of extraction are completely
primitive and output was 1,000 kilograms per day in 1914; the price was 50 paras a kilogram.
North of Baghdad, exploration carried out a few years ago by the Germans led to the discovery of abundant sources of naphtha, and also at Shanekuk; the deposits have been worked
since then and, in 1914, produced 175 tons, which were distilled at Baghdad.

Asphalt

This is found in its pure state [poit de Judée] in Palestine (near the Dead Sea), on
Mount Hermon, near Damascus, and at Latakia. Mean annual output:

	Tons	₺T
1907	5,266	13,194
1908	6,039	16,642
1909	4,487	11,736
1914	1,683	4,870

Sulfur

Large deposits near the Dardanelles, and also in the kaza of Balıkesir. Borings made
near Ginon (Panderma) seem to indicate a large sulfur deposit in that region.

Sulfur is also found mixed with the iron pyrites extracted from the mines of Kassan-
dra; it is exported in its crude state to Europe, where it is used for making sulphuric
acid. Similar pyrites are also found at Adana. Two mines near Halaç produced 11,830 tons
with a value of 19,900 Turkish pounds in 1910, and 12,820 tons with a value of 7,690 [sic]
pounds in 1911.

Chromium

The soil of Anatolia is very rich in chromium ore, which is to be found particularly in the vilayets of Bursa (near Mt. Olympus) and Smyrna, and also in the region around the Gulf of Alexandretta, between that town and Adana.

Several borings seem to indicate that the deposits of the vilayet of Bursa are the largest in the world: they have been estimated at 10 million tons of ore; unfortunately, lack of transport prevents the industry from achieving its potential scope. Chromium is also to be found in the vilayet of Kastamonu. In the vilayet of Smyrna, the deposits were, until 1914, worked by 13 concession holders: 2 English, one Italian, one Turkish and 9 Greek. The largest mines are those of Çukur (English) which, in 1911-1912, produced 6,000 tons with a value of ŧT16,875.

Total output in Turkey:

	Production		Export	
	Tons	ŧT	Tons	ŧT
1908-09	9,857	29,981	9,756	28,881
1909-10	16,830	42,280	16,828	42,275
1910-11	16,604	37,396	16,604	37,395
1911-12	17,095	39,565	14,676	34,122
1914-15	2,035	4,579	--	--

Arsenic

There are a few, rather small deposits in the vilayets of Sıvas, Van, and Kastamonu. The only ones that have so far been worked are those of Smyrna (Tireç) and Kastamonu, with an annual output of:

	Tons	ŧT
1908-9	2	26
1909-10	99	1,353
1910-11	28	467
1911-12	24	410
1914-15	23	233

Mercury

Mercury is found in the vilayets of Smyrna and Konya. The only two working mines belong to Englishmen and had the following output:

	Smyrna		Konya	
	Tepecik Mine (Karaburnu)		Pulary Mine	
	(Carabournou Mercury Syndicate Co.)		(Konia Mercury Co.)	
	Tons	ŧT	Tons	ŧT
1908-9	108	18,540	34	5,872
1909-10	90	16,353	35	6,690
1910-11	55	9,925	24	4,102
1911-12	46	6,281	10	2,711

Total Production:

	Tons	ŧT
1908-9	142	24,412
1909-10	124	23,043
1910-11	79	14,027
1911-12	56	8,992
1912-13	17	1,830

Antimony

This mineral is to be found in the vilayets of Bursa, Smyrna, and Sıvas. In Bursa: Kızıl-dağ, Demir-kapu, İrmidi, Tuluk-tüy; in Smyrna: near Ödemiş (Çinili-kaya mine, seam of 2 kilometers), Keranos and Kordelio; in Sıvas near Karahisar.

Annual output:

	Tons	ŧT
1908-9	162	2,144
1909-10	62	803
1910-11	374	4,863
1911-12	697	8,882
1912-13	143	1,720

Copper

Copper is to be found in:

Erzurum: 3 mines worked until 1914
Smyrna: one mine
Trabzon: 5 concessions (one German, one Greek, one Armenian, 2 Turkish, of which one is copper mixed with zinc).

Kastamonu: Küre-Nahiye (Turkish)
Dardanelles: Kayacık (Turkish)
Diyarbekir: Ergani—maden mines [6:3], one produces pure copper, the other copper mixed
with other minerals; worked by Ministry of Commerce and Agriculture

	Mixed Copper		Pure Copper	
	Tons	₤T	Tons	₤T
1908-9	239	16,537	1,201	54,127
1909-10	90	6,166	1,266	54,909
1910-11	246	15,000	560	22,972
1911-12	--	--	1,040	40,904

Total production of Turkey:

	Pure Copper		Copper Ore		Copper Slab	
	Tons	₤T	Tons	₤T	Tons	₤T
1907-8	46	2,785	1,052	48,558	23	91
1908-9	265	18,083	1,200	54,127	--	--
1909-10	92	6,529	1,266	54,909	2	25
1910-11	246	15,002	560	22,972	177	1,619

Zinc

Zinc is found either by itself or mixed with silver-bearing lead; the deposits discovered and mined until the outbreak of war were:

Adana (pure state)--Haydar-dağı mine
       (with silver-bearing lead)--Gökçe-bilan mine
                              --Orta-gümüş mine
Aydın (with silver-bearing lead)--Asab-dağı mines
                    Şeytan-dere mine
İzmit (pure state)--Kestane Pinar mine (Carassou Company)
Trabzon (pure state)--Latoun (Greek) mine
               Peroun (German) mine
       (with copper)--Simle (Turkish) mine
Dardanelles (with silver-bearing lead)--Papazlık (Greek) mine
Constantinople (with copper)--Kıç-dere (not worked).
Total output:

	Zinc Ore		Zinc mixed with Silver-bearing Lead	
	Tons	₤T	Tons	₤T
1908-9	2,231	5,980	130	1,040
1909-10	1,791	5,440	202	1,534
1910-11	6,927	24,667	222	1,773
1911-12	5,261	22,614	560	4,480
1914-15	1,879	5,890	428	1,712

Silver-bearing Lead

Lead is seldom found in its pure state; it is always mixed with silver or zinc. The
main deposits are:

Constantinople--near Kıç-dere (not worked)
Adana--Gökçe-bilan and Orta-Gümüş (with zinc)
Ankara--Denek (French concession; work stopped)
Aydın--Riff (French concession)
       Asab-dağı (English concession) with zinc
       Şeytan-dere (Greek concession) with zinc
İzmit--Kestane Pinar (Carassou Company)
Diyarbekir--Perçinen
Karasu--Ballia (in bars), Gükükte-gümüç
       Ballia-Karaid Co.), whose output was:

	Tons	₤T
1908-9	11,924	201,603
1909-10	12,773	202,844
1910-11	12,347	200,519
1911-12	11,543	212,836

constituting almost the whole of Turkey's production of silver bars.

Dardanelles--Papazlık (with zinc)
Konya--[illegible]--with copper and zinc
Total output of Turkey:

	Silver-bearing lead ore		Silver-bearing lead and zinc		Silver-bearing lead in bars	
	Tons	ŁT	Tons	ŁT	Tons	ŁT
1908-9	480	2,532	130	1,040	11,930	201,765
1909-10	604	3,407	202	1,534	12,797	203,305
1910-11	195	3,510	222	1,773	12,356	200,760
1911-12	666	8,480	560	4,480	11,544	212,870

For exports, see general table.

Manganese

This is found mainly in the <u>vilayets</u> of Bursa and Smyrna. The main deposits are at:

Karaca-Ören (Smyrna), English concession; 1,000 tons a year average, in normal times.
Serdi-köy
Kendros
In 1912, total output was 1,393 tons, with a value of ŁT8,882. In 1914-15, output was only 3 tons.

Gold

Among auriferous deposits, the one in the <u>vilayet</u> of Konya (near Bulgar-dağ) may be mentioned; it is worked by the Ministry of Commerce and Agriculture and produced:

1908-9	3 kilograms	940 grams,	ŁT	571
1909-10	0 "	700 "	"	112
1910-11	1 "	510 "	"	224
1911-12	0 "	060 "	"	10

Another small vein, containing gold mixed with silver, is also to be found in the <u>kaza</u> of Dardanelles (near Kartal-kaya). The concession belongs to a Frenchman and the deposit is not worked. Total output:

	Grams	ŁT
1902-3	5,284	775
1903-4	13,145	1,906
1904-5	8,123	1,178
1905-6	9,489	1,376
1906-7	6,536	948
1907-8	6,079	884
1908-9	3,938	571
1909-10	772	112
1910-11	1,509	224
1911-12	65	10

Silver

In Konya, near the gold mine of Bulgar-dağ (Ministry of Commerce and Agriculture). Output:

	Kg.	ŁT
1908-9	523	1,848
1909-10	110	392
1910-11	278	925
1911-12	14	64

Clay

Numerous deposits of fuller's earth are to be found in the <u>sancak</u> of Kütahya, stretching for over 100 kilometers along both banks of the Sakarya River. It is also to be found near Eskişehir. Before the war, it was thoroughly worked. Output was:

	Tons	ŁT
1908-9	5,965	12,262
1909-10	7,696	15,822
1910-11	6,144	12,631
1911-12	8,134	16,723

Mineral Waters

The <u>vilayet</u> of Bursa is the richest region in the world in mineral waters, the healing powers of which are universally recognized. Some of these waters are so hot that they are used only after they have gone over a long distance. If they were rationally operated, these springs could constitute one of the richest sources of revenue of the region. The waters may be distinguished thus:

1. Sulfurous waters--main bathing establishments at Bursa and neighborhood; temperature: 47° at the spring and 38°-40° at the bath.
2. Ferruginous waters--in the center of the town of Eskişehir and in its neighborhood; temperature varying between 38° and 56°.

3. Thermal waters: 57° at the spring and 37° at the bath.

Important springs of these three kinds are to be found in several localities in the sancaks of Bursa, Kütahya, Karasi, Bandirma, Edremit, Balıkesir, İzmit, and also in the regions of Karamürsel, Adapazari, and Geyve; the baths of the last named (Yalova) are universally known and have been celebrated since early antiquity.

HANDICRAFTS: TEXTILES AND LEATHER

Selection 11 is a good description of the structure of handicrafts in the first half of the nineteenth century and selection 12 shows to what extent they survived at its close in the remoter parts of Anatolia. This was in marked contrast to the European provinces where, by the 1830s, a great decline had already occurred because of the competition of European machine-made goods.[1]

In his journey through eastern Anatolia in 1835 Brant noted (FO 78/289) that Armenians of Arapkir "are principally engaged in manufacturing cotton goods from British yarns. The manufacture which has been introduced of late years only, has extended itself very rapidly and there are now nearly 1,000 looms at work."[2] Malatya and its neighborhood had 700-800 looms "employed in manufacturing native yarn alone, and a very excellent cloth is made; it is rather dearer than British but its durability ensures its preference. A great deal of blue dyeing is carried on here and there is a considerable consumption of indigo. British calicoes are constantly sent hither to be dyed and afterwards dispersed over the country for sale."[3] In the bazar of Sivas "European manufactures do not form the bulk of the stock of the traders" because of high transport costs due to bad roads and insecurity. And, more generally, "there is a great deal of manufacturing industry and various articles are made both of cotton and wool, which are consumed partly in the country and partly exported to Georgia and the Crimea. In some of the cotton manufactures native yarn is still used, but British is increasing very much in consumption."

On the other hand in Diyarbekir, which formerly had 2,000 looms, "there exist but a few hundred looms half employed," but this seems to have been due to insecurity rather than competition. Similarly in Mosul local manufactures "have been nearly annihilated" by oppression and foreign competition (Rassam to Brant, 21 December 1840, FO 78/401).

A few years later Bor was doing a good deal of weaving and dying (Trade of Konia, 1844, FO 78/615) but the weavers of Erzurum "cannot compete in price with our better made fabrics" (Trade, 1847, FO 78/752). Similarly in 1849 it was noted that imports of British cotton yarn to Salonica were rising, for use in "bath cloths which are much esteemed all over Turkey. . . . cotton stockings are more worn by the people of the country than formerly, hence an increased demand for twist" (Report, 1849, FO 78/831).

By the 1850s, however, the process of decay was unmistakable and can be followed quite closely in Bursa. In 1838 its manufactures of cotton and silk were "on the decline," in contrast to those of Istanbul (Cartwright to Bidwell, 21 March 1838, FO 78/335). In 1843 production was officially put at 18,000 pieces and may have actually been 20,000-22,000 (Report, FO 78/570). In 1845 output fell to 15,000 pieces and in 1846 again to 13,000 (ibid., FO 78/652 and 701). The 1850 report states that imports of yarn were rising and that local output had increased by 3,000-4,000 above the level of 14,000 pieces (of 7 yards each) last reported (ibid., FO 78/868). Following the destruction caused by an earthquake, production in 1857 rose to 20,000 pieces but in 1858 fell to 8,200.[4] By 1860, because of British competition, "Local Manufactures now employ but a very inconsiderable number of looms . . . these having successively decreased to 40 for the make of Brussa stuffs of silk and cotton and to 100 for both wrappers and towels" (ibid., FO 195/590) and in 1862 there was a further decline to 26 and 60 (ibid., FO 195/741). In 1863 output was only 3,000 pieces.[5]

Other crafts came under far less pressure than textiles, but even the latter survived for some time in the remoter parts of the country. In 1858 the population of Antep was "almost exclusively trading and manufacturing, the operations of weaving, tanning of leather and dyeing employing a great number of hands. There are also three soap manufacturies. . . . The native handlooms supply the middle and lower class of the population with the striped woollen garments usually worn in the East, whilst the richer inhabitants have contracted a taste for the finer textures of Europe."[6] In Balıkesir, in 1858, over 44,000 woollen abas were made; of these the government took 36,000, at the low rate of 34 piastres, the balance being secretly sold on the market at 65 piastres, leaving "a yearly loss to the manufacturers of about 700,000 piastres" (Trade of Samsun, FO 195/647). In Diyarbekir in 1863 there were 1,200 cotton looms and much leather work.[7] In Erzincan in 1886 there were some 800 looms, in Harput 1,000, in Malatya 1,000, in Adyaman 700, and in Bitlis 600.[8] As late as 1911 there were 1,940 looms in Mardin.[9] And domestic industries continued, e.g., in Konya in 1907 cottons were "very generally made in the houses and villages by women," using mainly British yarn.[10] But the pressure was relentless. By 1909 in Trabzon "local industries are on a general decline. Tanners, coppersmiths, joiners etc. may still find full work, but not so weavers, as native hand-made stuffs are being gradually superseded by the machine-made goods of Europe."[11] And even in distant Maraş, "In recent years the competition of Europe has proved too strong for the antiquated methods in use here. There are about 500 looms in the city but more than half are idle, with severe distress, consequently, in the families affected."[12] Nevertheless, up to the First World War, handlooms continued to operate in large numbers: an estimated 10,000 in the western parts, notably, Manisa, Kadiköy, Denizli, Burdur, Bolvadin, and Isparta and several thousands in the northeastern parts, e.g., Merzifon, Zile, Amasya, Karahisar, Erzincan, and Arapkir.[13]

Although affected by imports, copper work and earthenware, and other traditional crafts, fared better. Particularly noteworthy was the leather industry, as is shown by a survey made in 1909. Adapazar's tanneries, which used primitive methods, had suffered from the competition of factories in Istanbul, Ayvalık, Samos, Cyprus, and elsewhere, and their number had fallen from 50 in the 1880s to 15. Bursa had 37 small tanneries, Mytilene 6, Kastamonu 8, and Safranbolu 60, and the latter exported leather, as did Afyon.[14] Konya also had active tanneries.[15]

Shoes also remained a handicraft industry. In 1910 it was stated that there was not a single factory in the country; leading centers were Adapazar, which had 350 workshops, making some 500,000 pairs a year, and Bursa, where a great improvement in quality had taken place. The bulk of consumption was met by local output and imports were very small.[16]

---

1. EHME, p. 43, and, more generally, pp. 46–59.
2. This illustrates the fact that machine-spun yarn, while wiping out hand spinning, greatly helped hand weaving. "Cotton yarn in its application for the manufactures of the country is, like a two-edged sword, cutting both ways" (MacGregor, 4:156), quoting a consular report from Syria. For the same reason, in Britain the number of hand looms did not fall sharply until the 1830s—Phyllis Deane and W. A. Cole, British Economic Growth, 1688-59 (London 1962), p. 191.
3. It may be noted that around 1,800 European merchants imported white muslins to Turkey, had them dyed, and reexported them, paying 5 percent on the value of the dyeing—10 July 1801, HHS Türkei II, vol. 125.
4. A and P 1859, vol. 30, "Brussa," 1857 and 1858.
5. Ibid. 1864, vol. 61, "Brussa"; see also EHME, p. 50. It may be noted that the number of looms in Aleppo fell from 10,000 in 1852 to 2,800 in 1858 and 3,650 in 1862 (Report, FO 195/741).
6. A and P 1859, vol. 30, "Aintab."

7. Ibid., 1865, vol. 53, "Diarbekr and Kurdistan" for details.
8. Ibid. 1887, vol. 82, "Erzeroum" for details.
9. TJ, March 1911.
10. A and P 1908, vol. 116, "Konia."
11. Ibid., 1910, vol. 103, "Trebizond."
12. TJ, March 1909.
13. Stich, p. 92
14. RC, no. 268, 1909.
15. Ibid., 270, 1909.
16. RC, no. 274, 1910 and 1896.

SELECTION 11. HANDICRAFTS IN THE 1830s

A. D. Novichev, Ocherki ekonomiki Turtsii (Moscow-Leningrad, 1937), pp. 89-100

In contrast to mining, which only just subsisted in the 1830s and later, manufacturing was marked by a much greater degree of development. The Turks produced almost all objects of household use, and especially articles of dress. Fabrics of cotton, wool, silk, and silk mixed with other fibers, kerchiefs, shawls, bedspreads, morocco of various colors, vessels of copper or pottery, rugs, tools--all these made in large quantities; moreover, production was not only for local use but for export to other regions. There were distinct centers of production for each commodity.

Between the different towns there was a division of labor in the production of some goods. Thus the Zhurnal Manufaktur i Turgovli[1] stated: "Kindiak or Bogaz is a colored cloth used by the common people for kaftans. This fabric is woven in Amasia and Malatia, dyed in Aleppo and Tokat, and glazed in Mosul; in the latter town the cloth is also woven, finished, and prepared for sale."

Merchants would take goods from one place to another for finishing. "Astar and Borla are mostly made in the town of Zile and neighboring places in the paşalik. Merchants buy the cloth there and take it to Amasia and Tokat for finishing."

Some goods were exported abroad, and in particular to Russia through the Black Sea ports. Russian sources show that through these ports Astar or Borla, a rough cloth, used by the common people for shirts, baggy trousers, etc. was imported. In Feodosia, a piece of this cloth, 10 to 17 arshin long and 7.5 to 12 vershok wide cost 3-4 rubles.[2] The center of manufacture of this cloth was Zile, from where it was sent for finishing to Amasia and Tokat. Other items were glazed Borla, used for the same purposes as Astar, by the well-to-do; Basma, used for making baggy trousers (its centers of production were Amasia and Tokat); Kumach; sashes; printed kerchiefs (from Istanbul, Izmir, Bursa, Aleppo, and Tokat); towels; various kinds of silk fabrics (from Bursa and Diyarbekir); etc.

There were various centers for the production of rough cotton cloth: Egerdir, a town all of whose inhabitants were weavers, Kastamuni, Sinop, Kasaba (near Izmir), Denizli and others. Woollen cloth was produced in Ankara and its neighborhood.

However, already then production was confined to rough cloth, used by the common people. But "anyone who wishes to dress somewhat better, i.e., part of the handicraftsmen, all the merchants and all the higher classes, makes himself clothing from broadcloth imported from Belgium and partly (not more than 1/7 of total consumption) from Saxony."[3]

Among the textiles for which Turkey had long been famous, silk and mixed silk cloth were prominent. The center of this industry was Bursa. "The abundance and beauty of Bursa silk were known throughout the world," wrote in the 1830s the French traveler Charles Texier. According to him, at that time 100,000 pieces of Bursa silk were exported each year.[4]

Already at the beginning of the nineteenth century, the production of this cloth declined sharply. and it went on diminishing further and further. And this industry was struck a hard blow by the importation of European silk fabrics, made out of that same Bursa raw silk. Machinery made it possible to produce such fabrics from Turkish raw silk at a lower cost, notwithstanding the cheapness of Turkish labor using hand looms.

Another observer of this period, Ubicini, writes: "The numerous and varied manufactures, which formerly sufficed not only for the consumption of the empire, but which also stocked the markets of all parts of the Levant, and of several countries of Europe, no longer exist or have completely declined. . . . At Scutari and Tirnova there were two thousand looms of muslin in operation in 1812, whereas there were only two hundred in 1841. Five years ago Salonica possessed from twenty-five to twenty-eight silk-looms; this number has been reduced to eighteen. . . . In Anatolia, Diyarbekir, and Broussa, which were formerly so renowned for their velvets, satins, and silk stuffs, do not now produce a tenth part of what they yielded from thirty to forty years ago."

He goes on to state, along with other contemporary observers, that instead of cloth raw fibers were now exported, from which the imported cloth was made. "In our time [Bursa] scarcely manufactures 400,000 piastres worth of silk annually, whilst its exports of raw silk and of dry cocoons amount to a value of nearly nine million piastres."[5]

A similar decline occurred in other branches of Turkish industry. Among them, rug-making was perhaps the only one not to be hurt by foreign imports; on the contrary, its exports went on increasing. But the whole of this branch became dependent on foreign capital.

The production of black, red, and yellow morocco was widespread. Morocco was made in many places, principally in Izmir, Ankara, Kayseri, Niğde, Uşak, Ak-Hissar, Mardin, Burdur, and Isparta. Sole-leather was produced chiefly in Aydin. Hides and sole-leather were also exported. And along with leather, shoemaking was also developed. Shoes were produced, in the main, in towns and small settlements.

Domestic consumption of such household articles as knives, axes, locks, nails, various tools, cauldrons, etc. came to be met, in those years, mainly by imports. Glassware was also imported from Bohemia, which led to a decline in Kutahia pottery.

Already in the 1830s, one can observe that the importation of cheap European machine-made goods was striking a hard blow at Turkish industry, which was still in the handicraft and small-scale production stage, even though some branches produced not only for the local but for the whole Turkish market, and even exported to Europe. Turkish industry was enabled to survive thanks only to Turkey's backwardness in transport, which impeded the penetration of foreign goods more deeply into the country, and to a certain extent also thanks to the suitability of the products of small-scale industry to the peasant market.

With the coming of the railways, the flood of foreign goods into the interior of Turkey expanded, and whole branches of Turkish industry perished, with the exception, however, of rug-making which came to produce for export. Turkey became an exporter of raw materials, whereas formerly it had, on the contrary, exported manufactured goods such as silk, velvet, cloth, morocco, tools, etc.

There was a certain amount of trade with Russia. At the end of the eighteenth century, the Russian author Chulkov wrote about Turkish goods exported to Russia: "These goods are produced in leather workshops for all uses, even for scabbards, which are made out of calf and sheepskins. Their art of dyeing silk, wool, and leather is carried to a high degree of perfection, in particular as regards vividness and fastness of color. From their own wool they make their carpets, rugs, and wall-carpets, and if only they had had more artistic patterns, nothing in the world would have been more beautiful to behold than these carpets. Recently, taffeta factories have been introduced among them, using their own silk; they also make other cloth with their customary patterns, as well as cloth of gold or silver, especially in the island of Chio."[6]

But in spite of great transport difficulties in the first half of the nineteenth century—i.e., before railways were built—the importation of cheap foreign goods caused great and systematic damage to Turkish industry. And it was at this time that the view that Turks were lacking in "industrial spirit" began to circulate among European and Russian capitalists, and spread more and more widely as foreign capitalists enslaved Turkey in all respects, particularly in the field of industry.

Already in the 1840s the official Russian Zhurnal Manufaktur i Torgovli stated: "Turks never show an industrial spirit, particularly as regards manufactures and hence their factories have not followed the improvements of European industry, which every day invents new ways of lightening, improving, and diversifying human labor, and the Turkish government has shown no interest in promoting industry."[7]

That the feudal Turkish government not only showed no interest in developing industry, but in every possible way hindered it, is an incontestable fact. But in those same years foreign capitalists tried to suppress the role that foreign capital was playing as a factor impeding the industrial development of Turkey.

The Economic Structure of Turkish Industry

As we have already noted, the basic forms of Turkish industry in the first half of the nineteenth century were handicrafts and small-scale production. The traveler Vronchenko gives the following interesting description of the crafts of that period:

"The situation of the handicraftsmen is diverse. Some employ workers, produce in significant quantity, and are fairly prosperous. However, one should not expect to find among them people living on the level reached by some craftsmen in Europe, who have at their disposal men working under their supervision and only watch over the excellent articles delivered by them. This stage has not yet been reached by Turkish industry: the craftsman has to work himself and, in spite of all his labor, hardly attains the condition of the most insignificant merchant, for all superfluity is taken away from him, on one pretext or another. Other craftsmen only just manage to survive with the help of the labor of their families, who either work the land or in other ways lighten the task of the head of the household in obtaining the means of subsistence. There are, lastly, craftsmen who are in what one can call dire poverty: they sometimes lack shelter, spend the night where they can, and during the day repair clothes and shoes in the street or, carrying a few horseshoes and nails in a bag, look around for someone who wants to shoe his horse or donkey."[8]

On the basis of the evidence of this close and attentive observer, we can draw some inferences regarding the nature of the Turkish industry of that period. First of all, one can observe that there were three groups among Turkish craftsmen (a) craftsmen employing hired labor, (b) craftsmen who had not cut their ties with the land, which served them as a supplementary source of livelihood, and (c) hired laborers.

Although the author speaks only of craftsmen, we have already noted that several branches of Turkish industry produced goods for sale not only in local markets but also for export to other regions and even to foreign countries. Hence, we are dealing not only with handicraft industry but also with small-scale production of goods.

Turkish handicrafts were, as a rule, urban, although several craftsmen and small-scale producers lived in villages, close to industrial centers. One should also bear in mind that, at the time, a significant part of the inhabitants of towns farmed the land. And whereas in the towns we observe a link between craftsmen and farming, with the latter serving only as a supplementary source of livelihood, not as a source of raw materials, in the villages--where many goods were made at home--farming was also a source of raw materials. As a rule, villagers were engaged in spinning and weaving.

Among small-scale producers, there were some who were hired laborers. One can judge their wages by the following data: in Ankara in the 1830s, a woollen-cloth weaver received 1½ piastres daily; in one day he produced 2½ _arshin_ of cloth, the piece of cloth being usually 25 _arshin_ long. Therefore, for the manufacture of a piece he had to spend ten days, receiving for that 15 piastres, while the price of a piece varied between 80 and 500 piastres, depending on quality and color. In Kugla, workers in rug workshops received about ³/₄ of a piastre per day. In Egerdir, a weaver was paid about 1½ piastres a day. In Bursa, a silk weaver received about a piastre per ell; in one day a worker could produce 1½ to 2½ ells, and in rare cases a good weaver could make up to 3 ells.

While on the subject of hired labor, we should mention that the employer of such labor usually worked himself. This means that he did not own the minimum amount of individual capital which, according to Marx, was the initial sum required "in order that the number of labourers simultaneously employed, and, consequently, the amount of surplus-value produced, might suffice to liberate the employer himself from manual labour, to convert him from a small master into a capitalist, and thus formally to establish capitalist production."[9]

Given such conditions, the question arises: how were industrial products marketed, especially in distant markets? The history of Turkey gives us the following answer: the merchant-buyer-up was the person who put such goods on the market, and he also supplied craftsmen with raw materials. We have already mentioned the fact that, between different towns, there was a division of labor in the production of cloth. For example, cloth woven in Zile was sent by merchants for finishing to Amasia and Tokat. In this case it also appears that Turkish merchants supplied, in certain circumstances, raw materials to craftsmen in Tokat. The above-mentioned French traveler, Charles Texier, stated: "In the silk industry to which Bursa owes its fame there are no large factories. As in Lyon, workers work at home. The silk-cloth producers (kamaşciler) provide them with silk, by weight, which they return in a finished form, together with any leftover thread."[10]

Thus we must, first of all, note the domination of buyers-up in the Turkish industry of that period. In Turkey, as in other countries, in Lenin's words: "Thus, under commodity economy, the small producer inevitably falls into dependence upon merchant capital by virtue of the purely economic superiority of large-scale, mass-scale marketing over scattered, petty marketing."

The fact that the Turkish buyer-up also supplied raw materials is very important in revealing the stage of development of capitalist relations in Turkish industry at that time. As Vladimir Ilich pointed out: "When, however, the buyer-up of finished goods begins to pay for them with the raw materials needed by the "kustar" this marks a very big step in the development of capitalist relations. Having cut off the small industrialist from the finished-goods market, the buyer-up now cuts him off from the raw-materials market, and thereby brings the "kustar" completely under his sway. It is only one step from this form to that higher form of merchant capital under which the buyer-up directly hands out materials to the "kustars" to be worked up for a definite payment. The "kustar" becomes de facto a wage-worker, working at home for the capitalist; the merchant capital of the buyer-up is here transformed into industrial capital. Capitalist domestic industry arises."[11]

Hence we may note that in the period when, protected by Capitulatory rights, foreign capital began to devastate Turkish industry by means of imported goods (i.e., in the first decades of the nineteenth century), Turkey already had, in Marx's expression, not only the general preconditions of the capitalist mode of production--i.e., the production and circulation of goods--but capitalism itself in an embryonic form; it already had capitalist cottage industry and also separate large manufactory and factory enterprises. If, however, the capitalist mode of production did not become dominant in Turkish industry and the twentieth century found it in a state of extreme backwardness, this was because of both the internal and the external obstacles which were put in its path.

Internal and External Factors Impeding the Development of Turkish Industry

Among the internal obstacles mention should be made, first of all, of the feudal system, which plundered Turkish industry and commerce and gave no assurance whatsoever regarding the security of life and property. Moreover, the feudal government machinery intervened in the very process of production, regulating the kind of goods produced, the number of craftsmen working on them, the purchase of raw materials, sale prices, etc. This kind of regulation continued up to the nineteenth century, and even the beginning of the twentieth.

The regulations in force provided that the cost of labor for a silk-lined __kaftan__ should not exceed 15 aspers and for a silk __kaftan__ 20 aspers. Tailors were fined if they deviated from these prices, or from the models prescribed for the cut. Similar regulations were made for other crafts.[13]

All craftsmen were grouped in appropriate guilds (__esnaf__) which were a mechanism used for the feudal regulation of production and more closely connected with the Sultan's authority. In earlier periods, the head of the guild, the __kahya__, was nominated by the government. In the last decades of the nineteenth century guilds lost their function of regulating production but continued to form part of the machinery of the feudal system. The __kahya__ came to be elected from among the members of the corporation. Together with him a treasurer and a secretary were elected and all three constituted the administrative committee of the guild, which looked after the interests of the guild and retained the right to punish wrongdoers by forbidding them from working, imprisoning them for a few days, or beating them with sticks.

In 1894 instructions were given regarding the duties of guild committees, which included the registration of all craftsmen, the overseeing of their work, the transfer of a member from one guild to another, the granting of certificates giving the right to work in a given craft, the fining of craftsmen working without certificates or those who were overdue, etc.[14]

In all large industrial centers, each craft had its own street or set of streets.

The guilds survived even the Kemalist revolution and were liquidated only later. They constituted a significant obstacle in the path of the development of Turkish industry. A second great obstacle was the fact that the Turkish merchants gained control over production. For their own advantage and in order to preserve their dominant position, these merchants were interested in regulating all aspects of production, prices, and so on. In this connection, one is reminded of Marx's words regarding the two paths of transition to capitalist production. . . .

1. 1839, pt. 2, p. 325.
2. The __arshin__ equalled 28 inches, the vershok 1¾ inches, the silver ruble, at that time, about 3 shillings and 2 pence, and the assignat ruble about 11 pence.
3. Vronchenko, pt. 2, p. 275.
4. Texier, p. 247.
5. Ubicini, __Letters__, pp. 339-40; for fuller text, EHME, pp. 43-45.
6. Mikhail Chulkov, __Istoricheskoe opisanie rossiskoi kommertsii pri vsekh portakh i granitsakh__ (1786) vol. 2, bk. 2, p. 7.
7. __Zhurnal__, 1844, pt. 4, p. 284.
8. Vronchenko, pt. 2, p. 282.
9. Marx, __Capital__ [(New York, 1906), p. 362].
10. Texier, p. 221.
11. [Lenin, __The Development of Capitalism in Russia__ (Moscow, 1956) pp. 387, 396.]
12. Ibid.
13. Hammer, __Osmanischen Reich__ (Vienna, 1815) p. 154.
14. Young, __Corps de Droit__, 5:188.

THE GUILDS[1]

The origin of the Turkish guilds (__sinf__, pl. __esnaf__, __gedik__) is obscure. Some scholars trace them back to the __Ahi__ and __Fütüvvet__ movements, others to the Byzantine corporations.[2] What seems clear is that by the sixteenth century the whole urban population, except the higher bureaucracy and army, was organized in guilds. More specifically all craftsmen and merchants--who largely overlapped, since craftsmen sold their products to consumers--were enrolled in guilds. These were very numerous; in the nineteenth century there were fourteen guilds of shoemakers and seventy of hatmakers; generally, all members of a guild belonged to one religious community, but many had mixed membership. Their size varied greatly, from several thousand to a dozen members. Their structure was less rigid than in Europe but the threefold distinction of apprentice (__çırak__ or __şagird__), journeyman (__kalfa__), and master (__üstad__ or __usta__) was common. The guild was led by an informal élite of elders (__ihtiyarlar__) and the head of the guild (__kethüda__), assisted by various officers; the __kethüda__ was chosen by the members and confirmed by a kadı. Each guild could produce or sell only specified goods; they were usually concentrated in one street or quarter and membership was often passed down from father to son.

The guilds formed an administrative link between the government and the urban population, helping to implement regulations and representing the members before the authorities.
They controlled weights and measures and the quality of products, fixed prices and wages,
supplied services and goods to the government, and supervised the distribution of raw materials and products. They arbitrated disputes between their members and helped them in case
of need. All this was encouraged by the government, since it facilitated control of the
potentially dangerous urban population. But practices contrary to the government's interest were curbed: "enforcement of minimum prices by agreement among the guild's members,
for instance, did not prevail; in any case, no sign of their existence is shown in our
sources."[3]

For the foreign businessmen eager to open up markets and develop resources, the guilds
were an unmitigated nuisance. In Turkey, "Everything was made a monopoly, from the Governor-
Generalship of Syria and Mesopotamia, to the privilege of selling a handful of salt"[4] and,
armed with the 1838 Treaty (chap. 3) the foreigners set out to destroy these monopolies.
Hence there were numerous clashes, e.g., in 1847 in Istanbul the Grand Vizier closed five
wine shops belonging to British subjects because they infringed on the privileges of the
guild, which had 4,000 members operating 502 shops and paying a tax of 62,400 piastres, and
refused to grant permission for new shops; there was an exchange of correspondence between
the Embassy and the authorities (FO 195/289). Similar conflicts arose over the sale of
snuff, where the gedik included 94 shops (ibid).[5]

The government's support of the guilds was largely motivated by fiscal considerations.
In 1847 the consul in Bursa reported: "In general, however, I find the Turkish Authorities
latterly object more to British subjects carrying on any sort of Trade interfering with
that of their Esnafs, comprising the different bodies of Shopkeepers, Artisans and others
of almost every association, on the ground of the competition being detrimental to the
Revenue, by diminishing gains of those who pay Taxes" (Administrative Conditions, FO 78/652).
A few years earlier, Aali Paşa had spelled out the government's position in a memorandum to
Lord Aberdeen:

"In Turkey, as in most other countries, the exercise of _retail_ trade belongs, since
time immemorial and exclusively, to the subjects of the Sublime Porte. Each branch of this
trade is divided into corporations, which one enters under specified conditions. No one
can open a shop unless he has what is called a _gedik_, or license, of which every corporation has a limited number. The corporations are, in addition, subjected to various fiscal
dues.

"For some time now, in contravention of the laws of the Country and the spirit of the
Treaties, foreign subjects have opened small and large shops [boutiques et magasins] where
they sell, in retail, all kinds of goods.

"The result has been that the corporations, consisting of subjects of HM the Sultan,
being unable to withstand a competition which is not subjected to any taxation or regulation, find themselves forced to dissolve. This causes suffering to a large number of subjects and a reduction of the Treasury's revenues."

Aali then pointed out the political dangers, namely, that those affected might seek
foreign nationality for protection, and requested Aberdeen to instruct his ambassador to
put a stop to such proceedings, claiming that such action would not be in conflict with
the treaties (TE, Box 5, 1844-45).

The economic base of the guilds was undermined by the influx of foreign goods and the
change in tastes, while the bureaucracy became increasingly able to take over their

administrative functions. On 22 May 1860 an _irade_ decreed that no new _gediks_ would be granted and that personal (_havai_) _gediks_ that became vacant could not be sold. In the next few years many guilds were abolished, but others survived until the First World War, e.g., the dockers (see 4:11).[6]

(See also works by Nuri, Refik, Sidki and White, listed in Bibliography.)

1. The first part of this note is based on three well-documented articles by Gabriel Baer: in IJMES, January 1970; Israel Academy of Sciences and Humanities, _Proceedings_, IV, 10; and JESHO, April 1970.
2. EI(2), s.v. "Akhi" and "Futuwwa," and Angheliki Hadjimihali, "Aspects de l'organisation des Grecs dans l'Empire ottoman," _L'Hellénisme Contemporain_, May 1953.
3. Baer, in JESHO.
4. Neale, p. 11.
5. Two other examples may be given. In Izmir the _gedik_ of fruit-box makers, consisting of thirty-five Turkish and Greek carpenters, supplied poor quality boxes to fruit exporters. Some British subjects who were engaged in fruit export sought entry but were denied and warned that any attempt to make boxes outside the guild would be severely punished. In 1861 a British factory for printing muslins was forced to close down by the opposition of local craftsmen because its methods were more advanced--Kurmuş, pp. 169, 176.
6. In 1870 there were in Galata and Pera 140 guilds, with 13,500 members (FO 83/334, Constantinople). As late as 1891 a law on corporations was passed--texts in Young, 5:288-91.

SELECTION 11. HANDICRAFTS IN DIYARBEKIR, 1889

Report by Bertrand, "Turquie d'Asie" BC, 1889, pp. 431-432

. . . The main industries producing for export in Diyarbekir are: coppersmith work, iron foundries, tanning, silk and cotton weaving, and silkworm breeding. The other handicraftsmen, such as tinsmiths, smiths, saddlemakers, masons, timber workers, carpenters, shoemakers, etc. make only articles needed for local consumption. Except for saddlemaking, all these crafts are undertaken exclusively by Christians, who constitute half the population of Diyarbekir.

Coppersmith works--Formerly, this branch was very prosperous in Diyarbekir; 230 shops delivered, for local trade and export, 65,000 to 70,000 kilograms of wrought copper a year. Six hundred masters and workers, all of them Christian, earned their living in this industry, which yielded a net profit of 25 to 30 percent. Two-thirds of the copper was exported and the remaining third sold on the spot; the main destinations for exports were: Mosul, Baghdad, Harput, Malatya, and Erzurum. Of these 230 shops, only 30 survive, with about a hundred workers; only 16,000 kilograms are delivered for sale and profit has fallen to 5 to 6 percent. Exports of this commodity have almost entirely disappeared. The price of wrought copper is 9 piastres a kilogram, or about 2 francs.

Iron Foundries--There are 80 foundries, with some 300 masters and men. Some 40,000 kilograms of soft Russian iron and 60,000 of Swedish iron are processed. This commodity is consumed at Diyarbekir and in other localities in the province; it yields a profit of 12 percent. The average price of wrought iron is 15 piastres the _batman_, or 2 piastres (about 40 centimes) a kilogram.

Tanneries--Twenty years ago, there were 80 tanneries in Diyarbekir, employing not more than four to five workers each. They produced about 15,000 Turkish pounds' worth of leather a year, yielding a net profit of 25 to 30 percent. This leather was exported to Mosul, Baghdad, Harput, Malatya, Sivas, Erzurum, and Trabzon. Today, only seven tanneries remain in Diyarbekir, producing hardly 2,000 pounds' worth of leather which is consumed locally. A tiny amount is sent to Harput and Malatya. This industry now shows a profit of only 9 to 10 percent.

Weaving, silks--In Diyarbekir, there are 100 looms producing the gold-brocaded silk veils known as Çarçaf, with which women cover themselves when they go out. Each loom is tended by one worker, who can make one veil a week and earns 25 piastres a week. On average, these veils are sold at 2 Turkish pounds each. This industry yields hardly 5 percent profits. Of the total output, 20 percent is consumed in the _vilayet_, the rest being exported to Aleppo, Harput, Sivas, Bitlis, Van, Erzurum, and Trabzon. Another hundred looms produce a kind of watered silk known as _gezi_. Each loom is tended by one man, who can produce five pieces a week, each 6 meters long. These workers earn 5 piastres a piece, or 25 piastres a week. On average, this kind of silk is worth half a Turkish pound. One half of the output is consumed locally and the other half exported to Harput and Sivas. This kind of merchandise yields a profit of hardly 5 percent.

Silk and cotton fabrics--Thirty looms produce this kind of cloth. Each loom is tended by one man, who can produce eight pieces a week. The cost of labor is 2½ piastres a piece and profit only one piastre; on average, each piece sells for 20 piastres. Of the total output, 25 percent is sold on the spot and the rest exported to Harput and Sivas.

Cotton fabrics--This industry has 200 looms each of which is tended by one man, who produces eight pieces a week. The cost of labor is 2 piastres a piece. Each piece is sold, on average, at 10 piastres, yielding at most a profit of half a piastre. Of the total output, 12½ percent is sold in Diyarbekir and the rest exported to Harput, Van, and Bitlis.

Silkworm breeding--Formerly, production of and trade in silk were very flourishing; today it has fallen almost to zero. The state collects an annual tax of 600 Turkish pounds in tithes, which means that the output of silk can be put at 6,000 Turkish pounds.

From this brief account, it is clear that local industry is insignificant and is within course of disappearing. The methods of production being primitive, it is bound to give way to European products, even though it is superior as regards quality and durability [usage]. These regions will therefore not be able to raise themselves through their industry; their salvation would lie in agriculture and the extraction of minerals, if only economic and rapid means of transport were available.

CARPETMAKING

Carpets and rugs have been woven in Anatolia for many hundreds of years and already in the sixteenth century a few were exported from Uşak to Europe. In the first half of the nineteenth century the village weavers of the Izmir region--which was by far the largest producing area--sold their goods to a small number of Turkish merchants, some of whom bought and exported on a large scale.[1] A French report (CC Smyrne, vol. 50, Trade of 1862) states that carpets were brought to Izmir on camels and were generally "almost square, with border and medallion, but can be made to order in size and shape." Shortage of cotton had led to a rise in prices during the previous three years: first-quality carpets (dyed with cochineal) had risen from 47 piastres a pike (65 centimeters) to 65 and others (dyed with madder) from 36 to 50; the dyes had deteriorated considerably in the last thirty years. Most of the carpets were shipped from Izmir to other Turkish ports, but Britain took some and France came third.

Carpets and rugs were also made in several other regions, e.g., Sıvas (see following selection), Isparta, Bursa, Kastamonu, and Erzurum.[2] In Ankara province four types were made: first, Kırşehir carpets, of which there were many kinds, e.g., prayer carpets, side carpets for sofas, and cushion carpets; Kurdish carpets; Kurdish kilims; and cicims, with designs embroidered on plain woollen or woollen and cotton textures.[3]

In the 1860s British merchants from Izmir entered the business and by the 1880s six large houses had established control.[4] Already in 1871 the French consul reported: "Now that this industry has passed to the hands of Europeans, it knows how to adapt itself to all the luxury needs of the West and I can see a great future ahead of it." Output was expanding; much improvement had been made and exports amounted to 750,000 francs. Prices had risen considerably, to 31-34 francs a meter for first quality and 25-77 for others (CC Smyrne, vol. 51, Trade of 1871).[5] By 1881 the annual value of the carpets produced at Uşak was 1,400,000 francs, at Gördes 360,000, and at Kula 120,000.[6] The British merchants bought the woollen yarn from peasants, who spun it in their homes, or from Armenian spinners in Kasaba and Demirci, and distributed it to the dyers. There were fifteen small Greek dyeing factories in Izmir, all working for the British merchants, and one owned by a British subject in Demirci.[7] The colored yarn was then distributed to the villages through agents who fixed the size and pattern; in 1890 it was found that European patterns were more profitable, and they were imposed on the weavers; it was also found that a cotton backing gave greater durability, and small factories were set up for this purpose. Weavers were paid 6d. a day, during which the skilled ones could knot 5-6,000 knots. Agents were paid according to the area of the carpet and the number of knots.[8] Under this system, output expanded greatly: that of western Anatolia was put at 155,000 square meters in 1884 and 368,000 in 1894;[9] in 1900 it was estimated at 413,000 meters[10] and in 1910-13 at 456,000, with another 627,000 being produced in Kayseri, Kırşehir, and other parts of Anatolia, or 1,087,000 in all.[11] Exports had risen to 7.5 million francs in 1889 and in 1910 those of Izmir were Ł735,000 (18,375,000 francs), of which Ł530,000 went to the United Kingdom, much of it for re-export to the United States. By then it was reckoned that there were twenty-four centers of production in Anatolia and that the average wage for a weaver was 1s. a day, a skilful weaver earning over 2s.6d.[12]

In the meantime there had been important changes in the structure of the industry. At the beginning of this century an Austrian established a carpet factory near Uşak, employing eighty workers and producing 12,000 meters, and was followed by fifteen Turkish, Greek, Armenian, and Jewish firms. The British merchants responded by founding, in 1908, the Oriental Carpet Manufacturers, Ltd., with a capital of Ł400,000, subsequently raised to Ł1,000,000. They set up two wool-spinning and two dyeing factories in Izmir, with German and Austrian technicians, and opened a design office with British and French designers. They also replaced their brokers in the villages by agents in fourteen towns, drawing a salary with bonuses. This struck a severe blow at their competitors and by 1913 the syndicate was producing at least three-quarters of Turkey's carpets and handled a larger proportion of exports.[13] But this modern organization was superimposed on an essentially unchanged technological structure. The yarn was machine-spun and dyed but otherwise the old handicraft methods and traditional patterns remained.[14]

Carpetmaking was shattered by the First World War and the War of Independence. In the 1920s the Oriental Carpet Manufacturers, joined by other Turkish and foreign firms, restored production, but output and exports did not quite regain the prewar level and in the 1930s fell sharply; exports in 1913 had been 1,584,000 kilograms worth ŁT663,000; in 1928 they peaked at 1,552,000 worth ŁT6,364,000, and by 1935 stood at 207,000 worth ŁT431,000.[15]

(See also works by Cuinet, Stich, and Pretextat-Lecomte, listed in Bibliography.)

1. Kurmuş, p. 180.
2. A and P 1883, vol. 74, "Erzeroum."
3. Ibid. 1895, vol. 100, "Angora," which gives details and prices.
4. Kurmuş, p. 180.
5. A similar judgment was made by the Austrians--K. K. Handels Ministerium, Statiskik des Oesterreichischen Postwesens, Jahre 1872 (Vienna, 1874), p. 144.
6. BC 1881, Smyrne, p. 1062.
7. They started to use aniline dyes but in 1888 were forced by the governor of Izmir to return to native vegetable dyes.
8. Kurmuş, pp. 181-82.
9. Ibid., citing Georgiades and Cuinet.
10. A and P 1901, vol. 85, "Smyrna." Uşak's 1,200 looms produced about 190,000 square meters of carpets, worth Ł120,000; prices ranged from 7s.-8s.6d. a square meter for başana to 17-20s. for tekilme. Kula's 900 looms produced about 60,000 square meters worth Ł40,000 and varied in price from 9s. to Ł1-6s. At Gördes 1,100 looms produced 100,000 square meters worth Ł60,000 with prices from 10s. to 16s. Demirci had 450 looms producing 35,000 square meters worth Ł26,000, prices being 12-16s. Kütahya had 250 looms producing 18,000 square meters worth Ł16,000, prices being 18-21s. Isparta's 300 looms produced 10,000 meters, worth Ł12,000, "resembling Persian carpets and worth 18s. to 22s. the square meter."
11. Eldem, pp. 142-43; the total number of looms was 19,445 and of workers 60,000; the value of carpets produced was 108.5 million piastres.
12. TJ, June 1914.
13. Kurmuş, pp. 183-88.
14. TJ, June 1914.
15. Conker and Witmeur, pp. 99-100; in 1892-93 exports had been 862,000 kilograms and in 1893 739,000 kilograms (CC Smyrne, vol. 56, Trade of 1893).

SELECTION 13.   CARPETMAKING, 1889

United States Special Consular Reports, 1890

                                        Asia Minor

Report by Consul Emmet of Smyrna

Factories.--There are no factories, mills, or distinct establishments properly so-
called in the districts of Asia Minor where carpets are woven.

Looms.--Nearly every house at Ushak, Ghiordes, and Coula has a loom; some have even
two or three. These belong to the owners of the houses themselves. The weavers are all
women and girls. The mistress of the house superintends the work of her daughters, or hired
journeywomen and apprentices. The looms are of wood, roughly fashioned. A vertical or
slightly inclined frame supports two horizontal rollers about five feet apart; the warp divided into two sets of strands by leashes fastened to a horizontal pole is wound around the
upper roller and the ends secured to the lower one, from which the work is begun, and on
which the carpet is rolled in the process of manufacture.

The weavers kneel or sit cross-legged to their work side by side, each taking about
two feet of carpet width. The tufts that form the pile and pattern are tied to the warp
in rows, and the woof is passed over with the hand after every row without the help of a
shuttle; the pile and woof being then driven together or beaten down with a heavy wooden
comb, and the tufts clipped smooth with shears of native make.

Above the weavers are suspended the bobbins of colored yarn from which the pile tufts
are cut. There are now from 800 to 900 looms at Ushak, all worked by private owners in
the courtyards or main room of their houses.

At Ghiordes the number of looms is estimated to be about 300; at Coula, to be about
200.

Grades of Carpets Produced

The proportion at Ushak is 70 per cent. fully of carpets to 30 per cent. of rugs and
mats. The carpets vary in size from 12 feet by 9 feet to 50 feet by 25 feet, and in a few
exceptional instances more. For a very large carpet, exceeding the last-mentioned dimen-
sion, a special loom would have to be constructed.

The mats and rugs vary in size from 2 feet 9 inches by 1 foot 6 inches, to 11 feet by
8 feet.

At Ghiordes it is estimated that the manufacture of carpets and rugs is about the same
as at Ushak, while at Coula the proportion of mats and rugs is much larger, and it would
not be an overestimate to say that 80 per cent. of rugs and mats to 20 per cent. of carpets
is the correct output of that section. The bulk of the looms at Coula are not wider than
5 to 7 feet.

Labor and Wages

At Ushak, the number employed in the manufacture of carpets and rugs, including the
dyers, is from 5,000 to 6,000. At Ghiordes and Coula the number varies from 1,500 to 2,000
hands each. Forty-four rows of pile are considered an average day's work, for which an
ordinary weaver gets about 8 to 10 cents a day. Hours of labor from seven to eight per
day, according to the season of the year. The weavers live in the most frugal manner; a
meal consisting of bread, cheese, and a raw onion, is considered a good one. The number
of hands at work varies according to the season, as many work in the fields in summer and
manufacture carpets in winter.

Condition of the Industry

At Ushak the dyeing, save in rare instances, is no longer performed by the weavers
themselves, as in former times, but is carried on by a separate class (of men). Spinning
is carried on by elderly women at odd moments, when not occupied with their household
duties. The yarn is loosely spun, so as to allow the fibers to mix slightly together in
the pattern and present a blended appearance. The washing of the wool is performed by men
in the streams and combed and spun by women.

The bulk of the wool is spun in the outlying villages of Ushak, etc.

At Ghiordes the division of labor is similar to that of Ushak, while at Coula the
spinning and dyeing is usually done by the weavers themselves.

Marketing the Products

The carpet merchants in Smyrna have native agents at Ushak, Ghiordes, and Coula, who
act as intermediaries between said merchants and the owners of the looms. These native
agents are paid a commission varying from 3 to 4 per cent., and their duties consist in
superintending the carpets while in process of manufacture and accepting and delivering
the same when completed.

Advances are usually made to the owners of the looms, but total payment is not effected
until the carpet is taken from the loom and measured. The price is fixed per Turkish arsheen or pike of 26 $\frac{5}{8}$ inches square.

Where the Products Find Consumption

The bulk of the carpets and rugs made in the interior are for export and a very small portion of the whole remain in the country.

Ushak turns out about 300,000 arsheens or pikes of carpets and rugs per annum. Ghiordes and Demardjik about 65,000 pikes; Coula 20,000 pikes.

England imports about two-thirds of the whole product.

America ranks next in importance, then France and Austria, and lastly, Germany and Italy.

The Smyrna carpet dealers are either the special agents of the European consuming firms, and as such charge a commission varying from 3 to 5 per cent., or else they submit firm offers free on board at Smyrna, which would include such remuneration as they are able to secure for themselves.

The prices are regulated per arsheen or pike of 26 $\frac{5}{8}$ inches square--about 5 square feet.

Sivas

Report by Consul Jewett

Owing to the want of any system of collecting statistics by the government or otherwise, it is impossible to give any very definite replies to the questions asked as to the number of establishments, looms, and persons employed in the manufacture of carpets.

The carpets and rugs manufactured in this are, of course, only those known as Turkish. They are entirely of wool. The industry is carried on by families in their own houses. There are no factories. It is impossible to say how many persons are employed. In almost every village there are a number of families who make carpets. Hand-looms only are used. Most of the work is done by women and young girls. There is no system of rate of wages or hours of labor. The manner of living is the same as with all others of the laboring classes. Their food consists largely of rice and crushed wheat with meat (mutton) at rarest intervals. Three to four piasters (14 to 19 cents) is considered a good day's wages. Cost of living probably does not exceed 12 cents per day.

The dyeing, spinning, weaving, etc., are all conducted unitedly, the women of each family engaged in the business doing all the work from the spinning of the yarn by hand, dyeing it with vegetable dyes, to the weaving and completion of the carpet. The carpets seldom exceed 8 by 4 feet in size.

The product is sold usually at home, being placed on the market by the makers going from house to house, or by sending the carpets to Constantinople to be sold in the bazaars.

There has recently been started in this city by two or three families the manufacture of a new style of carpet which is quite remarkable for the beauty and novelty of the patterns and the excellence of the finish. The prices asked for these are higher than has been usual, and average about 32 cents per square foot.

It may be observed here that the common people invest their savings in carpets as the people of other countries do in savings-banks, handing them down from father to son, and selling one when hard pressed for money, so that one is often surprised to find in the poorest of houses a collection of very valuable rugs.

TEXTILE FACTORIES

The first textile factories in Turkey were the fez and cloth factories established by the state in the 1830s. At the 1856 Paris Fair the following state enterprises exhibited textile products: Izmit, cloth and military uniforms; Istanbul, cloth, fezzes, blankets; Zeytinburnu, cloth, stockings; Hereke, velvet, silk, satin; and a printing factory for flannels--to which should be added the cloth factory of Islimiye.[1]

The beginnings of private factories other than silk filatures (6:15) are more difficult to trace, since many were hardly distinguishable from handicraft workshops. Thus in 1850 a French subject in Bursa began the manufacture, on a small scale, of silk handkerchiefs, gauzes, and fancy articles, which he delivered to Istanbul cheaper than European imports (Trade, FO 78/868). In 1862 an Italian subject set up a chiffonerie near Izmir (CC Smyrne, vol. 50). There were probably other similar enterprises, but in 1872 a British report summed up the situation as follows: "There is no progressive increase of production in these factories in Turkey. The Imperial household has some few factories for spinning and weaving cotton, silk and woollen factories, and there are a few factories on a limited scale belonging to private individuals. The amount produced is inconsiderable."[2]

By 1898, however, the situation had changed. "Of recent years" seven cotton-spinning factories had been set up: at Yedikule in Istanbul, two in Salonica and two in Niaousta (Macedonia), in Izmir and Tarsus. Cheap labor and duty-free cotton imports had enabled them to compete successfully in coarser yarns, but Belgian competition was severe and labor turnover, e.g., of girls at Yedikule, was preventing the development of skills needed to produce the finer counts.[3] There was further growth in the Salonica region: "Of the two cotton mills at Salonica one has not been worked for some years past, but the other produced during 1906 about 1,500,000 lbs. of cotton twist. At Niaousta there are three mills producing a total of about 1,700,000 lbs. of cotton yarn. The mill at Caraferia, which produced 500,000 lbs. of yarn, is increasing the number of its spindles by half as many again. The Vodena mill produced some 600,000 lbs. of yarn. The raw cotton used in these mills is chiefly home-grown, though a little American is also used."[4]

But the main advance was at Izmir and Adana, both cotton-growing areas (5:15). In Izmir "two factories have recently started for dying yarns. Both are British enterprises," but the machinery and technicians were German.[5] In 1909 two spinning mills were recorded, the chief one, a Belgian firm with a capital of £100,000, was finding it difficult to compete with imports because of "the inferiority of native workmanship and the insufficiency of the 11 per cent import duty."[6] And in 1911 "a weaving mill has been opened with a production capacity of 500,000 meters, which will be increased this year to 1,200,000 meters. It will employ 300 to 400 hands."[7]

In the Adana region the first modern spinning mill was founded in 1887 at Tarsus. By 1908 it had 6,000 spindles, and a newly opened spinning and weaving factory had 22,000 spindles and 400 looms "to be increased to 1,400." In Adana there was a mill with 3,000 spindles, which had "ordered 2,000 more," and the spinning and weaving factory had 10,000 spindles and 180 looms.[8] The last-named was finding it hard to keep up with demand, that came from as far as Aleppo, and had a backlog of orders.[9] Much the same figures were reported for 1913, but it was stated that the industry was handicapped by the scarcity and increasing cost of labor.[10]

Other cotton factories are mentioned at Manisa, Mersin, and Mytilene, two weaving plants at Bursa, and one for dyeing yarn at Giresun.[11] In 1914 there were, within the present borders, 82,000 spindles, of which 68,500 were active, and 787 looms; the industry employed 3,000 persons and produced 3,700 tons of yarn and 6,600,000 meters of cloth, worth 80 million piastres (5:16).[12]

The woollen industry was somewhat smaller. In addition to three state factories (Defterdar, İzmit, and Hereke), three private ones were founded between 1892 and 1905 at Uşak (6:13) and one at Karamürsel. In 1909-11 three more were founded at Izmir and one each in Istanbul, Bandırma, and Bursa. The industry had 30,000 spindles, employed 2,400 persons, and had a gross output of 67 million piastres.[13]

Raw cotton has to be ginned and pressed for export. Already in the eighteenth century hydraulic presses, which reduced the volume by three-quarters, were used, but ginning was done manually.[14] "The native cotton gins are very clumsy--they will gin from 12 to 14 lbs. of cotton in the 12 hours at the rate of about 25 piastres or 4/5 per kintal of 120 lbs.," a figure raised to 60 piastres during the cotton boom of the 1860s. This saw the introduction, on a large scale, of mechanical gins "of the most approved principle from both England and America," which charged 1d per lb. (Trade Report Smyrna, 1863, FO 195/771--see 5:15 and 6:14). British merchants were largely responsible for this process, and in 1863 established eight ginning factories in Izmir, Manisa, Aydın, and Menemen; they charged less than the older gins and produced cleaner cotton.[15] Modern gins were also set up in 1863 in

Adana, Mersin, and Tarsus. In 1864 a Greek, Trypani, imported a gin and founded a firm
that, by 1909, had grown into a large complex including ginning, spinning, weaving, flour
mills, and agricultural machinery.[16]

By 1908 there were twenty-two large establishments with 550 gins in the Adana region,[17]
and by 1914 the number had risen to 800; there was also a modern German steam press. In
the Menderes plain there were twelve establishments with 270 gins (5:16).

1. Sarç, in EHME, pp. 55-56.
2. A and P 1872, vol. 68, "Turkey."
3. Ibid. 1899, vol. 103, "Constantinople"; the Tarsus factory was founded in 1887
and the Yedikule in 1890--Eldem, p. 131.
4. A and P 1907, vol. 93, "Salonica."
5. Ibid. 1908, vol. 116, "Smyrna."
6. Ibid. 1910, vol. 103, "Smyrna."
7. Ibid. 1912-13, vol. 100, "Constantinople." Eldem lists two firms, one for spinning and one for spinning and weaving, founded in 1914 and 1913 respectively. It is not
clear whether these are the ones described above.
8. Ibid. 1909, vol. 98, "Adana."
9. Almanach d'Orient, 1907 (Constantinople 1907), p. 129.
10. TJ, June 1913.
11. A and P 1910, vol. 103, "Smyrna"; Eldem, p. 131; RC, no. 290, 1911.
12. Eldem, p. 131.
13. Ibid., pp. 131-32.
14. Stich, p. 86.
15. Kurmuş, pp. 189-94. Many difficulties were encountered (6:14). In 1863 Gout's
factory at Izmir, with machinery worth ₤15,000 and warehouses ₤12,000, was deliberately
burned down because "the chimney resembled the minaret of a mosque"; it was rebuilt with a
less offensive shape--ibid. Gout showed much enterprise, even introducing electric tur-
bines, which failed to operate because of the weakness of the stream. Before being forced
into bankruptcy by the cotton failure of 1865, he owned ten factories in Western Anatolia--
ibid.
16. Details in Fraser, p. 19.
17. A and P 1909, vol. 98, "Adana."

SELECTION 14. COMPLAINTS OF COTTON GINNERS, 1868

TE, Box 105

> The Asia Minor Cotton Company Limited
> 9 Orange Court
> Liverpool, 15 September 1868

To the Cotton Supply Association
        Manchester.

Having a considerable stake in Turkey & having at the outset of the American War invested
large sums for the purpose of developing the cotton growing resources of that country, we
have read with special interest the portion of the report just issued by the Cotton Supply
Association referring to that country, & we can cordially reciprocate the regret expressed
of the "Ottoman Empire not having made such progress as a cotton growing country as there
seemed reason to anticipate" [5:14]. We must however join issue with the Association as to
the causes which have produced this disheartening result, & instead of attributing the
failure to the apathy and want of perseverence on the part of the people, we would throw
the whole blame upon the Imperial Government, the sincerity of whose earnestness our experience gives us every right to question; the Central authority is sufficiently powerful
in the provinces where cotton is grown to make its ordinances respected, it is therefore
undignified to throw the blame upon the local officials.

When the American War broke out no country was so well prepared to take advantage of
the circumstances. In all the centres of trade there was a body of merchants both foreign
and native with influential European connections ready and willing to invest capital to
assist cultivators and to introduce machinery into the country.

On the faith of the great promises of special protection from the Government many
merchants invested largely in various undertakings, & of such the Asia Minor Cotton Company
was the most extensive & what has been our experience for the past 5 years? Instead of being allowed free scope legitimately to employ our energies and capital we find petty impediments placed in our way on every side.

Once the Government offered encouragement to the introduction of cotton cleaning machinery by the remission of the import duty, we could not anticipate difficulties would be
placed in our way of its erection but in many instances after we had got our machinery up
the country, we were stopped putting it up for want of authority from Constantinople, much

time was lost in consequence. When these obstacles had been overcome and our machinery in motion other impediments constantly crop up, one season a tax collector insists upon levying double weighing tax upon cotton brought to our factories, is supported by the local authorities, seizes our books and thrusts our manager into prison; twelve months' time and about £400 is expended in removing the attempted impositions.

In two of the districts (Kirkukatch & Serres) where we have ginning establishments, lignite coal found in the neighbourhood, has been used for fuel and no other fuel is procurable it was lying unknown & never used until our factories were established at Kirkukatch; when we first opened the factory a charge per quintal was fixed by the local authorities and paid by us without demur for three years, but last year it was notified this tax would be increased fivefold equivalent to 20/- per ton, nearly the price of Newcastle coal delivered in Smyrna. At Serres until the spring of this year we have been using the coal with the knowledge and consent of the government, paying the owner of the soil a very handsome price; all at once when our factory is full of unginned cotton the government stops the supply, & our operations for the remainder of the season are at an end: not only do we loose [sic] our trade in consequence but we also have to pay an indemnity to the owners of the unginned cotton for not carrying out our engagements. Our representative begged & petitioned to be allowed the supply for the remainder of the season engaging to pay any tax the government should fix, to no avail. We have for the past four months been applying for authority to supply ourselves with these coals under the usual regulations, but little progress has yet been made; should this not be granted in time (with a large prospective cotton crop) our factories will remain standing for the next season.

If the Ottoman Government are really sincere in their desire to encourage & give facilities to those engaged in enterprises connected with cotton, one edict from Constantinople embodying strongly such sentiments couched in unmistakable language could put an end to these petty annoyances on the part of local officials which tend so much to dishearten & discourage further effort. . . .

Nathal Buckley
Chairman

SILK REELING

The increase in the production of silk (5:22) was made possible by the installation of modern filatures. The first improved ones were set up in Bursa in 1838. A filature "on the French model" was established in 1845 by the Russian vice-consul "and much extended"; in addition to the tithe on the product, he paid "a small tax on each reel employed, the same as levied on those of the country" (Report on Tariff, 31 August 1846, FO 78/652). In 1846 there were two factories, with 120 reels; in 1847 one of them, belonging to Falkeisen, the representative of "a mercantile house of Zurich" burnt down but was rebuilt and a third added (6 July 1847, FO 78/701). By 1851 there were 15 filatures with 910 reels;[1] local capital had been attracted, including that of Cezayirli, the contractor for customs and silk duties, but "in consequence of the defalcations in his affairs, his property having been sequestrated, three filatures of his at work and one in course of construction at Biligik have fallen to the disposal of the Government, and it is expected will be sold" (Report on Trade 1851, FO 78/952).

A few years later, the capital of British subjects "now directly engaged in filatures and other branches of trade in the District is now become more considerable and may not be under £50,000 to 60,000" and was yielding "large profits" (ibid., 1854, FO 78/1111). Several Frenchmen worked as "directors of filatures or otherwise concerned with them" (ibid.), and the skilled personnel came from France and Italy.

By 1858 there were 36 filatures, with 1,465 reels, in Bursa and 28 with 1,323 reels in neighboring villages (Trade Report, FO 195/674) and by 1862 there were 90 filatures with 4,345 reels; factory-reeled silk, which in 1846 had amounted to 7,600 lbs. or 8 percent of Bursa's output, had risen to 362,000 lbs., or 85 percent, and by 1870 constituted 95 percent.[2] In 1900 there were 87 plants with 5,400 reels.[3]

In Izmir a steam-powered filature was founded by a Frenchman in 1847 (Black to Canning 31 August 1848, FO 195/288). By 1862 there were two French and one Turkish plants, but the consul complained that wages were 1 franc to 1.50 higher than in France (CC Smyrne, vol. 50, Report on Trade, 1862). Two years later, of the five filatures in Izmir one had been destroyed and one other converted into a cotton gin (ibid., 1864) and in 1871 the silk industry was described as "almost entirely ruined" (ibid., vol. 51, Report on Trade, 1871).

Filatures were also built in other silk-growing areas, e.g., in Amasya in the 1850s, at the request of a German firm operating there[4] and in Lebanon.[5] In the Edirne region in 1872 there were 4 filatures with 7,000 reels.[6]

Labor conditions in Bursa are well described in an 1872 report.[7] Only 4 percent of workers were male (foremen, engine drivers, packers); 84 percent were female adults and 12 girls. Every hundred reels employed 100 winders or reelers and 54 auxiliary hands. Total employment in the 75 plants with 3,520 reels operating in 1872 was 5,415, of whom 95 percent were Armenians or Greeks; "the authorities endeavour to discourage and prevent the employment of Turkish women in the factories."[8] Working hours were 7 1/2 in winter and 13 1/2 in summer, an average of 52 1/2 a week. Daily wages for reelers had risen from 3–4 piastres in 1846–50 to 10 in 1857 and fallen back to 6–8; in 1872 they were 8 piastres in summer, 6 in spring and autumn, and 4 in winter, an average of 6 piastres.

During and immediately after the First World War the silk-reeling industry was severely disrupted. In 1918 there were, nominally, 103 filatures in the provinces of Bursa and Istanbul, "but the greater part belonging to deported Christians were out of working order, having been either totally pillaged or partly demolished. Only 39 were able to work more or less regularly against 67 in the preceding year."[9] After that, silk reeling declined along with the production of silk (5:22).

---

1. A and P 1873, vol. 68, "Turkey," for table covering 1846–72. The Report for 1851–52 (FO 78/905) stated: "Filatures--there are now eight in this city, one at Mundania and one in course of construction at Biligik. . . . one filature here belongs to the Sultan erected by express command--two others by Mons. Gesairli the noted Government Saraf at the capital who also owns those at Mundania and Biligik and works a fifth rented from the proprietor, our late governor Sarim Pacha. Steam power is used in four." The capacity of the completed plants was 91,000 lbs. of silk per annum.
    For much fuller details, Erder, pp. 95–131.
2. A and P 1873, vol. 68, "Turkey"; as early as 1858 the British consul had stated that steam-driven filatures were "more and more taking the place of the hand-reels of the country which are in course of being are long totally superseded" (ibid., 1859, vol. 30, "Brussa").
3. Stich, p. 96.
4. Ibid.
5. EHME, pp. 243 and 280.
6. A and P 1873, vol. 68, "Turkey."
7. Ibid.
8. Turkish girls were, for many years "shy of the employment, which requires them in great measure to be unveiled, but they found the wages [8 to 14 piastres] sufficiently attractive to overbalance their old customs and religious scruples" (Trade Report, 1858, FO 195/64).
9. TJ, February 1921.

SELECTION 15. SILK REELING IN BURSA REGION, 1870s

Dispatch of 3 June 1871 and report of 26 February 1877, CC Brousse

. . . The so-called Bilecik silk-reeling filatures number eighteen, divided as follows: 11 in Bilecik itself; one at Aşaga Köy, a village half an hour away from the town; one at Peldas, an hour away; 4 at Kuplu, a very large Turco-Greek village, also one hour away; and lastly one at Yenişehir, which is regarded as depending on Bilecik, no doubt because it is run by people from Bilecik.

All these plants, which are operated by steam-engines, include 750 reels [tours] and, if properly run, should be able to produce 360 bales of silk, or 36,000 kilograms, with a total value of 3,600,000 francs. But several of them are not working, notably that of Aşaga Köy (60 reels), which belongs to the Turkish government and which is in poor condition, and another one with 66 mills belonging to Swiss merchants from Constantinople.

Moreover, since crops have not been very good for the last few years and cocoons have been expensive while silk, on the other hand, has not sold well, work has not been very active and interruptions have been frequent. Hence, output does not reach the figure given above.

It may seem strange that two Frenchmen and a Swiss should own silk reeling plants in Bilecik, but they did not do so intentionally. It was because of business dealings with the local people, and after having lost their money, that they had, willy-nilly, to settle by taking up property whose value falls short of the amount owed to them.

The boilers of these filatures are heated with a small quantity of wood and a much larger proportion of mineral coal, extracted from a deposit four hours away from the town, which I was unfortunately unable to visit. This coal burns well and heats more economically than wood but it is not, properly speaking, coal but rather a kind of lignite in a very advanced stage of formation and thus very close to real coal; the latter is found in a perfect form only in much older soils.

This lignite deposit seems to be large. So far, only the surface has been worked, with very primitive methods, but the deeper one goes the purer and better seems to be the lignite. . . .

[The Report on Hüdavendigar province, 1877, stated that in good years cocoon production reached 1,500,000 okes (1 oke = 1.314 kilograms) and averaged 1,000,000; it was the main source of employment.]

. . . A silk-reeling filature with 60 reels producing about 30 bales of silk a year, employs 88 persons, as follows: 60 women for silk reeling, 15 women for carding and sorting [batteuses] 5 apprentices [élèves], two forewomen, one woman for twisting [plieuse] two men for stoking the boilers, one director, and two women for taking out the floss.

The French silk-reeling filatures, of which there are twelve, employ Greek women and sometimes Muslim women. The Armenian plants employ Armenian women and the Greek plants Greek women.

Including the plants at Bilecik and Panderma, there must be about 3,000 reels in the province. . . .

SELECTION 16. INDUSTRY IN ISTANBUL, 1863

Preussisches Handelsarchiv, no. 39, 23 September 1864

. . . Local industry in Istanbul was unable to withstand the powerful flow of imports in 1862 and 1863. Local industry, in the European sense of the term, does not in general yet exist. Nothing produced here is exported, except for a few fancy goods which, because of their oriental character, are bought by travelers as curiosities and souvenirs. Craftsmen work solely for local consumption; most of them are natives: Turks, Greeks, Armenians, and Jews. European master-craftsmen and work supervisors are to be found, in general, only in those trades catering to the needs of Europeans living here or temporarily resident in this place, and they too employ native workers.

Only one branch of industry has, strictly speaking, passed beyond the handicraft stage: milling. There are six steam mills, one of which produces 20 million kilograms of flour a year and the others between 500,000 and 1,500,000 kilograms. They belong, respectively, to two Frenchmen, a Greek, and three Turks. The machines are English and French, the foremen Europeans of various nationalities and the workmen, here too, natives.

In addition, there are some copper and iron foundries, workshops making furniture and billiard tables, breweries and distilleries, several printing presses, an oil factory, a sawmill, and a marble quarry in the Istanbul area. The activity of these enterprises, of which some are at present idle, is very insignificant. They produce only for local consumption and even in this field are outstripped by the importation of foreign goods, which recently has been delivering everything better and more cheaply.

Lastly, mention should be made of a few state enterprises, which produce solely for the needs of the Army and Navy: the imperial iron and cannon foundries, powder mills, dockyards, and workshops producing wearing apparel. These establishments are managed by Turkish officials and employ Europeans in technical jobs and natives for mechanical work. They are very important and are provided with all the equipment required for efficient operation. However, they produce at a cost far above that of private industry in Europe and, in a consideration of the state of private industry, do not have to be taken into account.

PAPERMAKING

Papermaking was brought to Iraq by the Chinese prisoners captured in Central Asia in 751, and in the course of the next two centuries spread to Byzantium.[1] There is evidence that in the fifteenth and early sixteenth centuries paper was made in Istanbul, and there are references to a Kağit Hane near the Sweet Waters. But it is clear that at least the bulk, and perhaps the whole, of consumption was met by imports from Europe (mainly Italy), China, and India; however some European paper was further processed in Istanbul, giving employment to hundreds of families. By the eighteenth century, Britain had become the main supplier of paper.

In 1746, a paper mill was set up at Yalova, but it did not last long. The ones established by Selim III in 1805 also did not flourish, nor did the factory opened at Beyköz in 1818 and the one at Bursa, because of foreign competition.[2]

Some time before 1852 a paper mill was established at Izmir by "a Mr. Duzoglu, a native of Turkey"—and probably a member of the prominent Armenian family. He received a monopoly for rags, which were used as raw material, but this was promptly, and one may presume successfully, challenged by the British consuls as an infringement of the 1838 Treaty.[3]

The following selection describes the largest and most up-to-date paper factory, built under a concession granted in 1889. In addition, the 1913 census shows that there were numerous small factories making cigarette paper or engaged in papermaking and printing.

----

1. Haussig, p. 169.
2. F. Babinger, "Appunti sulle cartiere . . . ," Oriente Moderno 11 (1931); A. S. Ünver, "XV yüzyilda Türkiyede kullanin kağitlar . . . ," Belleten 26 (October 1962).
3. Protest by Cumberbatch, March 1852, FO 195/382; Fisher to Brant, 7 May 1852, FO 195/389.

SELECTION 17. HAMIDIEH PAPER MILLS, 1908

FO 371/560

The following notes on the Concession, Mills and existing conditions at Hamidieh have been taken from reports made by Professor Schulte and Mr. Masson.
1. Concession granted by H. I. M. Abdul Hamid II, Sultan of Turkey.
2. Sole right to manufacture all kinds of paper in the whole Empire of Turkey for a period of 50 (fifty) years, dated March 2nd 1889.
3. Reports on the Mills have been made by Professor Herman Schulte, and Mr. Masson leading authorities on paper making and paper making machinery in Europe.
4. There are no taxes of any kind, nor rent for the 11 (eleven) acres of ground granted along with the Concession.
5. Abundance of raw material at very low cost can be procured.
6. Ad valorem duty of $12\frac{1}{2}$% on all kinds of manufactured paper coming into the Turkish Empire—packing same for export 5%—freight insurance &c. 5% making in all about $22\frac{1}{2}$% in favour of paper manufactured in Turkey.
7. Labour—plentiful and efficient and never gives any trouble.

    Rates for men   8/- to 15/- per week
    do. do. girls   4/- to 5/- do. do.

8. Everything required for the manufacture of paper comes into the country free of of all duty, with the exception of English coal on which there is an import duty of 1/- (one shilling) per ton.
9. Local coal of fair quality can be delivered into the boilerhouse at 15/- (fifteen shillings) per ton. English coal would cost about 18/- (eighteen shillings) per ton.
10. The mills are well situated, being close to the Bosphorous and some 10 (ten) miles from Constantinople. The Mills have their own jetty and tramline. Steamers drawing 23 (twenty three) feet can get to within a 100 (one hundred) feet of the jetty. The jetty could be easily repaired and extended so that large steamers could come alongside.
11. Sea freight from Mills to Constantinople about 2/6 (two and six pence) per ton.
12. Sufficient water for the whole Mill (four machines) could be brought in at a cost of about £4,000 (four thousand pounds).
13. The plant is new and in fair order. The Machinery consists
of 1 Cigarette paper making machine
    2 ordinary   "   "   "
The Cigarette paper making machine is complete.
The No. 1 paper making machine is complete and has been worked satisfactorily for six months.
The No. 2 machine is all complete with the exception of the beaters. The beaters for the No. 3 machine are there and could be utilised for the No. 2 machine.
14. The Mill is already altered for boiling straw, and wood pulp can be procured from the Danube.
15. The Engineers would overhaul the whole plant, equip three machines with all the

recent improvements, and bring the whole plant to a point of production, rearrange and bring in an ample supply of water for the sum of ₤10,000 (ten thousand). As soon as the present plant of three machines was working and the output meeting with ready sale, the Company could arrange for an additional machine to be built.

16. The Mills could be producing paper within three months of re-opening.

17. The output of paper is estimated as follows:

Cigarette Paper Making Machine   5 tons per week
No. 1 Ordinary"   "   "   "   35/40 "   "   "
No. 2   "   "   "   "   35/40 "   "   "

or a total output of 75 tons per week.

18. Disposal of output. It is possible that one firm alone would take all the cigarette paper. There is a very large market for paper for newspapers, as the weekly newspapers in Constantinople have been turned into dailies.

19. Seeing that the political conditions in Turkey have changed for the better, and that the English are held in very high esteem, the present time would be a most favourable one for re-starting the Mills.

20. The cost of the Mill buildings was ₤25,000 (twenty-five thousand) and of the Machinery ₤80,000 (eighty thousand).

21. The price asked for the Concession Rights, buildings, machinery, the Hamidieh First Mortgage Debentures, all the ordinary shares in the Turkish Company and all their assets is [left blank in original].

SELECTION 18.   STRUCTURE OF INDUSTRY IN 1915

Osmanlı Sanayii 1913, 1915 yılları sanayi istatistiki, A. Gündüz Ökçün, [Ankara, 1970], pp. v-xi, and information extracted from tables; footnotes omitted

Foreword

The Ministry of Trade and Agriculture took an industrial census for the years 1913 and 1915 in the province of Istanbul and in the cities of Izmir, Manisa, Bursa, İzmit, Karamürsel, Bandırma, and Uşak. In 1917, the results of this census were published under the title Industrial Statistics for 1329, 1331. In spite of the fact that this census covered a very small part of the large Ottoman territory, it is sufficiently sound to give a general idea of Ottoman industry. In fact, in those days, Istanbul and Izmir were the places where Ottoman industry was concentrated. As mentioned in the Industrial Statistics, apart from four cotton-yarn factories, and the flour mills and tanning shops which were generally to be found in cities, in other parts of Anatolia there were no important industrial enterprises. . . .

In addition to small commodity production, we observe that trade capital was putting small producers under its hegemony. This production system, which in the West is called the putting-out or verlag system, and which is defined as the last stage of the transformation of commercial capital into industrial capital by gradually putting production under its control, was quite widespread in certain fields in the Ottoman lands. In this system, as applied in the Ottoman Empire, the merchant gave the contractor raw materials and the manufacturing wages, which were calculated per piece; the contractor, in turn, distributed this material to the "workers," who generally worked in their houses, and after processing was completed collected the manufactured goods and delivered them to the merchant. In the Ottoman Empire, especially in big cities, in branches like carpets, shoemaking, dress, tie, shirt, hat, and umbrella manufacturing, piecework was quite widespread. The diffusion of this system is shown by the fact that before the First World War, 6,045 men and women "workers" of this type, went on strike in Istanbul. Besides, according to the same source, there were 3,000 shoemakers working for big firms in Istanbul. Moreover, there were many carpenters who worked for furniture workshops, and manufactured furniture was to be found. This system, which may be defined as the domination of commercial capital over production, had also spread into inner Anatolia, for example in carpetmaking. In fact, Oriental Carpet Ltd., which was a foreign company, had carpets manufactured by the local carpetmakers through the agencies it had opened in the towns of Demirci, Akhisar, Sivrihisar, Niğde, Kula, Kütahya, Simav, Manisa, Gördes, Uşak, Denizli, Milas, Akşehir, Zile, Isparta.

In addition to piecework, there was a factory system in the Ottoman Empire in its last years. For example, in the manufacturing of dresses, underwear, ties, shirts, and hats in Istanbul, firms like Karakaş, Selliyan, Anjel, Margarit, and Sigala had workshops of their own. In the Orozdi Back firm about sixty workers were employed. In Sigala and Partners (the store of 100,000 shirts) and Hayim Yeşula's shirt and tie factory, shirts, ties, and pajamas were manufactured. Statistics indicate that "in recent times (1917)" shoe workshops which employed 50 workers had come into being in Istanbul. In the same way Oriental Carpet Ltd. installed carpet workshops gathering together girls and women in the towns of Izmir, Sıvas, Burdur, Isparta, Haçin, Urfa, Maraş, Kırkağaç. In these places the company dealt directly with the workers. It is evident that, apart from agriculture, Ottoman production had passed to the manufacturing stage in certain branches.

As a last point, in the sections outside agriculture a very small portion of Ottoman output was produced in factories which used motor power and employed workers.

In the census which formed the basis for the <u>Statistics for 1329, 1331</u>, establishments that had an installed motor and employed at least 10 persons or establishments which, though they had no motor, employed at least 20 workers, and mills which ground at least 100 quintals [10,000 kilograms] of cereals in 24 hours, and soap factories which employed more than 10 workers continuously were taken into account. In the <u>Statistics</u>, detailed information is given about the equipment and buildings of such establishments, their production, the relation of production to exports and consumption, and the situation of the people working in them. Prior to repeating these details, which will be explained below, the general characteristics of Ottoman industry can be summarized as follows:

1. <u>In the Ottoman Empire basic industry was not established</u>.

In the Ottoman Empire, which had become an exporter of raw materials and food and an importer of manufactured goods, and was exposed to the overwhelming competition of developed European economies, the task of establishing basic industry could not be achieved. As was indicated in the Industrial Statistics, high furnaces and metallurgical factories did not exist in the Ottoman lands. The metal-goods industry, which produced for nearby markets, used scrap iron as raw material. On the other hand, we see that in the Ottoman Empire the machine-making industry had not been established either. In fact, the great majority of the machines in use in the Ottoman lands were imported from foreign countries. In this branch, only four factories in Izmir (Isigonis D. Imalathanesi, Rankin and De Mas, Rays Brothers, and Kalohretas K. and Partners) produced steam engines, internal combustion engines, flour, soap, fats, towels, and macaroni-making equipment. Nevertheless, we believe that this manufacturing was more of the nature of assembly. In the early twentieth century, we see German-made machines and equipment in use, whereas English-made machines had been prevalent in the nineteenth century.

2. <u>Ottoman industry could only develop to produce consumption goods for nearby markets</u>.

Ottoman industry developed in the face of the overwhelming competition of European industries and could grow only where this competition was not very intensive, generally producing consumer goods for nearby markets. In the cities and towns where the industrial census was held, 68.6 percent (in 1913) and 70.3 percent (in 1915) of the consumer-goods manufacturing industry consisted of the food industry. The food industry had seven sections, namely, milling, macaroni manufacturing, sugar and sesame oil manufacturing, canned goods, ice and tobacco manufacturing. The textile industry came second with a ratio of 14.9 percent in 1913 and 11.9 percent in 1915. . . .

Another aspect of Ottoman industry was that the raw materials and intermediate goods which were essential for industry were imported. For example, raw sugar for the sugar industry and sesame oil manufacture, paper for cigarette-paper manufacturing and printing, gasoline and motor oils for internal combustion motors were imported. According to the <u>Statistics</u>, 80 percent of the cotton produced in the Ottoman lands was exported raw, and yarn spun outside the country was imported to be used in the textile industry and especially in small industries (and in cottage industries) which were still widespread in those days. Ottoman industry had the capacity for processing into yarn only 18.6 percent of the existing cotton production.

3. <u>Ottoman industry could not achieve a healthy integration between mineral and agricul-</u>
    <u>tural production</u>.

The data in the Ottoman statistics show that all or a very great majority of the minerals produced in the Ottoman lands were exported. According to calculations we have madeon the basis of these statistics, the minerals which were almost wholly exported between the years 1902 and 1911 were: chromium, emery, lead with silver, manganese, iron pyrites, antimony, zinc, raw boracite, lead with zinc and silver, pyrites with lead, mercury, arsenic, crude copper, meerschaum, lead ingots with silver, and tar. A very small portion of lead with silver and tar and quite an important part of lignite and coal were consumed in the country. Lignite and coal were used in industry and by the navy as fuel.

We see that agricultural products which were used in industry were also generally exported without being processed. We have already mentioned that the cotton we exported as raw material was imported as thread. A similar situation existed in wool and leather manufacturing. In the same way, tobacco leaves were exported without being processed. . . .

[. . . In 1913 there were 269 establishments, of which 144 were in the Istanbul area and 60 in Izmir; in 1915 the figures were 282 and 155 and 62 respectively. Establishments included in the censuses were those with a capital of at least ŁT1,000, using motors of at least 5 horsepower and with an annual wage bill of at least 750 worker-days per annum.

A breakdown by ownership and horsepower of machinery is available for 264 establishments in 1915:

	Government	Joint Stock Co.	Individual	Total	HP
Food processing	1	8	66	75	7,893
Ceramics	1	5	11	17	3,837
Tanneries	1	1	11	13	961
Wood industries	--	--	24	24	513
Textiles	18	10	45	73	6,247
Paper & printing	1	--	50	51	705
Chemical	--	4	7	11	821
	22	28	214	264	20,997

The following table groups information regarding employment, average daily wages, and gross value of production in 1913 and 1915; it brings out the disorganization caused by the outbreak of war.

	Employees		Daily wage (kuruş)		Value of Production (Thousands of kuruş)	
	1913	1915	1913	1915	1913	1915
Food	4,281	3,916	11.8	14.2	531,896	459,645
Ceramics	980	336	13.8	..	2,684	13,382
Tanneries	930	1,270	13.6	13.9	62,577	31,983
Wood	705	377	16.9	16.0	5,920	11,063
Textiles	7,765	6,763	6.1	6.8	90,788	100,267
Paper & printing	1,897	1,267	11.7	13.6	46,185	37,541
Chemical	417	131	13.7	..	16,997	16,936
	16,975	14,060			757,047	670,817

EXEMPTION OF INDUSTRIAL MACHINERY

The first document in the following selection consists of a draft law and explanatory note for exempting from customs duties machinery imported by small industrial firms. A careful search through volumes 1 to 4 of Düstür, the official gazette, failed to find a law corresponding to the draft; it would seem that the main provisions of the latter were incorporated in Law 151, reproduced below.

Already, before the promulgation of the law, requests for exemption had been numerous. A cursory search through the Ministry's correspondence[1] during the last seven months of 1325 (1907) revealed the following requests within the present borders plus Salonica: olive oil presses in Ayvalık, Izmir, Mytilene (three), and Dokuz; mills in Edirne (two), Adana, Hasköy, İskeçe (Salonica region) and Ortakçı (Edirne region); textiles in Trabzon, hosiery and flannels in Izmir, and weaving in Salonica; beer in Büyükdere; building materials in Safranbolu; tanning at Ayvalık; steamboats on the Golden Horn; ore smelting in Konya, boracite in Karasu, and sulphur in Hüdavendigar.

1. BVA=BEO, Ticaret ve Nafia, vol. 551, various.

SELECTION 19.   DRAFT LAW AND LAW ON EXEMPTION OF MACHINERY
BVA=BEO 279009 and Düstür, 2d ser., vol. 3

Ministry of Commerce and
Public Works
Directorate-General for Industries
No. 58

To: the exalted presence of the Grand Vizier

Summary: Concerning a request for permission confirming validity henceforth of the first and second articles of the Law to Encourage industry, debated and accepted by by Chamber of Deputies.

Petition of your most humble servant.

To make known to Your Excellency:

The protection and development of the internal industrial base depends on the revocation and abrogation of the Capitulations.

Henceforth, for the expansion and development of industries as a whole in the Ottoman lands, with respect to the need for this opportunity, and in view of the fact that it appears necessary to give some help and encouragement in order to carry this out, to assure this purpose, a bill, approved by the Exalted Opinion, organized and presented as the Law to Encourage Industry, has been given over to the Chamber of Deputies.

The General Assembly, which set to work on debate, debated up to Article XII of the said law because of the approaching end of the session. Its completion is essential and it will be added to the work of the next session.

For the purpose of assuring the progress of industries in the country and encouraging their proprietors, the exemption from customs duties on machinery, tools, equipment, etc., which are imported specifically for the primary establishment of factories in the Ottoman lands has been valid by imperial rescript for 35 years.

The period of the above-mentioned law's confirmation of validity, which had come to completion on 3 Muharrem 1328, was not extended.

The encouragement of industry, at present an important matter which is lagging, is subjecting local industries to stagnation as well as damaging the initiative of (the) proprietors. They are in strong need of support and protection. In this fashion, the petitions and complaints which, for a year, have followed in uninterrupted succession and which have been made necessary by the deprivations and losses of facilities obtained in the Constitutional Period, are to be understood from the applications made every day to the Directorate of Industries.

Therefore, as a remedy for this situation, the case of the above-mentioned law, which has been debated and accepted by the Chamber of Deputies, concerns and is connected to this matter of exemptions.

Confirmation of the validity henceforth of the first and second articles is given over for the illustrious Grand Vizier's approval and his exalted, eminent, and worthy permission to execute this memorandum as required.

1 Cemaziyelâhir 1329/ 16 Mayis 1327

In the name of the Deputy Supervisor of
Commerce and Public Works

The Undersecretary

Ministry of Commerce and Public Works
Directorate-General for Industries

Copy of the first and second articles of the Law to Stimulate Industries, debated and accepted by the Chamber of Deputies.

Article One. In accordance with the special law, factories established to convert primary raw materials or half-manufactured materials to another form, with a minimum of five horsepower required for manufacture, and with building annexes, tools, and equipment of a value of not less than 1,000 liras on condition of a minimum of 900 daily wage workers employed per year, will benefit from the exemptions and facilities set forth in Article Two.

Article Two. The manner in which the said factories cited in Article One will obtain exemptions:

(1) As required for the establishment and expansion of factories and annexes, from one to five dönüms of vacant government property will be given up by the state and a free deed of disposal will be provided.

(2) Factories, land, buildings, and annexes will be exempted from all taxes, tithes, and other imposts.

(3) As required for the renovation and expansion of factories' initial establishment, iron, petroleum, machines, tools, equipment, and requirements will be exempted from customs duties.

(4) As required for factory manufactures, raw primary materials not found in the Ottoman lands will be exempted from customs duties.

(5) As required for factory manufacturers, if the total value of half-manufactured primary materials not found in the Ottoman lands is less than half the total value of articles manufactured from them--those materials will be exempted from customs duties.

(Seal of the Bureau of Industries)

Düstür, 2:434-435.

No. 151:   Law concerning exemption from customs duties for agricultural tools and chemical
           fertilizers and equipment for factories.
           6 Cumada II 1329/22 May 1327
           Published and announced in the Official Gazette (as no. 849) on 17 Cumada II
           1329/1 June 1327.

Sole Article

Out of consideration for the preliminary establishment and enlargement of factories,
as of the date of passage of an exalted order which concerns the exemption from customs
duties of equipment relating to the preliminary establishment and enlargement of factories,

as of the publication of this legal article which will make restitution for customs duties
obtaining on machinery and equipment for factories which will be established, constructed,
and expanded:

in order to facilitate transport of imported equipment, factory products, and primary equipment, customs duties will not obtain on décauville [narrow gauge railway], havai teller
[aerial cables] and its derivatives, agricultural tools and chemical fertilizers when imported from foreign countries.

I declare this bill, approved by the Council of Notables and by the Deputies, legal,
and to be added to the laws of the state.

6 Cumada II 1329/22 May 1327   Mehmed Raşad

          Nā'il   Ibrahim Hakki
Superintendent of Finance   Grand Vezir

7

Finance and Public Finance

In the first half of the nineteenth century the main financial development was the
continued debasing of the currency and the sharp rise in prices that had begun in the sixteenth (chap. 1 and 7:1,2). Various attempts at improving and stabilizing the currency had
only limited success, and until the First World War Turkey's monetary system remained seriously defective (7:3 to 5); but, helped no doubt by the downward trend in world markets,
prices showed little increase until the turn of the century, after which they rose again.[1]
Banking, which for centuries had been carried out by the Galata bankers and other sarrafs
(7:6), took a new turn after the Crimean War, with the foundation, by foreign capital, of
the Ottoman and other banks and the opening of branches of large European institutions.
These banks adequately financed Turkey's foreign trade but provided almost no help to its
agriculture or industry, a deficiency that was only partly remedied by the government (7:6).

Other financial institutions were also established. In 1873 a stock exchange was set
up in Istanbul, and regulations were drawn for it on 15 April 1886, but the volume of transactions was small.[2] The absence of insurance was for long a handicap to business[3] but this
was gradually remedied; by 1906 there were fifty-three foreign companies in Istanbul, and
they protested strongly against the government's attempt to regulate their activities and
require them to deposit guarantees and set aside not less than 20 percent of their annual
net income as reserves (29 May 1906, FO 368/59). Fire insurance proved to be an unprofitable business: in Istanbul in 1905-9 average premiums were ₤120,000-125,000 and losses
₤106,000; losses in Izmir averaged ₤42,000 in 1900-1909 and in 1911 fire losses reached a
record and premiums had to be raised by 50 percent.[4]

Finance was only one of the branches into which a large amount of foreign capital
flowed. In the first half of the century foreign investment had been confined to setting
up import-export houses, small processing plants for export products such as silk, and the
minor installations required to service steamships calling at the Turkish ports. In 1854
the Ottoman government contracted its first foreign loan, a process that led to the accumulation of a debt of ₤T212 million, the declaration of bankruptcy in 1875, and the setting
up, by the Great powers, of the Public Debt Administration that exercised a large measure
of control over Turkey's finances (7:16). With the Administration's consent, loans were
contracted for railways and other purposes and the debt, which under the 1881 settlement
had been reduced to ₤T116 million, had by 1914 climbed up again to ₤T139 million. It should
be added that, over the whole period, the bulk of the money received--which was only some

Table 1

Price of Wheat (piastres per Istanbul kile[a])

Year	Edirne	Salonica	Istanbul[a]	Bursa	Mytilene	Izmir	Rhodes	Kayseri	Samsun	Erzurum	Diyarbekir	Varna
1800	2[b]											
1828		10										
1834		30–33										
1835	6	13										
1836	9											
1837		13–16								12[c]		
1839	25											
1840	19								13[d]			
1841	12											
1842	11	12–16		16–21								
1843	10			11								
1844	13[e]	14		13				6				
1845	16	23		14			16–20	7				
1846	14			16		27				10		
1847							30					19
1848					18–22		16	7				15
1849							16	6				17
1850				16		18	15					16
1851				23		23	17	8				15
1852			(18)			23	18					15
1853			18–42		27		18					15
1854			40–48	40	34		20					19
1855				65	52		30				4	45
1856					34	43	40				8	45
1857											8	
1859											24	
1860				35							25	
1861											8	
1863	21			22						21	10[f]	
1864		19								19	28	
1865										21	29	
1866										12	28	
1867										9	14	
1868										8	12	
1872										17		
1876–80			25									

1876–80   25
1881–85   24
1886–90   19
1891–95   16
1896–1900   17
1901–05   17

Source: Various reports in FO 78 and A and P series.

[a]Rumelian hard wheat; 1876–1905 figures from Quataert, p. 366.

[b]Price of wheat from Edirne and Bulgaria at Enez; price of wheat at Volo 3 1/4 piastres, at Izmit 2 3/4, at Rodosto (Tekirdağ) 2 1/4 (FO 78/28).

[c]Price of average crop (FO 78/443).

[d]Price of former years 10 piastres (ibid).

[e]The price rose from 9 piastres in July on news of crop failure in England (Report 30 September 1845, FO 78/612).

[f]Locust infestation (A and P 1867–68 vol. 68, "Koordistan").

two-thirds of the debt contracted—was used to liquidate previous debts, cover budget deficits, or finance wars.

Foreign capital also began to flow to the private sector after the Crimean War; estimates of the total amount vary, but table 2 is probably the most reliable one available.

Table 2

Foreign Investment in Ottoman Empire around 1909-12 (ŁT millions)

	In Ottoman Empire					Amount Within Present Borders
	French	German	British	Other[a]	Total	
Railways	23.7	22.7	5.8	1.1	53.3	33.7
Mining	2.9	0.2	0.5	0.1	3.6	3.3
Manufacturing	2.0	1.0	2.5	1.0	6.5	6.5
Banks and insurance	3.2	1.3	2.9	0.9	8.2	5.6
Ports and quays					4.7	2.9
Electricity, tramways, water, etc.	5.1	3.5	2.5	2.0	5.7	3.1
Commerce					2.7	2.1
Total	36.8	28.7	14.1	5.1	84.7	57.1
Public debt	52.1	10.1	10.9	23.7	96.8	
Grand Total	88.9	38.8	25.0	28.8	181.5	

Source: Eldem, pp. 190-91.

[a]Belgian, United States, etc.

France was by far the largest investor in the Public Debt; the British gradually reduced their holdings while the Germans rapidly increased theirs in the two decades before
the First World War. Whereas in 1881 Britain and France owned, each, about a third of the
total, by 1914 the French share had risen to about 60 percent and the German to around 20
percent while the British was about 10 percent. In railways British capital took an early
lead but soon lost interest and sold the Izmir-Kasaba line to French and the Mersin-Adana
line to German interests;[5] Germany was by far the leading investor in Turkey proper but
France's holdings in Syria kept it ahead until almost the end of the period (4:Introduction).
In mining France was easily ahead and in industry and banking shared the lead with Britain.[6]

The large public debt reflects the imbalance between government revenues and expenditures. This became acute in the 1840s, and was at first met by issuing Treasury bonds
(7:8,9) and, after 1854, by contracting foreign loans. Central government revenue rose
from the equivalent of Ł2,250,000 in 1809 (Report by Canning, 25 March 1809, FO 78/63) to
about Ł3,000,000 in 1830, Ł6,200,000 in 1840, and Ł9,000,000 in 1855,[7] but expenditures increased even faster. No reliable budget figures are available until the 1870s, but the
main outlines are clear.[8] Even in peacetime, the bulk of expenditure was absorbed by the
armed forces, the bureaucracy, the court, and, increasingly, by debt servicing (7:7,8).[9]
The burden of the numerous wars in which Turkey was engaged, particularly in the first half
of the period (chap. 1) is impossible to measure, but must have been great. The direct cost
of the Crimean War was put at from Ł11.2 million (Report by Minister of Finance covering 15
May 1853 to 15 September 1855, FO 78/1157) to an estimated Ł13 million (Fuad paşa to Musurus,
13 December 1855, TE, Box 13). To this must be added the opportunity cost of the mobilization of hundreds of thousands of farmers and other workers. The period between 1878 and
1911, however, was quite peaceful and, with the scaling down of the debt in 1881, matters
gradually improved. Between 1887 and 1911 debt servicing declined from 30 percent of total
expenditure to 19, military expenditure from 44 to 38 (a figure higher than those of Britain,
France, and Germany) and the civil list from 5 to 2, while investment rose from 2.2 to 7.6

percent.[10]   But until the very end of the Empire, central government expenditure was of very little direct benefit to the people, and the same was largely true of provincial expenditure.

Central government revenue continued to rise rapidly (after adjustment for territorial losses), and just before the First World War caught up with expenditure. In 1863 it was ŁT15 million, in 1872 ŁT21.5 million, in 1887 ŁT15.6 million, in 1907 ŁT24.5 million, in 1911 ŁT31.2 million, and in 1913 ŁT29.2 million.[11] At the beginning of the nineteenth century revenues accruing to the central government probably formed only a fraction of the total raised in taxes, the greater part being kept by the various local authorities (7:7), but with the increase in centralization the balance shifted and by the 1890s provincial government revenues were a little over one-third of those of the central government, while municipal revenues were very small.[12]

Turkey's central tax burden of about ŁT1 per capita, or about 10 percent of national income, in the years immediately preceding the First World War (chap. 1) was quite heavy for a country at its level of development (7:11), and in the previous decades it must have been even heavier. But what greatly added to the weight was the nature of the taxes and their distribution. Tithes and taxes on livestock and other agricultural produce formed one-half of central government revenues around 1870 and nearly two-fifths around 1913 (and still higher proportions of provincial revenues), and their incidence was regressive. So was that of customs duties, which were levied at a flat rate and accounted for another fifth of central government revenues.[13] All observers agree, first, that the burden on farmers was much higher than was suggested by the nominal rate of taxes and, secondly, that only a fraction of the amount levied reached the government (7:12,15). They also agree that the incidence of taxation was very uneven and arbitrary, the towns being taxed much more lightly that the countryside and some localities and communities being very hard hit (7:10 to 13) while others got off rather lightly (7:14).[14] The vagaries of the currency added to the woes of the taxpayers and increased the opportunity for arbitrariness and extortion. There is no doubt that the Ottoman tax system was a major discouragement to development, the more so since the benefits derived by the mass of the population from government expenditure were negligible.

But it must be remembered that the Ottoman government's power to remedy this situation was strictly limited by the Capitulations and the Commercial Treaties. Tariffs could not be either raised or differentiated without the consent of the Powers, and this was withheld until 1911. And since taxes could not be imposed on foreigners without the consent of their governments, which was almost never given, and since it would have been unacceptable to tax Ottoman subjects only[15]--particularly in view of the fact that most of the modern sector was in foreign hands--the scope for new direct taxes that would have rendered the fiscal system less regressive was very small indeed.

All this was clearly realized, but efforts at reform produced only minor results, and only under the Republic was this question seriously taken up.

---

1. No overall price indexes are available, but table 1 gives an indication of the price of wheat (also table in 7:2). Bruce McGowan (see 2:10) gives two series of wheat prices per kile at unspecified ports in the southern Balkans:
        1780, 12 kuruş; 1804, 20; 1813, 45.
        1780, 1 1/2; 1800, 5 1/2 - 6; 1812, 14 1/2 - 15.
There was a sharp rise in prices until the late 1830s, but in the 1840s, partly in line with world prices and partly because of the effect of the 1838 Treaty and improved transport, import prices fell markedly and so did export prices (Cumberbatch to Canning, 17 March 1846, and to Wellesley, 14 August 1846, FO 195/255). The Crimean War sent prices sharply up, but they declined again in the following decade. Quataert's indexes of agricultural prices (pp. 23 and 366-70) show a drop of about 25-30 percent between 1876-80 and the end of the century, followed by a rise to 1906-8; Eldem, pp. 198-99, has a series of

agricultural prices that shows a further small rise until the war. As regards import prices, Imlah's index of British export prices dropped from 300 in 1815 to 100 in 1850 and from 141 in 1864 to a low of 83 in 1888, rising again to 97 in 1913--Mitchell, pp. 331-32; Sönmez's index of Turkey's import prices shows little change between 1878 and 1913, a 15 percent drop to 1895 being followed by an equal rise.

2. Almanach d'Orient, 1907 (Constantinople, 1907).

3. In 1851, the British consul-general, whose house and belongings had just been destroyed by fire, complained to Palmerston about "the impossibility of insuring houses and property in Constantinople against the risk of fire" (FO 78/866).

4. TJ, June 1910, A and P 1912-13, vol. 100, "Constantinople" and "Smyrna."

5. A and P 1896, vol. 96, "Report by Major Law on Railways in Asiatic Turkey."

6. Germany's investments in 1914 were put at 1,000 million marks (₤50,000,000) of which one-half was in the Public Debt, 225 million in railways, and 250-300 million in other enterprises--Wiedenfeld, p. 399. Aulneau, cited by Eldem, put French investments at ₤T111 million, German at 55 million, and British 33 million, for a total of ₤T200 million. This total is close to the one given by Hüsrev (EHME, p. 94). Thobie, pp. 305-308, discussing various estimates, puts the total outstanding public debt in 1914 at 3,347 million francs (₤134 million); the French share had risen from 46 percent in 1895 to 60 in 1914 and the German from 11 to 16, while the British had fallen from 18 to 14.

As for direct investments in the private sector, the French share had risen from 39 to 45 percent and the German from 19 to 25, the British falling from 24 to 16; the total amount invested had risen from 742 million francs (₤30 million) to 1,130 million (₤45 million)--Thobie, pp. 476-82.

7. Preussiches Handelsarchiv 16 September 1864. The 1809 figure is low compared to contemporary ones for Britain, France, Iran, and India--Issawi in Naff and Owen.

8. The first available budget, other than the one given in 7:7, was the incomplete one published in Ubicini. After 1861 a budget was sent each year to the foreign ambassadors, but not published (information kindly given by Professor Enver Ziya Karal). The 1869-70 budget was described by the Austrian ambassador as the first "serious" one (HHS, Türkei, Berichte 1869, VII-XII, 13 August 1869). For breakdowns for 1863 and 1911-12, EHME, p. 186, and Mears pp. 391-99; for 1880 and 1907, Shaw, History, 2:225.

9. In 1855 the Sultan's civil list was raised from ₤540,000 to ₤850,000 (Palmerston to Musurus, 16 December 1855, TE, Box 13). In 1872 debt accounted for 44 percent of total expenditure, armed forces for 22, administration 18, and civil list 6, while development took only 6 percent--table by Aktan in EHME, p. 111; also Shaw, History, 2:155-56, 221-26, 285-86.

10. Eldem, pp. 244-45.

11. Ibid., p. 243; EHME, p. 109.

12. The table on revenues of selected provinces in EHME, p. 110, suggests that in the 1890s they amounted to ₤6-7 million, while central revenues were ₤15 to 20 million.

13. Details in Eldem, p. 243; the balance of revenue came from monopolies, tribute (from Egypt, Cyprus, and other places), the temettü vergisi, a tax usually assessed on conventional indices of income, the musakkafat vergisi on urban land and buildings, and various stamp and other taxes (7:11).

14. In addition to the examples in the selections, the following may be given. In 1841 the British consul in Bursa judged that the salianeh or communal tax was moderate in large towns and cities but "so onerous to the rural population in some cases as to be completely insupportable" (29 May 1841, FO 78/441).

In 1850 the consul in Erzurum stated that the customs of that paşalık had been farmed for ₤230,000; if the duties "were fairly levied" they would bring in "little short of ₤1,000,000" (7 January 1850, FO 78/834).

In 1858 it was stated that "the cultivator who would comparatively pay less than in any other country in Europe, if the taxes be levied by the government itself, pays in reality the double" (Trade of Samsun, 1858, FO 78/1451).

In 1869 a careful calculation put the yearly taxation of the Anatolian peasant family at ₤2, compared to an estimated income of ₤7 plus some food grown on the farm--A and P 1870, vol. 64, "Anatolian Provinces."

15. For one of many examples, see the negotiations with Britain regarding the draft law on a Patente (temettü) tax in 1889. The British government stated judiciously that only when all the other Powers had agreed would it be in a position to declare its views (TE, Box 256, 19 June 1889).

CURRENCY

In the nineteenth century few countries had as unserviceable a currency as the Ottoman Empire, or one which constituted a greater obstacle to economic development. The trouble had begun much earlier, with the successive debasing of the akçe (first minted in 1327 and known to Europeans as the asper or aspre) and the para (introduced around 1620), the two silver coins that constituted the main medium of transactions. Around 1688 another silver coin, the kuruş (groschen, known as piastre), was introduced; it was modeled on the European dollars (Austrian thaler, Spanish piastre) but was only two-thirds as heavy and exchanged at about 4.5 to the pound sterling. The rate 1 kuruş = 40 paras = 120 akçes was soon established and maintained throughout the eighteenth century, all three coins depreciating together (see the following selection). These silver coins were supplemented by a small number of gold coins: pieces of 3.4 grams known as tuğralı, zencirli, or fındıklı, and of 2.5–2.6 grams, the zer-i mahbub.[1] A large amount of foreign coins--Austrian, British, Dutch, French, and others--also circulated. Finally there was a unit of account, the kes or kese (purse); the kese-i Rumi was the equivalent of 50,000 akçes and the kese-i Misri of 60,000 "regardless of the real values of the coins concerned,"[2] but by 1800 they tended to equal 500 piastres.

The debasing of the currency was the main force pushing up prices (7:2), and its inhibiting effect on trade was reinforced by the tendency of bad money to drive out good and the consequent speculation. In 1780, following rumours of further debasing, "trade is at a standstill" (Ainslie to Hillsborough, 2 November 1780, FO 78/1). In 1800, because of depreciation, "a considerable agio is given for specie in the neighbouring countries as at Vienna and Petersburg on which our bills are chiefly negotiated--and there is very little foreign trade carried on here" (Elgin to Grenville, 15 December 1800, FO 78/30).

The response of the Porte was to prohibit exports of specie and force people to give up good coins for bad (7:3).[3] On this particular occasion the Austrian Internuncio pointed out that such a prohibition "seems at once to violate property rights and to paralyse circulation," and wrote a memorandum explaining how currency depreciation raised prices in proportion. This lesson in monetary economics may not have been entirely wasted, for in April 1801 the Reis Efendi informed the Internuncio that he had removed the prohibition on the export of specie, because of complaints, but that the rates fixed in the order had to be maintained (correspondence in HHS Türkei, II:125).

During the Napoleonic Wars the decline in the exchange rate of the piastre was slowed down by the fact that sterling and other currencies also depreciated, but with peace it was resumed and then accelerated sharply during the War of Greek Independence and the struggles with Mehmet Ali. The introduction of new coins, the beşlik (5 piastres) in 1810 and the new beşlik in 1829, as well as coins of 2 1/2 and one piastre and fractions, did not help since they too were short in weight and heavily alloyed.[4] In July 1833 a note sent by the Porte to the embassies announced that as from 16 August only coins of 6 piastres (the altı lık), 3 piastres, and one piastre and fractions, with a higher silver content, would be minted (CC Constantinople, vol. 85, 27 July 1833). These coins were in fact issued and raised the exchange rate of the piastre but by September it had become evident that the government was continuing to mint the older coins and that the task of withdrawing the 500 million piastres in circulation was beyond its means (ibid., 7 September 1833).

But worse was to come. In 1839, to cover the deficit caused by the various wars, the government issued 25-piastre Treasury bearer bonds, carrying 12 percent interest, the Kaime-i Mutebere Nakdiye. The government had borrowed from Ricardo's, in London, against an understanding that not more than 60 million piastres of Kaime would be issued, but within a year some 160 million were in circulation, and moreover there was much counterfeiting.[5] Kaimes were soon at a very heavy discount.

In 1844 another attempt to stabilize the currency was made. A bimetallic gold and silver standard was adopted, at the ratio of 1:15.909, the new Turkish pound (lira) being worth 100 kuruş or 18 shillings, and an unsuccessful attempt was made to withdraw some of the old coins (7:5). Soon after, arrangements were made with the Banque de Constantinople (7:6,8) to furnish traders with bills of exchange on Paris and London at the rate of 110 piastres per pound sterling, a measure that stabilized the exchange for a few years, at considerable loss. But chronic financial difficulties, aggravated by the Crimean and other wars, an import surplus that drained away specie, continued overissue of paper and debased money, and the fall in world prices of silver starting in 1860--after a stability in rela- tion to gold that had lasted since 1780 and facilitated bimetallism everywhere--combined to wreck the new scheme.[6] An example of the magnitude of the fluctuations may be given: in Bursa in 1858 sterling dropped from close to 200 piastres to 140 on news that the Ottoman government had contracted a fresh loan.[7] The amount of Kaimes reached £12 million and their price ranged "within 10 percent above or below 185"; in 1865 this floating debt was funded, being replaced by 5 percent long-term bonds.[8]

The declaration of bankruptcy on 6 October 1875 (7:16) caused a great crisis among Galata bankers and, unable to borrow anywhere, the government once more resorted to Kaimes. Originally it was intended to issue only £T3,000,000 but between August 1876 and August 1878 the total rose to £T15,393,000, and the gold currency in circulation dropped from £T6,000,000 to £T2,500,000. In March 1878 the government's decree that Kaimes would "only be received in payment of taxes to the extent of one-fifth of the amount of the tax," at 400 to the lira, "destroyed its value as money" and its rate fell below 1,000.[9] In 1879-80 the government redeemed the outstanding £T14 million of Kaimes at one-fourth of their value in gold.[10]

A new attempt was made with the decree of 6 January 1881.[11] The Turkish gold lira of 7.216 grams, 91.65 percent fineness, equivalent to 18 shillings or $4.40, was the basic coin. It was subdivided into 100 gold kuruş saǧ, or sound piastres, known in the Arab provinces as qurush sahih. The main silver coin was the mecidiye, originally intended to be worth 20 kuruş saǧ but, since silver had depreciated, officially fixed at 19, giving an implicit ratio of 105.26 piastres to the lira. But the subsidiary coins constituted a fur- ther complication, the old silver ones being debased and the copper issued in excess of de- mand. Hence their market value fell well below par, and a new unofficial unit came into being, the kuruş çürük (Arabic qurush mu'ib) or defective piastre. This meant that the Ottoman Empire had two kinds of piastre, the gold (saǧ) used as a unit of account, at 100 to the lira, and the silver (çürük). The latter had three sets of value: the legal one of one-nineteenth of a mecidiye, or 105.26 to the lira; a conventional one for retail trade, mainly in Istanbul, of 108 to the lira; and a commercial one that varied according to place, to supply and demand, and to the kind of transaction, and that ranged between the official value and the intrinsic value.[12] Thus around 1905 the commercial rate was 108-9 in Istanbul, 124-25 in Beirut, 103-53 in Baghdad and 102-78 in Izmir; in Izmir official transactions were conducted at the implicit rate of 102.5, those involving oilseeds and cereals other than wheat at 110.75, for cotton, raisins, and some other exports 125, for tin, lead, and other hardware 151.25 and for wheat and licorice 178.[13]

Two further complications may be noted. The basic monetary unit of trade varied: in Istanbul it was the lira, in Izmir the mecidiye, in Armenia the altılık, in Syria the kuruş, and in Yemen the Maria Theresa dollar. Secondly, a wide variety of foreign coins was used, especially in the Arab provinces, including gold, such as the English sovereign, French Napoleon, Russian imperial, Persian tuman, and Dutch ducat; and silver, such as the Maria Theresa dollar, the crown, florin, silver ruble, rupee, and Persian kran.

The government made some attempts to improve the currency. No paper money was issued,

except for the notes of the Ottoman Bank (7:6), until the First World War. In 1880 the
value of the pre-1844 altılık was reduced from 6 piastres to 5, that of the beşlik from 5
piastres to 3 and that of the metalık from 1 piastre to 1/2, the fractions of all these
coins being reduced correspondingly. This made it profitable for money-changers to withdraw
some 60 million piastres of these coins from circulation and melt them down. And in 1888
the government, the Public Debt Administration, and the Régie signed an agreement for the
withdrawal of 50 million piastres of altılıks, replacing them by purer coins made by melting
down an equal amount of mecidiyes; by 1905 some 41.5 million piastres had been withdrawn and
130 million piastres of mecidiyes had been melted and struck in coins of 5, 2, and 1 piastres. To meet the shortage of small change, copper coins of 10 paras were issued in 1900.[14]

(See also works by du Velay, Morawitz, and Young, listed in Bibliography.)

1. For fuller details, EHME, pp. 520-21 and Barkan, "Price Revolution."
2. Shaw, Financial, p. xxii.
3. Forgery was also severely punished. In 1781 "two Turks of some consequence, inhabitants of Brusa" were brought to Istanbul and publicly hanged (Ainslie to Hillsborough,
26 July 1781, FO 78/2); also du Velay, p. 56, for a case in 1798.
4. Du Velay, pp. 56-57; Lewis, Emergence, p. 108.
5. Grunwald and Ronall, p. 14; du Velay, pp. 123-25; EI2 s.v. "Kaime."
6. For comparable developments in Iran, EHI, pp. 339-56.
7. A and P 1859, vol. 30, "Brussa."
8. Ibid., 1878-79, vol. 71, "Constantinople," which has a very good study of this
subject.
9. The price dropped from 124 on 18 December 1876 to 350 on 25 November 1878, and 860
on 2 December 1879--Maynard to Evarts, 2 December 1879, DSP, "Turkish Empire," p. 969.
10. EI2, s.v. "Kaime."
11. Texts and notes in Young, 5:1-12.
12. The intrinsic value of the silver content of the piastre fell from 110.6 a lira in
1875 to 129.4 in 1885, 210.5 in 1895, and around 236 in 1905--ibid., p. 2.
13. Ibid.
14. Ibid., pp. 3-5. Between 1844 and 1884, ₤T31,057,000 of gold liras were minted and
1,020 million piastres of silver coins. In 1885-1908, a further ₤T17,000,000 of gold liras
were minted. Around 1908, some ₤T30 million in gold and over 1,000 million piastres in
silver were in circulation--Biliotti, pp. 100-107.

SELECTION 1. EXCHANGE RATES, 1780-1844

Charles Issawi

Rate of Pound Sterling in Piastres (Kuruş)

Date	Place	Rate	Source (FO 78/)
1740	Istanbul	5-7	FO 195/152
1770	Istanbul	8.0	FO 195/152
1780	Istanbul	9.5	1
1790	Istanbul	11.1	11
1794	Istanbul	12	15
1795	Istanbul	13.5	195/152
1796	Istanbul	13.5	17
1799	Istanbul	15.8	195/152
1800	Istanbul	12.0	30
1802	Istanbul	14.1	37
1803	Istanbul	15	60
1804	Istanbul	15	60
1804	Istanbul	15	42
1805	Istanbul	15.9-17.5	48
1805	Istanbul	14.8	60
1806	Istanbul	15	60
1806	Istanbul	16.5	49
1806	Istanbul	16.5	50
1806	Istanbul	16.7	51
1806	Istanbul	15	60
1807	Istanbul	14.9	60
1808	Istanbul	19	62
1809	Istanbul	19	64
1809	Istanbul	20.5	68

Date	Place	Rate	Source (FO 78/
1810	Istanbul	19.6	68
1810	Istanbul	19.9	68
1816	Istanbul	19	87
1817–20	Istanbul	average 32	147
1822	Istanbul	about 40	106
1825	Izmir	53.5	147
1826	Izmir	58.5	147
1826	Istanbul	57.5–58.8	147
1827	Izmir	58	171
1827	Istanbul	60.8	FO 195/96
1828	Istanbul	57–57.5	171
30 June 1828	Istanbul	59.3	185
31 December 1828	Istanbul	61.8	185
12 January 1829	Istanbul	64	195
10 April 1829	Istanbul	66.3	195
30 June 1829	Istanbul	70.5	195
25 September 1829	Istanbul	70.5	195
31 December 1829	Istanbul	74.5	195
30 June 1829	Izmir	70	185
19 March 1830	Izmir	75	195
30 June 1830	Izmir	76	201
31 December 1830	Izmir	76.5	201
26 March 1830	Istanbul	76.8	201
25 June 1830	Istanbul	77.3	201
25 September 1830	Istanbul	75	201
31 December 1830	Istanbul	77.5	201
1830	Salonica	average 77.5	368
1831	Izmir	83.5	215
25 March 1831	Istanbul	78	215
25 June 1831	Istanbul	80.3	215
26 September 1831	Istanbul	82	215
31 December 1831	Istanbul	84.8	215
27 March 1832	Istanbul	87	229
30 June 1832	Istanbul	87.3	229
29 September 1832	Istanbul	87.5	229
27 December 1832	Istanbul	94	229
19 July 1832	Izmir	88.8	229
31 December 1832	Izmir	93.5	229
1832	Trabzon	100	265
1833	Trabzon	96	229
1834	Trabzon	97.3	241
26 March 1833	Istanbul	95	241
25 June 1833	Istanbul	96	241
25 September 1833	Istanbul	95.8	241
31 December 1833	Istanbul	96.9	241
1833	Salonica	96	265
1835	Salonica	100	290
1835	Trabzon	average 99	265
4 March 1835	Istanbul	98	286
30 June 1835	Istanbul	99.5	286
30 September 1835	Istanbul	98.5	286
31 December 1835	Istanbul	101.8	286
1835	Istanbul	average 98.7	286
13 January 1836	Istanbul	102	286
30 March 1836	Istanbul	98.4	286
29 June 1836	Istanbul	98.3	286
28 September 1836	Istanbul	100	286
31 December 1836	Istanbul	103.5	286
1835	Izmir	average 99	287
30 June 1836	Izmir	97.5	314
31 December 1836	Izmir	102.5	314
1836	Izmir	99	314
1837	Izmir	107	338
1836	Trabzon	average 100	286
1837	Edirne	average 108	335
11 July 1838	Edirne	109.5	368
9 January 1839	Edirne	104.5	368
1837	Istanbul	average 108.9	335
25 October 1837	Istanbul	105	335

Date	Place	Rate	Source (FO 78/)
22 November 1837	Istanbul	108.8	335
10 January 1838	Istanbul	104	335
1838	Trabzon	average 106.5	367
1839	Trabzon	average 106.5	401
1838	Salonica	average 104	368
1839	Salonica	average 104	411
1838	Izmir	average 105.5	369
30 June 1838	Izmir	109	369
31 December 1838	Izmir	101.3	369
27 March 1839	Istanbul	104.8	411
26 June 1839	Istanbul	106.5	411
25 September 1839	Istanbul	100	411
31 December 1839	Istanbul	104.8	411
1839	Istanbul	average 104	411
25 March 1840	Istanbul	109	440
24 June 1840	Istanbul	108.3	440
30 September 1840	Istanbul	108.3	440
31 December 1840	Istanbul	109.8	440
1840	Istanbul	average 107.3 (sic)	440
1840	Salonica	average 106.5	441
31 December 1841	Salonica	114	441
1840	Bursa	average 110–111	441
30 June 1840	Izmir	107.5	442
21 October 1840	Izmir	107.5	442
30 June 1841	Izmir	109	443
31 December 1841	Izmir	113.5	443
1840	Trabzon	average 105.5	491
1841	Trabzon	average 108	491
31 March 1841	Istanbul	110	489
30 June 1841	Istanbul	110.1	489
29 September 1841	Istanbul	109.6	489
31 December 1841	Istanbul	114.5	489
1841	Istanbul	average 110.5	489
1841	Bursa	average 111	490
1841	Edirne	average 110	490
1842	Salonica	average 116	490
1842	Edirne	average 118	531
1842	Bursa	average 117	532
30 March 1842	Istanbul	115.3	530
29 June 1842	Istanbul	117.5	530
28 September 1842	Istanbul	116	530
28 December 1842	Istanbul	118.1	530
1842	Istanbul	average 116.6	530
30 June 1842	Izmir	118.3	532
31 December 1842	Izmir	119	532
1843	Izmir	average 117	571
31 March 1843	Istanbul	123	569
30 June 1843	Istanbul	111.5	569
27 September 1843	Istanbul	108.3	569
31 December 1843	Istanbul	110	569
1843	Istanbul	average 114.3	569
27 March 1844	Istanbul	108.8	611
30 June 1844	Istanbul	109.3	611
30 September 1844	Istanbul	108	611
31 December 1844	Istanbul	110	611
1844	Istanbul	average 108.8	611
1844	Salonica	average 109	612
1844	Bursa	average 108.3	612
1844	Izmir	average 108	614
1844	Trabzon	average 111	614

PRICES OF FOODSTUFFS

It is extremely difficult to give precise indications of changes in the cost of living in Turkey in the period under review. For one thing, data on prices are scanty in published sources and in the European archives, except for times of sharp inflation, like the Crimean War, when the consuls asked for salary increases. However, one can be confident that a mass of information is to be found in the various Turkish records, and will eventually be used as effectively as has been done by Barkan for earlier times.[1] But, even more important, a price index presupposes a homogeneous market, and in the nineteenth century, because of poor transport and lack of storage, Turkey consisted--with respect to bulky and perishable goods like foodstuffs--of many small markets with few interconnections. This may be illustrated first by the sharp seasonal fluctuations in prices: in Diyarbekir in 1860 the highest annual wheat price was 270 percent of the lowest, 148 percent in 1861, 182 in 1862, and 276 in 1863.[2] In Ankara in 1851, the price of wheat went up in fifteen days from 15 piastres to 80, "the measure of 4½ killos, and even 90 to 100 piastres was demanded by holders from the hopeless appearance of the crops but which changed after abundant and still timely rains, reducing the market rate again to 40 piastres"; over the year, the price rose from 0s3d per imperial quarter to a peak of 34s4d and fell to 13s4d.[3] The narrowness of markets is also illustrated by the great differences in prices between years of poor harvests and those of good crops. In Kayseri wheat prices per quarter moved as follows: 1843 7/7, 1844 10/7, and 1845 29/6 (Report 1845, FO 78/655). Lastly, the compartmentalization of markets is shown by the wide range of prices in places not too far apart: in 1847, in the hinterland of Salonica, flour was sold at 6/- per sack but at 31/- in places 80 to 100 miles distant (Blunt to Palmerston, FO 78/700), and in 1867, wheat was selling at 18s a quarter in Diyarbekir, 12s in Erzurum 130 miles away, and 4s7d in Van, 233 miles away.[4] Before the railway was built, wheat cost ₺2 to ₺3 in Ankara and ₺6 to ₺10 in Istanbul.[5]

Finally, a cost of living index presupposes weights, based on sample family budgets, and no studies on the subject are available. The two following observations may however be noted. In Kastamonu province in 1879 "peasants live very poorly, rarely eating meat, and consuming only the products of their gardens. They have soup made of rice or flour, sour milk (yaourt) and bread baked in flat cakes. Milk is plentiful everywhere in the vilayet. The townsmen live better, often eating meat. Bread is cheap and not of very bad quality, 36 paras the oke. The peasants' living costs about 2 to 3 piastres per diem, mechanics 5 piastres and the better classes up to 20 piastres."[6]

In Ankara province, in 1893, the British consul classified the inhabitants into three groups and estimated their annual expenditure as follows:[7]

First class	₺120–200
Second class	50–60
Third class	20–30

A tentative estimate may also be made for earlier years. In 1828, the daily cost per patient at the French hospital in Izmir was: bread 24 _paras_, meat 18, wine 8, fresh vegetables 10, rice 10, salt, pepper, oil, vinegar, wood, coal 14, medicines 20, total 100 (sic); these figures had risen in "recent years" because of the depreciation of the _para_ (CC Smyrne, vol. 42). In 1840, the cost per patient at the British hospital in Izmir was: bread 24 _paras_, beef and mutton 42, vegetables for soup 10, charcoal 15, total 91 (FO 78/440 and 781/2). These diets were far better than those available to the mass of the people and it may be surmised that an expenditure of 40 _paras_, or one piastre, a day could provide adequate food for an adult. Assuming an average family to consist of 3.5 adult equivalents, a daily expenditure of food of about 3.5 piastres might be required. Further assuming that

two-thirds to three-quarters of family expenditure went on food, a minimum family budget of
5 piastres a day may be suggested.

Nevertheless, when all these reservations have been made, the trend in the cost of
living over the centuries is clear: it went sharply upwards. The main cause for this is
also plain: the steady depreciation of the currency. Barkan's index of prices of foodstuffs, measured in akçes, rose from 50 in 1490 to a peak of 631 in 1605, and then fell
back to 470 in 1650; in terms of silver the change was much smaller: from 50 to 265 and
187, respectively, but it must be remembered that the price of silver itself fell rather
sharply in this period.[8] Both the trend and its main cause continued: between 1591 and
1775, the prices of mutton rose eightfold and that of bread ninefold.[9] And in the second
half of the eighteenth century, as the following extract shows, the price of foodstuffs
rose about fourfold. The situation is summarized, impressionistically, in the Memorandum
on the Chaplain's Salary presented by the British embassy in Istanbul in 1828 (FO 78/171).
That salary had remained unchanged at £250 per annum since 1680; at that time, the chaplain
could live on £30-40 a year, saving the rest for retirement, but this was no longer true.
"150 years ago the price of butcher's meat was about 1 or 2 paras the oke, whereas at present it is from 30 to 45; a brace of partridges, which in 1670 is recorded to have cost only
2 aspers, two-thirds of a single para, now costs from 3 to 4 piastres, or nearly 200 times
as much. Bread, charcoal, oil, wine, servants' wages and labour are at least in relative
proportion to the butcher's meat."

The table below sets out the available figures on bread, meat, and other staple items
of food in the nineteenth century. The cluster of figures on bread and flour in 1844 came
in response to a questionnaire sent out by the British embassy. Discounting the exceptionally high prices in Kayseri, Aleppo, and Damascus caused by drought, they suggest a level of
1 piastre per oke of bread in the coastal cities of Izmir and Salonica--and presumably Is-
tanbul--and about half that amount in the interior. These figures are equivalent to under
1d. per lb. and less than half a penny per lb., respectively, and compare with a range of
1¾-3d. per lb. in England and Wales between 1840 and 1850.[10]

The scanty information available suggests that at the beginning of the century bread
and meat prices were only a third as high as in the 1840s. The more abundant data for the
years preceding the First World War show that bread prices were almost twice, meat prices
about three times, and butter prices one and half times as high as in the late 1840s and
early 50s. Rice showed very little increase and sugar actually declined over the period.
Another item, not shown in the table, whose price may have fallen was fuel, at least in
those areas where charcoal was replaced by imported kerosene. Altogether, the cost of food
probably less than doubled between the 1840s and 1906-14. Most of the rise occurred after
the turn of this century, and the available data show very little increase between the
1840s and the 1870-90 period.

This very sketchy outline may be partly filled in by information from the consular reports. The Russian envoy in Istanbul gave the following prices (in paras per oke) which
are comparable to those in the selection.[11]

	1798	1802	1806
Bread	9	12	18
Flour	12	16	30
Rice	14	20	38
Beef	12	38	80
Coffee	142	180	400
Egyptian sugar	149	160	300

A dispatch from Istanbul in 1805 (Arbuthnot to Milgrave, 25 November 1805, FO 78/46) mentions "the very alarming scarcity of all the more immediate necessaries of life. . . . complaints on account of the excessive dearness of provisions." In 1813 Istanbul had "one of the most rigorous winters that has been known in the memory of man. . . . And the dearth of every species of commodity is augmented by the attempts made by the Turkish Government to compell the dealers to part with their stocks at a fixed price. . . . The distress of the lower orders has therefore been great; discontent has been widely spread; and tumults have been repressed only the the exercise of a rigid and sanguinary police" (Liston to Castlereagh, 22 March 1813, FO 78/81). This dearth and the rise in prices is also mentioned by some Ottoman historians.[11]

The end of hostilities brought only a short respite, being soon followed by the Greek War of Independence. The continued and rapid devaluation of the currency (8:1) caused a sharp rise in prices. In 1834 the British dragomans in Izmir complained that their salaries, reckoned in piastres, had remained unchanged whereas there had been a "great augmentation in the cost of all articles of food as well as raiment in accordance with the rise in value of European monies" and pointed out that the exchange rate of the pound sterling had risen from 23 piastres in 1815 to 35 in 1822 and now stood at 100 (FO 78/242).

Between 1841 and 1853 the Empire was at peace and the currency remained relatively steady, while the trend in world prices was downward and Turkey was more closely linked to the world economy by the fall in transport costs and the reduction of tariffs brought about by the 1838 Commercial Convention (3:10). A table prepared by British merchants showed a considerable fall--ranging from 5 to nearly 50 percent--in the price of the main British imports while the price of the main articles of export fell as follows: opium 31 percent, valonea 29, silk 28, wool 22 (Cumberbatch to Wellesley, 14 August 1846, FO 781/2).

The outbreak of the Crimean War caused a very sharp rise in prices of "necessaries"-- in Istanbul "nearly threefold" (Calvert to Clarendon, 25 January 1855, FO 78/1105), in Izmir "more than doubled" (Chumaran to Brant, 4 June 1855, FO 78/1108), in Bursa "doubled" (Report on Administration, FO 78/1111). A detailed table prepared by the Austrian consul in Izmir (HHS--V/1/2, vol. 35, 16 November 1855) shows that the price of most foodstuffs at least doubled between 1853 and 1855. Another detailed table, by the British consul in Samos, shows that the price of the food products exported (raisins, wine, oil, almonds, onions, and vegetables) remained mostly constant between 1846 and 1852 but, with few exceptions, had risen two- to threefold by 1855 (Reply to Questionnaire, FO 78/1419). The end of the war was followed by a drop in prices, but its extent is not clear, and the data are too sparse to detect a clear trend in the 1860s and early 70s. After that, agricultural prices decreased sharply until near the end of the century, Rumelian wheat, for example, falling by about a third,[13] and it may be presumed that the cost of foodstuffs also showed a decline.[14] This trend was reversed in the first years of this century and accelerated after 1908, and all indications point to a sharp increase in the price of foodstuffs and the cost of living right up to the outbreak of the war. Eldem puts the rise in wholesale prices between 1897-98 and 1913-14 at 24 percent, with a sharp acceleration to 9 percent between 1913 and 1914, and believes that retail prices showed a similar trend.[15]

---

1. O. L. Barkan, "Price Revolution."
2. A and P 1865, vol. 53 "Diarbekr and Kurdistan."
3. Sandison to Canning, 18 June 1851, FO 78/868.
4. A and P 1867-68, vol. 68, "Koordistan."
5. Stich, p. 35.
6. A and P 1880, vol. 74, "Kastamuni."
7. A and P 1894, vol. 88, "Angora."

8. Braudel and Spooner, in Cambridge Economic History of Europe, 4:chap. 7.
9. Novichev, Istoriya, 2:137.
10. Lord Ernle, English Farming (London 1961), and Mitchell, p. 498.
11. Novichev, Istoriya, 2:55.
12. Cevdet, Tarih, vol. 9.
13. Quataert, p. 22.
14. However, the United States consul in Izmir stated in 1896: "There has been no especially marked change in prices recently, but the prices of commodities have been gradually advancing for the past ten years"--USSCR, 13 (1896-97), p. 209.
15. Eldem, p. 204; since the last set of figures in the table above refers to Istanbul it is worth noting that in 1913-14 the cost of foodstuffs was lower than in the neighboring European lands, though presumably higher than in Anatolia. Taking Istanbul as 100, the indexes were: Athens 140, Rumania 120, Salonica 117, Bulgaria 106, Cairo 117, Damascus 113, and Baghdad 86--ibid., pp. 203-4.

Prices of Foodstuffs (piastres, decimalized, per oke of 2¾ lbs.)

Year	Place	Wheat Bread	Wheat Flour	Rice	Beef	Mutton	Butter	Sugar	Source
1800	Istanbul	0.30	..	0.70	0.40	0.60	..	5.00	FO 78/31
1828	Istanbul					0.75-1.12[a]			FO 78/171
1828	Salonica	0.25	..	..		0.38[a]	..	..	FO 78/265
1834	Salonica	0.70	..	..		0.95[a]			FO 78/265
1835	Salonica	..	..	1.90					FO 78/265
1836	Keban Maden	0.40							FO 78/289
1837	Salonica	..	0.68	2.15	..	..	..	..	FO 78/314
1841	Bursa	..	1.88	..	..	2.40			FO 78/441
1842	Bursa	..	1.10	2.13	1.45	2.50			FO 78/490
1842	Salonica		1.15	1.55	..				FO 78/490
1844	Izmir	1.12	1.28						FO 78/614
1844	Erzurum	0.60	0.46						FO 78/614
1844	Salonica	1.05							FO 78/612
1844	Bursa	..	1.00	2.25					FO 78/612
1844	Edirne	0.35							FO 78/612
1844	Kayseri	1.00[b]	1.30[b]						FO 78/615
1844	Cyprus	1.24	1.10						FO 78/621
1844	Beirut	1.44	1.20						FO 78/621
1844	Aleppo	1.65[b]	1.58[b]						FO 78/621
1845	Bursa	..	1.00	2.13					FO 78/612
1846	Iskenderun	..	..	..	1.5	1.8			FO 78/1419
1846-53	Mytilene	..	..	..	2.0	2.50			FO 78/1419
1846	Damascus	2.00[b]	1.99[b]						FO 78/621
1847	Salonica	..	1.60						FO 78/700
1847	Salonica hinterland	..	0.35						FO 78/700
1849	Rhodes				2.50		12.00		FO 78/833
1850	Menteşe	1.28			2.56		10.24		FO 198/11
1852	Bursa	0.46							FO 78/905
1853	Izmir		1.50	2.50	2.25		12.00	5.50	HHS V/I-2, vol. 35
1853	Istanbul	..	2.40						FO 78/951
1854	Bursa	..			4.80				FO 78/1023
1854	Istanbul	..	5.00						FO 78/1016
1854	Iskenderun	0.50			1.50[a]		10.00	5.00	A&P 1859/30
1855	Mytilene	..	..	..	2.50	5.00	..	..	FO 78/1419
1855	Mytilene	..	..	..	3.50	5.00	..	..	FO 78/1419
1855	Izmir		4.00	4.50	4.00		22.00	7.00	HHS V/I-2, vol. 35
1855	Izmir	3.50		4.50	4.00	5.50			CC Smyrne 49
1856	Izmir	..	2.50	4.50	4.50	5.50			CC Smyrne 49
1856	Mytilene	..	..	..	4.50	5.00	..	..	FO 78/1419
1856	Diyarbekir	..	..	..	..	1-2	..	..	FO 78/1419
1856	Jaffa[c]				3.1	2.1			FO 78/1419
1856	Mosul	..	..	..	1.5-2[a]		..	..	FO 78/1419
1856	Rhodes[c]	..	..	..	2	..	..	..	FO 78/1419
1856	Rhodes	..	..	..	3	..	..	..	FO 78/1419
1856	Samos	..	..	..	3	3.5	..		FO 78/1419
1856	Varna				1.4[a]				FO 78/1419

Year	Place	Wheat Bread	Wheat Flour	Rice	Beef	Mutton	Butter	Sugar	Source
1856	Tripoli (Syria)	..	..	..	3-3.5	3-4			FO 78/1419
1856	Urfa	..	..	..	1	1.5	..	..	FO 78/1419
1856	Iskenderun	..	..	..	4.5	5.5	..	..	FO 78/1419
1856	Antakya	..	..	..	1.5	2-2.5	..	..	FO 78/1419
1856	Latakia	..	..	..	1.8	2.9	..	..	FO 78/1419
1856	Antep	..	..	..		2.9	..	..	FO 78/1419
1856	Maraş	..	..	..	1.5-3[a]		..	..	FO 78/1419
1858	Diyarbekir				1.0-2.0				FO 78/1419
1858	Iskenderun	1.0			4.5[a]		20.00	11.00	A&P 1859-30
1861	Bursa	..		..	..	..	..	7.25	FO 195/700
1863	Rhodes	1.0	2.00	3.25	3.50	5.00	16.00	5.50	A&P 1864-61
1863	Diyarbekir							9.00	A&P 1865-53
1865	Bursa		1.20		2.88	5.25	12.0-15.0	..	A&P 1866-69
1868	Rhodes	1.25	2.00	3.00	4.00	5.00	15.00	5.50	A&P 1868/ 9-60
1876	Trabzon	1.83	2.75		2.75	4.13	13.75		A&P 1882-70
1879	Kastamonu	0.90							A&P 1880-74
1881	Trabzon	1.83	2.75		2.75	4.58	13.75		A&P 1882-70
1882	Erzurum	0.92			1.60	2.29			A&P 1883-74
1891	Salonica	0.50			1.80				A&P 1893/ 4-97
1900	Average	1.42	2.84	2.22	6.82			2.39	Eldem,p.201
1906	Average	1.70	3.98	2.39	8.41			2.56	Eldem,p.201
1907	Kastamonu	2.00	..	..	3.00	5.00	..	..	A&P 1908-116
1908	Izmir					4.35[a]	15.00		A&P 1911-97
1911	Izmir				6.42[a]		20.00		A&P 1911-97
1912	Average	1.70	4.55	2.73	10.57			2.73	A&P 1911-97
July 1914	Istanbul	1.90		3.00		7.00	20.00	3.00	RC 328

[a]Butcher's meat, unspecified.

[b]Exceptionally high prices because of drought; that for Kayseri stated to be twice the normal level.

[c]Average of last ten years.

SELECTION 2. PRICES OF STAPLE ITEMS OF CONSUMPTION, 1756-1800 (averages in paras, index numbers added, 1779=100)

Elgin to Grenville, 25 March 1801, FO 78/31

	From 1756		To 1779		From 1780		To 1794		From 1795		To 1800	
	Price	Index	Price	Index	Price	Index	Price	Index	Price	Index	Price	Index
Beef	..	..	5	100	10	200	12	240	12	240	16	320
Veal	..	..	9	100	14	156	15	167	18	200	20	222
Mutton	8	80	10	100	16	160	18	180	16	160	24	240
Lamb	10	83	12	100	18	150	20	167	18	150	24	200
Fish of the best quality	20	83	24	100	40	167	50	208	80	333	100	417
Common fish	5	83	6	100	20	333	30	500	20	333	30	500
Bread	..	..	5	100	..	..	10	200	..	..	12	240
Common wine	..	..	3	100	7	233	8	267	..	..	14	467
Barley the cwt.	15	94	16	100	25	156	30	188	50	313	60	375
Straw the cwt.	13	87	15	100	30	200	40	267	..	..	90	600
Firewood	..	..	25	100	40	160	60	240	..	..	70	280
Charcoal the 100 weight	..	..	60	100	..	..	100	167	..	..	200	333
Chickens	4	80	5	100	10	200	20	400	16	320	18	360
Pigeons	..	..	4	100	10	250	12	300	16	400	18	450
Coffee of Moca	..	..	66	100	..	..	100	152	220	333	240	364
Rice	6	86	7	100	8	114	10	143	..	..	28	400
Oil	12	86	14	100	..	..	20	143	..	..	32	229
Soap	13	87	15	100	18	120	20	133	..	..	36	240
Tallow candles	13	81	16	100	26	163	28	175	28	175	40	250
Wax candles	..	..	100	100	..	..	130	130	..	..	160	160
Butter	12	71	17	100	40	235	45	265	40	235	50	294
Milk	..	..	4	100	..	..	6	150	8	200	12	300
Powdered sugar	20	80	25	100	..	..	30	120	110	440	120	480
Loaf sugar	..	..	50	100	..	..	70	140	160	320	200	400
Unweighted Mean		83		100		187		208		278		338

SELECTION 3. ATTEMPT TO PROHIBIT TRANSFERS OF GOLD COINS, 1801

Memorandum of the Porte of 2 July 1801, HHS Türkei II-125--original in French

The rate of the Istanbul sequins, otherwise known as zeri mahbub, fixed at 5 piastres, that of the halves, nisfiye, at 100 paras, of the quarters, rubiye at 50 paras; the old and new findik at 7 piastres, the quarter at 70 paras; the Missir sequin at 4 piastres, the half of the same at 2 piastres; the sequin of Hungary, Germany, and Holland [gulden or florin] under the name of Magiar altuni at 7 piastres; that of Venice at 7½ piastres; the taler at 3 piastres 10 paras--this rate having been thus fixed both for those who receive those currencies and for those who pay them, it is evident that the rise in the rate of exchange of all these different kinds of sequins and other coins relative to the fixed and prescribed rates must necessarily produce inequality in the mercantile operations of the public and cause at one and the same time a rise in prices and a scarcity of goods of all kinds.

Since it is also an admitted fact that some persons who are under the protection of the other honorable Powers and who are engaged in the trade of Aleppo, of Syria, of Baghdad, and of other provinces of this Empire in partnership with Franks have gradually introduced a completely separate kind of trade by sending sequins to the above-mentioned provinces and elsewhere, thereby destroying the internal organization [police] of this Empire; moreover following the principle that trade must be the same for all, if prohibitions are applied only to the subjects of the Sublime Porte and do not hold the protégés of the other Powers within bounds, the regulation cannot have any consistency; and being far from challenging the power which every state has to take measures concerning its internal organization, particularly when dealing with prohibitions in matters causing such prejudice; based on all this and the necessity in which the Sublime Porte finds itself to watch over the enforcement of the above-mentioned regulation, new orders have been issued and sent to Aleppo, to Syria, to Baghdad, and to the other provinces of the Ottoman Empire stating that henceforth no kind of sequin may be sent from the capital outside; that when sequins are discovered and seized with one of the protégés they will be confiscated by the Zarbhane [Mint], on payment however of the value fixed by Supreme Order; that from today such seizure will begin in Constantinople and its neighborhood; but that as regards those coins which are already on their way to be sent to a distant place and which might be subject to some delay, no obstacles will be placed for three months from the date of the present order in order to avoid too great losses and dissensions; but that after three months have passed, these sequins--no matter with whom they are found--shall be taken and confiscated, their kind and quantity and the name and description of the person who held them being noted and the sequins themselves being sent to Constantinople to be handed over to the Mint.

The present Memorandum has therefore been officially transmitted to the Imperial and Royal Internuncio, our friend residing at the Sublime Porte, in order that he may give his instructions to all the protégés and merchants of the Imperial Court as well as to any others who may need them. . . .

SELECTION 4. COMPETITION AND COMMERCIAL PRACTICES IN IZMIR, 1820

David to Under Secretary, Foreign Affairs, CC Smyrne, vol. 36, 3 January 1821

Among the abuses to which commercial rivalry has given birth, there is one that has become truly intolerable, that of the prolonged extensions [suréchéances] or unlimited delays in payment granted to the Levantine merchants by the European traders, who are jealous of each other and are required to sell superabundant quantities of merchandise which they offer at a discount. It hardly needs mentioning that it was the English who first granted these abusive facilities, to crush their competitors and remain sole masters of the markets of Asia.

A second, and no less unfortunate, abuse has also sprung from their speculations. It is the Agio of 2 percent exacted on payments made in good money here. The English, having found it profitable to pick up the foreign coins circulating in Asia--and even the gold coins of the Grand Signior--in order to melt them down, have granted premia of 2 and even 3 percent to those who provided them. The result was that the Levantines were no longer willing to make their payments in these currencies unless they received a premium, and paid in paras those who refused to give it them. To avoid the trouble and losses which would have been unavoidable if large payments were received in this detestable currency, the Europeans have preferred to grant a discount of 2 percent to their debtors in order to be paid in good money; this mutual Agio has become common among all Europeans, but in fact it is the Levantines alone who profit from it, since they have to pay much more than they receive.

When I came to Smyrna, I found these abusive practices in full swing. The prolonged extensions, which had been raised from 3 times 31 days to 3 times 62 and 3 times 93, then ran for 3 times one year and even 3 times 18 months; thus one had to wait 3 or 4 or 5 years to receive payments which should have been settled in three months.

Foreign currencies had completely disappeared from circulation. The export of large

quantities of beşliks[1] by our Frenchmen led to the disappearance of these Ottoman coins.
The mahmudiehs,[2] which had been partly melted down and recoined by the English and the
native counterfeiters, included many coins of low standard and were thoroughly distrusted.
All that remained in circulation were rubiehs,[3] mostly clipped, and paras[4] in bags of 29
piastres. Thus people were very glad to give up 2 percent in order to be paid in good
money, which had become very scarce. The Levantines made this a condition sine qua non for
Europeans, and the latter, forced to submit in order to receive payment after such long
periods, were obliged to impose the same condition on each other, i.e., allowing each other
a deduction of 2 percent.

It was this abuse, together with that of the prolonged extensions and many others that
we managed to abolish by the conventions of September, which in turn were abolished at the
end of October. Hardly one month had passed since the deplorable defection of the English
when four merchants of that nation, forming a committee, presented a request to their consul
asking for the suppression of the Agio in payments to be made by French protégés to English
firms. . . .

[There followed a spirited exchange between the French and British consuls; the matter
was settled by the abrogation of the convention of September 1820--see French Chargé
d'Affaires, Constantinople, to David, 29 January 1821.]

1. Silver coin of 5 piastres.
2. Gold coin of 25 piastres.
3. Gold coin of 2¾ piastres.
4. Small silver coin; 40 paras make one piastre, or 75 centimes.

SELECTION 5. ATTEMPT AT CURRENCY REFORM, 1844

Report on trade of Trabzon by F. J. Stevens, December 31, 1844 FO 78/614

. . . The restoration of the Current Coin of the Realm to a proper standard, was a
measure which could not but be approved; yet, like many Reforms in Turkey, it has been carried out in so objectionable a manner, as to have occasioned great inconvenience, and the
advantage to be derived from the measure seems to be indefinitely deferred. The monetary
circulation here was composed of a small proportion of Turkish Coin, and larger ones of
Russian and Persian; all passed above their legitimate value, and of all the current value
was very considerably reduced by the Sultan's Firman. This was so peremptory and the penal-
ties of disobedience so severe, that for a time every one was afraid to act in opposition
to it. The richer holders of specie, however, wouldnot submit to the heavy loss the Firman
would have imposed on them, and withheld their Coin; and those only whom necessity obliged
to pass the money they possessed, were sufferers; consequently the loss fell on the persons
least able to bear it; meantime specie became very scarce, and payments were suspended. At
length the Pasha set the example of an infringement of the Firman by paying the troops in
Coins at a higher value than that fixed, and they again circulated at nearly their former
rates. The Pasha has republished the Firman at intervals, and each time the same consequences ensued. Turkish Coin has since almost entirely disappeared, and for want of small
money, great difficulty is felt in the minute transactions of every day. Scarce a piece of
the new Coinage has been seen here, and there does not appear any prospect of a supply being sent from the Capital. In short, the results of the measure hitherto felt here have
been loss to the poorer classes, interruption to trade, and more or less embarrassment to
all.

BANKING AND AGRICULTURAL CREDIT

At the beginning of the nineteenth century banking activity in the Ottoman Empire was
concentrated in the hands of the Galata bankers, a group that had arisen shortly after the
conquest of Constantinople to serve the financial needs of the government. Its members
were Levantines, Jews, Armenians, and Greeks; until the seventeenth century the Jews had
been predominant but after that Armenians, and still more Greeks--who had widespread commercial and shipping contacts with Europe--played the major role (2:15).

"The Galata bankers performed three types of services: the exchange of currencies,
the granting of loans, and the discount of receivables. In dealing with the court or the
government, the collateral was often in the form of anticipated tax receipts, in cash or
in kind; and thus the banker eventually acquired the position of a tax farmer and tax collector."[1] Tax-farming contracts were auctioned by the Treasury, and the highest bidder
had to appoint a sarraf (money changer) as a surety; only sarrafs with a license from the
Treasury could be thus appointed. In addition to the interest earned from the sums paid to

the Treasury on behalf of the tax farmers the _sarrafs_ profited from the chronic needs of the Treasury, which met temporary deficits by borrowing from them repaying the following year.

The _sarrafs_ were also indispensable for the transfer of funds, as is clearly described in a _ferman_ of Muharram 1218 (May 1802) (HHS Türkei II, 132--1803, VII-XII): "It is impossible that all the sums provided by the tax farms of Miri [Land tax], customs duties, and other revenues levied and gathered by the collectors and agents appointed by my Sublime Porte in the vast stretch of the Ottoman provinces should be paid in cash into the coffers of the Sublime Porte. For this reason, the greater part of the said revenues is usually transmitted by bills of exchange, and all merchants, whether Muslim or Christian, whether subjects or Franks, established in Baghdad, in Egypt or Syria, in Aleppo, in Erzurum, Diyarbekir, Izmir, Salonica, Edirne, Belgrade, in Morea, in Jannina, and in other places subjected to Ottoman dominion, are in the habit of mutually settling their debits and credits by this means." The _ferman_ goes on to state that, recently, merchants who had accepted these bills had refused payment when due on various pretexts, and it ordered this practice stopped. Both the commercial transactions of the bankers and their dealings with the Treasury were facilitated by a _ferman_ of 1795 legalizing the collection of interest.[2]

The growth of trade and government expenditure necessitated a more developed banking system. In 1842 the Banque de Smyrne was founded, at the initiative of some British merchants; the shareholders included subjects of Britain, France, Austria, Russia (many of them Greek), Netherlands, Greece, Sardinia, the United States, Tuscany, Denmark, and Spain (see list in FO 195/178). The following year, however, the bank was closed by the government.[3]

The Banque de Constantinople survived only slightly longer. Founded in 1847 by two prominent Galata bankers, Alleon and Baltazzi (7:8), together with the government, its main objective was to stabilize the exchange rates (7:1). Its authorized share capital of 100 million piastres was not subscribed and it began operations with 25 million piastres supplied by the government. The French revolution of 1848, which disrupted Ottoman trade, struck it a mortal blow and it closed down in 1852. Between March 1848 and March 1850 it had issued bills and letters of credit totalling 810.3 million piastres and incurred a loss of 26.3 million.[4]

In 1856, following the promulgation of the Hattı Hümayun, which had proclaimed the need for "banks and other similar institutions," the Ottoman Bank was founded in London, with a capital of £500,000. At first its activity was purely commercial but, after the 1861 crisis, the government's need for an institution to help it manage its increasingly strained finances led to a change in 1863: French capital combined with British to transform the Bank into the Imperial Ottoman Bank, with note-issuing privileges.[5] The latter did not prove very important: note circulation rose to £T325,000 in 1874, fell sharply to 18,000 in 1878, and then rose slowly to a peak of £T1,300,000 in 1906, after which it dropped again.[6] But until the Public Debt Commission took over in 1881 (7:16) it helped the government service its debt, and after that it aided it in floating new loans. It opened branches in numerous towns[7] and by 1907 its current deposits amounted to £T10.4 million, its fixed-term accounts to £T1.4 million, and its advances to £T7.1 million.

The Ottoman Bank was followed by several others, e.g., Société Générale de l'Empire Ottoman in 1863, Crédit Général Ottoman in 1868, Banque Austro-Ottomane in 1871, Banque Austro-Turque in 1872 (the two latter representing an unsuccessful attempt by Austrian capital to replace French, temporarily affected by the defeat of 1870), Banque de Constantinople

and Société Ottomane de Change et de Valeurs, Russian Bank, Italian Oriental Bank, Banque
de Crédit Industriel, and others. Most of them did not survive the 1873 crisis, a few amal-
gamating with the Ottoman Bank and the rest being liquidated.

A new chapter started in 1887 with the opening of a branch at Izmir by the Crédit Lyonnais, soon followed by the Deutsche Bank. By 1912 the following foreign banks also operated
in Turkey: Deutsche Orientbank, Wiener Bank Verein, Banque Russe, Banco di Roma, Banque d'
Athènes, and Banque d'Orient. Banks incorporated in Turkey included: Banque de Salonique
(1888), Anglo-Levantine Banking Co. (1908), with a capital of ŁT100,000, one-quarter paid
up; Banque Nationale de Turquie (1909), capital ŁT1,100,000, one-quarter paid up, Banque
Commerciale Ottomane (1910), ŁT100,000, one-quarter paid; and Banque de Turquie (1910),
ŁT550,000, fully paid.[8] These banks rendered a great service to trade, and helped bring do
down short-term interest rates, which had been very high (7:6).[9] But only the Banque Nationale was primarily designed to finance industry and mining and none of them made any significant contribution to agriculture.

Farmers obtained short-term credit from landlords and moneylenders. The replies to a
circular in 1863 (FO 195/771) show the rates charged and procedures followed. In the Edirne
region interest was 2 percent a month or higher; "in some districts the lender, instead of
taking interest, makes an arrangement with the farmer to take his crop at a lower price than
market value at harvest time," thus leading him into debt. Near Istanbul the average was
20-30 percent a year; here too crops were sold in advance below market value, the usurer
"giving himself a very large margin to secure himself" against bad harvests and other eventualities. At Enez interest was 20-25 percent a year and at Gelibolu 20, "and glad to pay
it," but if badly in debt the farmer would pay "what the Greek or Armenian creditor exacts."
In Salonica loans were usually on personal security and interest was seldom below 20 percent;
Christian and lower-class Turks paid promptly, but upper class Turks, once they got into
debt, fell deeper and ended by having to sell their land; however "before they do so, [they]
give their creditors much trouble and put them to a great deal of expense."

Conditions in the Anatolian provinces were somewhat worse. In the Dardanelles farmers
borrowed 3-4 months before harvest and delivered the crop at 5-10 percent below the market
price, "which at harvest time is usually lower than at other times"; in some parts interest
was 15 or even 25 percent for a few months; "although the borrower is occasionally in arrears with the delivery of part of the produce, the lender very seldom incurs any losses."
"The people more rarely borrow on the security of title deeds of their landed property
though almost everyone in the country is a landowner"; such loans were seldom for less than
a year and carried 12-20 percent interest. In Izmir the normal rate was 1½-2 percent a
month, but in fact more was paid; loans were usually for Ł2 to Ł10 but when sums of Ł200 to
Ł300 were needed the title deeds were "transferred to the lender in the Turkish Court under
the title of 'Istillal' [istiğlal] Mortgage." In Diyarbekir landlords advanced funds according to the area sown, some 60-100 piastres per keyl; no interest was charged but at
harvest time they "share alike" with the peasant "who then also repays them the money borrowed"; in bad years the debt was transferred, without interest. "Capitalists" charged
2-3 percent a month, with no security except the right to sell the debtor's cattle; "losses
are however rare and then only when the lender presses for his money. With a little management and patience all great risks may always be avoided." Finally, in Cyprus rates were
12-20 percent, in Acre 24-40, and in Jerusalem 24-36 per annum; in Baghdad they were 15-20
percent, the cultivator undertaking to deliver produce at 15-20 percent below market price.
In Rhodes in 1858 money was "usually advanced on land at 18-24 percent" (Reply to Questionnaire, FO 78/1419).

To remedy this situation, the government, in 1844, ordered provincial agricultural councils (5:12) "to grant loans to qualified applicants engaged in agriculture, commerce, and industry,"[10] but the effect of this was negligible. In 1863 the reformer Midhat paşa started credit cooperatives (sandık) in the Danubian provinces; these spread rapidly, helped by government contributions, but were subject to abuse. In 1888, therefore, the government founded the Agricultural Bank with a capital of ŁT2,210,000, raised in 1900 to ŁT6,749,000 and in 1913 to ŁT11,223,000;[11] in addition to taking over the capital and outstanding loans of the sandıks the Bank received the proceeds of a surtax on the tithe. In 1889 the Bank had 331 branches and 466 by 1908. Its new loans rose from ŁT163,000 in 1889 to ŁT508,000 in 1900 and ŁT1,122,000 in 1913, and the total outstanding was ŁT2,924,000 in 1900 and ŁT5,869,000 in 1913.[12]

There is no doubt that the Bank, which charged only 6 percent, was a great help to many farmers.[13] But it suffered from two major defects. First, it could meet only a small fraction of agricultural credit needs. Secondly, its procedures were cumbrous: "The formalities, delays, and exigencies of the bank rules, and the unscrupulousness of the generality of the officials connected with those establishments keep the peasant away, as the inducements and advantages held out to him are not sufficient to make him close accounts with his 'outside' partner, whose terms of credit, though seemingly more onerous, are unaccompanied by any sort of formality, and who is more lenient and less exacting in case of a bad season. The consequence is that only about half the capital at their disposal is employed."[14]

Fifteen years later the funds of the Bank were judged to be inadequate, especially as some of the funds were being used by the government for other purposes. Moneylenders were still charging 5 percent a month and in addition had the right to buy the debtor's crop at a price below that of the market. Moreover the usurer was often a merchant who, instead of advancing money, sold the debtor goods at inflated prices. In such circumstances the real rate of interest was as high as 100 percent and a peasant could never free himself from debt but "in fact, works for him [the creditor] all his life."[15] Clearly, the problem of agricultural credit was still unsolved.

1. Grunwald and Ronall, p. 2.
2. Ibid., p. 10.
3. Kurmuş, p. 307.
4. Du Velay, pp. 126-29.
5. Biliotti, pp. 19-20; du Velay, pp. 189-96. Both before and after the foundation of the Ottoman Bank there were projects for an Imperial National Bank, with a capital of Ł2 million and branches all over the country, which would undertake all kinds of commercial business, issue notes, and help the government withdraw the paper money in circulation. Naturally, the Ottoman Bank was opposed to this project and in 1858 accepted, in principle, the doubling of its capital by adding Ł500,000 provided by the local capitalists supporting the Imperial National Bank project (TE, Boxes 18 and 27, 1856 and 1858). For much fuller details on the Ottoman Bank, Crédit Lyonnais, and some other banks, see Thobie, pp. 83-94.
    In 1857, there was another project, for a National Bank of Turkey. This seems to have received a concession in May 1858 which was cancelled in 1863, when the Ottoman Bank was enlarged (ibid., Boxes 23 and 62, 1857 and 1863).
6. Biliotti, p. 155.
7. In 1905 it had nine branches in the European provinces and twenty-six in the Asian, as well as in Cyprus and Egypt--Young, 5:30; for text of concession Young, 5:30-52.
8. Du Velay, pp. 197-205; Marouche and Sarantis, pp. 26-37; the Banque de Metelin was founded in 1891 and closed in 1911. Deposits in the main banks rose from ŁT5,540,000 in 1888 to ŁT10,580,000 in 1900 and ŁT22,790,000 in 1913, and advances increased correspondingly--Eldem, p. 234.
9. "At present [early 1860s] the Armenian saraffs have a monopoly of the business. For ordinary commercial discounts they demand the most usurious rates; while for small sums, at short dates, and with first rate security, they do not hesitate to charge from 3 to 6 percent per month" (Farley, Turkey, p. 195).
10. Quataert, p. 129; see pp. 129-54 for a thorough study of the Agricultural Bank.

11. Atasağun, p. 139; texts in Young, 5:342-54.
12. Atasağun, p. 261.
13. At the turn of the century the bank was making some 50,000 loans a year in Anatolia, of an average value of about 700 piastres—table in Quataert, p. 375.
14. A and P 1895, vol. 100, "Angora."
15. RC 1911, no. 293.

SELECTION 6. INTEREST RATES IN SALONICA, 1848

Report on Trade of Salonica, 1848, FO 78/794

. . . Taking the liberty of referring your Excellency to my remarks respecting usurious interests in my dispatch no. 34 of the 24th October last, I am happy in being able to report that His Excellency Riza Pasha has declared to the Council of Salonica, that he will no longer permit the onerous charges of Towaddieh (Commission), Kallemyieh (pen Money), Icramyieh (Service money) in all, amounting to 7½ p. Cent, charged by the Usurers in their banking accounts, over and above the rate of interest of 20 p. Cent. I may also add, that the money advanced by these Bankers, is always, what is termed, high money, that is Foreign Coin, but the payments are demanded (or it would be more correct to say, extorted) in Turkish 5 p. pieces, upon which there is a difference of 5 p. Cent and some times even 7 p. Cent so that the rate of Interest actually charged is Viz.

Interest	20 p. Cent.
Commissions	7½ p. Cent.
Average Agio	5 do.
	32 p. Cent.

added to which the bonds are renewed every three months, so that with the rate of Interest 20 p. Cent, commissions and Agio 12½ p. Cent, and compound Interest added thereto the security for the Capital is soon absorbed, hence further observations are needless as to the ruin of such a system. . . .

SELECTION 7. REVENUES OF OTTOMAN EMPIRE, 1800[*]

Lord Elgin to Lord Grenville, FO 78/29

Constantinople, May 28th, 1800

My Lord,
    I have the honour to inclose for Your Lordship's information a statement of the actual revenues of the Ottoman Empire - the administration of its finances, its public expenditure, and its Military Force.
    In a Government so little accustomed to regularity or precision in any branch of public business, Your Lordship must not rely on the perfect accuracy of the inclosed details. In our present connexion, however, with this country, I have thought it my duty to submit to Your Lordship the best accounts of these subjects, which I have hitherto been able to procure, as furnishing materials for any future enquiries to which You may wish me to direct my attention.

General Table of the Finances of the Ottoman Empire

Revenues of the Grand Signior, Tributes, Harac, Mukataa, Bedele Nusul (buying out of quarter [rachat de quartier]) Avariz-Hane (extraordinary or casual [casuelle] contribution on houses), Cebelaiyan (conscription), Evkaf-Humayun (royal bequest or royal foundation), Cebelaiyan-Emlak (real estate conscription) Havasi-Humayun (royal domain or royal revenues), Ceibi Humayun (royal purse), Peskies [peşkeş?]-Zaise [caize?] (customary gifts), Mevkuf-Taraphane-Amire (succession [échute] dues to Mint), Haramein Şerifein Hazinesi (Treasury of Mecca and Medina).

Revenues of Province of Rumelia	Purses of 500 piastres
For harac of Constantinople and surroundings, paid by rayahs who are not Turks	2,916
(360 purses are the yield of a new impost of the year 1786, of which only 100 go to the Public Treasury)	
For harac of Andrinople and surroundings	1,750
Sofia, idem	320
Tatar basargik [bazarcik]	250
Philipopoli [Plovdiv]	280
Salonica	530
Uschiup [Uskup, Skoplje]	260
Kiostendil [Köstendil]	226
Terhale	450
Yeniscehr-Kienar [Yenişehir-kenar]	270

[*][I owe this text to Prof. D. Skiotis.]

Avlonia [Valona]	350
Ohry [Ochrida]	250
Delvine	170
Elvisan [Elbasan]	160
Bania	450
Kisrie	250
Ozie [Ozü?]	90
Silistria	170
Varna	170
Babadagh	100
Paravadi [Provadie]	160
Karinabad	180
Eghri-bozuk	190
Ruschzuk [Ruschuk]	220
Hezargarad	90
Sciumna [Shumna]	170
Niceboli [Nigbolu?]	390
Harmen	260
Vidin	300
Islemie	150
Uzungi-abad Haskioy	176
Gallipoli	240
Napoli di Romanie [Nauplia?]	225
Orse	70
Inebauli	210
Negroponte	500
Isdien	96
Belgrade	180
Nissa [Nish]	196
Alassonia	170
Tif	45
Kiordos	70
Athens	90
Ienikie [Yeniköy]	220
Hatevmis	120
Calamata	130
Enghili-Kasry	170
Livadie	70
Tancara	90
Donige	80
Alexandria	290
Bosnia and its dependencies	1,495
Bender and Chotzim [Chotin]	200
Morea with its five jurisdictions yields annually	3,560
Total Revenues of Rumelia	20,515
Piastres 10,107,500 [sic]	

Revenues of the Provinces of Anatolia

Hudavendighiar sangiaghi	280
Province of Kiutahia	480
Jurisdiction of Eskischehr	120
of Sultanony	130
of Karahissar	160
Government of Angora	190
Jurisdiction of Tussia	180
of Kistin	75
of Boli	90
of Viranschehr	75
of Hissarony	120
of Aktcheschehr	110
Carasu [Karasu]	55
Ghiul-bazar	80
Government of Castimony	190
Jurisdiction of Sinop	150
Jurisdiction of Tyr	50
Sultanony	70
Ghiuzel hissar	90
Ala schehr	80
Metmen	90
Government of Mentesche	150

Of Smyrna	320
Of Akscha Schehr	120
Of Sahri hisar [Şehrihisar?]	125
Island of Kursch adassi	150
Jurisdiction of Ghiuzel hissar	160
Of Hamed	300?
Of Jali Kesri [Yalikasri]	80
Of Sandughi	50
Government of Beigha [Biga]	160
Carasse [Karasu]	40
Teke	27
Alaye [Alanya?]	210
Isenghemid	450
Ala	110
Sivas	490
Tokat	200
Nikde [Nigde]	120
Yenischehry	210
Ieni Il [Yeni il]	90
Amassia	180
Bozauk [Bozacik?]	70
Zuvem	150
Dsanitz	800
Dyunik [Canik?]	120
Arabkir	320
Province of Caramania	200
Askery	210
Kaisserie	120
Ac Serray [Ak sarai?]	120
Adana	200
Silis [Cilicia?]	110
Ic Il [Içel?]	300
Ekin	90
Tripoli of Syria	120
Damascus	400
Aleppo	600
Kelis	120
Agraz	70
Miras [Maraş]	200
Anitab [Aintab]	240
Government of Malatia	120
Rica [Rize?]	200
Ahmed	110
Hisni Mansur	80
Diarbekir	300
Mussil	300
Erzerum	450
Trebisonda [Trabzon]	300
Gelder	200
Van	110
Karis [Kars]	150
Baghdad, Basra, Mardin and surroundings	500
Island of Tenedos	45
Meteline	180
Schio [Chios]	380
Stanchio [Istanköy?]	150
Candie [Crete]	560
Cyprus	850
Tine	45
Islands dependent on Kapudan paşa	180
Cairo	1,350
Other revenues in separate account	<u>1,455</u>
	19,182

Piastres 9,591,000

Revenues of <u>Mukatas</u> or Tax Farms

<u>Mukatas</u> registered in the <u>Baş Muhasebe</u>, i.e., main Accounting Office, numbering 812, yield annually	4,791
The <u>ocalik</u> of the Bulgarians pays	520
The ağalik of the Turkomans	450
The Bohemian Corps [Gypsies?]	2,690
Revenue of <u>cebelaiyan-evkafi-humayun</u>	280
Idem <u>emlak-humayun</u>	350
Idem <u>cebelayan</u> of <u>timars</u> and <u>ziamets</u> belonging to old men or adolescents	470
Revenues of <u>bedeli nusul</u>, <u>timars</u> and <u>ziamets</u> of Rumelia and Anatolia	3,580
Of <u>avariz-hane</u>	2,959
Of tobacco tax farming, silver and tin mines and contributions of administrators of same	2,300
Revenues of Wallachia and Moldavia	450
Revenues of <u>mukata</u> dues and <u>mizan</u> [weighing] dues on silk, mastic, oil etc. of the fiscal office (<u>comptoire</u>) of Bursa	790
Revenue of dues paid by sheep merchants in Anatolia and Rumelia	780
Revenues of saltpans etc. registered in the fiscal office (<u>comptoire</u>) of Uuslar	1,200
Revenues of fish, forests, the ports [échelles] of Meteline and dues on weights of Constantinople	2,800
Revenues of department of Imperial kitchen, paid by cities, towns and villages to which they are assigned	1,300
Revenues on tax farms of butchers	600
Revenues of the customs house of Constantinople	1,872
Revenues of tobacco customs	1,287
(of which 855 purses are for the owners of <u>malikianes</u>, 232 to the <u>mufti</u> and 200 to the imperial treasury)	
Revenues of houses bequeathed to Arsenal	1,280
Dues of tobacco customs house of Arabia and on the (<u>stades</u>) of same (of which 400 to owners, as above, and the other 300 to the imperial treasury)	700
Revenues of tax farms of the towns of Mecca and Medina	2,800
Revenues of other small tax farms, given to charities	<u>2,995</u>
Total of fixed revenues of Ottoman Empire Piastres 18,622,000	37,244

Amounts Due (<u>Rentes éventuelles</u>)

From <u>muacele</u> (arrears) of <u>mukatas</u>	5,777
Due from confiscated properties and from estates	1,327
From <u>muacele</u> of tobacco customs	3,065
From tax farms of Cairo	1,650
From tobacco tax farms, according to new regulations	400
<u>Zaise</u> [caize] of Viziers and other Ministers	1,800
There are other revenues which will also be due, for example on the nomination of a vizier or other Minister of the Porte, etc.	
Total of revenues due Piastres 7,009,500	14,019

Annual Expenditure	Divani Purses
Pay of Constantinople troops	22,700
Pay of <u>bostancis</u> and those of kitchen of Grand Signior	700
Ağas, officers of Palace of Grand Signior	1,700
Harem of Old Palace	1,800
Eunuchs of Grand Signior	800
Ağa of Seraglio of Galata	501
Expenses of kitchen (in <u>rumi</u> purses)	1,800
To <u>kassab-başi</u> [meat supplier]	600
To <u>arpa-emini</u> [barley supplier] for expenses of imperial stables	600
Sundry (assignations arbitraires)	1,250
Gift to Mecca and Medina	9,000

Pay of sailors of the Fleet	2,700
For their provisioning	800
Expenses of Admiralty	1,800
Pensions to Sultanas, and to Khans of the Portes	1,372
Pay of garrison of Vidin	1,250
Pay of other fortress of Ottoman Empire	18,000
Of Bosnia	1,970
For upkeep of recruits	472
Expenditure of second fiscal agency (comptoire) or kuçuk kalemi	
Pay of guards along Danube	3,521
Upkeep of Posts	1,700
Total, Divani purses	75,036

Equals Piastres 31,714,176

N.B. Divani purses are valued at 50,000 aspers or
piastres 416, Rumi purses at piastres 500.

Debts of Public Treasury

To treasury of Mecca and Medina, piastres	1,350,000
To Privy Purse (Trésor Particulier) of Grand Signior	45,500,000
To Arsenal	6,500,000
Piastres	53,350,000

Owed to Public Treasury

From tobacco customs, piastres	3,786,000
From different revenues, still due	6,000,000
Balance of revenues due this year, 1786, to Treasury	7,280,480
	17,066,480

The Public Treasury, or miri, owes   36,283,520

N.B. To the Fixed Revenues should be added 300 purses given
by Wallachia and Moldavia as Zaise [caize?]

Total of Revenues of Ottoman Empire

Rumelia, purses	20,215	— piastres	10,107,500
Anatolia, purses	19,182	— piastres	9,591,000
Tax Farms,	37,544	— piastres	18,772,000
Amounts Due (rentes éventuelles)	14,019	— piastres	7,009,500
	90,960		45,480,000

State of Troops of Ottoman Empire

In peacetime, this Empire has 225,000 men, including the Cossacks and the Tatars of
Bessarabia, viz:

30,000 Janissaries and 20,000 Topcis (artillery) in Constantinople	50,000
Janissaries in Egypt	10,000
Artillery in provinces	8,000
Serhad-quli (frontier troops)	50,000
Sipahis (horsemen)	20,000
Horsemen in provinces	75,000
Horsemen on frontiers	12,000
	225,000

The Payment of the troops of the New System comes out of the Fund (Caisse) of the New
System (Iradi-Gedid) which has a separate administration known as Iradi-Gedid Tefterdari.
The said Fund receives all State Revenues destined for military purposes (aux Fraix de la
Guerre).

In Europe Wallachia and Moldavia, the Governments of Syria, Caramania and in general
all the provinces of Anatolia, the whole of Egypt in Africa--except for certain provinces
of Rumelia in Europe--constitute completely separate governments which, although subject
to the orders of the Grand Signior, nevertheless administer their finances apart and raise
from within their borders all the troops required for maintaining the internal and external
security of their province. For example, the Province of Baghdad (Babylon) with Basra,
Mardin etc. always keep 30,000 Janissaries under arms (sur pied) to man the frontier for-
tresses and to provide security against Persia, whose incursions are a threat; in times of
war against Persia, this province and other neighboring ones, organized in the same manner,

raise over 100,000 men, and have often carried on the war against the Persians and other tribes (peuplades) with no other help or subsidy.

In addition to the fixed revenues of the Empire, one should note the profits made by the Porte on Tithes, over the extent of the whole Empire; on Ziamets and Timars (military fiefs) which in the past were administered by private persons but are now only by the Head of the aforesaid Fund (Caisse); on the customs levied on goods; and on the Tobacco Tax Farms all over the Empire, the revenues of which have been paid since the year 1790 into the said Fund. The new tax on wine, at 2 paras per oke and on brandy at 4 paras; the tax on wool and goat hair, at one para per animal; the payments into the said Fund by the Farms on Cotton--formerly given to private persons--and which have been raised up to one para per oke on cotton fibre and two paras on yarn; the duty of one para per oke on Gall nuts and of two on Corinth raisins; the duty of one para per tree on silk mulberry trees--all these revenues put together make up, according to the most accurate calculations for the year 1798 (1212 A.H.) a total of thirty two million, two hundred and fifty thousand piastres, a revenue which is increasing very considerably each year.

Conclusion:

Revenue according to calculations made in 1786	45,480,000 piastres
Revenue of New System according to calculations made in 1798	32,250,000 piastres
Grand total	77,730,000

SELECTION 8. GOVERNMENT REVENUE AND EXPENDITURE, 1844

Observations de M. J. Alléon sur l'Etat Financier de la Turquie, CC Constantinople, vol. 80

. . . According to the statements drawn up in the Ministry of Finance, the whole of this year's revenue, including the tribute paid by Egypt, amounted to a total of 600,000,000 piastres of the Grand Signior.

Expenditure during the same year came up to:

Sultan's Civil List	60 million
Expenditure on 100,000 soldiers which the government must maintain each year, according to the statements, including clothing, arms, equipment, pay of paşas, generals etc.	300 million
Expenses of arsenal	25 million
Expenses of evkaf	12.5 million
Expenses of powder-mill and arms (harbiye)	10 million
Expenses of artillery (tophane)	14 million
To meet life annuities and arrears (mukata) taken over by the Government	72 million
Salaries of employees	55 million
Extraordinary expenditure, movement of troops, construction and repair of barracks	20 million
Amount due to trade by the Supplier-General (masraf)	55 million
Arrears due by provinces which will never be paid (bakaye)	35 million
Amount of interest at 10 percent paid on the 60 million of paper (kayme) in circulation	6 million
Expenses which are being and will be incurred to keep up the cadres of 50,000 men still to be recruited, of whom 40,000 in Syria, in order to reach the figure of 150,000 men and the expenses that will be incurred by these 50,000 men when they have been recruited	150 million
Total	814.5 million
Deducting Revenue	600 million
Deficit Balance	214.5 million

To this should be added the 75 million due to the Sultan on arrears to his Civil List, and which the Ottoman Ministry of Finance will be able to pay only when the Treasury will have the necessary funds

	75 million
	289.5 million
Amount of Paper Money[1]	60 million
Total Deficit	349.5 million

1. The Treasury has already received these funds; the paper is entirely held, at the present time, by capitalists which is why it is not in circulation (I myself hold over 10 million); but at any moment it could all be suddenly presented to the Treasury if, as is probable, the government should increase the amount in circulation in order to raise funds or if, on the other hand, it should successively reduce the annual interest paid by it below the present 10 percent, as has been suggested. If the rate should be reduced to 8 percent but the quantity of paper in circulation not increased, capitalists would probably continue to hold on to what they have—that is, assuming the country remains quiet. The danger of the existing paper being discredited and dumped on the Treasury would arise as soon as the government reduced the rate to, say, 6 percent. In that case it is likely that all the capitalists who held such paper (and I myself in the first place) would prefer to transfer their funds to Europe—particularly since that can be done at the favorable exchange rate of 110 piastres per pound sterling or 172 paras per franc. By doing this, they can be sure of finding investments far less subject to the risk of a sharp decline than is Turkish paper money, whose quantity can be increased by the government at will—not to mention the anxiety already felt in trading circles, and which will grow later, regarding the consequences that might result from the expiration of the contract we made with the government to prevent the pound sterling from exceeding the rate of 110 piastres. If, as I said, this contract is not renewed with us or with other bankers, the exchanges and commercial transactions will, as in the past, be subjected to perturbations as long as the beşlik and 20-para pieces continue to flood the country and as long as the new gold and silver currency has not replaced them, if not totally at least in part.

Constantinople, 1 April 1844

SELECTION 9. GOVERNMENT SALARIES AND EXPENDITURES IN THE 1840s

From Ahmet Cevdet Paşa, _Tezakir-i Cevdet_ (Ankara, 1953), 1:18-22

. . . The officials of cabinet (vizir) rank had excellent allowances in addition to their monthly salaries ranging from 60,000 to 100,000 kuruş. Other important officials, in addition to salaries ranging between 30,000 and 50,000, received adequate allowances for bread and meat. Furthermore, most ministries were allocated expense allowances. Especially, the revenues collected by the Ministry of the Treasury amounted to a great deal as, at that time, 1,000 kuruş were equal in value to 20 dirhems of gold or 320 dirhems of pure silver.

The chief litigation officer, the head of the chancery, the receiver of the correspondence, and the master of ceremonies at the Sublime Porte belonged to the highest grade, and earned monthly salaries ranging from 12,500 to 20,000 kuruş, and were given adequate allowances for bread and meat; some of them even had further expense allowances. The private secretaries of the Grand Vizir and the foreign minister, the chief scribe of the High Court, the first and second secretaries of the chief litigation officer, and the chief archivist were the second highest grade of officials, who earned monthly salaries ranging from 6,000 to 11,000 kuruş. Some had additional expense allowances and some were simultaneously appointed as representatives of provincial governors in Istanbul and received an additional salary of 1,000 to 2,500 kuruş from such appointments. In the government offices were scores of assistants and clerks who earned the third-grade salary of 3,000-5,000 kuruş per month.

According to the adopted custom, the receiving office of the Sublime Porte employed twenty clerks who were paid 2,500 kuruş monthly salary each, and those who had seniority, more. In the remaining offices of the Sublime Porte, there were clerks of various grades variously salaried within the range of 25 to 2,500 kuruş per month.

The clerks of the Imperial Chancery and of the independent offices of management, religious affairs, and fiefs held fiefs which brought annual revenues within the range of 20,000 to 80,000 kuruş. When such clerks died without children, the revenues of these fiefs were used to pay the salaries of clerks in these offices. Such is the summary of the state of affairs at the Sublime Porte, and the reader may compare the situation of the officials and clerks of other offices with those of the Porte.

The şaihulislam's salary and allowance amounted to 100,000 kuruş per month. At that time there were seventeen or eighteen _kadiaskers_ [chief judges], among whom the one with seniority, that is, the first one to be granted the rank of Rumeli, was called the head of the _ulema_, whether or not he was educated, and received a salary and allowance of 15,000 kuruş per month. The others of the Rumeli rank received salaries of 9,000 kuruş each, and the ones having the rank of Anatolia would receive salaries of 7,000 kuruş each. There were quite a few chief judges of the Istanbul rank who received salaries of 3,500 kuruş per month.

Other men of the pen with sinecures, and professors, received various salaries. While it was possible for public servants to live well on such salaries, dissipation increased day by day. Thus, some officials incurred debts and others received gifts in order to make payments on the residences they purchased in town or on the waterfront. The officials also had quite a substantial income from various donors.

'In addition to the above-mentioned sources of income, people with influence and connections made money through the leasing of tithes and other revenues. Thus, through a moneylender a person would guarantee the payment of a certain sum in lieu of the revenue of a district (multezim), and agree on the sum with an influential person in the government. The influential person, in turn, would request from the government a contract for the payment of the revenue at a lower price. If the Grand Vizir agreed, he received a contract from the minister of the treasury calling for payment of a few thousand purses less than the farmed-out revenue. Thus, much money was made easily. This mode of operation, however, did not benefit everybody: only high government officials got involved in such transactions, which they usually made openly. This, in fact, meant the stealing of the funds of the Imperial Treasury through ingenious machinations. Thus, people of foresight did not carry out such transactions openly, but worked secretly through a moneylender acting as an intermediary. Reşit Paşa received large gifts from the sultan and did not deign to make profit through other means. But only a few high officials were left who did not make money through the farming out of taxes. A great many of them made thousands of purses through such illegal means and spent their money in dissipation.

While Reşit Paşa's partisans had based their platform on fighting corruption, and serving to improve education and civilization, such unpleasant undertakings of theirs caused public opinion to turn against them. Public protests increased. Sultan Abdulmecit called these transactions "theft by contrivance." Hence, the giving of expensive presents to government officials, farming out of tax revenues, and the selling of tithe and tax revenue without public auctioning were banned. Since honorable public servants had never profited from such deeds, they were not adversely affected by the new prohibition. The corrupt ones, on the other hand, started taking bribes secretly and blocking the open auctioning of the tax revenues. People who earned money from such sources could not keep it, but squandered it away. Money easily made was easily spent.

Yet, buying and selling increased in Istanbul. Merchants became rich. At a certain time, many beys, paşas, and ladies from the family of Mehmet Ali of Egypt left that country and came to Istanbul, where they spent the great quantities of money they had brought with them and became an example to the bons vivants. They opened a new era in luxurious living. In particular, the Egyptian ladies preferred Western clothing and jewelry, and the ladies of Istanbul, notably the ladies of the Palace, started imitating them. A large number of the Egyptians purchased houses and villas on the shore and other real estate at high prices. Thus, real estate prices greatly increased and a false wealth developed in Istanbul. In fact, the balance of payments was hurt and trade deficits began. Great quantities of money began to flow to Europe. But, since the civil servants were getting their salaries at the beginning of the year and merchants were reaping great profits from the increased consumer market, nobody thought seriously about the future. Especially in summer, the shores of the Bosphorus and other resort areas were filled with bons vivants, and people avoided mentioning anything that would induce sombre thoughts and dark reflection. Istanbul became like a paradise and each corner of it became a place of pleasure and enjoyment.

Especially after the inception of the ferryboat service, the pleasures of the Bosphorus increased and the price of real estate on the shores of the Bosphorus also rose greatly. But economic balance was lost as the revenues of the state could not meet expenditures. Yet, since the Porte was not well aware of the situation at the Treasury, no serious thought was being given to the deficit. In 1267 [1850] Nafiz Paşa, the minister of the treasury, began complaining, and one day at a meeting of ministers he said that salaries could not be given on the first of the following month, that it was necessary to delay payment of salaries for a week. Those attending were confused and terrified. Everybody began thinking of what would befall them if the state could not meet its payroll demand on the first of the month and, therefore, the Treasury would be considered to have gone bankrupt. Even Reşit Paşa was alarmed and feared the consequences of His Imperial Majesty's reaction when he heard about this situation. A commission was appointed at the High Council of Judicial Ordinances to examine the matters relating to the Treasury. The minister of war Rüştü Paşa, foreign minister Ali Paşa, and the minister of the treasury Halit Efendi were appointed to this commission. Books were brought from the Treasury and examined. It was then seen that the expenditure of the state was much higher than the revenue. Treasury matters were indeed in bad shape. The Treasury was in a state of crise [crisis]. Yet there was no word in the Turkish language that conveyed the meaning of crise. Trying to find a word for crise became a problem. One night we were gathered in Fuat Efendi's kiosk on the Bosphorus and this matter came up. After some searching, the word buhran was found to convey the meaning of crise in Turkish and was accepted as such. In fact the word was used in the official memorandum, "The situation of crisis at the Treasury." In 1268, matters with regard to the Treasury became even more serious. Everybody at the Porte began talking about those matters. Although, to improve matters, the first precaution should have been to cut down on expenditure, it was decided to borrow money. It was mostly Fuat Efendi who recommended this solution. Finally, some gold was borrowed from France.

At that time discord between Reşit Paşa, Damat Fethi Paşa, and Mehmet Ali Paşa came to a head and consequently there was a constant shifting of cabinet members. Aali Paşa was appointed Grand Vizir and Fuat Efendi, foreign minister.

Right at that juncture, Fethi Pasa said to Sultan Abdulmecit, "Your father had two wars with the Russians and lived through many campaigns. He had many pressures on him, yet he did not borrow money from abroad. Your sultanate has passed in peace. What will the people say if money is borrowed?" Upon the which comment the imperial heart was saddened, and the sultan forbade the borrowing of money.

Meanwhile, the agreement to borrow money had already been signed and the Porte decided to go ahead with it. The French ambassador told Fuat Efendi, "I do not like the international climate. It is possible that a war will break out. Do not nullify the accord. You should have some gold in reserve." Thereupon, Fuat Efendi unsuccessfully tried to prevail upon the sultan to change his mind. His Imperial Majesty told Fuat Efendi, "I shall leave this state to my posterity in the same condition that I inherited it. I shall abdicate if this accord is not nullified." Thus, the accord was nullified and the security money that had to be paid was raised among the cabinet ministers. . . .

SELECTION 10. TAXES IN IZMIR REGION, 1844

Report upon the State of the Country around Smirna (1844), FO 195/241

It is a lamentable but undoubted fact, that great misery and destitution prevail among the Majority of the Inhabitants of the Towns and Villages situated in the surrounding Sanjaks of Aidin, Sarouchan, Sigala [Sugla] and Adala.

One of the chief causes of this state of things is the arbitrary and abusive manner in which the Tax on Houses, called "Salghin" is levied in these Provinces.

For example, the Town of Menemen and its dependant villages in this immediate neighbourhood contain about 1,800 Houses, or rather Hovels, each occupied by a single family, who are so extremely poor as to be almost in a state of indigence. No less a sum than p.563,000 is yearly exacted from this small District, which is further augmented by the charges of collection to p.600,000.

About 10 years ago, the amount of this Tax was fixed at p.503,000, but the Porte having at that time given orders that Barracks should be built at Magnesia, at the expense of the Province of Sarouchan, the sum of p.60,000 was added thereto as the proportion payable by the District of Menemen, and altho' the Barracks have long since been finished, this increased contribution continues to [be] levied up to this day, with the utmost rigour.

The mode of collecting this Tax, is as arbitrary and cruel, as the Tax itself is onerous and oppressive. When the unfortunate inhabitants are unable to pay it, they are thrown into prison, and their families, deprived of the means of Subsistence from their labour, are left to starve.

As the only means of regaining their liberty, they are obliged to resort to the ruinous expedient of borrowing money from Usurers, who lend it at the rate of 5 p.ct. p. month, or 60 p.ct. p. annum. It is quite clear that no profits derived from Agriculture can possibly support such a charge, and the natural consequence of so ruinous a system is, the gradual abandonment of the Soil by the Cultivators.

This accounts for the decrease in the Inhabitants of the District of Menemen, which 10 years ago contained, 2,400 Houses. If some salutary and effective measures be not speedily taken to remedy this evil, it is easy to foresee that this once fertile District will become a Desert.

To show in what an absurd and unjust manner Taxes are assessed, it is only necessary to state that the Inhabitants of the rich and flourishing city of Smirna, and its adjacent villages, containing at least 30,000 Houses, many of them of great value, are required to pay only p.1,200,000, while the small, impoverished District of Menemen is taxed at half that sum; the true proportion being only p.72,000.

But it is not to Menemen alone that these remarks are confined. They apply to four fifths of the Towns and villages situated in this part of the country, which are in the same, if not a worse predicament. The Inhabitants whereof are groaning under the exorbitant weight of Taxation imposed upon them, which they are unable to bear.

The Town of Magnesia and the villages in the adjacent District are moderately taxed, but the reason is that half the Town and many of the Villages, belong to the Family of Cara Osman Oglu, and one of its members being the Governor of the Province, he takes good care not to burden his own and his Relations' property too heavily.

Another cause of distress and ruin to the cultivators of the Soil, is the pernicious System, which has again been resorted to, of selling the Tythes (ushur) to the Governor or Mudirs of the Provinces. The Same persons who formerly purchased the Mucatas [Mukataa], so greatly reprobated in, and abolished by the Hatti Scheriff of Gulhane, are now the buyers of the Tythes.

It is a revival of the old vicious System, under a different name and the same abuses which formerly existed, are now again in full force.

When articles of produce are Sought after by Purchasers, and the prices consequently high, the Mudir takes the Tythe in kind, weighing or measuring the goods in a manner extremely advantageous to himself. If on the contrary, there is no demand for Produce, he estimates the Tythe at double its real value, and insists on the payment of the amount in money.

Should complaint be made against these arbitrary and unjust proceedings, to the Pacha of the province no redress would be obtained, and the complainant would perhaps be punished for his audacity, as the Farmers of the Tythes, being the Pacha's creatures and Dependants, he is interested in protecting and supporting them in all their exactions.

The sole object of these persons being to fill their Coffers, they employ the most unscrupulous means for this purpose, and it is to their avidity, that the ruin of the country, and the aversion of the population towards their Rulers, are in a great measure to be attributed.

The following fact may be cited as an example of the expedients to which the authorities resort, in order to enrich themselves at the expense of the people.

In January last the Governor of the Town of Eudemish near Aidin forced the Corporation of Bakers at that place to buy from him 5,000 Killos of wheat, at p.10 p. Killo, while its market price was only p.6½.

This act of injustice was committed with impunity, as the sufferers did not dare to complain of the conduct of the Governor of Eudemish to his Superior the Pacha of Aidin.

Another abuse has been introduced, and is now carried to a great pitch, in the neighbouring Pachaliks; about Two Years ago a Duty on produce sold for consumption in Turkey, called "Iktisabie" was established by a Firman, and fixed at 2½ p. cent.

This rate was not at first exceeded, but not long after the promulgation of the order, the Governors began to increase it, and they now extort as much as 8 p. cent from the Sellers of Produce of every description, whether for internal consumption or exportation. As they act in this respect without any control, and all they exact above 2½ p. ct. goes into their own pockets, there is no knowing how far their rapacity may extend.

The Treaty of 1838 is indirectly infringed by these proceedings, as the 9 p ct. duty was substituted for all other interior Duties (except the Tythe) and it is therein stipulated that its provisions "shall be applicable to all the subjects of the Ottoman Dominions" --the agriculturists are not bound to pay any other duty on these Articles produced by them which are not consumed in Turkey.

The Framers of the Treaty justly considered, that if the Turkish Government received 22 p. ct. Duty on the produce of the Soil, exported, it ought to be satisfied, and it was assuredly on that understanding that the concessions it contains were made, as well as with a view to encourage Agriculture, and thereby to increase the prosperity of the Empire, the resources of which had been diminished by a vicious system of Administration.

If however the grievous burdens which formerly weighed so heavily on Agriculture and Trade are again to be imposed in addition to the Duties stipulated for in the Treaty, that Convention will have proved abusive, instead of a blessing, and ought to be annulled, should this abuse be suffered to continue.

The venality of Turkish Judges (Mollahs) is proverbial, and the administration of Justice in this City, and in the neighbouring Provinces, is deserving of much censure on this score.

The Municipal Councils are no longer efficient. During the Administration of Reschid Pasha, the Members received salaries, but on his retirement from Office, they were abolished, and influential persons do not now think it worth while to belong to them. The consequence is, that the Governors and Mollahs determine all questions and the other Members, who are mere cyphers, and generally their creatures concur in their decision, without daring to offer any opinion of their own.

The manner in which the Haratch has of late been levied here, and in the neighbourhood, has given rise to great complaints.

Soon after the promulgation of the Hatti Scheriff of Gulhane Firmans were issued forbidding the collectors of this Tax to molest or imprison the poorer classes who were unable to pay it. Within the last six months however, the Commissioners charged with taking the Census of the population, have also been employed in levying this Tax. They have forced persons to pay it, who were formerly excused, and in many instances, arrears of 3 and 4 years have been extorted, by violent and harsh treatment.

Others who have not been able to produce the Receipts, for the last two or three Years, which they did not deem it necessary to preserve have been obliged to pay the Tax over again. There are three Rates or Classes of Haratch; the first is fixed at p.60, the second at p.30, and the third at p.15. Individuals of the third class are arbitrarily required to pay the Rate due by the Second, and those of the Second, that of the first. Whatever loss the Porte may have sustained by its leniency in former years, will now be amply compensated, through the zeal of the Commissioners, whose obnoxious proceedings will tend to alienate more and more the affections of the Rayah Population from the Government.

In Conclusion, it may be affirmed, without any fear of contradiction, that Abuses are as rife as ever, in this part of Anatolia, that the Authorities in the Interior, relying no doubt on the Support of their Patrons at Constantinople, are totally regardless of the orders of the Porte, and act in the most arbitrary and unscrupulous manner.

It is true that the punishment of death is no longer inflicted at the caprice of every petty Tyrant, and that exorbitant fines are not so openly imposed as formerly, upon false pretences, but barring those improvements, no other benefit has resulted from the promulgation of the Hatti Scheriff of Gulhane, which in all other respects, has become completely a dead letter.

TAXES

Not surprisingly in a country like the Ottoman Empire, where agriculture was by far the most important activity and where the urban population, particularly that of Istanbul, was exempt from most taxes, taxes on agriculture were the mainstay of government revenue.[1] These took two main forms, tithes (uşr or öşür) and animal tax (ağnam vergisi). Similar taxes had been levied since time immemorial and were taken over by the Ottomans. Under the tımar system peasants handed anything from a fifth to a half of their crops to their "feudal" lord, the sipahi. The gradual replacement of tımar by tax farming (iltizam) increased the scope for abuse, since the enfeebled state had much less control over the tax farmers than it had had over the sipahis, and by the nineteenth century tithes stood at 15-50 percent of crops, in addition to a small land tax.[2] The urban population's burden was much lighter, consisting of market dues (ihtisab resmi) as well as customs duties on exports, imports, and goods moving within the Empire. In addition, both urban and rural non-Muslims paid a head tax (cizye) in return for exemption from military service and retention of their traditional laws and customs.

"The main financial goals of the Tanzimat reformers involved shifting the tax burden from the land to urban wealth, supplanting indirect with direct tax collection by salaried agents of the state, replacing the excise taxes, which were levied mainly on households and land plots regardless of ability to pay, and abolishing many of the historic exemptions which had been granted over the centuries,"[3] e.g. to vakıfs, and various localities in return for special services such as providing soldiers, sailors, or labor for fortifications, roads, or forests, or for historic reasons (7:14). Effective reform began at the end of Mahmud II's reign. In 1830 the cizye was simplified. In 1839 it was decided that all taxes were to be collected by salaried agents of the state, and censuses and cadastres were taken for that purpose. In the cities a profits tax (temettü vergisi) replaced market and excise taxes; in practice, it was delayed till 1860, when it was applied at the rate of 3 percent, raised to 4 in 1878 and 5 in 1886, at which date it was extended to salaries and wages. Under the Young Turks, differentiated rates were imposed on various incomes. Foreigners remained exempt until the First World War, which further increased their competitive advantage over Ottoman businessmen.

As for agriculture, following the Hattı şerif of 1839, the ancient Muslim distinction between öşür and harac land was abolished and all land was subjected, in principle, to a 10 percent tax, as was livestock. But shortage of trained personnel made it necessary to return to tax farming in 1842, for two-year periods, which in 1847 were extended to five years; tax farmers were supposed to earn a profit of 2 percent a year and the basis of assessment was the average tithe paid in the previous three years. In 1853, owing to the financial strain of the Crimean War, tithes were put to auction. Various other methods were tried in the next thirty years but in 1885 tax farming was restored.[4] From that date until the First World War, some 90-95 percent of tithes were farmed and the rest collected by government agents.[5] The Tithes Law of 1889 and its subsequent modifications stipulated that payment of the tithes should be in kind, except for certain crops where payment was in specie.[6] Tax farms were to be granted for one year (two years for olives), and were to cover only one village, except in specified cases where several villages--or even a whole kaza or sancak--could be auctioned as a unit. If bids were too low the government could collect the tax directly. Farmers could not dispose of their crops until they had paid the tithe.

The basic rate of the tithe was 10 percent, but some provinces, e.g., Aydın, levied a

surtax. In 1883, a central surtax of 1 percent was imposed, to finance agricultural credit
institutions (7:6) and one of 1/2 percent for education. A further surtax of 1/2 percent
was added in 1897--probably in connection with the Greek war--and one of 0.63 per cent for
armaments in 1900, raising the total to 12.63 per cent which, in 1906, was reduced to 12.5
to simplify calculations and protect cultivators.[7]

But since the rate was applied to gross output, and did not allow for seeds, depreciation, and other inputs, the effective rate was very much higher and the system deterred
agricultural improvement. Moreover, abuses by tax farmers could not easily be checked;
thus when prices were high the tax farmers would insist on payment in kind and when they
were low on payment in specie. The cultivator's obligation to hold on to the produce until
payment of tithe was particularly onerous, given the absence of storage. The government
also suffered from the system. Various improvements were made after 1890, but things were
still essentially unchanged at the outbreak of the First World War.

Nevertheless, presumably because of the increase in agricultural output, the yield of
tithes rose markedly, from about ŁT2,500,000 in 1850 to ŁT4,000,000 in 1864 and ŁT4,500,000
by 1900 and in 1910 stood at ŁT6,500,000.

Until 1883 the animal tax was levied in kind, one animal in ten being taken. After
that a tax of 3 1/2 to 5 piastres, depending on the locality, was imposed and in 1903 the
rate was raised to 10 piastres on all animals more than two years old, except donkeys, for
which it was 3 piastres.[8] Lists of animals were prepared by village headmen and tribal
chiefs and the tax paid by the latter was "related more to the degree of state authority
over him than to the number of animals owned by his group."[9] The table below shows the
assessed amount of various taxes in selected years; with improving efficiency, actual receipts came to equal, and even exceed, estimates.

	Tithe	Animals	Profits	Military Service	(million kuruş) Customs	Salt	Land & Buildings	Total Estimates	Actual Collections
1862-3	434	88	317	60	283	75	..	1,661	..
1877-8	675	179	335	92	148	84	..	1,973	..
1887-8	428	190	70	61	198	66	246	1,902	1,556
1894-5	438	172	73	90	212	74	265	1,866	1,650
1909-10	738	207	53	--	427	118	295	2,508	2,693

Source: Shaw, "Tax Reforms," IJMES, October 1975.

In the early 1870s, when receipts from tithes and animal taxes were at their peak, they
supplied about 45 percent of central government revenues, and the addition of taxes on silk
and tobacco production would raise the total to one-half. Tithes and animal taxes formed
a higher proportion--nearly two-thirds--of provincial government revenues.[10] The growth
of customs and other revenues, however, brought down the share of tithes to 26 percent and
of the animal tax to 7 percent of central government revenues in the five years preceding
the First World War.[11] Of the other revenues the most important was the property tax
(arazi ve müsakafat vergisi) imposed in 1861, at the rate of 0.4 percent of the value of
cultivated land, urban plots, and buildings and of an additional 4 percent of rental income
therefrom: these rates were gradually raised. The tobacco tax, which was quite significant in the 1860s and 70s, was handed over to the Régie in 1883 (5:19). The military exemption tax (bedeli askeri), paid by non-Muslims, was abolished in 1909, with the imposition
of military service on all Ottoman subjects.[12]

Taken as a whole, the tax burden in Turkey was not too heavy; per capita it was about
half of what it was in Egypt and Greece, countries with roughly equal per capita incomes.[13]
But it was very unequally distributed between town and country. It has been calculated

that in 1872-73 farmers contributed 45 percent of central government revenue totally and 7 percent more than proportionately, whereas the share of government expenditure that benefited farmers specifically was negligible.[14] By 1913 the farmers' total and more than proportional contribution had fallen to about one-third and the increase in expenditure on education, public works, and agricultural credit and extension raised their share of benefits, but there seems little doubt that they continued to give the state far more than they received.

---

1. This note draws heavily on Shaw, "The Nineteenth-Century Ottoman Tax Reforms," IJMES, October 1975; see also Aktan, du Velay, Morawitz, and Heidborn.
2. Young, 5:302.
3. Shaw, "Tax Reforms," p. 421.
4. For details, ibid., pp. 422-30; Shaw, History 2:95-101; and Young, 5:305-7.
5. Quataert, pp. 28-30.
6. Text in Young, 5:310-41.
7. Quataert, pp. 28-30; Young, 5:310-41.
8. Texts in Young, 5:292-301.
9. Quataert, p. 31.
10. Aktan, in EHME, pp. 109-11.
11. Table in Eldem, p. 268.
12. For these and other taxes and fees see Shaw, "Tax Reforms," and idem, History, 2:101-5.
13. Sir E. Vincent's estimate for 1896, quoted in Quataert, p. 30.
14. Aktan, in EHME, pp. 110-12. In 1869 a careful calculation put the average tax paid by a peasant family in northern Anatolia, including the cost of forced labor, at nearly Ł2 per annum, whereas an urban family paid only 16 shillings, a ratio of 2.5:1—A and P 1870, vol. 64, "Anatolian Provinces"; in 1864 the average tax per family in the overwhelmingly rural paşalik of Kurdistan was about Ł1-10s.—ibid. 1865, vol. 53, "Turkey."

SELECTION 11.   TAX ASSESSMENTS IN ERZERUM, 1845

Report on the Trade of Erzeroom for the Year 1845, and on the state of the Pashalik, FO 78/654

. . . The new system of Taxation and of collection of the Revenue, called the Tanzimat-i-Hairieh, has been announced as a boon of the Sovereign, and no doubt it would be so, if fairly carried out. As far as I have learned anything of its operations, I know only one point in which it has brought relief. The Armenian Agriculturist formerly often paid 20 per Cent, while the Mohamedan paid only 5, or at most 10 per Cent; and it frequently happened, besides, that the latter, by favor, was exempted altogether from the Tax. This year, however, both classes have paid equally their legitimate 10 per Cent, and the Tax has been fairly levied. Free quarters on the Christians and forced labour are both prohibited by the Tanzimat; but, until Essat Pasha's time, the abuses continued; they probably will be abolished hereafter. The property of the inhabitants of the Town has been three or four times assessed, but always so unfairly, that the valuation has been rejected. At last, it was asked what the Mussulmans could bear and what the Christians. The answer given was, that the former (consisting of 9,000 families) could contribute 75,000 piastres or Ł750; and the latter (1,000 families), 32,000 piastres or Ł320; this sum, the Armenians had usually paid for Salian, while the Turks had never contributed at all. The Government, then, ordered that the Mussulmans should pay 75,000 piastres, and the Christians 35,000; but it abated from the two 10,000 piastres, and directed the Chiefs of the nations to distribute the tax justly and conscientiously among their co-religionists. The Turks here took, however, the whole abatement on their own contribution; so that they pay 65,000 piastres = Ł650, and Christians 35,000 = Ł350. The assessment on the Mohamedans has not been fairly levied. Each parish was apportioned its contingent; but the distribution was left to the Imaum, who made as much out of it as he could. This is an evil of the system and not an injustice of the Government; and it is an improvement for it to have enforced the principle, that Mohamedans are liable to taxation on an equality with Rayahs. The Defterdar is not such a man as should hold so responsible a post; he is a notorious Debauchee, very corrupt, and without those qualifications which would entitle him to such an office; and the sooner he be changed for a more respectable man, the better it will be for the Government as well as for the governed. I may observe, however, that he is underpaid, considering the responsibility he has to bear and the temptation to which he is exposed; but, while integrity should be better rewarded, venality should be more severely punished than by a mere removal from his office. . . .

SELECTION 12. TAX FARMING IN ERZURUM, 1850

Vice Consul to Minister of Foreign Affairs, 28 March 1850 and 10 April 1850, CC Erzerum, vol. 1

The apalto of the customs of the whole province of Erzurum is put to auction each year at Constantinople. Only five years ago, this tax farm was granted for 600,000 piastres (150,000 francs). Since then, imports from Persia have increased so much that the price of the farm has risen to 1,500,000 piastres (375,000 francs), at which it was given out last year. The customer admitted to me that, even at that price, he had made a net profit of about one million piastres (250,000 francs). It is therefore at a price of 2,500,000 piastres (625,000 francs) that the Porte should have sold the farm for the current year, and last year's customer would gladly have offered such a price, but that was not what happened.

Instead of being, as usual, put up to public auction and given to the highest bidder, the tax farm was given to Tevfik Bey, the Kiateb Effendi of the Ministry of Foreign Affairs who, exerting all his influence, spontaneously presented himself as a buyer, and to whom it was granted on payment of only 1,700,000 piastres (425,000 francs). A firman of concession was therefore given to Tevfik Bey, but his name doesnot feature in the firman, which is made out in that of one of his servants, Ali Aga.

Wishing to make a large profit without incurring any expenses, Tevfik Bey immediately got in touch with a few Armenian bankers, offering to sell them his privilege. And indeed several persons offered a price considerably above the buying price and Tevfik Bey finally decided to sell his firman for 2,500,000 piastres (625,000 francs), thus making a net gain of 800,000 piastres (200,000 francs) . . . [The concession was taken up by two Armenian bankers and a alim, Cennet Zadeh. The latter forms the subject of the next dispatch.]
. . . The sale of the farm of these taxes [on agricultural products] for this year took place in Erzurum, two months ago. It was carried out by public auction, in the presence of the Governor General and the Tax Collector [Receveur Général] of the province. The large number of buyers who had come from all parts of the province, and the competition that should have ensued, would have led one to expect a large profit for the Treasury. But here, as so often when the financial interests of the State are at stake, the sales were carried out with an unheard of degree of favoritism, and most often it is the most influential who gets the tax farms, not the highest bidder.

The alim Cennet Zadeh, whom I have had the honor to mention to your Excellency in several of my dispatches and whose conduct I have denounced, is a man who, for some ten years, has been able to use his influence with the authorities to acquire, so to speak, a monopoly of tax farming. . . . Here is an example. . . .

A few days before the auctions Cennet Zadeh mentions clearly, and spreads around through his numerous agents, the names of the districts or villages whose tax farms he wishes to buy. The other buyers immediately understand the meaning of this unofficial statement, which for them is a formal order to abstain. However, they do turn up at the auction, to bid for the few villages which he is willing to leave to them, either because they seem to him too meagre a prey or because they do not offer much chance of gain. It goes without saying that it is precisely those farms that give the State a relatively higher profit.

At the auction, the public cryer puts up a village or a district at the previous year's selling price. Cennet Zadeh stands up and raises the bid by a few hundreds of piastres. The numerous buyers, who know very well that that village or district gaveits last buyer a profit, would be glad to enter a competitive bid, but the stern look of Cennet Zadeh and the terror he inspires makes them all keep perfectly silent. Woe to anyone who would have bid higher. He would soon pay for his temerity with certain ruin, for Cennet Zadeh has a thousand means at hand to undo such a man. Cennet Zadeh is therefore proclaimed tax farmer of that village or district. That evening the other bidders come to his house in crowds, and it is then that a real and regular auction takes place. Each bids and the highest gets the farm. Thus Cennet Zadeh obtains, at no expense, an enormous profit.

I have it, Sir, from Mehmet Reşid paşa himself, that last year Cennet Zadeh made a profit of about 1,800,000 piastres on the 2,000,000 piastres of tax farms that were granted to him, almost without having to lay out anything. The Treasury's loss is therefore indicated by the amount of his enormous gain. This year, Cennet Zadeh was also granted about 2,000,000 piastres' worth and at prices very close to those of last year, but his gain will be much higher for it is certain that the tax revenues are increasing by a large fraction each year.

The Governor General and the Tax Collector of the Province are fully aware of these manipulations but they say nothing because they too profit from the situation. Cennet Zadeh is not the kind of man who would be ungrateful towards them; he needs them too much and his influence with these officials is too profitable for him not to reward richly--in spite of his avarice--the kind of connivance that has multiplied his wealth. Besides, he is very well informed of the peccadillos which they commit at the expense of the State funds in other instances. They can therefore count on his discretion, but only on the condition--tacit but clear--that they will be equally indulgent towards him. . . .

SELECTION 13.   TAXES IN CYPRUS, 1858

Translation of Report, in Italian, by A. Palma, Vice-Consul in Larnaca, 25 February 1858,
FO 195/647

In compliance with the instructions contained in your dispatch No. 5 of the 13th ultimo, I hasten to give you a short report on the taxes and imposts paid in this Island.

Ihtisabie. This tax ought to have been abolished in conformity with the existing
Customhouse Tariff, established between the European Powers and the Sublime Porte, which
tax was abolished only in part, and which is collected according to the old custom, not
only on the articles of consumption, but in general on all articles which are brought for
Sale from the interior into the town, the greater part of which are intended for exportation. The produce of industry such as shoes, clothing, cloths etc., and every other manufacture of the country have to pay this tax, which is fixed at one para per Piastre on the
value of the object taxed, namely 2½ per cent. The value, however, being calculated at
Caprice, this tax becomes in consequence much heavier.

Bashi Bazar [Bac-i Bazar]. This tax is levied indiscriminately on the produce intended
for the daily consumption of the town such as vegetables, fruits, firewood, and is paid in
kind or in money, for instance vegetables pay 10 paras per load, fruits 1 oke per load,
charcoal P.1 per bag, wine 5 paras per skin, acquavitae 10 paras per Barrel, Flour 1 oke
per bag. As, however, there are abuses in the collection of these sums, much more money is
taken than is just.

Tenths. They are sold to the highest bidder. The contractors commit all kind of
wrongs; with arrogance and threats, and often with beatings they tax the peasants arbitrarily, and forcibly take away from them not the tenth, but the third part of their produce.
Their remonstrances pass unheeded, owing to the connivance of the Government functionaries
the greater number of whom are interested in the matter.

Fruits are tithed on the trees at the risk of the peasant. Wine is tithed many months
after the vintage, so that whatever drainage or loss there may be, is at the cost of the
proprietor.

Custom-house. As the Tariff fixes the duty on each article, abuses cannot be committed. The wine called Commanderia is taxed by the Tariff at 20 paras per oke, a very
exorbitant tax for the commanderia of one year, which is principally exported, as the exportation of the old commanderia of from 2 to 10 years is very limited, being rather an
article of luxury than otherwise. The price of the new being usually from P.1 to 1½ an
oke, the duty of 20 paras per oke, makes in reality from 40 to 50 per cent. instead of 12
per cent, which last is the general basis of the Tariff for the articles of exportation.
It would be very desirable now that the Tariff is about to be reformed, to fix the value
of the new commandaria of from 1 to 2 years at the rate of P 1½ an oke, according to the
market price, and the old of from 3 to 10 years from P.5 to 8, and to fix on these valua-
tions the duty of 12 per cent called Amede and Reftie.

Calamie [Kalemiye]. The contractors of the Customs collect under this denomination
10 per cent on the amount of the Custom duties on the goods exported to Turkey. The Consular body with the intervention of the Governor, considering that this duty is not specified
in the Tariff, have unanimously refused that their subjects should submit to this arbitrary
payment until fresh orders are received from their respective superior Authorities, which
orders His Excellency has been in hopes of obtaining since the month of June last, but
which he has not yet received. The Ottoman subjects are obliged to pay this tax.

Imposts. From investigations made, it results that the excessively large sum of about
14 millions of Piastres for taxes, imposts, customs, tenths, salt pits, etc. etc., as
stated in the following detailed note, is paid by this Island to the Treasury, while the
expenses of the Government for salaries of public functionaries of every grade, artillery-
men, health officers, etc. etc. do not amount to but about one million of Piastres. Those
contributing are obliged to pay in Beshliks (the only money which the Government receive)
which has in trade an aggio of 9 to 10 per cent, in consequence thereof this not unimportant loss falls on the population.

Direct contributions	P.3,000,000
Do. for arrears of debt	600,000
Do. for conscription	750,000
Tenths	6,000,000
Customs and tenths of silk	2,100,000
Salt works	300,000
Ihtisabie, weight, measure & Bashi Bazar	150,000
Stamped paper	250,000
Tapi, and duty on transfer inland	450,000
	P 13,900,000

SELECTION 14.   TAX EXEMPTIONS AND TAX REFORMS IN SPORADES, 1860s

Biliotti to Cumberbatch, 5 April 1898, FO 78/5446

. . . It results from these reports, and indeed I was myself aware, that the islands in question, namely: Patmos, Nikaria, Leros, Calymnos, Symi, Tilos, Nissiros, Stampalia, Halki, Scarpanthos, Cassos and Castellorizo, have from early times enjoyed certain privileges at the hands of the Imperial Government but is is rather difficult to ascertain authentically the nature and dates of the various Charters by which the privileges now invoked were conferred on, or confirmed to, those islands.

I beg, however, to inclose the Copies of a selection from the mass of correspondence which I find in the archives and which bear more particularly on this point, namely two despatches addressed to Her Majesty's Embassy at Constantinople on December 5th 1867 and will be observed that the first two of these documents mention the privileges in question as having been granted by a Firman of Sultan Mahmoud in the Year 1834, whilst the last states that they date as far back as the time of Sultan Suleiman the Conqueror of Rhodes in 1523.

I have been informed by the Russian Vice Consul at Rhodes Mr. Galinos (a Greek by birth and long resident in this island) that he has in his possession photographic copies of five documents purporting to be Imperial Firmans and Bouyourldis (Government orders) of an earlier date than the reign of Sultan Mahmoud, relating to the grant of privileges to Rhodes as well as to the other islands of the Sporades, but Mr. Galinos does not, he says, feel at liberty to give me copies of these documents without the authorisation of his official superiors.

On the other hand I have been told that the Demogerondia of Symi pretends to possess the following Firmans and Bouyourldis:
Firman from Sultan Mehmed the IV dated 16 Redjeb 1062 (1652)--
Firman from Sultan Ahmed the III dated Chaban 1132 (1720)--
Firman from Sultan Osman the III dated Chaban 1168 (1755)--
Firman from Sultan Abdul-Hamid the I dated Cheval 1188 (1775)--
Firman from same Sultan, dated Rebiul Ahir 1189 (1776)--
Firman from same Sultan, dated Rebiul Ewel 1189 (1776)--
Bouyourldi from Dilaver Pasha dated 23 April 1836.
Bouyourldi from Ahmed Kaiserli Pasha dated 17 October 1867.
Bouyourldi from same Pasha dated 26 Djemaziul Ewel 1284 (1869).

A friend of mine has promised to obtain from Symi, if they really exist there, photographic copies of these different documents, and will not fail to transmit them to you as soon as they may be in my possession.

The privileges enjoyed by the above islands consisted of exemption from capitation (Kharatch) afterwards called military service exemption tax (Bedeli askerie), custom dues, tithes, land tax and all other dues in force in other parts of Turkey. In lieu of these exemptions the Islands had to pay to the Porte a moderate annual fixed sum. With an economical view, apparently, instead of being administered in the usual way by a staff of Turkish officials, the islands were at the same time allowed a certain degree of autonomy by being left to the government of locally constituted administrative bodies called Demogerondia (Council of Elders), and by having their own tribunals, the Imperial Government being represented by a simple Mudir, paid by the local Communities and whose duties consisted of little more than the appending of his seal of Office to the acts passed by the Demogerondia.

It is to be noted that the above mentioned fixed annual tribute came to be, from an early period, gradually augmented, without however raising great objections on the part of the Islanders, whilst on the other hand they energetically strove to maintain their other privileges.

It further appears from the correspondence of this Vice Consulate with Her Majesty's Embassy at Constantinople that insubordination on the part of the natives towards the Imperial Government prevailed in the privileged islands, that the orders of the Governor of Rhodes were seldom attended to, and especially that nobody from outside the islands, whether foreigners or Ottoman Subjects, could obtain justice at the hand of the tribunals in the islands of the Sporades.

In consequence of this state of things, it can hardly be denied that compulsory measures became desirable as regards these particular abuses, although this does not imply that it necessitated or excused interference with the other privileges conferred on the islanders, especially as regards their immunity from ordinary taxation.

In any case the Ottoman Government made a first attempt in September and October 1867 to introduce administrative reforms, but without success. It was only in 1869 that Ahmed Kaiserli Pasha, then Vali of the Archipelago, having at his disposal some ships of War and soldiers, succeeded in carrying them out. In order to calm the apprehensions of the islanders, the Pasha at the same time gave them the assurance that his object being administrative reforms only, he would not interfere with their other privileges.

The reforms thus introduced were: the appointment of Caimakams and Mudirs (sub Governors) with more extended powers than they exercised until then, the establishment of more regular tribunals, the imposition of dues on salt, tobacco and teskeres (passports) and of fines, stamp duty and a fee of 5 per cent (including judicial fees) on amounts encashed through the Authorities.

The islanders submitted with great unwillingness to these innovations naturally fearing that they would be followed by further encroachments on their remaining privileges. And in fact since that time (1869) the Government has successively imposed on the Sporades, in 1873, the levying of Custom dues on imports and exports, as in other parts of the Empire, and in 1876 a new tax was established and has since been levied by the Porte on all boats leaving the islands for the sponge fishery, even if these boats are bound for Crete or Cyprus where they are subjected to a further duty as a condition for being allowed to fish for sponges in those localities. This tax is as follows:

Boats with diving apparatus	₤T32
Boats with naked divers	₤T10
Boats with tridents	₤T 4
Boats with dragnets	₤T 3

It is also to be remarked that the boats of the Sporades which principally proceed to the coast of Egypt to fish for sponges have to pay the above mentioned tax to the Ottoman Government--before their departure from their islands, whereas the sponge fishing boats starting from Greece for Egypt are exempt from any sort of tax, and whilst the Egyptian Government levies no tax of any sort on sponge fishery.

The islanders especially complain that the above taxes levied on their sponge fishing boats, which are their principal source of livelihood are exorbitant, and that the value of their sponges are arbitrarily and unfairly estimated in the levying of Custom dues on the same.

A duty of 3 per cent on the value of sponges sold is levied from the buyer and seller, but this due is encashed exclusively by the Demogerondia and goes to support the expenses of schools, medical doctors, medicines, etc. as also towards the annual tribute to the Porte.

It is generally understood that the original motive for the exemption of these particular islands of the Sporades from the usual taxation was one of consideration for their exceptional poverty, and their administrative privileges went along with that exemption.

These favours were subsequently confirmed in reward for their fidelity to the Porte during the Greek revolution. The eventual disregard of the first named immunities was probably in consequence of several of these islands having in the course of time attained a certain degree of relative prosperity, chiefly through the development of the sponge fishing industry, whilst the invasion of their administrative privileges was certainly caused by the abuse of these privileges, by the local bodies, as above stated.

In conclusion there is no doubt that the administrative reforms imposed on the privileged islands were necessary and even imperatively so, but the Porte has availed itself of the opportunity to gradually encroach on the other privileges enjoyed by the Sporades and although the complaints of the Islanders are often exaggerated it cannot be denied that there is some foundation for them.

SELECTION 15. TITHES IN ANKARA PROVINCE, 1878

Gatheral to Layard, 7 September 1878, FO 195/1161

I beg to call attention to the following facts and details regarding the sale and collection of tithes now proceeding in this province with reference specially to the injury inflicted thereby on commerce of all kinds. The mode in which the sale proceeds is as follows. The Imperial Treasury instructs the local government to encash or collect the tithes and advises them at the same time to whom the money proceeds are to be paid, as for some years past the tithe of this province has been hypothecated as security for loans or advances made to the Imperial Government. This year they were assigned as security for an advance of TL100,000 (one hundred thousand Turkish Liras equal to ninety thousand pounds sterling) made by a group of Constantinople capitalists, and the proceeds are accordingly being collected on their behalf by a British merchant resident here. The Provincial Council appoints a day and invites all those willing to bid to attend; printed forms are prepared, on which the previous year's sale is specified as a minimum and those present are asked to put down the additional sums they are prepared to give. These forms are then hawked about by the public criers for sixty days and the Council meets weekly to ascertain and report progress. Last year caimés or paper money was accepted but for the current year payment in specie is insisted on. At the expiry of the term fixed by law the highest bids are accepted and the districts allotted; those for which there is no offer or the Council regarding the offers as unsatisfactory are retained by Government and revenue officers and clerks sent out to collect the produce in kind. The Province is divided into four "Cazas" or cantons and those are subdivided into a large number of districts. The Caza of Angora that is the canton round the capital at distances of from 2 to 72 miles is subdivided into thirteen districts and has realized the following sums and as Turkish proper names seem uncouth the literal translation is added.[*]

---

[*][Present-day names added in brackets.]

1.	Istanos (Riverside) [Incesu]	TL1260
2.	Ayash (Mountain Pass) [Ayaş]	1770
3.	Beybazar (Princes Market) [Beypazari]	2856
4.	Nullihan (Horseshoe Inn) [Nallihan]	1923
5.	Mohallitch (Little District) [Mihallicik]	2800
6.	Sivrihissar (Turretted Castle) [Sivrihisar]	2903
7.	Heymana (Upper Plateau) [Haymana]	1640
8.	Balaman (The Place of Honey) [Bala]	1800
9.	Yabanova (The Stranger's Field)	1299
10.	Tchibukova (Reedy Plain) [Çubuk]	1800
11.	Tchorbu (Cottage) [Kalecik?]	900
12.	Moutani Abad (Upper Springs) [Yabanabat]	890
13.	Itchneya (Within sight, i.e. what can be seen from the walls of the city [Zir?]	780
		TL22,621
	equivalent to	₤ 20,566 Stg.

This amount represents the tithe values of wheat and barley only. The tithes of opium, yellowberries and gum tragancanth are assessed at their values and commuted for a money payment made by the growers.

The evils of this system are as follows:

1. The injury inflicted on commerce of all kinds. The population naturally regards the refusal of the Government to accept its own paper-money as a virtual repudiation and in consequence use every means to dispose of what they hold and as specie of every kind is leaving the Province, caimé has depreciated more than 70 per centum and the price of all articles whether of necessity or luxury being abnormally increased business of every kind comes to a standstill.

2. The prejudicial effects on the administration and the officials connected with it. During the time when tithes are on sale the government building becomes a huge auction-mart and courts are all either deserted or closed, causing much injustice and many vexatious delays. A stringent law prohibits all officials from becoming either buyers or guarantors for purchasers. Under former Governors-General this was openly ignored but the present ruler Said Pasha wisely insists on the letter of the law being respected. Means are taken to evade his vigilance, however, in order to secure the large profits this traffic realizes and the buyers are for the most part either the partners or employees of officials. Much intrigue and jobbery results and the government practically loses for a time the services of members of Council although they are paid large salaries in order to free them from temptations of this kind.

3. The expense and loss to government of this mode of collecting the revenue. As it is always uncertain whether the tithes will or will not be sold the authorities have to appoint and pay a large staff of officials in readiness to collect in kind. As this kind of appointment is only temporary these officers are under great temptation to understate or embezzle and are notoriously addicted to bribery and the consequence is that only a portion of the taxes reaches the exchequer, the rest being consumed in expenses of collection and irregularities of every kind.

4. The damage to the cereals thus tithed. As the crops cannot be taken from the fields till the revenue officer has made his rounds and as much time is lost in the manner described, unfavourable weather often sets in and the grain is damaged in consequence. The Government when collecting in kind also suffers loss as wet grain becomes rapidly unfit for food. There are in the Province 11 government granaries most of them filled to overflowing and the amount they represent appears as a credit in official books but as it cannot be realized nor exported owing to the want of carriage the amount thus represented is fictitious.

The cure for these evils would be found in a comprehensive measure commuting these tithes and accepting in lieu of them a money payment. Such a measure would undoubtedly be looked upon as a great boon and would of itself go far to reform the whole administration and give the poor peasantry a stimulus towards greater industry and the use of improved appliances instead of the antiquated and barbarous implements at present employed. Meanwhile such progress is hopeless as the farmers fear and with good reason that they would be deprived of the fruits of their industry and they prefer leaving their fields fallow rather than expose themselves to further risk and loss.

The local newspapers having given great prominence to articles notifying that the British Government intends including this among projected reforms the writer is constantly implored by the peasantry and farmers to report the facts of the case and they desire me to express in advance their gratitude for the immense amelioration in their condition the anticipated change will bring about.

PUBLIC DEBT

Although its finances had been under strain for at least two centuries, it was not until well on in the nineteenth that the Ottoman government incurred a regular and permanent
debt. When revenue fell short of expenditures, the currency was debased (7:1) or money
was borrowed from the Galata bankers (7:6) and repaid from the following year's revenues.
Esham, or transferable annuities, were also issued starting in the 1760s or 70s.[1] Under
Abdül Hamid I (1774-89) "a foreign loan of 50,000 to 100,000" purses of 500 piastres was
considered, but not concluded.[2] In 1785 a project for raising a large sum by granting
"annuities on some branches in the European Provinces, without distinction of religion or
even nation, at five years purchase" was proposed by the Grand Vizier. One of the advantages of the scheme was that it would absorb local funds and check emigration: "The Rayas,
who lend their money secretly at an exorbitant profit, have no method of placing their fortunes when they retire from Trade. This inconvenience has induced many rich Greeks, Armenians and Jews to place money in the foreign Funds, and even to follow it into Italy, Germany,
France and Russia." The project was, however, defeated by the Vizier's enemies (Ainslie to
Carmarthen, 10 January 1785, FO 78/6). At Selim's accession, to cover rising military expenditure, "it was certainly proposed [in the Divan] to raise money by a Loan which could
easily be done at a moderate interest had it not been opposed on religious grounds, as was
also an increase of Taxes or an appropriation of Church Revenues (as has already been practised) as inauspicious at the commencement of the present Reign," and instead the currency
was debased (Ainslie to Leeds, 22 September 1789, FO 78/10).

Mahmud's constant wars against rebellious subjects and foreign powers involved a huge
outlay of funds.[3] This was met by issuing currency and Treasury bearer bonds, carrying 12
percent interest (Kaimes), for 160 million piastres (7:1)[4] In 1850 a foreign loan was seriously considered but finally rejected,[5] and 130 million piastres were borrowed from the
Banque de Constantinople.[6] In 1854, however, during the Crimean War, Turkey launched its
first foreign loan, for ŁT3,300,000; carrying 6 percent interest and issued at 80, it
brought in ŁT2,515,000. In 1855 a ŁT5,500,000 4 percent loan was issued at 102⅝ and
brought in 5,644,000. Several loans followed, in quick succession and at increasingly adverse terms, as Turkey's credit deteriorated; thus the ŁT44,000,000 5 percent loan of 1874
was issued at 43.5 and brought in only 19,140,000. Including the 1877 loan (ŁT5,500,000,
which raised only 2,860,000) the total amount contracted was ŁT268.8 million, of which just
over half, ŁT135 million, had been actually received.[7] Annual service charges amounted to
some ŁT14 million, out of a total revenue of under 18 million. And practically the whole
proceeds of the debt had been used for military operations, building of palaces and other
court expenditure, the covering of budget deficits or the funding of floating debt.

On 6 October 1875 an official commission declared that the budget showed a deficit of
over ŁT5 million, and in mid-1876 the government announced that it was suspending interest
and amortization payments. The 1877 loan--taken up by the Ottoman Bank and other local
banks--gave only a temporary respite, while the Bulgarian insurrection and war with Russia
imposed huge additional burdens.[8] At the Congress of Berlin the Powers recommended that an
international commission be set up to settle claims on the Ottoman government; the latter
rejected the suggestion and, on 22 November 1879, sought to satisfy its local creditors by
ceding to the Galata bankers the receipts from excise taxes and monopolies (Rüsumu Sitte)
for ten years and assigning other revenues for servicing the debt. But soon representatives
of the foreign creditors were invited to Istanbul and negotiations resulted in the "Decree
of Muharrem" of 20 December 1881.[9] This set up the Public Debt Administration, consisting

of representatives of Britain (who also represented Dutch bond holders), France, Germany, Italy, Austria, and Turkey, to which the Rüsumu Sitte revenues were transferred and other important ones assigned and which played a major part in the economic life of the Empire until 1914.[10] Its first task was to scale down the debt. The loans of 1854, 1855, 1871, and 1877, for which the Egyptian Tribute had been pledged as security, were left unchanged, with a principal of ₤T17,200,000 and an annual charge of 938,000; the principal of the privileged 1881 debt to the Galata bankers was also kept unchanged at ₤T8,170,000, but the charge was reduced from ₤T1,100,000 to 590,000. The other loans were grouped in four series (A to D) and Lots Turcs (issued for construction of European railways); the principal outstanding on 20 December 1881, ₤T211,769,000,[11] was reduced first to 117,081,000 and subsequently to 116,135,000--in other words just about what Turkey had in fact received from those loans. The service charge was drastically cut down, from ₤T12,955,000 to 1,463,000, consisting of 1 percent interest (with the possibility of raising this to 4 percent if sufficient revenue was available) and 1/4 percent amortization. The addition of the excluded loans enumerated above raised the total funded debt to ₤T141,505,000 and the charges to 2,991,000. There was also a floating debt of about ₤T19,000,000, which by 1900 had been reduced to about 7,000,000.[12]

The revenues ceded to the Debt Administration constituted 12 to 15 percent of total government revenues, and rose from ₤T2.2 million in 1882 to 3.3 million in 1908.[13] But under the terms of the Muharrem Decree, any surplus in the Administration's revenues was to be used to raise the interest paid to bondholders to a maximum of 4 percent. This created a conflict of interest between the government and the Administration since the former could use the increase in revenues neither to amortize the debt more rapidly nor for other purposes; and an increase in interest rates would naturally raise the market price of the bonds, making redemption more expensive. The ensuing friction had adverse effects, including a delay in imposing new taxes such as stamp duties and temettü and in negotiating new commercial treaties. Various projects were put forward for the conversion of the debt and that of Rouvier, the future minister of finance of France, was implemented by the decree of 14 September 1903. This converted the ₤T76,050,000 of series B to D bonds (series A had been already amortized) into a Unified Converted Debt of ₤T31,088,750 bearing 4 percent interest, and 0.45 percent amortization. The Lots turcs were added to the Unified Debt, at ₤T13,448,796, as were the privileged 1881 bonds, which had already been converted to 4 percent in 1890, at 7,161,264. In all, the Muharrem debts had been reduced to ₤T53,349,000.[14]

In the meantime, however, new loans had been contracted. "The loans taken between 1881 and 1908 amounted to 120,314,473 liras, of which 107,858,796 was actually received. It appears that in the conversions and consolidations made by the loans of 1890, 1891, 1894, 1902, 1903 and 1906 [which are included in the above figures], the debt amounted to 51.5 million and the amount received to 45 million. In 1908-14 a debt of 46 million was incurred, but only 39 million received."[15] In 1914, the total Ottoman debt in circulation was ₤T139,100,000, with a service charge of 8,998,000; to this should be added municipal loans of 2,197,000 with a charge of 128,000, guaranteed by the government, a total of ₤T141,297,000 and 9,126,000.[16] Of this, ₤T16,550,000 represented the outstanding amount on railway loans (4:Introduction). Most of the rest of the money received was spent for military purposes or to cover budget deficits.

Taking the whole period from 1854 to 1914, a recent study has put the gross amount borrowed at ₤T399.5 million. Of this, ₤T135.5 million, or 34 percent, represents

commissions and the difference between nominal and issue price; 178.9 million, or 45 percent, was used to liquidate previous debts; 22.3 million, or 6 percent, for military expenditure; 20 million, or 5 percent, to cover budget deficits; 18.1 million, or 5 percent was
invested; and the balance was paid to the Treasury or put to other uses.[17]   Clearly, Turkey
derived very little benefit from its huge public debt.

1. EI(2), s.v. "Asham."
2. Suvla, in EHME, p. 97; du Velay, p. 135.
3. Noteworthy was the indemnity paid to Russia after the 1828-29 war. Originally
fixed at 400,000 purses (Shaw, History, 2:32), in March 1836 it was reduced to 160,000
purses and paid off within a few months (Sturmer to Metternich, 30 March and 31 August
1836, HHS Türkei, 1836, vols. 64-65). There were, however, occasional compensations; the
loot taken from Ali paşa of Jannina consisted of 29 mule-loads of gold, estimated at 16,000
purses (Stangford to Londonderry, 23 March 1822, FO 78/107).
4. EI(2), s.v. "Kaime."
5. See 7:9 and EHME, pp. 98-99.
6. Grunwald and Ronall, p. 13.
7. These figures are the sum of the loans listed by Suvla in EHME, pp. 100-101; Eldem
gives a slightly different list denominated in francs and totalling 5,298.7 million and
3,012.9 million; converting at 22.8 francs to the Turkish pound and adding the 1877 loans
would give totals of 237.9 million and 135.1 million. Quoting the Maliye Vekaleti Mecmuası,
Suvla states "the amount of the debt is 251,209,758 liras and the amount received is
135,015,751."
8. Young, 5:55-56. The Russian war indemnity was fixed in 1882 at 802.5 million
francs, or ŁT35.3 million, payable in annuities of ŁT350,000. These annuities were, by
and large, paid but the fact that the Ottoman government was almost always in arrears gave
the Russians a means of exerting much pressure (Young, 5:118 and 3:26).
9. Text in Young, 5:61-95.
10. Blaisdell, passim.; EI(2), s.v. "Duyun-i Umumiye" and sources cited; for its promotion of agricultural development, Quataert, pp. 245-77.
11. Figure given by Suvla in EHME, p. 103.
12. Young, 5:61.
13. Quataert, p. 60.
14. Note and text in Young, 5:98-110; to effect the conversion, a loan of ŁT32,738,772
was floated, leaving a surplus of ŁT1,687,207 paid to the Treasury.
15. Suvla in EHME, p. 106; see pp. 104-05 for detailed list of loans; see also Thobie,
pp. 119-25.
16. Eldem, table facing page 274.
17. K. Fişek, "Osmanlı Dış Borçları Üstüne," Siyasal Bilgiler Fakültesi Dergisi, vol.
22, June 1962.

SELECTION 16. OTTOMAN DEBT, 1903

The Present Position of the Ottoman Debt - Note by H. Babington-Smith, FO 78/5314

The present moment is a somewhat critical one in the history of the Ottoman Debt, and
in order to make clear the situation it is necessary to enter into some detail.

The Decree of Mouharrem and its Defects

"The Decree of Mouharrem" (Signed the 8/20th December, 1881) gave effect to the arrangement under which certain revenues were assigned by the Ottoman Government for the
benefit of its creditors and the Council of the Debt was instituted for the purpose of
collecting and administering those revenues. The capital of the loans included in this arrangement was reduced in proportions varying according to the circumstances of each loan,
and the reduced capital was classified in four Series (A., B., C., D.), with identical
rights as to interest, but different rights as to the application of the Sinking Fund. A
first charge of LT.590,000 per annum on the assigned revenues was created in favour of the
"Priorities," and the "Lots Turcs" or Lottery Bonds were also included separately in the
arrangement. The following table gives the nominal capital of the four Series under the
Decree of Mouharrem, and also of the Priorities and of the Lottery Bonds; while the last
column gives, approximately, the nominal capital which will remain outstanding on March 14,
1903, that is to say, at the end of the current financial year.

Under the Decree of Mouharrem the service of the Priorities is a first charge of
LT.590,000 on the revenues, four-fifths of the balance of the net receipts being applied
to interest and the remaining fifth being applied as Sinking Fund. A minimum rate of interest of 1% on the Series was practically guaranteed by the stipulation that the sum required for payment of interest at this rate should have priority over the Sinking Fund.
The result of these provisions is that a net receipt of LT.2,053,512 is necessary in order

	Nominal Capital under Decree of Mouharrem	Nominal Capital outstanding March 14, 1903 (approximate estimate)
	ŁT	ŁT
Priorities	8,609,640	7,300,000
Series A	7,902,259	--
Series B	11,265,153	4,456,000
Series C	33,915,762	27,945,000
Series D	48,365,235	44,617,000
Total of Series	101,448,409	77,018,000
Lots Turcs	15,632,547	13,521,300
Total	125,690,596	97,839,300

to pay 1% on the Series and the corresponding Sinking Fund in full; while a net receipt of LT.2,419,390 is necessary to pay interest at $1\frac{1}{4}$% and the corresponding Sinking Fund. These sums would be distributable as follows:

		Interest at 1%	Interest at $1\frac{1}{4}$%
		LT.	LT.
Priorities	LT.430,000		
Economy resulting from conversion of the Priorities applied as Extraordinary Sinking Fund	160,000	590,000	590,000
Four-fifths of remainder equal to 1% or $1\frac{1}{4}$% on nominal capital of LT.117,081,000		1,170,810	1,463,512
One-fifth of remainder, applied as Sinking Fund		292,702	365,878
Total		LT.2,053,512	2,419,390

The following table gives the net receipts for the last 10 years and the estimated receipts for the current year:-

1892-3	LT.2,184,545
1893-4	2,189,405
1894-5	2,196,319
1895-6	2,138,357
1896-7	2,069,216
1897-8	2,104,530
1898-9	2,131,082
1899-1900	2,154,702
1900-1	2,067,909
1901-2	2,126,591
1902-3 (estimate)	2,500,000

It will be seen that since 1892-3 the net receipts have always exceeded the above-named sum of LT.2,053,512. Of the surplus, one-fifth has formed part of the Sinking Fund, and the remaining four-fifths have been set aside as a reserve for increasing the rate of interest. This reserve at present amounts to LT.638,536.

The interest is paid half yearly and cannot be raised by fractions smaller than $\frac{1}{4}$% per annum. The provisions of the Decree relating to the rate of interest to be paid are not free from obscurity. There is, however, no doubt that the rate is to be fixed half-yearly by the Council of the Debt; and, in my opinion, it is clearly laid down that, if the receipts of the year are sufficient to raise the interest by $\frac{1}{4}$%, the Council is obliged to make the payment at the higher rate.

The Sinking Fund is usually applied by the purchase of bonds in the market. So long as the interest remains at 1%, $66\frac{2}{3}$ is the maximum limit of the price that can be paid for the purchase of bonds; that is to say, if the market price rises above this level, amortisation is effected by drawings and by repayment of the drawn bonds at $66\frac{2}{3}$. If the rate of interest is increased to $1\frac{1}{4}\%$, the limit of $66\frac{2}{3}$ is automatically raised to 75.

This arrangement has, on the whole, worked well during the twenty years of its existence. The revenues have largely increased under careful and honest administration; the Bondholders have received their 1% regularly; Series A., and nearly two-thirds of Series B., have been extinguished, while Series C. and D. have been materially reduced, with the result that the market value of the bonds remaining in circulation is much higher now than it was when the arrangement first came into force. As yet, however, the Bondholders have not realized the hope held out to them of obtaining a rate of interest higher than 1%. The Ottoman Government, too, has derived very solid advantages from the regularity introduced into that portion of its finances with which the Council of the Debt is concerned. Ottoman credit stands far higher in the European markets than it ever did before, and is little inferior to that of Austria or Italy.

Thereis, however, one serious defect in the arrangement from the point of view both of the Bondholders and of the Government; namely, that the Government has no share in the increase of the assigned revenues, however great that increase may be. The result is that the Government has no direct interest in promoting the growth of the revenues; on the contrary, its interest lies in the other direction, since any increase of receipts would take more from the tax-payer and give more to the Bondholders, and far from benefiting the Imperial Treasury would, in consequence of the increase in the market value of the bonds, retard to some extent the amortization of the Debt. This absence of motive for co-operation on the part of the Government is prejudicial to the Bondholders, since the assigned revenues can only reach their full development if the Council of the Debt can obtain the assent of the Government, both to administrative measures and also to necessary amendments of the law. This consideration applies with special force to the new resources which would be produced by the revision of the Customs Treaties. This revenue is assigned by the Decree of Mouharrem for the service of the Debt, but under existing conditions there is no prospect of realising it; for so long as the assignment remains in full force the Government has no interest in bringing about the revision of the Treaties and thereby raising a large amount of revenue for the benefit, not of the Imperial Treasury, but of the Bondholders. It is evident, therefore, that the Council of the Debt, as representing the interests of the latter, has good reason to endeavour to modify the existing arrangement.

The Ottoman Government, on the other hand, having urgent need of new sources of revenue, has been brought to consider the means of obtaining for itself the whole or part of the increases of the revenues assigned to the Debt; and, in a similar manner, those who are interested in the Bagdad Railway and who desire to find revenues hitherto unpledged and available for a guarantee, have been brought to consider the same problem.

Unification

The solution which has been suggested from time to time for a number of years is the Unification of the Debt. The scheme put forward about a year ago by Monsieur Rouvier, representing a group of French and German Banks, contemplated the conversion of the Bonds of the existing Series into 4% bonds of a uniform character, at the rate of LT.66 of the new security for LT.100 nominal of Series B.; LT.37$\frac{1}{2}$ for LT.100 nominal of Series C.; and LT.35 for LT.100 nominal of Series D. These new bonds were to have a Sinking Fund of 1%. The annuity necessary for their service, together with that of the Priority Bonds, which were to remain on their present footing, and that of the Lottery Bonds, which were to receive an increased sum annually, would have amounted to LT.2,290,000, and was to be provided from the sources of revenue already assigned by the Decree of Mouharrem. . . .

Epilogue

The Turkish Economy, 1914-75

During the First World War and the War of Independence, Turkey's losses were enormous. Military casualties have been put at 1,800,000.[1] Massacres, deportations, and flights and exchanges of population (including the exodus of 1,260,000 Greeks and influx of 400,000 Turks from Greece and the Balkans) had by 1927 reduced the population to 13,648,000; the number of Christians was 257,000 and of Jews 82,000, heavily concentrated in Istanbul.[2] The effect on the urban population is clearly shown in 2:5. Agriculture suffered from direct hostilities, as in Western and Eastern Anatolia and Cilicia; from the mobilization of the rural population; from the flight of hundreds of thousands of Greek and Armenian farmers; and from the drastic reduction of draft animals--the number of oxen and buffaloes in 1919 being only 15 percent of 1913 and that of horses 40 percent.[3] As a result, by 1917 the area under cereals had shrunk to 30 million dönüms, compared to 64 million in 1913.[4] Cash and tree crops were particularly hard hit: by 1918 output of tobacco had fallen to 38 percent of the 1913 level, of cotton to 8, of raisins 40, of figs 83, and of silk cocoons 31[5] (see also 5:22 and 6:15). Most branches of mining (6:10) and industry were adversely affected and equipment was run down.[6] So were the railways, roads, and ports, but some important stretches of the Baghdad railway were completed (4:17).

Foreign trade fell off sharply: in 1918 the value of imports was only 11 percent of 1913 and of exports 25 percent.[7] Huge budget deficits were incurred: by 1915 authorized expenditure was more than twice estimated receipts, and the latter fell off sharply after 1916.[8] Paper money expanded correspondingly; a total of £T160 million was issued in 1915-20, and by 1920 the gold pound was worth 436 piastres, depreciating further to 763 by 1923.[9] So did the public foreign debt, from £T154 million in 1914 to 465.7 million in 1918, mainly thanks to loans from Germany.[10] Inflation was rampant: the cost-of living index (July 1914 = 100) stood at about 300 in 1916, 1,675 in November 1918 and 2,200 in February 1919.[11] These high prices persisted after the end of hostilities: in October 1920 the cost of the main foodstuffs and articles of clothing was nearly 15 times as high as in 1914.[12]

Turkey's gains from the wars were indirect and intangible but nonetheless real and in the long run perhaps more important than the losses: the end of the futile and exhausting effort to hold down recalcitrant subject peoples and defend the Empire against European encroachment; the shattering of obsolete social institutions and practices, opening the way for greater participation of women in economic and social activity,[13] and the emergence of a leader of genius, aware of Turkey's needs and able to guide it along a new path.

I. RECOVERY AND ECONOMIC NATIONALISM, 1923-29

Turkey's most urgent need was for peace and peace was what it got (with the brief exceptions of the Korean and Cyprus expeditions, it has enjoyed peace since 1922--by far the
longest period in its history). This, and the resilience of a growing population operating
a primitive agricultural system (in 1927 there were only 211,000 iron ploughs, against
1,187,000 wooden ones) in a country with abundant land, enabled the economy to recover and,
by the late 1920s, to regain its prewar level. Table 1 illustrates the progress achieved.[14]

Economic recovery owed little to direct help from the government, which had neither
the financial means nor the political freedom of action to promote a vigorous development
program. Nevertheless, many important measures were taken. The abolition of the tithe and
the reduction of the military burden lifted a great weight off the peasants, but taxation
remained heavy, absorbing some 12-15 percent of GDP, and consisted mostly of regressive
taxes on mass consumption.[15] The laws of 1929 and 1935 that made it easier to register
land as private property probably encouraged development,[16] as did the raising of the capital of the Agricultural Bank.[17] Otherwise, hardly anthing was done to promote agriculture
in this period.

The urban sector received more attention. The adoption of a civil code patterned on
the Swiss, in 1926, followed by commercial, penal, and maritime codes based on German,
Italian, and other models, stimulated capitalist development, as did the replacement of the
Arabic script by the Latin[18] and the adoption of metric weights and measures. The marked
expansion in the school population, particularly at the secondary level, took place mainly
in the towns,[19] and the same was true of medical services. The establishment of the Iş
Bank in 1924 and Sanayi ve Maadin Bank in 1925 increased commercial and industrial credit.
The Law to Encourage Industry, of 1927, which granted tariff exemptions, lower transport
rates, and other benefits, led to the foundation of many new enterprises.[20] But by far
the greatest government contribution to economic development--which of course also benefited the rural section--was the investment of hundreds of millions of liras in transport,
resulting in the extension of the railway network by over 3,000 kilometers and some improvement of the roads.[21]

The most drastic change in the economic structure was Turkification, the regaining of
economic control by the Turkish government and citizens. Under the Lausanne Treaty of
1923, the Capitulations and Public Debt Administration were abolished and coastal navigation was reserved for Turkish ships. The Public Debt--of which 67 percent was allotted to
Turkey and the rest to the Successor States--was, by successive steps, greatly reduced.[22]
Turkey was not allowed to increase customs duties on imports from the powers signing the
Treaty but, starting in 1924, rates on goods from nonsignatories--which accounted for nearly half the total--were raised severalfold and in 1929 Turkey recovered its full tariff
autonomy.[23] And, from 1928 onward, eight railway and dock companies, twelve enterprises
in municipal services, and four mining and manufacturing companies were repurchased, generally on very favorable terms, for a total of ŁT154.7 million.[24]

DEPRESSION AND ETATISME, 1930-39

The Depression caused Turkey, along with many other countries, to veer sharply from
the course it had been following for nearly a hundred years, that of an open economy pro-
pelled by exports and foreign investment. The drop in world agricultural prices worsened
the terms of trade and reduced exports from a high of ŁT192 million in 1925 to 92 million
in 1934, necessitating an even greater reduction of imports, to balance trade.[25] The

prostration of the capitalist democracies, the lack of interest of Western and timorousness
of Turkish private capital, the achievements of the Soviet and later the Nazi economies, and
the growth of bilateralism had a strong impact on Turkey. There was a revival of government
suspicion of, and desire to guide and control, private economic and social activity. The
1930s and 40s saw the growth of étatisme, adopted as official policy in 1931 and aptly defined as "the intervention of the state as a pioneer and director of industrial activity,
in the interests of national development and security, in a country where private enterprise was either suspect or ineffective."[26]

Exchange control was introduced in 1930 and import quotas in 1931, and soon over 80
percent of Turkey's trade was carried out under bilateral agreements; this made it easier
for Germany to become the main supplier and market, accounting for nearly half the total
trade.[27] The government also intervened more vigorously in agriculture, expanding agricultural credit, promoting credit and marketing cooperatives, implementing small irrigation
schemes, founding research and training centers, and importing machinery and modern implements. Some 300,000 hectares were distributed to refugees or landless peasants. Wheat was
bought from farmers at support prices and storage capacity was increased.[28] The growth in
output is shown in Table 1.

Table 1

Indicators of Development, 1913-1938

	1913	1923	1928	1933	1938
Population (millions)	(15.7)	(12)	13.8	15.5	17.2
Foreign trade (million dollars)	179	137	202	83	234
GDP per capita (1948 prices ŁT)[a]	...	254	330	370	474
Agricultural production (millions of liras at 1940 prices)[a]	...	1,522	2,254	2,490	3,791
Industrial production (millions of liras at 1948 prices)[a]	...	421	662	1,019	1,423
Wheat (million tons)[a]	3.4	1.0	1.9	2.3	3.6
Tobacco (thousand tons)[a]	49	45	50	36	68
Cotton (thousand tons)[a]	30	44	51	40	64
Coal (million tons)	0.8	0.6	1.3	1.9	2.6
Refined sugar (thousand tons)	...	...	4.3	65.1	42.5
Cement (thousand tons)	...	...	59	143	287
Electricity (million kwh)	(20)	(40)	(90)	152	312
Railways (thousand kilometers)	3.6	4.1	4.8	6.1	7.2
Students in schools (thousands)	...	359	517	657	944

Sources: Istatistik Yilliği; League of Nations, Statistical Yearbook; UN, Statistical
Yearbook; Tezel.

[a]Averages of 1923-25, 1926-30, 1931-35, and 1936-40, compiled by Tezel.

The table also shows the expansion in railways and electric power in those years.
But the most noteworthy government intervention was in industry and mining.[29] With Soviet
technical assistance and loans of $11 million, the ŁT44 million first Five-Year Plan was
launched in 1934; with British help and credits aggregating over $60 million, a draft
ŁT112 million second Five-Year Plan was drawn up in 1936 and, in substance, adopted in
1938. The Sümer Bank was founded in 1933 and the Eti Bank in 1935, to promote industry
and mining, respectively. Eventually, the first plan was to cost about ŁT100 million

($77 million) and the war prevented the implementation of most of the second, but the
plans introduced important new industries, such as steel and basic chemicals, and greatly
expanded older ones such as textiles, paper, glass, and various mineral products. Special
efforts were made to disperse the new factories, to diffuse their impact. Some private industries also expanded, as a result of direct protection and linkages with the state industries. The industrialization program was marked by inefficiency and technical and financial
imbalances, the cost to both the Treasury and consumer was high, and some branches of private industry suffered from unfair competition on the part of state enterprises; but Turkey
certainly benefited from both the expansion of the manufacturing and mining base and the
training given to industrial managers and workers.[30] Turkey's industries were to stand it
in good stead during the coming war years.

WAR, 1939-45

During the Second World War Turkey remained neutral and, unlike other parts of the
Middle East, was not occupied by foreign troops. Trade was conducted with both Axis and
Allies, whose competitive buying drove up the price of chromium and other products, resulting in a cumulative net export surplus of ₤T326 million and a corresponding rise in foreign
exchange reserves.[31] But in all other respects the war imposed a heavy strain. The mobilization of about 1 million men reduced agricultural output and created budget deficits. The
quantum of imports fell by half, further reducing supply, and import prices more than
doubled. Industrial production increased by some 50 percent, but investment declined and
industrial and transport equipment deteriorated. Per capita income fell by about a quarter.
The cost-of-living index rose from 100 in 1939 to 350 in 1945, causing great hardship to
large sections of the population. And, as in other countries, state intervention increased.
One deplorable aspect of this was the Varlık Vergisi (capital tax) of 1942, which was intended to tax war profits. It was applied in a highly discriminatory way, the ₤T315 million collected being levied to a large extent on non-Muslims, many of whom were bankrupted
and considerable numbers deported. It constituted a decisive blow against the remaining
economic influence of minorities in Turkey, since those who could do so hastened to transfer their funds abroad after the war.[32]

LIBERALIZATION, UPSURGE, AND ACCUMULATING DIFFICULTIES, 1945-60

The defeat of Germany and Russia's territorial demands turned Turkey towards the
United States, and for nearly thirty years American influence was predominant. Lend Lease
was followed by the Truman Doctrine and the Marshall Plan and in 1947-75 Turkey received
$2,823 million in U. S. grants and credits, and probably more in military aid. This was
accompanied by economic and political liberalization--facilitated by the devaluation of the
lira in 1946 from 1.28 to 2.80 to the dollar--and a more determined effort to develop agriculture, particularly after the 1950 elections and change of government. The land reform
of 1945, although it did not seriously affect large estates, by 1960 transferred 1,800,000
hectares of state, communal, or unclaimed land to farmers who could work it better.

Some 6,500 kilometers of surfaced, and nearly 14,000 of all-weather, roads were built,
putting thousands of villages in touch with markets for the first time in history. Advances by the Agricultural Bank increased about tenfold. World demand for agricultural
produce was high and the government supported farm prices. About 40,000 tractors were imported under the Marshall Plan and constituted a significant addition to the 566,000 iron
and 1,803,000 wooden ploughs in use in 1950. As a result, and thanks to good weather, the

under cereals expanded from 7 million hectares in 1945 to 11 million in 1953, output doubled
to 14 million tons and Turkey became the world's fourth largest exporter of wheat. Industrial crops, such as sugar beets and cotton, increased even more. Industrial output rose
equally rapidly and continued to do so, and investment in infrastructure was maintained at
a high level. The growth of the business sector is shown by the fact that whereas in 1943
there were only 421 joint stock companies, with a capital of ŁT245 million, and in 1950
782 with ŁT875 million, in 1951-June 1957 no less than 1,703 companies, with a capital of
ŁT1,500 million, were founded, and bank deposits rose from ŁT750 million in 1946 to
ŁT7,350 million in 1959.[33] But the series of bad crops beginning in 1954 (it was not until
1958 that the 1953 level was regained), rapidly rising inflation because of budget deficits
and over-investment, deteriorating terms of trade, growing deficits in the balance of payments, and accumulating foreign debts led to an increasingly acute crisis which was not al-
leviated by the government's reluctant and belated devaluation, in 1958, to 9 liras to the
dollar for most transactions. Economic ineptitude as well as increasing repression led to
the military coup of 1960.[34]

Table 2

	1945	1950	1960	1970	1975
Population (millions)	18.8	20.9	27.8	35.6	40.2
Foreign Trade (million dollars)	263	574	789	1,475	6,140
GNP (ŁT billion, 1961 prices)	(20)	28.5	49.9	86.4	(124)
Energy consumption (million tons coal equivalent)	(4.5)	5.4	6.8	17.1	24.1[a]
Index of Agricultural Output (1952-56 = 100)[b]	61[c]	92[d]	130	(177)	(201)[a]
Index of Manufacturing Output (1958 = 100)	(30)	40	116	..	..
Cereals (million tons)	4.0	7.8	12.6	15.9	22.0
Cotton (000 tons)	54	99	176	400	457
Steel (000 tons)	64	91	265	1,300	1,100
Sulphuric acid (000 tons)	5	11	24	28	22[a]
Refined sugar (000 tons)	90	186	618	643	(800)
Cement (million tons)	0.3	0.4	2.0	6.4	10.9
Electricity (million kwh)	470	676	2,815	8,616	15,569
Automobiles (000)	9	33	134	311	610
Licensed radios (000)	179	362	1,352	3,072	4,033[e]
Students in school (million)	1.4	1.8	3.4	6.5	7.0[e]

Source: UN Statistical Yearbook; FAO, Production Yearbook; İstatistik Yilliği;
Central Bank of Turkey, Annual Report.

[a] 1974

[b] Spliced index.

[c] 1944-48

[d] 1950-52

[e] 1973

SUSTAINED EXPANSION, 1960-75

After a hesitant start in 1960 and 1961, rapid growth was resumed and in 1962-75 the average annual increase in real GNP was over 7 percent, compared to 6.3 in 1950-60 and 4.7 in 1960-63. The high rate of population growth, 2.5 percent, reduced per capita increase to a little over 4.5 percent, a figure exceeded by only a dozen or so countries.[35] Physical indexes of economic activity, such as use of energy, steel, and cement, and of levels of living, such as consumption of textiles, sugar, and radios, also show a sharp increase.[36] But Turkey's per capita income of nearly $700 in 1974, although well above that of nonoil Middle Eastern countries, lies far below that of its Balkan neighbors which, in the past, had not been much more developed economically.

Foreign aid played a significant part, Turkey receiving government loans and grants from the United States, Western Europe, and the Soviet Union. The inflow of private capital, mainly West European, was much smaller, £T1,479 million in 1951-73.[37] In the early 1960s, the resource gap (net imports of goods and services) rose to 4 percent of GNP[38] and covered more than a quarter of investment. But the huge expansion of remittances from Turkish workers in Europe from $50 million in 1965 to a peak of $1,426 million in 1972,[39] greatly improved the balance of payments, and in 1965-73 the resource gap narrowed to 2.3 percent of GNP, covering less than 10 percent of gross investment. After that, however, the sharp rise in the price of imported oil, food, and manufactured goods caused a deterioration in the balance of payments and in 1974 Turkey's outstanding debt reached $4,300 million[40] and has undoubtedly increase since then.

But the main thrust of the economy was internal, and took the form of a rise in the investment rate from 13 percent in the late 1950s to 20 in 1973. The government provided a framework, in the form of three five-year Plans beginning in 1962, expanded the infrastructure, and invested large amounts in certain industries; in all it accounted for just over a third of total investment in 1960-73. The private sector contributed nearly three-fifths of total investment[41] and most of the driving force in the economy. Perhaps the most important social change in Turkey has been the growth of the middle class, which now accounts for about 20 percent of the population. "By the late 1940's, the new managerial skills that had developed from the bureaucratic nucleus and the capital resources acquired primarily through commercial profits permitted a growing number of entrepreneurs to enter various economic fields," notably industry and banking.[42] There was also a severalfold expansion in the salaried middle class, whose skills are indispensable for the increasingly complex economy--engineers, technicians, economists, statisticians, and accountants.[43]

Hardly less important was the growth in the urban labor force and the great improvement in its quality. Employment in industry and construction rose from 450,000 in 1927 to 846,000 in 1950 and 2,309,000 in 1975, of whom over a third worked in large public or private enterprises.[44] Meanwhile, the vast expansion in education, which by now is available to practically all children of primary school age and about a third of secondary, has raised the adult literacy rate from 11 percent in 1927 to 35 in 1950 and 55 in 1970,[45] and almost all male factory workers can by now read and write. An active labor movement, helped by the labor laws of 1947 and 1963,[46] has developed. Of particular significance has been the migration of hundreds of thousands of workers to Germany and other parts of Western Europe; in 1973 the total number of Turks working in Europe, including illegal immigrants, was around 900,000.[47] Many of these have returned, bringing with them capital, skills, habits or work, and new ideas that should have an immensely beneficial effect on the economy.

Turkey's development may be further traced in its directly productive sectors. In 1960-75 industry (manufacturing, mining, and power) grew at an average rate of over 11 percent, to account for 24 percent of GDP and over 12 percent of the labor force.[48] Output of intermediate and investment goods has been growing much faster than that of consumption goods, and Turkey now has a wide range of metal products, machinery, transport equipment, electric, electronic, and chemical industries. Trade figures show that Turkey has achieved a very large measure of import substitution in consumer goods, but it is still dependent on outside sources for many raw materials and investment goods.

Agriculture, which still employs 60 percent of the labor force and forms about 25 percent of GDP, is growing much more slowly--averaging under 2.5 percent a year, but fluctuating very sharply because of weather. Much has been done to intensify agriculture by extending irrigation, introducing improved seeds, including high-yield Mexican wheat, shifting to more valuable crops, such as sugar beets and cotton, using more machinery and better tools (there are now about 160,000 tractors), and, above all, greatly increasing the application of fertilizers; use of nitrogenous fertilizers increased from 54,000 tons of nitrogen content in 1961-65 to 430,000 in 1973 and 383,000 in 1974. A land reform law was enacted in 1973 and is being slowly implemented.[49]

Turkey is undoubtedly facing many difficulties.[50] Its rapid population growth is imposing a heavy economic and social burden; this is in marked contrast to its Balkan neighbors and partly explains their superior performance; however, the relatively low birth rate of Istanbul and Izmir gives hope that with development, and thanks to greater government efforts at family planning, population growth will slacken in the next decades.[51] The bureaucracy is rigid and authoritarian. The educational system is not well-adapted to the country's needs. Agriculture is sluggish, and output barely keeps pace with population growth; here, too, Turkey's performance may be expected to improve in the near future.[52] Unemployment and underemployment remain high. The gap between the more prosperous western and the backward eastern regions shows no signs of narrowing. Lack of oil has put a heavy strain on the balance of payments, but some relief will be provided by the newly opened Iraqi-Turkish pipeline. Like other countries, Turkey is suffering from inflation. Many industries are uncompetitive and their economic contribution is small or even negative. And, more generally, Turkey's foreign trade policy has been unduly restrictive and it would greatly benefit from liberalization and greater integration in the European Common Market.[53] Lastly, distribution of income is still very unequal although, judging by the Gini concentration ratio, there was an improvement in the 1960s.[54]

But no one who has followed developments in the last sixty years can fail to be impressed by the great progress achieved. Turkey has increased its per capita income almost threefold since the Second World War, and has significantly raised the level of living of its inhabitants and provided them with adequate food and clothing, and life expectancy at age five has risen to sixty-five years. The great bulk of its consumer goods is made locally. It has a rapidly growing investment and capital goods sector. Its infrastructure has been vastly expanded and improved. Thanks to workers' remittances and tourist expenditures, its current account was, until recently, close to balance and its military expenditures have remained low. It has generated a rapidly growing supply of entrepreneurial, managerial, and technical skills, and all this has been achieved within a framework that, during the last thirty years, has ensured a large degree of civil rights and political freedom. Turkey has, indeed, come a long way since the dark days of 1914-22.

---

1. Tezel, p. 71, citing an unpublished paper by Eldem; Shaw, _History_, 2:373, puts total Turkish losses during the war at 2.5 million.

2. Tables in Webster, pp. 49–52.

3. Mears, p. 289.

4. Novichev, Ekonomika, p. 19.

5. Ibid., pp. 20–25.

6. Ibid., pp. 53–68.

7. Ibid., pp. 85–86.

8. Ibid., pp. 110–11.

9. Hershlag, p. 42.

10. Novichev, Ekonomika, p. 121; Eldem, p. 266; Trumpener, passim.

11. Emin, p. 151; also table in Novichev, p. 97.

12. Table in TJ, February 1921.

13. For a vivid picture of the impact of the war on a middle-class family, see Orga.

14. See similar tables, comparing Turkey, Egypt, and Iran in 1925–68 in EHI, pp. 374–82; an excellent study of the sociopolitical transformation of Turkey, with abundant statistical series, is Karpat, "Structural Change," in Karpat et al., pp. 11–92.

15. Tezel, pp. 322–31; Hershlag, p. 78.

16. Tezel, p. 285.

17. Atasağun, pp. 191–207; Hershlag, pp. 47–51.

18. Lewis, Emergence, pp. 266–74, and sources cited therein.

19. Webster, pp. 210–39.

20. Hershlag, pp. 52–57.

21. Tezel, pp. 92 and 337–40; Webster, pp. 135–36; Conker, passim.

22. Hershlag, pp. 19–21.

23. Tezel, p. 117.

24. Ibid., p. 157.

25. Hershlag, pp. 43, 61.

26. Lewis, Emergence, p. 464.

27. Hershlag, pp. 115–17; Tezel, pp. 125–34.

28. Hershlag, pp. 78–79; Thornburg, pp. 43–75; Tezel, pp. 284–315.

29. UN, Development of Manufacturing, passim.

30. Hershlag, pp. 80–84; Thornburg, pp. 91–131; Land, passim; Tezel, pp. 210–43; Osman Okyar, "The Concept of Etatism," Economic Journal, March 1965; all five authors, particularly Okyar and Thornburg, have apt criticisms.

31. UN, Review of Economic Conditions in the Middle East, 1949–50, pp. 20, 76.

32. Lewis, Emergence, pp. 291–96; Shaw, History, 2:398–99; E. C. Clark, "The Turkish Varlik Vergisi Reconsidered," Middle Eastern Studies, 1972.

33. Rozaliyev, pp. 192–3.

34. The above account has drawn on Hershlag, Robinson, Griffin, UN, Economic Developments in the Middle East, 1945 to 1954 (New York, 1955), and other UN and FAO sources.

35. World Bank, Atlas, 1975; idem., World Tables, 1976 (Washington, D. C. 1976), and Central Bank of Turkey, Annual Report, 1975.

36. For these and other indexes for Turkey and other countries, C. Issawi, "The Economy of the Middle East and North Africa: An Overview" in A. L. Udovitch, ed., The Middle East: Oil, Conflict and Hope (Lexington, May 1975), pp. 59–100; also K. Karpat, "Structural Change," in Karpat, Social, pp. 11–92.

37. Breakdown and analysis in K. Göymen and G. Tüzün, "Foreign Private Capital in Turkey," METU Studies in Development, Spring 1976.

38. Krueger, p. 12.

39. Central Bank of Turkey, Annual Report 1974; this sum almost equalled earnings from exports.

40. World Debt Tables, vol. 1, October 31, 1976, p. 36.

41. World Bank, World Tables, p. 235.

42. N. Neyzi, "The Middle Classes in Turkey," in Karpat, Social, pp. 124, 127; also Hershlag, pp. 216–25, and Rozaliyev, pp. 177–238.

43. I. Aydinoglu, "Manpower and Employment Policies," in Abadan-Unat, pp. 104–32.

44. Tezel, p. 210; Central Bank, Annual Report 1975.

45. World Tables, p. 522.

46. Bülent Ecevit, "Labor in Turkey," in Karpat, Social, pp. 151–81; Hershlag, pp. 312–22.

47. Abadan-Unat, pp. 7–8.

48. UN, Statistical Yearbook, 1975; Central Bank, Annual Report, 1975.

49. For details, Aresvik, passim.

50. For a good analysis, Cohn, passim.

51. Hill in Udovitch, The Middle East, pp. 31–32.

52. See Aresvik.

53. For the last two points, see the excellent analysis in Krueger.

54. This matter is being thoroughly studied by the Princeton University Income Distribution Project.

Appendix

Weights and Measures

As in other parts of the Middle East (EHME, pp. 517-19, EHI, pp. 389-90), weights and measures in Turkey were very diverse in the past. They varied not only from place to place but often also according to the nature of the object being weighed or measured. The following were the units most commonly used in the nineteenth century.[1]

WEIGHTS

For precious metals and stones: the <u>denk</u>, 0.05 grams; <u>kırat</u>, 4 <u>denks</u> or 0.2004 grams; <u>dirhem</u> (dram), 16 <u>kırats</u> or 3.2074 grams; and the <u>miskal</u>, 1.5 <u>dirhems</u> or 4.811.

For merchandise, the basic unit was the <u>okka</u> (oke), 400 <u>dirhems</u> or 1.2828 kilograms (2.83 lbs.); the Adana <u>okka</u> equalled 1.212 kilograms. Another unit was the <u>ritl</u> or <u>rotol</u>; the Istanbul <u>ritl</u> equalled 876 <u>dirhems</u> or 2.81 kilograms; the Orfa <u>ritl</u>, 2,400 <u>dirhems</u> or 7.698 kilograms and the Sivas <u>ritl</u>, 1,440 or 4.619 kilograms.

The <u>batman</u> equalled 6 <u>okkas</u> or 7.698 kilograms; the Adana <u>batman</u> equalled 4.848 kilograms.

The <u>lodra</u> or <u>londra</u> equalled 176 <u>dirhems</u> or 564.432 grams.

The <u>kintar</u> or <u>kantar</u> equalled 44 <u>okas</u> or 100 <u>lodras</u>, i.e., 56.44 kilograms; a less commonly used <u>kintar</u> in Anatolia equalled 180 <u>okkas</u> or 230.922 kilograms; in Izmir the <u>kintar</u>, or <u>quintal</u> as it was called by foreigners, varied according to the kind of merchandise from 39 <u>okkas</u> or 50.033 kilograms for British goods to 180 or 230.922 kilograms for special goods, the most common being 80 <u>okkas</u> or 102.616 kilograms for ordinary merchandise and 78 <u>okkas</u> or 100.066 kilograms for European goods.

Another highly variable unit was the <u>çeki</u>, usually 176 <u>okkas</u> or 225.79 kilograms, but ranging from 100 to 195 <u>okkas</u> or 128 to 250 kilograms; for gold and silver, the <u>çeki</u> equalled only 100 <u>dirhems</u> or 320 grams, for opium in Izmir 763 grams and for mohair 4.564 kilograms.

LENGTH

The <u>parmak</u> (inch) equalled 3 centimeters and the <u>ayak</u> or <u>kadem</u> (foot) 12 <u>parmaks</u> or 36 centimeters, both measures being used for heights.

The main unit of length was the <u>dira</u> or <u>zira</u> (ell) or <u>arşın</u>, also known to Europeans as the <u>pic</u>. The <u>çarşı arşını</u>, or market ell, used for measuring cloth, equalled 68 centimeters. The <u>mimar arşını</u>, or architect's ell, equalled 75.8 centimers. The subdivision of the <u>çarşı arşını</u> were the <u>rub</u> (1/8 or 8.5 centimeters) and the <u>gire</u> (1/16 or 4.25 centimeters).

374

Distances were measured in mil (mile) of 2,500 mimar arşını or 1,895 meters or in fersah (parasang); the İran fersahı equalled 6,232 meters; the Arap fersahı, 5,763; and the Mısır fersahı, 2,250 meters.

AREA

The square mimar arşını was equal to 576 square parmaks or 0.575 square meters.

The evlek equalled 400 square dira mimaris or 229.825 square meters.

The dönüm varied but was eventually standardized at 4 evleks or 1,600 mimar arşını, equal to 918.667 square meters.

CAPACITY

For liquids, the most widespread measure was the binlik or gallon, equal to 1,000 dirhems; the same name was also applied to a unit used to measure cereals, being equal to 100 okkas or 128.2 kilograms for maize and 111 okkas or 141.1 kilograms for wheat.

Other measures of capacity used for cereals were the kile (bushel) and the mudd, with their subdivisions. The Istanbul kile was equal to 4 şiniks or 8 kutus, or 36.8 liters; its weight equivalent varied as follows: barley, 17 to 20 okkas; wheat, 22 to 26; oats, 14 to 16; maize, 23 to 25; beans, 19 to 20; rye, 23 to 24.[2] In addition, there was a wide array of local kiles, ranging from 17 okkas in Izmir to 240 in Mardin; the Rumelian kile was equal to 4 Istanbul kiles.

The mudd was equal to 18 liters; it was divided into nisf-i mudd and rubuye, or a half and a quarter mudd, respectively.

---

1. For fuller details, see Young, 4:367-75, Hinz, passim, and Eldem, pp. 321-23, on which this account is mainly based. I have checked the conversions into metric units and found minor inconsistencies but have reproduced the figures in Young.
2. For somewhat different figures, Quataert, p. 364.

Bibliography

Abadan-Unat, Nermin, et al. Turkish Workers in Europe. Leiden, 1976.

Abu-Lughod, Ibrahim, et al. Settler Régimes. Wilmette, Ill., 1974.

Ahmad, Feroz. The Young Turks. Oxford, 1969.

Ainsworth, W. F. Travels and Researches in Asia Minor, Chaldaea and Armenia. 2 vols. London, 1842.

Akbal, Fazıla. "1831 . . . Taksimat ve Nüfus." Belleten, vol. 15. 1951.

Akdağ, Mustafa. Celali İsyanları. Ankara, 1963.

_____. Türkiyenin İktısadi ve İçtimai Tarihi. Ankara, 1973.

Aktan, Reşat. "Agricultural Policy of Turkey." Ph.D. diss., University of California, 1950.

Anhegger, Robert. Beitrage zur Geschichte des Bergbaus im Osmanischen Reich. 2 vols. Istanbul, 1943-45.

Annuaire Commercial Turc, 1924-1925. Istanbul (n.d.).

"Empire Ottoman. 1. La situation intérieure et la crise internationale. II. Les rayas chrétiens, les étrangers et le commerce européen en Turquie." Annuaire des Deux Mondes. 1852-53 (1853).

Aresvik, Oddvar, The Agricultural Development of Turkey. New York, 1975.

Arpee, L. The Armenians Awakening 1820-1860. Chicago, 1909.

Artinian, Vartan. "A Study of the Historical Development of the Armenian Constitutional System in the Ottoman Empire." Ph.D. diss., Brandeis University, 1970.

Atasağun, Yusuf. T. C. Ziraat Bankası. Istanbul, 1939.

Avcıoğlu, Dogan. Türkiyenin Düzeni. Ankara, 1969.

Aybar, Celal. Osmanlı Imparatorluğunun Ticaret Muvazenesi 1878-1913. Ankara, 1939.

Bailey, Frank. British Policy and the Turkish Reform Movement. Cambridge, Mass., 1942.

Baltzer, F. Die Kolonialbahnen. Berlin, 1916.

Banse, E. Die Türkei. Brunschweig, 1915.

Barkan, Ömer Lütfi. Çiftçiyi Topraklandırma Kanunu. Istanbul, 1946.

_____. "Les problèmes fonciers dans l'Empire Ottoman." Annales d'histoire sociale. 1939.

_____. "Essai sur les donnees statistiques des registres de recensement." JESHO. 1957.

_____. "The Price Revolution of the Sixteenth Century." IJMES. 1975.

Barker, James. Turkey. New York, 1879.

Başgöz, İ. and Wilson, H. E. Educational Problems in Turkey. Bloomington, Indiana, 1968.

Basmadjian, K. J. Histoire moderne des Arméniens. Paris, 1917.

Basse, Alfred de. The Turkish Empire. Philadelphia, 1854.

Bazili, Konstantin. Ocherki Konstantinopolya. 2 vols. St. Petersburg, 1835.

Beaufort, F. Karamania. London, 1817.

Beer, Adolf. Die osterreichische Handelspolitik im neunzehnten jahrhundert. Vienna, 1891.

Belin, F. A. Essai sur l'histoire économique de la Turquie. Paris, 1865.

Benedict, Peter. Ula, an Anatolian Town. Leiden, 1974.

Benedict, Peter et al. Turkey, Geographic and Social Perspectives. Leiden, 1974.

Berkes, Niyazi. 200 Yıldır Neden Bocalıyoruz. Istanbul, 1964.

_____. The Development of Secularism in Turkey. Montreal, 1964.

Bernardakis, A. "Aperçus économiques et Statistiques sur la Question d'Orient, la Grece, la Turquie, etc." Journal des Economistes. 1878.

Biliotti, A. La Banque Ottomane. Paris, 1909.

Bonné, Alfred. State and Economics in the Middle East. London, 1948.

Boue, Ami. La Turquie d'Europe. 4 vols. Paris, 1840.

Bouvier, Jean. Le Crédit Lyonnais de 1863 à 1882. 2 vols. Paris, 1961.

Brandt, Orhan. Dix ans de régime républicain. Istanbul, 1933.

Braudel, Fernand. The Mediterranean and the Mediterranean World in the Age of Philip II. 2 vols. New York, 1972.

_____. Capitalism and Material Life, 1400-1800. New York, 1975.

Brooks, Jerome E. The Mighty Leaf: Tobacco through the Centuries. Boston, 1962.

Bruck, W. F. Die türkisch-Baumwollwirtschaft. Jena, 1919.

Brünner, E. R. J. De Bagdad spoorweg. Groningen-Djakarta, 1957.

Brunschvig, R. "Coup d'oeil sur l'histoire des foires à travers l'Islam." Recueils de la Société Jean Bodin. La Foire. Brussels, 1953.

Bulliet, Richard. The Camel and the Wheel. Cambridge, Mass., 1975.

Bursal, Nasuhi. Die Einkommensteuer--Reform in der Türkei. Winterthur, 1953.

Çalgüner, Cemil. Türkiyede Ziraat İşçileri. Ankara, 1943.

Campbell, Sir George. The Races, Religions and Institutions of Turkey. London, 1875.

Çark, Y. Türk Devleti hizmetinde Ermeniler. Istanbul, 1953.

Carles, G. La Turquie économique. Paris, 1906.

Chandler, R. Travels in Asia Minor. Oxford, 1775.

Chapman, Maybelle. Great Britain and the Bagdad Railway. Northampton, Mass., 1948.

Choiseul, Gouffier, M. de. Voyage pittoresque dans l'Empire Ottoman. Paris, 1842.

Cillov, Haluk. "Les Recensements industriels en Turquie." Revue de la Faculté des Sciences Economiques de l'Université d'Istanbul. 1951-52.

Clark, Edward C. "The Ottoman Industrial Revolution." IJMES, 1974.

Clarke, Edward D. Travels to Russia, Tartary and Turkey. New York, 1970.

Clogg, Richard. The Movement for Greek Independence. London, 1977.

Cohn, Edwin. Turkish Economic, Social and Political Change. New York, 1970.

Collas, M. B. La Turquie en 1861. Paris, 1861.

_____. La Turquie en 1864. Paris, 1864.

Collignon, M. de. Notes d'un voyage en Asie Mineure. Paris, 1897.

Conker, Orhan. Les chemins de fer en Turquie et la politique ferroviaire Turque. Paris, 1935.

_____. and Witmeur, Emile. Redressement économique et Industrialisation de la Nouvelle Turquie. Paris, 1927.

Cook, M. A., ed. <u>Studies in the Economic History of the Middle East</u>. London, 1972.

_____. <u>Population Pressure in Rural Anatolia, 1450-1600</u>. New York, 1972.

Cooke, W. S. <u>The Ottoman Empire and Its Tributary States</u>. London, 1876.

Cuinet, Vital. <u>La Turquie d'Asie</u>. 4 vols. Paris, 1890-95.

Dadian, Mekitar. <u>La Société arménienne contemporaine</u>. Paris, 1867.

Dakin, Douglas. <u>The Greek Struggle for Independence, 1821-1833</u>. Berkeley, 1973.

Dalsar, Fahri. <u>Bursada İpekçilik</u>. Istanbul, 1960.

Davison, Roderic. <u>Reform in the Ottoman Empire</u>. Princeton, 1963.

De Dreux, Robert. <u>Voyage en Turquie</u>. Paris, 1925.

Delaygue, Louis. <u>Essai sur les finances Ottomanes</u>. Paris, 1911.

<u>Deutsche Bank, 1870-1970</u>. Frankfurt, 1970.

Dewdney, J. C. <u>Turkey: An Introductory Geography</u>. New York, 1971.

Dietrich, Karl. <u>Hellenism in Asia Minor</u>. New York, 1918.

Diouritch, G. <u>L'expansion des banques allemandes a l'étranger</u>. Paris, 1909.

Draganof. <u>La Macédoine et les Réformes</u>. Paris, 1906.

Ducruet, Jean. <u>Les capitaux Europeens au Proche-Orient</u>. Paris, 1964.

Dunstan, Wyndham. "Report on Agriculture in Asia Minor." A and P, 1908.

Earle, E. M. <u>Turkey, the Great Powers, and the Bagdad Railway</u>. New York, 1923.

Earle, Peter. <u>Corsairs of Malta and Barbary</u>. London, 1970.

Eldem, Vedat. <u>Osmanlı Imparatorluğunun iktisadi şartları hakkında bir tetkik</u> (Istanbul, 1970).

Emin, Ahmed. <u>Turkey in the Great War</u>. New Haven, 1930.

Emmanuel, I. S. <u>Histoire des Israélites de Salonique</u>. Paris, 1936.

Engelhardt, E. <u>La Turquie et le Tanzimat</u>. Paris, 1882-84.

Erinç, S. and Tunçdilek, N. "The Agricultural Regions of Turkey." <u>Geographical Review</u>, 1952.

Erder, Leila. "From Trade to Manufacture in Bursa. Ph.D. diss., Princeton University, 1976.

Eren, Ahmet Cevat. <u>Türkiyede Göç ve Göçmen Meseleleri</u>. Istanbul, 1966.

Ergin, Osman. <u>Türkiye Maarif Tarihi</u>. 5 vols, Istanbul, 1939-43.

Erişçi, Lüftü. <u>Türkiyede İşçi Sınıfının Tarihi</u>. Istanbul, 1951.

Eton, W. <u>A Survey of the Turkish Empire</u>. London, 1798.

<u>The Famine in Asia Minor: Its History</u>. From the <u>Levant Herald</u>. Constantinople, 1875.

Farley, J. Lewis. <u>The Resources of Turkey</u>. London, 1862.

_____. <u>Turkey</u>. London, 1866.

_____. <u>Modern Turkey</u>. London, 1872.

_____. <u>The Decline of Turkey, Financially and Politically</u>. London, 1875.

_____. <u>Egypt, Cyprus and Asiatic Turkey</u>. London, 1878.

Fellows, C. <u>A Journal Written during an Excursion in Asia Minor</u>. London, 1838.

Fesca, M. <u>Anatolien über die landwirtschaftlichen Verhaltnisse</u>. Beihefte zum Tropenpflanzer, 1902.

Field, James A. <u>America and the Mediterranean World, 1776-1882</u>. Princeton, 1969.

Fickendey, E. <u>Der Oelbaum in Kleinasien</u>. Leipzig, 1922.

Finnie, David. <u>Pioneers East</u>. Cambridge, Mass., 1967.

Fisher, S., ed. <u>Ottoman Land Laws</u>. London, 1919.

Franco, M. <u>Essai sur l'histoire des Israélites dans l'Empire Ottoman</u>. Paris, 1897.

Fraser, David. <u>The Short Cut to India</u>. London, 1909.

Galanté, Abraham. _Histoire des Juifs d'Anatolie_. Istanbul, 1939.

_____. _Histoire des Juifs d'Istanbul_. Istanbul, 1942.

_____. _Turcs et Juifs_. Stanbul, 1932.

Genç, Mehmet. "Osmanlı Maliyesinde Malikane Sistemi." In Okyar, ed.

_____. "A Comparative Study of the Life Term Tax Data." In _La Révolution industrielle_ (see below).

Georgiades, D. _Smyrne et l'Asie Mineure au point de vue commercial_. Paris, 1885.

Gibb, H. A. R. and Bowen, H. _Islamic Society and the West_. London, 1950.

Giraud, Hubert. _Les origines et l'évolution de la navigation à vapeur à Marseille 1829-1900_. Marseille, 1929.

Gödel, Rudolf. _Ueben den pontischen Handelsweg_. Vienna, 1849.

Goodblatt, M. S. _Jewish Life in Turkey in the XVIth Century_. New York, 1952.

Goodell, William. _Forty Years in the Turkish Empire: Memoirs_. New York, 1876.

Gordon, Leland James. _American Relations with Turkey, 1830-1930_. Philadelphia, 1932.

Grenville, Henry. _Observations sur l'état actuel de l'empire ottoman_. Ed. A. Ehrenkreutz. Ann Arbor, 1965.

Griffin, Keith. _Land Concentration and Rural Poverty_. New York, 1976.

Grothe, H. _Die asiatische Türkei und die deutschen Interessen_. Halle, 1913.

_____. _Länder und Völker des Türkei_. Berlin, 1915 et seq.

_____. _Turkisch - Asie und seine Wirtschaftswerte_. Frankfurt, 1916.

Grunwald, Kurt. _Turkenhirsch: A Study of Baron Maurice de Hirsch_. New York, 1966.

Grunwald, Kurt and Ronall, Joachim. "The Bankers of Galata." Unpublished paper.

Günyüz, Süleyman. _Entwicklung und Bedeutung dem Tabakproduktion in der Türkei_. Istanbul, 1951.

Guseinov, A. A. _Profsoyuzy v Turtsii_. Moscow, 1975.

Hagemeister, Julius von. _Der Europäische Handel in der Turkei und in Persien_. Riga and Leipzig, 1838.

Hamilton, W. J. _Travels in Asia Minor, Pontus and Armenia_.

Haussig, H. W. _A History of Byzantine Civilization_. New York, 1971.

Hecker, M. "Die Eisenbahnen in der asiatischen Türkei." _Archiv für Eisenbahnwesen_. Berlin, 1914

Heidborn, A. _Manuel de droit public et administratif de l'Empire Ottoman_. 2 vols. Leipzig-Vienna, 1908-12.

Hellauer, J., ed. _Das Türkische Reich_. Berlin, 1918.

Hellferich, Karl. _Die Deutsche Türkenpolitik_. Berlin, 1921.

Hepworth, George. _Through Armenia on Horseback_. London, 1898.

Herrmann, R. _Anatolische Landwirtschaft_. Leipzig, 1900.

Hershlag, Z. Y. _Turkey: An Economy in Transition_. The Hague, 1960.

_____. _Introduction to the Modern Economic History of the Middle East_. Leiden, 1964.

Hommaire de Hell, Xavier. _Voyage en Turquie et Perse_. Paris, 1854.

Horton, Thomas. _Turkey: The People, Country and Government_. London, 1854.

Hoskins, H. L. _British Routes to India_. London, 1928.

Houille, René. _La politique monétaire de la Turquie depuis 1929_. Paris, 1937.

Hourani, A. H. _Minorities in the Arab World_. London, 1947.

Huart, C. _Konia_. Paris, 1897.

Hüber, R. _Die Bagdadbahn_. Berlin, 1943.

Hurewitz, J. C. _Diplomacy in the Near and Middle East_. 2 vols. Princeton, 1956.

Hüsrev, İsmail. Türkiye Köy İktisadı. Ankara, 1934.

İnalcık, Halil. "Tanzimat nedir," Tarih Araştımalari. Ankara, 1941.

_____. "Land Problems in Turkish History." Muslim World (Hartford, Conn.),

_____. "Capital Formation in the Ottoman Empire." JEH, 1960.

_____. The Ottoman Empire in the Classical Age, 1300-1600. London, 1973.

Inan, Afet. Aperçu général sur l'histoire économique de l'Empire turc-Ottoman. Istanbul, 1941.

Indzhikyan, O. G. Burzhuaziya Osmanskoi Imperii. Erevan, 1977.

International Bank for Reconstruction and Development. The Economy of Turkey. Baltimore, 1951.

_____. Turkey: Prospects and Problems. Washington, D.C., 1975.

Issawi, C. and Yeganeh, M. The Economics of Middle Eastern Oil. New York, 1962.

Itzkowitz, Norman. Ottoman Empire and Islamic Tradition. New York, 1972.

Jelavich, Charles and Barbara, eds. Balkans in Transition. Berkeley, 1963.

Johnson, Clarence R., ed. Constantinople Today. New York, 1922.

Junge, R. Die deutsch-türkischen Wirtschaftsbeziehungen. Weimar, 1916.

Kahyaoğlou, H. S. Le Tabac turc et son importance économique. Fribourg, 1937.

Karadenizli, Kemal. Trabzon Tarihi. Ankara, 1954.

Karal, Enver Ziya. Osmanlı imparatorluğunda ilk nüfus sayımı, 1831. Ankara, 1943.

Karamursal, Ziya. Osmanlı mali tarihi hakkında tetkikler. Ankara, 1940.

Karpat, K. H. Turkey's Politics: The Transition to a Multi-Party System. Princeton, 1959.

_____. "An Inquiry into the Social Foundations of Nationalism in the Ottoman State," The Woodrow Wilson School, Princeton University, 1973.

_____ et al. Social Change and Politics in Turkey. Leiden, 1973.

_____, ed. The Ottoman State and Its Place in World History. Leiden, 1974.

Kay, J. E. de Sketches of Turkey in 1831 and 1832. New York, 1833.

Kazamias, Andreas M. Education and the Quest for Modernity in Turkey. London, 1966.

Keddie, Nikki R. "Is There a Middle East?" IJMES, 1973.

Kinneir, Macdonald. Journey through Asia Minor. London, 1878.

Kolerkinç, E. Osmanlı imparatorluğunda para. Ankara, 1958.

Kollektiv Avtorov. O Genesise Kapitalizma v Strnakh Vostokie. Moscow, 1962.

Köymen, Oya. "The Imperialism of Free Trade." Paper presented to International Congress of Economic History, Leningrad, August, 1970. Moscow, 1970.

Kurmuş, Orhan. "The Role of British Capital in the Economic Development of Western Anatolia, 1850-1913." Ph.D. Thesis, London University, 1974.

Kutal, Metin. Le Syndicat devant la législation turque et le movement syndical en Turquie. Grenoble, 1959.

Ladas, S. P. The Exchange of Minorities: Bulgaria, Greece and Turkey. New York, 1932.

Land, James. "The Changing Role of Government in the Economic Development of Turkey." In G. Ranis, ed., Government and Economic Development. New Haven, 1971.

Landau, Jacob M. The Hejaz Railway and the Muslim Pilgrimage. Detroit, 1971.

Leake, W. M. Journal of a Tour in Asia Minor. London, 1824.

Leart, Marcel. La question arménienne à la lumière des documents. Paris, 1913.

Lecomte, Prétextat. Les arts et les métiers de la Turquie et de l'Orient. Paris, 1902.

Lemonidi, Alexandre. Du Commerce de la Turquie. Constantinople, 1849.

Lewis, Bernard. The Emergence of Modern Turkey. London, 1961, rev. ed. 1965.

_____. Istanbul and the Civilization of the Ottoman Empire. Norman, Okla., 1963, rev. ed. 1968.

Lewis, Rafaela. _Everyday Life in Ottoman Turkey_. London, 1971.

Lisenko, V. K. _Blizhnii Vostok kak rynok Sbita russkikh tovarov_. St. Petersburg, 1913.

Longrigg, S. H. _Oil in the Middle East_. London, 1961.

Lynch, H. F. B. _Armenia: Travels and Studies_. London, 1901.

MacFarlane, Charles. _Constantinople in 1828_. London, 1829.

_____. _Turkey and Its Destiny_. London, 1850.

MacGregor, John. _Commercial Statistics_. 4 vols. London, 1847.

Mansur, Fatma. _Bodrum: A Town in the Aegean_. Leiden, 1972.

Mantran, R. _Istanbul dans la seconde moitié du XVIIe siècle_. Paris, 1962.

Ma'oz, Moshe. _Ottoman Reform in Syria and Palestine, 1840-1861_. London, 1968.

Mardin, Şerif. _The Genesis of Young Ottoman Thought_. Princeton, 1962.

Marmont, Marshal. _The Turkish Empire_. London, 1839.

Marouche, P. and Sarantis, G. _Annuaire Financier de Turquie_. Pera, 1912.

Martineau, A. _Le Commerce français dans le Levant_. Paris, 1902.

Masson, Paul. _Histoire du commerce français dans le Levant au XVIIe siècle_. Paris, 1896.

McCarthy, Justin. _International Historical Statistics: The Late Ottoman Empire_ (in press, Boston).

McCulloch, J. R. _A Dictionary of Commerce and Commercial Navigation_. Philadelphia, 1852.

Mears, E. G., ed. _Modern Turkey_. New York, 1924.

Michaud, J. and Poujoulat, Baptistin. _Correspondence d'Orient_. Paris, 1834, 1835.

Michelsen, E. H. _The Ottoman Empire and Its Resources_. London, 1853.

Mikhov, Nikolai. _Naselenieto na Turtsiya i B'lgariya_. Sofia, 1915-35.

Miller, A. F. _Mustafa Pasha Bairaktar_. Moscow-Leningrad, 1947.

Mitchell, B. R. _Abstract of British Historical Statistics_. Cambridge, 1962.

Moiseev, P. P. _Agrarnye Otnosheniya v Sovremennoi Turtsii_. Moscow, 1960.

Moltke, Helmuth von. _Briefe über Zustände und Begebenheiten in der Türkei_. Berlin, 1911.

Morawitz, Charles. _Les Finances de Turquie_. Paris, 1902.

Mordtmann, Andreas. _Anatolien, Skizzen und Reisebriefe_. Hannover, 1925.

Morier, James. _A Journey through Persia, Armenia and Asia Minor_. London, 1812.

Moutal, Mosche. _L'Avenir Economique de la Turquie Nouvelle_. Paris, 1924.

Müller, Hermann. _Die Baghdadbahn, Bodenschätze und Bodenkultum in Kleinasien_. Hamburg, 1916.

Muratet, A. _Le Chemin de Fer de Baghdad_. Avrillac, 1914.

Mussler, Wilhelm Julius. _Die Turkei_. Ph.D. thesis, University of Freiburg (1924?).

Naff, T. and E. R. J. Owen. _Studies in the Eighteenth Century_. Carbondale, Ill., 1977.

Namikawa, Ryo and Banri. _Istanbul: Tale of Three Cities_. California, 1972.

Neale, F. A. _Turkey Redeemed from Existing Abuses_. London, 1854.

Nechama, J. _Histoire de Israélites de Salonique_. Paris, 1934-39.

Newton, C. T. _Travels and Discoveries in the Levant_. London, 1865.

Novichev, A. D. _Ekonomika Turtsii v period mirovoi voiny_. Leningrad, 1935.

_____. _Ocherki ekonomiki Turtsii_. Moscow-Leningrad, 1937.

_____. _Istoriya Turtsii_. 3 vols. Moscow, 1963.

Novo, John A. de. _American Interests and Policies in the Middle East, 1900-1939_. Minneapolis, 1963.

Nuri, Osman. _Mecelle-i Umuru Belediye_. Istanbul, 1922.

Ohsson, Mouradgea, Ignatius, d'. _Tableau général de l'Empire Othoman_. Paris, 1790.

Ökçün, A. Gündüz. _Osmanlı Sanayii, 1913, 1915, yılları_. Ankara, 1970.

Okyar, Osman. "L'Industrialisation en Turquie," _Economies et Sociétés_. Paris, 1973.

Okyar, Osman, ed. _Türkiye İktisat Tarihi Semineri_. Ankara, 1975.

Onar, Ahmet. _Türkiye Demiryolları Tarihi_. Istanbul, 1953.

Ongley, F. _The Ottoman Land Code_. London, 1892.

Oppenheim, Baron M. von. _Vom mittelmeer zum Persischen Golf_. Berlin, 1899-1900.

Orga, Irfan. _Portrait of a Turkish Family_. New York, 1950.

Padel, W. and Steeg, L. _La Legislation foncière Ottomane_. Paris, 1904.

Papadopoulos, S. A. _The Greek Merchant Marine, 1453-1850_. Athens, 1972.

Pech, E. _Manuel des Sociétés Anonymes Fonctionnant en Turquie_. Constantinople, 1911.

Pepper, C. M. _Report on Trade Conditions in Asiatic Turkey_. U. S. Department of Commerce
    and Labor, 1907.

Pere, Nuri. _Osmanlılarda Madeni Paralar_. Istanbul, 1968.

Philips, E. B. _Der türkische Tabak_. Munich, 1927.

Philippson, A. _Das türkische Reich_. Weimar, 1915.

Pitcher, Donald. _An Historical Geography of the Ottoman Empire_. Leiden, 1972.

Planhol, Xavier De. _De la plaine pamphylienne aux lacs pisidiens_. Paris, 1938.

Pococke, R. _A Description of the East and Some Other Countries_. London, 1743.

Ponteil, Félix. _La Mediterranée et les Puissances, depuis l'Ouverture jusqu'a la nationali-
    sation du Canal de Suez_. Paris, 1964.

Porter, James. _Turkey: Its History and Progress_. London, 1854.

Poujoulat, M. Baptistin. _Voyage à Constantinople_. Paris, 1840.

Poulgy, Grégoire. _Les Emprunts de l'Etat Ottoman_. Paris, 1915.

Pressel, W. von. _Les chemins de fer de Turquie_. Zurich, 1902.

Pretextat-Lecomte, M. _Les Arts et Métiers de la Turquie_. Paris, 1902.

Puryear, Vernon John. _International Economics and Diplomacy in the Near East_. Stanford,
    1935.

Quataert, Donald. "Ottoman Reform and Agriculture in Anatolia." Ph.D. diss., University
    of California, Los Angeles, 1973.

Ragey, Louis. _La Question du chemin de fer de Bagdad_. Paris, 1936.

Raymond, André. _Artisans et Commerçants au Caire au XVIIIe siècle_. 2 vols. Damascus,
    1973-74.

Refik, Ahmet. _Osmanlı Devrinde Türkiye Madenleri_. Istanbul, 1931.

Reinach, J. _Voyage en Orient_. 2 vols. Paris, 1879.

Renner, R. _Der Aussenhandel der Türkei vor dem Weltkriege_. Berlin, 1919.

La Révolution industrielle dans le sud-est européen-XIXS. Sofia, 1976

Rigler, Lorenz. _Die Türkei und deren Bewohner_. Vienna, 1852.

Robeff, Theodossi A. _Die Verkehrs-und Handelsbedeutung von Saloniki_. Lucka, 1926.

Robert, L. and Robert, J. _La Carie: Histoire et Géographie historique_. Paris, 1954.

Robinson, R. _The First Turkish Republic_. Cambridge, Mass. 1963.

Rohrbach, P. _Die Bagdadbahn_. Berlin, 1902.

Rosen, Georg. _Geschichte der Türkei_. 2 vols. Leipzig, 1866.

Roumani, A. _Essai historique et technique sur la dette publique ottomane_. Paris, 1927.

Rozaliyev, Yu. N. _Osobennosti Razvitiya kapitalizma v Turtsii_. Moscow, 1962.

Rustow, Dankwart. "The Modernization of Turkey." In Karpat et al.

Ryan, C. W. _Guide to the Known Mineral Resources of Turkey_. Ankara, 1954.

Saint-Yves, G. _Les chemins de fer français dans la Turquie d'Asie_. Paris, 1914.

Salaheddin, Bey. _La Turquie à l'exposition universelle 1867_. Paris, 1867.

Salmaslian, A. _Bibliographie de l'Arménie_. Erevan, 1969.

Sanjian, Avedis. The Armenian Communities in Syria under Ottoman Domination.   Cambridge,
    Mass., 1964.

Sarç, Ömer Celal. Türkiye Ekonomisinin Genel Esasları. Istanbul, 1949.

Sarim, Hüsnü. Über die Opiumgewinnung.

Sarkissian, A. O. History of the Armenian Question to 1885. Urbana, 1938.

Sarre, F. Reisen in Kleinasien im Sommer, 1895. Berlin, 1896.

Saul, Norman. Russia and the Mediterranean, 1797-1807. Chicago, 1970.

Schaefer, C. A. Deutsch-Türkische Freundschaft. Berlin, 1911.

_____. Ziele und Wege für die jungtürkische Wirtschaftspolitik. Karlsruhe, 1913.

Scherka, B. The Turkish Mining Regulations. Constantinople, 1917.

Scherzer. Smyrna. Vienna, 1873.

Schmidt, H. Das Eisenbahnwesen in der asiatischen Türkei. Berlin, 1914.

Schweinitz, Hilt von. In Kleinasien. Berlin, 1906.

Sencer, O. Türkiyede işçi sınıfı. Istanbul, 1969.

Senior, N. W. Journal Kept in Turkey and Greece in the Autumn of 1857 and the Beginning of
    1858. London, 1859.

Shaw, Stanford J. The Financial and Administrative Organization and Development of Ottoman
    Egypt. Princeton, 1962.

_____. Between Old and New: The Ottoman Empire under Sultan Selim III, 1789-1807.
    Cambridge, Mass., 1971.

_____. History of the Ottoman Empire and Modern Turkey. 2 vols. Cambridge, 1976.

Shorter, F. C., ed. Four Studies on Economic Development in Turkey. London, 1967.

Shwadran, Benjamin. The Middle East, Oil, and the Great Powers. New York, 1959.

Sıdkı Bey. Gedikler. Istanbul, 1909.

Slaars, Bonaventure. Etude sur Smyrne. Paris, 1868.

Slade, A. Record of Travels in Turkey, Greece, etc. London, 1854.

Sönmez, Attila. "Ottoman Terms of Trade, 1878-1913," METU Studies in Development. Ankara,
    1970.

Sousa, N. The Capitulatory Régime of Turkey. Baltimore, 1933.

Spratt, T. A. B. and Forbes, E. Travels in Lycia. London, 1847.

Stephenson, R. Macdonald. Railways in Turkey. London, 1859.

Stich, Heinrich. Die weltwirtschaftliche Entwicklung der anatolischen Produktion seit An-
    fang des 19 Jahrhunderts. Kiel, 1929.

Stirling, Paul. Turkish Village. London, 1965.

Stoianovich, Traian. "The Conquering Balkan Orthodox Merchant." JEH, 1960.

Strange, G. Le. The Lands of the Eastern Caliphate. Cambridge, 1905.

Sülker, Kemal. Türkiyede Sendikacılık. Istanbul, 1955.

Svoronos, N. G. Salonique et Cavalla (1686-1892). Paris, 1951.

_____. Le commerce de Salonique au XVIIIe siècle. Paris, 1956.

Szyliowicz, Joseph. Political Change in Rural Turkey: Erdemli. Paris, 1966.

_____. Education and Modernization in the Middle East. Ithaca, 1973.

Tanzimat. Istanbul, 1940.

Tate's Modern Cambist. A Manual of Foreign Exchanges and Bullion. London, various
    editions.

Tshihatchef, P. de. Bosphore et Constantinople. Paris, 1864.

_____. Une page sur l'Orient. Paris, 1868.

_____. Klein Asien. Leipzig, 1887.

Testa, I. de. _Recueil des traitésde la Porte Ottomane_. Paris, 1864-1901.

Tezel, Yahya. "Turkish Economic Development, 1923-1950." Ph.D. diss., Cambridge University, 1975.

Thobie, Jacques. _Intérets et impérialisme français dans l'empire ottoman_. Paris, 1977.

Thornburg, M. et al. _Turkey: An Economic Appraisal_. New York, 1949.

Thornton, Thomas. _The Present State of Turkey_. London, 1807.

Tischendorf, P. _Das Lehnswesen in den Moslemischen Staaten_. Leipzig, 1872.

Todd, John. _The World's Cotton Crops_. London, 1915.

Todorov, N. "The Genesis of Capitalism in the Balkan Provinces." _Explorations in Entrepreneurial History_, 1970.

Tosbi, S. _Anonim Şirket_. Ankara, 1943.

Townshend, A. _A Military Consul in Turkey_. London, 1910.

Trask, Roger R. _The United States Response to Turkish Nationalism and Reform, 1914-1939_. Minneapolis, 1971.

Trietsch, Davis. _Levant-Handbuch: Eine Übersicht_. Berlin, 1910.

Trumpener, Ulrich. _Germany and the Ottoman Empire, 1914-1918_. Princeton, 1968.

Tümertekin, E. "The Structure of Agriculture in Turkey." _Review of the Geographical Institute of the University of Istanbul_, 1959.

Türk Ticaret Salnamesi. _İktisadi Tetkitat, Neşriyat ve Muamelat Türk Anonim Şirket_. Istanbul, 1340-1341.

Tute, R. C. _The Ottoman Land Laws_. Jerusalem, 1927.

Ubicini, A. _La Turquie actuelle_. Paris, 1855.

————. _Letters on Turkey_. London, 1856. Translated by Lady Easthope.

Ubicini, A. and Pavet de Courteille, A. J. _Etat présent de l'Empire Ottoman_. 1876.

Ülgener, S. _İktisadi İnhitat Tarihimizin Ahlak ve Zihniyet Meseleleri_. Istanbul, 1951

Umur, Hasan. _Of Tarihi_. Istanbul, 1951.

United Nations, _Economic Conditions in the Middle East_. New York, 1950-63.

————. Economic Commission for Europe. _Economic Survey of Europe_. Geneva, 1954.

————. _The Development of Manufacturing in Egypt, Israel and Turkey_. New York, 1958.

————. Food and Agriculture Organization. Center of Land Problems in the New East. Salahuddin, Iraq. 1955. Papers and Reports.

Urquhart, David. _Turkey_. London, 1833.

Vacalopoulos, Apostolos. _A History of Thessaloniki_. Thessalonike, 1963.

————. _The Greek Nation, 1453-1669_. New Brunswick, 1975.

Velay, A. du. _Essai sur l'histoire financière de la Turquie_. Paris, 1903.

Wallach, Jehuda, ed. _Germany and the Middle East, 1835-1939_. Tel-Aviv, 1975.

Ward, Robert E. and Rustow, Dankwart A. _Political Modernization in Japan and Turkey_. Princeton, 1964.

Warriner, Doreen. _Land and Poverty in the Middle East_. London, 1948.

Warsberg, A. von. _Ein Sommer in Orient_. Vienna, n.d.

Webster, D. E. _The Turkey of Atatürk_. Philadelphia, 1939.

Wiedenfeld, Kurt. _Die deutsch-türkischen Beziehungen_. Munich, 1915.

White, C. _Three Years in Constantinople_. London, 1845.

Williamson, John. _Karl Helfferich_. Princeton, 1971.

Wittman, William. _Travels in Turkey, Asia Minor, Syria and Egypt_. New York, 1971.

Wolf, John Baptist. _The Diplomatic History of the Bagdad Railroad_. Columbia, Mo., 1936.

Wood, Alfred Cecil. _A History of the Levant Company_. London, 1935.

Worms, Dr. "Recherches sur la constitution de la propriéte territoriale dans les pays
    musulmans." _Journal Asiatique_, 1842.

Wright, Walter L. "American Relations with Turkey to 1831." Ph.D. diss., Princeton Univer-
    sity, 1928.

Yalman, Nur. "On Land Disputes in Eastern Turkey." In G. L. Tikku, ed., _Islam and Its
    Cultural Divergence_. Urbana, Ill., 1971.

Yasa, I. _Hasanoğlan: Socio-economic Structure of a Turkish Village_. Ankara, 1957.

Yeniay, Hakkı. _Osmanlı borçları tarihi_. Ankara, 1936.

————. _Yeni Osmanlı borçları Tarihi_. Ankara, 1964.

Young, G. _Corps de droit Ottoman_. 6 vols. Oxford, 1905-6.

Index of Place Names

Adana, 7-10, 12, 16, 17, 33-34, 41-43, 58,
  61, 78, 82, 88, 129-33, 149-50, 189,
  191, 193, 195, 202-7, 209, 213, 216,
  234-35, 240, 242-46, 255, 270, 276-78,
  294, 296, 310-11, 318, 324, 345
Afyon Karahisar, 34, 149, 186, 189, 191,
  262, 263
Aleppo, 40-41, 61, 64, 78, 83, 101-2, 124,
  129, 131, 133, 145-46, 149-51, 177,
  179-81, 188-91, 193-94, 196, 209,
  224, 254, 259, 275, 299-300, 305,
  310, 333, 335, 338, 340, 345
Alexandria, 83, 101, 102, 105, 109, 118,
  161, 163-64, 209, 344
Ankara, 7, 16, 34, 36, 41, 82, 96, 114,
  120, 144, 148-50, 179, 188-89, 191-93,
  195, 197, 202, 207-8, 213, 215, 224,
  230, 261-62, 268, 270, 278, 291, 296,
  300-302, 306, 316, 332, 334, 344, 349,
  359
Austria-Hungary, 53, 54, 57, 79-81, 83, 87,
  105, 107, 109, 112, 133, 135, 138-39,
  142-43, 145, 151, 154, 164, 174, 176,
  210, 214, 233, 241, 246, 261, 264,
  265, 269, 275, 285, 293, 309, 338,
  340, 365

Baghdad, 8, 40-41, 58, 79, 101, 115, 121,
  149-50, 172, 178, 183, 188-96, 210,
  219, 224, 231, 233, 235, 259, 294,
  305, 328, 335, 338, 340-41, 345, 347,
  365-66
Batum, 121-22
Beirut, 40-42, 101-2, 115, 133, 141, 147,
  151, 161, 162, 168, 174-75, 214, 248,
  328, 335
Berlin, 250, 361
Bulgaria, 4, 17, 81, 140-43, 176, 234, 247,
  250, 323, 335
Bursa (Brusa), 2, 7, 8, 12, 16, 23, 33-34,
  37, 40, 42, 44-45, 56, 58, 61, 96,
  100-1, 106, 109, 114, 120, 146-47,
  149-50, 152, 191, 196-98, 204-6, 210,
  221-22, 227-28, 235, 239-41, 247,
  250, 252, 255-56, 259, 261-68, 275,
  277-79, 284, 288, 291, 293, 295,
  297-300, 302, 304, 306, 309-10, 312,
  313, 315-16, 322, 326, 328-29, 331,
  334, 336

Constanza (Kustenje), 148, 162, 167
Cyprus, 18, 19, 42, 61, 81, 101, 203, 210,
  213, 233-34, 236, 239, 299, 326, 335,
  341-42, 345, 357, 367

Diyarbekir, 17, 34, 40-42, 61, 121, 129-30,
  133, 146, 149, 151, 177-81, 189, 191,
  195-96, 199, 202-3, 206-8, 210, 213,
  215, 219-20, 234, 245, 270-71, 278,
  283-84, 296, 298-300, 305, 322, 332,
  334-36, 340-41, 345

Edirne (Adrianople), 10, 25, 29, 33-34,
  38-39, 41-42, 63, 74, 83, 92, 101,
  113-14, 118-20, 145, 150-51, 163,
  177-78, 197, 199, 203-4, 207-9, 211,
  215, 224, 233-34, 240, 254, 259, 278,
  294, 313, 318, 322-23, 330-31, 335,
  340-41, 343
Egypt, 3-7, 17-18, 23-24, 53-54, 58, 61,
  74, 76, 82-83, 86, 89, 96, 100, 106,
  108-9, 139-43, 156, 162, 170, 205,
  210-11, 214, 236-37, 239-40, 242-43,
  246-47, 250, 253-54, 264, 277, 281,
  326, 340, 342, 347-48, 350, 354, 359,
  373
Erzurum, 11-12, 16-17, 34, 55, 58, 61-62,
  64-65, 78, 101-2, 120-23, 127-29,
  146-47, 149-50, 177-78, 180, 195-96,
  202, 206-7, 209, 215-18, 224, 235,
  245, 254, 270, 278, 284, 293, 295,
  298, 300, 305-7, 322, 326, 332,
  335-36, 340, 345, 355-56

France, 3, 4, 63, 64, 75, 78-83, 86-90,
  105, 107, 109, 112, 115, 118-19,
  122-23, 133-36, 138, 142, 144-45,
  149, 151, 174-76, 190, 211, 229, 233,
  235-38, 242, 246-47, 254-56, 259,
  261, 264-65, 267, 269, 275, 280-81,
  289, 306, 309, 312-13, 324, 326, 340,
  350, 361-62

Germany, 54, 57, 75, 78-79, 87, 89, 105,
  109, 112, 118-20, 133-35, 138-39, 142,
  145, 149, 151, 174, 176, 233, 236,
  246, 250, 262, 309, 324, 338, 361-62,
  366, 368-69, 371

387

Index of Subjects